SCHOOL OF ORIENTAL AND AFRICAN STUDIES

University of London

TEACHING COLLECTION SHORT LOAN

This book is due for return before the last time below. A fine will be charged for late return.

Principles of Visual Anthropology

World Anthropology

General Editor

SOL TAX

Patrons

CLAUDE LÉVI-STRAUSS
MARGARET MEAD
LAILA SHUKRY EL HAMAMSY
M. N. SRINIVAS

MOUTON PUBLISHERS · THE HAGUE · PARIS
DISTRIBUTED IN THE USA AND CANADA BY ALDINE, CHICAGO

Principles of Visual Anthropology

Editor

PAUL HOCKINGS

MOUTON PUBLISHERS · THE HAGUE · PARIS
DISTRIBUTED IN THE USA AND CANADA BY ALDINE, CHICAGO

13/4/76

General Editor's Preface

Anthropologists have traditionally sought, welcomed, and accepted new research methods and techniques from any source. The development of chemical methods for the absolute dating of prehistoric objects and sites (beginning with the atomic-age knowledge that carbon-14 decays at a regular rate after the death of an organism) is only the most famous of many instances. If the elders are slow in adapting new techniques to their uses, a new generation in academia is only five years away. It is, therefore, remarkable — and a matter for discussion in this book — that this first full treatment of the use of motion pictures and television techniques in anthropological research and teaching is only now being published. Though the field has suffered because there has been no such book to use, clearly the book is different from anything that could have been written even a few years earlier. It is a better book, too, because its impetus was a unique Congress which demanded a planetary view of every problem discussed.

Like most contemporary sciences, anthropology is a product of the European tradition. Some argue that it is a product of colonialism, with one small and self-interested part of the species dominating the study of the whole. If we are to understand the species, our science needs substantial input from scholars who represent a variety of the world's cultures. It was a deliberate purpose of the IXth International Congress of Anthropological and Ethnological Sciences to provide impetus in this direction. The *World Anthropology* volumes, therefore, offer a first glimpse of a human science in which members from all societies have played an active role. Each of the books is designed to be self-contained; each is an attempt to update its particular sector of scientific knowledge and is written by specialists from all parts of the world. Each volume should be read and reviewed individually as a separate volume on its own given subject. The set as a whole will indicate what changes are in store for anthropology as scholars from the developing countries join in studying the species of which we are all a part.

The IXth Congress was planned from the beginning not only to include as many of the scholars from every part of the world as possible, but also with a view toward the eventual publication of the papers in high-quality volumes. At previous Congresses scholars were invited to bring papers which were then read out loud. They were necessarily limited in length; many were only summarized; there was little time for discussion; and the sparse discussion could only be in one language. The IXth Congress was an experiment aimed at changing this. Papers were written with the intention of exchanging them before the Congress, particularly in extensive pre-Congress sessions; they were not intended to be read at the Congress, that time being devoted to discussions — discussions which were simultaneously and professionally translated into five languages. The method for eliciting the papers was structured to make as representative a sample as was allowable when scholarly creativity — hence self-selection — was critically important. Scholars were asked to both propose papers of their own and to suggest topics for sessions of the Congress which they might edit into volumes. All were then informed of the suggestions and encouraged to re-think their own papers and the topics. The process, therefore, was a continuous one of feedback and exchange and it has continued to be so even after the Congress. The some two thousand papers comprising *World Anthropology* certainly then offer a substantial sample of world anthropology. It has been said that anthropology is at a turning point; if this is so, these volumes will be the historical direction-markers.

As might have been foreseen in the first post-colonial generation, the large majority of the Congress papers (82 percent) are the work of scholars identified with the industialized world which fathered our traditional discipline and the institution of the Congress itself: Eastern Europe (15 percent); Western Europe (16 percent); North America (47 percent); Japan, South Africa, Australia, and New Zealand (4 percent). Only 18 percent of the papers are from developing areas: Africa (4 percent); Asia-Oceania (9 percent); Latin American (5 percent). Aside from the substantial representation from the U.S.S.R. and the nations of Eastern Europe, a significant difference between this corpus of written material and that of other Congresses is the addition of the large proportion of contributions from Africa, Asia, and Latin America. "Only 18 percent" is two to four times as great a proportion as that of other Congresses; moreover, 18 percent of 2,000 papers is 360 papers, 10 times the number of "Third World" papers presented at previous Congresses. In fact, these 360 papers are more than the total of ALL papers published after the last International Congress of Anthopological and Ethnological Sciences which was held in the United States (Philadelphia, 1956). Even in the beautifully organized Tokyo Congress in 1968 less than a third as many members from developing nations, including those of Asia, participated.

The significance of the increase is not simply quantitative. The input of scholars from areas which have until recently been no more than subject matter for anthropology represents both feedback and also long-awaited theoretical contributions from the perspectives of very different cultural, social, and historical traditions. Many who attended the IXth Congress were convinced that anthropology would not be the same in the future. The fact that the next Congress (India, 1978) will be our first in the "Third World" may be symbolic of the change. Meanwhile, sober consideration of the present set of books will show how much, and just where and how, our discipline is being revolutionized.

This description of the state-of-the-art in visual anthropology is well grounded in papers commissioned in advance of the Congress. These were discussed for four days in a special conference, the conclusions of which were presented (with simultaneous translation) to a worldwide audience at the Congress itself, and the discussion was recorded for possible future study. From beginning to end, the whole creative process was coordinated by the editor of what turns out to be a remarkably fresh book.

Chicago, Illinois   SOL TAX
September 6, 1974

Foreword

The masterly introduction which Margaret Mead has written for this volume makes it unnecessary for me to emphasize either the promise that visual anthropology offers us today or the reserve with which it has been considered in the past. The present collection of papers will, I trust, serve to put visual anthropology into its proper perspective as a legitimate sub-discipline of anthropology and at the same time a contributor to the history of cinema.

A few words about the editorial procedure may not be out of place here. Nearly all of these papers were written in 1973 for discussion at the International Conference on Visual Anthropology, which was held in Chicago at the University of Illinois as part of the IXth I.C.A.E.S. A few were written or drastically revised afterwards as a result of that Conference. And the brilliant paper by Colin Young was produced six months later.

Visual anthropology is clearly the product of a dozen Western countries. Being familiar with many of the people active in this new field, I solicited nearly every paper with a view to how it would fit into the entire volume. To this end I sometimes suggested alterations and the excision of points duplicated in several of the papers. Where time has not permitted a long editorial dialogue, alternative viewpoints have simply been added as "comment" at the end of some papers. Only three papers were submitted in foreign languages: that by Peterson was translated by Russian experts, and those by Rouch and Lajoux were translated by me.

It is a matter of great satisfaction that nearly all of the key persons in visual anthropology have contributed to this volume. I should add that we are all indebted to the National Endowment for the Humanities, which made the International Conference possible; to Margaret Mead and Sol

Tax for their continuous interest in the project; to Jean Block and her staff for their valuable editing services; to Bill Hintz, the film Librarian at this University, for his help with problems in the Filmography; and to Karen Tkach of Mouton Publishers for easing my way to the press.

University of Illinois, Chicago   PAUL HOCKINGS
May 1974

ERRATUM

After page 504 the pagination of this book starts again with page 499, instead of continuing with page 505.

These page should have been numbered:

Biographical Notes	should begin on page 505 instead of page 499;
the Index of Films	,, ,, ,, ,, 511 ,, ,, ,, 505;
the Index of Names	,, ,, ,, ,, 515 ,, ,, ,, 509;
the Index of Subjects	,, ,, ,, ,, 521 ,, ,, ,, 515.

These pagination changes should also be applied to the Table of Contents.

Table of Contents

Introduction

Visual Anthropology in a Discipline of Words

MARGARET MEAD

Anthropology, as a conglomerate of disciplines — variously named and constituted in different countries as cultural anthropology, social anthropology, ethnology, ethnography, archaeology, linguistics, physical anthropology, folklore, social history, and human geography — has both implicitly and explicitly accepted the responsibility of making and preserving records of the vanishing customs and human beings of this earth, whether these peoples be inbred, preliterate populations isolated in some tropical jungle, or in the depths of a Swiss canton, or in the mountains of an Asian kingdom. The recognition that forms of human behavior still extant will inevitably disappear has been part of our whole scientific and humanistic heritage. There have never been enough workers to collect the remnants of these worlds, and just as each year several species of living creatures cease to exist, impoverishing our biological repertoire, so each year some language spoken only by one or two survivors disappears forever with their deaths. This knowledge has provided a dynamic that has sustained the fieldworker taking notes with cold, cramped fingers in an arctic climate or making his own wet plates under the difficult conditions of a torrid climate.

In the light of this record of devoted, tedious, often unrewarded work under trying and difficult conditions, it might be expected that each branch of practitioners of anthropology would eagerly avail itself of new methods which could simplify or improve its fieldwork. Thus, methods of dating became progressively available to archaeologists; phonograph, wire, and tape recording to musicologists and linguists; and still and moving pictures and video to ethnologists. The fantastic advances that have been made in each field when the new instrumentation became available (as carbon 14 replaced tree rings, tape recorders replaced wax cylinders, sync-sound and filming replaced the wet plate camera) would seem to be so self-validating that a world congress in 1973 would only have to concern itself with a discussion of the latest theoretical advances, based upon the newest instrumentation, coupled with exhibits and demonstrations of the most trustworthy instruments — an approach exemplified by Joseph Schaeffer's article on videotape in this volume. Instead, we are faced with the wretched picture of lost opportunities described in Emilie de Brigard's article and the picture of what can still be done in the face of many lost possibilities in Alan Lomax's worldwide survey and synthesis.

All over the world, on every continent and island, in the hidden recesses of modern industrial cities as well as in the hidden valleys that can be reached only by helicopter, precious, totally irreplaceable, and forever irreproducible behaviors are disappearing, while departments of anthropology continue to send fieldworkers out with no equipment beyond a pencil and a notebook, and perhaps a few tests or questionnaires — also called "instruments" — as a sop to scientism (Plate 5). Here and there, gifted and original filmmakers have made films of these behaviors, and here and there anthropologists who could make films or arrange for them to be made have appeared, labored, been complimented and cursed in the perverted competitiveness of the unstable and capricious market place... but that is all. What we have to show for almost a century's availability of instruments are a few magnificent, impassioned efforts — the Marshall films on the Bushmen, Bateson's Balinese and Iatmul films, the Heider-Gardner expeditions to the Dani, Jean Rouch's tireless efforts in West Africa, some films of Australian aborigines, Asen Balikci's Netsilik Eskimo series, the Asch-Chagnon series of the Yąnomamö, and, on the archival and analytical side, the gargantuan efforts of the Columbia Cantometrics Project, the Child Development Film Project of the National Institutes of Health, the Research Unit at the Eastern Pennsylvania Psychiatric Institute, the Encyclopaedia Cinematographica, and the Royal Anthropological Institute in London.

I venture to say that more words have been used, spoken and written, disputing the value of, refusing funds for, and rejecting these projects than ever went into the efforts themselves. Department after department and research project after research project fail to include filming and insist on continuing the hopelessly inadequate note-taking of an earlier age, while the behavior that film could have caught and preserved for centuries (preserved for the joy of the descendants of those who dance a ritual for the last time and for the illumination of future generations of human scientists) disappears — disappears right in front of everybody's eyes. Why? What has gone wrong?

A partial explanation of this clinging to verbal descriptions when so many better ways of recording many aspects of culture have become available lies in the very nature of culture change. Much of the fieldwork that laid the basis of anthropology as a science was conducted under conditions of very rapid change, where the fieldworker had to rely on the memory of the informants rather than upon observation of contemporary events. The informant had only words in which to describe the war dance that was no longer danced, the buffalo hunt after the buffalo had disappeared, the discontinued cannibal feast, or the abandoned methods of scarification and mutilation. Thus ethnographic enquiries came to depend upon words, and words and words, during the period that anthropology was maturing as a science. Lévi-Strauss has devoted all of his mature years to an analysis of that part of myth and folklore caught with a written translation of a written text. Lowie, working on Indian reservations, demanded how you could know that an individual was someone's mother's brother unless someone "told" you so. Relying on words (the words of informants whose gestures we had no means of preserving, words of ethnographers who had no war dances to photograph), anthropology became a science of words, and those who relied on words have been very unwilling to let their pupils use the new tools, while the neophytes have only too often slavishly followed the outmoded methods that their predecessors used.

Another explanation has been that it takes more specialized skill — and gift — to photograph and make films than it does to set a tape recorder going or to take written notes. But one does not demand that a linguist, carefully tape recording in the field, be able to construct a symphony out of his materials when he returns. Samples of filmed behavior can be made, just as adequately as can taped texts, by any properly trained ethnologist who can load a camera, set it on a tripod, read an exposure meter, measure distance, and set the stops. Surely any ethnologist with the intelligence to pass examinations based on a critical knowledge of the current sacred texts and worthy of being supported in the field can learn to make such records, records which can then be analyzed by our steadily developing methods of microanalysis of dance, song, language, and transactional relations between persons. We do not demand that a field ethnologist write with the skill of a novelist or a poet, although we do indeed accord disproportionate attention to those who do. It is equally inappropriate to demand that filmed behavior have the earmarks of a work of art. We can be grateful when it does, and we can cherish those rare combinations of artistic ability and scientific fidelity that have given us great ethnographic films. But I believe that we have absolutely no right to waste our breath and our resources demanding them. That we do is the unfortunate outcome of both the European tradition of the overriding importance of originality in the arts and the way in which the camera has replaced the artist's brush and so developed film as an art form.

Thus the exorbitant demand that ethnographic films be great artistic productions, combined with the complementary damnation of those who make artistic productions and fail in fidelity to some statistically established frequencies of dramatic events, continues to clutter up the film scene, while whole cultures go unrecorded.

A second explanation of our criminal neglect of the use of film is cost. It is claimed that the costs of film equipment, processing, and analysis, in both time and money, are prohibitive. But as every science has developed instrumentation, it has required more expensive equipment. Astronomers did not give up astronomy because better telescopes were developed, nor did physicists desert physics when they needed a cyclotron, nor did geneticists abandon genetics over the cost of an electron microscope. Instead, each of these disciplines has stood behind its increased and expanded efficiency, while anthropologists not only have failed to support their instrumental potentialities but have continued to use questionnaires to ask mothers how they discipline their babies, words to describe how a pot is made, and a tangle of ratings to describe vocal productions. To add insult to injury, in many cases they have disallowed, hindered, and even sabotaged the efforts of their fellow research workers to use the new methods.

I think that we must squarely face the fact that we, as a discipline, have only ourselves to blame for our gross and dreadful negligence. Much of this negligence has resulted in losses that can never be regained. But there is still time, by concerted, serious, international effort, to get at least adequate samples of significant behaviors from every part of the world and to underwrite more full-scale records of whole cultures to add to the paltry few that we have.

There is, then, a second issue, and one variously addressed in the pages of this volume — how best to train ethnologists to understand filmmaking and film analysis, how best to train those who start as filmmakers and wish to learn ethnographic filming, and how to organize teams for massive fieldwork. A half century of inspired and unrewarded stabs at this problem has provided us with a fair amount of usable experience. It is possible to direct a cameraman who has no real knowledge of the significance of what he is filming, especially when much scene-setting has to be done, as in the kind of participatory reconstruction used by Asen Balikci in his

Eskimo series. It is possible for the filmmaker to use the work of an ethnographer who precedes him in the field, as Gardner did with Heider's work and as Craig Gilbert and his team did with my work on Manus. But I believe the best work is done when filmmaker and ethnographer are combined in the same person, although in many cases one interest and skill may outweigh the other. We have long insisted that the cultural ethnologist learn to take into account aspects of a culture in which he lacks personal interest and specialized technical training for recording. If he learns a language, he is expected to bring back texts; if the people make pots, he is expected to record the technique; whatever his problem, he is expected to bring back the kinship nomenclature. The requirement that certain minimum tape recording, filming, still photographic records, and video (where technically practicable) be brought back from every field trip can be added quite simply to the single field expedition. Such a requirement will not produce magnificent, full-scale, artistically satisfying, humanistically as well as scientifically valuable films — these, perhaps, will always be few in number. But recent work in New Guinea, such as the fieldwork of William Mitchell and Donald Tuzin, has demonstrated that it is possible to combine good traditional analytical ethnography with photography, filming, and taping. Assembling, mastering, transporting, maintaining, and using the equipment do add extra burdens. But in the past, the fieldworker had to contend with a great deal of illness that is now preventable with vitamins and minerals, and with immense gaps in communication between home base and field station that have now shrunk from months to days. The diaries of earlier fieldworkers like Malinowski (in the Trobriands), Deacon (who died of blackwater fever in the New Hebrides), and Olsen (ill days on end in the Andean highlands) are quite sufficient to document the savings that modern technology has given us. The time and energy made available by modern medical and mechanical technologies can now be diverted to using that same technology to improve our anthropological records.

A third problem is that of the relationship between the ethnologist, filmmaker, or team and those whose behavior (so precious and so trembling on the edge of disappearing forever) is being filmed. Although no film has ever been made without some cooperation from the people whose dance or ceremony was being filmed, it has been possible, in the past, for the filmmaker to impose on the film his view of the culture and people that are to be the subject of this film. This cannot, I believe, ever be entirely prevented. Still, the isolated group or emerging new nation that forbids filmmaking for fear of disapproved emphases will lose far more than it gains. In an attempt to protect a currently cherished national image, they will rob of their rightful heritage their descendants, who (after the recurrent spasms of modernization, technological change, and attempts at new forms of economic organization) may wish to claim once more the rhythms and handicrafts of their own people. Not only the whole world of science and the arts, but their own future generations will be impoverished. However, there are contemporary steps that can be taken by the ethnographer, by those who are filmed, and by governments newly alerted to the problems of culture change in a world arena. Agreements can be made so that neither book reproductions of stills nor prints of films of ceremonies that are either sacred and esoteric, or illegal and therefore rejected under the new governmental system, may be shown within that country. Filming for television may be forbidden; in such cases, films may be restricted for scientific use only. This is one set of safeguards.

There is a second set of safeguards which does not (although it is often sentimentally claimed to do so) replace these formal safeguards on dissemination or use. This is the articulate, imaginative inclusion in the whole process of the people who are being filmed — inclusion in the planning and programming, in the filming itself, and in the editing of the film. We have just the beginning of such activities, not yet fully integrated, in Adair and Worth's films made by Navaho Indians; in the types of participation accorded Peter Adair in *Holy Ghost People*; in the training of local assistants and critics (such as those we trained in Bali, who could view the films in the field, for example, and discuss whether or not they believed that a trance dancer was "in trance"); and in the filming being done by some of Jean Rouch's former assistants in Niger. An ideal toward which we might set our sights would be a combination of films made by ethnographic filmmakers from different modern cultures — e.g. Japanese, French, American — combined with sequences photographed and edited by those who dance or enact the ceremonies or sequences of everyday life that are being filmed. The hazards of bias, both in those who film from their own particular cultural framework and in those who see their own filmed culture through distorting lenses, could be compensated for not by shallow claims of culture-free procedures, but — as in all the comparative work which is the essence of anthropology as a science — by the corrective of different culturally based viewpoints.

We must, I believe, clearly and unequivocally recognize that because these are disappearing types of behavior, we need to preserve them in forms that not only will permit the descendants to repossess their cultural heritage (and, indeed, will permit present generations to incorporate it into their emerging styles), but that will also give our understanding of human history and human potentialities a reliable, reproducible, reanalyzable corpus. We need also to consider that we would have no comparative science of culture without the materials generated by comparative work in all parts of the world (studies of the isolated peasant skills and movement styles in literate cultures as well as of the preliterate peoples who have maintained very ancient forms of behavior); the human sciences would still be floundering, as is much of our culture-bound, specialized social science, within an inadequate framing of experience which assumes that history and civilization as inaugurated by the Greeks form the pattern of culture.

As we approach a planetary communications system, there will inevitably be a diffusion of shared basic assumptions, many of which will be part of the cultural repertoire of members of all societies. We may hope, and it is part of anthropology's task to see to it, that before such planetary systems of thought are developed, the Euro-American tradition will have been broadened and deepened by the incorporation of the basic assumptions of the other great traditions and by the allowance for and recognition of what we have learned from the little traditions.

Nevertheless, the time will come when the illumination of genuine culture shock will be harder to attain, when the cultural diversity will be far more finely calibrated, and when greater and subtler educative experience will be required to perceive it and make constructive use of it. How then, in the future, will we be able to provide materials as contrastive as those from Europe, Asia, Africa, and the Americas today and as comprehensive and comprehensible as the entire culture of an isolated Eskimo or Bushman group? It is by exposure to such differences that we have trained our students to gather the materials on which we have then developed our body of theory. The emerging technologies of film, tape, video, and, we hope, the 360° camera, will make it possible to preserve materials (of a few selected cultures, at least) for training students long after the last isolated valley in the world is receiving images by satellite.

Finally, the oft-repeated argument that all recording and filming is selective, that none of it is objective, has to be dealt with summarily. If tape recorder, camera, or video is set up and left in the same place, large batches of material can be collected without the intervention of the filmmaker or ethnographer and without the continuous self-consciousness of those who are being observed. The camera or tape recorder that stays in one spot, that is not tuned, wound, refocused, or visibly loaded, does become part of the background scene, and what it records did happen. It is a curious anomaly that those against whom the accusation of being subjective and impressionistic was raised — those, in fact, who were willing to trust their own senses and their own capacity to integrate experience

— have been the most active in the use of instrumentation that can provide masses of objective materials that can be reanalyzed in the light of changing theory. Those who have been loudest in their demand for "scientific" work have been least willing to use instruments that would do for anthropology what instrumentation has done for other sciences — refine and expand the areas of accurate observation. At the present time, films that are acclaimed as great artistic endeavors get their effects by rapid shifts of the cameras and kaleidoscopic types of cutting. When filming is done only to produce a currently fashionable film, we lack the long sequences from one point of view that alone provide us with the unedited stretches of instrumental observation on which scientific work must be based. However much we may rejoice that the camera gives the verbally inarticulate a medium of expression and can dramatize contemporaneously an exotic culture for its own members and for the world, as anthropologists we must insist on prosaic, controlled, systematic filming and videotaping, which will provide us with material that can be repeatedly reanalyzed with finer tools and developing theories. Many of the situations with which we deal, situations provided by thousands of years of human history, can never be replicated in laboratory settings. But with properly collected, annotated, and preserved visual and sound materials, we can replicate over and over again and can painstakingly analyze the same materials. As finer instruments have taught us more about the cosmos, so finer recording of these precious materials can illuminate our growing knowledge and appreciation of mankind.

Ethnographic Filming and the Cinema

The History of Ethnographic Film

EMILIE DE BRIGARD

Ethnographic films have been produced ever since the technological inventions of nineteenth-century industrial society made possible the visual recording of encounters with other societies. Since its beginning, ethnographic film has been burdened with the expectation that it will reveal something about primitive cultures – and ultimately, all of culture – which can be grasped in no other way. The fulfillment of this expectation is what concerns us here. It is usual to define ethnographic film as film that reveals cultural patterning. From this definition it follows that all films are ethnographic, by reason of their content or form or both. Some films, however, are clearly more revealing than others.

Since the simultaneous inventions in Europe and America of motion pictures, shortly before the turn of the century, almost every people in the

I am indebted for information about Haddon to Peter Gathercole and James Woodburn. Many others have generously helped me in countless ways. Among those not named in the text are: Charles Weaver and the staff of the American Museum of Natural History; Jacques Ledoux and the staff of the Cinémathèque Royale de Belgique; Ernest Lindgren and the staff of the British Film Institute; and Tahar Sheriaa, Executive Secretary of the Journées Internationales Cinématographiques de Carthage. This paper has benefited from discussions with Erik Barnouw, Jean Rouch, and Richard Sorenson, who called certain inaccuracies to my attention; and from the editorial scrutiny of Paul Hockings and Timothy Thoresen, the chairmen of the sessions on Visual Anthropology and the History of Anthropology. I alone am responsible for the views expressed, and for errors of fact and omission. I am especially grateful to the Wenner-Gren Foundation for Anthropological Research, The Museum of Modern Art, the Smithsonian Institution, and the Choreometrics Project of Columbia University for support, and to the Directors of these bodies for their encouragement.

world has been filmed in one way or another, and a few groups have been filmed repeatedly, intensively, and brilliantly.[1] Examination of the corpus of ethnographic film and its literature shows that filmmakers have been guided (and also limited) by the technical means available to them, by the theoretical formulations of anthropology and cinematic art and by the intended and actual uses of their films. The history of technical progress, theoretical advance, and increasing sophistication in the use of film runs counter to a long-standing reluctance on the part of social scientists to take film seriously. The overwhelmingly verbal bias of anthropology was naively, and ineffectually, challenged by the innovators of ethnographic film in the years before World War I. The period between the wars saw solid if isolated achievements in theory and application, and, outside the academic sphere, the creation of an audience for social documentary films; but ethnographic film became an institutionalized scientific field, with recognized specialists and a body of criticism, only during the 1950's. In 1973, on the twenty-first anniversary of the formation of the International Committee on Ethnographic and Sociological Film, its members recognized that their discipline was in process of reinterpretation and unprecedented growth.

It is no accident that respect for film in the scientific community in recent years has been equaled by interest in the concerns of anthropology among the viewing public. The postwar revolution in communications technology is responsible for this. Today's young citizens have grown up with the new freedom of 16-mm synchronous sound filming, the impact of television transmission, and the possibility of computerized videotape storage of records. This technological revolution has facilitated development of ethnographic film from the fragmentary and idiosyncratic to the systematic and thorough; it has also caused the disappearance of much of its traditional subject matter. But the irony of the situation is superficial. Although the inclination to capture "the conspicuous, the traditional and the bizarre" is still present, both in scientific and in commercial films, it has gradually been giving way to a more thoughtful tendency to try to record, as coherently as possible, items of unspectacular but significant behavior. We now turn our cameras on ourselves for a good hard look at our own societies, thus redressing an imbalance which the "native" subjects of ethnographic films have found highly offensive.

---

[1] A definitive filmography of ethnographic films, invaluable for determination of filming priorities, has not yet been published. The International Committee on Ethnographic and Sociological Film has to date completed catalogues of ethnographic films of Subsaharan Africa (1967), the Pacific (1970), Asia and the Middle East (in press), and is assembling material on films of Latin America.

Ethnographic film began as a phenomenon of colonialism, and has flourished in periods of political change: socialist revolution, democratic reform, independence for developing nations. Its problems bear comparison with those of the new cinemas in former colonies: like these it enjoys an essential seriousness (sometimes ideologically tinged) and suffers from technical and financial handicaps by comparison with the established film industry. Like these it struggles to overcome Hollywood conventions; and it does without mass acceptance. But a few ethnographic filmmakers have influenced important movements in the cinema, and thus shaped the way in which generations of viewers saw life on the screen (cf. Young's paper, *infra*). Moreover, there are indications that some films have aided cultural renewal. The most exciting possibility of ethnographic films is to enable many who would not otherwise do so — amongst them, those whose specialized knowledge directs men's affairs — TO SEE, newly and richly, the range of patterns in the behavior of man. Its essential function, however, was stated by its very first practitioner and remains unchanged today. Film "preserves forever all human behaviors for the needs of our studies" (Regnault 1931:306).

The first person to make an ethnographic film was Félix-Louis Regnault (Plate 2), a physician specializing in pathological anatomy who became interested in anthropology around 1888, the year in which Jules-Étienne Marey (Plate 1), the inventor of "chronophotography," demonstrated his new camera, using celluloid roll film, to the French Académie des Sciences. In the spring of 1895, Regnault, aided by Marey's associate, Charles Comte, filmed a Wolof woman making pots at the Exposition Ethnographique de l'Afrique Occidentale. The film showed the Wolof method of making pottery, using a shallow concave base which is turned with one hand while the clay is shaped with the other. Regnault claimed that he was the first to note this method, which, he said, illustrates the transition from pottery made without any wheel at all to that made on the primitive horizontal wheel used in ancient Egypt, India, and Greece. He wrote up his experiment, including several line drawings taken from the film, and published it in December, 1895; the same month that the Lumières gave the first public projection of "cinématographe" films, a successful commercial experiment which launched the motion picture industry (Lajard and Regnault 1895; Sadoul 1966: 11).

Regnault's subsequent films were devoted to the cross-cultural study of movement: climbing a tree, squatting, walking, by Wolof, Fulani, and Diola men and women (Regnault 1896a, 1896b, 1897). He championed the systematic use of motion pictures in anthropology, and proposed the formation of anthropological film archives (Regnault 1912, 1923a,

1923b). Toward the end of his life he seems to have felt that his urgings had not been effective. In fact the Anglo-Saxons and Germans soon overtook the French in ethnographic filming; nonetheless, Marey's countrymen continued to excel in filming physiology (Michaelis 1955: 87).

One of the events marking the transformation of nineteenth-century speculative anthropology into a discipline with standards of evidence comparable to those of natural science was the Cambridge Anthropological Expedition to the Torres Straits, which Alfred Cort Haddon, a former zoologist, mounted in 1898. The expedition was conceived as a team effort of systematic salvage ethnography covering all aspects of Torres Straits life, including physical anthropology, psychology, material culture, social organization, and religion. A whole battery of recording methods was used, some of them new, such as W. H. R. Rivers' genealogical method, which has since become standard, and photography, together with wax-cylinder sound recording and motion pictures. Haddon's ethnographic films, for which a Lumière camera was used, are the earliest known to have been made in the field. What remains of them (several minutes' worth) shows three men's dances and an attempt at firemaking.

Haddon encouraged his colleagues to array themselves for fieldwork with photographic equipment (Plate 5). In 1901 he wrote about filming in a letter to Baldwin Spencer, who was about to undertake an expedition to Central Australia. Spencer and his associate, F. J. Gillen, spent the next thirty years studying the Australian Aborigines, and they produced monumental ethnographies copiously illustrated with photographs, but Spencer filmed on only two occasions, in 1901, and in Northern Australia in 1912. Despite flies, difficulties of transport, and the shyness of the Aranda, he collected over 7,000 feet of film, chiefly of ceremonies, and a number of wax cylinders. The scale of this effort (running time more than an hour) was large for its time, and the films are still legible enough to be used in research today. One long sequence of a Bugamani ceremony on Bathurst Island is even eerily beautiful. Notwithstanding the merit of what had been done, Spencer apparently made no further use of his films once they were housed in the National Museum at Victoria. Another colleague of Haddon's, Rudolf Pöch of Vienna, saw the Torres Straits films at Cambridge in 1902, and then took motion picture and stereoscopic cameras on his field trips to New Guinea and Southwest Africa in 1904 and 1907. Pöch's attempts at filming met with mechanical snags – underexposure and loosening of the lens through rough handling. Nearly half of the footage exposed in New Guinea failed to come out. Pöch ruefully advised developing film in the field whenever possible, or at least testing a strip from each roll, in order to catch and correct technical problems as they came up. He managed to film dance in Cape Nelson, girls carrying water and children playing in Hanuabada (Port Moresby), and a man being shaved with an obsidion razor (Pöch 1907: 395 ff.).

Pöch's films were restored and published by the University of Vienna in 1960, and Spencer's were shown in a retrospective of Australian ethnographic films which attracted world-wide attention in 1967. To be unused and unknown has been the fate of all too many ethnographic films stored in the vaults of museums or in the garages of anthropologists' families. Many were destroyed as fire hazards, and others will soon be beyond saving, unless the programs of restoration which have been carried out on an *ad hoc* basis since the 1950's are rationalized, centralized, and well funded.

Of the pioneers of ethnographic film, only Regnault is known to have made use of it over a period of years. Why were the efforts of others without a sequel? Filming has always been far more expensive than writing, and it was, relatively speaking, even more so in the early years of the century.[2] There was real danger in working with highly inflammable nitrate film; gruesome fatalities occurred as late as the 1950's, and taking the necessary precautions, for example building a fireproof projection booth, added expense and inconvenience. Filming in the field resembled a wrestling match with protean equipment: cumbersome cameras fixed on tripods, with or without panning heads, viewfinders, or extra lenses, and using film whose low exposure index demanded shooting in broad daylight. These technical difficulties were serious enough; when problems of theory were also taken into account, the prospects for ethnographic film seemed bleak indeed (Plates 6 and 7).

Regnault had a theoretical focus for his filming: "the study of physiology proper to each ethnic group" (Regnault 1931: 306). Haddon's motive was apparently the urgent one of salvage, and cannot be faulted as such; but ethnographic salvage, however valuable, is not a substitute for a program of scientific inquiry. Moreover, interest in the material expressions of culture, which occupied Haddon's generation, began to be supplanted, early in this century, by emphasis on psychologistic traits and the intangibles of social structure. For many years it was beyond the technical capabilities of cinematography to follow this shift.

Up to this point the exposition has been concerned with ethnographic research films, which were made by scientists and were not intended to be

[2] For examples of budgets, see Hilton-Simpson and Haeseler (1925: 330) and Collier (1967: 127-135).

seen by laymen. But if we were to limit ourselves to what has been filmed by scientists, our history would appear poorer than it is. Comparative study of human behavior on a global scale, by means of the World Ethnographic Film Sample, would be severely hampered if all commercial and sponsored films were excluded.

Edgar Morin (1956) has described the transformation of motion pictures, the plaything of inspired *bricoleurs*, into the cinema, the dream machine of the masses. From its earliest days, two tendencies in the cinema can be made out: the documentary or *actualité* film, originated by the Lumières, and the fiction film, invented by Méliès in 1897 to win back to the box office a public which had speedily become bored by motion pictures (Sadoul 1966: 32). Actuality is generally less expensive to film than fiction. At various times and places, producers and public have preferred one of these tendencies to the other, but the distinction is often blurred to take advantage of both. The hybrid *documentaire romancé* – the story film set in a genuine exotic background – made its appearance by 1914.

Among the earliest commercial films were some autobiographical documentaries of the Lumière family: *Le déjeuner de Bébé, La partie d'écarté, La pêche à la crevette*, etc. (1895).[3] In 1896–1897, their *opérateurs* fanned out across the globe, showing films to curious crowds on all continents and shooting items to be sent back to Lyon for the Lumière catalogue (Sadoul 1964). The American firm of Edison sent cameramen to film Samoan dancers at Barnum and Bailey's Circus, Walapai snake dancers in the pueblo (Plate 7), and Jewish dancers in the Holy Land. From 1905, Pathé Frères produced and distributed 35-mm *actualités* with an average length of 300 feet on a variety of subjects in Europe and abroad; other firms engaged in this activity were Warwick, Urban, Kineto, and Gaumont.[4]

Georges Méliès' firm, Star Film, which was known for its fantastic productions (as a trip to the moon was then considered), suffered chronic financial difficulty after an initial period of success. In 1912, Gaston Méliès, a brother, sought to cash in on the vogue for films of faraway places by producing melodramas in the South Seas. He assembled cameras, film, and a troupe of actors, and took ship for Tahiti and New Zealand. On his return to New York in 1913, Star Film released five two-reel *documentaires romancés*, none of which has survived. The best of

---

[3]   For further information on the films cited, see the item on "Filmography" in this volume.

[4]   The national archives of many countries contain film catalogues which repay close study.

Plate 1. Étienne-Jules Marey (1830–1904).

Plate 2.   Félix-Louis Regnault (1863–1938).

Plate 3.   Robert Flaherty (1884-1951) on location in Samoa.

Comité international des films de l'homme

Plate 4.   Jean Rouch.

Indische Reisebriefe (Berlin, 1883)

Plate 5.   Ernst Haeckel in Ceylon (1882).

Plate 6. Eskimo sketch of Robert Flaherty in three different acts of film making –
directing, setting up, and shooting – all shown simultaneously. This may come from
the shooting of *Nanook of the North*, 1920–1922, or from an earlier film venture in the
Hudson Bay area.

Royal Ontario Museum

Edmund Carpenter

Plate 7.   Hopi snake dance, Oraibi, 1898. Photographer Adam Clark Vroman. Note movie camera. Filmmaker probably Thomas Edison, believed to be the first person to film this dance; though tourists, even at this early date, sometimes numbered in the hundreds and many brought still cameras, possibly even movie cameras.

Plate 8.   Mark McCarty (right) in Ireland (1967).
Note sophisticated Éclair and Nagra tape-recorder.

Paul Hockings

Plate 9.   Mothering among the Foré. Research film footage from New Guinea reveals the range of mothering behavior within a community.

Adelaide DeMenil

Plate 10.   Biami, Papua, 1969.

Plate 11.   Authentic Zuñi Katchina, circa 1945.

them, from the point of view of ethnographic production values, was probably *Loved by a Maori Chieftainess*, in which an English explorer of the 1870's, about to be killed by a headhunter, escapes to an island with the help of a beautiful princess, marries her, and is accepted as her husband by the Maori. The action took place against a background of genuine village life, dancing, and war canoes (O'Reilly 1970: 289–290). Méliès planned to distribute a whole series of these tropical entertainments, but he discovered that most of his film had been ruined by a year of South Seas humidity. Star Film never recovered from the blow. Georges Méliès sold his company and eventually died a pauper (Sadoul 1966: 39).

Apart from entertainment, what is the value of nonscientific films of peoples and customs? Availability of information supplementing the film is of critical importance. *Actualités* and newsreels, often short and sometimes falsified, seldom give a systematic view of anything, although dance fares better than most categories. Human behavior in documentary and fiction films is subject to directorial distortion to such an extent that the film may be scientifically worthless. However, authenticity can be found on levels untouched by dramatic action (cf. Weakland's paper, *infra*).

A case in point is Edward Curtis' remarkable 1914 film, *In the Land of the Head-Hunters*. (The beginnings of visual ethnography of the American Indian, incidentally, are not in the films of Edison or Thomas Ince, but in still photography [Taft 1938: 249 ff.][5] The photographers of the Indians were not trained anthropologists, but the best of them did their work with enthusiasm, extraordinary dedication, and sensitivity.) Curtis, a prolific still photographer, spent three seasons with the Kwakiutl filming a drama of love and war in settings painstakingly reconstructed for precontact authenticity. Curtis had learned the same lessons as D.W. Griffith, and he handled suspense well. What gives his film its lasting appeal is the way in which Indian elements are used to tell the story visually. Its plot, which concerns a wicked sorcerer, a hero, and their respective factions battling for a girl, was to recur twenty-five years later, in H. P. Carver's Ojibwa melodrama, *The Silent Enemy*.

Toward the end of the pioneer period of ethnographic film came the first use of film in applied anthropology, the origin of the colonial cinema. By 1912, it had occurred to the Americans who administered the Philippines that films might serve a purpose in native education: where a language barrier prevented giving lessons successfully by word of mouth,

[5] For surveys of photography in anthropology, see Rowe (1953); Mead (1963); and Collier (1967).

films would convey the message. Worcester, the Secretary of the Interior for the Philippines, devised a program of sanitary education for the provinces. To hold the interest of the Bontoc Igorot, Ifugao, and Kalinga between health films, Worcester's subordinates projected scenes of native and foreign life. The program achieved the desired result; when shown moving pictures of better conditions, the people showed a disposition to change. Moreover, Worcester reported, "the old sharply drawn tribal lines are disappearing... At the same time that all of this has been accomplished, the goodwill of the people has been secured" (Donaldson 1912: 41–42).

The generation before World War I was a time of innovation; the period between the wars was a time of popularization. In 1931, Regnault surveyed the status of film in anthropology, formulated a typology of film according to its use for entertainment, education, or research, and asserted that the importance of film in scientific research had been forgotten (Regnault 1931: 306). In fact, this was not the case; film had an established place in the laboratory (Michaelis 1955). But until Mead and Bateson's work of 1936–1938, the films made by anthropologists in the field, though intrinsically valuable, were not original in conception. What was new was the spread of film in anthropological teaching, fostered by museums and universities. Alongside the development of the teaching film, educational motion pictures, in the broadest sense, found a new dimension in the documentary. The technical advance of miniaturization of the 16-mm teaching film made possible the unprecedented fluency of Mead and Bateson's visual research. The aesthetic development of the documentary profoundly influenced the shape of the ethnographic film when it came into its own after World War II (cf. Young's paper, *infra*).

The history of the teaching film can be traced from the origins of motion pictures, but its great spurts occurred during the World Wars and in the periods following them, when film equipment and personnel were diverted to civilian life (Anderson 1968). By the mid-1920's, the anthropological teaching film evolved its canonical forms: the single-concept film of ceremonial, crafts, and the like; and the filmed cultural inventory, more or less complete. Another form, the comparison film (of houses of the Arctic and the tropics, for example) was less common. In format the anthropological teaching film was from ten minutes to over an hour long, silent, with intertitles which sometimes took up more than half of the film. After the adoption of sound in 1927, voice-over narration gradually replaced titles.

Museums were well-suited to produce films on anthropological subjects, since they had the possibility both of sending cameramen on their expeditions and of attracting steady audiences to their programs. An excellent series about the Zuñi was made in 1923 by F. W. Hodge, ethnologist, and Owen Cattell, cameraman, for the Heye Foundation-Museum of the American Indian. An overview film, *Land of the Zuñi and Community Work*, shows planting, threshing, water carrying, children at play, and gambling, by men, women, and children who appear to be going about their daily occupations with complete absorption, oblivious of the camera. Three films of ceremonials show dancing and the planting of sacred wands. The rest of the series covers hairdressing, housebuilding, baking bread, and tanning and wrapping deerskin leggings. Despite occasional awkwardness in the technical process films, these compare favorably with the series directed by Samuel Barrett at the University of California more than thirty years later.

Sensing the possibility of profit, commercial film producers entered into association with museums and universities; the Harvard-Pathé project produced a number of short, straightforward films on the *Battacks of Sumatra, Mongols of Central Asia, Wanderers of the Arabian Desert*, etc. (1928), before the relationship was dissolved. Nordisk Films Kompagni and Svensk Filmindustri coproduced the Svarta Horisonter (Black Horizons) series (1935–1936) directed in Madagascar by Paul Fejos, the Hungarian director. Later, as Director of Research of the Wenner-Gren Foundation, Fejos trained film crews in anthropology (*Nomads of the Jungle*, 1952) and anthropologists in filming (at Yale and Columbia Universities), but his excellent anthropological documentaries (*A Handful of Rice*, 1938; *Yagua*, 1941) are not as well known as his theatrical films, *Lonesome* (1928) and *Légende hongroise* (1932) (Bidney 1964; Dodds 1973).

Eastman Kodak developed the 16-mm format (1923) expressly for the school market, but by the 1950's most educational films were still being filmed in 35-mm and reduced for distribution. A certain stiffness marred even the best of these films. And the format of the visual lecture, now in color, is with us still.

However successful teaching films might be (and it should be remembered that Eastman Teaching Films was a subsidized operation, designed to bolster the parent firm's sales of film stock), they were surpassed in visibility and profitability by explorer films and by fiction films set in exotic locations, which enjoyed great popularity between the wars. Among explorers, Martin Johnson was the durable producer of *On the Borderland of Civilization* (1920), *Simba, Congorilla, Baboona*, and *Borneo* (1937). Frank Hurley's *Pearls and Savages* (1924) was probably the first film made in New Guinea. The makers of *Grass* (1925), Merian Cooper and Ernest Schoedsack, went on to film Lao villagers and elephants in

Chang (1927), before their greatest success, *King Kong* (1933). Léon Poirier's *Croisière noire* (1926), the first feature-length French film made in Africa, did its job (advertising Citroën trucks) so well that it was released in a sound version in 1933. The Marquis de Wavrin's *Au pays du scalp*, record of an Amazon expedition edited by Cavalcanti and with music by Maurice Jaubert, appeared in 1934. Fiction films of the period include episodes of the *Perils of Pauline*, filmed in the Philippines in the 1920's, and Cecil B. de Mille's remake of *Squaw Man* (1931), which is all the more poignant since it is unclear which locale is meant to be more exotic, the studio interior of an English country house or the Wild West. W. S. Van Dyke directed the singularly offensive *Trader Horn* (1930), which was partly filmed in Africa, and *Tarzan, the Ape Man* (1932). Jean Mugeli's *Rapt dans la jungle* (1932) was the first Melanesian talking picture. And André-Paul Antoine and Robert Lugeon produced what was to become the first publicly exposed ethnographic film hoax, *Les mangeurs d'hommes* (1930). Antoine and Lugeon engaged a village of Christianized Small Namba to enact a terrifying drama of cannibalism, supposedly set in the "unknown region" of the interior of Malekula, where the authority of the white man was "entirely nominal." The deception was unmasked by their host in the field, the Bishop of Port Vila, but not before a celebrity-studded première had taken place in Paris (Leprohon 1960).

Although he transcended these genres, Robert Flaherty began his filmmaking career as an explorer, and he continued by directing a South Seas love story for Hollywood. *Nanook* (1922) was described by a spokesman for the Asia Society as "drama, education, and inspiration combined"; and of *Moana* (1926) John Grierson wrote: "*Moana*, being a visual account of events in the life of a Polynesian youth, has documentary value." Both films were technically innovative. For *Nanook*, Flaherty used a tripod with gyro-movement, which allowed him to follow and anticipate his subjects with the delicacy which became his trademark; and while filming *Moana* he discovered that the panchromatic film intended for his special color camera gave excellent skin tones in black and white, and his improvement became industry standard. (Unfortunately, Flaherty's interest in the problems of sound did not equal his visual gifts.) As an artist, Flaherty is of the first rank; as an anthropologist (which in any case he did not pretend to be) he leaves much to be desired (Plates 3 and 6). Iris Barry's attack on the authenticity of *Nanook* can never be well answered, since Flaherty, always the raconteur, did not leave a systematic record of its making. Mrs. Flaherty's 1925 account of the conditions under which *Moana* was filmed is sufficient to dismiss its value as a record of interpersonal behavior, although its sequences of crafts are acceptable. Alas for Flaherty! *Man of Aran* (1934) was denounced for being escapist, for ignoring the political realities of the tenant system; *The Land* (1942) was shelved because it was considered too pessimistic, too grimly realistic to be circulated in wartime. Flaherty's gift was not that of a reporter or recorder, but rather that of a revealer.

The social documentary film, which came into being in the 1920's and flourished in the 1930's, was a mass education medium sensitive to the needs of government policy or of opposition politics in various countries. "Of all the arts," Lenin told his Commissar of Education, Lunacharsky, "for us the cinema is the most important" (Leyda 1960: 161). "I consider *Las Hurdes* one of my surrealist films," remarked Buñuel (Taylor 1964: 90). Scientific data are to be found amidst the actuality, but they are clothed in argument more subtle than fiction. If the explorer film cannot escape its exploitative nature, neither can the documentary desist from visionary exhortation.

Concern with the transformations in society is a trait common to Soviet anthropologists and filmmakers; as Marxists, they have tried not only to describe social change, but also to cause it to happen (Debets 1957; Krupianskaya, *et al.* 1960). What is striking about the first generation of Soviet filmmakers is the closeness of their ties to science, as well as to the *avant-garde* in art. Theoretical explicitness and candor about how they produced their effects distinguished Eisenstein, Pudovkin, and other Soviet filmmakers from their Western contemporaries, from whom they had learned much (cf. Temaner's paper, *infra*). Dziga Vertov, the pioneer of Soviet documentary, directed the *Kino-pravda* series (i.e. "cinema truth"; "*cinéma vérité*") (1922) and expressed the following theory of montage, or "the organization of the seen world":

1. Montage during the observation period (immediate orientation of the naked eye at al times and places).
2. Montage after observation (logical organization of vision into one or another definite direction).
3. Montage at the time of filming (orientation of the ARMED eye — the moving picture camera — during the search for the appropriate camera position, and adjustment to the several changing conditions of filming).
4. Montage after filming (rough organization of the filmed material according to main indications, and ascertaining what necessary shots are missing).
5. Judgment of the montage pieces (immediate orientation to link certain juxtapositions, employing exceptional alertness and these military rules: judgment – speed – attack).
6. Final montage (exposition of larger themes through a series of smaller

subtler themes; reorganization of all material while keeping the rounded se-
qunce in mind; exposure of the very heart of all your film-objects) (Belenson
[1225] quoted in Leyda [1960:178–179]; cf. Rouch's paper, *infra*).

Three Songs of Lenin (1934) is considered to be Vertov's best film. It ends
with a lyric section on the progress "from past to future, from slavery to
freedom" of the Soviet Union's Central Asian ethnic minorities. The
Soviets encouraged the development of regional filmmaking in Uzbekistan,
Armenia, Georgia, and elsewhere. Mikhail Kalatozov's *Salt for Svanetia*
(1930) shows past hardships of life in the Caucasus ("tormenting hunger for
salt") overcome by Soviet technical aid (tractors construct an all-weather
road). The Svans took offense at the film, and denied that the old customs
portrayed in it had ever existed. Another "before and after" film, Viktor
Turin's *Turksib* (1928), shows the building of the Turkestan-Siberian
railway and the reactions of people along its path.

In Eastern and Central Europe, documentary filmmakers approached
traditional life with a reverential attitude. Karel Plicka directed *Za
Slovensky ludem* [Games of Slovak Youth, 1931], *Večna piseň* [The
Eternal Song, 1941], and *Zem spieva* [Earth in Song, 1933], which he
considered to be his "hymn to the Slovak people." Drago Chloupek and
A. Gerasimov filmed a Croation *zadruga* in 1933 (*Dan u jednoj velikoj
hrvatskoj porodici* [A day in a large Croatian family], anticipating later
peasant symphonies by Henri Storck in Belgium and Georges Rouquier in
France. German filmmakers were also attracted by folklore and ethnographic subjects, which they fashioned into *Kulturfilme*. The more ambitious of these trace the development of a trait from primitive beginnings
to its advanced form. Wilhelm Prager's *Wege zu Kraft und Schönheit*
(1925) compares Greco-Roman with modern German athletics, and
illustrates the development of dance from Hawaiian and Burmese,
through Spanish and Japanese, to Russian ballet and the dance dramas
of Rudolf Laban. It concludes with shots of famous sportsmen, including
Lloyd George golfing and Mussolini on horseback. The UFA publicist
claimed that this film would promote "the regeneration of the human
race" (Kracauer 1947: 143).

French documentary, unlike Soviet and German documentary, was
individualist, largely anti-establishment, and undeveloped (cf. Rotha *et
al.* 1963: 268). Noteworthy, even brilliant beginnings were made, but they
were to mature later or elsewhere. In 1926, Alberto Cavalcanti made *Rien
que les heures*, the first of the city symphonies. In 1929, Georges Rouquier
made *Vendanges*, forerunner of *Farrebique* (1946) and his other films of
peasant life. An obscure film, *Coulibaly à l'aventure* (1936), made by G.

H. Blanchon in French West Africa, preceded Rouch's *Jaguar* by twenty years, both in theme (migrant labor) and treatment (improvised acting). Documentary techniques found their way into fiction films, such as Jean Renoir's *Toni* (1934).

In Spain, Luis Buñuel used money won in a syndicalist lottery to produce that succinct masterpiece of dreamy outrage, *Las Hurdes* (1932). The stuff of Buñuel's argument is not only the misery of the inhabitants of Cáceres, but also our curiosity, never innocent, because human.

No such dark scruples are to be found in British and American documentaries, which were meliorist in tone and popular in scope.[6] A film of North Sea herring fisheries, John Grierson's *Drifters* (1929), was the beginning of the British documentary movement, which had as its purpose the formation of a more aware citizenry by means of the "creative treatment of actuality" (Hardy 1966). Production was supported by government and industry, and dealt with the broad topics of Empire capitalism, domestic social reform, and (with the coming of war) colonial propaganda. Rotha (1936) describes two stages of British documentary: the first, "impressionistic" stage peaked with Basil Wright's exquisite *Song of Ceylon* (made for the Ceylon Tea Propagation Board in 1935), with its symphonic structure and Eisensteinian views of Sinhalese working the fields. The second, or "realist," stage quietly anticipated the social reporting of the 1960's, by making use of spontaneous, unrehearsed speech, filmed with synchronous sound. In *Housing Problems* (produced for the British Commercial Gas Association in 1935), Edgar Anstey and Arthur Elton took camera and microphone into the working-class districts of South London. The residents pointed out the vermin and other signs of dilapidation "without prompting" (Rotha 1936: 255). In this way the film not only gained credibility but disarmed potential criticism of the makers' motives: "When the subjects raised more obvious social issues, facts and people were made to speak for themselves" (Broderick 1947: 50). To Rotha's stages must be added a third, beginning with the formation, in 1939, of the National Film Board of Canada, under Grierson, and the Colonial Film Unit (CFU), directed by William Sellers. Both were propaganda organizations, concerned with the war effort, Grierson from a stance inside European culture, Sellers from the outside. The CFU, for example, made a film designed to present the British way of life to Africans, *Mister English at Home* (1940). In the decade after the war,

---

[6] Until McCann (1973), the British movement was the better documented, thanks to John Grierson and his editor, Forsyth Hardy. Grierson's writings, when collated with an account of Britain's domestic situation between the wars, constitute a primer on the politics of film.

Sellers and his group were instrumental in developing television in Anglophone Africa.

Whatever the ideological angle of filmmakers in the 1920's and 1930's, their films share a new quality: for the first time since the Lumières, ordinary people in their everyday surroundings were seen on the screen. At the same time, the mass medium of cinema was becoming demystified through technology. Amateur filming in 16-mm was no longer an oddity. Armed with the ciné-Kodak, Major P. H. G. Powell-Cotton and his family filmed systematically in Africa during the 1930's and 1940's. In a single year, 1937–1938, the impresario, Rolf de Maré, collected an estimated 49,000 feet of 16-mm film of dance, in Sumatra, Java, Bali, and the Celebes. Film, the toy of scientists and the instrument of fantasists, was coming of age.

In anthropology, the middle of the 1930's was the watershed between film's unimportance and its acceptability. To W. D. Hambly, Melville Herskovits, Patrick O'Reilly, and Marcel Griaule, film was an illustration, not an integral part of research to be used in understanding and cited in publication. Quality, in this kind of filming, still meant 35-mm and, if possible, a trained cameraman. (But Norman Tindale, in Australia, and Franz Boas, in British Columbia, took their own 16-mm films.) By contrast, Gregory Bateson and Margaret Mead's decision to use cameras in Bali and New Guinea, in 1936–1938, was dictated by the needs of their research. They innovated both in the scale of their filming and photography (22,000 feet of 16-mm film, 25,000 stills) and in its aim, the description of the "ethos" of a people.

The shift in scale was directed primarily at recording the types of non-verbal behavior for which there existed neither vocabulary nor conceptualized methods of observation, in which the observation had to precede the codification (Mead 1963:174).

Harris states that Mead turned to photography as a direct result of criticism of her previous works, challenged over their "soft" unverifiable data (Harris 1968:417). Mead's own account of the events leading to the "quantum leap" of research in Bali and Iatmul emphasizes personal and intellectual factors (Mead 1972). Whatever its causes, the effect of methodological originality in *Balinese Character* was to make photography a respected tool in anthropological research (Bateson and Mead 1942).

The expedition to Bali was financed by the Committee for the Study of Dementia Praecox, who recognized an opportunity to cast some light upon the etiology of schizophrenia. The anthropologists brought complementary abilities to the project: Mead's unsurpassed note-taking skill and her interest in babies and family life, Bateson's grounding in natural science (he had been a student of Haddon, another former zoologist) and interest in communication and context. His was the task of taking pictures, while Mead and a Balinese secretary, equipped with chronometers, recorded events verbally, and carefully cross-referenced the pictures and notes. They were without means of recording sound.

We tried to use the still and the moving picture cameras to get a record of Balinese behavior, and this is a very different matter from the preparation of a "documentary" film or photographs. We tried to shoot what happened normally and spontaneously, rather than to decide upon the norms and then get the Balinese to go through these behaviors in suitable lighting (Bateson and Mead 1942:49).

For the greater part of their two years' stay, Mead and Bateson lived in the mountains at Bajoeng Gede, where "everything went on in a kind of simplified slow motion," owing to the poverty and hypothyroidism of the villagers. Bateson took pictures "as a matter of routine," without asking special permission. Habitually he directed attention to his photography of small babies, and the parents came to overlook the fact that they were included in the frame as well, so that the angular viewfinder, for photographing sensitive subjects, was seldom needed or used. Some theatrical performances were specially staged in daylight, as a concession to the camera. As the corpus of photographed data grew, it "was used consciously to compensate for the changing sophistication of the viewer" (Mead 1963:174), by comparing photographs taken before a hypothesis was formulated with those made afterwards.

On their way home from the field, Bateson and Mead spent six months in New Guinea, collecting comparative data among the Iatmul. Then World War II made fieldwork impossible, and other urgent research priorities demanded attention. Despite these, Bateson and Mead prepared *Balinese Character* and edited several films, which were released, after the war, in the Character Formation in Different Cultures Series (1952). In discussions of film, Mead often fails to distinguish it from still photography, a usage which reflects her method in dealing with both (Mead 1963). After viewing the 25,000 stills sequentially, Bateson and Mead chose and arranged 759 of them in 100 plates, thematically juxtaposing related details without "violating the context and the integrity of any one event" (Mead 1972:235). The films were edited chronologically (*Trance and Dance in Bali*) or by presenting contrasting items of behavior (*Childhood Rivalry in Bali and New Guinea*) (cf. Plate 9).

While Bateson and Mead were in Bali, Jean Rouch was in Paris, studying engineering and forming the associations which would lead to his be-

coming a leader of the ethnographic film wave in Europe, and an indefatigable producer and popularizer. At the Musée de l'Homme, Rouch heard
the lectures of Marcel Mauss and Marcel Griaule. He encountered Henri
Langlois, now the director of the Cinémathèque française. His decision
to study anthropology seriously was made during the war, which he spent
in French West Africa supervising the construction of roads and bridges.
"Culture conflict struck me from the start," he said (Desanti and Decock
1968:37). Rouch was not among those chosen, in 1946, for the Ogooué-
Congo Expedition, a well-equipped (in 35-mm) group of explorer-film-
makers (Francis Mazières, Edmond Séchan, and Pierre Gaisseau) and
anthropologists (Raoul Hartweg, Guy de Beauchêne, and Gilbert Rouget).
Instead he floated down the Niger with two friends, making films by trial
and error with a 16-mm Bell and Howell from the flea market. The tripod
soon fell overboard, and necessity nudged Rouch toward an original
shooting style (Rouch 1955). In order to film a hippopotamus hunt on the
river, he enlisted the help of Damouré Zika, a Sorko who was to collab-
orate with Rouch in research and filming (*Les maîtres fous*, 1953), as did
Oumarou Ganda (star of *Moi, un noir*, 1957; director of *Le wazou poly-
game*, 1971) at a later date. Rouch's career has been described as one of
"inveterate amateurism" and "incurable dilettantism" (Marcorelles
1963: 18). Rouch is, in fact, the first full-time ethnographic film professional (Plate 4).

The only film that Rouch had to show for those months on the Niger
was sufficiently well done to be bought by Actualités Françaises, blown up
to 35-mm, embellished with narration and shown as *Au pays des mages
noirs*, on the same bill as Rossellini's *Stromboli*. There was a grander
sequel in 1955, when a number of Rouch's short films in color were enlarged, combined, and released as a feature, *Les fils de l'eau*. This was
rapturously reviewed in *Cahiers du cinéma* by Claude Beylie, who compared Dogon cosmogony to the philosophy of Thales, Empedocles, and
Timaeus, and asserted: "WE are the monsters" (Beylie 1959). Rouch by
this time was Executive Secretary of the International Committee on
Ethnographic Films (CIFE), which had been formed in 1952 at the International Congress of Anthropological and Ethnological Sciences at
Vienna, to further preservation, production and distribution. The French
section of this organization prepared analyses and critiques of 106 films,
and in 1955 UNESCO published this catalogue as part of its series on
Mass Communication. Thus, under Rouch's care, the genre of ethnographic film acquired scientific and political as well as artistic stature in
the postwar decade.

Others besides Rouch were active in this transformation (or, as Rouch called it, "renaissance"), and there were other conceptions besides that of CIFE as to what an ethnographic film should be. In Germany, the Institut für den Wissenschaftlichen Film was reorganized immediately after the war, and soon German anthropologists were again filming in Melanesia, Africa and Europe. The Institute's approach to anthropological film was characterized by emphasis on scientific purity (Spannaus 1961:73–79). Subjects and treatments that might have ideological significance were to be avoided, along with the tendency to admit laymen to the field. The Institute conducted intensive courses in film technique for anthropologists preparing to do fieldwork, and supplied equipment for expeditions supported by the Deutsche Forschungsgemeinschaft, provided the applicants had taken the course. On the basis of this program, the Institute published its "Rules for film documentation in ethnology and folklore" in 1959. These require that filmmaking be done by persons with sound anthropological training or supervision, and that an exact log be kept; that the events recorded be authentic (technical processes can be staged for the camera, but not ceremonies), filmed without dramatic camera angles or movement, and edited for representativeness.

In 1952, the Institute's director, Gotthard Wolf, was the first to implement what had repeatedly been proposed, by establishing at Göttingen the first systematic anthropological film archive. Films meeting the Institute's scientific criteria were first solicited from anthropologists in Germany and then, with growing success, from abroad. At the start, Konrad Lorenz worked on assembling and arranging the *Encyclopaedia cinematographica* and others have added several thousand films on anthropological and biological subjects. To facilitate comparative research, each film consists of a single "thematic unit," such as dance, work, or ritual, and the films are arranged in natural science categories, biological subjects by phylum, genus, and species, ethnological ones by geographical location and social grouping, e.g.:

SOUTH AMERICA
BRAZIL

  E75 Tukurina (Brazil, Upper Purus River) — Curing the sick by
  medicine men. 1950 (Color, $2^{1}/_{2}$ minutes) H. Schultz, São Paulo.

This natural science treatment of ethnographic film contrasts with and complements CIFES' social science orientation. (The Committee added the "*Sociologique*" to its name in 1959.) Several countries have institutional affiliations with both CIFES and the *Encyclopaedia cinematographica;* CIFES has been less active than its counterpart, however, in making films routinely available to scholars. Wolf's efforts in this regard have been major and prescient. Since 1966, an American archive of the

Encyclopaedia cinematographica has been housed at Pennsylvania State University; and in 1970, a Japanese archive was established at Tokyo.

As ethnographic film became institutionalized, it quickly accumulated a literature. Definitions and typologies of ethnographic film were devised. Griaule sustained Regnault's conception of ethnographic filming as a scientific activity concerned with traditional ethnographic subjects. He distinguished three film types: archive footage for research, training films for anthropology courses, and public education films (including, occasionally, "works of art") (Griaule 1957). (Although Griaule was hardly a film enthusiast, he became in death the subject of a "public education" film — of his own Dogon funeral.) André Leroi-Gourhan expressed a more original view of things in an article, "Le film ethnologique existe-t-il?", in which he applied the term "ethnological" to another tripartite classification: the research film, the "exotic" travel film (to be abhorred as superficial and exploitative), and the "film of environment... produced with no scientific aim but deriving an ethnological value from its exportation" (Leroi-Gourhan 1948). These contrasting typologies of ethnographic film, one exclusive in tendency and the other inclusive, survive to this day. Griaule's view has been echoed by many who differ among themselves chiefly as to the degree of prophylaxis necessary against the "contamination" of the commercial cinema. On the other hand, it has been pointed out by Sol Worth that definitions of ethnographic film are tautological, since no film can be called ethnographic in and of itself (Worth 1969). Much depends upon the uses to which a film is put, regardless of the intentions of its author. A single film can be used in a variety of ways. It's a simple matter, when film represents the confrontation between "us" and "them" (Europeans and natives; scientists and laymen), for the filmmaker and the viewer to negotiate the conventions. But especially since World War II (though even long before it), neither "we" nor "they" have ceased to change.

The "steady inertia" *vis-à-vis* new technical devices in anthropology, of which Rowe complained in 1952, has since been supplanted by steadily accelerating activity, heightened, in recent years, by the availability to anthropologists of videotape. We are now waiting for videotape storage of data, in a central location servicing far-flung terminals, to be implemented (Ekman *et al.* 1969). But the existence of technology has never been a sufficient condition of scientific advance.

Although Kuhn (1962) has questioned the existence of paradigms in the social sciences, a fair degree of consensus exists as to what constitutes normal anthropological research using film. The state of the field a decade ago can be glimpsed in Michaelis (1955), Spannaus (1961), and Mead

(1963); today's situation is exposed in the papers in this volume, and, often more revealing, in their overlapping bibliographies. New uses of film, and refinements of old ones, are constantly occurring. Semiotic analysis and evocative techniques have joined the following long-established uses of film by anthropologists: as a note-taking tool for events which are too complex, too rapid, or too small to be grasped with the naked eye or recorded in writing; as a means of salvaging data for future generations of researchers, either because the behavior is about to disappear, or because the theoretical equipment to deal with it does not yet exist; and for comparisons. These may be either synchronic (cross-cultural, emic-etic, macro-micro) or diachronic (individual maturation or cultural change).

The use of film to elicit responses, which occurred in psychological research as early as 1909, became fairly common in psychiatry during World War II (Moreno 1944; Saul 1945; Prados 1951), and was adapted to sociological research by Rouch and Morin in the early 1960's. (In 1925, Mead used still photos taken during the filming of *Moana* to elicit responses from Samoan children.) Rouch not only recorded his actors' comments and exclamations at seeing themselves on the screen (in *Jaguar*), but also used the presence of cameras and cameramen to provoke psychodramas in *La pyramide humaine* (1959) and *La punition* (1962). Worth and Adair carried the process still further in 1966, when they experimented with eliciting films AS RESPONSES. They undertook to teach a group of Navaho men and women to make their own motion pictures, on any subject they wanted, in order to elicit a "visual flow" that could be analyzed semiotically, i.e. "in terms of the structure of images and the cognitive processes or rules used in making those images."

A working hypothesis for our study was that motion picture film, conceived, photographed, and sequentially arranged by a people such as the Navajo, would reveal aspects of coding, cognition, and values that may be inhibited, not observable, or not analyzable when the investigation is totally dependent on verbal exchange – especially when such research must be done in the language of the investigator (Worth and Adair 1972:27–28).

The Navaho filmmakers learned to use 16-mm Bell and Howell cameras with amazing rapidity, and within two months produced short exercises and seven silent films. These were shown to the Navaho community, analyzed by the researchers (who compared them with films made by Philadelphia teenagers), and eventually placed in distribution, where they have acquired a renown in experimental film circles.

The use of videotape as an experimental agent in urban anthropology, by George Stoney, the Rundstroms, the Videograph project and others, has added synchronous sound (namely, speech) to the resources available to informants for their productions.

Reinterpretation of "ethnographic film" as a process of communication between filmers and filmed is among chief developments in this kind of filming since the war. The Balinese experience has never been replicated, but it served to open up the whole communication field, which has been so fertile that only a few of its works can be mentioned in this short account. When war and cold war destroyed some cultures outright and made others inaccessible, Columbia University's Research in Contemporary Cultures Project, directed by Ruth Benedict, gathered together a team from various disciplines to study cultures "at a distance," by means of interviews, films (preferably Grade B films, less idiosyncratic), literature, art, and other types of material. During the war, Bateson worked at the Museum of Modern Art on an analysis of the UFA film, *Hitlerjunge Quex* (1933), in order to derive some of the "psychological implications of Nazism." Martha Wolfenstein went on to apply the principles of thematic analysis to the content of films made in Western nations (England, France, Italy, and the United States), and discovered national patterns in fantasy. These studies gave rise to others dealing with personal and formal levels of filmic communication, exemplified in the *"politique des auteurs"* expounded in *Cahiers du cinéma* from 1950, and the anthropology and semiology of the cinema (Powdermaker 1950; Morin 1956; Metz 1974; cf. Weakland's paper, *infra*).

One would assume that the study of nonverbal communication would demand the use of film, and the members of the American linguistic school have used not only film but also videotape in their research. But Ray L. Birdwhistell, who adapted the methods of descriptive linguistics to the study of culture, at first used film less to study communication than to communicate about it; he mapped the kinesics of American English by eye, using a written notation system (Birdwhistell 1952). Other researchers in choreometrics have from the start depended upon rater consensus and successive refinements of parameters discovered by repeated inspection of a large sample of dance films. The musician and folklorist, Alan Lomax, has since 1961 directed a cross-cultural study of expressive style, of global proportions, involving song, dance, and speech; his Choreometrics Project, which is concerned with movement style, has collected for analysis films of dance and work from nearly two hundred cultures. Most of the footage analyzed by Lomax and his collaborators was filmed by others, both scientists and laymen, for a variety of reasons. Each extract found to be acceptable for research was coded, using a descriptive system based on the Laban Effort-Shape theory. The ratings thus obtained were computerized for multifactor analysis, into summaries identifying the most "potent classifiers" of cultural style. The aim of Lomax's research is the development of an evolutionary taxonomy of culture (Lomax 1968; Lomax, Bartenieff, and Paulay 1969; Lomax and Berkowitz 1972). In applied terms, it is also the renewal and revitalization of cultures, threatened by mass media "greyout," which spring to life again when confronted with self-expression (Lomax 1973; cf. his paper, *infra*).

The method of the research film can be summarized by the statement that the ratio of analysis to observation is high at this end of a continuum which extends, at the other extreme, to the purest, most uninterpretable aesthetic experiences. Research film technique is expected to behave with a modesty befitting the handmaid of the mind. Where research use of film involves production, the technology is in general that which can be mastered by a nonprofessional cameraman. Film costs in research budgets are modest compared with documentary or theatrical production, and the proportion of usable footage is greater. Videotape, in use since the late 1960's, offers advantages of easy handling, immediacy, and economy (the tape is reusable; cf. Hockings' paper, *infra*). If an image of high quality is required, conventional filming is called for. At present, this means shooting 16-mm with or without the recording of synchronous sound on quarter-inch tape. It's possible, though unusual, for a single person to be a complete film crew, by using, for example, a zoom-equipped Beaulieu connected to a Nagra (Polunin 1970).

In the course of research into ecology, epidemiology, and child development in New Guinea and elsewhere, E. Richard Sorenson has developed a conception of the "research cinema film" which is, together with the *Encyclopaedia cinematographica*, a leading attempt at rationalization of ethnographic film archives. Such systematization is essential if future research involving film is to be carried out efficiently — or at all (Sorenson and Gajdusek 1966; Sorenson 1967; cf. his paper, *infra*).

The uses of ethnographic film in education range from scholarly communication, such as Birdwhistell's *Lecture on Kinesics* (1964), to elementary-school social studies, for which the multi-media *Man, a Course of Study: the Netsilik Eskimos* was designed. Since World War II, the social sciences have received an increasing share of academic importance, and markets for textbooks and educational films have grown enormous. Until the mid-1960's, the bread-and-butter of ethnographic film in education was the descriptive documentary, used as an adjunct to lectures and "relevant readings" in college courses on ethnology. The best of these filmed ethnographies are very good indeed: Robert and Monique Gessain's *Obashior endaon* (1964) and William Geddes' *Miao Year* (1968) spring immediately to mind. Both films were by-products of the fieldwork of their authors.

The most spectacular and influential of all visual ethnographies is John Marshall's record of the Bushmen, filmed on several expeditions to the Kalahari desert in the 1950's and still being edited. After collaborating with Robert Gardner to produce *The Hunters* (1958), Marshall photographed the celebrated *Titicut Follies* (directed by Fred Wiseman), and filmed the activities of the Pittsburgh police for the Lemberg Center for the Study of Violence. Concurrently, he was developing a theory of reportage and pedagogy as he structured the Bushman material (over 500,000 feet in all) into short sequences. He became dissatisfied with *The Hunters*: it had not been filmed with synchronous sound, and its synthetic story depends heavily on narration; furthermore, it gives undue importance to hunting in Bushman subsistence, which is in fact more dependent upon gathering. *Men Bathing*, *A Joking Relationship*, and *An Argument about a Marriage* concentrate, instead, on the details of interpersonal interaction during a short time span; the dialogue was hand-synched and translated by means of subtitles. These film episodes were shown in the introductory anthropology course at Harvard to illustrate concepts such as avoidance and reciprocity. The police series (*Three Domestics, Investigation of a Hit and Run*, etc.) was filmed in long uninterrupted shots with synchronous sound, representing virtuoso camera performances under difficult conditions for which Marshall's work in the Bridgewater State Hospital had prepared him. They have been used for police training and in law school and junior high school discussions. With Timothy Asch, Marshall in 1968 formed the Center for Documentary Anthropology, where Asch and Napoleon Chagnon, using the "sequence concept" which they had developed, are collaborating on a series of more than forty films of the Yąnomamö (*The Feast, Magical Death*, and others). The films are being subjected to curriculum experimentation during the editing process.

Instruction in ethnographic filming, initiated by Mead at Columbia in the 1940's has of late become extremely popular with undergraduates, many of whom have used home movie cameras since childhood. Rouch and Gardner have trained individually a number of filmmakers. In Rouch's words, only "one in a hundred" turns out to have the capacity for combining scientific rigor with cinema fluency. How can this capacity be developed? A "how-to" literature exists (Dyhrenfurth 1952; Collier 1967; sections in *Research Film* and the *Program in Ethnographic Film Newsletter*). Gatherings such as the International Film Seminars (from 1955), the Festival dei Popoli (from 1959), the Conferences on Visual Anthropology organized by Jay Ruby (from 1968), Venezia Genti (1971–

1972), several UNESCO round tables, and the UCLA colloquium (1968), provide opportunities to learn from new films. University programs are effective in teaching film strategies, but much work remains to be done on the theoretical underpinning of ethnographic film, beginning with the problem of reconciling often rivalrous systems of science and art. Too many social scientists still feel uncomfortable about following the advice of Luc de Heusch, the anthropologist-filmmaker:

Ethnographers should make themselves familiar with contemporary film theories and abandon the notion that the camera purely and simply shows reality (de Heusch 1962:25).

Finally, accessible film collections (such as the Museum of Modern Art's and the Royal Anthropological Institute's) are essential if students are to profit fully from accumulated experience.

Unlike the specialized uses of film in research, where conclusions are expressed verbally, and unlike the uses of film in education, where effectiveness is dependent upon context, the use of ethnographic film as public information depends upon the presence, in self-contained form, of visual attractiveness and intellectual substance — a most demanding format. But this use, by making it possible for many to view the richness of human resources, makes it slightly more possible that we will preserve and encourage them in the years to come (cf. Sorenson's paper, *infra*).

The personal film statement on a universal theme is a durable public information format. Robert Gardner, whose film *Dead Birds* (1963) was praised by *Variety* and Robert Lowell, first expressed his theory of film while he was engaged in producing *The Hunters* at the Film Study Center at Harvard. Gardner's cinematography is conservative (he filmed *Dead Birds* using a battery-driven Arriflex, without synchronous sound), and much of the expressive power of his films is produced by editing of images and by the commentary. Gardner's binnacle has been his own sensibility, applied to universal themes such as the relationship of men and women, and death.

I saw the Dani people, feathered and fluttering men and women, as enjoying the fate of all men and women. They dressed their lives with plumage, but faced as certain death as the rest of us drabber souls. The film attempts to say something about how we all, as humans, meet our animal fate (Gardner 1972:35).

Other nonintrusive sensibilities have produced anthropological documentaries with forms recognizable by those steeped in European tradition, hence readily accepted by lay audiences. Jorge Preloran's *Imaginero/Hermógenes Cayo* (1970) and *Araucanians of Ruca Choroy* (1971) employ a biographical model. Of Cayo, Preloran remarked, "I was not interested in the details of his situation, but rather in the image of his soul" (Suber 1971:48). Although the audience for these films may feel that "its humanity is confirmed" (in Gardner's words) by viewing them, the films can also be employed to reaffirm and reinforce European cultural hegemony (cf. Preloran's paper, *infra*).

A film which caused a scandal when shown to African students in Paris marked Rouch's turning from conventional documentary to what he and Edgar Morin, resurrecting Vertov's title, were to call *cinéma vérité*. ("Vertov and Flaherty are my masters," Rouch declared in 1963). While studying Songhay religion in Accra in 1953, Rouch was invited by the priests of the Hauka sect to document sequences of a possession cult. The result was *Les maîtres fous*, a short film showing Hauka adepts, possessed by spirits of generals, doctors, and truck drivers from the British power structure, as they slaughter a dog, cook and eat it, march back and forth, dance violently and foam at the mouth. By including shots of the Hauka going about their menial daily work in the city, Rouch implies that the cult helps its members to cope with the strains of everyday life, particularly in the colonial situation (cf. Muller 1971:1473). The film is not fully comprehensible without Rouch's written treatise on the subject (Rouch 1960); nonetheless it excited such strong reactions that both Europeans and Africans urged him to destroy it. He demurred, and *Les maîtres fous* went on to win a prize at Venice. However, after this experience Rouch began the "cinema of collective improvisation" with *Jaguar*, his "ethnographic science fiction" collaboration with Damouré, Lam, and Illo playing three young migrant workers in search of fortune on the Ghana coast. By the time the film was completed, Rouch sensed that the period of freedom of movement between the newly independent West African nations was over, and that the experience could never be duplicated. In a sense, what Rouch and Morin accomplished in 1960 with *Chronique d'un été* was a condensation of the *Jaguar* process: instead of planning a dramatic improvisation before shooting, and recording the dialogue and comments of the actors afterward, the characters in *Chronique d'un été* were instantly created, with the help of the prototype Éclair camera, the Nagra recorder, and the question "Are you happy?"

Well might one ask such a question. While *Chronique d'un été* was being filmed in Paris, France was undergoing the painful disengagement from Algeria. Much has been made of the new portable synchronous sound filming rig (Plate 8), which enabled cameraman Michel Brault to follow the subject for ten minutes or more without stopping the camera, as if this hardware in itself had caused *cinéma vérité* to happen; but the motivations of the filmmakers are at least as important in its history. In addition to the leftist political message of much of *cinéma vérité*, the films of Rouch, Ruspoli, and Marker demanded renegotiation of the existing conventions governing the roles of filmmaker, subject, and audience: the filmmaker appeared to become a transmitter of "truth," the subject would henceforth be judged by his own words and actions, and a heavy burden of interpretation was now placed on the viewer. It is no coincidence that the other home of *cinéma vérité* — the place, in fact, where it all began, according to one critic, with Brault's photography of *Les raquet-teurs* (1958) (Madsen 1967) — was Québec, where cultural and political differences are still a problem. In the 1960's the superpowers, after more than a decade of colonial crisis, were redefining their stance *vis-à-vis* the minorities. Culture contact was implicit in *cinéma vérité*; and the function of *cinéma vérité* was politicization.

This use of film encountered opposition, and long before it arrived in Hollywood, *cinéma vérité* had gone on the defensive. Financing was hard to come by (Marcorelles 1963). Rouch has known the discomfort of being ridiculed by Europeans and shut out by Africans. The "new kind of journalism" which Richard Leacock and his colleague D. A. Pennebaker developed for television in 1960 was resisted by critics (Bluem 1965) and sponsors. *Cuba si! Yanki no!* was withdrawn from circulation in 1961, and *Happy Mother's Day*, a report of the commercial pressures to which the parents of quintuplets were subjected, was broadcast by ABC television in an altered version (cf. Young's paper, *infra*).

Even traditional ethnography has had a hard time getting on television in an intellectually reputable form. Thanks to an unusual decision of the head of programming at CBS television, the Netsilik became known to millions who saw *Fight for Life!*, a specially edited presentation of the material embellished with narration and background music. In television the Europeans and Japanese seem to be far in advance of the United States.

One of the major changes in motion pictures since World War II has been decentralization of production, as professional equipment became available on an unprecedented scale. Georges Sadoul's *Histoire du cinéma mondial* gives an account of the development of national cinemas. When Sadoul laid down his pen in 1966, after writing, "in fifty countries, the nation and its people became, in all their diversity, the material for ever more numerous films," only Africa remained without a cinema. This is no longer the case. Senegal's Ousmane Sembene, known to American audiences for *Mandabi*, *Tauw*, and *Emitai*, is one of a growing number of artists who are gaining fluency in all film genres (Hennebelle 1972). The effect of African production has not yet been felt outside, and until it is, returnees from the festivals at Tunis and Ouagadougou can only try to describe what Europe and the United States are missing — what Rouch has labelled with justice "spiritual assistance for the overdeveloped countries" (Desanti and Decock 1968).

Film is such a rich trove of data that its usefulness depends upon a happy choice of level of analysis. The retrospective significance of a film often differs from the prospective significance intended by its maker. Films can be put to more than one use and should thus be preserved with written records. The most striking change in ethnographic film since its beginnings, and especially since World War II, has been the shift in the orientation of the camera, which no longer looks out at the world, but rather inside one's world. In Mali, Cisse has made *Cinq jours d'une vie*, a film of boys growing up, learning the Koran, migrating to the city, and returning to the village. In the United States and elsewhere, filmmakers are hard at work filming cultural enclaves, family life, and even their own biographies; autobiography, veiled in Flaherty's *Louisiana Story*, is now explicit. Recently some scholars in the field of semiotics have rediscovered Eisenstein's fascination with Freud and Malinowski, and his interest in myth which he planned to express in *Que viva México!* A flowering of ethnographic films fulfilling Eisenstein's promise would indeed be as important as drama or the novel have been in the past in helping people understand themselves. The history of ethnographic film is rich in examples of film's unique capacity to record the multileveled nature of events, of its usefulness in teaching new ways of seeing, and of its power to evoke deeply positive feelings about mankind by communicating the essence of a people.

REFERENCES

ANDERSON, JOSEPH L.
   1968   "The development of the single-concept film in a context of a general history of educational motion pictures and innovation in instructional media." Unpublished master's thesis, Ohio State University.
BALIKCI, ASEN, QUENTIN BROWN
   1966   Ethnographic filming and the Netsilik Eskimos. *Educational Services Incorporated Quarterly Report* (Spring-Summer): 19-33.
BATESON, GREGORY
   1943   "An analysis of the film *Hitlerjunge Quex* (1933)." New York: Museum of Modern Art Film Library, and Institute for Intercultural Studies (typescript).
BATESON, GREGORY, MARGARET MEAD
   1942   *Balinese character: a photographic analysis.* New York Academy of Sciences, Special Publications 2.

BEYLIE, CLAUDE
 1959   Review of Rouch: *Les fils de l'eau. Cahiers du Cinéma* 91:66-67.
BIDNEY, DAVID
 1964   Paul Fejos 1897-1963. *American Anthropologist* 66:110-115.
BIRDWHISTELL, RAY L.
 1952   *Introduction to kinesics.* Louisville: University of Louisville Press.
BLUEM, A. WILLIAM
 1965   *Documentary in American television.* New York: Hastings.
BRODERICK, A.
 1947   *The factual film: a survey sponsored by the Dartington Hall Trustees.*
        London: Oxford University Press.
COLLIER, JOHN, JR.
 1967   *Visual anthropology: photography as a research method.* New York:
        Holt, Rinehart and Winston.
COMITÉ DU FILM ETHNOGRAPHIQUE
 1955   *Catalogue of French ethnographical films.* Reports and Papers on Mass
        Communication 15. Paris: UNESCO.
COMITÉ INTERNATIONAL DU FILM ETHNOGRAPHIQUE ET SOCIOLOGIQUE
 1967   *Premier catalogue sélectif international de films ethnographiques sur
        l'Afrique noire.* Paris: UNESCO.
 1970   *Premier catalogue sélectif international de films ethnographiques sur
        la région du Pacifique.* Paris: UNESCO.
DEBETS, G. F.
 1957   Forty years of Soviet anthropology. Washington: National Science
        Foundation / Smithsonian Institution. (Originally Sorok let sovetskoi
        antropologii. *Sovetskaya Antropologia* 1:7-30.)
DE BRIGARD, EMILIE
 i.p.   *Anthropological cinema.* New York: Museum of Modern Art.
DE HEUSCH, LUC
 1962   *The cinema and social science: a survey of ethnographic and sociological
        films.* Reports and Papers in the Social Sciences 16. Paris: UNESCO.
DESANTI, DOMINIQUE, JEAN DECOCK
 1968   Cinéma et ethnographie. *Arts d'Afrique* 1:37-39, 76-80.
DODDS, JOHN W.
 1973   *The several lives of Paul Fejos.* New York: Wenner-Gren Foundation.
DONALDSON, LEONARD
 1912   *The cinematograph and natural science.* London: Ganes.
DYHRENFURTH, NORMAN G.
 1952   Film making for scientific field workers. *American Anthropologist*
        54:147-152.
EKMAN, PAUL, W. FRIESEN, T. TAUSSIG
 1969   "VID-R and SCAN: tools and methods for the automated analysis
        of visual records," in *Content analysis.* Edited by G. Gerbner *et al.*
        New York: Wiley and Sons.
FLAHERTY, DAVID
 1925   Serpents in Eden. *Asia* 25: 858-869, 895-898.
FLAHERTY, FRANCES HUBBARD
 1925a Setting up house and shop in Samoa. *Asia* 25: 638-651, 709-711.
 1925b Behind the scenes with our Samoan stars. *Asia* 25: 746-753, 795-796.

1925c   A search for animal and sea sequences. *Asia* 25: 954-963, 1000-1004.
1925d   Fa'a-Samoa. *Asia* 25: 1084-1090, 1096-1100.

GARDNER, ROBERT G.
1957   Anthropology and film. *Daedalus* 86:344–350.
1972   "On the making of *Dead Birds,*" in *The Dani of West Irian.* Edited by Karl G. Heider. Andover, Mass.: Warner Modular Publications 2.

GRIAULE, MARCEL
1957   *Méthode de l'ethnographie.* Paris: Presses Universitaires de France.

HARDY, FORSYTH
1966   *Grierson on documentary* (second edition). Berkeley: University of California Press. (Originally published 1947.)

HARRIS, MARVIN
1968   *The rise of anthropological theory.* New York: Crowell.

HEIDER, KARL G.
1972   *Films for anthropological teaching* (fifth edition). Washington: American Anthropological Association.

HENNEBELLE, GUY
1972   *Les cinémas africains en 1972.* L'Afrique Littéraire et Artistique 20. Paris and Dakar: Société Africaine d'Édition.

HILTON-SIMPSON, M. W., J. A. HAESELER
1925   Cinema and ethnology. *Discovery* 6:325–330.

INTERNATIONAL SCIENTIFIC FILM ASSOCIATION
1959   Rules for documentation in ethnology and folklore through the film. *Research Film* 3:238–240.

KRACAUER, SIEGFRIED
1947   *From Caligari to Hitler: a psychological history of the German film.* Princeton: Princeton University Press.

KRUPIANSKAYA, V., L. POTAPOV, L. TERENTIEVA
1960   "Essential problems in the ethnographic study of peoples of the USSR." Paper presented at the Sixth International Congress of Anthropological and Ethnological Sciences, Paris.

KUHN, THOMAS S.
1962   *The structure of scientific revolutions.* Chicago: University of Chicago Press.

LAJARD, J., FÉLIX REGNAULT
1895   Poterie crue et origine du tour. *Bulletin de la Société d'Anthropologie de Paris* 6:734–739.

LEPROHON, PIERRE
1960   *Chasseurs d'images.* Paris: Éditions André Bonne.

LEROI-GOURHAN, ANDRÉ
1948   Cinéma et sciences humaines – le film ethnologique existe-t-il? *Revue de Géographie Humaine et d'Ethnologie* 3:42–51.

LEYDA, JAY
1960   *Kino.* New York: Macmillan.

LOMAX, ALAN
1968   *Folk song style and culture: a staff report on cantometrics.* Washington: American Association for the Advancement of Science. Publication 88.
1973   Cinema, science, and culture renewal. *Current Anthropology* 14: 474–480.

LOMAX, ALAN, IRMGARD BARTENIEFF, FORRESTINE PAULAY
1969   Choreometrics: a method for the study of cross-cultural pattern in film. *Research Film/Le Film de Recherche/Forschungsfilm* 6:505–517.

LOMAX, ALAN, NORMAN BERKOWITZ
1972   The evolutionary taxonomy of culture. *Science* 177:228–239.

MCCANN, RICHARD DYER
1973   *The people's films.* New York: Hastings House.

MADSEN, AXEL
1967   Pour la suite du Canada. *Sight and Sound* 36 (2):68–69.

MARCORELLES, LOUIS
1963   *Une Esthétique du réel, le cinéma direct.* Paris: UNESCO.

MEAD, MARGARET
1963   "Anthropology and the camera," in *Encyclopedia of photography.* Edited by W. D. Morgan. New York: National Educational Alliance.
1972   *Blackberry winter: my earlier years.* New York: Morrow.

MEAD, MARGARET, RHODA MÉTRAUX
1953   *The study of culture at a distance.* Chicago: University of Chicago Press.

METZ, CHRISTIAN
1974   *Language and cinema.* The Hague: Mouton.

MICHAELIS, ANTHONY R.
1955   *Research films in biology, anthropology, psychology and medicine.* New York: Academic Press.

MORENO, J. L.
1944   Psychodrama and therapeutic motion pictures. *Sociometry* 7:230-244.

MORIN, EDGAR
1956   *Le cinéma ou l'homme imaginaire.* Paris: Les Editions de Minuit.

MULLER, JEAN CLAUDE
1971   Review of *Les maîtres fous. American Anthropologist* 73:1471–1473.

O'REILLY, PATRICK
1970   (orig. 1949). "Le 'documentaire' ethnographique en Océanie." In *Premier cataloque sélectif international de films ethnographiques sur la région du Pacifique.* Edited by Comité International du Film Ethnographique et Sociologique, pp. 281–305. Paris: UNESCO.

PÖCH, RUDOLF
1907   Reisen in Neu-Guinea in den Jahren 1904–1906. *Zeitschrift für Ethnologie* 39:382-400.

POLUNIN, IVAN
1970   Visual and sound recording apparatus. *Current Anthropology* 11:3-22.

POWDERMAKER, HORTENSE
1950   *Hollywood, the dream factory.* Boston: Little, Brown.

PRADOS, MIGUEL
1951   The use of films in psychotherapy. *American Journal of Orthopsychiatry* 21:36-46.

REGNAULT, FÉLIX-LOUIS
1896a   Les attitudes du repos dans les races humaines. *Revue Encyclopédique* 1896:9–12.

1896b La locomotion chez l'homme. *Cahiers de Recherche de l'Académie* 122:401; Archives de Physiologie, de Pathologie et de Génétique 8:381.
1897   Le grimper. *Revue Encyclopédique* 1897:904–905.
1912   Les musées des films. *Biologica* 2 (16) (Supplement 20).
1923a Films et musées d'ethnographie. *Comptes Rendus de l'Association Française pour l'Avancement des Sciences* 11:880–881.
1923b L'histoire du cinéma, son rôle en anthropologie. *Bulletins et Mémoires de la Société d'Anthropologie de Paris* 7-8: 61-65.
1931   Le rôle du cinéma en ethnographie. *La Nature* 59:304-306.

ROTHA, PAUL
1936   *Documentary film.* London: Faber and Faber.

ROTHA, PAUL, SINCLAIR ROAD, RICHARD GRIFFITH
1963   *Documentary film* (third edition). London: Faber and Faber.

ROUCH, JEAN
1953   Renaissance du film ethnographique. *Geographica Helvetica* 8:55.
1955   Cinéma d'exploration et ethnographie. *Connaissance du Monde* 1: 69–78.
1960   *Essai sur la religion songhay.* Paris: Presses Universitaires de France.

ROWE, JOHN HOWLAND
1953   "Technical aids in anthropology: a historical survey," in *Anthropology Today.* Edited by A. L. Kroeber, 895–940. Chicago: University of Chicago Press.

SADOUL, GEORGES
1964   *Louis Lumière.* Paris: Seghers.
1966   *Histoire du cinéma mondial des origines à nos jours* (eighth edition). Paris: Flammarion.

SAUL, LEON S., HOWARD ROME, EDWIN LEUSER
1945   Desensitization of combat fatigue patients. *American Journal of Psychiatry* 102:476–478.

SORENSON, E. RICHARD
1967   A research film program in the study of changing man. *Current Anthropology* 8:443-469.

SORENSON, E. RICHARD, D. CARLETON GASDUSEK
1966   The study of child behavior and development in primitive cultures. *Pediatrics* 37 (1), part 2, Supplement.

SPANNAUS, GUNTHER
1961   "Der wissenschaftliche Film als Forschungsmittel in der Völkerkunde," In *Der Film im Dienste der Wissenschaft,* 67–82. Göttingen: Institut für den Wissenschaftlichen Film.

SUBER, HOWARD
1971   Jorge Preloran. *Film Comment* 7 (1):43–51.

TAFT, ROBERT
1938   *Photography and the American scene: a social history, 1839–1889.* New York: Macmillan.

TAYLOR, JOHN RUSSELL
1964   *Cinema eye, cinema ear.* New York: Hill and Wang.

WOLF, GOTTHARD
1972   *Encyclopaedia Cinematographica 1972.* Göttingen: Institut für den Wissenschaftlichen Film.

WOLLEN, PETER
    1969   *Signs and meaning in the cinema.* London: Thames and Hudson.
WORTH, SOL
    1969   The development of a semiotic of film. *Semiotica* 1:282–321.
WORTH, SOL, JOHN ADAIR
    1972   *Through Navajo eyes: an exploration in film communication and anthropology.* Bloomington: Indiana University Press.

McCarty's Law and How to Break It

MARK McCARTY

There is good reason for us all to be concerned with the standards developing in the highly specialized (perhaps too highly specialized) field of
cinematic observation in which so few people are trained professionally.
Many of the more primitive cultures will be gone in a few years, and it
is to be hoped that a large portion of the film material on these disappearing cultures will be obtained (if anything at all is captured) by non-
professionals — reasonably accomplished 16-mm movie makers who,
whether by design or accident, find themselves in an important place at a
critical time, have the sense to realize this, and use their cameras in such a
way as to capture human behavior that would otherwise be forever lost.
There is much heart to be taken from the history of ethnographic film:
some of the earliest and most valuable material was shot by amateurs,
among them Sir Baldwin Spencer:

There was a native camp out in the scrub...containing some thirty or forty men
and women who had come in to perform a rain ceremony...this rain dance gave
us the opportunity of experimenting with the cinematograph. It was a Warwick
machine, and, if not actually the first, was amongst the earliest cinematographs
to be used in Australia. It was certainly the first used amongst the Aboriginals.
A diagram showed how to fix the film in the machine, so as to make it run round,
but no instructions had been sent out as to what rate to turn the handle, so I
had to make a guess at this. The focussing glass was, of necessity, small and you
could only get a sideways and not a direct view of it, but after a little practice
with a blank spool, I felt equal to the first attempt in real life. This was in 1901
(Dunlop 1967:3).

For all the technical crudities, Spencer's material is still important.
Because of the respect he had for his subjects, and the interest he had in

them as a scientist, he produced records which give us at least the exterior look and feel of a now-vanished way of life. Later on, Spencer encountered the main problem of more intimate and detailed accounting:

I spent some time trying to get cinematograph pictures of camp life. It would be quite easy to do this with a small hand-held machine of which, after a while, they would take little notice, but a large one attracts too much attention and makes their actions rather unnatural (Dunlop 1967).

Today, anyone with thirty dollars has more versatile equipment at his disposal than Spencer had, but the problems of intimacy, naturalness, and the relevance of the filmmaker's perception are still bothering the experts, just as they did at the time of the medium's invention.

The Village (McCarty and Hockings 1967), an early experiment in observational film (i.e. cinema presentation of an on-going culture which is not directed, staged, reconstructed, or fictionalized) was addressed to what we framed as the critical problems in the use of this kind of film:

1.   How can we differentiate between un-affected behavior and responses caused by reaction to the camera's presence? Or, stated another way: How intimate is it possible to be with the mechanical impedimenta of camera and recorder?

2.   What kind of soundtrack can contribute most in documenting a culture whose language is unintelligible to the film's audience?

3.   How long does it take an outsider to penetrate, identify, and capture the relevant life patterns of a strange community?

From the concerns of practical logistics, let us look at the last question first — how long does it take? We have found that a detailed visual and aural representation of a discrete community demands a minimum of three months' fieldwork. Now this seems a long time for the amateur cinematographer, vacationer, or "educational" producer, and it would bankrupt Lowell Thomas. But consider that all these types are dealing with the surface impressionism of the better travelogue. As we shall see later, THREE WEEKS is probably enough to get all the exterior views and "picture postcards" which make up this kind of film, but we are after something a great deal more: to capture the feeling, the sounds, and the speech of a culture from the intimate ground of those inside it — and to present this culture to others for serious and intelligent evaluation.

Therefore the filmmaker must deal with the same problems that face the conventional ethnographer — getting over culture shock, learning a language, searching out informants, etc. In conventional anthropological research, the preparation time in the field for this process is something like NINE MONTHS, and this BEFORE any definitive work is attempted.

Obviously, the conventional wisdom on this subject must pale before the exigencies of limited funds and personal (as opposed to institutional) interest, but it should be clear that we are into something which goes beyond a summer's vacation with the Kodak Brownie. Nevertheless, three months are available to many of you, and they will probably go by in the following rough periods:

Culture Shock and Language Familiarity: The First Month

Culture shock can be defined as that period when all arrangements for food and lodging go wrong; you are ill with irritation and/or dysentery; the locals smile patronizingly at your attempts to become one of them; and the only English-speaking informant you've found is discovered to be unreliable and himself an outcast from the community. There is not much to be said about this grim period — it simply must be endured.

Toward the end, however, several important things will have happened: the community's interest in you will have changed from a casual regard for the pass-through tourist or trader to genuine curiosity; your struggles with the language will be rewarded with patient attempts at dialogue by increasingly friendly individuals — and you will begin developing the sharpened sensitivity to local lore which is impossible to gain from library research, and is so crucial for later success.

One of the fundamental precepts in ethnographic film work is that you do not shoot during this period — for obvious reasons: the most you are supposed to do is break out the equipment and, perhaps, pretend to shoot (without film in the camera) so that people get used to seeing it and relax any fear as to its function. Now, although the theory behind all this is perfectly clear, I'm not sure that strict observance in practice is altogether desirable.

First of all, the miserable frustrations in language and acculturation which go on during this time produce a powerful need to roll some film (in your misery you tend to revert to the one thing you, by God, know how to do right); and then, you've spent a lot of money and you've been there a long time already; and besides, rigging up the camera and sound crew is a lot of work. The temptation to shoot is one to which we always succumbed.

Be prepared to throw away everything shot in this period, but also be prepared for some surprises. Your acute disorientation tends to lead you toward recording odd surface elements of the culture which seem unlikely, or at variance with your own practice. Small things — like the way sheep are sheared, or boats rowed, or the way men milk their cows — elements which, when later and more intimate familiarity with the culture make them seem commonplace, you may forget to document.

And then, in filmmaking as in life, an early and genuine curiosity on both sides of the camera can produce a kind of spontaneity of its own; it sometimes leads to a kind of hearty and direct response to the camera (as when the pub owner drives up to the camera and puts on a performance) which can be extremely revealing. In any case, the fact that you don't know exactly what you're getting and they don't know exactly what you're up to should not keep you from beginning.

I would like to be more specific about this early period, but in point of fact much depends on luck, accident, and intuition — all of which may be in direct ratio to the degree your "antennae" are sensitized to the culture. Suffice it to say that a great deal of the best material in *The Village* came from this period; as a matter of fact, afterwards the rushes went downhill in relevance and technical achievement the more knowledgable we became, until at the end the material rose again to match our final intimate acculturation.

In other words, the most revealing film we got came from the very beginning and the very end of a long continuous effort — a rhythm I find unnerving as well as contrary to theoretical assumption. At any rate, the end of this early period marks the point of readiness for the kind of material which usually makes up the whole of anthropological film — a thorough documentation of the external aspects of a culture.

Tripod Methodology: The Second Month

It was in this next three to four weeks that we shot the agricultural round of activities in the village: harvesting of oats, hay, peat-cutting, sheep-shearing and dairying. Here too, we shot the accessible archaeology of ruins, architecture, and field ownership patterns, as well as the general landscape of the community; social rituals involving groups of villagers, like the gathering at the pub, after-hours carousing, people standing around trading gossip at the creamery and post office — this kind of material is available at this stage of rapport. All of it tends still to be distant and rather general; if you stopped shooting at this stage (as traditional travelogue films usually do) the material would probably require a narration of some kind to tell you why you're looking at it (as traditional ethnographic films usually do).

The artistic credo in our cutting room was that any such supplementary information must come from the culture itself; it must be material actually gathered in the field and not composed later from a world outside the film. Thus, the scene in *The Village* where the three boatmen are digging rabbits out of ancestral walls might have stood by itself as a visual symbol of the past. But in the context of past generations of emigration and the slow dying of the culture, the story of Tomás' uncle digging his grandfather's skull out of a rabbit-warren seemed to add resonances of the typical Irish humor in the face of tragedy. Likewise, the scene of the Englishman struggling with Gaelic in the pub might stand alone as offhand comedy, or the Irish lesson going on in the background of the sequence where the old lady is making bread might just be another accidental detail; but in the context of the village philosopher's rather poetic theories of Gaelic revival ("... the language is a part of the body, and it must die before it gets new life into it again..."), all these elements work together to give us some idea of how seriously this culture takes its language, and the village its status as sole repository of linguistic purity. The critical point here is that you don't get material like these intimate stories and personal revelations until a later period in the shooting; if you stop at this tripod stage, you won't get it at all.

Close Portraiture of Everyday Life: The Last Month

Oddly enough, it is the minutiae of any one character's day that we found hardest to capture; what people do when they are at home, uninvolved in some structured social event; what they do in their kitchens, what they talk about over tea, or the slow round of daily tasks. Perhaps it is because what they are doing seems so commonplace that they wonder why you're shooting it, and thus try to put some other face on it, to match their own image of a movie. In any case, no trick of direction, staging, hidden camera or film technique will help you here; if this material is natural, it is because you are no longer a stranger doing something mysterious, but an acquaintance whom they trust, are interested in, and accept as their equal though you seem always to have that gadget on your shoulder.

During the past eight weeks or so, you must have developed the kind of friendship with key individuals that makes this possible, and it strains all your resources of language, patience, and plain calculated social engineering. And it strains the filmmaking process too, since you have to get rid of the tripod, lights and crew, and wing it alone, with a hand-held camera and available light in casual cinema portraiture; Jane Austen with a combat camera, if you will.

But after a time, the rewards are gratifying — you begin to get material that is simple, natural, and unaffected by the camera's presence. Or rather, the camera is just another person; as in the fishermen's hut, where they offer it a cup of soup; or wink at it, including it in the evening's drinking; or talk to it in the post office. And inclusion of this kind of material seems to us vital for another reason; it gives the film's eventual audience a constant frame from which to judge the relevance of the filmmaker's bias or perception. It allays the kind of nagging question (which so much of ethnographic film is open to) which usually takes form as "...now, did the director ask them to do that, I wonder?" or "...I bet they wouldn't do that if the camera wasn't there..."

Filmmaking will just never be the window to reality that the social sciences are always hoping for. It is an art of abstraction and therefore the bias, temperament, and predilections of the makers need to be made evident if the thing is going to pretend to insight, or at least honest reportage. The real question is what kind of abstraction is relevant, or might contribute to the task of ethnographic film. This task we have defined as: *To capture the feeling, the sounds, and the speech of a culture from the intimate ground of those inside it, and to present this culture to others for serious and intelligent evaluation.*

As filmmakers we will naturally choose the abstractions most accessible to our methods (i.e. picture and sound) and in *The Village* these may be listed broadly as the visible archaeology of the past, the present landscape of faces, gesture, occupation, and language (including lore), and the visible future of slowly encroaching tourism. Are these preoccupations less contributive than more traditional concerns in the social sciences? Field ownership? Distribution of wealth? Kinship patterns?

A sociologist of my acquaintance is convinced that in any given discipline the questions asked are those its own methodology can answer. What I am suggesting here is not that the filmmaker be ignorant of or disregard the more traditional abstractions of anthropological literature. I'm saying that if you immerse yourself in the hurly-burly of Irish village life with a camera, waiting for a kinship system to present itself with the clarity of Arensberg and Kimball, you will never roll a foot of film. And further, if you close your eyes to everything else and contrive to photograph only those aspects of the village which are a function of kinship, or somehow reflect it, you will wind up with a film abstraction of an original abstraction, and the results are probably going to be so thin that you'll be needing the old narration again. When the filmmaker knows what a culture is at the same time the scientist knows what a scene is, only then does ethnographic film begin.

All of the above is an attempt to describe how it actually feels to be struggling with the process in the field and what some of the critical problems are. And this description is itself an abstraction, rather-too-neatly simplified; in practice you will get some very intimate things very early, and some exasperatingly clumsy junk at the end, banal and useless. Cultures other than your own tend to bustle along regardless of the honor you are trying to pay them, unaware of the elegance of previous scientific analyses, and innocently deranging the purity of your intended cinema. It's an incredible hassle at best, with a constant aggravation that came to be known among our group as *McCarty's Law:* most simply stated,

1. Relevant action takes place when you are set up elsewhere.
2. In case of accidental coincidence of camera and action, the action will (a) stop being relevant, or (b) become relevant only when you are out of film.

This condition never entirely disappears, nor should you worry excessively about it. More pointedly, worry when things go smoothly, because that only happens in the cinema of prearrangement; discarding both fiction and reconstruction, yours is the film of discovery.

REFERENCES

ARENSBERG, CONRAD M., SOLON T. KIMBALL
  1968   *Family and Community in Ireland.* Second edition. Cambridge, Mass.: Harvard University Press.
DUNLOP, IAN
  1967   *Retrospective review of Australian ethnographic films (1901–1967).* Pamphlet. Lindfield, N. S. W.: Australian Commonwealth Film Unit.
MCCARTY, MARK, PAUL HOCKINGS
  1967   *The Village.* Black-and-white 16-mm documentary film, 70 minutes, with sound, English subtitles, no commentary. Produced by Colin Young for the UCLA Program in Ethnographic Film. Distributed by University of California Extension Media Center, Berkeley. Reviewed in *American Anthropologist* 74:1577–1581.

Cinematic Social Inquiry

GERALD TEMANER, GORDON QUINN

In the production of films for ethnographic record, research totally controls the filmmaking process. Framing is fixed by quite definite research goals, and cuts occur only where the film runs out. In the production of ethnographic instructional films, research is usually done before the filmmaking process begins, determining beforehand what the filmmaker should shoot and what the finished film should present. In the production of ethnographic documentaries, however, research and filmmaking interpenetrate in a more complex fashion.

The following description of the process of making the *cinéma vérité* documentary *Home For Life*, although not in the traditional domain of ethnography, would, we thought, be useful to anyone interested in an example of a process of integrating research and filmmaking. We have called this process cinematic social inquiry. Depending on the kind of ethnographic documentary being produced, there are other ways of relating these two activities. The method we describe tinkers as little as possible with the collected material; consequently it results in relatively long takes and relatively few cuts; and it depends on the position that, "For the movies, as for modern psychology, dizziness, pleasure, grief, love, and hate are ways of behaving "(Merleau-Ponty 1964:58). *The Nuer*, a successful example of a much more expressionistic use of film, must have required a very different process of research and making. Jean Rouch,

In its original form, this description was part of a proposal submitted to the Wieboldt Foundation, entitled "A Cinematic Social Inquiry into the Educational Process in an Urban Low-Income School Community, 1967," 6–15. It was later presented at the American Sociology Association's meeting, 1971, under the title, "Making a Documentary from the Inside."

when he modifies elements in the filmed situations in order for them to yield richer truths about the reality of which they are a part, had to develop another relationship between research and filmmaking. The MacDougalls' excellent *To Live With Herds* (although its makers may not feel our process describes their production) is in its finished form an ethnographic documentary of the sort that could result from the process of cinematic social inquiry.

Our task was to make a film about the Drexel Home, a home for the aged in Chicago. The sponsor agreed to grant us freedom in all aspects of the production. Such freedom, obviously desirable in the making of any film, was particularly necessary for us because we had decided to make a film according to the principles of what is called *cinéma vérité*.

This meant that we would not script the film. It meant that we would not be directing actors, or non-actors, but capturing real events with the people who were truly involved in them. It also meant that the film would be organized by a "found structure," such as an event, or process, or theme inherent in the people's lives, and not by the imposed structure of an artifical story or a geriatric theory. What we were after was a film as close to having a plot and characters as possible, without our staging anything or changing the meaning of footage by editing. Freedom is a necessary condition for the production of such a film because the ideas that would guide us in the selection of material and the ideas that would structure the finished film must be ideas that emerge from the situation. They cannot be agreed upon beforehand, and they cannot be changed for reasons extrinsic to the situation.[1]

Apart from these conditions, we had little idea of what the finished film would be. We also had little idea of what Drexel Home was. Research, then, was our first step, but research of a special sort. For in addition to having to learn all we could about the general problems of old age; the functions and nature of homes for the aged in our society; the aims, structure, and services of this particular home; and the sociology and psychology of the residents of this home; we also had to look for people who could be "characters" in the film; places that could be "locations"; and interactions that could be "scenes." We used the methods of an anthropologist to study this community systematically while we kept the goals of a fiction filmmaker.

With most documentary productions there are clear-cut stages: research, script (or treatment or some very determinate idea of the finished

[1] Although some critics have liked the narration that is sparsely employed in the film, it was our solution to the sponsor's insistence on the incorporation of material about the facilities.

film), shooting, and finally editing. There is almost always a sharp separation between these stages. Research is all of the reading, writing, interviewing, and observing before scripting. The research team is then replaced by the writer. After a script has been written, the film goes into
production and shooting begins. Then the crew replaces the writer. When
the editing begins, the shooting has ended, and the editor tries to approximate the script or original plan with the footage he is given. In this
traditional way of making a documentary, there are four quite distinct
operations, so distinct that frequently different people perform them. The
operations are in a dependent succession, and they are discontinuous —
one does not begin until the previous one is finished. Perhaps most importantly, all gathering of knowledge occurs at the research stage, while the
decision of how to present this knowledge occurs at the scripting stage.
(Indeed, sometimes the script is first and research is merely employed to fill it in and illustrate it.) Many documentaries are not made in
this manner; sometimes the same people are directly involved in each
stage; sometimes, as in rock festival movies, the process begins with the
shooting and the film is totally put together at the editing stage. Enough
documentaries, however, are still being made this way for this method
to serve as a legitimate contrast to our method.

These stages were not sharply distinguished in our production. We
continued to interview and systematically observe after we began to run
film through the camera; and we continued to shoot, as well as to interview and observe, after we began editing the film. More important than
these stages not being discontinuous was that, in an interesting sense, they
were not distinct operations. Because we do not consider research an
activity that cannot be done on film and because we do not consider filmmaking to be limited to handling film, we believe that our filmmaking was
research and that our research, after a first step, was filmmaking.

The following description of the stages in our production should support this claim. Since they are continuous, and since the same activity will
have to be described in one respect as filmmaking and in another as research, or inquiry, the stages can only be identified, but not adequately
described as: (1) non-film research, (2) film research, (3) heavy shooting,
and (4) heavy editing.

We began, then, by reading what we could about old age and institutional life generally. Fortunately, a small unpublished study was available
on the home which collected various vital statistics about its population.
We also went through minutes of meetings, the home's newspaper, poems
by the residents, etc. We interviewed all of the residents (approximately
250) as well as the professional and administrative staff. These interviews,

some of which we taped, were structured by questions concerning the film: what should be shown in the film; what should not be shown? Such questions created a willingness to participate in the project at the same time that they revealed, with or without the awareness of the speaker, a great deal about old age at this home. We were observers or participant-observers at staff and residents' meetings, home events, medical examinations, therapy sessions, and the like. This went on for a period of about two months. For a good part of this time, while we systematically roamed the home, we carried our equipment so people could become accustomed to it. (This technological initiation, as well as our using equipment that can follow people, and using film stock (double X negative) which did not require astonishing people with lighting, accounts for the absence of camera shyness that most viewers have remarked on.) In short, we developed a fairly thorough community study. These activities of reading, observing, and interviewing, as well as making index cards to manage the material, can be considered the first stage in our inquiry.

Every filmmaker, or anyone behind the camera and in front of the editing table, faces three questions. What to shoot? How to shoot it? How to put it together? All of this first stage and the goal of the second stage could be viewed as trying to answer the question, "What should we shoot?" From this filmmaking point of view, in stage two, strategies for shooting (and intensive observation for shooting purposes) began to take shape. These were provisional hypotheses about what and how to shoot, not decisions about what would be in the finished film. We felt we knew enough about the subject to decide what would or would not be fruitful to film, but not enough to decide what would be in the finished film. (At this stage, relevance and then fruitfulness were the dominant considerations; completeness was a later consideration). As a natural extension of some of our strategies, still in this stage, we began occasional shooting. Thinking about shooting became shooting.

Another way of describing this stage, which more adequately captures the process than does a description in filmmaking terms, is that the movement from the stage of non-film research to that of film research is like what takes place in anthropology when a field of inquiry is narrowed and examined more intensively. But we narrowed our field according to cinematic as well as anthropological criteria, so once it was narrowed, we observed, interviewed, and thought in cinematic terms. As a result of our earlier research, we could make a number of true assertions about old age and this home, but we now discarded all those that were abstract or, if concrete, not observable in behavior. The problem of making the film moved from the stage of abstract ideas and indiscriminate collection of data to that of concrete phenomena and more focused collection. We began to gather only "cinematic knowledge." Consequently, because thinking in cinematic terms is filmmaking, we were filmmaking even when we were not shooting.

At this point filmmaking and research began to become one process. First, our field for research was now limited to what was filmable. Within this field, then, meanings of events, intentions, and feelings evidenced themselves in observable behavior. The behavioral accessibility of meanings for research and presentation is a familiar problem to philosophers, sociologists, and filmmakers. Philosophically, a position like that represented by Merleau-Ponty's remark quoted earlier must be taken in order for filmmaking and research to be integrated in this process. Some remarks of William Foote Whyte can serve as an example of a sociological version of this position.

...you could examine social structure directly through observing people in action... (Whyte 1961:285)

...I could explain Cornerville better through telling the stories of those individuals and groups than I could in any other way... Instead of getting a cross-sectional picture of the community at a particular point of time, I was dealing with a time-sequence of interpersonal events (ibid.: 357–358).

To a filmmaker the issue becomes, "That's a good idea, but can it be filmed?" Accepting this position, then, if research is the organized capturing of relevant meanings, our research became filmmaking.

Second, since our filmmaking was a continuation of our research, since it became the means of our inquiry and was controlled by the same considerations which control a social scientific observer (at least, in the Whyte tradition), filmmaking became research. We employed the shooting, the viewing of our footage, and the editing as methods of study. (Even at this early stage, when we did do some shooting, we immediately edited the material to help us learn more about our subject and to help us decide on further shooting.)

Third, the questions, "What should we shoot for our film?" and "What should we observe for our research?" began to receive the same answer. Shooting strategies were the same as hypotheses — conceptions which directed our observations and later served to discriminate and order our data. Shooting thus became the collection of data. We would then reject the strategy, or hypothesis, or more frequently modify it, on the basis of the data.

To give a simple example, we filmed, quite early, a Seder (a Jewish dinner at Passover), thinking that it would embody and reveal material about the social and religious life of the residents and, since their relatives also attended, about their relation to the outer world. It did not. After editing, it revealed, supported by other information, that formal religion played almost no part in most of the residents' lives; that there was little feeling of community in such large group events; that participation was in every respect so "mute" that little of the residents' characters, their relation to one another or their relatives, was revealed.[2] Not only did we learn such things about our subject, but we then decided that it would not be fruitful to shoot any more such events.

A final way of describing stages one and two:

But the Ethnographer has not only to spread his nets in the right place, and wait for what will fall into them. He must be an active huntsman, and drive his quarry into them and follow it up to its most inaccessible lairs (Malinowski 1932:8).

What we were doing up to this stage was laying the nets. At this point we became active huntsmen, using the camera, either in imagination or in fact, to track our quarry. Stage one is relatively passive and absorptive. You are not looking for anything because you do not yet know what to look for. You are watching for something to look for. Stage two is relatively active; it begins the pursuit. You begin to look for things, which at this stage you may or may not find. If stage one is complete openness, stage two begins to focus this openness.

We have an advantage over the ethnographer. Once he has caught his quarry, he has to describe it. Usually his inquiry is separate from his presentation. We do not have to describe our data after we collect them. We employed a tool for inquiry which is also a medium of communication. Our tool, cinematic social inquiry, is a continuous process wherein filmmaking and research become identical and the natural result of the process is a presentation.

Keeping in mind that when the distinctions that rest on observing with a camera or with a pencil are recognized as inessential then the two become alternative ways of describing the same activity, we can say that stages one and two have been described in two principal ways: in one, our descriptive language was that of filmmaking— shooting strategies, shooting, etc; in the other, that of inquiry — observation, collecting data, discoveries, hypotheses. The third description, based on the Malinowski quotation, was, we thought, an interesting look at the subjective aspect of

[2] This assumes we could judge the effects of the camera, which in this case we felt we could.

this process. To describe the last two stages — heavy shooting and heavy editing — we shall continue to employ these two descriptive modes, one in terms of inquiry, or making discoveries about a subject matter; the other, in terms of filmmaking, or shooting and editing plans, adding to them a description in terms of the finished film or "scripting."

In terms of discovery, our investigative hypotheses for cinematic discoveries about our subject became more and more directed and intensive until we were finally following only a few lines of inquiry into our subject. We had some major foci. In terms of making the film, our provisional hypotheses about what would be good film material led to some provisional shooting plans and we began our heavy shooting. These plans were also modified and sometimes suggested other provisional hypotheses which in turn became definite plans. (Once more, to stress the identification between making and research, since the film was being made out of realities, these plans were also hypotheses about our subject whose referential truths could be "tested" by further shooting and whose coherence could be checked by editing.) This stage lasted about a month and a half.

In our shooting we were observers. We filmed the data of a situation as it developed. Our shooting could be called cinematic observation. Our camera, however, was not passive in the candid camera style but responsive to the situation. We did not pretend that we were filming through a one-way mirror. Sometimes we would stand back and record the intensity of an argument almost unobserved by the participants, but at other times we would move in and participate in the argument ourselves. In a number of situations, the cameraman or soundman initiated responses. In a few cases, we modified the situation by arranging meetings between people who did not ordinarily meet, or by arranging that a topic of interest to us be discussed at a residents' meeting. Twice, we showed people films of themselves or others and filmed their responses. In all of these cases, when they were used, we included these stimuli in the screen presentation of the situation.

Also at this stage, although our inquiry was far from complete, problems of presentation began to emerge. To describe how we thought about these we would like to employ Pudovkin's notion of a "keystone."

In a work of fiction, when thinking leaves the abstract plane and begins to work itself out and organize itself around ideas expressed, or expressible in a medium, the keystone stage is reached.

A writer, when he plans out a future work, establishes always a series of, as it were, key-stones, significant to the elucidation of the theme and spread over the whole of the work in preparation. ...to them belong the elements characteristic of the various persons, the nature of the events that bring these persons together, often the details conditioning the significance and strength of the elements of crescendo and diminuendo, often even just separate incidents selected for their power and expressiveness.

Exactly the same process occurs certainly in the work of the scenarist.... Before the discovery of a definite concrete form that, in the scenarist's opinion, will affect the spectator from the screen, the abstract idea...has no creative value and cannot serve as a key-stone in the constitution of the action (Pudovkin 1949:13).

The novelist expresses his key-stones in written descriptions, the dramatist by rough dialogue, but the scenarist must think in plastic (externally expressive) images. He must train his imagination, he must develop the habit of representing to himself whatever comes into his head in the form of a sequence of images upon the screen. Yet more, he must learn to command these images and to select from those he visualises the clearest and most vivid; he must know how to command them as the writer commands his words and the playwright his spoken phrases (ibid: 14).

In a fiction film, then, a keystone is a plastically expressive possibility around which cinematic thinking organizes itself. In the kind of film we are describing a keystone is a behaviorally observable possibility around which film data collection and cinematic thinking organize themselves. Since we were aiming at a film which would formally resemble a fiction film, our keystones were the same as those of a fiction filmmaker — the traits of various persons, the nature of the events that bring them together, separate incidents, etc. The fiction filmmaker creates his key-stones out of his imagination; we made ours out of the material of social reality.

One of our keystones was the entrance of residents. We imagined, as if we were scripting a fiction film, that we could represent the crucial themes and concerns of old age, as well as the essential elements of this environment, and that we could relate the incidents of this representation in a cinematic plot by following two residents entering the home, an obvious idea which came up before we did much research and was dismissed at that point as over-used. Our reasons, briefly, were that this embodied the transition from the larger society to the institution, that this was a period during which the feelings of the residents would be most visibly expressed, and that the institution would be forced to reveal its nature in this encounter with people unfamiliar with it. We could imagine their coming into the home; meeting the volunteer greeter; putting away their belongings in their new "home;" eating in the dining room; participating in an orientation meeting; and being examined, interviewed, and discussed in a staff meeting. The particular scenes we envisioned did not have to happen — some did and some did not. Some scenes that were filmed were even better than we imagined. But many things that were filmed were not foreseen at all. We could not have envisioned anything without an intimate familiarity with the home's entrance procedures. After deciding on this keystone, we then waited until we found two new residents who were visually and verbally expressive themselves, and who embodied a rich contrast in their attitudes, their relation to the outside world, their reasons for entering the home, etc. (male and female, medical problems and domestic problems, complaining and stoic). After applications were made, potential residents were interviewed before their entrance, so we were able to meet possible subjects before filming them and, once we made our decision, we were able to explain what we wanted to do and still film their actual entrance. Casting, both for expressiveness and for the embodiment of the elements to be explored and expressed, is a crucial matter in a documentary which must remain faithful to the situations it films.

During this heavy shooting stage, interviewing and observing without filming slowly decreased, while viewing and discussing our shot footage increased and had a significant effect on further shooting. We also rough-cut more sequences.

At the last stage, heavy editing, we felt certain enough about our shooting plan, after modifications because of the material we had shot, to stop and face the problem of selection. Our lines of inquiry got to the point where the collection of data ceased and the problem of significantly relating the data came to the foreground. We had filmed enough scenes based on our keystones and were able to see enough rich and dramatic connections between the scenes to deal with the problem of a significant dramatic unity.

The editing, just as the shooting, was guided by the human expressions and activities that developed before the camera. Because we were following out lines of inquiry, very little of the footage was so irrelevant that we could easily discard it before editing it into some rough-cut form to ascertain fully its meanings. We edited each scene first by itself so that its integrity could be preserved and would have to be taken into account as we organized and edited the film into its final form. Sometimes sequences were allowed to run on with little or no editing; other times, they were edited to reveal meanings that were present but not evident in the situation. As the meanings of a scene were revealed in editing, the scene shortened itself and we derived further criteria for selection, both for other scenes and for deciding which scenes would have to go. We edited in a "plain style," avoiding fancy juxtapositions and editorial intrusions, and allowing the people to express themselves.

Thus we found ourselves with a four-hour film which was organized by an interweaving of three strands. One strand followed the two residents; the second conveyed the attitude and the formal and informal tasks of an occupational therapist; the third explored the administrative hierarchy and the way institutional decision-making took place in the home. Residents, a staff member, and the institution were strands which when woven together presented a fairly adequate view of Drexel Home. Because of our process of inquiry, these were not merely related by intercutting, i.e. they were not in themselves unrelated to one another. People central in one strand appeared in other strands; scenes in one strand were talked about, as events, in another strand. It would have been an organized film in the epic manner, but unfortunately it was too long. Moreover, a shorter film, if it were to have a proper unity, could not, we thought, be made by condensing it. We solved this problem by extracting one of the strands, that of the entering residents, and by adding some of the relevant material from the other strands. A film in the dramatic manner was the result, eighty-three minutes long, moving along according to the chronology of these residents' encounter with the home and the home's responses to them. The editing took four months. Although the total shooting ratio was eight to one, the ratio on the strand that became the final film was only three to one.

If research and inquiry have to be carried on and stated in statistical terms or in terms of explicitly conceptual models, we were not doing research. Such a view would probably grant that our film is a case study. We carried on our inquiry in phenomenological terms and presented its discoveries in phenomenological structures. If research has to be replicable, we were not doing research. Someone with better eyes and better ideas would have made better discoveries and a better film. What has been outlined here is not a universal method of discovery and proof. In the last analysis, it may be that we were functioning as some sort of social artists. From that standpoint, the method of cinematic social inquiry is a means of intelligently surrendering to a situation without losing creative identity. It is a way of trying to assure that the basic meanings and values which are the stuff of the maker's imagination, out of which a work's form and matter emerge, are primarily derived from the situation. Further, as you surrender yourselves to the situation, the situation surrenders its meanings to you. You express its expressions.

For inquiry to be successful it must become knowledge, and this means that people must learn from it. The administrators of Drexel Home, who had themselves frequently observed their entrance procedures, changed a number of them on the basis of studying this film. Professionals at work in

Drexel Home modified some of their techniques after seeing themselves at work. The initial reaction from social scientists and medical experts was surprise, because they customarily thought of films as either a way of communicating what was common knowledge in the field to lay audiences or, at best, as a way of making a few points to students, but not as a way of learning something. Since then, *Home For Life* has been used by anthropologists, psychiatrists, sociologists, psychologists, social workers, and gerontologists at their conventions and in their courses. (It has also been shown at a number of American and European festivals, receiving favorable critical notices in film journals, *Variety*, and various newspapers).

From the reasons these experts gave for themselves having learned from the film, as well as their being certain of its value for classrooms, for training situations and the general public, and from our discussions with lay audiences, we realized that the film is effective because of the KIND of film it is. And this is a result of cinematic social inquiry. Because the film is not organized around a few points to be made, it is much richer than most documentaries. Because it is not structured by a particular interpretation of old age, it has been used by experts in a variety of fields holding a variety of positions. Because of the way it used the completeness and complexity of film for recording behavior, *Home For Life* has been used as a primary source for experts and their students to interpret. By dealing with the same data that the expert usually deals with, but concretely and not conceptually, the film is able to put the general audience directly in contact with the expert's problem. For similar reasons, the film seems to manage more topics and coherently present more behavior with fewer concepts than written documents. This makes it particularly valuable for use in discussion with lay audiences. Because there is no mediating narrator, and because of the way we shot and edited *Home For Life*, people's concerns — the inside view — are directly presented to the audience. At the same time, because the film has a "plot" and "characters," it is much more interesting than the typical social problem documentary.

As one anthropologist has said,

The language used by "sociology" is frequently abstract, even enigmatic and sometimes positively incomprehensible, whereas the ethnographer displays a marked preference for concrete experiences which are always unique. This type of approach no doubt explains why it is traditional — or exotic — ethnographic research which in recent years has provided the greater number of film documents on man's social condition (de Heusch 1962:27).

But strangely enough, this human approach of ethnography has from the first been that of the documentary cinema, even before sociologists took any notice of the employment of cameras or the existence of films. This immediate contact with man which the camera restores is clearly destined to become one of the important elements in sociological communication. In this connexion, the film can already be seen as a necessary counterweight to the disordered and sometimes frenzied extension of current sociological jargon. A smile or a frown on the screen restores the living presence of man buried beneath the arid treatises which we are all guilty of writing (ibid: 28).

REFERENCES

DE HEUSCH, LUC
  1962   *The cinema and social science*. Reports and Papers in the Social Sciences 16. Paris: UNESCO.
MALINOWSKI, BRONISLAW
  1932   *Argonauts of the Western Pacific*. London: George Routledge & Sons, Ltd.
MERLEAU-PONTY, MAURICE
  1964   *Sense and non-sense*. Translated by Hubert L. Dreyfus and Patricia Allen Dreyfus. Evanston, Illinois: Northwestern University Press.
PUDOVKIN, V. I.
  1949   *Film technique and film acting*. Translated and edited by Ivor Montagu. New York: Lear Publishers, Inc.
WHYTE, WILLIAM FOOTE
  1961   *Street corner society*. Chicago: The University of Chicago Press.

Observational Cinema

COLIN YOUNG

When shooting westerns..., use real Indians
if possible; but if Indians are not available,
use Hungarians.[1]

After 1963 the new documentary filmmakers abandoned the interview as
an appropriate component of *cinéma vérité*. About that same time Jean-
Luc Godard started using "interviews" in his fiction. Richard Leacock
tried to do without the interview because he was imposing the discipline
upon himself to look for other ways of gathering information about the
subjects of his films: "I want to discover something about people. When
you interview someone they always tell you what they want you to know
about them" (Marcorelles 1973:55). This was the rebirth of the observational style of shooting. Godard used the interview because, being a common
device from current affairs or news programs, it lent apparent authenticity
to his fiction. But just as fiction was raiding the territory of documentary,
documentary had to move further towards its subject and further away
from fictional forms.

Television mixes things up – editorialising, reporting, reconstruction,
fiction, non-fiction, advertising. It has the tendency to make everything
of equal value. A lot of people tend to believe audiences can tell the
difference, but can they? The BBC makes a point in its programs to
LABEL things for what they are, believing that it is important not to lose
the distinction between fact and fiction. British commercial television

---

[1]   Richard Leacock quoting the advice of a classic American text on lighting in Marcorelles (1973):54.

has to have a visual device on the screen separating commercials from the programs, and commercial radio has a tell-tale signature tune to set them apart. This provides a context, but it also acknowledges that there is nothing in the content of the advertisement nor is there necessarily anything in the form of it that sets it apart from fantasy or "the news."

By comparison, the faith that many social scientists have in film as providing them with an "objective recording instrument" is touching and almost sentimental. Much of the energy that anthropologists have poured into film in the last decade has been based on the hope that they could be rescued from the subjectivity of their field notes, but they have not stopped to consider the problems that exist within film aesthetics about selectivity and subjectivity.

When we organised a conference of filmmakers and ethnographers at the University of California (Los Angeles) in 1968, we decided that one of the points to be made should be that film is not objective. It may OBJEC-TIFY, but that is a different matter. The first implies a quality of the finished film; the second describes what film does to the viewer. We wanted to emphasise the structuring that went not only into filmmaking, but into every selective process.

To put it at its bluntest – the camera tends to lie but the audience tends to believe: David MacDougall (cf. *infra*) includes examples of why this is true. Film has a tendency to appear plausible, and thus to diminish the importance of what it ignores. But it was looking at only a very small part of the problem that led anthropologists in the early days to ask film-makers to preserve all the footage exposed and not "edit" it into a "film." Their argument had a lot of moral weight when the finished films they had in mind were highly editorialised versions of the footage obtained in the field. But raw footage itself requires a great deal of contextual explication, and it should be possible, within limits, to provide that in the framework of a film.

There are two points at which we can "go wrong." The filmmaker can either misrepresent the total event or situation by what he films or he can misrepresent the footage by how he edits. But language of this sort – "misrepresent," "objective," "subjective," or even "interpret" — presupposes an epistemology and an aesthetic. OBSERVATIONAL CINEMA is an attempt to develop a practical approach to these problems which has many things in common with the traditional role of the note-taking field researcher, but also has much that distinguishes it from former methodologies.

When an anthropologist, guided by his training and his informants, observes behavior in a village, takes notes, transcribes these notes, and draws inferences from them, he is following a method suggested to him by precedent and refined by experience. He publishes the results of this note-taking method – not the notes themselves. But his descriptive as well as his observational powers will have been severely stretched by this process. He can write down only so much and remember only so much more, and he is forced to apply a system of cognitive priorities in deciding what will be noted, these priorities coming at least in part from his training. Potentially the decision to record some event with the camera might follow the same system of priorities, but it would at least allow the postponement of detailed analysis. The decision to shoot the arrival of a stranger into a village can be made but the detailed observation of all the things that happened can be postponed until later when the film has been developed.

This appears, superficially, to give film an advantage that I referred to earlier. However, if you distinguish between using the camera as a surveyor's instrument and as a method of examining human behavior and human relationships in detail, you cannot afford in the latter case to stand back and get distant panoramas of human behavior – you have to be close to it and follow it intimately. This is very much the style of observational cinema (and of Rouch), but the difference between this and simple note-taking is that the final film CAN represent the original event or situation directly. The filming process can be as much like observation as possible; the finished film can represent the event observed.

What has to be studied by people using the cinema, however, is the way that film acts as "representative." It is after all an artifact, a system of images. There are conventional rules governing these systems, and the cinema is as likely to influence a filmmaker in his choice of shots as is the prior training of an anthropologist; that is, not only what is the proper subject of film but also what, within that subject, is the proper way to record it.

David MacDougall (cf. *infra*) has introduced doubts about the passion for pretending to be invisible while filming. In certain situations having a camera draws attention to the filmmaker; in others, or in the same ones after time has passed, the camera makes him invisible by giving him a justification for being there. But the fly-on-the-wall philosophy always was a conceit. In fact, the ideal never was to pretend that the camera was not there – the ideal was to try to photograph and record "normal" behavior. Clearly what finally has to be understood by this ideal is that the normal behavior being filmed is the behavior that is normal for the subjects under the circumstances, including, but not exclusively, the fact that they are being filmed. If we observe, as a matter of fact, that our filming CHANGES the behavior, then we have to decide whether or not that change is relevant to the total portrait we are trying to make. In one set of circumstances, the subject might have to be abandoned or postponed. In another, the alteration introduced by the camera might have to be accepted. MacDougall worries about the subjects being asked to be open to the cameraman when the latter remains closed to his subjects. But they might not want it any other way. If they do, or if more interesting things might be revealed with a different relationship, then the kind of participation of the filmmaker in the events of his subject might turn out to be the most revealing method to adopt. What remains common to all such approaches is that the mandate is coming from the subjects, not only from some preconception of the subjects introduced by the filmmaker. These are cultural matters both for the subjects and for the filmmakers.

Godard, according to James Blue, referred to *cinéma vérité* as a technique like oil painting. When filmmakers are developing a new approach, they tend to become fanatical about it. They invest in their method to the exclusion of all others. The method defines them and they define it. In this way advances are made, although at the cost of mortgaging the future and fracturing the present. There are, nevertheless, real issues involved.

In the early sixties, some filmmakers in North America and France were doing what film artists rarely do – demanding new technology. In the past, filmmakers were more conservative than engineers. Synchronous sound, wide screen processes, and color were all available long before the filmmaker wanted them. He was still struggling to control the earlier forms of cinema: silent, "academy" aperture (the old postage stamp shape), black-and-white films. But groups of documentary filmmakers went ahead of the available technology in the early sixties and produced for themselves portable, relatively quiet professional cameras with synchronous sound units. They did so because they wished to shoot people in natural surroundings doing what came naturally.

As a result of their early work (Leacock, Pennebaker, the Maysles, groups at the National Film Board of Canada, and Jean Rouch), it was possible about the same time to put into words our disaffection with two kinds of cinema: highly manipulative classical melodrama and didactic educational films.

What these two kinds of films shared was omnipotence. Like the hairdresser in the Clairol advertisements, only the filmmaker knew for sure. He kept all the aces, controlling the flow of information and letting us see only what he wanted and what fitted his story or his thesis.

Take an example. If Hitchcock had a wider angle lens on his camera and I could see the lights or the script girl, the tension in the scene would disappear. As the cinema became more familiar and therefore more conventional, it was possible to anticipate its manipulative devices and to resent them for their inevitable effect. We preferred Flaherty and Renoir out of the classical cinema and, when the new French cinema of Truffaut and Godard and Bresson and, later, Rohmer came along, we rushed to it. Many of them, having analyzed the American cinema to see how it got its effects, stopped short of the stab at the jugular vein, stopped short of making us cry, and left it to our imagination. They were not so much unconventional as restrained. They left us space to fill and we participated.

The difference is between TELLING a story and SHOWING us something. Take Rohmer's *Chloe in the Afternoon.*[2] The young husband tells us, as he rides the commuter train into Paris, that he has reached the point in his emotional life when all women appear to him the same — equally beautiful. The camera then shows us different women he sees in the train, equally beautiful as he says but, more to the point, *all* beautiful. So the theme of the film is established. The hero, despite his intelligence, will deceive himself. We have not been told the theme, we have been shown it.

In the classical educational film we are also locked into a single argument. We inherit someone else's views of the subject (not always the filmmaker's) and are given a take-it-or-leave-it option. Other parts of the culture make us sceptical.

In *Bitter Melons* John Marshall illustrates songs composed and sung by a blind old man. Towards the end, children and then a whole family group dance an ostrich mating-dance. Marshall simply runs his camera and lets us look at what he saw. Apart from reloading or rewinding, he does nothing except watch. We watch too. He tells us only what it is called; we then see what it is. We will need help in understanding its significance, but we are allowed to feel it without interference.

The Nuer by Hilary Harris, George Breidenbach, and Robert Gardner is altogether different. There is no single sequence in the film in which we are allowed to watch an event develop without interference. I do not know enough about the shooting to know whether that possibility existed in the footage. But as it is edited, we are struck by the way it has been chopped up to reveal a particular analysis of what is happening, rather

---

[2] For further information on the films cited, see the item "Filmography" in this volume.

than being allowed to experience the event and make our own analysis.

When you think of it, it is extraordinary that films are so often like that – more often than not, in fact. In the field of documentation you would think there would be an irresistible urge to do with the camera what only the camera can do, that which even the fastest speed writer or stenographer in the field could never do – record actuality in a form which, when replayed, allows a viewer elsewhere to have a sense of experiencing the event. Instead, they play the game of being the artist or the scientist with the camera. If, as in the case of Robert Gardner's *Dead Birds*, the artistic side comes off, we can accept him as an artist and we don't look for actuality. But here, in *The Nuer*, the view is too fragmented and we are given a take-it-or-leave-it option.

After seeing David and Judith MacDougall's *To Live With Herds*, you get very impatient with films that don't let you see.

When the equipment available to filmmakers now is compared with that of fifteen or twenty years ago, it is easy to see why film will change and why with portable, synchronous units we had to go back to the beginning with film and start all over again. The earliest filmmakers had portable cameras which could operate with clockwork (spring-wind) motors and could be completely independent of power supply. But whenever anyone wished to record the sound along with the picture, power was needed and the equipment became very bulky (cf. Plates 6 and 8).

The dominant aesthetic of film was its narrative strain, and the successful documentaries of the thirties and forties more often than not used the devices of fiction and were based on many of the same aesthetic assumptions. That was what cinema was to the people; anything else would have looked unreal. And people who otherwise might have been attracted to poetry or sculpture or architecture came into film as artists. Magic was created, like Basil Wright's *Song of Ceylon*, one of the most beautiful films ever made, or *Louisiana Story*, directed by Flaherty and photographed by Leacock in an earlier incarnation.

Finally we came back to the Flaherty of *Nanook* and to the stories of how he made it (Plate 7). But for a while the documentary filmmaker controlled his environment at the time of shooting and controlled his film at the time of editing in order to permit his film to be compared favorably to wholly contrived fiction. (It was really hard in those days to define "documentary.")

Other kinds of film, unless they were about spectacular events, were considered dull. Film was so impressive and its plastic beauty so innovative that people's ordinary lives were diminished by comparison. Ordinary behavior, which is quite bearable and may even be exciting for the participant, becomes dull under this aesthetic, when a frame is put around it.

The first big post-war shift was to neo-realism, especially as practised by Rossellini, the early Visconti, and De Sica working with Zavattini. De Sica's *Umberto D* can look a bit romantic now but at the time opened our eyes to a new subject. Building on what Renoir had been doing earlier in the French cinema (*La règle du jeu*) this new breed of filmmakers did more than push the pendulum back from romantic, chauvinistic wartime subjects. They minimised their dependency upon melodrama as the source of their structural conventions. Like all good fiction of the time, their films still had an overall dramatic form, and had a general metaphorical power. What was unusual was the low key of the drama, the attention to lifelike detail, and the willingness to have the dramatic development, in its details, verified by us against our own experience as the film progressed. This was quite different from the so-called genre film (the Western, the thriller, the musical) where we verify against our experience of the *genre*, a matter of artistic convention and not of "normal behavior".

The neo-realist's film, like every good description, obeyed its own syntactical laws and was internally consistent (logical), but it also obeyed that species of semantic laws which in a culture permits us to verify pictures as being authentic.

We did not suspend our disbelief.

Neo-realism was the god-father of *cinéma vérité*. In the new style of documentary there was at least a desire to make films without any of the controls a director usually assumed were indispensable. If the filmmaker missed something because he was not ready, he tried to improve his skill, but at that moment he let it go by on the assumption that his subject was the people or the events themselves (the process of their lives, in David Hancock's phrase). If the filmmaker started asking for repetition, the subjects of his film might one way or the other start acting for him instead of for themselves. Thus the filmmaker can agonize over losing some priceless "action," but he would try to console himself that something equally revealing would occur later.

It is obviously not only a case of "missing" things, but of being excluded from them because of uneasiness about the relationship. Herb Di Gioia, who worked with Hancock in New England and Afghanistan, came to the conclusion that each occasion of being shut-out or of missing things dramatized the limitation of the observational method and justified a more fictional approach.

In the early stages of *cinéma vérité*, the Maysles were so certain of the new morality that they argued against shooting with more than one camera – the essential subjectivity of the person seeing the events being filmed was necessary for the unity of the film. Two or three cameras would perpetuate the style of so-called "continuity cutting" in which actions in fiction appear to be continuous because of the illusion created when the camera angle is changed or someone goes through a door out of sight, only to reappear in another shot. At the same time, television was in the golden years of "live" drama, but paradoxically its camera style was based precisely on the stop-go shooting of film. *Cinéma vérité* changed all that. It was obsessed with the idea that we could get, for the first time, real people in front of the camera, talking to each other and living out their lives with the minimum of interference. The doubts about the particular merit of invisibility came later (cf. MacDougall, *infra*).

As Marcorelles (1973) points out, the decision to shoot everything with accompanying sound led to dramatic changes. In the silent cinema and in the classical cinema based upon it, the shot could be used as an element in a montage without consideration being given to the sound that existed when that shot was taken. Thus it could be independent of any anchor to a precise concrete event and could be exploited. In *cinéma vérité* (or direct cinema, as Marcorelles prefers to call it) the sound is taken with the shot and the two are considered together in the editing. Thus, within the fabric of the original camera material there is more dependence on the structure of the event than on the impulse of an idea.

In the immediate enthusiasm for *cinéma vérité* it suddenly became crucial that we were hearing people speak. It was almost as if "talkies" were starting all over again, but this time in the right way. This was crazy, of course, because we had seen newsreels on television as well as other sorts of precedent. But "real people talking" had seldom been the reason for making whole movies before. Although nothing spectacular was going on, filmmakers stopped the self-censorship which came from comparing what was in front of the camera with what usually got into movies. What people said (and did not say) and how they said it became of crucial importance. For this to have any impact, it had to be seen in the context of a total process, not simply as a bit of a montage.

What we did not notice right away was that the subject for movies, in the dramatic sense, often had not changed. The basis of conventional drama is conflict or danger or frustrated ambition. This was at the heart of the Drew Associates' films like *Chair, Mooney vs. Fowle* and *Primary*. *Primary* contained its own system of EXPOSITION (the candidates, Kennedy and Humphrey, introduce themselves to the people of Wisconsin), contained its own CONFLICT STRUCTURE (the contest for the Democratic presidential nomination), and its own inevitable RESOLUTION (the result of the election). Outside this type of structure filmmakers were at a loss to know what to shoot and, having shot, how to edit.

Pete and Johnny had no script. The teams of Drew Associates went out into the streets of Harlem whenever they heard something interesting was happening. Although the footage was fascinating, as observations of life going on, it did not seem to be heading for a finished film. Drew, the producer, had to step in and shape the movie around scripted material in order to come close to meeting his television audience's expectations for a conventional film. (Even now, *To Live with Herds* gives some people trouble: Rouch, while admiring it and supporting its receiving the grand prize award at Venice in 1972, said to James Woodburn that it wasn't really a MOVIE).

It is possible that if given the time, Leacock and his colleagues at Drew would have moved away from the narrow requirements of narrative structure and would have found a way of using their material which would have anticipated new observational cinema by a decade.

Since the original material did not fall around a single person or event there was no way of organizing it. One of the other networks did a similar show at the time, but they built it around a social worker who was about to leave his precinct. This was enough to guide the shooting, to suggest what was "relevant," and to shape the editing structure.

Thus at that stage what had happened was a change in morality and tactics during shooting, but not yet a change in overall aesthetics. That change had to come when filmmakers went after more open-ended subjects. *Pete and Johnny* may have been a failure (see Pat Jaffe's [1965] crucial article on editing *cinéma vérité*) but in *Happy Mother's Day* Leacock and Joyce Chopra had to do something different.

A national magazine sent Leacock to Aberdeen, South Dakota to make a film about the live birth of quintuplets:

We were simply observers. You can't have a director with this kind of film. You even have to edit your film as the event is actually happening. You have to decide: it's this and this and this I want to look at; and not this and this and this.... you can't alter anything afterwards; nothing can be reshot. You're doing an entirely different thing: you're a social observer. Your own ingenuity becomes less important than the fact of how interesting the subject is; and whether your own approach to it is interesting enough. You don't show the whole of a subject; you select; and your selection matters (Marcorelles 1973:53).

The whole reason for transforming the filmmaker's approach is the hope that new information about people of a novel and exciting kind will come into the cinema if the subject directs the filmmaker, rather than the other way around. DiGioia's concern is appropriate. Does this method leave us too much on the surface; are too many things hidden; can intervention (of certain types) pull back the shades without changing the situation intolerably?

Of course not only the observational film is truthful and not only fiction is art. Nothing is so simple. In observational cinema the camera is not used randomly but in fact the opposite – very purposefully and self-consciously. David Hancock gave me some notes about how he and Herb DiGioia worked in Afghanistan (where they made *Naim and Jabar*, *An Afghan Village* and *Afghan Nomads*):

> We shoot in long takes dealing with specific individuals rather than cultural patterns or analysis. We try to complete an action within a single shot, rather than fragmenting it. Our work is based on an open interaction between us as people (not just film-makers) and the people being filmed. Their perspectives and concerns shape and structure the film rather than our emphasis on a particular topic or analysis of their culture which would distort or overemphasize, perhaps, the importance of that topic to those people and that culture.
>
> We feel it is both limiting and naive to pretend the camera isn't there (after all we are there) and believe that the interaction of the film-makers with their subjects is a part of the event or process being filmed and as such should be included — not as a superficial narcissistic acknowledgement of filmic illusion; but as part of the film's evidence in which the impact of the film-makers' presence can be related to the apparent authenticity of what is documented.

It then becomes crucial to know how a filmmaker prepares himself to shoot in a particular situation. Until anthropologists are their own filmmakers, this means that they must help a filmmaker choose his subject.

But what is the proper subject of an observational film? In the old days, more often than not, Grierson would have said an idea was the subject of documentary. Social scientists too often choose very abstract subjects. When Hancock came back from Afghanistan he said to me, "This kind of film is very good at being specific — no good at all at making generalisations." At least one anthropologist we know, after one such experience, now regrets he gave the filmmakers a "shopping list" of things to film, instead of helping the filmmaker make a selection within the overall topic of a specific subject for his film, which would then reveal many of the other things which interested him.

The details of our films must be a substitute for dramatic tension, and the film's authenticity must be a substitute for artificial excitement. This does not rule out the possibility that a film's events will have the weight of general metaphor, but first and foremost they will have meaning within their own context. In any case, life is oversimplified in drama. The task is to break down into details the constituents of drama and find these cues in human behavior.

MacDougall refers to the time he and James Blue asked Guyo Ali to make a statement in their film *Kenya Boran* — not to camera in the form of an interview, but to another man in his village, Iya Duba. In that scene, Guyo Ali may be playing the devil's advocate, but he seems uneasy; he is certainly routed by the older man's arguments. I end up being ambivalent about him and this affects my reading of a subsequent scene where he "instructs" his son, Peter Boro. He questions Peter about his chances of a successful education, and Peter is extremely cocky. Thus the emphasis in the film shifts to the boy. Later, his father instructs him in a different sense — showing him how to hold and throw a spear. Here Peter is uneasy, and I conclude that his father is better at doing things within the village than he is at talking, arguing, or conceptualizing. Later Peter does badly in an examination at school and slinks back home to the village, also out of place there. He is at greater risk than his father. None of this was predicted or predictable. A scenarist might have plotted it, but it happened anyway. By having each episode provide a context for the others, Blue and MacDougall in their editing allow us to see what they saw over a longer period and could have elaborated upon in other material.

Hancock's notes also cover this process of selection and organizing the material.

If you have shot in the observational style and wish to edit in a way which respects the integrity of the shooting, all you are doing is providing fewer events and less information than the rushes give. This is why we end up by dropping whole scenes or sequences rather than trying to keep them all, but at shorter length. Each scene is made up of discrete pieces of information and behavior and shortening it for dramatic effect would lose the resonances (to use Blue's phrase) and misrepresent the material.

More and more we seem to be finding scenes that have no crisis, no main structural or dramatic point, but are composed of the bits of behavior which are the ingredients of our daily lives. Scenes in which nothing appears to be happening dramatically can gradually be revealing.

Thus a decision to drop an entire scene does not misrepresent the material to the same extent — we have simply provided less information.

As it turns out, there is a fairly strong narrative line to *Naim and Jabar*. The events of these two boys' lives during one summer lend themselves to dramatic interpretation. But they are not treated sensationally. Each component scene is as close as possible to the behavior of the two boys. The relations of the total footage to the event and of the film to the total footage should, according to Hancock, be the product of a consistent attitude towards what the filmmaker is doing. Observational cinema has its laws of editing along with its rules for shooting.

It is normally during the editing period that all the pressure of making the footage into a MOVIE builds up, and all the fictional devices to involve the audience come into play. At that stage, our long takes which match the duration of events take on another appearance when the duration of the event seems out of all proportion to a conventional sense of editing time. This is when the capitulation to fiction occurs.

In some ways, *Naim and Jabar* is more conventional in its narrative structure than some of our earlier material in Vermont, whose openendedness perhaps represents a greater movement away from traditional dramatic structure.

Thus we bring the argument up to date. Among the many different types of film we can make, ordinary behavior can be the subject of filmmaking and we can identify the best way to approach it. From neo-realism at the beginning through *cinéma vérité* to observational cinema, the way of looking at behavior is gradually changing. The temperament of individual filmmakers has influenced the way they have used their new opportunities — some have been quite shy while others have acted as catalysts in social situations. It is extraordinary (and tragic) that the people who edited the huge National Educational Television series in America, *An American Family*, seemed to be totally unaware of the debate going on about film. By never dealing properly with the problem of the crew's relationship to their subjects (the Loud Family) and by systematically excluding from the material any analysis of the filmmaker's possibly manipulative role, an opportunity for social documentary has been squandered and sensationalized. For too many people this represents a dead-end for observational cinema but, in fact, the editing style very seldom lets us look for very long and work out what is happening. We are told, we are not shown. The tragedy is perhaps best illustrated by reference to one remarkable scene when Bill Loud returns home from a business trip, is met by a son (and the crew) at the airport, and is given his marching orders by his wife when he reaches their house. From all accounts the original material, as it came out of the camera, was extraordinary; Alan Raymond simply watched Bill Loud. But in the film the scene is truncated and the chronology changed. The power goes out of it, and it appears implausible and manipulated. If we had seen it all without cuts it might still have been difficult to believe but, finally, it would have been compulsive and irresistible.

A possible weakness in the observational approach is that in order to work, it must be based on an intimate, sympathetic relationship between the filmmaker and the subject — not the eye of the aloof, detached observer but of someone watching as much as possible from the inside. It would thus be immoral and a betrayal of trust to make a film of this sort about people you disliked. If the diary (true confessions) is a form of suicide in literature, observational cinema can be a form of homicide on the screen.

But the edges of *An American Family* are blurred. There was little contact between the producer and his crew much of the time (Ward *et al.* 1973) and even less between the crew and the editors.

Far closer to what was needed can be seen in Roger Graef's series *The Space between Words* (for the BBC and KCET Los Angeles), which was similar to Leacock's approach in *Happy Mother's Day*, but which (with largely English crews) seems to have been a quite separate development. Graef took five situations: an English family in therapy, an English secondary school teacher at work, an English factory in the middle of management-labor troubles, a U.S. Senate Committee hearing, and a U.N. treaty meeting in Geneva. The style of shooting (much of it by Charles Stewart) was observational and non-participatory. The films all had to be about an hour in length and they came as close as anything in British television has to the objectives which have been discussed here. What is extraordinary is how little effect the series has thus far had. Graef's British contemporaries are still too aware of the advantages of directed cinema to wish to take up direct cinema.

When Rudolph Arneim writes about communication, he uses the concept of "authenticity." I used it earlier when describing how we deal with information given to us in pictures. But what happens to history if photographers fake still photographs and fake the ageing process? David Wolper, a Hollywood producer of television documentaries, has recently been staging his own "stock footage." It is probably cheaper than buying someone else's rare shot from the library and, in any case, the shot has probably been over-used. The staged shot could easily be of something which was never filmed; it could just as easily be of something which never happened. Watkins' films, *Culloden, The War Game* and *Punishment Park* look to some people like documentaries; they are intended to, of course. This raises problems for the documentary.

If we are spending time perfecting our ability to see straight, shoot straight, and edit the sections so that the parts of our film have a sense of the whole, we resent the fiction boys coming along and cheapening the currency. Of course, fiction has to use the cultural methods available to it. Television has made such inroads into our patterns of perception that fiction cannot ignore the influence. But observational films have to be believed to be seen. Their authenticity cannot afford to be little more than apparent.

So we raise problems for the anthropologist. First, he must either become the filmmaker or he must help the filmmaker with his choice of subjects. Second, he must assist in the analysis of the structure of events and learn to use film as representative of these events. This could involve challenging the entire way education uses film in twenty or twenty-five minute chunks. It also involves challenging the whole system of packaging information in education (cf. Asch's paper, *infra*).

I will take only one example. Some sociologists have been working on the difference between the structure of actual and reported conversation, between the structure of complex events and the reportage of these events. In journalism, compression is usually inevitable, either because of space (in a newspaper) or of time (on television). The same is true in education.

This compression introduces orderliness to the proceedings, and closes out in the mind of the viewer the need to make any further analysis. The job has been done for him, but again in the style of the privileged author who conceals the evidence for his analysis. Thus the events appear to be more coherent or more rational than they probably were.

A lot of this goes on in education in materials packaged for the classroom hour, the school term, the education committee policy, and the degree requirements. It should be possible to do all this more imaginatively, without spending vast amounts of money on the new packages. But if filmmakers have to learn their subject, teachers have to learn how to look at film.

This whole argument could have been about one film by Jean Rouch, *Chronique d'un été* — a watershed in documentary. Nothing can ever be the same after it. In it the invisible wall between the filmmaker and his subject collapsed. We see it falling in the scene with the garage mechanic as he explains how he fiddles his books to make ends meet. He is quite matter of fact about it, unconcerned that he is being recorded. Behind him stands his wife, trying to shush him. But she smiles too, embarrassed, because they are also being photographed. The microphone takes away a man's words, but the camera takes away his soul. Clearly such an important procedure should not be concealed. It is an old-fashioned notion that the camera should not be looked at since the effect of the camera pointing at people can often be measured by watching the way they deal with it.

Rouch puts his participation at the core of his film and makes it easier for us to evaluate the result. The moment we try to have our work include evidence of its own manufacture the rules change drastically. We can read Baldwin Spencer's early aboriginal studies without wondering what he had for lunch, but we cannot resist wondering about the crew's diet during the last stages of Marshall's *The Hunters*. Trying to conceal our act is defeatist. We are throwing away the most important advantage of the non-scripted, observational approach and lending support to the fiction that our work is objective.

Any intellectual discipline will outgrow its early enthusiasms and change its methodologies. At one time it was enough to set about recording dying cultures before it was too late, but this form of "urgent anthropology", as MacDougall argues (cf. *infra*), is itself accessible to a number of different strategies. There is no need to argue exclusively for one method. Conferences about method are arguments about power; representatives of one approach are racist about all others. This is obviously a waste of time. If different languages are being used, we just have to learn their rules to avoid confusion.

REFERENCES

JAFFE, PATRICIA
  1965 Editing cinéma vérité. *Film Comment* 3 (3):43–47.
MARCORELLES, LOUIS
  1973 *Living cinema — new directions in contemporary film-making.* London: George Allen & Unwin Ltd.
WARD, MELINDA, SUSAN RAYMOND, ALAN RAYMOND, JOHN TERRY
  1973 The Making of *An American Family. Film Comment* 9 (6):24–31.

COMMENT *by Gerald Temaner*

A simple sign of a basic agreement between Colin Young's position and the position Gordon Quinn and I maintain in our article is our both choosing the MacDougalls' *To Live With Herds* as the kind of film we think should get made. After seeing it, as Young says, "You get very impatient with films that don't let you see." He has marked off in terms of completed films a kind of film which is the same kind that what we have called cinematic social inquiry leads to; we have tried to schematize (perhaps too much so) the process of making that leads to a piece of observational cinema, while he has distinguished examples of observational cinema from other kinds of film, along with tracing its development. His article is, I believe, an important statement.

There are a few observations about it I'd like to make. He distinguishes between being "objective," which is "a quality of the finished film," and "objectify," which "describes what film does to the viewer". This distinction has a function in his nicely practical criticism of the notion of objective films. Although it might have been better made by maintaining that "being objective" has to do with the relation between the film and its object — the situation it is about; while "objectify," as he says, has to do with the relation between the film and its viewers — its seeming real. But once it is accepted that like any made thing, including census data and journal articles, films — whether ethnographic or documentary — are still not objective, I think it might serve Young's position better if he pointed out that while a film like *The Nuer* objectifies, observational cinema because of its fidelity to the situation (not a mindless fidelity to everything in the situation) is, if you will, humanly objective. Or tries to be objective. At least in the sense that the filmmaker tries not to intrude his smaller thoughts and smaller feelings into his film.

A second point. I do think that the distinction between telling and showing is important to Young's demarcation of observational cinema. But unless I misunderstand his example, something is unclear here. The important difference is not between verbal telling and visual showing but between telling, whether verbal or visual, when it is the total and only possible viewpoint, telling us what is important, telling us who is right; and showing, whether verbal or visual, when it allows us to take viewpoints, make sense of a character and discern what is important. In his example, if we have to believe, as far as the film's structure is concerned, precisely what the husband says, that would be "telling"; being put in a position to make inferences from what he tells makes this "showing".

In conclusion, Young says, "A possible weakness in the observational approach is that to work, it must be based on an intimate, sympathetic relationship between the filmmaker and the subject — not the eye of the aloof, detached observer, but of someone watching as much as possible from the inside. It would then be immoral and a betrayal of trust to make a film of this sort about people you disliked."

I should first point out that there is absolutely no contradiction between being committed to the inside view and being, or trying to be, objective. It simply means that the filmmaker makes a film about an inside view of the world other than his own; and that being an aloof and detached observer has little to do with being truly objective.

However there is a stance which, while it looks to some like being aloof and detached, is I think more appropriate to observational cinema than the one this passage suggests. It is a stance in which liking or disliking are not particularly important. In my own experience, while disliking is the more serious problem, ethically and practically, liking can also be a problem as a stance. Laughing with someone, because you like them, at a joke they themselves do not endorse is the kind of problem liking, or trying to like, leads to. Liking and having a close relationship with the subject is a bonus of sorts: I don't think it is the more ethical relation. Being unjudging and open to the values of others, and within that stance remaining true to those of your own views that are good enough to survive that stance — this would allow a filmmaker to make a film with any subjects. Unless, as it happens for many of us, we cannot achieve that stance with some people. Then it WOULD be immoral to make such a film about people you disliked. But if one continues to try to do observational cinema, such people should number less and less.

Approaches to Anthropological Film

The Camera and Man

JEAN ROUCH

When André Leroi-Gourhan (1948) was organizing the first ethnographic film conference at the Musée de l'Homme, he asked himself, "Does ethnographic film really exist?" He could only answer: "It does exist, because we project it..."

Luc de Heusch (1962:9) wrote quite correctly:

To brandish the concept of "sociological film", to isolate it in the huge international production of films, is surely a chimerical and academic enterprise. The very concept of sociology is fluid and varies according to the countries concerned and local scientific traditions. It does not refer to precisely the same kind of research in the Union of Soviet Socialist Republics, in the United States of America and in Western Europe. Moreover, is it not a distressing craze of our time to catalogue, to cut up into arbitrary categories, the confused mixture of ideas, ethical values and aesthetic research on which those complex artists who make films feed with such extraordinary avidity?

In 1974, these two statements take on special significance which on the one hand arises from the shame felt by ethnographers and, more recently, sociologists about their own discipline, and on the other hand from the filmmakers' refusal to accept their creative responsibility. Never has ethnology been such a disputed field, and never has the "authored" film been so extensively questioned... And yet the number and quality of ethnographic films increase each year.

We are not interested here in continuing some sort of polemic. We wish merely to note the existence of the following paradox: the more often these films are attacked from the outside or from within (by the actors and spectators or by the producers and researchers), the more they develop and come into their own. It appears that their completely marginal nature is a way of saving them from simply being classified within the reassuring orbit of all the daring experiments of today.

For example, since 1969 in Montreal (Congress of Africanists) or in Algiers (Pan-African Festival), when ethnographers were compared (with much skill, it might be noted) to "salesmen of Black culture," and sociologists were likened to "indirect exploiters of the working class," there have been more students enrolled in university departments of anthropology and sociology than ever before.

For example, ever since young anthropologist-filmmakers declared that films on rituals or traditional life were out of date, there have never been so many films made on traditional systems and so few on problems of development.

And again, since the creation of production cooperatives, there have never been so many "authored" films in the fields of both cinema and human sciences (nor has there been such decadence of filmmakers as of those working in these cooperatives).

In a word, if ethnographic film is under attack, it is only because it is in good health, and because the camera is finding its place among men.

ONE HUNDRED YEARS OF FILM

The Pioneers

However, since 1872, the road taken by ethnographic filmmakers has been a tough one. It was in that year near San Fransisco that Eadweard Muybridge made the first stop-action photograph sequence to solve a dispute over the way horses trot. By splitting up the movement involved, he managed to reconstruct it as a sequence as well, i.e. to transform it into cinematography (cf. Prost's paper, *infra*).

From the very beginning, after animals – after the horses – it was man. First came the horseman or the horsewoman (nude for purposes of muscular observation), and then the walker, the crawling woman, the athlete, or Muybridge himself, all nude, spinning around in front of thirty still cameras. In these furtive images the society of America's west coast is revealed, a century ago, as no Western film will ever reveal it again! It was a society of horsemen, to be sure, but also one which was essentially white, robust, violent, immodest, ready to give the world the virus of good will, and, first and foremost, the American way of life.

Fifteen years later, in 1887, when Étienne-Jules Marey (Plate 1) encompassed thirty individual machines of Muybridge with his chronophotographic rifle, and used the celluloid film invented by Thomas Edison (Plate 6), MAN became the subject once again. And in 1895, Dr. Félix Regnault (Plate 2), a young anthropologist, decided to use time-sequence photography in his comparative study of body behavior (some forty years before Marcel Mauss wrote his unforgettable essay on "*Techniques du corps*"). He photographed the "ways of walking, squatting, climbing," of a Peul, a Wolof, a Diola, and a Madagascan (Regnault 1896, 1897).

In 1900, Regnault and his colleague, the anthropologist L. Azoulay, (who was the first to use Edison sound-record cylinders to record sound; Azoulay 1900a, 1900b) conceived the FIRST AUDIOVISUAL MUSEUM OF MAN:

Museums of ethnology should add time-sequence photographs to their collections. It is not enough to have a loom, a lathe, or a javelin; one must also know how these things are used; and, we cannot know this precisely without using time-sequence photography" (Regnault 1900:422).

Unfortunately this ethnographic museum of visual and sound documents is still a dream three-quarters of a century later!

While the cinematographer Louis Lumière is known for his introduction of the animated image in filmmaking, he still focused on man as his principal subject:

The film archives of this century begin with his first naive productions. Was the cinema to be an objective instrument which would capture the behavior of men from the life? The marvellous ingenuity of *Sortie des usines* [Leaving the factories], *Déjeuner de Bébé* [Baby's mealtime] and *La Pêche à la crevette* [Shrimp-fishing] made it seem likely. (De Heusch 1962:13).

But from the beginning the camera has shown itself to be a "thief of reflections." The workers leaving Lumières' factories scarcely paid attention to the small crank-box camera, but a few days later when they attended the presentation of these brief films, they suddenly became conscious of an unknown magic ritual. They experienced that ancient fear of fatal contact with one's double (cf. Carpenter's paper, *infra*).

Next came "the illusionists [who took] this new sort of microscope away from the scientist and transformed it into a toy..." And cinema-goers preferred Méliès' artificial reconstruction of the eruption of the Mt. Pelée volcano in the Antilles to the frightening documentaries done by the Lumières' team on the wars in China.

The Inspired Precursors

It took the great torments of 1914–1918, the questioning of all human values, the Russian revolution and the European intellectual upheaval to bring camera and man together once again.

At that time two forerunners of our discipline were working in the field. One was a futurist poet, and the other a geographer-explorer, but both of them were cinematographers who were concerned with expressing reality. The Soviet (originally Polish) Dziga Vertov was doing sociology without knowing it and the American, Robert Flaherty, was doing ethnography also without knowing it. They never met one another, nor did they ever have any contact with the ethnologists or sociologists who were developing their new sciences seemingly unaware of the existence of these indefatigable observers. And yet, it is to these two filmmakers that we owe all of what we are trying to do today.

For Robert Flaherty, around 1920, filming the life of the Eskimo of Canada meant filming one particular Eskimo, not an object, but a person (Plate 7). His basic honesty required that he show the subject what he was doing. When Flaherty set up a developing room in a cabin on Hudson Bay and projected his brand new pictures on a screen for his first spectator, the Eskimo Nanook, he did not know that, with absurdly inadequate means, he had just invented both "participant observation" which would be used some thirty years later by sociologists and anthropologists, and "feedback" with which we are still so clumsily experimenting.

If Flaherty and Nanook succeeded in recounting the story of the struggle of one man against a nature which is rich in both benefits and pain, it is only because there was a third party with them. This capricious but faithful little machine, which has an infallible visual memory, let Nanook see his own pictures from the very moment of their conception. The camera became what Luc de Heusch has appropriately called "the participant camera."

And, without a doubt, when Flaherty was developing his rushes inside his igloo, he must have realized that he was sounding the death knell for over 90 percent of the filmed documentaries which would be produced later on. We had to wait forty years before people would follow the still current example of the old master of 1921.

For Dziga Vertov, who was working in the same period, the job was to film the revolution. Thus it was no longer a problem of shooting in a hostile setting, but rather of recording small elements of reality. So the poet-turned militant, noticing the archaism of the cinematographic structure in filmed diaries, invented the *kinok*, the 'cine-eye':

I am the "cine-eye," I am the mechanical eye; I am the machine that will show you the world as only the machine can see it. Henceforth, I shall be liberated from human immobility. I am in perpetual motion. I can approach things, back away from them, slide under them, enter inside them; I can move up to the very nose of a race horse, pass through crowds at great speed, lead soldiers into battle, take off with airplanes, turn over on my back, fall down and stand up at the same time as bodies which fall and stand up again... (Vertov 1963 [1923]: 34).

Thus, this pioneer visionary foresaw the era of *cinéma vérité*.

Cinéma-vérité is a new sort of art, the art of LIFE ITSELF.
The "cine-eye" includes:
all techniques of filming;
all moving pictures;
all methods, without exception, which permit one to reach out and record REALITY: a reality in motion (Vertov 1963 [1923]:34).

The "camera in the purest state," not in its egotism but in its willingness to reveal people with absolutely no pretense, to catch them at any moment, to stop as soon as they leave off complaining, to imprison their thoughts...
But is not sufficient to present fragments of reality on the screen to represent life by its crumbs. These fragments must be elaborated upon so as to make an integrated whole which is, in turn, the thematic reality... (Vertov 1968 [1940]: 443-444).

Within these impassioned statements resides all the cinema of today, all of the problems of ethnographic film, of research films done for television and of the creation of the "living cameras" we use today, so many years later.

And yet, no filmmaker in the world has been so poorly accepted, no inspired explorer has been so alone or misunderstood. It was not until the 1960's that producers and theoreticians took up again the notion of the *kinoki* from these two who made "films which produced films."

When, in the 1920's, Flaherty and Vertov had to resolve those problems which always present themselves to the filmmaker when faced with the people he must film, techniques of shooting were still quite elementary. The production of a film took more skill — indeed, more art — than hard work. The camera of Nanook, ancestor of the Eyemo, had no motor, but did already have a "reflex" viewer coupled mechanically to the camera lens. The camera of the "cine-eye," as seen in *The Man with the Movie Camera*, was also hand cranked and was kept permanently upon a tripod. The "eye in motion" extolled by Vertov could only move about in an open vehicle. Flaherty worked alone (as cameraman, producer, lab-technician, editor, projectionist – Plate 7); Vertov only worked through another cameraman and had a small crew (a curiously familial group: his brother Mikhail on the camera, his wife at the editing table; later Flaherty also had a familial crew: his brother David on the second camera, and his wife Frances as the assistant).

It is probably because of this simplicity and naiveté (even in "cine-sophistication") that these pioneers discovered the essential questions we are still asking ourselves: should we put reality on film ("the real life setting") as Flaherty did, or should we film it as Vertov did, without planning a particular setting ("life caught unawares")?

The Eclipse of the Cinema Industry

But in 1930, technical progress (the recent passage from "silent films" to "talkies") had transformed the cinematic art into an industry, and no one really had the time to think about what he was doing. No one even questioned what anyone else was doing. White cinema became canniba-listic. It was a time for exoticism, and Tarzan, a white hero among black savages, was not far away.

To make a film then was to head a group of a dozen technicians, to use several tons of sound and filming equipment, to be accountable for hundreds of thousands of dollars. Rather than sending the camera out in search of people, it seemed simpler to make people come to the camera – the indomitable Johnny Weismuller, the most famous king of the jungle, never left the sacred forest of Hollywood. Instead, the wild beasts of Africa and the feathered Tubi came to the studio to be filmed there.

One almost needed to be crazy to try using (as did some ethnographers) a tool as forbidding as the camera. When we see today the first clumsy attempts to use it correctly in Marcel Griaule's *Au pays des Dogons* [In the land of the Dogon; 1935] and *Sous le masque noir* [Beneath the black mask; 1938] or in Patrick O'Reilly's *Bougainville* (1934) which was later changed to *Popoko, île sauvage* [Popoko, the wild island], we can understand their discouragement with the results of their efforts. Their admirable documentation was put through the filmmaking machine. There was wild, insensitive editing, oriental music, commentary in the style of a sportscast... It is this sort of travesty that Margaret Mead and Gregory Bateson were able to avoid when they produced their series at about the same time (1936-1938): *Character Formation in Different Cultures: 1. Bathing Babies; 2. Childhood Rivalry in Bali and New Guinea; 3. First Days in the Life of a New Guinea Baby.* They were successful because they had the financial aid of American universities which understood before others did that it is absurd to try to mix research and business.

The Post-War Technical Revolution: Light-weight Cinema

The new technical development precipitated by the war brought about the revival of ethnographic film. The advent of the 16-millimeter reduced format was a breakthrough. The light cameras used by the American forces in the field were no longer 35-mm monsters, but instead they were accurate and hardy tools which came directly out of amateur cinematography. In the late 1940's young anthropologists followed to the letter the manual of Marcel Mauss ("you will film all of the techniques...") and brought the camera closer to man once again. Though some expeditions continued to have dreams of super-productions in 35-millimeters (e.g. the admirable *Pays des Pygmées* [Land of the Pygmies] which in 1947 brought back the first authentic sounds recorded in the equatorial forests on wax discs), the 16-millimeter camera was rapidly gaining ground.

From then on, things developed quite quickly. In 1951, the first portable tape recorders appeared. In spite of their weight (thirty kilograms) and their cranked motors, they replaced an equipment truck of several tons. No one would believe in the new sound equipment at first except for a few anthropologists who taught themselves how to manage these bizarre tools which no professional from the film industry would even look at. Several of these ethnologists made themselves into producers, cameramen, sound engineers, editors, and directors. Quite curiously, Luc de Heusch, Ivan Polunin, Henri Brandt, John Marshall and I realized that, as a sideline, we were inventing a new language. In the summer of 1955 at the Venice film festival in a magazine called *Positif, Revue du Cinéma*, I presented ethnographic film in the following manner:

What are these films? What barbarian name can distinguish them from any others? Do they really exist as a separate form? I still don't know, but I do know that there are a few rare moments when the filmgoer suddenly understands an unknown language without the help of any subtitles, when he participates in strange ceremonies, when he finds himself walking in towns or across terrain that he has never seen before but that he recognizes perfectly...

A miracle such as this could only be produced by cinema, but it happens without any particular aesthetic telling us how it works, or any special technique which provokes it. Neither the brilliant counterpoint of good cutting nor the use of stereophonic cinerama could work such wonders. More often than not, in the middle of the most banal film, amid the wild collage of random events, in the meanderings of amateur cinema, a mysterious contact is established. Perhaps it is a close-up of an African smile, a Mexican winking at the camera, the gesture of a European which is so everyday that no one would dream of filming it. All of these force the crystallization of a bewildering facet of reality. It is as if the shots, the sound track, the photo-electric cell, the mass of accessories and technicians who form the great ritual of classical cinema no longer existed. But today's filmmakers prefer not to venture along these dangerous paths, and only masters, fools, and children dare to press the forbidden buttons... (Rouch 1955:14).

But soon, the quick development of television gave our ridiculous tools the status of professional nobility. It was in the attempt to satisfy our demands (lightness, solidity, quality) that excellent portable tape recorders and portable silent cine cameras were perfected around 1960 (Plate 8). The first ones to use these were, in the United States, Richard Leacock (*Primary* and *Eddie*), and, in France, the team of Edgar Morin, Michel Brault, and myself (*Chronique d'un été* [Chronicle of a summer]).

ETHNOGRAPHIC CINEMA TODAY

Thus, today, we have quite extraordinary equipment available and, ever since 1960, the number and the quality of the ethnographic films produced throughout the world has increased yearly (more than seventy films were submitted to the selection committee for the first Venezia Genti in 1971). However, ethnographic film, in spite of its marginal and yet quite specific aspects, has really not yet found its proper path. After having resolved all the technical problems, we must seemingly re-invent, like Flaherty or Vertov in the 1920's, the rules of a new language which might allow us to cross the boundaries between all civilizations.

It is not my concern here to evaluate all of the experiments and trends in the field of ethnographic film, but rather to reveal those which seem to me to be the most pertinent.

Ethnographic Film and Commercial Cinema

Although there are no technical factors preventing it, wide distribution of ethnographic films is extremely rare. However, the majority of ethnographic films produced within the last few years have ALWAYS been made with the techniques of commercial cinema: credits, original music, sophisticated editing, commentary for the masses, appropriate length, etc...

Most of the time, then, what results is a hybrid product satisfying neither scientific rigors nor film aesthetics. Of course, some masterpieces or original works escape from this inevitable trap. Ethnographers consider film to be like a book, and a book on ethnology appears no different from an ordinary book.

The result is a notorious rise in the prime cost of these films. This makes the almost total absence of commercial distribution even more harshly felt, especially when the market for films remains so open to "sensational" documentaries like *Mondo Cane*.

Obviously, there will always be exceptions: *The Hadza* made by the young filmmaker Sean Hudson in close collaboration with the anthropologist James Woodburn, or *Emu Ritual at Ruguri* and the whole Australian series of the producer-filmmaker Roger Sandall in collaboration with an anthropologist again, or *The Feast* in which Timothy Asch immersed himself completely in the research of Napoleon Chagnon among the Yạnomamö (cf. Sandall's and Asch's papers, *infra*).

The solution to this problem is the study of the distribution network of these films. When universities, cultural institutes, and television stations can show these films without having to make them conform to commercial productions but rather can accept their differences, a new type of ethnographic film with its own specific criteria may be developed.

Ethnographer-Filmmaker or Team of Filmmaker-plus-Ethnographer?

It is for similar reasons, to "take advantage of all technical skills available," that ethnologists over the past few years have preferred not to do the filming themselves but instead to call upon a team of technicians for the job (actually, it is the technical crew — sent out by a television production unit — who call upon the ethnologist).

Personally — unless forced into a special situation — I am violently opposed to film crews. My reasons are several. The sound engineer must fully understand the language of the people he is recording. It is thus indispensable that he belong to the ethnic group being filmed and that he also be trained in the minutiae of his job. Besides, with the present techniques used in direct cinema (synchronic sound), the filmmaker must be the cameraman. And the ethnologist alone, in my mind, is the one who knows when, where, and how to film, i.e. to do the production. Finally, and this is doubtless the decisive argument, the ethnologist should spend quite a long time in the field before undertaking the least bit of filmmaking. This period of reflection, of learning, of mutual understanding might be extremely long (Robert Flaherty spent a year in the Samoan Islands before shooting the first foot of film there), but such a stay is incompatible with the schedules and salaries of a team of technicians.

The films of Asen Balikci on the Netsilik Eskimo or the recent series of films by Ian Dunlop on the Baruya of New Guinea are for me good examples of what must not happen again. For these productions a superior crew of technicians intruded into a hostile land in spite of the presence of an anthropologist. Every time a film is shot, privacy is violated; but when the filmmaker-ethnologist is alone, when he cannot lean on his group of foreigners (two whites in an African village already form a community, a foreign body which is solid and thus risks rejection), the responsibility for any impurity can only be assumed by this one man. I have always wondered how that small group of Eskimos reacted to those crazy white men who made them clear their camp of good canned food.

This ambiguity probably did not appear in the *Desert People* series because the filmmakers and the aboriginal family they were filming spent time making their way through the desert together. But it is naturally apparent in the film on New Guinea, at the extraordinary end of the ceremony, when the group responsible for the initiation does not actually reject the filmmakers but asks their anthropologist friend if he can limit the distribution of the film. They asked that the film be seen only outside New Guinea (*a posteriori* rejection). At any rate, the complexity of the technical procedure was an obstacle to the "participant camera."

This is why it seems indispensable to me to initiate anthropology students into the techniques of recording both pictures and sound. Even if their films are technically quite inferior to the work of professionals, they will have the irreplaceable quality of real contact between the person filming and those being filmed.

Tripod Camera or Hand-held Camera — Zoom or Fixed Lens?

When American television networks were looking for films after World War II (particularly the *Adventure* series of Sol Lesser or of CBS), films shot without a tripod were almost unacceptable because of the consequent lack of stability. However, most of the war reporting done on 16-mm film (e.g. the extraordinary *Memphis Bell*, actual adventures of a Flying Fortress filmed in 16-millimeter and the first film to be enlarged to 35-mm) had been done with hand-held cameras. But in fact, if some of us were to follow the example of these pioneers and film without a tripod, it was to economize and allow quick magazine changes between shots. The camera was stationary most of the time, panned sometimes and, on exceptional occasions, moved about ("crane" effect achieved by squatting, or traveling in a car).

It took the audacity of the young team from the National Film Board of Canada to free the camera from this impossibility. In 1954, *Corral* by

Koenig and Kroitor pointed out a path later opened up more defini-tively in 1959 by what has become today's classic model of the traveling shot, i.e. when the camera follows the revolver of the bank guard in *Bientôt Noël* [And soon it will be Christmas]. When Michel Brault came to Paris to shoot *Chronique d'un été* [Chronicle of a summer], it was a revelation for all of us and for the television cameramen as well. The shot from *Primary* in which Leacock follows the entrance of John F. Kennedy was without a doubt the masterpiece of this new style of filming.

Since then camera designers have made considerable efforts to improve the manageability and balance of cine cameras. And today, all direct-cinema cameramen know how to walk with their cameras, which have thus become the living cameras, the "cine-eye" of Vertov.

In the area of ethnographic film, this technique seems to me to be par-ticularly useful because it allows the cameraman to adapt himself to the action as a function of space, to generate reality rather than leave it simply to unfold before the viewer.

However, some producers continue to use tripods most of the time. This is probably done for technical reasons, and it is, to my mind, the major fault of the films of Roger Sandall and especially of the latest films of Ian Dunlop from New Guinea (it is not an accident that these are both Australian-based producers, since the best tripods and the best "panora-mic heads" are made in Sydney!) The immobility of the filming apparatus is compensated for by the extensive use of zoom lenses which give the optical effect of a dolly shot. In fact, these artificial techniques for simulating movement back and forth do not really succeed in letting one forget the rigidity of the camera which only sees from a SINGLE POINT OF VIEW. Despite the obviously intriguing nature of these casual ballets, we have to remember that the forward and backward movements are only optical and that the camera does not move closer to the subjects. The zoom lens is more like a voyeur who watches and notes details from atop a distant perch.

This involuntary arrogance of the camera is not only felt *a posteriori* by the attentive audience, but the subjects themselves perceive it even more strongly as an OBSERVATION POST.

For me, then, the only way to film is to walk about with the camera, taking it to wherever it is the most effective, and improvising a ballet in which the camera itself becomes just as much alive as the people it is filming. This would be the first synthesis between the theories of Vertov about the "cine-eye" and those of Flaherty about the "participant camera." I often compare this dynamic improvisation with that of the bullfighter before the bull. In both cases nothing is given in advance, and the smoothness of a *faëna* (strategy of play) in bullfighting is analogous to the harmony of a traveling shot which is in perfect balance with the movements of the subjects.

Here again, it is a question of training, of the kind of mastery of the body that proper gymnastics might allow us to acquire. Then, instead of using the zoom, the cameraman-filmmaker can really get into his subject, can precede or follow a dancer, a priest, or a craftsman. He is no longer just himself but he is a "mechanical eye" accompanied by an "electronic ear." It is this bizarre state of transformation in the filmmaker that I have called, by analogy with phenomena of possession, the "cine-trance."

EDITING

The producer-cameraman of direct cinema is his own first spectator thanks to the viewfinder of his camera. All gestural improvisation (movements, centerings, duration of shots) finally leads to editing in the camera itself. We can note here again the notion of Vertov: "the 'cine-eye' is just this: I EDIT when I choose my subject [from among the thousands of possible subjects]. I EDIT when I observe [film] my subject [to find the best choice from among a thousand possible observations...]" (Vertov 1923).

Actually this work done in the field is what specifically marks the filmmaker-ethnologist. Instead of waiting until he has returned from the field to elaborate upon his notes, he must try, under threat of failure, to synthesize them at the very moment he observes particular events. He must conduct his cinematic study, alter it or cut it short, while on location. It is no longer a question of cuts written down in advance, nor of cameras determining the order of sequences, but instead it is a sort of risky game in which each shot is determined by the preceding one and itself determines the next. Certainly shooting with synchronous sound demands perfect correlation between the cameraman and the soundman (and the latter who, I repeat, must understand perfectly the language spoken by the people filmed, plays an essential role in this adventure). If this "cine-eye" and "cine-ear" crew is well-trained, the technical problems will be resolved by means of simple reflexes (focus, F-stop) and the filmmaker and his soundman are left free for this spontaneous creation. "'Cine-eye' = cine-I see [I see with the camera] + cine-I write [I record on film with the camera] + cine-I organize [I edit]" (Vertov 1923).

During the filming, thanks to the viewfinder and headphones the production crew will immediately know the quality of what has been recorded. They can stop if they aren't satisfied (so as to try another way), or if it is going well, they can continue to connect together the sentences of the story which is created at the very moment that the action transpires. And that is, for me, the real "participant camera."

The next spectator is the editor. He must never participate in the filming, but be the second "cine-eye"; not being acquainted with the context, he must only see and hear what has actually been recorded (whatever the intentions of the filmmaker might have been). Thus, the editing between the subjective author and the objective editor is a harsh and difficult dialogue, but one on which the whole film depends. Here again, there is no recipe:

> Association [addition, subtraction, multiplication, division and bracketing together] of film strips of the same sort. Incessant permutation of these pieces of film until they are placed in a rhythmic order in which all of the cues for meaning coincide with all of the visual cues (Vertov 1923).

But there is another step not foreseen by Vertov that seems indispensable to me. This is the presentation of the first rushes ("from beginning to end" in order) to the people who were filmed and whose participation is essential. I will come back to this later.

Commentary, Subtitles, Music

It is not possible to transmit two auditory messages simultaneously. One will be understood at the expense of the other. The ideal would therefore be a film in which the sound would be the synchronous sound that accompanied the action. Unfortunately, ethnographic films generally present us with complex alien cultures whose people speak an unknown language.

A commentary, as in silent films or a film shown along with a lecture, seems to be the simplest solution; it is the direct discourse of the filmmaker who becomes the intermediary between self and others. This discourse, which should be subjective, is most often objective. It usually takes the form of a manual or a scientific exposition which brings together the maximum amount of associated information. So, strangely enough, instead of clarifying the pictures, the film commentary generally obscures and masks them until the words substitute themselves for the pictures. It is no longer a film, but a lecture or a demonstration with an animated visual background. This demonstration should have been made by the images themselves. Rare indeed, then, are ethnographic films whose commentary is the counterpoint of the pictures. I shall cite two examples here: *Terre sans pain* [Land without bread] by Luis Buñuel, in which Pierre Unik's violently subjective text carries the vocal cruelty necessary to sights which are often quite unbearable; and *The Hunters* by John Marshall, in which the filmmaker leads us with a very simple narrative along the trails of giraffes and their hunters. The film therefore becomes as much the adventures of the hunters and their prey as the adventure of the filmmaker himself.

When new equipment came into use which allowed shooting with synchronous sound, ethnographic films, like all direct-cinema films, became talkative, and the commentary was subjected to the impossible operation of dubbing into another language. More and more, actors were called upon to speak the "commentary" in the hope of approximating the quality of commercial cinema. The result, with a few rare exceptions, was pitiful. Far from translating, transmitting, and approximating reality, this sort of discourse betrayed the subject and drifted away from reality. Personally, after some bad experiences (American version of *La chasse au lion à l'arc* [The lion hunters]), I have preferred to narrate my own films even with my own bad English accent (e.g. *Les maîtres-fous* [The mad masters]).

It would be quite interesting to study the style of the commentaries of ethnographic films since the 1930's. One would note how they passed from a colonial baroque period to one of exotic adventurism, and then on to the dryness of a scientific report. More recently they are characterized either by the shameful distance of anthropologists not wanting to confess their passion for the people they study, or by an ideological discourse through which the filmmaker exports notions of revolution that he has not been able to act upon in his own country. We would thus obtain both a series of profiles characteristic of various times and places, and insights into the scholars of our discipline that no book or lecture could reveal better.

Titles and subtitles therefore appear to be the most effective means of escaping from the trap of commentary. John Marshall was, in my estimation, the first to use this process in his *Kalahari* series for the Peabody Museum. His very simple film *The Pond* about the chatting and mild flirting of Bushmen around a waterhole remains a model of the genre. The difficulties involved in the procedure must not be discounted, however. Besides mutilating the picture, the most difficult obstacle to overcome is the time needed to read titles. As in commercial cinema, the subtitle can be no more than a condensation of what is said. I tried to use it for a sync-sound film on lion hunters (*Un lion nommé l'Américain* [A Lion called 'the American']). However, it was impossible to transcribe satisfactorily the difficult translation of the essential text (praises of the poisoned arrow) declaimed at the moment of the lion's death, because there was not enough time to read everything. The time needed to hear information is much shorter, so I spoke the text which became a voice-over of the original text. Actually the result is also deceptive, for even if this esoteric text takes on a poetic value at that moment, it offers no complementary information. I have returned today to a version without either commentary or subtitles. In essence it would be quite miraculous to be able to give the audience access to so much knowledge and so many complex techniques in twenty minutes when it requires decades of apprenticeship on the part of the hunters themselves. In these circumstances, the film can only be an open door to this knowledge. It is a free pathway and those who wish to learn more can refer to the short pamphlet (an example of the "ethnographic companion to film") which should henceforth accompany every ethnographic film.

To complete this discussion of titling and subtitling, I shall mention the excellent effort by Timothy Asch in *The Feast*. In a preamble made up of stills from the principal sequences, the indispensable explanations are given first of all. The film is then discretely titled so as to indicate who is doing what. Of course, this procedure de-mystifies the film from the very beginning, but this is in my estimation the most original effort made so far.

I shall say little about background music. Tape recordings of original music were (and still are) the basis of the soundtracks of most documentary films (and of all the ethnographic films of the 1950's). It was a question here, once more, of "making movies". I noticed at a fairly early period (1953) the heresy of this sytem when I was showing the film *Bataille sur le grand fleuve* [Battle on the great river] to the Nigerian hippopotamus hunters who had been its subjects two years earlier. On the soundtrack I had overlaid the hippopotamus hunt with a quite moving "hunting air" of string music which had a chase theme. It had seemed to me to be particularly appropriate for this sequence. The result was deplorable; the leader of the hunters asked me to leave out the music since the hunt had to be completely silent... Ever since that adventure, I have paid careful attention to the use of music in films, and I am convinced that even in commercial cinema it is a totally theatrical and outdated convention. Music envelops one, can put one asleep, lets bad cuts pass unnoticed, or gives artificial rhythm to images which have no rhythm and never will have any. In brief, it is the opium of cinema and, unfortunately, television has exploited the mediocrity of this process. I feel that admirable Japanese ethnographic films such as *Papua, a New Life* and especially *Kula, Argonauts of the Western Pacific* are spoiled by the musical sauce with which they are all served, necessary though it may seem.

On the other hand, we must value music which really supports an action, whether it be profane or ritual music, the rhythm of work or of dance. And although it is beyond the scope of this study, I must note here the considerable importance that the technique of synchronous film has and will have in the area of ethnomusicology.

The editing of sound (whether environment, words, or music) is doubtless just as complex as that of pictures, but here again I believe we must make some real progress and get rid of those prejudices which undoubtedly stem from radio. They result in our treating sound with more respect than we treat pictures. Many recent films of the direct-cinema type are thus spoiled by incredible regard for the chatting of the people filmed, as if oral testimony were more sacred than the visual sort. While that kind of filmmaker will not hesitate at all to cut off a gesture in the middle of a motion, he will never dare cut off a speech in the middle of a sentence or a word. Even less often will he dare cut off a musical theme before its final note. I believe that this archaic habit (which television uses a great deal) will disappear quite soon and that pictures will once again take priority.

The Audience of the Ethnographic Film: Films for Research and Distribution

This last point (a final link which could equally well be the first one of a chain if we were asked to justify our intentions) is in my estimation essential for ethnographic film today. Everywhere — in Africa, in universities, in cultural centers, on television, at the Center for Scientific Research of the *Cinémathèque française* — the first question that is asked after the screening of an ethnographic film is: "For whom have you produced this film, and why?"

Why and for whom do we put the camera amongst people? Strangely enough, my first response to this will always be the same: "For myself." It isn't that I am addicted to a particular drug whose "lack" would make itself quite regularly felt, but rather that, at certain times in certain places and around certain people, the camera (and especially the sync-sound camera) seems to be necessary. Of course, it will always be possible to justify its use for scientific reasons (the creation of audiovisual archives of cultures which are rapidly changing or in danger of disappearing), or political ones (sharing in a revolt against an intolerable situation), or aesthetic ones (discovery of a fragile masterpiece in a landscape, a face, or a gesture that we simply cannot let fade away unrecorded). But actually, we make a certain film because there is suddenly that necessity to film, or in some quite similar circumstances, a certainty that filming must not occur.

Perhaps our frequenting of cinema theaters and our ill-timed use of audiovisual methods might make some of us into mad *kinokis* in Vertov's sense or into "cine-eyes" like the "pen-hands" (Rimbaud) of earlier times who could not keep from writing: "...I was there..., such-and-such a thing happened to me..." (La Fontaine). If the cine-voyeur of his own society could always justify himself by this sort of militancy, what reason could we as anthropologists give for the glances we cast over the wall at others?

Without a doubt, this word of interrogation must be addressed to all anthropologists, but none of their books or articles has ever been questioned as much as have anthropological films. And that would be my second response: film is the only method I have to show another just how I see him. In other words, for me, my prime audience is (after the pleasure of the "cine-trance" during the filming and editing) the other person, the one I am filming.

So the position is much clearer: henceforth, the anthropologist has at his disposal the only tool — the "participant camera" — which can provide him with the extraordinary opportunity to communicate with the group under study. He has the film that he made about them. Admittedly we do not yet have all of the technical keys to this, and projection of a film in the field is still at an experimental stage. Without a doubt, the perfection of an automatic super-8 sound projector which runs on a 12-volt battery will be an important step forward, but the experiments that I have been able to carry out with a rebuilt 16-millimeter projector and a small portable 300-watt generator have already proved conclusive: the projection of the film *Sigui 69* in the village of Bongo where it was shot brought considerable reaction from the Dogon of the Bandiagara cliffs together with a request for more films, a series of which is now being made there. The projection of a film called *Horendi* on the initiation rites of possessed dancers in Niger has allowed me, by studying the film on a viewer with priests who had participated in the ritual, to gather more information in a fortnight than I could get from three months of direct observation and interviews with the same informants. And here again we were asked to make more films. This *a posteriori* information on film is still only in its early stages, but it is already producing completely new relationships between the anthropologist and the group he is studying. This is the start of what some of us are already calling "shared anthropology". The observer is finally coming down from his ivory tower; his camera, his tape recorder, and his projector have led him — by way of a strange initiation path — to the very heart of knowledge and, for the first time, his work is not being judged by a thesis committee but by the very people he came to observe.

This extraordinary technique of "feedback" (which I translate as "audiovisual counter-gift") has certainly not yet revealed all of its possibilities, but we can see already that, thanks to feedback, the anthropologist is no longer an entomologist observing his subject as if it were an insect (putting it down) but rather as if it were a stimulant for mutual understanding (hence dignity).

This sort of research employing total participation, idealistic though it may be, seems to me to be the only morally and scientifically possible anthropological attitude today. Today's camera designers should try their hardest to further the development of its technical aspects (super-8 and videotape).

But it would obviously be absurd to condemn ethnographic film to this closed circuit of audiovisual information. This is why my third response to that question "For whom?" is: "For the greatest number of people possible, for all audiences." I believe that if the distribution of our ethnographic films is limited (except for rare exceptions) to a select network of universities, learned societies, and cultural organs, it is due less to the wide distribution of commercial films than it is to a fault in the films that we are producing. It is time for ethnographic films to become cinema in their own right.

I do not think that this is impossible as long as their essential quality of being the privileged records of one or two individuals can be carefully preserved. If lectures by explorers and if television series done in travelogue style have been successful, it is only because — and I repeat this — behind the clumsily taken shots there lurks the presence of the person who took them. As long as an anthropologist-filmmaker, out of scientism or ideological shame, hides himself behind a comfortable sort of incognito, he will ruin his films irreparably and they will join the documents in archives which only the specialists see. Recently ethnographic works, which had previously been reserved for a very small group of scientific libraries, have been published in paperback editions. Their success gives the ethnographic filmmaker an example to follow.

While waiting for the production of real ethnographic films, i.e. films which, according to the obvious definition we gave them nearly twenty years ago, "tie cinematic language to scientific rigor," the International Committee for Ethnographic and Sociological Film decided, at the last Venice film festival (Venezia Genti 1972) to create a veritable network of conservation, documentation, and distribution of "the films of man," with the aid of UNESCO. For we are people who believe that the world of tomorrow, this world we are now in the process of building, will only be viable if it recognizes the differences among various cultures and if we do not deny the existence of these cultures by trying to transform them into images of ourselves. In order to achieve this, we must know these other cultures; to acquire this knowledge, there is no better tool than ethnographic film.

This is not a pious vow, for an example comes to us from the Far East. A Japanese television company, hoping to bring the Japanese out of their insularity, decided to broadcast once a week, for three years, an hour of ethnographic film (cf. Ushiyama's paper, *infra*).

CONCLUSION: SHARED CINEMA-ANTHROPOLOGY

Here we are at the end of our survey of the various uses of the camera among men of yesterday and today. The only conclusion that can be drawn at this point is that ethnographic film has not even passed through its experimental stages yet, and that, while anthropologists have a fabulous tool at their disposal, they do not yet know how to use it properly.

At this stage there are no "schools of ethnographic film"; only trends. Personally, I hope that this marginal situation will last for a while to avoid freezing a young discipline into immutable norms and to keep it from developing a sterile bureaucracy. It is good that American, Canadian, Japanese, Brazilian, Australian, Dutch, British, and French ethnographic films are so different. We can contrast this multiplicity of conception with the universality of concepts characteristic of the scientific approach. If the "cine-eyes" of all countries are ready to unite, it is not to create a universal point of view. I have already stated that films of human science are, in a certain sense, in the forefront of cinematic research. In the diversity of recent films, similar tendencies are appearing because our experiments have led to the same conclusions in different places. The multiplication of shot sequences is new, (and I have asked a designer of light cameras to produce a 16-mm 1000-feet magazine which will permit continuous filming for half an hour). We are thus giving birth to a new filmic language.

And tomorrow? Tomorrow will be the day of the self-regulating color videotape, of automatic video editing, of "instant replay" of the recorded picture (immediate feedback). The dreams of Vertov and Flaherty will be combined into a mechanical "cine-eye-ear" which is such a "participant" camera that it will pass automatically into the hands of those who were, up to now, always in front of it. Then the anthropologist will no longer monopolize the observation of things. Instead, both he and his culture will be observed and recorded. In this way ethnographic film will help us "share" anthropology.

REFERENCES

AZOULAY, L.
   1900a L'ère nouvelle des sons et des bruits. *Bulletins et Mémoires de la Société d'Anthropologie de Paris* 1:172–178.
   1900b Sur la constitution d'un musée phonographique. *Bulletins et Mémoires de la Société d'Anthropologie de Paris* 1:222–226

DE HEUSCH, LUC
   1962 *The cinema and social science.* Reports and Papers in the Social Sciences 16. Paris: UNESCO.

LEROI-GOURHAN, ANDRÉ
   1948 Cinéma et sciences humaines: le film ethnologique existe-t-il? *Revue de Géographie Humaine et d'Ethnologie* 3:42–51.

REGNAULT, FÉLIX
   1896 Les attitudes du repos dans les races humaines. *Revue Encyclopédique* 1896:9–12.
   1897 Le grimper. *Revue Encyclopédique* 1897:904–905.
   1900 La chronophotographie dans l'ethnographie. *Bulletins et Mémoires de la Société d'Anthropologie de Paris* 1:421–422.

ROUCH, JEAN
   1955 À propos de films ethnographiques. *Positif, Revue de Cinéma*, numbers 14–15.

VERTOV, DZIGA
   1923 Kinoki Perevorot. *Lief*, June; republished in part in *Cahiers du Cinéma* 144:32–34 (1963).
   1940 History of the newsreel [in Russian]. *Kino*; cited by Jean Rouch, in "Le film ethnographique," in *Ethnologie générale.* Edited by Charles Samaran (1968):443–444. Paris: Éditions Gallimard.

Documenting the Human Condition

JORGE PRELORAN

In 1968, I was invited to a colloquium on ethnographic film in Los Angeles. There I was told that I make ethnographic films. Actually, to this day I really wonder if that term applies to my work; but if my films serve ethnographic purposes, so be it.

There seem to be two approaches to the documenting of the human condition:

1. Simply using footage as another tool for the anthropologist, in order to record data for future analysis, but not structuring it in any way to form a film.

2. Shooting so as to put together a film that will try to convey to an audience the FEEL of the people, the ambiance in which they live, the ways by which they have adapted to a certain pattern of living according to innumerable factors, among them topographic, climatic, economic, political, traditional, genetic, and so on. Thus the filmmaker faces an almost impossible task: to bring it all together in a tidy hour of projection.

Inasmuch as most of my work has been done without the help of anthro-pologists — and when I have called on them it was generally at the end when the script was being written — I think that I fall into the filmmaker category. This is my training, and I certainly feel like a communicator, making films to convey to an audience what I've lived through while shooting.

During the fifteen years in which I've been making films, isolated in Argentina — on my own and without having teachers or guidelines on hand — perforce I've had to find a meaning in my work, which has never been scientific in approach. But because it has not been in the enter-tainment field either, I was always on a middle ground, and my films are only now starting to become known — after making almost thirty of them — and more so outside than in my own country, where they should be USED. Their adoption is a slow process that has to do with cultural and political conditions in Latin America.

However, the process of evolution in my filming is quite evident: at first the films were simply travelogues, remote documents of places and events with no real involvement. Then slowly I seem to have lost my shyness in getting nearer to people; this is evident in the photography, with the action shown now in more detail, and in our getting to see the people's faces. But the one element of profound change was to be in the sound track. Little by little the people themselves started to talk, to share their thoughts with us, explaining how they did the things we saw, and why. Eventually, I tried to almost do away with the narrator, that outsider who with a careful script and an antiseptic voice explains dispassionately what we see, or what we are supposed to look for in the film. And this always from OUR middle-class westerner's point of view, an impersonal barrier, a wall of incommunication between the protagonists and ourselves. It's so much more rewarding to listen to people, to find out that they are human beings, and even more so, become quite amazed that they are extraordinary human beings at that!

So after all this time, I've evolved a philosophy that guides my work, something I feel is essential in any creative process. The films I make are all part of a path towards a goal I've set for myself: to try to understand the human experience, the "Human Comedy" that Balzac so relished. But at the same time, if I may be permitted a cliché, to give a voice to people who have none.

I think that wherever there is an urban society, people will find ways of being heard, be it through labor unions, associations, clubs, churches, petitions, or some other voluntary medium so that an urbanite can really exert pressure when he feels he's been unjustly treated. Yet there are millions of human beings who are lost in the rural areas all over the world, who have no representation, no pressure groups, no economic power, no imagination to cope with urbanites, no physical stamina to fight for what they wish, perhaps even no fixed goal for themselves. And I thought that if I gave them a chance to communicate to us their plight, and we learned how other people live, we would be better able to understand, rather than strengthen our basically separatist or racist notions of all the "other" world around us. In other words, I wanted to put at the disposal of those people the most sophisticated — indeed THE most sophisticated — medium of communication in the world, and record what they want to tell me, with no preconceived ideas, no pressure to get what WE would see in the situation, with no paternalistic attitudes towards them — and yet, not being objective, but rather subjective and involved. Let us try to think in THEIR terms as much as possible, and be clued by them all the way. For me, the experience has been fascinating. I think that when one is willing to LISTEN, he learns far more than he bargained for.

And my audience? Well, it's the widest I can get: no specific group of scientists, no narrow path of specialization, no movement breakdown... just human communication at its broadest. But that's perhaps why so much can be read into the films.

My films are conceived as a MEANS of communication, and not as a GOAL in themselves. I've worked on single films sometimes over a period of seven years! I am driven by no real urge to finish films, but rather the idea that through films I can convey an experience that I've lived through. The experience is mine: a quest for knowledge, a delving into human possibilities removed from my own, in which human beings just like myself have tried to explain the world they live in, and have become ecologically balanced with their surroundings. This can assume so many different forms, it's absolutely fascinating. The film, then, boils down into a short span of time what I've lived through during several years. And there is a digesting, a sedimenting of things; the subconscious works and comes up with hidden meanings. And eventually, after sifting out what seems to be the fundamental — that which is basic to all human experience that we can relate to — the film emerges and is ready for that magic moment when individual viewers will relate to those people on the screen: they will come up with diverse interpretations but never be indifferent. That is FILM, not simply footage which lacks a soul.

After seeing dozens of films on ethnographic subjects, one thing stands out clearly for me: the majority of them create a gulf between us and the "primitive" people they usually depict. This to me is a racist approach because unless we have a chance to listen first-hand to those people, letting them explain to us WHY they act as they do, WHY they have those extraordinary rituals, those fantastic colorful, exotic, disgusting, fascinating — you label it — ceremonies that are shown to us, we will only think of them as savages, and never as human beings who are striving for something that is fundamental to all human nature. I believe that if we delve deep into human needs, they boil down to shelter, clothing, and food; socially, they include a need for companionship, a biological urge to have children, and a quest for a transcendental world that eludes us all. During these last thousands of years, in adapting to the various environments in which he found himself, man has tried innumerable ways of explaining the world around him. It's worth our while to try to understand all of these ways, and understand the richness of the human experience.

Outstanding films such as David MacDougall's extraordinary work *To Live with Herds*, the remarkable documents by John Marshall, Timothy Asch, Michel Brault, and just a handful of other sensitive and humane filmmakers, or extraordinary team work such as that of Brian Moser and the anthropologist Bernard in the making of *The Last of the Cuiva*, are truly landmarks in a kind of film that should be the foremost effort of our civilization: to celebrate man as the most extraordinary spirit we know. Not defame him, but rather admire his variety of adaptations.

When filming folk cultures as I've been doing — because in Argentina there are no truly isolated cultures left — there is no exotic or fascinating action that one can use to give a punchy ending to the film. But this in itself is a challenge that is exciting. And sometimes dramatic undercurrents can be found in the course of filming during long months: the process of a drought, the slow transculturation patterns, the feeling that evil exists, but can't be pinned down — and thus the need for atonement through religious beliefs — the friction between local authorities, and the staid ways of traditional behavior. All this may seep through the material as one documents, and through long months of elaborating it in the editing room, trying to extract those elusive fundamental threads of our humanness in its quest for balance and survival.

It has been an extraordinary experience for me up to now. But somehow, unless there is a firm conviction behind what one does, and above all, some kind of overall goal that one strives to fulfill, there is no real satisfaction in any accomplishment. I was once told a definition of decadence: "when the means become the goal"; when the reason for filming is simply to make a good living; when a culture becomes so satisfied that there are no further goals to achieve but personal satisfaction; when anthropology has no goal but anthropology itself. My films, I like to think, are made for SOCIAL CHANGE. They are films that are meant to help the people I film, and whom I love. And they are made for them, not for us, nor for us to dissect or watch as we'd watch an ant colony, "objectively". My films are SUBJECTIVE, CONCERNED and INVOLVED. I think there is no more time for science just for science's sake. The world is marching at an accelerated pace towards a crisis the like of which no man has lived through; and all our efforts should be put to mitigate and solve those problems, rather than sit back and look on, content with a safe, comfortable and lucrative position of superiority that science somehow affords.

My films are gentle documents of people that need help; they are not aggressive nor dogmatically ideological. My conviction is that people relate to each other through feeling, rather than through intellectual exercises, theories, discussions, and debates. These can easily be dislodged by other theories, discussions, and exercises, if strongly enough stated. And so man flips from one point of view to another with few qualms. But when a man FEELS, through emotion, this is indelible; and it is our duty to make him more sensitive to feeling than to theories.

Beyond Observational Cinema

DAVID MacDOUGALL

Truth is not a Holy Grail to be won: it is
a shuttle which moves ceaselessly between
the observer and the observed, between
science and reality.

EDGAR MORIN

The past few years have seen a recommitment to the principle of observation in documentary filmmaking. The result has been fresh interest in the documentary film and a body of work which has separated itself clearly from the traditions of Grierson and Vertov.[1] Audiences have had restored to them the sense of wonder at witnessing the spontaneity of life that they felt in the early days of the cinema, seeing a train rush into the Gare de Ciotat. This sense has not grown out of the perfection of some new illusion, but out of a fundamental change in the relationship that filmmakers have sought to establish between their subjects and the viewer. The significance of that relationship for the practice of social science is now beginning to be felt as a major force in the ethnographic film. This would seem an appropriate moment to discuss the implications of the observational cinema as a mode of human inquiry.

In the past anthropologists were accustomed to taking their colleagues'

---

[1] Many consider Vertov the father of observational cinema, and to the extent that he was committed to penetrating the existing world with the "kino-eye" there can be no doubt of his influence. But Vertov's films reflected the prevailing Soviet preoccupation with synthesis, taking their temporal and spatial structures more from the perceptual psychology of the observer than from structures of the events being filmed. His was not a cinema of duration, in the sense that Bazin attributes it to Flaherty.

descriptions on faith. It was rare to know more about a remote people than the person who had studied them, and one accepted his analysis largely because one accepted the scholarly tradition that had produced him. Few monographs offered precise methodological information or substantial texts as documentary evidence.

Ethnographic films were rarely more liberal in this regard. The prevailing style of filming and film editing tended to break a continuum of events into mere illustrative fragments. On top of this, ethnographic filmmaking was a haphazard affair. It was never employed systematically or enthusiastically by anthropologists as a whole. *Moana* (Flaherty 1926) was the work of a geologist and explorer, *Grass* (Cooper and Schoedsack 1925) of casual adventurers who later went on to make *King Kong* (1933). Until very recently most ethnographic films were the by-products of other endeavors: the chronicles of travelers, the political or idealistic visions of documentary filmmakers, and the occasional forays of anthropologists whose major commitment was to other methods. In most cases these films announced their own inadequacies. When they did not, neither were they wholly persuasive. One often wondered what had been concealed or created by the editing, the framing, or the narrator's commentary.

Even as good a film as *The Hunters* (Marshall 1958) left important areas of doubt. Could one accept that this was how the !Kung conducted long hunts, given the fact that the film was compiled from a series of shorter ones? In Robert Gardner's *Dead Birds* (1963), how could one know that the thoughts attributed to the subjects were what they might really have been thinking?

Over the past few years ethnographic filmmakers have looked for solutions to such problems, and the new approaches to filming within our society have provided most of them. By focussing upon discrete events rather than upon mental constructs or impressions, and by seeking to render faithfully the natural sounds, structure, and duration of events, the filmmaker hopes to provide the viewer with sufficient evidence to judge for himself the film's larger analysis. Films like Marshall's *An Argument About a Marriage* (1969), Sandall's *Emu Ritual at Ruguri* (1969), and Asch's *The Feast* (1969) are all attempts of this kind. They are "observational" in their manner of filming, placing the viewer in the role of an observer, a witness of events. They are essentially revelatory rather than illustrative, for they explore substance before theory. They are, nevertheless, evidence of what the filmmaker finds significant.

To those of us who began making ethnographic films at the time that *cinéma vérité* and American direct cinema were revolutionizing documentary filmmaking, this approach to filming other cultures seemed all but inevitable, Its promise for social science appeared so obvious that it was difficult to understand the years of unrealized potential. Why, we often wondered, with time running out to document the world's vanishing cultures, had it not been anthropologists rather than journalists who had first fashioned such a use for the cinema and struggled for its perfection?

The observational direction in ethnographic filmmaking had, after all, begun vigorously enough. The very invention of the cinema was in part a response to the desire to observe the physical behavior of men and animals (Muybridge 1887; Marey 1893). Regnault and Baldwin Spencer quickly went beyond the popular interests of Lumière, making essentially observational film records of technology and ritual in traditional societies. Flaherty's work, for all its reflection of his own idealism, was rooted in the careful exploration of other people's lives. It heralded the achievements of such diverse filmmakers as Cooper and Schoedsack among the Bakhtiari of Iran, Stocker and Tindale in Australia, and Bateson and Mead in Bali. From then on, the ethnographic film fell heir to the fragmentation of image that had originated in the Soviet cinema and that began to dominate the documentary film with the coming of sound.

It could be said that the notion of the synchronous-sound ethnographic film was born at the moment Baldwin Spencer decided to take both an Edison cylinder recorder and a Warwick camera to Central Australia in 1901. It became a practical possibility in the late 1920's only to be neglected in documentary films until the 1950's. In 1935 Arthur Elton and Edgar Anstey demonstrated what could have been done more widely by taking sound cameras, bulky as they then were, into the slums of Stepney and documenting the lives of the inhabitants.[2] To say that they were ahead of their time is only to note with regret that they should not have been.

When highly portable synchronous-sound cameras were finally developed around 1960, few ethnographic filmmakers jumped at the chance to use them although long awaiting this event. Two exceptions were Jean Rouch in France and John Marshall in the United States. Indeed, Rouch's influence was to become a major force in European filmmaking. Marshall had already practised a makeshift kind of synchronous-sound filming in the 1950's among the !Kung and Gwi of the Kalahari. His observational approach foreshadowed the discoveries of the Drew Associates group and the Canadian Film Board in North America,

[2] *Housing Problems*, made for the British Commercial Gas Association.

although the originality of his early work only became evident with the release, long after *The Hunters*, of additional material from his Peabody-Harvard-Kalahari expeditions.

Filmmakers who followed an observational approach quickly divided along methodological lines. Unlike the followers of Rouch, those in the English-speaking world were hesitant to interact in any way with their subjects, except occasionally to interview them. Their adherence to this principle had an almost religious fervor and asceticism, as distinct from the speculative European approach as Calvinism is from Roman Catholicism.

It is this self-denying tendency of modern observational cinema that I should like to examine in particular. It is the tradition in which I was trained, and it has an obvious affinity to certain classical notions of scientific method. But this very orthodoxy could well make it a dangerously narrow model for ethnographic filmmakers of the future.

Many of us who began applying an observational approach to ethnographic filmmaking found ourselves taking as our model not the documentary film as we had come to know it since Grierson, but the dramatic fiction film, in all its incarnations from Tokyo to Hollywood. This paradox resulted from the fact that of the two, the fiction film was the more observational in attitude. Documentaries of the previous thirty years had celebrated the sensibility of the filmmaker in confronting reality; they had rarely explored the flow of real events. Although this style had produced such masterpieces as Basil Wright's *Song of Ceylon* (1934) and Willard Van Dyke and Ralph Steiner's *The City* (1939), it was a style of synthesis, a style that used images to develop an argument or impression.

Each of the discrete images of such documentaries was the bearer of a predetermined meaning. They were often articulated like the images of a poem, juxtaposed against an asynchronous soundtrack of music or commentary. Indeed, poetry was sometimes integral to their conception, as in *The River* (Lorentz 1937), *Night Mail* (Wright and Watt 1936), and *Coalface* (Cavalcanti 1936).

In contrast to this iconographic approach, the images of the fiction film were largely anecdotal. They were the pieces of evidence from which one deduced a story. The audience was told little. It was presented with a series of contiguous events. It learned by observing.

It seemed that such a relationship between viewer and subject should be possible with materials found in the real world. In our own society this had indeed become the approach of filmmakers like Leacock and the Maysles, who were fond of quoting Tolstoy's declaration that the cinema would make the invention of stories unnecessary. For the few of us interested in filming in other cultures, the films of the Italian neorealist period, with their emphasis upon the economic and social environment, seemed like mirror-images of the films we hoped could be made from real events in the ongoing lives of traditional peoples.

The natural voice of the fiction film is the third person: the camera observes the actions of the characters not as a participant but as an invisible presence, capable of assuming a variety of positions. To approximate such an approach in the nonfiction film, the filmmaker must find ways of making himself privy to human events without disturbing them. This is relatively easy when the event attracts more attention than the camera — what Morin (1962:4) calls "intensive sociality." It becomes difficult when a few people are interacting in an informal situation. Yet documentary filmmakers have been so successful in achieving this goal that scenes of the most intimate nature have been recorded without apparent embarrassment or pretense on the part of the subjects. The usual method is to spend so much time with one's subjects that they lose interest in the camera. Finally they must go on with their lives, and they do so in their accustomed ways. This may seem improbable to those who have not seen it happen, yet to filmmakers it is a familiar phenomenon.

In my own work I have often been struck by the readiness of people to accept being filmed, even in societies where one might expect a camera to be particularly threatening. This acceptance is of course aided by de-emphasizing the actual process of filming, both in one's manner and technique. While making *To Live With Herds* (1972) among the Jie of Uganda I used a special brace which allowed me to keep the camera in the filming position for twelve or more hours a day over a period of many weeks. I lived looking through the viewfinder. Because the camera ran noiselessly, my subjects soon gave up trying to decide when I was filming and when I was not. As far as they were concerned I was always filming, an assumption which no doubt contributed to their confidence that their lives were being seen fully and fairly. When I took out a still camera at the end of my stay everyone began posing —a clear sign that they had understood an essential quality of the cinema.

I would suggest that at times people can behave more naturally while being filmed than in the presence of an ordinary observer. A man with a camera has an obvious job to do, which is to film. His subjects understand this and leave him to it. He remains occupied, half-hidden behind his machine, satisfied to be left alone. As an unencumbered visitor, he would have to be entertained, whether as a guest or as a friend. In this, I think, lies both the strength and the weakness of the observational method.

The purpose behind this curiously lonely approach of observational cinema is arguably to film things that would have occurred if one had not been there. It is a desire for the invisibility of the imagination found in literature combined with the aseptic touch of the surgeon's glove — in some cases a legitimization, in the name of art or science, of the voyeur's peephole. It has even been reduced to a formula for anthropology:

Ethnographic film is film which endeavors to interpret the behavior of people of one culture to persons of another culture by using shots of people doing precisely what they would have been doing if the camera were not there (Goldschmidt 1972).

Invisibility and omniscience. From this desire it is not a great leap to begin viewing the camera as a secret weapon in the pursuit of knowledge. The self-effacement of the filmmaker begins to efface the limitations of his own physicality. He and his camera are imperceptibly endowed with the power to witness the TOTALITY of an event. Indeed, they are expected to. Omniscience and omnipotence.

It is an approach that has produced some remarkable films. And for many filmmakers it has in practice a comforting lack of ambiguity. The filmmaker establishes a role for himself which demands no social response from his subjects, and he then disappears into the woodwork. Allan King's *Warrendale* (1966) and *A Married Couple* (1969) make the audience witnesses of scenes of private emotional anguish without reference to the presence of the film crew. In a film like *At the Winter Sea Ice Camp, Part II* (Balikci 1968), from the Netsilik Eskimo series, the people seem altogether oblivious of Robert Young's camera. And in Frederick Wiseman's *Essene* (1972), a study of people striving painfully to live communally in a religious order, one has at times the curious sense of being the eye of God.

When films like these are functioning at their best, the people in them seem bearers of the immeasurable wealth and effort of human experience. Their lives have a weight that makes the film that caught but a fragment seem trivial, and we sit in a kind of awe of our own privileged observation of them. That emotion helps us accept the subjects' disregard of the filmmaker. For them to notice him would amount almost to a sacrilege — a shattering of the horizons of their lives, which by all rights should not include someone making a film about them. In the same way, some scholars are disturbed by descriptions of traditional societies in which the anthropologist is a feature of cultural contact.

Audiences are thus accomplices in the filmmaker's voluntary absence from his film — what Leacock calls "the pretense of our not being there" (Levin 1971:204). From a scientific standpoint, the priorities of research also keep the filmmaker out, because to pay attention to him is to draw valuable time from the subject at hand. Finally, the literature and films we have grown up with have shaped our expectations: Aeneas is unaware of Virgil; the couple on the bed ignores the production crew of twenty standing round. Even in home movies people wince when someone looks at the camera.

Filmmakers begin as members of an audience and carry part of that inheritance with them. But the act of filming tends to interpose its own barriers between the observer and the observed. For one thing, it is difficult for a filmmaker to photograph himself as an element in the phenomenon he is examining — unless, like Jean Rouch and Edgar Morin in *Chronique d'un été* (1961), he becomes an "actor" before the camera. More often it is through his voice and the response of his subjects that we feel his presence.

Perhaps more important, the filmmaker exhausts most of his energy making his camera respond to what is before it. His concentration induces a certain passivity from which it is difficult for him to rouse himself. Active participation with his subjects suggests an altogether different psychic state. This may explain the rather frequent success of film as a contemplative art.

Among ethnographic filmmakers, another restraint is the special reverence that surrounds the study of isolated peoples. The fragility of these cultures and the rarity of filming them turns the filmmaker into an instrument of history — an obligation which, if accepted or even felt, must necessarily weigh down his efforts to pursue specific lines of inquiry.

This lofty view is often reinforced by an identification with his audience that may cause him to mimic, consciously or otherwise, their impotence. As members of an audience we readily accept the illusion of entering into the world of a film. But we do so in complete safety, because our own world is as close as the nearest light switch. We observe the people in the film without being seen, assured that they can make no claims upon us. The corollary of this, however, lies in our inability to reach through the screen and affect their lives. Thus our situation combines a sense of immediacy with an absolute separation. Only when we try to invade the world of the film do we discover the insubstantiality of its illusion of reality.

In his attempt to make us into witnesses, the observational filmmaker often thinks in terms of the image on the screen rather than his presence in the setting where events are occurring. He becomes no more than the eye of the audience, frozen into their passivity, unable to bridge the separation between himself and his subjects.

But it is finally scientific objectives that have placed the severest strictures on ethnographic film. Inevitably, the extraordinary precision of the camera-eye as a descriptive aid has influenced conceptions of the use to which film should be put, with the result that for years anthropologists have considered film pre-eminently as a tool for gathering data. And because film deals so overwhelmingly with the specific rather than the abstract, it is often considered incapable of serious intellectual articulation.

Certainly there are enough ethnographic films containing crude or dubious interpretations to explain, if not to justify, such a conclusion. Films risking more legitimate, if more difficult, kinds of analysis are often flawed in the attempt. Still others receive no credit because their contribution exists in a form that cannot be assessed in the terms of conventional anthropology. Each of these instances adds weight to the common impression that attempts to use film as an original medium of anthropology are simply pretexts for self-indulgence. What is more, each attempt that fails can be viewed as an opportunity lost to add to the fund of more routine ethnography.

With data-gathering as the objective, there is of course no real need for the making of films, but merely for the collection of footage upon which a variety of studies can later be based. Indeed, Sorenson (1967) suggests that footage might be collected with only this broad objective in view. Yet much bad anthropological writing is a similar gathering and cataloguing of information, deficient in thought or analysis. This is not far from the criticism that Evans-Pritchard levels at Malinowski:

The theme is no more than a descriptive synthesis of events. It is not a theoretical integration,... There is consequently no real standard of relevance, since everything has a time and space relationship in cultural reality to everything else, and from whatever point one starts one spreads oneself over the same ground (1962:95).

The same criticism could be made of many existing ethnographic films. If it is a valid criticism, if ethnographic film is to become anything more than a form of anthropological note-taking, then attempts must continue to make it a medium of ideas. There will inevitably be more failures. But it seems probable that the great films of anthropology, as distinct from ethnography, are still to be made.

Curiously, it is the survival of the data within the context of thought, inescapable in the cinema, that is responsible for the impatience of many social scientists with film as a medium for anthropology. The glimpse gained of the original field situation may be so immediate and evocative that it proves tantalizing to those who would like to see more, and infuriating to those whose specific theoretical interests are not being served. Thus an ecologist may well dismiss as shallow a film in which the study of social relationships takes precedence over ecology.

Films prove to be poor encyclopedias because of their emphasis upon specific and delimited events viewed from finite perspectives. Yet surprisingly, it is often the supposed potency of film in this capacity that has led to its downfall. At first glance, film seems to offer an escape from the inadequacies of human perception and a factual check on the capriciousness of human interpretation. The precision of the photographic image leads to an uncritical faith in the camera's power to capture, not the images of events, but the events themselves — as Ruskin once said of some photographs of Venice, "as if a magician had reduced reality to be carried away into an enchanted land" (1886–1887:341). So persuasive is this belief in the magic of photography that it is assumed by scholars who in the rest of their research would challenge far more circumspect assumptions. When disillusionment comes, it is therefore profound.

The magical fallacy of the camera parallels the fallacy of omniscient observation. It may result from a tendency in viewing films to define what has been photographed by what one is seeing. The film image impresses us with its completeness, partly because of its precise rendering of detail, but even more because it represents a continuum of reality which extends beyond the edges of the frame and which therefore, paradoxically, seems not to be excluded. A few images create a world. We ignore the images that could have been, but weren't. In most cases we have no conception of what they might be.

It is possible that the sense of completeness created by a film also lies in the richness of ambiguity of the photographic image. Images begin to become signs of the objects they represent; yet unlike words or even pictographs, they share in the physical identity of the objects, having been produced as a kind of photochemical imprint of them. The image thus continually asserts the presence of the concrete world within the framework of a communicative system that imposes meaning.

The viewfinder of the camera, one could say, has the opposite function of the gunsight that a soldier levels at his enemy. The latter frames an image for annihilation; the former frames an image for preservation, thereby annihilating the surrounding multitude of images which could have been formed at that precise point in time and space. The image becomes a piece of evidence, like a potsherd. It also becomes, through the denial of all other possible images, a reflection of thought. In that double nature is the magic that can so easily dazzle us.

Observational cinema is based upon a process of selection. The filmmaker limits himself to that which occurs naturally and spontaneously in front of his camera. The richness of human behavior and the propensity of people to talk about their affairs, past and present, are what allow this method of inquiry to succeed.

It is, nevertheless, a method that is quite foreign to the usual practice of anthropology or, for that matter, most other disciplines. (Two exceptions are history and astronomy, which the barriers of time and distance require to function in the same way.) Most anthropological fieldwork involves, in addition to observation, an active search for information among informants. In the laboratory sciences, knowledge comes primarily from events that the scientist himself provokes. Thus the observational filmmaker finds himself cut off from many of the channels that normally characterize human inquiry. He is dependent for his understanding (or for the understanding of his audience) upon the unprovoked ways in which his subjects manifest the patterns of their lives during the moments he is filming them. He is denied access to anything they know but take for granted, anything latent in their culture which events do not bring to the surface.

The same methodological asceticism that causes him to exclude himself from the world of his subjects also excludes his subjects from the world of the film. Here the implications are ethical as well as practical. By asking nothing of his subjects beyond permission to film them, the filmmaker adopts an inherently secretive position. He has no need for further explanation, no need to communicate with his subjects on the basis of the thinking that organizes his work. There is, in fact, some reason for him not to do so for fear it may influence their behavior. In his insularity, he withholds the very openness that he asks from his subjects in order to film them.

In his refusal to give his subjects access to the film, the filmmaker refuses them access to himself, for this is clearly his most important activity when he is among them. In denying a part of his own humanity, he denies a part of theirs. If not in his personal demeanor, then in the significance of his working method, he inevitably reaffirms the colonial origins of anthropology. It was once the European who decided what was worth knowing about "primitive" peoples and what they in turn should be taught. The shadow of that attitude falls across the observational film, giving it a distinctively Western parochialism. The traditions of science and narrative art combine in this instance to dehumanize the study of man. It is a form in which the observer and the observed exist in separate worlds, and it produces films that are monologues.

What is finally disappointing in the ideal of filming "as if the camera were not there" is not that observation in itself is unimportant, but that as a governing approach it remains far less interesting than exploring the situation that actually exists. The camera IS there, and it is held by a representative of one culture encountering another. Beside such an extraordinary event, the search for isolation and invisibility seems a curiously irrelevant ambition. No ethnographic film is merely a record of another society: it is always a record of the meeting between a filmmaker and that society. If ethnographic films are to break through the limitations inherent in their present idealism, they must propose to deal with that encounter. Until now they have rarely acknowledged that an encounter has taken place (cf. McCarty's paper, *supra*).

The main achievement of observational cinema is that it has once again taught the camera how to watch. Its failings lie precisely in the attitude of watching — the reticence and analytical inertia it induces in filmmakers, some of whom feel themselves agents of a universal truth, others of whom comment only slyly or by indirection from behind their material. In either case, the relationship between the observer, the observed, and the viewer has a kind of numbness.

Beyond observational cinema lies the possibility of a PARTICIPATORY CINEMA, bearing witness to the "event" of the film and making strengths of what most films are at pains to conceal. Here the filmmaker acknowledges his entry upon the world of his subjects and yet asks them to imprint directly upon the film their own culture. This should not imply a relaxation of the filmmaker's purposefulness, nor should it cause him to abandon the perspective that an outsider can bring to another culture. By revealing his role, the filmmaker enhances the value of his material as evidence. By entering actively into the world of his subjects, he can provoke a greater flow of information about them. By giving them access to the film, he makes possible the corrections, additions, and illuminations that only their response to the material can elicit. Through such an exchange a film can begin to reflect the ways in which its subjects perceive the world.

This is a process that goes back to Flaherty. Nanook participated in creating the film about himself, "constantly thinking up new hunting scenes for the film" (Flaherty 1950:15). During the filming of *Moana*, Flaherty projected his rushes each evening, building upon the suggestions that came from his subjects. Yet with the exception of Jean Rouch, few filmmakers today are able or willing to invite such insights.

To the degree that the elements of one culture are not describable in the terms of another, the ethnographic filmmaker must devise ways of bringing the viewer into the social experience of his subjects. This is partly an act of analysis, partly what Redfield called "the art of social science". But it can also be a process of collaboration — the filmmaker combining the skills and sensibilities of his subjects with his own. This requires that they and he, whatever their differences, be moved by at least some common sense of urgency.

Rouch and Morin's *Chronique d'un été*, about a disparate group of young Parisians, explores their lives within the context of their interest in the film itself. Despite the anonymity of the actual cameramen[3] (which is unfortunate), there is no pact made with the audience to ignore the role of the film's makers. On the contrary, it is the making of the film that binds them and their subjects together.

Chronique d'un été is an elaborate experiment which one would probably not expect to see transferred intact to a traditional society. Yet it is remarkable how few of the ideas of this extraordinary film managed to penetrate the thinking of ethnographic filmmakers in the decade after it was made. The approach proved too alien to an effort preoccupied with the needs of teaching or the urgency of preserving overall records of imperiled societies.

It is, of course, the value of such records that is open to question. They may be unable to answer future anthropological questions except in the most general manner. An exhaustive analysis of a social phenomenon usually requires that the data be collected with the full extent of that phenomenon in mind. It is clear from the body of Rouch's work that he views broad salvage anthropology, based upon no defined perspective, as more hazardous to the future understanding of extinct societies — and therefore to an understanding of man — than a study in which the investigator is passionately and intellectually engaged. If acutely perceived, he seems to say, the part may stand more accurately for the whole than the survey, which succeeds only in capturing the most superficial aspects of the whole. This is at odds with the view of Lévi-Strauss (1972) that anthropology is like astronomy, seeing human societies from afar and only discerning their brightest constellations.

In Rouch's approach anthropology must therefore proceed by digging from within rather than observing from without, which all too easily

---

3   Roger Morillère, Raoul Coutard, Jean-Jacques Tarbès, and Michel Brault.

gives an illusory sense of comprehension. Digging necessarily disturbs the successive strata through which one passes to reach one's goal. But there is a significant difference between this human archaeology and its material counterpart: culture is pervasive and expresses itself in all the acts of human beings, whether they are responding to customary or extraordinary stimuli. The values of a society lie as much in its dreams as in the reality it has built. Often it is only by introducing new stimuli that the investigator can peel back the layers of a culture and reveal its fundamental assumptions.

In the film that James Blue and I made among the Boran of Kenya (MacDougall and Blue 1973), some of the information revealed resulted from just such a process. Without the participation of our subjects, certain aspects of their situation might well have remained unexpressed. Once, during a typical men's conversation over tea, we asked a man named Guyo Ali to raise the subject of the government's advocacy of birth control. The result was an explosion of disagreement from Iya Duba, the most conservative old man present. In his reply, he set forth his view of the logic of having many children in a pastoral society, followed by an impassioned defense of cattle and cattle herding, which he was unlikely to have delivered without some such strong provokation. It was in fact the clearest expression of Boran economic values that we encountered during our stay.

Involvement with one's subjects can become a kind of pose — the fleeting recognition of the film crew which gives a sense of candor but really reveals nothing. For a film to gain meaning from the breakdown of old narrative conventions, that recognition must develop into a genuine conversation.

Sometimes one hears only half of the conversation. The oldest examples go back to those ruminative testimonies of lonely people, of which *Paul Tomkowicz: Street-Railway Switch Man* (Kroitor 1954) is perhaps the archetype and Jorge Preloran's *Imaginero* (1970) the most convincing document. Sometimes it becomes a performance — the compulsive talking of a subject stimulated by the camera, as in Shirley Clarke's *Portrait of Jason* (1967) or Tanya Ballantyne's *The Things I Cannot Change* (1967). The out-of-work father in the latter film cannot resist the offer to control the image of himself presented to the world. Yet he bears out Rouch's dictum: whatever he tries to be, he is only more himself.

Sometimes role-playing provides the necessary stimulus. In Rouch's *Jaguar* (1958–1967) his young protagonists respond to the invitation to act out an adventure for which they have long been eager. They use the pretext of the story to reveal a private image of themselves, just as Marcelline in *Chronique d'un été* uses the pretext of a film role to speak of her painful return from a concentration camp.

This is a kind of participation, but it remains one in which the film manipulates its subjects. A further step will be films in which participation occurs in the very conception and recognizes common goals. That possibility remains all but unexplored — a filmmaker putting himself at the disposal of his subjects and, with them, inventing the film.

The promise of a useful relationship between film and anthropology is still crippled by timidity on both sides. Its fulfillment will require an enlarging of the acceptable forms of both film and anthropology. Anthropology must admit forms of understanding which replace those of the written word. Film must create forms of expression reflecting anthropological thought. Films, rather than speculation, will finally demonstrate whether these possibilities are real. Ethnographic filmmakers can begin by abandoning their preconceptions about what is good cinema. It is enough to conjecture that a film need not be an aesthetic or scientific performance: it can become the arena of an inquiry.

REFERENCES

Literature

EVANS-PRITCHARD, E. E.
    1962   *Social Anthropology and other essays.* Glencoe: Free Press.
FLAHERTY, ROBERT J.
    1950   "Robert Flaherty talking," in *The cinema 1950.* Edited by R. Manvell. Harmondsworth: Penguin.
GOLDSCHMIDT, WALTER
    1972   Ethnographic film: definition and exegesis. *PIEF Newsletter of the American Anthropological Association* 3 (2):1–3.
LEVIN, G. ROY
    1971   *Documentary explorations.* New York: Doubleday.
MAREY, ÉTIENNE
    1883   Emploi des photographies partielles pour étudier la locomotion de l'homme et des animaux. *Comptes Rendus de l'Académie des Sciences* (Paris) 96:1827–1831.
MORIN, EDGAR
    1962   "Preface," in *The cinema and social science; a survey of ethnographic and sociological films,* by Luc de Heusch, 4–6. Reports and Papers in the Social Sciences 16. Paris: UNESCO.

MUYBRIDGE, EADWEARD
1887 *Animal locomotion: an electro-photographic investigation of consecutive phases of animal movements*, 16 volumes. Philadelphia: J. B. Lippincott Company.

RUSKIN, JOHN
1886–1887 *Praeterita: outlines of scenes and thoughts, perhaps worthy of memory, in my past life.* (New edition 1949, London: R. Hart Davis.)

SORENSON, E. RICHARD
1967 A research film program in the study of changing man. *Current Anthropology* 8:443–469.

Films[4]

ASCH, TIMOTHY
1968 *The Feast.* Center for Documentary Anthropology.

BALIKCI, ASEN
1968 *At the Winter Sea Ice Camp, Part II.* Educational Development Center.

BALLANTYNE, TANYA
1967 *The Things I Cannot Change.* National Film Board of Canada.

CAVALCANTI, ALBERTO
1936 *Coalface.* GPO (General Post Office) Film Unit.

CLARKE, SHIRLEY
1967 *Portrait of Jason.* Produced in association with Film Makers Distribution Center.

COOPER, MERIAN C., ERNEST B. SCHOEDSACK
1925 *Grass.* Famous-Players-Lasky.
1933 *King Kong.* RKO.

ELTON, ARTHUR, EDGAR ANSTEY
1935 *Housing Problems.* British Commercial Gas Association.

FLAHERTY, ROBERT J.
1922 *Nanook of the North.* Revillon Frères.
1926 *Moana, a Romance of the Golden Age.* Famous-Players-Lasky.

GARDNER, ROBERT
1963 *Dead Birds.* Film Study Center, Harvard University.

KING, ALLAN
1966 *Warrendale.* Allan King Associates.
1969 *A Married Couple.* Allan King Associates.

KROITOR, ROMAN
1953 *Paul Tomkowicz: Street-Railway Switch Man.* National Film Board of Canada.

LÉVI-STRAUSS, CLAUDE
1972 Interview with Edwin Newman, on *Speaking Freely.* ORTF- NET.

LORENTZ, PARE
1937 *The River.* Farm Security Administration.

MACDOUGALL, DAVID
1972 *To Live With Herds.* Film Images.

---

[4] See Filmography, *infra*, for details.

MACDOUGALL, DAVID, JAMES BLUE
  1973   *Kenya Boran*. American Universities Field Staff.
MARSHALL, JOHN
  1958   *The Hunters*. Film Study Center, Harvard University.
  1969   *An Argument About a Marriage*. Center for Documentary Anthropology.
PRELORAN, JORGE
  1970   *Imaginero*. Image Resources.
ROUCH, JEAN'
  1958–1967   *Jaguar*. Les Films de la Pléiade.
ROUCH, JEAN, EDGAR MORIN
  1961   *Chronique d'un été*. Les Films de la Pléiade.
SANDALL, ROGER
  1969   *Emu Ritual at Ruguri*. Australian Institute of Aboriginal Studies.
VAN DYKE, WILLARD, RALPH STEINER
  1939   *The City*. American Documentary Films, Inc., for American Institute of Planners.
WISEMAN, FREDERICK
  1972   *Essene*. Zipporah Films.
WRIGHT, BASIL
  1934   *Song of Ceylon*. Ceylon Tea Propaganda Board.
WRIGHT, BASIL, HARRY WATT
  1936   *Night Mail*. GPO (General Post Office), Film Unit.

Ethnographic Film Documents

ROGER SANDALL

Ethnographic films are today at a watershed. On the one side, falling away
to the broad and level plains of general education, are the traditional
teaching films which take it upon themselves to assimilate the raw
materials of alien cultures to the needs of the classroom, the mental world
of the student, and to lecture periods lasting about an hour. On the other
side the terrain is much more rugged and the films are similar. Instead of
being smoothly adapted to the educational plains they tend to have the
awkward craggy forms of the cultural topography they record, the unique
events they show, a tendency which follows from their consistently favor-
ing observation rather than interpretation, validation rather than illustration, a holistic concern for intact units of social behavior which contrasts
with the reductionist bias of older cinematic techniques, and a respect for
the claims of the subject of ethnographic enquiry to his own identity and
language rather than the assimilative claims of the educator and his needs.

To some extent these new priorities reflect changing priorities in the
world at large. If a quasi-economic vocabulary was appropriate to
describe the traditional relation of ethnographic films to their users, if it
seemed only natural to speak of "assimilating" the "raw materials" of
primitive culture to a classroom's interests and needs, then this was because that's what such films entailed. Such a vocabulary and such an
attitude seem much less fitting now. We're more sensitive to the claims of
raw material, especially in human form, and we're more sensitive to the
natural reluctance of tribals and other minorities to being assimilated, no
matter how benevolently, to the Western world's cultural or curricular
needs.

This is partly because we have found that such people have "voices of their own," a development which has come about as much for technical as for political reasons. Twenty years ago if filmmakers had wanted to know what the thoughts of tribal people in some remote location were on certain issues — or on no issues at all — the machinery then existing didn't permit it. Today all this is changed: the lightweight camera which shoots synchronous sound, the portable tape-recorder, the zoom lens which permits the uninterrupted but variably selective coverage of a scene — these have all vastly augmented cinematography's descriptive and observational powers (Plate 8). The result of new techniques, reinforced by the new and more sensitive attitudes, is a kind of film better described as a "film document" than a "documentary film." This emphasizes that we are dealing with the class documents, sub-class films, rather than simply a class of films having certain documentary characteristics. In the vocabulary of filmmaking a documentary is likely to be something with a strong manipulative and interpretative bias; whereas in the vocabulary of science a "document" is first and foremost a piece of evidence. The class "films" includes presentations in which elision, omission, and rearrangement for dramatic effect are common features. The class "documents" requires above all that things remain intact. While of great value for instructional purposes, what we call documents can in no sense be regarded as merely teaching aids. And once this is better understood it should be easier for both teachers and students to cope with some of the problems the new film documents entail.

First, there are the practical ones. Suppose you film a group of men discussing a proposed marriage. As each man says his piece you must follow him with both camera and microphone. The talk has a logical order which must be preserved at a later stage. You may have no chance to film the bride and groom. You may not be allowed to. Though the historical background to the occasion may be awesomely complex you find you have no material which shows this. In the older type of documentary almost any length would be gone to to obtain an "illustrative" shot of the bride and groom or a sequence suggesting the history of their relationship. But here the ethnographic intention is not illustration but documentation, and whoever makes films in this way is bound to the exigencies of what actually happens and what can actually be filmed. In film documents, gaps and omissions are circumstantial evidence of authenticity.

Or take the question of sound itself. The effect of adding synchronous sound is often to produce an extreme crowding of the time and space available for explanation. Given certain fixed quantities — language as the means of explanation, the natural speed of events — descriptive input and explanatory output tend to be inversely proportional. In film documents the extra channel of information provided by synchronous sound has greatly expanded the first: as a result the second has noticeably shrunk. In plain language, the new techniques enable us to see and to hear far more than it may be possible to explain simultaneously.

In these circumstances presentation and interpretation may have to be separated. This can be done within the film itself. A prologue which reviews the action to come may introduce the film, as in *The Feast*. A "rolling title" of descriptive text may set out facts which need to be known in advance, as in *Gunabibi — An Aboriginal Fertility Cult*. Part and chapter headings with explanatory text may divide one section from the next, as in *To Live With Herds*. Yet internal textual matter is very much of a *pis aller*. It tends to be both clumsy and inadequate, a forlorn attempt to incorporate material best acquired from books. What this inevitably implies is that for film documents to be used most effectively an instructor may have to give his class a more than usually thorough preparation. They are always most wisely situated in a curricular matrix of readings and related coursework without which much of their significance will be lost.

Could it be argued that synchronous sound is more of a liability than an asset? For those who require a document to be self-explanatory — who demand, as it were, an interlinear interpretation — it might seem so. Of course when the sound is non-linguistic the problem is trivial: should a film showing the making of a dugout canoe entirely obliterate the noise of axes with interpretative commentary, the loss would be atmospheric more than anything else. But when one turns from the visible and mechanical to the partly invisible or the wholly esoteric then the problems of simultaneous interpretation become acute. If we take *The Mulga Seed Ceremony*, for example, and freely concede the justice of Gould's wish for more narrated information than it now contains, it's still not clear how far one could usefully go with this (Gould 1972:190).

We might start by noting that the Aboriginal men are singing beside a rock representing one of the totemic Mulga Seed Men. Next we are led to try and explain how the rock got that way; how it is that by rubbing sacred ceremonial boards particles of fertility are created which pass into the bodies of women; all of which leads inescapably to the whys and wherefores of totemic identity itself. But before such a disquisition is much advanced it is likely that the men will have stopped their singing and walked away. The trouble is that ritual needs its own explicative structure, one much at odds with the behavior it regulates or the beliefs it helps sustain.

The practical objections to the simultaneous explanation of film documents are plain: are there others? One derives from the common expectation that the filmmaker owes it to his audience to provide a firm theoretical foundation for what is shown. Thus a reviewer of the Netsilik Eskimo series describes the absence of narration as a drawback which can "be overcome by a fully informed instructor who knows Central Arctic Eskimo ethnography... and has a theoretical framework... suitable for analysing hunting and gathering societies" (Honigmann 1970:722–24). To be sure, theoretical frameworks have an important place. But is it in the middle of documents? Experience teaches that in any film which hopes to be of enduring value the absence of intrusive theorizing is more often a virtue than a fault. Indeed, the contemporary theory of Aboriginal ritual is so highly speculative that in the series of films of ceremonies made by the Australian Institute of Aboriginal Studies it has seemed essential to avoid imposing notions which may very soon sound distinctly out of date. Such a "hands off" attitude may be less appropriate for the theory of hunting and gathering. Even so, ethology is revising many assumptions we have long taken for granted, and just how durable any given framework will prove is something only time will tell.

As an example of contemporary tendencies in the theory of ceremonial one may note a recent publication by Andrew and Marilyn Strathern, *Self-Decoration in Mount Hagen*. The authors seek to establish a color code explaining the Hagener's system of decoration, and conclude that its essence lies in a pervasive contrast of opposites, a scheme which they acknowledge finds "no exact replica in what Hageners themselves say." Reviewing the book from the standpoint of an art historian E. H. Gombrich mischievously imagines some anthropologists being invited to apply the same principles to the explanation of our own Christmas celebrations:

The first thing to tell them would be that both "explanation" and "meaning" are slippery terms: explaining a ceremony demands a knowledge of origins, of the historical dimension which eludes the anthropologist. Nor can the meaning of a ritual be identified with possible unconscious determinants. The fact that trees can be classed with phallic symbols will not tell our visitors what Christmas celebrations mean to us — provided, indeed, one can speak of such a collective meaning at all. In any case we would have a right to object if these investigators were to come up with a system of meanings "that has no exact replica" in what we ourselves have told them (Gombrich 1972:37).

Such considerations plainly apply just as stringently to document films of ceremonial events where gratuitous theorizing has implications almost as much ethical as scientific.

For reasons such as these in most of the films made by the Australian Institute of Aboriginal Studies explanation is confined to a minimum of sub-titles. These signal the main action, and have the notable advantage over commentary — important in the case of dance and song — that they leave the rich natural sound intact. This often consists of speech, and increasingly ethnographic film documents translate this at the foot of the screen. This familiar procedure has certain drawbacks; it easily arouses expectations which cannot always be fulfilled. Audiences accustomed to foreign feature films have sometimes regarded the Aboriginal talk they hear in the A.I.A.S. films as analogous to "dialogue" and expect it to be translated with equal facility. In fact this can rarely be done. Most of the scenes in these records of religious ceremonies show collective activity, and the talk heard on the soundtrack is a natural blend of several voices at once. A keen-eared linguist might disentangle them; but even so, the highly saturated input greatly exceeds the explicative output of the subtitle writer's art.

In her review of *Emu Ritual at Ruguri*, Nancy Munn sensitively notes that the subtitles successfully delete the "'foreign' voice of a commentator that inevitably intrudes upon the relationship between observer and film action" (Munn 1970:1202). Two things are noteworthy in this remark. A leading reason for not using commentary has been accurately identified — the intrusive assimilative effect of foreign narrators with foreign voices. At the same time the term "observer" is used instead of the more expected "audience" or "class." Here, perhaps unconsciously, the reviewer has drawn attention to a fundamental distinction between the film document and the traditional teaching aid. *Emu Ritual at Ruguri* does not try to bring back to the classroom pictorial glimpses of the Aboriginal world. Instead it takes students on a field trip to the desert and enables them to witness events at first hand.

Such films are primarily observational: if this were realized then users of film catalogs might be prepared for more arduous and demanding experiences than usually await the instructor who rents a teaching film. Unprepared, unaware of this distinction, the user of one of the A.I.A.S. records of Aboriginal ritual could well have the kind of reaction foreseen by Gould in the case of *The Mulga Seed Ceremony*, a "reinforcement of general prejudices about Aboriginal life." The film he refers to contains scenes of ritual blood-letting of a potentially disturbing kind. But regardless of content it's apparent that not all audiences wish to be observers, just as many students recoil from actually working in the field. Accustomed to safe guided tours through alien cultural territory they do not take kindly to finding themselves unescorted and far from home. It may not be too much of an exaggeration to say that film documents which vividly succeed in recreating ethnographic reality risk producing one of that reality's more notorious side effects — culture shock.

Is this a bad thing? If it results merely in reinforcing prejudices the answer would have to be yes. Yet it's possible that in our overprotected world a draft of culture shock might also prove intellectually bracing. Should it really be considered unendurable for a student to be suddenly set down in an alien environment when for centuries this was the lot of every traveller? Perhaps abrupt confrontation with difference compels closer attention to cultural idiosyncrasy than the bland world of the budget tour. Nevertheless it is true that while shock may brace the mind and mystery may stimulate reflection, educationally these are secondary virtues. Understanding is the main goal; and as remarked above, this can be most satisfactorily achieved through sound instruction and extensive preparatory reading.

Much of the above discussion of meaning in the document film has referred to the kind of material in which this presents inherent problems — the esoterica of religious ritual. But a growing number of films present informal as well as formal activities, and the meaning of activity in which informal talk can be heard and understood is plainly more accessible to audiences. Informal discussions are to be found in some of John Marshall's !Kung Bushman series and in David MacDougall's recent *To Live With Herds*. In the latter, comparatively long conversations, sometimes biographical, sometimes economic in implication, are rendered intact; and the most common audience response to such scenes is one of delight that the cameraman has succeeded in showing tribal people being so spontaneously themselves. "Intimate" is the word reviewers reach for, often using it as if intimacy were a value in itself. But is it? Or is this merely a reaction to its undeniable novelty on the screen? We do not express surprise at the intimacy of tape recordings in which informants tell about their lives. Nor are we awed by memoirs, no matter how personal or deeply felt, related to an anthropologist who pencils them on paper. One suspects that intimacy is admired on the screen more because it is unexpected than because it constitutes a distinctive ethnographic resource. Beyond it the critical ethnographic task remains: as with any other document one must try to establish, on the basis of data gathered in other ways, the relevance and pertinence of what is being said.

Related to this question is another — the merits of training the usual human subjects of ethnography to make ethnographic films themselves. Much of the thinking on this matter seems rather naive. One line of theory has concerned perception: this has led to the unsurprising discovery that if it's a man's business to notice animal tracks he's likely to notice them photographically as well; and if it's in his interest to study clouds and forecast weather he's also likely to read the sky with a cine-camera lens. Another more significant line of thought seems original only because of the reassuringly democratic sound such phrases as "self-generated data" have in certain ears. Yet the issues are surely as old as the choice between autobiography and biography; the choice between the evidence of interest versus disinterest. Each source of information provides something the other leaves out; but it's a rare autobiography which is not so disfigured by protective concealments and egotistical ploys that any claim to impartiality would be absurd.

What one can reasonably hope for in film documents made by communities themselves is not a greater objectivity in the selection of what is shown; it is the greater objectivity which results from a natural resistance to certain assimilative conventions of the cinema — conventions of photographic and editorial structure which, surprisingly, even anthropological audiences often confuse with "art." For example, a reviewer writes of *People of the River Neretva* "the film is a string of impressionistic vignettes, laudable as an art form but not as a coherent ethnographic document" (Halpern 1970:1203). It happens that this film was never intended as ethnography, coherent or otherwise; but there are scores of similar films made by and for anthropologists which deserve the same criticism and there is no reason at all to grant them the privileged immunity of art. After all, impressionism is only the aesthetic counterpart of reductionism in science; it favors the part as substitute for the whole, the needless close-up, the fragment which suggests, without showing, the entire action.

Hundreds of films recording such highly structured events as collective rituals and dances use a single wide-angle shot to "set the scene" and then plunge into a medley of kinetic closeups, all frantically shaken knees and wrists and thighs. These sequences reduce the event to a confusion of irrelevant details and offer the wrong level of action for analysis. Heuristically, impressionism leads to explanatory totals which are less than the sum of their parts. In their opposition to this, in their respect for the integrity of events and for the identity of their human subjects, ethnographic document films enable both beholders and beheld to take a stand on common ground.

REFERENCES

GOMBRICH, E. H.
  1972   Zebra crossings. *New York Review of Books* 18(8): 35–38.
GOULD, R. A.
  1972   Review of '*The Mulga Seed Ceremony.*' *American Anthropologist* 74: 189–191.
HALPERN, JOEL, BARBARA HALPERN
  1970   Review of '*People of the River Neretva.*' *American Anthropologist* 72: 1202–1203.
HONIGMANN, JOHN J.
  1970   Review of '*Caribou Hunters at the Crossing Place.*' *American Anthropologist* 72: 722–724.
MUNN, NANCY
  1970   Review of '*Emu Ritual at Ruguri.*' *American Anthropologist* 72: 1201–1202.
STRATHERN, ANDREW, MARILYN STRATHERN
  1971   *Self-decoration in Mount Hagen.* London: Duckworth.

Idea and Event in Urban Film

JOHN MARSHALL, EMILIE DE BRIGARD

Urban film is the coeval of anthropological film, for both first appeared in 1895, the year of *La Sortie des usines* (Lumière)[1] and *Poterie crue et origine du tour* (Regnault). Unlike anthropological film, which soon developed its own private currents of specialized research and exotic divertissement, urban film has throughout its history been primarily educational in the broad — i.e. public — sense of the word. The urban symphonies of Ruttmann, Cavalcanti, and Mizoguchi in the late 1920's were characterized by political liberalism, impressionistic montage, and faith in the magic of the cinema. The urban film proceeded through a stage of technical refinement without accompanying theoretical advance, in which filmmakers made films about what they assumed audiences thought about people, rather than about the people themselves. Editorial traditions presided and still preside over the form of the documentary, despite the development of portable synchronous-sound equipment which would allow people in a film to speak and act for themselves.

Sequence filming is an attempt to prevent the words and actions of people in a documentary film from being confused with what the audience wants to see and what the filmmaker wants to say. A sequence may be thought of as the verifiable film record of a small event. Sequence filming replaces the ordinary process of shooting and editing a thematic film, or overview, with the attempt to report the events themselves in as much detail and for as long as possible. Sequences may be combined in a variety of ways, but the connections between them cannot be made editorially

1 For further information on the films cited, see the article "Filmography" in this volume.

with film. Introduction of film sequences as primary data in the human sciences, or in professional training, or as vehicles enabling these disciplines to reach and inform a wider public, could place film in a context in which it can be analyzed as well as experienced. Seeing is believing, but thinking is finding out, and accuracy of reporting is important for purposes of inquiry.

As visual data, film can assist the microanalysis of interaction, and it has been so used by Birdwhistell, Byers, I. DeVore, and Lomax. Better understanding of gesture, stance, social space and movement style may help filmmakers to find angles and distances more responsive to nonverbal communication, but it cannot affect the few rules of perspective that enhance a camera's limited and subjective viewpoint. As record of an event, film is an instrument of discovery that depends on these rules of perspective, established in a moving window, which maintain relationships between content on the screen and content in the immediate vicinity. For instance, it is useful for a cameraman to remember that if he adopts a point of view approximating that of a spectator at an event, his audience will not be surprised to see spectators, should he wish to film them, at approximately his distance. (The audience would, of course, be taken aback at seeing the Spectator of an overview incarnate.) Or if the cameraman wishes to film people closely, he can speed up and condense his record of an event, but he should count heavily on the actual interactions and points of view of his subjects to tell him where to look next, or he must be prepared for many unexplained presences and absences of people and things in his record. Events have their own pace and content. The participants, if not guilty, embarrassed, or under indictment, will generally agree on the boundaries in time and space of small events, and will even share a rudimentary consensus of what happened. (As the size of the event increases, the degree of consensus diminishes.) Film can follow small events closely, letting them take their own time and produce their own content. The result is a sequence notable for the lack of conceptual and contextual framework which other forms of film attempt to supply.

Most filmmakers would be unwilling to call a sequence a film, and would probably be right. But a sequence can be verified if it is made properly, and valid intimate reporting can be corroborated by independent evidence.

To some extent, verification of a film can be accomplished internally. The appearances of people and things are either accounted for in some way by the content on the screen, or they require further explanation — like (though not, of course, equivalent to) the train that came through the waiting room at Union Station in Washington in 1961. Its engineer had a heart attack several hundred yards from the terminal, the dead-man brake failed, and the engine plowed into the lobby, broke through the ceiling of the baggage room and surprised a porter who said, "Right away, I knew something was wrong."

Preserving original footage intact, or keeping a print, and — cheaper and often more revealing — keeping intact sound will ensure a degree of verifiability to anyone interested. The effect of the camera's presence upon the subjects can be estimated by asking them about it, talking to them later about what they remember about being filmed, asking knowledgeable informants to evaluate the material, participating in similar situations without a camera, and comparing the film with independent descriptions of similar events. A filmmaker's choice of which events to film can likewise be evaluated by evidence both intrinsic and independent. Did the cameraman follow up events? Did he try to record what the participants said and did about the situations in which they were involved? Was his selection of events guided by people knowledgeable in the area of his interest, and was he aware of the biases of his informants? Many simple tests are available to a filmmaker to estimate the approximation of his material to the norm, or the validity of his sequences as records of key events in an ongoing situation — a "breaking story" in the trade. If there is a large body of film material, it can be evaluated statistically. Ultimately a film record, like a written ethnography, depends for its validity on the likelihood that two observers, with broadly similar interests, would describe generally similar events and detect similar patterns, if their visits to the same people were not separated by many years.

Film, however, is primarily a communicative medium, and questions of verifiability seem to pale in the face of montage.

Montage as described by Eisenstein (for the fictional film) and Vertov (*Kino-pravda*) is simply an editorial process: the cameraman chooses the angle and distance of his shots (if he has the time and opportunity to do so), the editor selects the shots which in juxtaposition seem to tell the story he has in mind (if the script doesn't do this for him), the director picks a location or mounts the actions for his sequences, and the producer decides whether the major elements of a film — the action and the story — will appeal to an audience. Most of what is written about montage is related to pictorial content, and except for studies of various interesting optical illusions, there are few intrinsic regularities that stem from pictorial content to govern the common meaning of an angle or a cut, and none to explain a producer's decisions. (That sex and violence attract attention is a fact that determines, rather than explains, these decisions.) Besides the possibility of culturally determined concepts of space that make some camera angles and distances more acceptable to certain audiences than others, there may well be regularities of rhythm in cutting, as Kirsch (n.d.) suggests, that stem from cultural patterns. The fad of extreme closeups of faces and mouths that seems to have swept documentary film may express turmoil about conventional social space, and the consistent timing in some genres of entertainment film may stem, like rock music, from a shared sense of rhythm. But a picture of the Archduke Franz Ferdinand is ultimately a picture of a man, not a symbol, and we are reminded by the author of *The Making of Americans* that "a rose is a rose is a rose."

Film may be said to possess tense — the present tense; a rudimentary future or anticipatory tense; and a somewhat longer and more stable past. It possesses a kind of person — a "he, she or it" which is the camera observing from somewhere between the subjective "I" — which filmmakers have tried to use but which is never fully convincing, even in *Metamorphosis*, and the collective "they," which requires many cameras and screens and demands editing by the audience. Film is composed of an endless supply of assertions with which we are entertained, edified, and bombarded (Metz 1974). If montage is editorial rather than reportorial, if verifiability is unimportant, objects juxtaposed in a picture, or pictures juxtaposed in a film will have as many different meanings as there are orders and arrangements in which they can appear. The ordering and arranging which take place prior to shooting, consciously or inadvertently, are sometimes called "conceptualizing," but the trade usually talks of "the treatment."

A conceptual point of view is necessary to interpret large or complex subject matter. Verbal interpretation, provided by such techniques as commentary or interview, organizes the impressions resulting from montage as much as it simplifies the subject matter. Urban documentary films exhibit a range of conventional styles and occasional insights, but the remarkable differences between *The City* (Steiner and Van Dyke 1939) and *Tenement* (CBS 1968) lie in changed values and circumstances that affect the filmmaker's interpretation, or treatment, more than the film form.

The City appeared during a time of architectural and social innovation. The United States, beginning its recovery from the depression, was regaining confidence, and urban planners, supported by a strong and progressive administration and Congress, saw no contradiction in steering America toward tomorrow in concert with architects, construction companies, finance, and the building trades unions. Few demographers were heard regarding the realities of population pressure, and the vast northward migration of the forties was still in the future. Ethnic politics, while remaining the municipal reality, had somewhat abated during the years of common cause in the labor movement, and racism was simply taken for granted. It isn't surprising that the filmmakers regarded the city as a whole. What may be a little surprising to the modern viewer is that *The City* seems to hate cities — but on reflection, that isn't strange either, since the rural fantasy and "land of one's own" have always been values near the surface of an immigrant country, underlying the suburban sprawl. Filmmakers, particularly documentary filmmakers in those days, felt a magic in the film that we are now, fortunately, beginning to question. To make a movie was to make the thing itself. To make a statement on film was to shock, enlighten, encourage the "masses" toward social change. (Was it a time to think big? Germany produced Riefenstahl and Hitler warmed himself before plaster models of the capital of the Thousand-Year Reich.) Perhaps it took the astounding effects of real propaganda, the stunned and blinking morning after, and eventually, with the television set, the realization that the masses wanted pleasure, not enlightenment, at the end of the day, for us to begin to have a more cynical and realistic view of the power of film.

Tenement is as much a montage as *The City*, except that people talk to the camera in place of a script by Lewis Mumford, and the concern of the film is to show a predicament rather than a solution. (In 1968, nobody really dared to say "Tear it down!", low-cost housing being an awesome, if symbolic, issue.) To make a film is no longer to create a reality; the times change. Now, to expose a problem in a film is to dispose of it. In both *Tenement* and *The City*, film retains a satisfying magic, and our response can only be uncritical involvement or — when the magic wears thin — ineffectual detachment.

The reverberation theory of communication (Schwartz 1968), which in its essentials is at least as old as Plato, postulates that the public is already in possession of the necessary information, and that the objective of the media is not to convey new information or insight (the transportation theory of communication), but to stimulate existing bits in the somnolent whole, by means of a kind of guided message that will make people aware of, and possibly even act upon, what they already know. Commercial television's livelihood, of course, is to sell products and candidates, and in such a closed system it is chancy to introduce a new thought. A program director once told John Marshall, "We don't feel that our purpose is to confuse our viewers with the facts."

The progression from impressionistic montage, through focus on a few people in related situations, to the reporting of directly related events just short of sequence filming is illustrated by Wiseman's *High School* (1968), the Maysles' *Salesman* (1969), and Leacock's *Happy Mother's Day* (1963).

Frederick Wiseman has tracked the "cultural spoor" of our society in an insane asylum, a high school, a police force, a hospital, and a monastery. Each of his films purports to show something of the use of power in the institution under examination. Wiseman describes his "quests for natural history" as "totally subjective," and *High School*'s incidents do, in fact, take on the hue of Wiseman's view of education — its factory setting, its irrelevant promises. Like the formal expectation that the comic sets up with his introduction, so that anything that follows is funny, Wiseman prepares the viewer at the beginning with Otis Redding's song, "Dock of the Bay," for the disappointment of education, for the contrast between the formal values and ideology of the high school and the actual practice. But the predicament of the high school students, captives of an authoritarian faculty which pays lip service to sensitivity, openness, and democracy, ends up by being perpetuated in the viewing situation, in which the audience becomes aware that any attempt to come to a conclusion about Wiseman's "neutral" data — the shots themselves — will be frustrated. Unlike *The City*, *High School* is free from the omniscient narrator, but the sequences themselves, edited and shaped to fit the theme of the film, ask many questions that are unanswered, and some that cannot be answered with film. In *High School*, we rarely see the same people in different situations, we see different people in different situations. What became of the boy who was disciplined by the dean? What else did the English teacher do with class periods besides reading "Casey at the Bat" out loud? What did the staff really think about the letter written by a grateful ex-pupil in Vietnam?

Wiseman's objective — to film institutions — determines the way in which he uses montage, since "institution" is a concept, and specific institutions have important invisible arrangements of values and other intangible relationships. What links people and situations in *High School* is the passivity of the students and the authoritarianism of the faculty, but this may be Wiseman's view of things. The sequences are not rich enough, and people and situations are not followed closely enough, to permit inferences to be drawn about what anyone really thinks or does about the predicament suggested in the film. There is no way of knowing the real consequences of any of the film's real situations. It's all right for audiences to be moved by *Titicut Follies*, *High School*, and *Essene*, but they are not permitted to think independently about them.

In terms of the impact of documentary compared with theater, *Salesman* is to *Death of a Salesman* what *Titicut Follies* is to *Marat/Sade*. Filmically,

Salesman is extraordinary in the subtlety with which it handles the silences between people and the poignant delicacy of the occasional relationships between subjects and camera. *Salesman* shows the anomie of non-institutionalized man in an institutionalized society. "The Rabbit," "The Bull," "The Gipper," and "The Badger" are the descendants of mountebanks and hucksters, who in an age of individual opportunity as late as the turn of the century could call themselves entrepreneurs, put elixirs into bottles, and go into business. They are in a position which is increasingly hopeless in an age of controlled markets, organized labor, and even more organized management; there is no bargaining organization that could represent them, except perhaps an actors' union for the illegitimate stage. Management tells them: "Some of you, at one time or another, may or may not have had a higher income, but you have never held a higher position of esteem in the minds of the world, or in your own self-satisfaction, than you now hold, knowing that you are going about your Father's business." The four salesmen peddle expensive Bibles to people who can't afford them.

Perhaps because Jimmy, Ray, Charlie, and Paul cling to the fancy that their independence is their dignity, and have an actor's scorn for the play, they blame their own failing powers when they can't make a score. But "thinking negatively" is to be avoided at all costs; the Great American Denial is still functioning, even if the dream has passed. Only Paul Brennan, "The Badger," allows himself to doubt what he's doing, and he is the worst salesman of the group. Al and David Maysles started by filming all four men at their work of selling Bibles — here was an American metaphor, they felt — but David Maysles and Charlotte Zwerin, the editor, ended by structuring the film arround Paul's disintegrating career. This involved removing the selling situations which didn't contain Paul, but Zwerin retained one sequence in which "The Bull," Ray Martos, makes a sale on his own, and his ease and speed are played against Paul's lack of control in the previous sequence.

The City, made about a vast subject, is inevitably a collage, while *Salesman*, concerned with a few people involved in related situations, who share their common experiences together, has a narrower, deeper theme. One way to distinguish the varieties of montage is to consider the kind of detail with which shots in the film are treated, and the relationships between sequences. The possible relationships between shots are:

1.   The content in one scene is the same in the next, but seen from another angle.

2.   Something of the content in one scene (less, more) is repeated in the next scene, and what the viewer is NOT seeing remains where it was, as

illustrated in Figure 1. A and C stay where they were, doing what they were doing when the viewer saw them last.

3.   Some element of the content in one sequence is repeated in the next. For example, a person appears in a new context, or a conversation is continued later in the film.

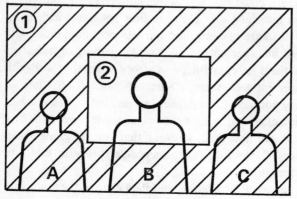

Figure 1.   Possible relationship between shots

If we regard REPEATED CONTENT as the INHERENT CONTENT of a film, and the impressions created by unrelated scenes (in the minds either of viewers or of filmmakers) as the THEMATIC content, then obviously *The City* is highly impressionistic and thematic.

Though it is far from *The City*, *Happy Mother's Day* is intentionally editorial, and it is instructive to compare the two versions of the film, the network version (brought to you by Gerber's baby food), and the film-makers' version. The events that *Happy Mother's Day* shows are directly related, part of the larger situation of commercial pressures on the Fisher family of Aberdeen, South Dakota, who have been blessed with quin-tuplets. Declared Mrs. Fisher: "We won't be on display to anyone." The Fishers successfully vetoed a proposal to add a special observation wing to their home, but financial need (they were already parents of a large family) made them give in to commercial exploitation by *The Saturday Evening Post*, countless baby-supply firms, and the Aberdeen Chamber of Commerce. (After the civic celebration of the quint's one-month birthday, Mrs. Fisher suffered a nervous breakdown.) The film by Richard Leacock and Joyce Chopra shows these relationships by means of acute shooting and editing, supplemented by commentary. The network version suppressed some of Leacock's material and added other sequences. For example, Leacock shows Mr. Fisher's Model T Ford — his one hobby —

and then films him climbing into the car and driving it, following the cues of *The Saturday Evening Post's* photographer. The same sequence in the ABC film is edited so that the viewer cannot perceive the irony which struck Leacock in the situation. He later said: "Now, the ABC film is all perfectly 'true'. It's just uninteresting. They are not distorting except by omission. They simply were not aware of what was going on. They didn't see it in the material. It just became a mish-mash about sweet little children lying in cradles and girls singing songs and nurses telling you in interviews how the babies were born and all that sort of stuff. All of which was 'true' and perfectly fine. It just missed what I found significant" (Blue 1965).

The events in many of Leacock's films — crises with wide implications — are interesting in themselves, apart from the filming. His work contains many sequences. Leacock's celebrated shot of John F. Kennedy in Wisconsin, moving from his car into the meeting hall to address a rally, is a landmark in cinema. But montage is inevitable when events or sequences are connected in a film, unless the cameraman walks around affixed to his instrument like a mad anarchist to his bomb. It is unlikely that such a man would be present at the most interesting events of his realm or time (cf. Young's paper, *supra*).

Sequence filming is concerned with small, manageable events. The subjects in the film recognize the boundaries of these events during, or shortly after, their conclusion. Scholars may debate the dates of the Renaissance, but we do not need the hindsight of history to know when a meeting is over, a game won, a debt paid. Film has number and tense, and with these the filmmaker can find manageable units in the flow of life and replace impressionistic statements by verifiable ones. Within film sequences, thematic montage is partly replaced by the visual implications of camera angle, distance, and screen direction, which form the framework within which the filmmaker can condense his material, rather than select it according to its thematic relevance. This condensation is cognitive, and it depends on the fact that human communication is so redundant (as every good editor knows) that within events people will offer each other and the cameraman as many opportunities to record their message as they can. Events are designed by the subjects, if they have a chance and aren't surprised by the locomotive in the baggage room. Within a sequence, people off-camera can be located by the viewer, and their behavior accounted for. When a sequence decays and a new sequence begins, behavior is unpredictable on an intimate level, and unseen people can't be located.

Good reporting is social research. The urban filmmaker probably has more knowledge of the culture he is filming than the anthropologist-filmmaker watching the unfamiliar, but the basic problem is still the choice of event to be filmed. A reporter starts with an event and follows the story — he may have to dig among unnamed informants to follow it — and seeks a pattern. An ethnographer usually starts with a hunch or hypothesis about a pattern. He may discuss it interminably with informants; eventually it is tested against events. Good ethnographers are the best observers of all.

Ethnographers and anthropologists who, like reporters, start with events, and who permit their case histories to appear as evidence in their publications (Bohannan 1957), find that the conflict between persons, interest groups and interests ("hard news") opens the widest cracks through which can be seen the social and economic engine at work. Lineages become collections of people with common interests; marriage regulations become matters of political convenience and arbitration; ritual is argued. When they deal with events, reporters and ethnographers share the need to understand the current issues in a society. Whether the aim of understanding is to challenge or confirm existing theory, or to awaken the public and get a story on the air, the excitement and interest in what people are actually saying and doing, and in what they recently did or soon will say and do, is common to both. This is the point where sequence filming, which is certainly reporting and may or may not be ethnographic, merges with anthropological practice.

In its capacity as an eyewitness report, film is an experience. The object of using film is to untangle impressions, to analyze the facts and implications of an event. Sequence films can be used both in education and in research for multiple discoveries rather than single-purpose demonstration. The question of the level of study is resolved by the user when he selects the issues in which he is interested.

The researcher involved in semiotics is concerned with film form and content and the *signifiant/signifié*. But if we are studying behavior, i.e. the denotative level of the film, then the behavior that we are allowed to see had better be authentic and the record faithful. Events that are unstaged, or if set up at least spontaneous, are greeted by film viewers with delighted recognition. When the teacher uses film rather than the written word, he involves the audience; and if the film is accurate, he can ask them to think about it. He can say to his captive classroom audience, "This happened, and it had real consequences; things happened to those people because of what someone did and said in that very scene."

Investigation of a Hit and Run was filmed by Marshall in 1969 as part of a study of the police department of Pittsburgh. The sequence is of a pregnant teen-age girl, Carol, and Pumpkin, her boyfriend, after they run afoul of the law. Pumpkin, who is driving without a license, speeds down Eloy Street and strikes a three-year-old boy, leaving him with a broken arm. Carol is in the car, and together they drive away, hide the car, and report it stolen. Many witnesses identify the car and driver; Pumpkin's brother claims that Pumpkin was at work; Carol has witnesses to say that they were swimming at the time of the accident. Pumpkin is arrested and denies all. Carol is asked to come to the police station, where she is threatened with being charged as an accessory to the crime and is subjected to intense questioning. After lying steadfastly, she eventually confesses, having been read her rights under the Miranda decision.

Harvard Law School students in James Vorenberg's class saw the sequence and discussed the following points:

— What happened to Carol? to Pumpkin?
— Is Carol an accessory? For being in the car? For not making Pumpkin stop and help? For knowing Pumpkin was constructing an alibi? For witholding information from the police?
— If the police had witnesses, why did they badger and threaten Carol? To rebut her alibi? Is that the job of the police? Because her lie challenged their authority? To be sure that they had the right suspect? Because they wanted to get somebody convicted, irrespective of his guilt, to clear the case?
— Can Pumpkin be charged with fornication and bastardy because the couple aren't married?
— Should Carol talk? Is she afraid of Pumpkin or of the law?
— Should police lie to get information? How can police get the information they need?
— Did Carol in fact "confess," or did she make a statement incriminating Pumpkin? Can her statement be used in court? Does Miranda apply?

And so on. Every one of these questions engages a wide area of custom, law, kinship, love, power, urban condition, and the matter of good faith. The content of the sequence can be addressed from any of these perspectives. In the course of untangling their impressions of the event, the viewers learn something about the situation, as opposed to their private reactions to the people in it. They can draw conclusions about cause and effect that surpass the bounds of the sequence. Ideas precede events, and remain after them.

Investigation of a Hit and Run has been used both in law school and in junior high school classes. Can this kind of view within, through the window of conflict, illuminate foreign societies and intrigue the students that anthropology would like to reach? Much is riding on the answer. In an armed and industrial world man can little afford elaborate comparisons between himself and people he knows nothing about if he doesn't want to scotch the last possibilities for cultural equity. There is some negative evidence regarding the enlightenment of American students and their acceptance of alien life as presented in *Man: a Course of Study*, the most impressive anthropological film curriculum ever devised (for which developing the supporting multimedia materials cost even more than the films themselves). Hearn and DeVore (1973) report that a majority of their college students, when exposed to the Netsilik Eskimo films in *Man: a Course of Study*, giggled, repudiated, and turned off.

But perhaps a coin is still wavering down through the waters. These Netsilik Eskimo films are not, strictly speaking, film sequences. However in *Man: a Course of Study* there is a written case of a bad, violent man who, judged dangerous by his Netsilik relatives and peers, and understanding his condition, asks his brother to kill him. In another case, an old woman is provided with a day's food and abandoned. In one of the Bushman sequences by Marshall, *An Argument about a Marriage*, two !Kung fathers-in-law square off over the legitimacy of an affair that produced a child. Each stands to lose the services and allegiance of a son-in-law. On several recorded occasions, high school students and teachers have understood and accepted the familial and economic underpinnings and transactions in all three events.

Moreover, the possibility of synchronous sound sequence filming is within the reach of more researchers, teachers, and students than ever before. Leacock, who is outspoken in his displeasure with the high cost of film and the consequent stultifying monopoly enjoyed by organized media, has designed and M.I.T. is distributing an 8-mm cordless sync-sound filming and editing system with cheap, high-quality transfer capability to videotape. "I want every student in every school in every state in this Union to be able to make the films they want, and I hope to God the little darlings make them about something besides themselves."

Still, no real evidence is in to demonstrate the educational utility of film sequences of events as opposed to interpretative films and other varieties of overview. Sequences and the case-study method they entail have scarcely been tried in the schools. Sequences proceed slowly; the events are small and cannot be connected with a fade or a dissolve or even a jump cut. The teacher must supply informational as well as interpretative context to connect events. Many teachers like to shine as much as TV emcee Johnny Carson, and they control the materials with which they make their statements just as firmly. Sequence filming could never portray in its totality a city or a high school, or provide the stuff for grand interpretations of

Constitutional Rights, or of Kinship or Labor or Exchange. Sequence filming deals with usage: the way people use their social forms as they experience or know them. If the sequence filmmaker has struck a rich vein among the people he observes, or if the teacher assembling collections of sequences to show to his class has a good clear argument and, above all, tolerance enough to watch with his students what is not explained, then abstract pattern may be seen underlying usage.

A big order, but consider the alternative. Consider the prospect of endless overviews about which you cannot think in your own way because you cannot hear what people are saying or see enough of what they are doing to be able to build your case on evidence that you can describe to someone else. The citizen who is exposed to urban film needs the kinds of knowledge, warnings, skills, and insights that permit responsible political life in an urban, industrial society. If sequence filming could provide these, how big the result would be, how true, how complicated.

REFERENCES

BLUE, JAMES
 1965   One man's truth: an interview with Richard Leacock. *Film Comment* 3 (2): 16–22.
BOHANNAN, PAUL
 1957   *Justice and judgment among the Tiv.* London: Oxford University Press.
HEARN, THOMAS, PAUL DEVORE
 1973   "The Netsilik and Yąnomamö on film and in print." Paper delivered at Film Studies of Changing Man, sponsored by Anthropological Film Research Institute and the Smithsonian Institution's Center for the Study of Man and Office of Elementary and Secondary Education. Washington, D.C.
KIRSCH, SANDER
 n.d.   "An approach to the nature of natural units: motion pictures as temporal analogues." Unpublished manuscript. New York.
LOMAX, ALAN
 1968   *Folk song style and culture: a staff report on cantometrics.* Washington: American Association for the Advancement of Science. Publication 88.
METZ, CHRISTIAN
 1974   *Language and cinema.* The Hague: Mouton.
ROSENTHAL, ALAN
 1971   *The new documentary in action: a casebook in film making.* Berkeley: University of California Press.
SCHWARTZ, ANTHONY
 1968   *Politeia.* Washington: American Association of Political Consultants.

Ethnographic Observation and the Super-8 Millimeter Camera

RICHARD LEACOCK

The idea of going out into the real world with a movie camera and observing society has been with us for a long time; in the early nineteen hundreds Lumière and his disciples went all over the world filming real people and real events. As early as 1904 Leo Tolstoy is quoted as saying "It is necessary that the cinema should represent Russian reality in its most varied manifestations. For this purpose life ought to be reproduced as it is by the cinema: it is not necessary to go running after invented subjects." But somehow this ideal was never achieved. The end results were almost always centered on process: this is how we build our boats, this is how we catch fish, this is how we divide the spoils. Valuable though these records are, they are a far cry from what Tolstoy had in mind. The inability to record verbal communication was, in my opinion, the central frustration.

When Dr. Eleanor Leacock and I first tried to make an ethnographic film during a long summer in central Labrador, living with our two children and a group of Naskapi Indians, I remember the consciousness that we were missing the point. It was the relationships, the decision-making processes, the emotions that were fascinating us, but inevitably it was the canoe-making, fishing, berry-picking, etc., that got filmed.

Around 1960 equipment was developed that made a radical change possible, and since that time those that could afford tens of thousands of dollars for cameras, recorders, and 16-mm film have been making films that occasionally transcended this frustration when no language barrier existed between the subjects and the observer and audience. However, these people not only needed lots of money, they had to be as strong and stubborn as mules to carry out their resolve. Hiking around the wilderness with some sixty pounds on your back is not particularly conducive to sensitive observation. This has resulted in the emergence of a very small group of film-oriented ethnologists who are closely allied with the "*cinéma vérité*" or "direct cinema," filmmakers who do not call themselves ethnologists but spend their time and lose their shirts observing our own society. The rules of this game are often very strict: never ask a question; never ask anyone to do anything; never ask anyone to repeat an act or a phrase that you missed; never pay anyone; etc. If the same people film the material and edit it, the results can be summarized as "aspects of the observer's perception of what happened in the presence of a camera." Such a definition gets us out of a fruitless bag of silly arguments about "absolute" truths, etc., and allows us to settle for something quite useful.

Recently there have been two technological leaps that can alter this situation considerably. First, the development of portable, relatively cheap video recorders which have a fascinating ability to play back on the spot but require access to some place where you can charge batteries and, at this stage of the game, a handy repair shop. Second is the development here at M.I.T. of a cheap, very sophisticated but easy to use super-8 synchronous sound filmmaking system. Both these systems are very easy to learn to use. The video camera and recorder weigh about 20 pounds. The film camera weighs 6 pounds and the separate sound recorder about 7 pounds.

With these two systems available, the technical and financial problems have been solved to the point where a much more general use of these techniques can result.

The degree of expertise required to make ethnographic films in the past resulted as already noted in this very special group of "filmmaker-ethnographers." I think it can be said that this group became specialists who did no other kind of observation. A chasm developed, to my dismay, between the film group and the non-film group, and further splits have developed between schools of filming, some claiming that closeups or details should be avoided at all costs, or the orientation to the general scene is a necessity; others advise one to "pretend film" with no film in the camera for the first month. Personally I reject dishonest behavior whatever the cost. I do not want to get into the details of these schisms. I merely want to suggest that perhaps non-filmmaker ethnologists might want to use these simple and at this point much cheaper techniques of recording behavior in a non-exclusive way perhaps, as they continue their customary forms of observation; they might, in particular instances where film and video seemed especially appropriate, make use of these techniques, without having to dedicate the rest of their lives to becoming "filmmaker-ethnographers". Perhaps they should depend on their own judgement as to how they use these techniques.

To this end we have designed systems here that try to cut out all the complexities and hassles of traditional filmmaking. A three-to-six week intensive course should give adequate training and obviate reliance on special technicians.

Research Filming of Naturally Occurring Phenomena: Basic Strategies

E. RICHARD SORENSON, ALLISON JABLONKO

The unique value of film records in many kinds of phenomenological research has been understood almost from the earliest days of the camera (see Michaelis 1955; de Brigard i.p.). However, only in the last decade (largely in response to the rapid environmental and cultural change since World War II) has much attention been given to making visual records of passing natural events maximally useful as a permanent scientific resource (Sorenson and Gajdusek 1963, 1966; Jablonko 1967; Van Vlack 1965; Sorenson 1967a, 1967b, 1968b).

The concept and method of the research film that have emerged are compatible with a variety of research and filmmaking goals and have now been used by more than twenty scientists and filmmakers to document vanishing cultures. They specify a format for turning exposed footage into research documents after filming and deal primarily with the assembly and annotation of film footage taken by anyone for any purpose in order to maximize its scientific potential. However, even though the stated aim and philosophy of the research film method may be extrapolated to help to guide filming, they do not tell how to use the camera in the field to increase the research value of the film record.

Although no generally applicable guidelines for research FILMING have yet been stated, basic theoretical and methodological considerations have been raised and discussed (Sorenson 1968b, 1973). Here we turn our attention to formulation of practical guidelines for research filming. Drawing from insights we have gained during a decade of collecting visual data from disappearing cultures for continued study and use, we present here the basic strategies we have learned.

What makes research filming such a powerful tool of inquiry into past events is the unique ability of film to preserve an objective chemical facsimile of visible phenomena. Because we have film, we may make windows, however small, through which we can review past events. But the value of these windows depends on how they are made and documented. For example, it is difficult to make many deductions from what is seen through windows on the past unless we know something about how, where, and when they were placed. For this reason the established research film methodology requires documentation of time, place, subject, and photographer's intent and interests. However, when actually engaged in research filming, we also face the problem of how, where, and when to place these camera windows in order to obtain a potentially more productive or representative sample. It is to this latter problem that we address this paper.

A great wealth of visual information emanates from all natural events. To attempt a "complete" record of even a small event would be a fruitless pursuit of an unachievable fantasy. Many more than thousands of "channels" would be needed to show "all" micro and macro views of everything from all angles and perspectives. We can only SAMPLE. In our own research filming efforts, we have found that we increase the potential scientific value of visual records of passing phenomena by adopting a basic tripartite sampling strategy based on OPPORTUNISTIC SAMPLING, PROGRAMMED SAMPLING, and DIGRESSIVE SEARCH.

Opportunistic Sampling

Seize opportunities. When something interesting happens, pick up the camera and shoot. Opportunistic filming, a freewheeling yet indispensable approach to visual documentation of naturally occurring phenomena, takes advantage of events as they develop in unfamiliar settings.

Some degree of opportunistic filming is useful in filming any natural event. The world in its dynamic diversity continually churns out transformations. We can never fully anticipate what is going to happen, when or how it will occur. What is "normal" here and now may not be so later or elsewhere. Expectations, insofar as they are constructed from past experience and circumscribed sophistication, are not completely reliable as guides to what will come. Opportunistic filming documents unanticipated and poorly understood phenomena as they occur. It relies on that most basic tool of discovery and the source of all our knowledge, the individual human mind. It uses to advantage the selective interests and perceptive eye of individual workers by tapping intuition, impression, and partially formulated ideas.

When a photographer is filming opportunistically, he flows with the events of the day and cues into them at some personal level, suddenly noticing that "something" is about to happen and following such events intuitively, without a worked-out plan. He takes it as it comes. Thus, the visual data sample achieved reflects the personality of the filmer: it takes its form and content from his interests, inclinations, and style. But by linking the camera to the pattern-recognizing capability of the human mind, the visual data sample reflects prearticulated stages of discovery. Such footage may not always be directly relevant to a predetermined scientific study, but it can be a powerful resource in the quest for knowledge.

Because observers with or without cameras always affect what is observed opportunistic film records made during early contact help to reveal the nature of the influence. As a setting reacts to the presence of fieldworkers, subtle transformations and adaptive restructuring of relationships, attitudes, and responses begin to take place. The kinds of information fieldworkers get often depend upon the nature of the relationships that they develop with selected persons and things within the community. An early record, continued through the familarization period, makes it easier to see the nature of the change and thus to gauge the effect of their own presence on the situation being documented.

In spite of its advantages, opportunistic sampling remains an unformulated sampling procedure. It allows us to cope with an unfamiliar situation profitably but according to a personal style that is not always, and never completely, obvious. Its major strength as well as its weakness is that selection of the sample is controlled by the interests and personality of the photographer. One of its most important advantages is that it allows the cameraman to flow with and in fact be controlled by the events — as an integral part of the scene.

Programmed Sampling

Programmed sampling is filming according to a predetermined plan — deciding in advance what, where, and when to film. It is therefore based on a cognitive framework and a concept of significance. Pictures are taken according to a preconceived structure; there are pigeonholes to fill.

A program can be very simple (e.g. taking pictures of a single category of activity, such as nursing behavior or agricultural practice) or it can be a complex attempt to sample broadly (e.g. Hockings and McCarty [1968] programmed their sampling of an Irish village to obtain some film coverage of every household type, every economic activity, every architectural style, every economic condition from richest to poorest, all key figures in the communication network, a visual suggestion of the age pyramid, every type of transport, every kind of farming device, the daily sequence of typical activities, each center of public interaction, etc.)

Like opportunistic sampling, the programmed approach also relies on human interests and ideas, but instead of unstated personal impressions and inclinations, a formulated statement governs the filming. This makes programmed visual samples easier to interpret and more scientific. They extend beyond the narrower personal inclinations and preoccupations of an individual to take advantage of the accumulated, systematized, and articulated knowledge that unites him with colleagues and a cultural heritage.

Programmed sampling depends on structured information rather than intuitions and inclinations to guide the filmer. This structured information takes its form from our articulated way of viewing things according to the concepts, ideas, and values bestowed upon us by our training and background. It provides us with a means of symbolically dealing with the undifferentiated phenomena about us by relating them to discrete categories manipulable through rules of language and logic. Structured information gives us an intellectual grip on experience and enables us to plan our own movements relative to it. It provides an anchor for discussion, conjecture, and study, and is the KNOWN to which we relate discovery in order to learn its significance.

A postulated uniform flow of time and a defined geometry of space are indispensable structural concepts in the scientific analysis and description of phenomena. They are fundamental in the construction and validation of scientific knowledge. In studies dealing with development, differentiation, diffusion, or communication, physical and temporal separation are the critical functions. Time and space parameters are essential in any research filming program.

Programming the sampling procedure according to any stated conceptual model is also useful. Not only do such models bring order into our minds and help us to "see" into the muddle of the real world, but they also enable us to place the footage shot in a more clearly defined context both for ourselves and for others.

Thus programmed sampling helps to break the egocentrism of opportunistic sampling by imposing a comprehensible structure over the often hard-to-grasp vagaries of human inclination. It does this by drawing from the public knowledge of a culture. Programmed samples represent ethnocentric distillations of human interests, desires, and inclinations. Because of the more public nature of ethnocentric bias, especially in cultures with written histories, the skewing effect may more readily be taken into consideration than in the case of opportunistic samples.

Digressive Search

Neither programmed nor opportunistic sampling solves the problem of how to branch out beyond our personal predilections or the structural concepts of our culture. Programmed sampling is limited to preconceived ideas about what is important to document. In essence, it prejudges importance and therefore misses categories of events not considered. Opportunistic sampling avoids this problem by deliberately taking advantage of unanticipated events, but because it is subject to the personal inclinations and vision of the photographer, it too prejudges and skews the sample, but in a less decipherable way.

A digressive search helps to solve these difficulties by deliberately intruding into the "blank areas," i.e. those places and events outside our range of recognition or appreciation. This tactic allows us, somewhat blindly at first, to expand our vision as we visually sample and document events alien to our structured formats and habitual shooting instincts. By digressing inquisitively, we may penetrate areas and situations peripheral to our attention, beyond our range of awareness or comprehension, and interstitial to our points of view and predilections.

This kind of sampling requires that we turn our attention away from the obvious to the novel — even to what may seem pointless, aberrant, or meaningless. We have to be purposefully digressive, in both space and subject matter turning our gaze from the familiar and "important" to events that appear incoherent and insignificant. A randomness must be intruded into the way we direct attention (the digressive search has also been called semirandomized [Sorenson 1973]). We must sample in places we know nothing of or which lie between the kinds of locales and events to which our sampling program or interests are anchored.

Digressive tactics such as these can broaden a visual data sample beyond the originally defined scope of a programmed sample and the undefined scope of habitual and unstated shooting predilections. To extend our observations and visual data sampling into fringe areas of understanding and attention, and thus beyond presumption and habit, is deliberately to add unanticipated, interstitial visual information to the research film sample. It is in this aspect that the greatest potential of research filming as a tool for discovery may lie.

DISCUSSION

The theoretical format underlying research filming presented here relies on three basic general strategies: (1) seizing the opportunity we "see," (2) taking advantage of the collective knowledge of our culture, and (3) looking into the unknown. These strategies take advantage of the unique ability of film emulsions to objectively record unrecognized and unappreciated visual information. They parallel three basic elements of scientific inquiry: (1) the significance-recognizing capability of the human mind, (2) an accepted, rationalized body of knowledge, and (3) the desire to learn.

Byers (1966) said that "cameras don't take pictures ... people take pictures". This statement is useful because it cleverly stresses the subjective aspect of photography. But it is only half accurate. While it is true that cameras do not take pictures, it is not true that people take pictures. People only select the pictures to be taken. Quite literally it is the film that TAKES the picture. Its light-sensitive emulsion takes light energy emanating from a scene to produce objective chemical changes that capture a permanent record of the pattern of light received. Because of this, the basic condition in any approach to research filming is the mutual dependence of (1) human selection of what to film and (2) the ability of film to preserve an objective chemical facsimile of the pattern of light it receives. In this equation the camera is only a facilitating device. Its sole purpose is to form under human guidance an image on the film and to control the amount of light admitted in order to produce a readable chemical image of the scene selected.

Each of our three basic strategies has its own merits. Opportunistic sampling can be quite easy, particularly in unfamiliar or novel situations. (However, when we want to flow well with the events developing around us by getting more intimately into them, considerable energy and ingenuity may be required.) Opportunistic sampling also permits a flexibility in approach which allows greatest advantage to be taken of personal impressions and insights.

On the other hand, programmed sampling enables us to take advantage of the parameters and structural concepts that have already been developed and proved significant (at least in our own culture). Such programs, drawing from sources broader than just ourselves, help us to sample more comprehensively and lead us to types of events that would otherwise escape attention. They also give us a starting point in an unfamiliar situation and the needed explanation of what we are doing among the people we may be filming. The articulated existence of such filming programs makes the visual samples obtained more widely intelligible and interpretable. Furthermore, when a program asks for things that cannot be found, attention is directed to an absence that in itself may be significant.

Both programmed and opportunistic sampling rely on forms of mind and habit which reflect the past: they depend either on the state of publicly accepted knowledge as developed through history or on the sensory abilities, interests, and habits provided by man's evolutionary background as programmed by his life experiences.

We may begin to move away from these limitations by adopting a deliberately digressive (or semirandomized) search and, with camera in hand, by recording what we may neither appreciate nor "see." Such an approach allows us to increase the content of unrecognized information in a visual record by moving, even if blindly, beyond the constraints of either personal intuition or sophisticated program, to document ahead of understanding and awareness. A digressive search makes it possible deliberately to impregnate the visual sample with information yet to be discovered.

Each of the three strategies has advantages and disadvantages. Each skews the sample in a different way. But in concert, they begin to balance one another so as to increase the informative potential of the visual records.

Although we originally moved somewhat intuitively in this direction (Jablonko 1968; Sorenson 1967, 1971, 1973), an analytical look at what we were doing suggested that the basic strategies are broadly applicable. They are compatible not only with the nature of scientific inquiry but also with such recent, more specific anthropological field filming endeavors as: demonstrating culturally standarized behavior (Bateson and Mead 1942; Gesell 1946; Mead and McGregor 1951; Mead 1954, 1956; Jablonko 1968; Lomax, Bartenieff, and Paulay 1969; Sorenson 1968a, 1971, n.d.); analyzing micromovements in human interaction and communication (Birdwhistell 1952, 1960, 1972; Van Vlack 1966); sampling human movement style as a means of characterizing and classifying culture (Jablonko 1966, 1968; Lomax, Bartenieff, and Paulay 1968, 1969); studying child handling in order to discover developmental dynamics and culturally specific patterns of behavior (Sorenson 1968a, 1971, 1973, n.d.; Lilly and Sorenson 1971); inquiring into socio-ecological processes and outlining the ecological basis of a hitherto unidentified type of society (Sorenson 1972; Sorenson and Kenmore 1974); investigating an indigenous economic organization and nutrition in an isolated culture (Sorenson and Gajdusek 1967, 1969; Sorenson *et al.* 1968); comprehensively documenting disease occurrence and management in its natural cultural and environmental setting (Gajdusek, Sorenson, and Meyers 1970); preparing a visual adjunct to an expedition log or travel diary (Stirling 1926; Gajdusek 1957); documenting life crises and ceremony in order to more closely reexamine ritual process and thus discover ways in which unarticulated cultural *gestalts* are transmitted to successive generations (Rundstrom and Rundstrom 1970; Rundstrom, Rundstrom, and Bergum 1973); documenting life crises and ceremonial events in order to more closely reexamine events that reflect and anchor cultural organization (Gibson 1969); revealing the social and procedural context of law enforcement practice (Marshall 1969a, 1969b); documenting the procedural and nonverbal components of litigation in order to show the effect of culture on resolution of social conflict (Nader 1970; Gibbs and Silverman 1970); analyzing the effect of culture on the facial expression of emotion (Ekman, Sorenson and Friesen 1969; Sorenson 1975); visually presenting a cultural setting while eliciting a culturally determined view of it through camera interview (Mac-Dougall 1972, *supra*; revealing how people in a culture view their lives and surroundings by letting them film themselves and their activities (Worth and Adair 1972); discovering the effects of diverging paths to socialization in changing society by filming boys and their discussions as they move apart toward different kinds of lives (DiGioia, Hancock, and Miller 1973); revealing to students the knowledge developed by anthropologists (Asch and Chagnon 1969; Asch, *infra*); reconstructing the past by filming persons reenacting the old ways (Balikci and Brown 1966; Sandall 1971); revealing the lives of others through the selective eye and particular awarenesses of an individual observer (Rouch 1955; Gardner 1957; Marshall 1958).

A single photographer may be guided by the basic strategies we have presented in order to increase the scientific usefulness of the visual sample he obtains. But these strategies also provide a means to balance a continuing sample involving several filmers. It would probably be preferable to have different filmers each contributing to a growing overall sample.

Accumulation of visual samples in a systematic way would increase the value of any record by putting it in a broader perspective. For example, effects of the diverse patterning and programming of human behavior by culture, background, and experience can only begin to be studied with increasingly comprehensive samples of increasing depth and breadth.

Because we still lack such records or a place to accumulate them, we can only start to scratch the surface of the various ways man's behavior has been programmed and organized under a variety of natural conditions. The preparation of an increasingly comprehensive and continuing human behavior sample across time, place, and culture in a central film study center will immeasurably further the study of such vital concerns as the behavioral potential of our own species under the varying social and environmental conditions that the world provides and alters.

REFERENCES

BALIKCI, A., Q. BROWN
  1966 Ethnographic filming and the Netsilik Eskimos. *Educational Services Inc. Quarterly Report* (spring-summer): 19–33.
BATESON, G., M. MEAD
  1942 *Balinese character: a photographic analysis.* New York Academy of Sciences, Special Publications 2. New York.
BIRDWHISTELL, R. L.
  1952 *Introduction to kinesics.* Louisville: University of Louisville Press.
  1960 "Kinesics and communication," in *Explorations in communication.* Edited by Edmund Carpenter and Marshall McLuhan, pp. 52–64. Boston: Beacon Press.
  1972 *Kinesics in context.* New York: Ballentine,
BYERS, PAUL
  1966 Cameras don't take pictures. *Columbia University Forum* 9:27–31.
COLLIER, J., JR.
  1967 *Visual anthropology: photography as a research method.* New York: Holt, Rinehart and Winston.
DE BRIGARD, EMILIE
  i.p. *Anthropological cinema.* New York: Museum of Modern Art.
EKMAN, P., E. R. SORENSON, W. V. FRIESEN
  1969 Pan-cultural elements in the facial expression of emotion. *Science* 164:86–88.
GAJDUSEK, D. C., E. RICHARD SORENSON, JUDITH MEYERS
  1970 A comprehensive cinema record of disappearing kuru. *Brain* 93:65–76.
GARDNER, ROBERT
  1957 Anthropology and films. *Daedalus* 86:344–350.

GESELL, ARNOLD
1946   Cinematography and the study of child development. *American Naturalist* 80:470–475.

JABLONKO, A.
1966   "Ethnographic film and movement analysis." Paper presented at the American Anthropological Association Meeting, November, 1966.
1967   "Ethnographic film as basic data for research" in *VII-me Congrès international des sciences anthropologiques et ethnologiques. Moscou (3 août–10 août 1964)*, 168–173. Moscow: ledatelgstvo "Nauka".
1968   *Dance and daily activities among the Maring people of New Guinea: a cinematographic analysis of movement style.* Doctoral dissertation, Columbia University, New York.

LOMAX, A., I. BARTENIEFF, F. PAULAY
1968   "Dance style and culture," in *Folk song style and culture*. Edited by Alan Lomax, 222–247. New York: American Association for the Advancement of Science, Publication 88.
1969   Choreometrics: a method for the study of cross-cultural pattern in film. *Research Film/Le Film de Recherche/Forschungsfilm* 6:505–517.

MEAD, MARGARET
1954   "Research on primitive children," in *Manual of child psychology* (second edition). Edited by Leonard Carmichael, 735–780. New York: John Wiley & Sons, Inc.
1956   "Some uses of still photography in culture and personality studies," in *Personal character and cultural milieu* (third edition). Edited by D. G. Haring, 78–105. Syracuse: Syracuse University Press.

MEAD, M., F. C. MACGREGOR
1951   *Growth and culture: a photographic study of Balinese childhood.* New York: Putnam.

MICHAELIS, ANTHONY
1955   *Research films in biology, anthropology, psychology, and medicine.* New York: Academic Press.

ROUCH, JEAN
1955   Cinéma d'exploration et ethnographie. *Connaissance du Monde* 1:69–78.

RUNDSTROM, D., R. RUNDSTROM
1970   "The path." Unpublished M. A. thesis, San Francisco State University, San Francisco.

RUNDSTROM, D., R. RUNDSTROM, C. BERGUM
1973   *Japanese tea: the ritual, the aesthetics, the way.* Andover, Massachusetts: Warner Modular Publications.

SORENSON, E. R.
1967a A research film program in the study of changing man: research filmed material as a foundation for continued study of non-recurring human events. *Current Anthropology* 8:443–469.
1967b "The concept of the research film." Paper presented at the Annual Meeting of the Society for Applied Anthropology, May 5, 1967, Washington, D. C.
1968a *Growing up as a Fore.* Paper and film presented at the Postgraduate Course in Pediatrics, Harvard Medical School, September 19, 1968.
1968b The retrieval of data from changing culture: a strategy for developing

research documents for continued study. *Anthropological Quarterly* 41:177–186.

1971 "The evolving Fore: a study of socialization and cultural change in the New Guinea Highlands." Unpublished doctoral dissertation, Stanford University, Stanford, California.

1972 Socio-ecological change among the Fore of New Guinea. *Current Anthropology* 13:349–383.

1973 Research filming and the study of culturally specific patterns of behavior. *PIEF Newsletter* of the American Anthropological Association 4(3):3–4.

1975 "Culture and the expression of emotion." in *Psychological anthropology*. Edited by Thomas R. Williams. The Hague: Mouton.

n.d. "The edge of the forest: land, childhood, and change in a New Guinea proto-agricultural society." Manuscript.

SORENSON, E. R., D. C. GAJDUSEK

1963 The investigation of non-recurring phenomena. *Nature* 200:112–114.

1966 *The study of child behavior and development in primitive cultures: a research archive for ethnopediatric film investigations of styles in the patterning of the nervous system.* Supplement to *Pediatrics* 37(1), Part II.

1969 Nutrition in the Kuru region I: gardening, food handling, and diet of the Fore people. *Acta Tropica* 26:281–330.

SORENSON, E. R., D. C. GAJDUSEK, J. MEYERS, J. SHOLDER

1968 "Nutrition in the Kuru region III: a research-special cinema study of the nutrition of the Fore people of New Guinea." Mimeographed manuscript.

SORENSON, E. R., P. E. KENMORE

1974 Proto-agricultural movement in the Eastern Highlands of New Guinea. *Current Anthropology* 15:67–73.

VAN VLACK, J. D.

1965 The motion picture as a research tool. *Audio Visual Notes from Kodak* 65–1.

1966 "Filming psychotherapy from the viewpoint of a research cinematographer," in *Methods of research in psychotherapy*. Edited by L. A. Gottschalk, and A. H. Auerback. New York: Appleton-Century-Crofts.

WORTH, SOL, JOHN ADAIR

1972 *Through Navajo eyes: an exploration in film communication and anthropology.* Bloomington: Indiana University Press.

Films[1]

ASCH, T., N. P. CHAGNON
  1969   *The Feast.* Somerville, Massachusetts: Documentary Educational Resources.
DIGIOIA, H., D. HANCOCK, N. MILLER
  1973   *Naim and Jabar.* Hanover: American Universities Field Staff.
GAJDUSEK, D. C.
  1957   *People of the Kuru Region.* Archive of the Study of Child Behavior and Development, National Institutes of Health, Bethesda, Maryland.
GIBBS, J., M. SILVERMAN
  1970   *The cows of Dolo Ken Paye: resolving conflict among the Kpelle.* New York: Holt, Rinehart and Winston.
GIBSON, G.
  1969   *Himba Wedding.* Produced by the Center for the Study of Man, Smithsonian Institution. Distributed by National Audio-Visual Center, Washington, D. C.
HOCKINGS, P. E., M. MCCARTY
  1968   *The Village.* Produced by Colin Young for Extension Media Center, University of California, Berkeley.
JABLONKO, A.
  1968   *Dance and Daily Activities among the Maring People of New Guinea: A Cinematographic Analysis of Body Movement Style.* Doctoral dissertation, Columbia University.
LILLY, J., JR., E. R. SORENSON
  1971   *Children of the Toapuri.* Produced by J. Lilly, Jr. and E. R. Sorenson for the National Institute of Mental Health, Rockville, Maryland.
MACDOUGALL, D. C.
  1972   *To Live with Herds.* Produced by David MacDougall, Media Center, Rice University, Houston.
MARSHALL, JOHN
  1958   *The Hunters.* Produced by the Film Study Center, Peabody Museum, Harvard University.
  1969a   *Three Domestics.* Produced by the Center for Documentary Educational Resources, Somerville, Massachusetts.
  1969b   *Investigation of a Hit and Run.* Produced by the Center for Documentary Educational Resources, Somerville, Massachusetts.
NADER, LAURA
  1970   *To Make the Balance.* Distributed by Extension Media Center, University of California at Berkeley.
SANDALL, ROGER
  1971   *Pintubi Revisit Yaru Yaru.* Berkeley: University of California Extension Media Center.
SORENSON, E. R.
  1968a   *Growing up as a Fore.* Paper and film presented at the Postgraduate Course in Pediatrics, Harvard Medical School, September 19, 1968.

---

[1]   See Filmography, *infra,* for details.

SORENSON E. R., D. C. GAJDUSEK
   1967 *Nutrition in the Fore People of New Guinea: A Comprehensive Study
         Document Compiled Chronologically from the Research Film Library.*
         The Archive of the Study of Child Behavior and Development in
         Primitive Cultures, National Institute of Neurological Diseases and
         Stroke, Bethesda, Maryland.

STIRLING, M. W.
   1926 *Surabaja-Mamberamo, Takutamesa Papuan, Rouffaer Papuan, and
         the Dem.* The Archive for the Study of Child Behavior and Devel-
         opment in Primitive Cultures, National Institute of Neurological
         Diseases and Stroke, Bethesda, Maryland.

Visual Anthropology and the Past

Ethnographic Film and History

JEAN-DOMINIQUE LAJOUX

Anthropological research is currently passing through a difficult period, a period of self-examination that parallels its increasing self-awareness. The ethnologist, practicing a scientific discipline that had its origins in the colonial period, is assailed by guilt feelings. He tends to criticize the actions of expansionist nations and to defend those of developing ones.

In a different realm, but in a similar development, anthropological texts are gradually giving way to images. Film is becoming a major mode of expression, and some ethnologists find in it a new medium with which to present the results of their work (cf. Plate 9).

Ethnographic cinema was invented at the same time as cinematography. With unconscious cynicism, those first strips of film restore to us today the image of the colonizers of yesteryear, wearing white clothes and headgear, and being carried in sedan chairs.

Troubled by its own image, ethnographic film has begun to question itself, and in the hands of some directors it is becoming a new means of political propaganda. No longer is anything merely shown in these films; rather, thanks to cinema (it is said), ideologies are affirmed by uninteresting images and long speeches.

However, we must consider that, as time passes, so do fashions; ideologies and civilizations change and, inexorably, the harangues fade into silence and make room for newer echoes. In contrast with this, filmed documents will remain to serve history.

Aware as I am of these problems, I nevertheless side with those anthropologists who recognize the urgency for establishing vast archives of filmed ethnographic documents, as well as for creating film consultation centers to promote mutual understanding and self-recognition among human societies. We hope this will arrest the trend in Western society toward cultural, religious, and economic colonialism; accentuate the riches inherent in each culture and in each human group; and gradually eliminate all of the prejudices which isolate and separate these human groups (cf. Sorenson's paper, *infra*).

THE UTILIZATION OF ETHNOGRAPHIC FILM

It will not be my concern here to undertake a panoramic review of the place of ethnographic film in the world today. Other articles in this volume do that. Only some of the possibilities for utilizing ethnographic film will be considered here.

In France, ethnographic film still remains a product of standard projection techniques, and each screening results in interminable debates on whether cinema is or is not a mode of objective expression. All concern is directed toward proper angles of shooting, or new techniques and apparatus for recording in the field; research is never focused on projection or on the perception of the film by spectators. Except for two researchers[1] who studied dancing, frame-by-frame or shot-by-shot, on 8-mm film, there is no other study using this method that has been undertaken by French anthropologists.

In the United States, on the other hand, studies are being carried out which analyze documentary films exclusively.[2] For example, in doing research on world dance, Alan Lomax[3] and the choreometrics team of Columbia University only use clips from films, or at most just a few sequences. It goes without saying that the way in which these shots are used is totally independent of the content of the edited film from which they have been taken. The information obtained from these analyses, once correctly recorded, is examined and compared by computer (Lomax 1969). In Italy, under the auspices of the Institute for Research on Mass Commu-

---

[1] Jean-Michel Guilcher, whose work on folk dances in France is based exclusively on the study of 8-mm film on a viewer, mainly in his doctoral thesis, "*La tradition populaire de dance en Basse-Bretagne*," and Francine Lancelot, for her research work on "*Les sociétés de Farandole*." All the necessary choreographic transcriptions in her thesis have been made from analyses of Super-8-mm film.

[2] Ray L. Birdwhistell has developed the science of kinesics. Scheflen studied the behavior of several different families. One camera filmed a forty-eight hour period in the kitchen of one of these families (Birdwhistell 1952, 1970). William Condon, through analyses at 1/25 and 1/40 of a second has provided evidence on the synchronization of movements in the bodies of speaker and listeners (Condon 1970; Condon and Ogston 1971).

[3] Cf. Lomax 1969, and his paper in this book.

nication, studies were made on different spectators' perceptions of the content of film images by using some experimental films (Calisi 1972).

Generally, however, ethnographic film is not considered to be a research tool; and French students of the human sciences seem especially hostile to this form of scientific investigation. On the whole, researchers think that nothing they do not already know will appear during the viewing of a film. Thus, cinema can only be a means of expressing the results of various research efforts in the form of a lecture illustrated by animated images, a lecture that is then called an "ethnographic film." Similarly it is presumed that a film, whatever its nature, may only be seen and understood in a single way, namely that which was intended at the time of its production.

However, nothing could be further from the truth. This is partly because each spectator sees in a film those details which most appeal to his sensibilities and to his scientific or intellectual preoccupations. And it is also because projection is not absolutely necessary in the perception of film images. There are in fact many different ways to view the images recorded on the emulsion:

1. By attending a public screening that has no interruptions or variations in projection speed (the viewing of a work conceived in time, produced with those technical skills appropriate to the cinema: cutting and editing, scoring, and titling, etc.); or

2. By seeing the film on an individual viewing apparatus, with many interruptions and variable speed or even stop-frame viewing (the analysis of filmed documents in order to study movement, the content of individual frames, the interaction, etc.).

In the first case, the objectivity that an isolated frame might have becomes more subjective when placed between the preceding and following frames. Hence, some objectivity can be recovered only after repeated viewing of the entire film.

In the second case, close analysis will focus on two units, the shot and the frame.[4] Both become totally independent of the story line of the complete film, and thus can be examined for the facts that they alone relate.

It thus appears that if only one way of viewing the film is possible, this is

---

[4] Without changing the angle of shooting, the camera movement will miss certain actions on the left or right edge of the screen which are occurring apart from the main subject. Thus two distinctly separate actions linked by a single camera movement are necessarily authentic, since no trick of compression, expansion, or changing of time can affect them both. We will thus have even more than "photographic objectivity"; we will have the "temporal truth" of the shot.

because it has been dictated by the cameraman, who chose his camera positions for what he wanted to reveal through his shots. His "scientific procedure" consists in finding the angles and framing that are best for observation and recording of the chosen scene.

Every shot made by starting and then stopping the camera action becomes the basic unit of a film. The shot may be considered the element which most authentically describes a moment of one reality. In summary, when these are used as filmed documents in the social sciences, continuous projection in a dark room leads to artistic cinema with themes that may be more or less ethnographic or sociological.

In contrast with this, discontinuous projection of a film might aid scientific research and allow for the criticism of the sources which are in filmed documents. Indeed, through this method of viewing, the film can become a source of ethnographic data, whether the shots are recent, or of historic events, or whether they are simply early films.

Thus the elements of a new genre can be perceived, elements too fleeting to have been already directly observed. The way has thus been cleared for the creation of a history and anthropology of gesture, postures, and human behavior.[5] Finally, due to the permanence of data recorded on film which can be repeated at leisure at any time, all filmed ethnographic documents will become in time documents of incomparable value for history.

ETHNOGRAPHIC FILM IN RELATION TO HISTORY

The viewing of Louis Lumière's short film segments from the end of the nineteenth century already lets us see the wealth of information he put into each shot, a concentration of data that no other document — written, drawn, or photographed — has been able to equal.

In the book *L'Histoire et ses méthodes*, Georges Sadoul presents a similar theory regarding documentary or news film sequences: "The images and soundtrack of a film are the best means of fixing forever aspects of the daily life (work, entertainment, festivals, family customs,

---

[5] In his research on "gesture," Bernard Koechlin uses a shot-by-shot movie projection technique to make rough sketches showing the positions of the limbs, bodies, and heads of the actors he is studying. In his comparison of film with movement notation, B. Koechlin remarks (1968:46–47): "The idea often held that camera shots can replace symbolic notation is erroneous. Film is, however, a definite aid, to the extent that it allows the accumulation of documents to be encoded later, and especially since it permits exhaustive description of the environment and the set-up."

manners, etc.) of all types of people in all lands and in all climates" (Sadoul 1961:1400). We have thus been provided with a description of those ethnographic subjects that will take their place within the category of sources for the writing of history.

If Georges Sadoul did not devote a special chapter in his analysis to ethnographic film, it is probably because in 1959 such film had not yet acquired the importance that it now enjoys.

Furthermore, all types of cinema contribute to history, or more precisely, to the various areas of historical research. However, it might be feared that the concurrent existence of sources as different as the entertainment film, the autobiographical film, the documentary, the newsreel, television, scientific film, advertising film, animated cartoons, etc., as well as ethnographic film, could provide complications that might limit or impede the use of any one of them. Actually, however, this complexity is only an apparent one: it depends to a great extent upon technical considerations.

In my concluding section, I shall propose a distribution system for films[6] which, by extreme oversimplification, permits the reduction to a common denominator of all the technical factors which until now have hindered the regular use of cinema in anthropological or historical research. However, it must be remembered that viewing a film is different from reading a text in more than one way. There are in fact several levels of viewing film. In historical research, the information gleaned from different viewings will be different or even contradictory, depending on whether the film is considered as a whole (uninterrupted projection, image, sound, and commentary) or as a juxtaposition of separate sequences to be studied successively (analytical viewing). Different interpretations will also depend on how sound and commentary are perceived.

What then can be expected from a science whose sources seem to have questionable authenticity? Actually, on the one hand, an edited film exhibits truly authentic facts (as was emphasized above) while on the other, that film is the filmmaker's interpretation of these facts, achieved by editing. Such editing reveals value judgements that differ according to the filmmaker's ideological or political orientation regarding his subject. History is interested in both of these types of information; it thus establishes the existence of an event (through shot-by-shot analysis) and of the idea formed of this event at the time of the film's production (through analysis of the complete film). And finally an interesting point

---

6   One needs a videotape machine which permits the viewing on a television set of the pictures recorded on magnetic tape.

with regard to the relative importance of film as a source of historical data is the spontaneity of these documents no matter who might have made them.

Film exhibits "realities" which are relatively independent of the culture and consciousness of the cameraman. Thus, the cinematographer who passes through a country without knowing anything about it can put together a series of shots resulting in the production of a film whose ethnological content will probably be very superficial. However, because each shot is representative of a season, of a period in the visited country, it will be of value as evidence. (Consider, for example, Louis Lumière's several films on Egypt made around 1897.)

CRITICISM OF FILMED DOCUMENTS

The shot-by-shot analysis of a film quite often allows a sort of reestablishment, through critical study, of the reality of the data presented. It can also shed light on the use of special effects and direction when the film deals with ethnography, reportage, or news.

Thus, to take the example of Flaherty's *Nanook of the North* — often cited as the first of the ethnographic genre — the analysis of the film as a series of sequences instead of as a whole will lead us to some curious conclusions. We wonder, among other things, whether "Nanook" is a film about the Eskimo or about the dogs of the Great North![7]

But, as a more serious criticism, a study of the seal hunting sequence will reveal a truly classic style of direction which is not really compatible with the labored efforts made by Flaherty in the production of his film. The arguments supporting such a claim are contained in the very images of this sequence, where we see the "ballet" of the Eskimo trying to land the seal he has harpooned.[8] After two superlative slides, Nanook, assisted by other Eskimos, succeeds in pulling the seal out from under the

[7]   The following remarks are anecdotal, but it is interesting to note that among the 236 shots (with 45 titles) that make up the copy which was analyzed, there are only five close-ups of the Eskimo as opposed to eighteen very close-up shots of the dogs. To these can be added thirty-one closely related shots and twenty-one more general ones in which the dogs also appear. Thus, almost 40 percent of the shots in the film are devoted to the animals.

[8]   Nanook pulls on the rope, walking backward and forward, and is dragged through several slides by the seal which is apparently struggling under the ice. Slides and tumbles are repeated for several long minutes. Then, simply by chance, some travelers pass across the horizon above the ice floe. Nanook gives distress signals and immediately the group is there to lend a strong hand to our hunter. After one last group slide, they succeed in hoisting the seal out from under the ice.

ice. Then (an unexpected consequence) after its removal from the water
the seal is seen to be absolutely amorphous, totally inert, and without
the slightest move of a bristle. And just ten seconds earlier it had been
dragging the Eskimos across the ice!

But there are even worse anomalies in this film. As a matter of fact,
the seal hunt, at this breathing hole in the ice, would only be carried out
in the winter when food ran out.[9] But in the winter the nights are long
and the sun does not rise. Thus, how did Flaherty manage to film the hunt
under a brilliant sun at its zenith? In fact, this sequence is not even a reconstruction,[10] but a scene mimed almost to the point of burlesque and
even played without a seal. There is definitely not a single action in this
sequence which can be considered an authentic part of seal hunting.

The point of this discussion is not to criticize Flaherty's film, for which
filmic renown came as soon as it was released, and was then perpetuated
in the human sciences by ethnologists who had never really LOOKED at
this work. Rather, we are arguing that a meticulous analysis of a film's
images will permit the reestablishment, to a large degree, of the truth of
the data presented and also of the interpretations of that data given by
the filmmaker.

The shots should definitely not be reduced to just a few images for
analysis, as they are, for example, in Marcel Griaule's film *Masque
Dogon*, where the masked dancers appear only for two-thirds of a second; i.e. in shots too short to permit any careful analysis of either the
dance or the context. At this level of sophisticated elaboration,[11] the film
holds out no possibility for research. On the contrary, it presents only a
series of drawbacks; and the study of the rushes that have produced the
film will be greatly preferable even in a debased state.

[9] Here is a short description of seal hunting of the Hudson Bay Eskimo, written in
1917: "Seal. Nippatok. Motionless, lying in wait during the long nights for up to thirty-
six hours in the middle of winter, either near land, or far out to sea, or over a hole in the
ice, waiting for the seal to come up to breathe, the Eskimo wants to harpoon the seal
without being seen. And since the hole is barely perceptible, only the dogs have noticed
it, and the hunter has no other means of discovering it." (Turquetil 1926).
[10] Direct ethnographic research can give us "historical data." Thus the re-creation
before the camera of outmoded techniques and practices that are known by a few elderly
specialists, allows us to record work methods or ways of using tools and utensils that are
of basic interest to science. Intellectual honesty demands (unless the manner of this re-
creation is flagrant) that the filmmaker specify in one way or another how he plans to
re-create things. Thus, I have shot several technological sequences to demonstrate
the ways of using certain utensils that are no longer in use (but whose uses are still well-
known) which I had earlier borrowed from a museum (cf. Peterson's paper, *infra*).
[11] "Editing becomes an interpretation of history. But it goes without saying that each
shot, when considered separately and independently of the sound, will be its own
authentic and direct source [as in newsreels]" (Sadoul 1961: 1394).

THE IMAGE AND THE TEXT

A text consists of a sequence of signs, the reading of which calls for vision. It has, however, an equivalent, which is speech. These two systems that serve thought and expression are totally independent of each other even when the text is the transcription of the speech. In present-day civilizations, the image has nothing corresponding to this.

An image — or, more precisely, a photograph — is the expression of a certain three-dimensional reality, recorded and compressed onto a flat, two-dimensional surface which vision alone allows us to perceive. The photograph is the transcription of the "reality" in front of the camera lens that has recorded it.

The text can only be the evocation, through the intermediary of words, of this reality surrounding the observer. At the other end of the scale, reading appeals to the reader's imagination, and thus literary description necessitates two successive transpositions whose immediate result[12] is directly proportional to the length and the precision of the text which embodies the description.

The image contains an infinity of details, whatever its format. Theoretically, a photograph of a peasant working his field will also reveal certain peculiarities of dress; and with close-up shots we might even distinguish the way in which the various articles of clothing are put together, the woven pattern in which they have been made, and perhaps even microscopically[13] the texture of the thread used to weave the material, and so on. Furthermore, viewing the image is an instantaneous act. A photograph is perceived immediately in its entirety and according to its basic meaning.

Although the written word is also perceived and understood instantly, groups of words and — even more so — pages of text can only be understood after reading each one of their component elements, i.e. by staggering visual perception through time. Two photographs of laborers, in which one man is seen working with horses in mountainous country and the other with a tractor on the plains, will be perceived as differing in these respects within a fraction of a second, as soon as they are shown to the observer. A comparison of the perception of two pages of text describing these same laborers will only lead to comparison of their material presentation, the typographic composition of the two pages, and not to a contrast of their respective content. Only after spending a certain amount of time

[12]   That is, the closest correspondence between reality and its description.
[13]   This view is theoretical. In the current situation this is still not possible, because of a lack of definition of emulsions and of thresholds in the resolution of lenses.

reading these pages will one be able to conclude that they concern two different laborers. The photographic image is therefore incontestably superior in achieving rapid perception of the reality recorded.

The image alone allows the possibility of research on modifications of this reality in time, whether over long periods or short. Because it is instantaneous, the process of vision also permits a simultaneous comparison of two, three, or many animated photographic images. Such comparison can help us to analyze their differences, to understand their modifications, to grasp their subtleties, and to isolate the influence of the time factor on their respective presentations.

In contrast to this, however, the reading of a text, temporally defined by its length and the speed of reading, impedes any sort of simultaneous comparison of two events. Texts are circumscribed in space and time, and their content described separately.

From these very general claims a certain number of considerations follow relative to the selection of one or the other of these means of expression. The following two factors will allow us to choose between text and image according to their respective communication potential.

First of all, we should note the quality of universality characteristic of photographs. By writing with light instead of words, photographic or cinematographic images are immediately understood by speakers of any language. Learning how to view films in an elementary fashion[14] requires only a few minutes, whatever the culture and degree of literacy of the viewer (cf. Carpenter's paper, *infra*).

Texts, on the other hand, utilize a particular means of expression, that of the author; all international communications require translation (into a minimum of about a hundred languages for worldwide consumption). Thus because of its documentary nature the medium of photography, whether animated or not, is designed to record events of all sorts. These recorded phenomena become ethnographic data when on film, and then subsequently become historical data. In contrast to this, written material is most effective in its discussion of facts, elaboration of theories, and development of concepts.

UNCUT FILMED DOCUMENTS

In order to be widely usable, filmed ethnographic or historical data

---

[14] Reading is an attribute of culture. Indeed, the elements that make up the picture are only perceived to the extent that the reader recognizes them.

require only a chronological presentation of the shots as they were taken. However, the sort of objectivity of the facts visible in these data can only depend upon their quality and duration.

Thus the editing of the current type of ethnographic film can be achieved only by eliminating some of the available filmed material and by adding commentary which will quite often distort the information presented.[15] Besides, regular films are usually projected in an uninterrupted fashion, although content analysis can only be done by examining the shots separately and sequentially.

These two different ways of viewing films lead to two alternative ways of using them: (1) film used as a means of expression, or (2) film used as a means of research.

However, the two uses need not be incompatible. It is not unreasonable to generate research films while producing creative ones on ethnographic themes, as long as certain precautions are taken with respect to original documents and with regard to the question: Do filmed documents have a "sacred character"?[16]

All of the preceding considerations might be seen to have already led to an affirmative response here; and other arguments can be added.

Thus, in order to resume the comparison between the respective values of text and film, we shall evaluate the research potential of field notes and of raw, unedited footage relative to this same question.

Raw footage, a set of different shots made of a single subject, constitutes the primary material from which the complete film is made that will be looked at by the researcher. These are some of the filmed records representing what we call "ethnographic data." The treatment they undergo during editing quite often puts them out of their original sequence, and alters both their continuity and length appreciably.

Manuscript notes are memory aids, often conveying ideas or recording important observations, quantification, etc. When he reports upon his research findings, the ethnologist will start off with this information but will be obliged to make important amplifications and digressions so as to render it intelligible to the future reader. When the material is being worked up, then, these two methods will be seen to determine two different procedures. The film will necessarily be of shorter duration than

---

[15]   In addition, Georges Sadoul says (1961:1393): "...editing of pictures and sound can, in the manner of photomontage, lead to a real counterfeiting of authentic documents."
[16]   Cf. Rouch (1971). There was an interview with Jean Rouch during the meeting of the Film Commission, August 26, 1971. To the question which he himself posed: "Is a filmed document sacred?" Rouch replied, "no," judging that rushes have no great value, and that one has the right to do with them what one wishes with the single condition that they not be lost.

that shot in the field, but the text, with rare exceptions, will be considerably longer and will either refer to or discuss the findings of other authors.

This means that without much difficulty a good filmmaker will be able to splice together an edited film from any given set of rushes from ethnographic filmed documents. But this cannot be done with the notes of an ethnologist, and it is hard to imagine that a systematic report could be garnered from the notes of an ethnologist who is no longer working with them. Hence the universal character of the image is again made incontestably clear. Because film research can only be done through shot-by-shot or image-by-image methods, it does not then seem worthwhile to do this by using edited films that present truncated information.

Private groups can (for all sorts of reasons and in the absence of pertinent national regulations) destroy the surplus footage from a documentary film's production. This should not be done, however, with scientific film, which is paid for by public funds in the interest of research. These latter films contain material which is perhaps the scholar's own intellectual property but which at least partially belongs to the people who have subsidized it, insofar as the material can also be of immediate value to other researchers.

For example, it is quite obviously impossible for an historian to retake the shots he might need in his films of certain events that happened at the beginning of the century, ten years ago, or even yesterday. Thus, from these observations it should be clear that rushes are extremely valuable for research, especially if we use certain formal devices (such as a chronology and identification of the events) that will render them even more fruitful.

That a researcher should do what he wants to with these filmed documents is not only normal but crucial. However the editing of the particular work must not prove detrimental to public viewing or to science. It should only be done once the conservation of the whole technically valuable document has been assured and it has been fully catalogued.

The fundamental problem is therefore the following: How can we make the rushes useful to a group of researchers? And what sort of investments are needed for such use? It is difficult to use rushes in their original form; at least some prior information is necessary for scientific evaluation of the data they provide: a note of the event filmed, and of the place and date of its occurrence (for example: the Bear Festival — France, Eastern Pyrenees, Prats de Mollo — February 3, 1970) can begin to give the reel some value as a scientific document.

With regard to this, Sorenson has already proposed a solution to the problem.[17] He provides indispensable instructions for the use of the rushes in any sort of scientific endeavor using film. His method does have the drawback of being painstakingly slow, and, as everyone knows, the lifetime of cine film is limited to some one or two hundred showings, after which is has been destroyed.

However, Sorenson's method is compatible with what we will propose here, which calls simply for abandoning cine film in favor of videotape as the basic tool of research. It should be understood that reference material on videotape can be shown several thousand times before any trace of perceptible wear appears.

COPIES FOR REFERENCE AND THE ARCHIVE

The method advocated hereafter is carried out chronologically after the the two operations of shooting and editing the film.[18] It is based on rational use of the work print. The latter is necessary in any use of filmed documents that are to be edited. Thus, as a first step, the work print, prepared by duplicating all of the original footage from one expedition and then developing it, is rid of any imperfections which might disturb a viewing such as stretches of hazy or light-struck film; black or white spots; a few repeated frames caused by false camera starts; indistinguishable blurry images, etc.

Next, the different sets of shots are regrouped according to the time sequence of the events filmed. They are put onto reels of various sizes, with each reel constituting a monograph whose subject is a single aspect of the event. If the reels relating to a particular event are all short, it is advantageous to group them together on a larger reel of up to 1,000 feet and to separate each section with black leader or, even better, with

---

[17]   Sorenson (1967: 448). He describes a process of editing of sequences in chronological order in the original or in a copy, and then printing from a copy or from a duplicate of the chronological edit. This last copy, marked with titles and subtitles, immediately receives magnetic track in the margin for recording information useful for scientific reasons. All of these operations are done on regular cine film.

[18]   All of these propositions are applicable in the first place to research works in progress or those to come, and also to documents already extant. Technical considerations can always be formulated with a larger or smaller percentage of applications, in the course of research. However, we need have no illusions, for experience in numerous realms has already demonstrated how much various attempts at standardization have posed problems.

Although they would be highly desirable in the short run, group campaigns to gather ethnographic data on film are not to be relied on in the long run, for they have only been successful in a few countries and remain nothing but a dream in most places.

a title. With this format all scenes would retain their proper length and time-sequencing within a particular series of shots. At this point the picture and sync-sound are put onto videotape. Thus, a reference copy of the rushes can be made at minimum expense. The recording devices used (videotape recorder or magnetoscope) allow for later recording and superimposition of a commentary without erasing the picture. Instead, the commentary can be recorded while the picture is being examined through a monitor. It must be noted, however, that for shot-by-shot or frame-by-frame analysis of a film, commentary is no longer of primary importance and only the synchronous sound is useful, especially for analysis of dance, song, speech, or body language.

When the videotape copy is archived and catalogued, the filmed work-print is once again available for further editing. Because videotape is so inexpensive, each stage in the editing process can be transposed all the more easily with the necessary video equipment available. The cost of this equipment for black-and-white film is about double that of a standard cine projector.

At the Centre d'Ethnologie Française at the Musée National des Arts et Traditions Populaires (French National Museum of Folk Arts and Traditions), I have been using a method of referencing and cataloguing material which groups the magnetic and photographic systems in the following ways:

1. Taking a work print from the original rushes;
2. Preparing and time-sequencing the work print;
3. Transposing this work print into videotape;
4. Storing and cataloguing the videotape, and making it available for reference;
5. Conforming the original film with the work print;
6. Printing the archive copy, called the maroon or security copy (a positive print for black-and-white films, and a black-and-white negative for color film) from the original stock and at the same time transposing the sync-sound on the archive tape to a 16-mm magnetic film stock;
7. Storing and labeling the sound version of the archive film in double-system;
8. Repeating the procedure used for the work print obtained in step one; that is to say, editing, adding a soundtrack, mixing, etc.

Having an archive copy on cine film allows printing of new negatives from which positive copies (in black-and-white) can be printed that will be of a quality close to that obtained by printing from the original negative. The advantage of our system is that we leave for posterity all of the documents on a particular subject, no matter what the aims of the original filmmaker were.

In this plan, then, I am considering that 16-mm film must remain the basis of most film recording. Videotape (whose popularization will provoke a revolution in the transmission of pictures) will on the other hand provide us with the most extraordinary means of promoting cross-references — mostly individual — among all sorts of extant films.

THE VIDEOTAPE VIEWER AND INDIVIDUAL REFERENCING

Because cinematography is now a leading means of investigation for anthropological research, it is inevitably attracting more and more young scholars. Until quite recently, these anthropologists had only very limited and difficult access to filmed documents, owing to the high cost of duplication and especially to the expense of the viewing equipment. It therefore seems desirable for us, at least in the early stages, to think of the most economical method and means possible for easy and rapid consultation of extant film documents, on equipment that is both technically new and easy to manipulate.

This will answer a deep and urgent need, for while it may be relatively easy for the researcher to shoot and edit films, it is much more difficult for him to view, project, or compare them with other films dealing with the same topic.

We remain frustrated with the slowness with which filmed documents have been put to use, especially when we compare this progress with that made for written and spoken documents. Whereas numerous libraries are being developed everywhere offering their users bigger, older, and more specialized collections; and while phonograph records and cassettes are everywhere accessible, there still does not exist, to my knowledge, any center devoted to film analysis and reference (cf. Appendix).

Ethnographic film must no longer be an inaccessible and peripheral instrument of research. It must enhance, with no further delay, the common heritage already at the disposal of all sorts of scholars. These sentiments are shared by a good number of anthropologists and historians. But one difficulty remains, that which we mentioned earlier, of finding a workable method for using the information contained in both completed films and rushes. In this regard, I shall cite the conclusions reached by historians who attended the three seminars devoted to ethnographic film and anthropological research by Professor H. Braudel at the Collège de France.

At the three seminars, the sentiments shared by the group of historians mingled admiration (so great did the wealth of information contained in the films seem to them) with a kind of confusion provoked by that sense of impotence which results from watching films normally shown in a public theater. In such situations, the pictures will follow each other in an inexorable sequence and the spectator is absolutely incapable of intervening to stop or review them, or analyze an interesting passage as he might while reading a text.

It is quite probable that these sentiments are also shared by numerous anthropologists who do not know how they can use the information in films and who therefore condemn the use of cinema in the human sciences.

A NEW PROCEDURE

If there is at the present time no system for making extant film documents available to researchers who want to consult them, this is very much due to the complexity and seriousness of the technical and financial problems posed by handling and projection. The difficulty results in part from the diversity of available procedures (optical or magnetic) and from the varying recording speeds of the soundtrack accompanying the picture. Practically every system will require the use of a different playback apparatus.

Classical films have always required costly and cumbersome multipart equipment that needs delicate and constant maintenance. Duplication and changes of format become very expensive for these films. The recent advent of a different procedure, however, has changed the situation. The magnetic recording of pictures has in effect most of the inconveniences inherent in systems using photographic copies on film.

The videotape recorder has proved to be the simplest and most suitable apparatus that might facilitate individual consultation of film documents and make possible their analysis for all conceivable uses. Experience with this technique makes it clear that the video system is perfectly reliable and will quickly and economically solve the problem of setting up a reference center for film documents.[19]

The videotape recorder alone provides the cheapest way to establish an important film library, and will eventually make available a set of copies

[19] Since 1969, I have been using and experimenting with this system of film presentation: first in the temporary exhibits of the Musée de L'Homme, and then, since September, 1971, in the continuous exhibits of a gallery of the Musée National des Arts et Traditions Populaires, where ten automatic machines are running permanently.

of the same film document for various scholars. Copying classic films onto magnetic tape does not really present any great difficulty (other than perhaps a legal one) and they can be shown on a standard film viewer (for looking at the original or the work print).[20] The videotape copy, at a reasonable price, can only be looked at through the intermediary of a televison set. But all the copies produced in such a manner from films of different format, projection, or sound processes will now be of a standardized type, and it will be possible to view them on a single apparatus[21] with all the current practical improvements: rapid forward and reverse, freezing a frame, and extremely simple operation (especially if a cassette recorder is involved).

And last but not least, a final advantage comes from using light and supple magnetic tapes. Indeed, videotapes or cassettes take up little space[22] compared with their length; they can be handled like books and be filed easily on shelves similar to those of a library.

Individual reference work is therefore now an immediate possibility. Its integration into research methodology depends on the establishment of film reference centers and on the setting up of film and video archives.

In conclusion, the filmed ethnographic document is one of the basic sources for modern history. As a result, certain measures must be imposed with great urgency, among them being the establishment of film and video libraries, and of film reference centers serving the human sciences.

The Ninth International Congress of Anthropological and Ethnological Sciences, along with the Anthropological Film Research Institute of which Margaret Mead is president, have asked for the immediate creation of a Center for Anthropological Film. Since 1964, within the framework of my activities at the Musée National des Arts et Traditions Populaires, I have been trying to set an example by storing and classifying all of my filmed ethnological research work (about a hundred hours of work print on rural France).

But in view of the great efforts that must quickly be made to save innumerable cultures from oblivion, I have already expressed my opinion on the need to set up ethnographic film archives in every country as

20   The film is projected into a television camera. This camera, relaying data to one or more videotape recorders, transforms the photographic image visible to the eye into a single invisible electronic image which is registered on as many magnetic tapes as there will be video copiers simultaneously in service.

21   The size of our videotape recorder is approximately 45 by 35 by 20 centimeters.

22   A video cassette with a volume of 20 by 10 by 3 centimeters weighs 400 grams, carries one and a half hours of color and sound film, or the equivalent of 40 kilograms of 35-millimeter film in cans, representing a cylindrical volume of 70 centimeters in height and 30 centimeters in diameter!

soon as possible (Lajoux 1970). I also proposed a program for the establishment of a library of films on French ethnography within the framework of the Musée National des Arts et Traditions Populaires.

In the United States, in 1970, Alan Lomax and Margaret Mead were making similar appeals for the creation of worldwide archives of ethnographic film (Lomax 1971). Because of such efforts, the National Anthropological Film Center became a reality at the Smithsonian Institution in Washington in 1974.

Quite recently, I have proposed a complete and detailed program for the creation of a center for the reference and storing of scientific film under the general direction of the Centre National de la Recherche Scientifique (CNRS). At the same time, the creation of a cinema library for the human sciences was proposed to UNESCO, to be at the Comité International du Film Ethnologique et Sociologique, under the direction of Jean Rouch. The latter will be examined during the UNESCO General Conference. These programs are currently under study. Certain decisions are urgently needed to safeguard particular aspects of the life of numerous ethnic groups. There must be no further delay. The resolutions passed unanimously during the Ninth International Congress are an important step in the right direction (cf. Appendix).

REFERENCES

BIRDWHISTELL, RAY L.
  1952 *Introduction to kinesics.* Louisville: University of Louisville Press.
  1970 *Kinesics and context.* Philadelphia: University of Pennsylvania Press.
CALISI, R.
  1972 "Il film di ricerca in etnologia e antropologia." Multigraph document. Venice: Biennale di Venezia.
CONDON, WILLIAM S.
  1970 Method of micro-analysis of sound films of behavior. *Behavior Research Methods and Instrumentation* 2:51–54.
CONDON, WILLIAM S., W. D. OGSTON
  1971 "Speech and body motion synchrony of the speaker-hearer," in *The perception of language.* Edited by D. L. Horton and J. J. Jenkins, 224–256. Columbus, Ohio: Charles E. Merrill.
GUILCHER, J. D.
  1963 *La tradition populaire de danse en Basse-Bretagne.* Paris and The Hague: Mouton.
KOECHLIN, BERNARD
  1968 Techniques corporelles et leur notation symbolique. *Langages* 10: 36–47.

LAJOUX, J. D.
  1970   L'ethnologue et la caméra. *La Recherche* 1:327–334.
  1972   Venezia Genti. Réflexions sur un festival et tendances actuelles. *Ethnologie française* 2:190–198.
LANCELOT, FRANCINE
  1972   "Les societés de Farandole." Unpublished doctoral dissertation, Paris.
LOMAX, ALAN
  1969   Choreometrics: a method for the study of cross-cultural pattern in film. *Sonderdruck and Research Film* 6:505–517.
  1971   Toward an ethnographic film archive. *Filmmakers Newsletter* 4(4): 31–38.
ROUCH, JEAN
  1971   "Montage et réalité du film ethnologique." Paper presented at the First Congress of European Ethnology, Paris.
SADOUL, GEORGES
  1961   "Témoignages photographiques et cinématographiques," in *L'histoire et ses méthodes*. Edited by Charles Samaran, 1390–1410. Encyclopédie de La Pléiade. Paris: Gallimard.
SORENSON, E. RICHARD
  1967   A research program in the study of changing man. *Current Anthropology* 8: 443–469.
TURQUETIL, A.
  1926   Notes sur les Esquimaux de la Baie Hudson. *Anthropos* 21:419–434. (Written in 1917.)

Some Methods of Ethnographic Filming

ALEXEI Y. PETERSON

The work on an ethnohistorical atlas of the Soviet Union that began in the sixties has demanded a thorough use of old and an extensive search for new material on various problems of ethnographical science (Bruk *et al.* 1968).

Today, the classical methods of collecting ethnographic materials (description, photography, drawing, etc.) have been complemented with ethnographic filming. This type of filming has been used by a number of Soviet research institutions including the Department of Ethnography of the Institute of History, the Academy of Sciences of the Latvian Soviet Socialist Republic, the State Museum of History and Ethnography of the Lithuanian Soviet Socialist Republic and the Institute of Art Criticism, Ethnography and Folklore, the Academy of Sciences of the Ukranian Soviet Socialist Republic. At the State Ethnographical Museum of the Estonian Soviet Socialist Republic, filming began to be used for scientific purposes in 1961. Over the next decade, the following films were made:

1961 Netting and fishing in the Gulf of Pyärnu; Flailing;

1962 Net-fishing through ice-holes in winter; Counterpane weaving methods in Rannu;

1963 Old farm buildings on Hiiumaa Island; Weaving ropes and baskets and making bow-staves;

1964 Villages and farm buildings on Saaremaa Island;

1965 Old tilling methods of the Southern Vepses;

1966 Villages, homes and farm outbuildings of the Southern Vepses;

1967 Old flailing methods of the Southern Vepses and initial drying of grain in the field;

1968 Making a dug-out in Southern Vepses;

1969 Making a dug-out boat in Estonia;
1970 Harvesting and flailing in Southern Estonia; and
1971 Old flax-growing methods in the southeast of Estonia.

In addition, a number of specific labor processes have been filmed. The total length of films made by the Museum over the past eleven years amounts to 50,000 meters.

Ethnographic field filming is a complicated process which requires special skill, yet there are still relatively few works on its methods (A. Jablonko 1967; M. Jablonko 1967; Simons 1969). This report contains some observations drawn from the experience of the Tartu Ethnographical Museum stuff.

A film's overall success and scientific value depend on a number of factors. One of the most important factors is the choice of a cameraman who is to work in close contact with or preferably under the direct supervision of an ethnographer who acts as a director or a consultant. This is because even an experienced professional cameraman, good at making educational science films, as a rule does not know all the peculiarities of making an ethnographic film which is to be used as a scientific document. For example, while filming some labor process, it is absolutely necessary that it be shown in a comprehensive manner and reflect in the minutest detail every operation and the role of every tool used in the process; the aesthetic side of the work, montage effects, etc., are all relegated to the background. For an ordinary audience, such a film is just a bore, while for an ethnographer, it is a source of rich, and sometimes unique, information. Hence, an ideal thing would be to have a cameraman who is also an ethnographer. Such persons do not grow on trees, however, so we have to contract ordinary cameramen from film studios. As our experience has shown, in this case, only a close cooperation between the cameraman and the scientific advisor results in a full fledged scientific documentary film.

We learned from experience that the filming of, say, old farm buildings requires a thorough methodological preparation. We tried to use the camera in such a way that our film could give one a comprehensive idea of the building techniques, the peculiarities of the design of houses and furniture, the arrangement and uses of living premises and outbuildings, etc. We learned that the way the camera moves is of utmost importance: first, the cameraman has to take a general view of a house and then, proceed to the door and, via the kitchen, go on to the living quarters. In the course of this work, we tried to film the most essential and typical features of any given object. Of course, that required hundreds of meters of film and much time.

We learned that it is extremely difficult to show the entire arrangement of outbuildings of a homestead, for a camera lens (even a wide-angle one) cannot take in all of them at once. For that reason, we started the filming with the most important structures. The functional purposes of outbuild- ings were shown by filming people working in them the way it used to be done in the past. The final stages of the work included the filming of general views, diagrams of details, and a general plan of the homestead. Of course, other approaches can be just as effective. However, the fewer auxiliary data required to explain a film and the more accurate the field filming of an object, the more effective the film is as a document.

To make a trustworthy and valuable ethnographic film, it is essential to create favorable conditions on the site. For example, in making a film devoted to harvesting and flailing the scientific advisor for the team of the Tartu Ethnographical Museum, together with the cameraman and the scientific advisor for the team of the Estonian Academy of Agriculture, studied in advance the conditions in the area selected for filming. One of the chief problems they faced was reproducing old working techniques. In Estonia, such an implement as the sickle has not been used in harvest- ing for as long as seventy or eighty years, so it was necessary to find older people used to this kind of work. It is essential that the worker be able to perform the process that is being filmed professionally, or we might say, mechanically. That allows us to avoid all kinds of unexpected things that may occur while a person is working in unusual conditions: in front of a camera and in an overheated place flooded with light. It is also essential to avoid, if possible, repeating demonstrations of labor techniques. The less interference on the part of the filming team, the more natural is the process on film. A lack of time and a nervous atmosphere are liable to make a worker simplify or reduce the working process, which sometimes is overlooked even by experienced ethnographers in charge of the filming. We agree with Simons who says that such an important advantage of an ethnographic film as its ability to record and reproduce labor techniques must not be marred by simplification; it is essential to take in every movement of a worker. Only then can a film become a documentary source that can promote the solution of such a complicated and thus far largely untouched problem as the interrelationship between the shape of a tool and the worker's movements (Simons 1969:58).

Sometimes it is difficult to find people who are good at some specific work. For instance, while shooting a film on flailing in Southern Estonia, we could not find enough men among the local folk who knew the job. At least four men were needed for such a film, so we invited some from other places. It turned out, however, that their techniques were somewhat different. Such a situation is indicative of a certain methodological problem. There are a great number of ethnographic labor processes and elements of material culture that have complicated local features; these features are often hardly noticeable, yet they are highly important. Apparently, ethnographers must deal exclusively with labor processes of a specific area (the site of filming), without bringing into them elements typical of other places. This is most important for the Soviet Baltic republics where different elements of material culture are concentrated in a comparatively small territory; for example, there are different techniques of harvesting, different types of flails, etc. Simultaneous filming of several types of tools or implements and several labor processes is only justifiable when we want to show a variety of types (for instance, in the latter half of the nineteenth century two types of sickle were used in Estonia for harvesting). However, if simultaneous demonstration of a number of tools of different types is attempted, an ethnographic film may be deprived of accuracy and clarity, which are its strongest points.

This brief report does not allow us to dwell on a script for an ethnographic film. It should be noted, however, that filming often has to be done within a short period and without any preliminary preparation, which calls for a great versatility and initiative on the part of filmmakers. During the filming of Veps farm buildings, for instance, the filmmakers learned that one of the oldest dug-out experts in the vicinity was going to make a new boat. The head of the filming team decided to finish the shooting of the farm buildings and start the filming of boat-making immediately, which was absolutely correct. As no research had been done in the field, the filming was for the most part directed by the boat-maker. Subsequent surveys showed that the boat had been made strictly in accordance with the tradition.

Finally, while shooting a film, we never forget the basic principle of Soviet ethnography which is the historical method, that is the showing of objects in their dynamic development. This requirement proves to be quite easy to fill, as we can invite for filming people of different generations and show labor processes and tools at different chronological levels.

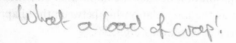

REFERENCES

BRUK, S. I., W. K. GARDANOV, K. G. GUSLISTYJ, M. G. RABINOWITSCH,
T. A. ZHDANKO, L. N. TERENTJEWA
  1968   Grundsätze und Methoden beim Zusammenstellen regionaler ge-
         schichtlich-ethnographischer Atlanten in der UdSSR. *Proceedings,
         VIIIth Intranational Congress of Anthropological and Ethnological
         Sciences, 1968, Tokyo and Kyoto,* 2:3–6. Tokyo: Science Council of
         Japan.

JABLONKO, ALLISON
  1967   Ethnographic film as basic data for analysis. *VII-me Congrès inter-
         national des sciences anthropologiques et ethnologiques. Moscou (3
         août–10 août 1964),* 4:168–173. Moscow Iedatelgstvo "Nauka".

JABLONKO, MAREK
  1967   Technical problems of field filming. *VII-me Congrès international des
         sciences anthropologiques et ethnologiques. Moscou (3 août–10 août
         1964),* 4:162–167. Moscow: Iedatelgstvo "Nauka".

SIMONS, GABRIEL
  1969   "Die Erscheinungen des werktätigen Lebens und die volkskundliche
         Filmdokumentation," in *Arbeit und Gerät in volkskundlicher Dokumenta-
         tion.* Edited by Wilhelm Hansen, 54–63. Münster: Verlag Aschendorff.

Reconstructing Cultures on Film

ASEN BALIKCI

Reconstructing cultures on film is a practice as old as the medium itself. Any feature production illustrating a precise historical event such as a Napoleonic battle scene or a fictional story on the conquest of the American West implies substantial efforts at cultural reconstruction. This can be more or less successful depending on a variety of factors such as the availability of good historical records and the producer's intention to interpret the historical past accurately. In any case, in feature presentations the reconstruction effort centers on a particular historical event along a given story line.

In visual anthropology cultural reconstruction acquires a different meaning. The general aim is to partially reconstruct sequences of traditional behavior as part of the routinized social process. No attempt is made to portray the extraordinary or the unique. There are no explicit story lines, rigid scenarios, professional actors or stage rehearsals. With this in mind we can ask, why reconstruct at all and to what purpose? It is common knowledge that for many decades Western culture has had a profound influence on countless indigenous societies. In recent years with rapid advances in Western science, industrial technology and communications the process of cultural levelling has speeded up tremendously, pointing in the direction of a world culture. The loss of original content among indigenous cultures has assumed dramatic proportions. The visual anthropologist who is reconstructing cultures tries in a sense to reverse the acculturative process and salvage elements of traditional behavior for posterity.

A first category of filmmakers, not necessarily anthropologists, seems fascinated by the ancient ways of a people which acquire a kind of mysterious aura. These ancient ways emerge on the screen to give added depth and meaning to a particular life style. A lyrical music score may intensify the emotional impact and expand the romantic ambiance. *Man of Aran*, for instance, is constructed, or reconstructed, as the perennial hero fighting hostile elements.

A second category of visual anthropologists have adopted a more sober attitude. A classic culture such as the Australian Aborigines has disappeared, yet it seems possible to find a few isolated families in the Western Desert who have subsisted traditionally in the bush until very recently. The filmmaker is motivated by an anthropological rationale, successfully reconstructs the traditional pattern and obtains a valuable ethnographic record. The visual record supplements, partially at least, the monographs of early anthroplogists.

A third class of visual anthropologists are motivated by purely educational imperatives. The Netsilik Eskimos, a classic culture, despite strong acculturative pressures remember vividly their traditional past. The old pattern is reconstructed and filmed for the specific purpose of providing instructional materials for classroom use. The reconstruction acquires full significance only when compared with the acculturated setting. The contrast is used to explicate the notion of social change in all its complexity. Clearly, this filmed reconstruction is part of a well organized social science curriculum.

Cultural reconstruction for filming purposes is obviously a very selective process. The range of reconstructed subjects may vary along a continuum from a single cultural trait to a cultural complex and to a "whole" culture. The first category usually comprises reconstructions of vanishing traditional technologies: step-by-step an old Algonquin Indian makes a birchbark canoe, or an Australian Aborigine carves and polishes a boomerang. Such reconstructions are very successful because the elderly informant has been selected specifically for his knowledge of the traditional technique. Filming such a subject is easy enough since the task accomplished is simple, involving only a single actor in a progressive relationship with a technical activity. In a sense the anthropologist-filmmaker is in total control of the subject.

The second category refers to reconstructing cultural complexes involving a large personnel. I have seen several films made in Eastern European countries on group dancing and singing and shot either *in situ* or on the stage. No doubt both choreography and music are traditional. Yet in an effort to make things nice, only pretty girls have been selected and the traditional costumes are of standard design and color and of course perfectly clean. If the performance takes place in the village, houses are immaculate. The dancing place is garden-like and the elders watching are all dignified and content. The presentation is elegant, well ordered and definitely pleasing to the eye. Yet I have seen similar performances in Southern Macedonia which are full of variety, contrast, uncontrolled spontaneity, explosive dynamism, disharmony, indifference and exuberance all at the same time. The reconstructed performance seems dull and artifical in comparison. Here we can see the main danger in reconstructing complex cultural settings. The scenario, if rigidly followed, by concentrating obsessively on the traditional (the reconstructed) takes away all spontaneity from the field of action and produces an effect of museum sterility.

The third category of reconstructions is the most ambitious in scope and concerns "whole" cultures. By this we mean that a large number of traditional culture traits and complexes are included in the filming plan with the aim of giving a rounded illustration of the indigenous way of life. I know of three such attempts, *Man of Aran* by Flaherty, *Desert People* by Ian Dunlop and Robert Tonkinson and the Netsilik Eskimos Film Series produced by Education Development Center and the National Film Board of Canada.

Man of Aran as a film classic is by far the best known of these productions and at the same time in my opinion the least "ethnographic." In order to understand this assertion it is necessary first to distinguish between the two major styles of anthropological filming.

Most anthropologists consider the camera as strictly a recording and research tool, an addition to the fieldworker's notebook. The camera, handled by the anthropologist is supposed to record directly spontaneous social reality, unrehearsed, within the total natural setting. The basic assumption is that the camera is a passive and objective recording device which does not distort the flow of social action. The individuals filmed are anonymous or just people from a particular society. Their behavior is culturally patterned and in a sense filming any individual from this group will lead to the same results. The camera becomes a wonderful tool for discretely recording the complex raw data of culturally patterned behavior. The viewer when screening the long sequences is supposed to make his own analyses of the behavior patterns.

This approach implies the belief in an obvious fallacy, which is the objectivity of the camera. First, the camera never records by itself, it is operated by a filmer who selects *a priori* the sequences to be filmed. This he does following a number of factors and assumptions, conscious and unconscious, which are not clearly stated. Second, the camera by its very nature — the limited range of vision of the lens — imposes a selectivity of its own. Third, the pruning done by the editor's blade determines a new sequencing. The net result is a filmed construction of a few aspects of the local culture implying a high degree of subject selectivity, and this despite the caution and care of the anthropologist-filmer.

The second approach in anthropological filmmaking admits right from the beginning that there is no such thing as the objectivity of the camera. A film is always a construction. Anthropological films are no exception, they are similar to monographs which are selective syntheses of cultural data. The creative, constructive contribution of the filmmaker cannot be ignored. This approach gives much freedom to the filmmaker in all phases of production; the anthropological film becomes an admittedly personal interpretation of the local culture. With this in mind, Flaherty developed a specific method for constructing (and reconstructing) cultures on film. Flaherty observed closely and for prolonged periods the way of life of the indigenous people he was to film and then selected an "actor" or a small number of "actors," all local folk who in front of the camera became the interpreters of their own culture. Flaherty filmed his actors in a series of locally typical or highly dramatic episodes which gave the local culture sharp contours and extraordinary intensity. One of Flaherty's favorite themes was the continuously heroic struggle of total, primordial man against infinitely powerful and hostile elements. Nanook and the man of Aran are portrayed in a succession of humble occupations and dramatic feats, this alternation revealing both the profound humanness of the actors and the originality of the cultures. One should not forget however that it is Flaherty who defines the Eskimo character of Nanook and creates the man of Aran.

While *Nanook* contains only a few staged sequences (barely perceptible) *Man of Aran* includes much prearranged and reconstructed material. John C. Messenger who has carried out recent field work among the Aran islanders writes:

Flaherty was so deeply influenced by primitivism and his philosophy of esthetics that he created new customs, such as shark fishing — a central theme of the work, and seriously distorted numerous indigenous ones in order to make the "man of Aran" fit his preconceptions and titillate his camera. As to the soil building and associated seaweed collecting technique it is faulty to the point of being ridiculous. And for the most dramatic scene depicting the wrecking of the craft on shore while landing, local informants agreed that weather conditions were not as severe nor the situation as perilous as illustrated on the film (Messenger 1966:21).

Clearly in his efforts to construct and reconstruct Aran island culture Flaherty introduced inventions of his own, plus exaggerations and distortions. In this sense we feel that *Man of Aran* is not an ethnographically valid reconstruction of the local culture.

Desert People and the Netsilik Eskimo Film Series do not seem to suffer from the same weaknesses. The reconstructive strategy implied in the production of *Desert People* was simple enough. The film director Ian Dunlop and his anthropological adviser Robert Tonkinson located at a mission station a family of Aborigines who until very recently had been living off the land. The family was invited to return to its traditional grounds for a period of time with the specific aim of being filmed. In accepting the contract the family apparently left whatever imported goods it owned at the mission station and left for the bush armed only with traditional tools. The director concentrated on the various daily routines: hunting small game, gathering wild plants, searching for water, eating practices, children's games, sleeping postures, etc. Dramatic effects are absent, the various activities are filmed in great detail, and when the behavioral segments involving one individual and his family are put together the viewer begins to get the feeling of a meaningful cultural totality. In the Flaherty tradition this sense of totality emerges from the principal "actor" who is the leader and the integrator of the family's activities. He slowly becomes a person with a distinct personality and the viewer has enough time to develop feelings of empathy for him. Unlike Flaherty however Ian Dunlop fails to exploit to the fullest the personality of his principal actor who doesn't have the humanistic depth of Nanook. At the same time the controlling supervision of the anthropologist is clearly felt, the routine activities filmed are of the same scale, there is balance in the harmonious succession of native tasks which excludes monotony. At no moment does the viewer feel the intrusion of the camera in the regular flow of subsistence and social activities. The reconstruction of the traditional family microcosm is so successful that even the critical ethnographer remains completely oblivious of the powerful intrusive society encircling this Aboriginal group.

Reconstructing the traditional life of the Netsilik Eskimos was a considerably more ambitious, dangerous and difficult task. During the winter of 1959–1960 I had carried out anthropological fieldwork among the eastern Netsilik Eskimos living around Pelly Bay. At that time the band numbered about a hundred individuals and had gone through several acculturative stages. The introduction of the rifle in the area had produced profound changes in settlement pattern, subsistence techniques and economic organization; it was the single most important acculturative factor. In traditional times seal hunting was necessarily a group activity, it took place around the large winter settlements on the flat ice, the hunters armed with harpoons keeping a watch for seals at the breathing holes. Associated with these collective hunts was a complex system of meat sharing at the community level. In August salmon trout were speared along the rivers inland at specially constructed stone weirs. Later in August the vitally important caribou hunts were conducted at the crossing places. The beaters drove the herds into the narrow lakes where they became easy prey to the fast paddling kayakers. In October fishing was resumed with the leister through the thin river ice.

In the 1950's the rifle had profoundly transformed this subsistence pattern. Sealing at the breathing holes was still done occasionally, but the hunters preferred to shoot seals at the ice edge, a much more efficient technique. The seals killed with a rifle were not shared; they belonged to the hunter. Caribou hunting from kayaks had been completely abandoned; with rifle in hand a Netsilik could search for herds in the vast tundra and make a kill in any season. Fishing techniques remained unchanged.

With a larger supply of seal meat, bigger dog teams became common; this increased the mobility of the hunters. Further, as the families were not obliged to follow the men on their hunting trips, the trend toward sedenterization became increasingly strong. In 1940 a Catholic missionary arrived in the area and established a permanent mission with a trading store. The band quickly converted to Christianity, abandoned shamanistic practices and ritual observances, and gradually the families settled more or less permanently around the mission.

In the 1950's the Pelly Bay people still lived in igloos, drove dog teams, preferred caribou leather for clothing and relied exclusively on local food. Yet they regularly attended mass, smoked pipes and drank tea. The middle aged and older people however remembered vividly the old ways and were very eager and proud to communicate their knowledge of local traditions to the anthropologist.

In 1962 I received an assignment to reconstruct on film the traditional migration pattern of the Pelly Bay band with the aim of preparing instructional materials for social science courses at the elementary level. No further limitations were imposed at the time. Right from the beginning I had to make two basic decisions concerning, first, the historical baseline as a guide for cultural reconstruction and second, the subject matter of each film unit. The historical baseline was to be the last year prior to the introduction of rifles in the area, namely 1919. For that period I had substantial information relative to the migration cycle of one particular family. As for the subject matter of the series of films it seemed most natural to make a particular film for each camp site within the annual migration circuit.

It was not easy to explain our objectives to the Eskimos. In the Flaherty tradition I decided to select one principal "actor" and relate most community activities to him and his small family. The Pelly Bay people were by no means ignorant at that time about picture-taking. So when the cameraman and I arrived at the Pelly Bay mission station in early August, I explained to Itimanguerk, a man about fifty years old, who was to be our principal actor, that a friend of mine had decided to accompany me for the purpose of taking pictures. The pictures we were to take, however, should depict the old ways of the Netsilik, from the time when Itimanguerk was a young man. All the new artifacts such as rifles, teapots, cigarettes, frying pans and canvas tents were to be kept in hiding when shooting or replaced. To this Itimanguerk readily agreed, for a consideration of course. Further, as a camp headman, Itimanguerk was free to select his camp fellows and if they were young to instruct them in the old ways. In a sense Itimanguerk was to be the head of the operations; it was his task to reconstruct the traditional ways, select camp sites and hunt the game he wished to hunt. The anthropologist's role was a subordinate one, namely to help with logistics and act as an intermediary between the Eskimo community and the cameraman.

I believe that Itimanguerk did not realize at the beginning the magnitude of the task he had accepted. He assumed probably that the exercise would take a few days instead of a whole year. As a matter of fact I was also ignorant of the prolonged efforts and hardships of the enterprise; our initial contract with the producer was for just a few weeks. With the best of intentions and no precise plans we proceeded to the stone weir for the fishing season and almost immediately upon arrival were able to film systematically.

It soon became apparent that reconstruction amounted to little more than "cleaning the camp," removing from the filming site the few imported objects. Itimanguerk, unsolicited, insisted on making fire by friction of wooden sticks and his wife took pride in using the old soapstone pot. Initiative for reconstruction was left entirely with Itimanguerk. The Eskimos behaved just as they would behave in any ordinary situation, paying little attention to the light, hand-held camera. The anthropologist became more and more involved with the recording procedures, preoccupied with the question: what should be filmed? To that basic question no easy answer could be given; there was of course the essential subsistence activity which was the *raison d'être* of the camp; this was filmed in the greatest possible detail. For the rest the anthropologist "fished" for subjects, evaluating on the spot the significance of this or that activity and the way it could be related to the rest. Obviously this is a highly selective and in a sense arbitrary process, the successful outcome of which depended mostly on the anthropologist's knowledge and understanding of Eskimo traditional ways. It should be remembered that the anthropologist as a rule did not interfere in and direct the flow of social action; he just selected. Reconstruction here did not mean in any way telling the Eskimos how to act; on the contrary, all our efforts were concentrated on capturing on film the spontaneity of behavior.

When the three major films dealing with cultural reconstructions are compared, it becomes apparent that in *Man of Aran* Flaherty consciously and strongly emphasized specific reconstructed aspects of the local culture; it is clearly Flaherty who ordered the reconstructions. In the case of *Desert People* Ian Dunlop was fortunate enough to deal with a society which was close enough to the traditional pattern to make the reconstruction effort relatively easy and safe. In the case of the Netsilik Eskimo Film Series the cultural reconstruction was carried out entirely under the initiative of the Eskimos who willingly acted as traditional Netsiliks.

It might be interesting to note the impact produced by these films on two types of audiences: high school and college classrooms in Western societies, and indigenous societies who shared the reconstructed culture.

J. W. Berry and E. Sommerlad have shown *Desert People* in three high schools in Sydney and administered an Australian ethnocentrism test. A significant positive correlation was found between ethnocentric attitudes and the evaluation of the film; that is, ethnographic film material seems to provide documentary evidence to confirm the prior attitudinal positions of positively and negatively ethnically prejudiced persons (Berry and Sommerlad, n.d.:3). Within the framework of a more complex experiment conducted at the University of Massachusetts, Nicholas Lazaris using Netsilik Eskimo films in four freshmen classes obtained essentially the same results: "The effects of emotional reactions on students' attitudes was measured by the semantic differential test. In general these test results showed little attitudinal change over the five-week (experimental) interval." Strangely enough, stereotypes pertaining to ethnic characteristics seem particularly resistant, and simple exposure to ethnographic films does not affect the content of the stereotypes. The situation changes entirely, however, when written materials are used together with films within the framework of a more active pedagogy.

As for *Man of Aran*, it seems that this film has created a kind of a mystique; in the Western public it has "idealized" the folkways of the islanders and has attracted many tourists to Aran who seek acceptance from the islanders, boast of their intimate knowledge of Aran customs and try to "go native" (Messenger 1966:22).

Now concerning the impact of these films on the local societies, it was stated already in relation to *Man of Aran* that the islanders considered the film somewhat ridiculous and resented the sequences depicting them as "savages." We don't know whether *Desert People* has been shown to Australian Aborigines and if so what their reaction was. As for the Netsilik Eskimo films they are at the present time being definitely disfavored in the Canadian North. Young Eskimos today point to their girls wearing mini-skirts and their shiny motorcycles and say: "We don't live like these Eskimos in the films; they are savages, we are civilized people." Attitudes are radically different in Alaska where acculturation has gone far enough to make the Netsilik Eskimo films highly appreciated as an invaluable record of the people's own history.

Films dealing with cultural reconstruction have greatest value, in my opinion, when they are accompanied by secondary productions depicting the modern, acculturated ways of the same actors. In 1970 the National Film Board of Canada produced a film on Itimanguerk and his family living in a three-bedroom frame house. The contrast between old ways and new ways is dramatic and no audience can remain indifferent. Lazaris writes in reference to the Netsilik Eskimo films:

Film materials are very important in the affective area of education: emotions, values and empathy. When students saw the same actors on every film, they began to empathize with the images on the screen who became real people to them. The acculturation film was able to upset students and make them react emotionally in a classroom where emotions are rarely revealed (Lazaris, n.d.: 57)

Considering that culture change is a worldwide process affecting all societies, comparisons between reconstructed traditional and acculturated settings become centrally important and invite the audience to ask basic questions about the future of mankind.

REFERENCES

BALIKCI, ASEN, QUENTIN BROWN
    1966   Ethnographic filming and the Netsilik Eskimos. *Educational Services Incorporated Quarterly Report* (Spring–Summer): 19–33.
BERRY, J. W., ELIZABETH SOMMERLAD
    n.d.   Ethnocentrism and the evaluation of an ethnographic film. Unpublished manuscript, Queen's University.
LAZARIS, NICHOLAS
    n.d.   "The Netsilik Eskimos on Paper and Film." Unpublished B.Sc. thesis, Massachusetts Institute of Technology, Cambridge.

MESSENGER, JOHN C.
  1966   Man of Aran revisited: an anthropological critique. *University Review* (Dublin). 3 (9).
SALZMANN, MONIQUE
  1967   Introduction à une filmographie des Aborigènes australiens. *Journal de la Société des Océanistes* 23:123–134.

The Role of Film in Archaeology

STUART STRUEVER

Film has two major roles in modern archaeology: (1) to document field research, and (2) to communicate the activities and results of archaeological research to a broader audience. I will argue that film's contribution to archaeology will be of greater importance to the second of these two potential roles.

A BRIEF ACCOUNT OF THE WRITER'S EXPERIENCE WITH FILMING ARCHAEOLOGY

I am not a cinematographer nor have I had any technical role in the production of films. I am, however, an archaeologist who, for the last fifteen years, has been involved in long-term, programmatic archaeological research in the central Mississippi River drainage. In the process I have made or been party to numerous films produced by various agencies for various audiences; the present paper attempts to describe why these films were made and what effect they have had on the archaeological research program.

The Mississippi Valley archaeological program emphasizes inter-disciplinary cooperation among specialists concerned with prehistoric culture, human biology, and physical environment. As many as fifteen different academic disciplines have been involved (Struever 1968). This research program maintains major facilities on the Northwestern University campus in Evanston, Illinois, and in west-central Illinois, specifically at the small village of Kampsville. Kampsville has become a permanent headquarters for the archaeological field program; it embraces five permanent and three to six temporary laboratory operations. These field laboratories process artifactual, botanical, zoological, and other classes of data as they are recovered by the excavators (cf. Brown and Struever 1973).

Large-scale, programmatic archaeological research now requires a high level of funding; it also requires continuity of funding. To date, it has been impossible to achieve this funding exclusively through traditional scientific granting agencies. The amounts of money required, and the need to hold the funding level as constant as possible require the development of a diverse funding base. Here the idea is to draw support from both the public and private sector and to diversify the funding sources to a point where the withdrawal of even a major donor agency or individual does not have a crippling effect on the research program. To achieve this, we have established a formal concept of the Northwestern Archaeological Program which in 1973 had a membership of more than 3,000 foundations, corporations, and individuals. In addition to membership fees ranging from $5 to $5000 each, the Northwestern Archaeological Program obtains support from the National Science Foundation and, in the area of salvage archaeology, from the National Park Service. Additional funds have been obtained on special occasions from various divisions of the Illinois state government. Except for National Science Foundation grants, the largest single source of funding supplied only 3 percent of the Northwestern Archaeological Program's budget in 1973.

A large budget supplied by a diverse membership has been developed by the Northwestern Archaeological Program, largely through an active effort at public communication, to maintain its research and educational programs and its Evanston and Kampsville facilities. Film, in the form of television documentaries and news stories, as well as film rentals and sales, has been one of the most important aspects of this communication effort.

Before we treat this important but generally overlooked application of film to archaeology, it is appropriate that we discuss film's research applications.

THE USE OF FILM IN ARCHAEOLOGICAL FIELDWORK

The Northwestern Archaeological Program has, over the past five years, been engaged in the excavation of the Koster Site. Koster has yielded evidence of at least 15 habitation levels superimposed one upon the other in more than 35 feet of soil. Heavy slopewash conditions at Koster have produced a situation of interbedded habitation and sterile levels, an ideal context for segregating the assemblages associated with each specific cultural component that is represented at the site. Radiocarbon dates from Koster range between 5,200 B.C. and A.D. 820.

Large-scale excavations were conducted each summer at Koster between 1970 and 1973, with another major excavation planned for 1974. Field crews of students and other archaeologists working at Koster at any one time range from 25 up to 55 individuals.

After an initial test phase, a major block excavation was made in the most productive area of the site. Major parts of this excavation were carried down to a depth of 34.5 feet below modern ground surface. During the 1972 and 1973 excavation seasons research was being conducted on four to six different habitation levels at any one time. Though a fulltime photographer was on hand to document any specific feature, profile, floor, or other unit for which still photographic documentation was desired, the "moving picture" turned out to have an essential, if supplementary, role in the documentation process.

The value of the film in archaeological research lies in documenting the excavation PROCESS in a way that neither words nor still photographs can achieve. One of the difficulties of photographing a very large, complicated excavation like the main trench at Koster is that it is almost impossible to demonstrate visually the spatial relationships between the specific areas included in the various photographs. If there are dozens of excavators working on a half-dozen different habitation levels in a trench that is 180 feet long and up to 90 feet wide, it is difficult to obtain a single photograph that will encompass all of the excavation operations without so reducing their scale as to make them almost invisible. It is possible, of course, to take several intermediate range photographs, each of which encompasses a portion of the excavation. By looking at these pictures together it becomes possible to identify areas of overlap, allowing the archaeologist to develop in his mind a composite picture of the total excavation. However, this is at best difficult — and there are always major areas of the excavation that are accidentally omitted — with still photographs. The value of the cine-camera is not only that the photographer can juxtapose, through his sequence of filming, those areas of the major excavation he wishes to show, but also that he can, with careful control of camera movements, document the areas to be shown while at the same time relating these areas to each other in space. For example, if it is desirable to show the relationship between a major section of wall on the north side of the trench and a section of the south wall, he can set up the camera so that it films one and then moves slowly to the other. If done correctly, this conveys a sense of the relationship between the two walls that is not achievable in even the best still photography.

Another research application of film lies in its ability to accentuate or dramatize specific points within a larger frame. For example, the cine-camera can shoot a sequence which begins with an overview of the entire trench at Koster and then zooms in on a specific living floor or wall section. By this means film gives the archaeologist the capacity to add emphasis to his photo documentation, an element missing from still photography.

A third research application for the film is in conveying information about the digging CONDITIONS that cannot be easily caught in the still photo. Two minutes of film at a particular juncture in the 1973 Koster excavation season conveyed clearly the difficulties of piece-plotting individual artifacts in Horizon II due to groundwater seepage in the excavation area. A minute or two of film quickly conveys the cement-like quality of the profile walls at Koster, impressing upon the viewer how difficult it has been to obtain the kind of flat, straight walls that are necessary to document the position and thickness of each habitation layer.

Clearly film can make important contributions to the documentation of archaeological excavations. However, the cost of film and film pro-cessing, not to mention original equipment costs, makes the still photo-graph a more practical mechanism for visual documentation. In addition there are limitations inherent in viewing a film. It is usually more feasible to look at photographs than to find a projector and screen for film view-ing. It is mainly the cost differential that makes still photographs the most practical means of documenting archaeological research at present.

THE FILM AS A COMMUNICATIVE DEVICE FOR ARCHAEOLOGY

The greatest potential contribution of film to archaeology lies in the area of communication. It is the most effective means of communicating the activities and tone of an archaeological excavation to a broad audience. It is much more difficult to use still photographs to catch the excitement of an excavation than it is to use a movie for this purpose. This has not been fully appreciated by the archaeological profession which is today growing increasingly aware of the importance of communicating its goals and techniques to general audiences. Archaeologists are realizing more and more that financial support, student recruitment, and other aspects of the development of the discipline are contingent on an acceptance by administrators, foundation boards, and other persons or groups with decision-making responsibilities.

North American archaeology, with its strong tie to anthropology and with its emphasis on sites that lack architectural grandeur and portable art works, has a continuing problem with credibility. Despite the major growth of archaeology in anthropology departments throughout the United States since World War II, there remains a strong popular belief that archaeology is the search for temples and tombs and artifacts that express the highest artistic achievement of an extinct people. North American archaeologists pulling chipping debris, stone artifacts, simple bone tools, and food remains from a midden deposit in a site that altogether lacks ruins above the ground or any other signs of grand achievement have a continuing problem of making potential funding agencies understand the importance of their work.

Film can, in essence, dramatize "the search" and so gain the attention of the viewer for a discussion of the goals and methods that give modern archaeology its importance. The entire emphasis on interdisciplinary research in archaeology, with focus on the reconstruction of prehistoric human biological, cultural, and physical environmental systems and their interaction in prehistory, can be — but has not yet been — conveyed to a broad audience with exciting results. It is my belief that film has more potential than any other medium for conveying the newly-evolving problems and techniques of today's archaeology.

In truth though, film has seldom been used effectively in this manner. Most television documentaries, whether from educational or commercial networks, tend to be lowcost, "quicky" productions. To my knowledge no serious attempt has been made to create a film that describes the developing scientific and cultural-ecological orientations of modern archeology. Such a film would be difficult and costly to produce. It would require in-depth research by the producer and a well-constructed script to translate the new directions of archaeology into a visually exciting yet accurate product. But in my view this is precisely where film can make its greatest contribution to modern archaeology. My own experience with attempting to introduce the goals and results of the "new archaeology" to a broad audience indicates that archaeology is intrinsically exciting to people and that many of its new goals and methods are as exciting to the layman as a temple or a royal tomb would be. But they are less visually exciting. It will take a clever filmmaker to convey the activities of today's interdisciplinary archaeology and still keep the air of drama and anticipation that has always made archaeology popular.

SUMMARY

In this paper I argue that film has two roles in archaeology: (1) to document the activities and results of excavations, and (2) to convey the goals and techniques of a rapidly changing discipline to a broad audience which includes the decision-makers upon whose judgments the continuing growth of the discipline depends. Certain aspects of an excavation are best documented in film, but many other aspects are equally well—or better—documented in still photographs. Furthermore, the cost of producing films greatly exceeds that of making photographs, and thus the extent to which archaeologists with limited budgets can justify film documentation of their research is sharply restricted. Even viewing the results of film documentation is more restrictive than looking at the results of still photography.

This paper argues that the most important application of the film to archaeology lies in the area of conveying the rapidly changing goals, techniques, and results of the discipline to audiences of non-archaeologists. It is argued that the dramatic qualities inherent in the film medium make it potentially the most effective means of telling the story of a rapidly changing academic discipline. Large-scale, programmatic archaeological research requires a scale and continuity of funding that exceeds the capacity of any single agency. The capacity of archaeology to engender the increased support necessary to conduct forms of research now being devised makes it important that the discipline broaden its communication — look outward to a much wider range of organizations for the increased support it requires. And film has a greater potential for achieving this result than any other medium.

REFERENCES

BROWN, JAMES A., STUART STRUEVER
  1973 "The organization of archeological research: an Illinois example,"
      in *Research and theory in current archeology*. Edited by Charles
      L. Redman, 261–280. Somerset, N. J.: Wiley-Interscience.
STRUEVER, STUART
  1968 "Problems, methods and organization: a disparity in the growth of
      archeology," in *Anthropological archeology in the Americas*. Edited by
      Betty J. Meggers, 131–151. Washington, D. C.: Anthropological
      Society of Washington.

COMMENT *by Paul Hockings*

There is an intermediate use of film that falls somewhere between the research and the publicity uses described in this paper, and which laps over into both. This use — which I first encountered in India — amounts to the creation of a rapid and dramatically clear summary on film of what might be a very complex stratified excavation. Such a summary has its research uses: it is made by exposing a few feet of film at each significant stage in the process of excavation. It may bring to light relationships between various parts of the site that are otherwise lost in a welter of photographs, plans, and notebooks; and it certainly may help the scholar organize the writing of his site report. The film will be equally useful in explaining quickly the significance of the excavation to funding agencies or to visiting government officials who in some cases would prefer not to be visiting. Intermediate between these two uses of such a summary film is its teaching application: it may be presented both in the classroom to underline the general importance of the excavation, and in the field to indoctrinate a new season's crew and help them find greater significance in what they are about to undertake.

Specialized Uses of Film and Videotape

Photography and Visual Anthropology

JOHN COLLIER, JR.

It is difficult to look at the scope of visual anthropology without considering all the research functions of photography, for methodologically the camera has made visual analysis a reality for the behavioral sciences. The still camera explored the area of nonverbal communication, but the moving picture camera has been able to integrate this language fluently. Because of this interlocking development, it is shallow to review still camera research without also considering the blossoming that took place when the still image began to MOVE. This paper will deal with both still and film data as photography's composite contribution to anthropology.

Photographic observation opened wholly new theoretical considerations in anthropology. As an example, Edward T. Hall's behavioral dimension, "proxemics," – how people regulate themselves in space and how they move through space – was recognized first in stills and then refined in film. The most recent application of visual anthropology is Alan Lomax's "choreometrics," which can be creatively defined as the choreographic melodies of culture. Lomax developed this dimension entirely through film study of world dance forms. His breakthrough has left the door wide open for study of cultural rhythmics in all fields of ethnic activity. It is important to recognize that the research opportunity afforded by the camera record has allowed us to consider, often for the first time, materials either too complex or too baffling in relationships for the human mind-eye to encompass, of circumstances too baffling in motion to track and analyze.

Photography's unique contributions to anthropology lie in three basic areas: Ray Birdwhistell's "kinesics," the significance of body expression;

Edward T. Hall's "proxemics," the meaning of space in human behavior; and also Alan Lomax's "choreometrics," the choreography of culture. Still photography laid the foundations for these three territories. As one example, Paul Ekman of the Langley Porter Clinic and his collaborator, Wallace Friesen, defined nonverbal aspects of psychiatric behavior. This language was first stabilized in still images and then further refined with computerized analysis of film and video. The reality that should be kept in mind is that much film research still comes from frame-by-frame detailed analysis, which methodologically continues the research potential of the frozen image of the still camera. As pointed out in Ekman's research, the photographic opportunity has been accelerated by film simply because the nonverbal record is consolidated into flowing relationships. This allows us to see static detail in the context of whole functioning schemes of culture.

A striking analogy can be made here to the static investigations of human anatomy through dissection of preserved human material. The foundations of physiological anatomy were established through this kind of dissection and observation. But what a revelation in terms of understanding it would be if the cadaver could come to life, flex its embalmed muscles, sit up and communicate to us as a living man or woman! Our anatomical study would suddenly move together in a state of synchronized life. Certainly this would allow us to see the functions of organs and muscle bundles very differently.

The same thing would happen if we raided the insect-proof vaults of ethnographic museums, reclothed the native in his true garments, and placed authentic tools in his hands. Even though we have a thorough knowledge of many artifacts studied piece by piece, our understandings would change and relate into a different kind of conceptualization were we able to see realistically how detail relates to cultural time and motion function.

RESEARCHING THE STILL CAMERA IMAGE

The potential of still image research was recognized before the development of the cine-camera. Archaeologists were using photography even when recordings had to be made with cumbersome 11-by-14-inch view cameras. They dealt with photographs as ARTIFACTS which integrated the camera record into their research. They worked with the fine detail of photographs as studiously as they analyzed spearpoints or architectural detail. The cultural anthropologists of this period simply recognized the illustrative value of the camera record. Archaeologists, in their need for definitive detail and accurate association of materials, genuinely established the three basic ways that photographs can be used scientifically, to MEASURE, to COUNT, and to COMPARE.

Eighty years later these three dimensions remain our basic research opportunities even in the most complex film analysis. There really are no other ways to use photographic records scientifically, except to use photographs as stimuli in interviewing. Certainly the projective use of photographs offers a rich recovery of data, but so do old maps and ink blots. In terms of direct research, projective use of photographs is a secondary research potential and will be reviewed later in this writing.

To return to the archaeological dig, the still camera record offers the archaeologist an invaluable mapping process that supports his explorations at many points. Photo reconnaisance is important in many fields. As an example, aerial photographs help the oil geologist discover oil-bearing subsurface structure just as successfully as they help archaeologists locate sites. Prehistoric sites in England that have been plowed over for centuries and are invisible to ground-level surveying can stand out boldly in aerial photographs taken at an appropriate hour of the day. In the same way many important sites have been located in the sandy wastelands of the Peruvian coast.

Sites in process of excavation are also mapped regularly on many digs. John Paddock of the University of the Americas in Mexico City states that he regularly surveys the progress of excavations so that the exact relationships of structure and stratification can be carefully recorded each day before descending to lower levels. Interestingly, Paddock makes these photographs before sun-up and before dust has risen so that he gets a clear shadowless record of the excavation. Paul Martin of Chicago's Field Museum mounted a 10-foot camera stand over important areas of his digs and regularly recorded the progress of excavation with an 8-by-10 inch view camera. This afforded him a measured record of exact relationships of all materials. Many archaeologists make careful records of exposed burials before removal so that exact *in situ* relationships can be accurately preserved. In opening tombs there may be hundreds of items to be recorded spatially – shards, bone fragments, charcoal fragments, as well as funerary offerings of pots or whatever. The camera record can hold all of these precisely in place and allow for a later check on the spatial and numerical patterns.

Archaeological excavation necessarily disturbs many aspects of a site. In Peru, where as many as six cultural horizons are found in one excavation, a photographic log allows for reconstruction of a site and further analysis of how and where the cultural time periods are interlocked. Photographs have also aided in tracking cultural drifts from one area to another. Influences can be visually obvious, but often they are to be found in subtle comparisons of structure, the arrangement of a burial, the construction of walls. Archaeological photographs make very refined comparison possible during the excavation or years later in laboratory analysis.

General anthropology is faced with as many mapping needs as archaeology. Consider the challenge of mapping social and ecological patterns in community studies. Hand-drawn maps are not only laborious to make, but they represent an ordering of data collected by various other means rather than a source of data themselves. On the other hand, even from ground level, photographs present undisturbed relationships which offer broad research opportunities. Especially important are photographs that show the relation of homes to the surrounding environment of field, forest, or sea coast. Trail patterns and field patterns can be realistic designs of social structure. Usually any village informant can identify the movement of trails and the ownership of fields on the photographic record.

Photographic mapping of terrain was exploited by military intelligence long before anthropologists used the camera as a survey tool. Aerial reconnaissance is the most general source of cartographic accuracy. George Collier and Evon Vogt (1965) used aerial photographs as their basic data source in land-use surveys in Chiapas. They found the Indians astute in reading photographs made at 10,000 feet above the valley floor. Key informants from villages were paid to work with the staff at a central point, reading the aerial photographs to the field workers to make an accurate detailed count of various elements of village structure. The field team was able to survey in one year an area that might have taken ten years of ground surveying. Only in a few instances was it necessary to send a field party to a particular village to complete the survey.

Even from ground level, photographs can speed up understanding of ecological relationships, while housetop or hilltop give even broader vistas. Black and white film can record fields, pasture, brush, and forest patterns in great detail. Using color film, crop patterns and fertile and starved soil can be read clearly. Panoramic photographs can be framed to form overlapping images that can give the field worker a 360° vista that relates all the ecological associations – valley, mountain range, areas of agriculture, and the village itself in one visual sweep.

Mapping and surveying usually fall into the orientation phase of a community study. By direct examination of photographs and by collaboration with native informants, volumes of encyclopedic data can be gathered in a few days or weeks, for example, listing of regional names for rivers, hills, and neighborhoods, boundaries of tribal and political territories, ownership of fields and grazing lands as well as the association of the family's dwelling place with their agriculture.

As the field experience deepens, the next general use of the camera is for inventorying. On one level this is another variety of surveying, but it may be applied to a wide range of content. We can illustrate this approach again by a community study. When we photograph every house in a town we can make an inventory of types and conditions of homes. Information in great volume can be gathered in a few days' work and a few rolls of 35-mm film. A town of 400 people can be surveyed photographically in a day. Photographic mapping of village dwellings constitutes a visual model in which all personalities can be placed with more assurance of accuracy than on sketchy diagrams. Photographs showing spatial relationships and the visual character of homes offer sociometric understandings, qualifications of affluence and poverty, older areas and new development, and often social subdivisions within a community. In the Stirling Project in Nova Scotia, Alexander Leighton had me photograph the front of every house in a community being studied for the epidemiology of mental disorder. When I questioned the expenditure of time and film, his reply was something like this: "When we know the mental health variables of each family in the community, we should be able to see correlative evidence in the character of each house."

A county-wide sampling of houses in the Stirling study reflected exact demarcation lines between French-Acadian and English settlements as well as economic differences. In San Francisco, a study of housing on a single street that ran from the industrial lowlands to the affluent heights of Twin Peaks revealed that social and cutural variables could be charted precisely along topographic lines.

Community photographic studies can leave the physical surroundings and streets and survey the interior culture of stores, churches, schools, and homes. When we leave the public domain and study the INTERIOR of culture, visual research becomes far more complex and the problems of rapport increasingly challenging.

It is not too soon to discuss the protocol problems of community photography. There is an area that the native defines as public. In Latin countries particularly this might include the village square and marketplace. Usually with reasonable tact a stranger can record in these areas without arousing hostility. Nevertheless, the "public domain" can change from culture to culture. Private space and public space vary enormously in cross-culture. Even in the public square if we move within the private airspace of the native we can encounter hostility and spark an "incident."

On the other hand, there are in every culture certain locales and activities that the natives consider representative of their public image, areas and structures which they expect the stranger to recognize and enter and take pictures of – sites like public buildings, parks, or the town waterworks, that are the pride image of a community. Sometimes when you fail to attend to these prestige structures, this omission can damage your rapport. Entering and observing within the area that the native considers private require patience and empathy and of course prior consent. In our own culture, as in many others, the home is private and all pictures made within this sanctuary of the family must remain private, to be shown only within the family, for they may carry a high degree of personal stress. At the other extreme, photographs made in public places are for all the public to see, and generally they contain a very low level of interpersonal stress. The most delicate recording is in the center of the family home.

It may strike the reader as presumptuous for the field worker to "invade" this privacy with a camera. Yet a Columbia University study of low income Puerto Rican households secured the consent and cooperation of families to set up closed-circuit television cameras to monitor what was happening in their homes twenty-four hours a day over an extended period (cf. Schaeffer's paper, *infra*). Sociologists manage to complete such samples constantly. For anthropologists, obviously, this accomplishment may be more difficult as their concerns may be more intimate, more personal, less abstract. You make a sound research design and hew as close to it as rapport will allow. Even a sketchy inventory sample offers a community study very stabilized insights.

As in any valid sampling process, we begin an inventory study by deciding what can be photographed in the same way through the community so that we get the understandings needed. In an inventory of household possessions, if we try to record every item in every home in a village, our study might go down in the sheer exhaustion of detail. Methodologically we might meaningfully limit the recording to selected rooms in the house – livingroom, kitchen, and one bedroom, or just the living room and kitchen. Within these sampled rooms we would have to decide on WHAT will be covered in all the houses in our sample. Where rooms are rectangular we might decide to make four photographs, one of each wall in each room, and simply work with all visible property. Or we might decide to include closets or storerooms as spots of great significance.

The sample might be every third house in a small village, or a selected sample of top, middle, and bottom in the socioeconomic scale in a larger community. But even in a limited sample we might end up with over a thousand negatives. To lower the over-burden of disorganized data, we begin analysis of the inventory by setting up categories and rapidly relating items of property to these categorical schemes so that we can arrive at a distinct pattern that would be representative of the social structure. The research movement in working with an inventory is to MAKE PATTERNS. If patterns do not emerge from analysis of the data, then it may be that the choice of categories is only compounding the disorganization.

Methodologically the photographic inventory can be read and analyzed systematically into statistics that make the contents of the home and their configurations into indices of the personal and shared culture of the community. Everywhere homes are programs of culture in which the individual must find his image. Cultural deviance is nowhere more clearly reflected than in the selection and arrangement of material objects in a home. Acculturation as well as tenacious nativism can be seen in the home setting. As the inventory proceeds patterns take shape, and we see the nonverbal contours of culture and the visual symbols of personality.

Edward T. Hall comments on the cultural significance of the home setting:

...the inside of the Western house is organized spatially. Not only are there special rooms for special functions – food preparation, eating, entertaining and socializing, rest, recuperation and procreation – but for sanitation as well. IF, as sometimes happens, either the artifacts or the activities associated with one space are transferred to another space, this fact is immediately apparent. People who "live in a mess" or a "constant state of confusion" are those who fail to classify activities and artifacts according to a uniform, consistent, or predictable spatial plan (1966:97).

Ten years ago I used a photographic inventory to analyze the dynamics of adjustment or failure for relocated Indians who came to the San Francisco Bay Area seeking employment. In a sample of twenty-two Indian homes we photographed all visible property in living room, kitchen, and bedroom. From this sample we recovered a strong profile of how these migrants readjusted their styles to urban living. How the home was organized, the nature of order and disorder, and the treatment of cultural symbols: all spoke of why they succeeded, and at other times how they failed. Their possessions and the use of space also spoke of the acculturation process, what they could afford to leave behind, and what was important to re-employ in the urban setting.

In Peru, I carried out a sweeping inventory of every eighth house in an Indian community of 2,000 people. The goal of this study was to establish a baseline of material culture against which to measure rapid change brought on by a project of applied anthropology. This was the Cornell-Peru Project at Vicos, a community development project that eventually resulted in the sale of a colonial *hacienda* to its Quechua-speaking peons. In two months, a sample of more than eighty households was covered, in which the walls of every room were photographed, including the interior of storerooms. With around 2,000 frames of $2^1/_4$-by-$2^1/_4$-inch film, the content of the study was comprehensive. We had a reliable measure of relative affluence and poverty in the Andean setting, the technology of both home and field, and evidence of public health practices, literacy, political awareness, and religious participation. All homes could be rated for these elements. Where would change come? Would it come first in technology, or would hygiene and public health change first? The photographs hold the evidence for future comparison.

Inventories offer data that can be mapped, charted, and compared in space as well as time. In the Vicos inventory the location of dwellings took on cross-cultural significance. The Vicos Project was just two years under way, yet already the presence of the new *haciendados*, the anthropologists, was clearly visible in the properties of the Indians. The extent and zones of influence created by the innovative living of the new *hacienda* staff, students, and administrators, could be accurately charted. Influence could be seen as extending waves of innovation circling the *hacienda* and flowing out along transportation routes. It was plainly recorded in what areas of the *hacienda* Indian households were as yet NOT affected by the presence of *gringo* (North American) and Peruvian innovators.

I have been describing inventories of static characteristics and properties. But the concept of photographic inventorying extends as well to sociometric analyses, studies of people in relation to other people, and people in motion. A community lived in is not an archaeological site but consists of changing, yet repetitive, patterns of human distribution and mingling. The human sense of a community is how people use space, how they distribute themselves, and how and where they flow together in sense of time and motion. The human mapping of a town would realistically appear as a scheme in time and space, changing from dawn to sunset, from Sunday to Saturday.

Sociometric charting and tracking are also forms of inventorying. Who comes to the Saturday market? How many from here, how many from there? Inventory the shoes worn in an Ecuadorean village market, and you have counted out a certain social class. Or count the poncho-wearing visitors and you have counted the Indian men in attendance. Details of costume and style identify people from different surrounding communities.

Systematic recording of streets can establish the flow patterns of community life. What happens at six in the morning, at five in the afternoon, or on Main Street on a Saturday? Record the foyer of the Saturday night movies, and you will recover a specialized cut of personalities in interaction. With the help of a native expert (anyone in the village is an expert) you can assemble exact personality inventories of the various locales of interaction, and often detailed information of the social dynamics of personal and group interaction.

Direct eye observation, without technology, has always been able to follow the rough dimensions of social movement, but the complexity of circumstances and also problems of identification of individuals can leave such observations incomplete and impressionistic. Camera observation offers accuracy of identification and objective detail upon which to base judgments. As an example Michael Mahar was studying caste relationships and interaction in a village in India with direct observation. This approach became practically impossible, for there was no way he could note down precisely the hundreds of people in motion who, in view of his short field experience, looked very much alike with their dark faces and white clothing. The camera allowed Mahar to record what he could see, and with the photographs as reference, a village informant helped him sort out personality and caste. With this key experience Mahar's research became possible.

The flow of people in time and space defines programmed relationships that are the human dimensions of cultural interaction. Edward T. Hall isolated some of these programs in his study of Americans overseas when he was assigned the task of providing cultural orientation for American diplomatic personnel. This involved direct observation of American diplomacy in interaction with its overseas counterpart. Out of this study came an understanding of many aspects of nonverbal communication, including the culturally different ways in which people regulate themselves in time and space, which he later developed into the concept of "proxemics" (1959, 1966).

Hall's nonverbal research has examined communication curves. Body signals seem always present at a communication peak. Hall has made slide studies of cross-cultural differences in communication, including a study of how Black Americans signal they have arrived at a communication shift or at the terminus of a message. Correlating photographs with sound tape and photographic reading by native speakers has isolated these nonverbal signals with precision.

Facial signaling has been extensively studied in psychiatric behavior. Paul Ekman of the Langley Porter Clinic has spent eight years clarifying a visual grammar of emotional behavior as an aid to psychiatric diagnosis. Much of this recognition rests in facial expressions which Ekman feels "leak" what is really going on in the person, as compared to the way people behave and speak in outward obedience to social expectations.

In a study with Margaret Mead on the dynamics of group behavior, Paul Byers traced the significance of proxemics within a conference of Fulbright scholars (Mead and Byers 1967). Byers found what Hall had experienced, that we all are highly programmed in HOW we use space and that the programs are highly specific for constantly changing social circumstances. As cultural creatures we are trained to respond to the cues and therefore change our behavior predictably when social signals change.

But what are these cues? How are programs communicated? Byers found through analysis of photographs of the conference that a sequence of ceremonial agreements and the pragmatic containers of space were largely responsible for patterns of programmed interaction. The Fulbright conference had a distinct schedule of formality and informality of behavior and interaction: the "getting-acquainted" introductory phase with ceremonial hospitality at the college president's home; lectures, exemplifying the one-to-many relationship, and seminars with everyone in the circle equal; and the relaxation phase with intimate interpersonal communication after the meetings were over. Each one of these phases took place in a specific matrix of space: large meeting rooms, formal living rooms, and finally a small intimate lounge that invited informality and physical togetherness.

With a few selected photographs Byers demonstrates that precise behavior consistently took place from the moment the Fulbright scholars arrived to the close of the day when the seminars were over. All behaviors were protocols of culture cued by common understanding. One photograph shows people getting acquainted in the lounge of the small college. Most participants were sitting facing one another in groups of two and three, the men with their legs crossed over their knees, leaning forward to communicate. An inventory of space shows nearly perfect regulation of distance throughout the room, close enough for direct verbal communication but no closer. The coffee cups also reflect regularity of behavior: on one table all the cups are placed about two inches from the edge, while on another all are placed precisely at the edge.

A second photograph, a gathering in the college president's home, shows the group circled round a folk singer. The event signaled a circle, the communication one-to-many, entertainer to audience. The room size controlled the size of the circle. The formality of the occasion signaled suits and sports coats ON and distinct (though small) airspace between the circled guests. No one was touching anyone else.

A third photograph was made after the scholarly events of one day were finished and the scholars were relaxing and drinking beer. The signal was informality, ALL coats OFF. The intimacy of the room ordered people to move in close. Everyone was touching someone else. In small or very large social gatherings the photographic record can offer a definitive measure of all visible behavior of a group and of individual units.

As visual anthropology develops it becomes evident that human behavior can be analyzed from many different variables. People are mobile and can be seen most realistically in the ebb and flow of their lives in motion. People don't move about like manikins. Eyes, hands, and posture all together signal further qualifications of the meanings of interchanges between one and another. Ray Birdwhistell's initial refinement of kinesics breaks down the components of every human interaction (1970; cf. Prost's paper, *infra*).

My own recent research has been in the kinesics of schoolroom behavior as recorded on Super-8 film (Collier 1973). Proxemics and kinesics have cued team analysts to the emotional state and learning intensity of students and also the intensity of their teachers. This has allowed us to make definitive observations of the effectiveness of various circumstances and styles of school culture. Though this research has been done with film rather than stills, the variables of kinesics and proxemics remain the same.

Whether it be ethnographic film or a file of still photographs of a community, the value of the camera record is its literacy which allows diverse people to extract a significant level of information from photograph or film. As researchers we may read our own visual data by ourselves or be assisted by a variety of interpreters. Clearly photography's aid to human understanding is its ability to evoke reality. Photography offers a reflex reportage of real circumstance, and its recognizable life messages make it a bridge of communication to the students watching film in a classroom, to the native informant, and between the informant and the researcher.

The photographic interview is based upon this communication. Photographic interviewing is like a can-opener into complex community involvement, even before the field worker has had time to acquire a background for his own understanding. Later, often much later, the field worker himself will be able to see and understand these territories, but a file of photographs can place him in the heart of a community in one evening's interviewing. The camera is able to record, at once, on the very first day of community study, specific evidence that can give the native points of reference to speed the understanding of the field worker.

The volume of information that can be gleaned by photo-interviewing is encyclopedic, but it is working knowledge essential to a penetrating study of human organization and activity. Generally speaking, these are the sorts of things you can expect to recover:

1. Precise identification of people – name, status, role, personality.
2. Identification of place: political, ethnic, and tribal boundaries; where people live, ownership of homes; ownership of fields and grazing areas, agricultural patterns.
3. Identification of all ecological elements: explanation of processes and technology; explanation of ceremony.
4. Historical happenings associated with places or people — contrast of present and past, the way things used to be.

The knowledge suggested here is usually made more valuable by the informant's emotional involvement with the content of the photographs, so that his information is qualified by a scale of values that reflects the system of the community. You get not only facts but feelings as well.

Projective methods are used in psychological testing to get at submerged content within the patient or subject. Photographs CAN be used this way, but their realistic definition limits their value as strictly projective probes. On the other hand, when the informant deals with concrete photographic circumstance, we find that he not only gives back distinct information, such as names of people and functions of process; he also can respond psychologically with deep emotions, though not about his submerged feelings of self but precisely about what is OUT THERE in the concrete circumstances of his life. The rich recovery in photographic interviewing is the tangible data of environmental reality as psychologically and emotionally qualified by the informants' projective responses.

This combination of emotional as well as strictly informative response was obtained in Picuris Pueblo by Bernard Siegel of Stanford University. Siegel was trying to gauge the significance of the annual saint's day fiesta which included a Catholic Mass, a superbly performed deer dance, and a community foot-race. White visitors to the fiesta would be inclined to see the deer dance as the high point of ecstasy simply because of its aesthetic appeal to our conventional eyes. For the White audience the foot-race was undramatic, not to be compared with one of the most beautiful deer dances in the Rio Grande Pueblos. When Siegel reviewed the fiesta photographs with his informants, their responses to the deer dance were informative, practical, and detached: "He's out of step,"or "His kilt is slipping." but when the pictures showed the fiesta crowd leaving the plaza for the old race track down on the other side of the river, the response was, in very emotional nuance, "Now the solemn time begins!" Without the photographs before him it is unlikely that a Picuris man would have revealed this depth of religious feeling. It was clear that the less impressive foot-race was the center of the religious mystique, not the exquisite deer dance.

George and Louise Spindler, also of Stanford, tried to use photographs projectively to find out what Blood Indians thought were ideal roles for modern Indians. The photographs failed to elicit this information, but Indian-made drawings of modern Blood life were given clear responses as to what jobs Bloods feel are good. This experience defined sharply the difference between drawings and photographs as projective tools. Photographs are precise and wholly readable in terms of concrete reality, whereas drawings are NOT precise records but an expression created by the hand of the artist from generalized experience. This very lack of documentary precision is the strength of drawings as projective probes. Photographs definitely limit the informants' responses. Drawings are open-ended and invite personalized responses directly from the emotions of the viewer.

When the Spindlers used a photograph of a trading post on the reservation to see what the Indians thought of trading as a job, the responses they actually got were: "Say, you see that guy walking up to the post, he owes me twenty dollars!" or "Yes, I know that post. That trader is a real thief!" Later, when the Spindlers showed a DRAWING of a trading post, and asked questions about the role of trading, the response was, "No, I would never want to run a trading post. My relatives would eat me into bankruptcy." The photograph was specific and the drawing was general. The vague and generalized nature of drawings, especially some of the blurred ones in the Thematic Apperception Test cards, offer the informant an open-ended opportunity, which is the character of most projective testing, including the Rorschach.

Almost anyone can master the rudiments of making photographic records, and through photographs we can recover a very wide sweep of data. But as in all data gathering, unless we are able to process, organize, and compute these data, nothing much happens for research or human understanding. The challenge of visual anthropology is to move from the visual finally to the verbal and the conceptual, to writing and the creation of ideas.

Much vivid anthropology has been based on limited data. Much important anthropological thought is conjecture, compounded of vividly gathered impressions, often from a single informant, or of an event seen only once and never to be seen again as old men die and ancient cultural patterns grow weaker.

The support photography offers anthropology is that it provides for the peculiar research environment of anthropology a scientific tangibility in studies of human behavior. Anthropology is not a clinical science, but it is always striving for scientific significance, for reliability, for valid comparability, that are so difficult to achieve in the often open-ended and uncontrolled domain of culture. Modern anthropology has devised extreme methodologies to close this open end by analysis of minute components and other massive analytic methods. But much of anthropology is not approachable by the kinds of gathering processes that allow computerized conclusions which APPEAR to be wholly scientific. To a degree these means can defeat the very enriched opportunities of anthropology. Eminent anthropologists have written very moving accounts on roving surveys, on samples of one, on basically empirical observations.

Vivid insights in our field may represent highly imaginative projections from relatively few points of scientific tangibility. Research is designed to get as many tangibles as field circumstances permit. As observers and conceptualizers of the human circumstance we wish to present the most objective rational account of culture we possibly can. We use every scientific opportunity possible and then we WRITE.

The camera can support the necessarily limited field encounter. The eye can keep track of only a limited range of phenomena, whereas the camera can record unlimited detail precisely. Also the camera eye is not subjective, does not become confused with the unfamiliar, and does not suffer from fatigue. The empirical encounter must be checked against human memory only, and the research must stop at the borders of memory. Photographic memory holds detail not even seen in the original encounter. It is a genuine part of the concrete event, and therefore it DOES offer an expanding research opportunity. This possibility can transform an empirical impression into many areas of sound deduction. Photographs immeasurably increase the fixed points of factual reality and therefore speed up and give projective breadth to reliable conclusions.

But these things will never happen if we fail to process and analyze our visual data rigorously. The photographic record can remain wholly impressionistic UNLESS it undergoes disciplined computing.

FILM FLOW AS RESEARCH AND EDUCATION IN VISUAL ANTHROPOLOGY

What happens when the still image begins to move? We asked earlier what would happen when the anatomical cadaver sat up, flexed his muscles, and communicated with the medical student. The dead would come to life, and we would see wholly new relationships in what had been only a frozen model. Still photographs only suggest life motion. Even organized time and motion studies, a still frame every few seconds, give only a static approximation of life. Time and motion studies give all the facts; film breathes life into the record. A skillfully organized and precisely timed still photograph can suggest past, present, and future; but film moves realistically through time with a genuine past and present and a concrete future. Time and motion studies record slices of time, but an invaluable fluency is missing that seriously limits researching with still photographs.

On a number of occasions I have tested the significance of motion with visual anthropology students. Objectively, I made a family study on film and had a colleague pace the footage, scene for scene, with well-made still photographs. Every bit of ethnographic information is contained in these stills. Students can critically define the life style of the family and all the domestic and craft technology. Then I screen the film for them. What can now be added to the record? Very little of content, but what IS added is vital. After students have viewed the film the general comment is, "Now we can define love, we can describe HOW the family relates emotionally." The frontier of film research lies in the emotional and the psychological. The still record holds psychological data, but film itself is a psychological experience.

When I accepted the research opportunity to photograph Eskimo education for the National Study of American Indian Education, I decided to use film for the precise reason that it COULD record in a measurable way the psychic state of students and teachers. I wanted to learn from photography whether Eskimo children were happy or repressed by White schools: I was sure film could reveal these states.

Stills can tell you precisely what is happening, but film can qualify the happening and present the nuances of human relations. To clarify this character of film I present a hypothetical situation read from stills and then read from film. (This is from an article published in *Program in Ethnographic Film Newsletter* 2(3):5-6.)

The Still Record

* Let us turn to the native stirring himself at sunrise. Still records made every few minutes would show the native lying under a hand-woven blanket, with hands under his head, eyes open staring upward. If we are trigger quick, we can see the woolen blanket being thrown off in a blur – or we would simply catch him standing up fully dressed by the bed. (Our motion memory would remind us that he had slept in his clothes, but the still sequence in itself might barely suggest this.)
* Now the camera shows him standing at the door. Maybe he is looking up and down the trail outside, but unless we take split-second exposures this would not be photographically observed.
* A further exposure shows his hand on his head as he looks out.
* Now the camera records our man sitting hunched by the fire as if preparing to eat. If we trigger quickly he can be seen smiling at his wife. Camera records shows wife toasting corn in a covered *olla* and looking intently at her task.
* Now our man has a handful of toasted corn. Right hand is to mouth.
* Wife stops the task and looks out of door.
* A girl is now seen near the father. Second shot shows child in father's hunched lap. Hand of father is touching child's head.
* Now father looks at door of hut. Wife is also looking out the door.
* Father stands before tools stacked under hut's eaves. Second picture: Father, tools in hand – two iron hoes. Third picture: shows tools on his shoulder, two hoes and an iron digging stick. Wife seen making up carrying cloth. It contains tortillas and a small cloth bundle.
* Man is now shown leaving house, approximately fifteen feet ahead of his wife. Next shot shows child has joined the mother. Distance between man and wife now about six feet. Girl is very near mother.

The Film Record

In our film sequence we see all these details, though they pass swiftly before our eyes.

* Film opens showing our man awake, LYING WITHOUT ANY MOVEMENT under hand-woven woolen blanket.
* Now he places hands under head and STARES THOUGHTFULLY at the thatched roof of the hut. We say "thoughtfully" because he seems in no hurry and his face is fully awake. He squints his eyes, frowns a little, then appears to smile.
* He THROWS OFF his woolen blankets, which reveal he has slept fully clothed, rises to his feet WITH A BOUND, walks SWIFTLY to the hut's door, and PEERS UP AND DOWN the trail outside his dwelling. His eyes are squinting, and as he looks he SLOWLY SCRATCHES tangled long hair. Then MOVING QUICKLY he squats down at the fire pit and stretches out a hand to the glowing coals. HE DOESN'T SEEM IN A HURRY, puts out another hand over the fire, APPARENTLY SPEAKING, and smiles warmly at his wife, who is ABSORBED in toasting corn in a closed clay *olla*. SHE DOESN'T LOOK UP, but SHAKES THE DISH as a few fluffs of corn POP OUT OF THE WARMER.

* The man reaches for the toasted corn with his left hand and slowly puts kernels into his mouth one by one with his right, as he CONTINUES TALKING with his wife.
* SUDDENLY THE WOMAN STRAIGHTENS, BRUSHES the hair back from her face, and peers with scrutiny out of the doorway. The man's head turns, and HIS EYES FOLLOW HERS, and as they look out together they CONTINUE TO TALK. (We can see face and lips forming sounds.)
* A small child who has been up to now in the shadow CRAWLS up to the man, her father. He WELCOMES the child with an outstretched arm as he CONTINUES TO LOOK out the hut door. Now he turns to the child who AGGRESSIVELY SETTLES herself in his crouched loins, as the father GENTLY DRAWS HIS FINGERS through her tangled hair.
* Father arises and stands before an array of tools stored under the hut's eaves. HE GAZES AT THE TOOLS FOR A MINUTE, as if considering which to select. He draws down two hoes and RUNS HIS FINGER OVER THEIR IRON BLADES as if contemplating the tool's condition. Now he shoulders the two hoes and an iron digging stick and passes SWIFTLY from the hut.
* His wife looks up from her hunched position by the fire, HURRIEDLY EMPTIES the remaining toasted corn into a square of cloth, TIES THE CLOTH BY ITS FOUR CORNERS, places cloth in larger carrying cloth and adds a pile of *tortillas*. Now she stands up, DRAWS THE CARRYING CLOTH TO HER SHOULDERS, knots it across her chest, and HURRIES AFTER THE MAN. The small child RUNS after mother, and the camera records the man STRIDING AWAY SWIFTLY with the mother, followed by the little girl, RUNNING after. Last shot shows the man still in front about six feet ahead, and the little girl is closely following her mother's footsteps.

What Film Does

The film has accomplished several very important types of observation:
1. Film has recorded a definitive measure of TIME in an unbroken flow.
2. Film has established for us by "time-flow" a character of PACE, which exemplifies HOW the day begins.
3. Film has qualified all behavior movements – SWIFTLY, SLOWLY, EVENLY, JERKILY.
4. The qualified character of movement in film has invited tangible emotional or psychological considerations that would have been relatively invisible on the still records. We can observe that the man is REFLECTIVE. He stares at the ceiling, quite awake with a keenly focused expression. He stands at the door and looks long in all directions. We see the man is RESPONSIVE AND AFFECTIONATE; when the baby gets near he puts out his right arm and allows the child to crawl into his crouched lap. He pets the child GENTLY: the film clearly identifies JUST HOW HE TOUCHES HIS CHILD. The film shows him walking away SWIFTLY and wife and child hurrying after him.

All these qualified observations would be demonstrated POSITIVELY on film.

In the still records, even with time and motion studies, these states would only be SUGGESTED, for the still record can't truly show HOW a man caresses his child, or HOW a man gets up from his bed. At best the still records are TIME SLICES, which the investigator must link together by conjecture.

A FINAL NOTE

Is anthropology research for its own sake, or is it education? Certainly we carry out research in part to relate the world's people into one human family. We explore primitive cultures to understand better where civilization is sweeping. Films of ancient people bridge this humanity over millennia. A stunning example is the work of John Marshall.

Marshall's film vignettes of the Bushmen of the Kalahari Desert can change one's attitudes about aspects of civilization. How civilized was "primitive" man? Did his crude technology also mean limited human sensitivity? With synchronized sound, color, and close-up zoom focus we see five Bushmen giving each other a ceremonial bath in a desert pool. We see the gentleness of the way they help each other bathe, see the delicacy of body touching, and hear the melodious singsong of conversation. Indeed, on film these Bushmen, whom Elizabeth Marshall Thomas wrote about as *The harmless people* (1959), appear far more sensitive in communication than we might expect in any male gathering in the usual American community.

The fulfillment of ethnographic film as education is not just its ability to present the cultural drama, but more importantly to present man's humanity, modern or ancient. This is also the effort, I believe, in all photography for anthropology – to deal honestly and realistically with the human condition and the sensitivity of men in all environments. The camera record can accomplish this image, where the strictures of scientific abstracts can fail.

REFERENCES

BIRDWHISTELL, RAY L.
   1970   *Kinesics and context*. Philadelphia: University of Pennsylvania Press.
COLLIER, GEORGE, EVON Z. VOGT
   1965   "Aerial photographs and computers in the analysis of Zinacanteco

demography and land tenure." Paper presented at the 64th Annual Meeting of the American Anthropological Association, Denver. (Mimeographed.)

COLLIER, JOHN, JR.
1967 *Visual anthropology: photography as a research method.* New York: Holt, Rinehart and Winston.
1973 *Alaskan Eskimo education: a film analysis of cultural confrontation in the schools.* New York: Holt, Rinehart and Winston.

EKMAN, PAUL
1957 A methodological discussion of nonverbal behavior. *Journal of Psychology* 43:141–149.
1964 Body position, facial expression and verbal behavior during interviews. *Journal of Abnormal and Social Psychology* 68:295–301.
1965 "Communication through nonverbal behavior: a source of information about an interpersonal relationship," in *Affect, cognition and personality.* Edited by Silvan S. Tomkins and Carroll E. Izard, 390–442. New York: Springer.
i.p. "Universals and cultural differences in facial expressions of emotion," in *Nebraska symposium on motivation.* Lincoln: University of Nebraska Press.

EKMAN, PAUL, *editor*
i.p. *Darwin and facial expression.* New York: Academic Press.

EKMAN, PAUL, WALLACE V. FRIESEN
1968 "Nonverbal behavior in psychotherapy research," in *Research in psychotherapy,* volume three. Edited by J. M. Shlien, 139–216. Washington D. C.: American Psychological Association.
1969a Nonverbal leakage and clues to deception. *Psychiatry* 32:88–105.
1969b The repertoire of nonverbal behavior: categories, origins, usage and coding. *Semiotica* 1:49–98.
1971 Constants across cultures in the face and emotion. *Journal of Personality and Social Psychology* 17:124–129.

EKMAN, PAUL, WALLACE V. FRIESEN, P. ELLSWORTH
1972 *Emotion in the human face: guidelines for research and an integration of findings.* New York: Pergamon Press.

HALL, EDWARD T.
1959 *The silent language.* New York: Doubleday.
1966 *The hidden dimension.* New York: Doubleday.

LOMAX, ALAN
1968 *Folk song style and culture: a staff report on cantometrics.* Washington: American Association for the Advancement of Science. Publication 88.

LOMAX, ALAN, IRMGARD BARTENIEFF, FORRESTINE PAULAY
1969 Choreometrics: a method for the study of cross-cultural pattern in film. *Research Film/Le Film de Recherche/Forschungsfilm* 6:505–517.

LOMAX, ALAN, NORMAN BERKOWITZ
1972 The evolutionary taxonomy of culture. *Science* 177:228-239.

MEAD, MARGARET, PAUL BYERS
1967 *The small conference.* The Hague: Mouton.

PADDOCK, JOHN, *editor*
  1966   *Ancient Oaxaca: discoveries in American archeology and history.*
      Stanford: Stanford University Press.
SPINDLER, GEORGE, LOUISE SPINDLER
  1965   The instrumental activities inventory: a technique for the study of
      acculturation. *Southwestern Journal of Anthropology* 14 (3):1-23.
THOMAS, ELIZABETH MARSHALL
  1959   *The harmless people.* London: Secker and Warburg.

Feature Films as Cultural Documents

JOHN H. WEAKLAND

There is a considerable, and probably a growing, anthropological interest in the making and study of film records, as this present symposium on visual anthropology itself demonstrates. And it is even more evident that feature films, which here may be understood to include television dramas, are taken seriously as cultural products by many people, from general audiences (possibly even including, in their private capacity, some anthropologists) to various special groups, among them filmmakers, critics, moralists and politicians.

Anthropological interest in feature films as cultural documents, however, is another matter. More accurately, it is two other matters. First, in spite of apparent similarities or common elements with the two areas of interest mentioned, this field of interest and study is quite separate and different from both of them, in ways to be described. Second, while enough work has been done in this area over the past thirty years to indicate some approaches and potentials, it currently stands as a quite small and neglected field.

Any consideration of the anthropological study of feature films must thus be a minority report in relation to both its filmic and anthropological contexts, and minority reports are seldom very influential. Nevertheless, this kind of film study is still worthy of promotion and development. It is interesting in itself, partly because it is different and special, yet partly also because basically it is surprisingly close to traditional anthropological interests and methods. And it has both theoretical and practical potentials, especially in the otherwise difficult study of large and complex contemporary cultures; but these potentials can only be tested by much intensive empirical work.

In this situation, then, a minority report seems better than none. It will consider, in order: (1) main lines of current interest in films, and the contrasting nature of anthropological feature film study; (2) previous work of this kind and its significance; (3) principles and problems in the study of film content; and (4) the uses and prospects of feature film study.

One further point should be made explicit at the outset. Although my report aims to present a broad view of what has been and might be done in this special field, this account must necessarily be limited in certain respects. It will set forth a view, grounded in my own experience, of the main points of intersection between fundamental anthropological interests and methods and the nature of feature films; but there might be other possible ways in which feature films could be culturally informative, or other possibly useful methods for their examination. That is, this present viewing of a field is significantly similar to what happens in the study of any film, or group or films — or indeed in any cultural study.

Selectivity — to some extent personal, but not just subjective — must be involved, since the whole can never be encompassed in a verbal account, and there is never even a final standard defining what should be chosen for attention. This always depends on purposes, preferences, and circumstances, both intellectual and practical. Further, since the purpose of this account is to present a focused view of what appears central in an area that is not well known, it will aim to be clear and concise about basic matters, rather than risk obscuring these by attempting exhaustive and detailed coverage of even this limited field.

VARIETIES OF FILM CONSIDERATIONS

In the broadest sense, feature films are cultural documents by definition — what product of any culture is not? The relevant questions are narrower: what sort of cultural documents are such films, and what significance can they have for cultural anthropology? These questions cannot be settled *a priori*. Answers can only be usefully approached — and even then never finally reached — empirically, by examining films and cultures and seeing what features and relationships are discernible. Correspondingly, this report will center around consideration of the nature, methods, and findings of actual anthropological studies of feature films, and possible further studies. Initially, however, some basic orientation — a general viewpoint — is needed to begin either such research or an account of it. Such a general viewpoint constitutes in effect a broad hypothesis about films and culture, towards which specific studies provide evidence of varying sorts. The essentials of this viewpoint can perhaps be conveyed best by the analogue of mapping by triangulation, in which they are specified and located in comparison with the two better-known areas already mentioned: work with anthropological films, and various appraisals of feature films.

As already mentioned, anthropologists have been and continue to be interested in the making and study of film records of culture. The subjects of this filming and study of film vary greatly, but there is a rather consistent general orientation amid this variety: to preserve and study, by objective and careful systematic examination, visual and sound records of samples of actual behavior. That is, one might say that the usual aim of such work is more accurate and detailed examination of certain overt behavioral realities or facts.

Anthropological study of feature films is consistent with this in several important respects. It also involves an appreciation of the value of permanent records, and the careful, systematic and objective study of their visual and sound (verbal, musical and other) content. But there is an equally important difference, related to the basic nature of the material. Feature films are fictional, and they are frankly viewed as such in anthropological analysis. That is, although fictional films may at times portray aspects of behavior accurately in a factual or documentary sense, this is not the main focus of their study. Rather, these films are taken as projecting IMAGES of human social behavior, and these images are the first object of study.[1] Such images, of course, may also be "real" in important senses (Boulding 1956), though differing from the reality of detailed records of actual behavior. They may reflect cultural premises and patterns of thought and feeling. They may influence the behavior of viewers and they may throw light on actual behavior, whether they are similar or different from it. Again, all of these are potentials. Actual significances can only be determined, once film images are discerned, by studying these in relation to the filmmakers, their audiences, and to other information about their subject matters.

In another corner there is a very mixed bag of filmmakers, ordinary reviewers, high-level critics and theorists, and political and moral guardians of society who are all especially interested in feature films. Certainly

---

[1] The converse approach is also possible, though probably more difficult for comparable results, in both cases. Fictional films can be studied with a concern about actual behavior, and documentaries — since at the least they must involve selection and emphases — can be examined in terms of the images they project, as expressive rather than descriptive records (e.g. Kracauer 1942).

they have already produced a vast literature of serious — including considerable over-serious — writing on fictional films. This literature appears to vary over a wide range. There are works with a primarily technical, commercial, sociological or critical focus, and various combinations of these. Attention may be centered on the making, showing, the nature or significance of the films. Yet except for the most narrowly technical or commercial considerations, which are not relevant here, there is a remarkable consistency in the general focus of this literature, both as to what it is concerned with and what it scants.[2]

By and large, this literature on feature films is focused on categorizing and evaluating. That is, it is concerned with labeling or classifying a given film, a group of films, or even films in general, and making statements about their goodness, truth, or beauty, whether this evaluation be in terms of entertainment, technical, artistic, or social-moral values. Even the considerable number of works concerned with defining the "essence" of film as a medium, though they may openly appear less evaluative, usually are covertly and sweepingly so.

These observers also are often concerned with labeling and evaluating relationships between films and reality. Their views on this matter, however, are complex and polarized. Some, such as the social and moral critics of films, are most apt to criticize films for not depicting reality accurately. In this one respect, they resemble the makers and students of anthropological and other documentary films — except that they may also criticize film depictions, for instance those of sex and violence, for being too realistic. Others, especially those who view films as works of art, are apt to view factual realism dimly, believing that films should portray a higher reality and truth.

Since such a concern to evaluate surely implies that films are considered important, it is remarkable how little explicit attention is given to film content in these writings. Content, of course, has not gone completely unmentioned, and there have been many intelligent and perceptive observers among these writers on feature films. Many of them, also working under restrictions of time and space, may have observed much more than they have reported. Nevertheless, especially in relation to the amount of visual and verbal material presented in even a single film, descriptions of film content in this literature are brief and selective.

Though the basis of this selectivity is often unstated, two main lines

---

[2] Since this literature is so extensive and is relevant here only in terms of its contrasting general approach, it will not be reviewed specifically. A useful guide to much of it, however, is provided by the lengthy annotated bibliography in Jarvie (1970), and two mimeographed supplements to this which he has subsequently produced.

appear to be dominant. Most commonly, observations on content are superficial and general, noting only what is dramatically obvious, in terms of commonly accepted categories. In the artistic or highbrow converse, maximum attention may be given to noting and interpreting apparently minor or obscure details. The common element in these two approaches is that existing criteria of some kind are applied to characterize and judge the nature and significance of the film content matter.

Along with this body of critical writing there is a fairly large amount of reported research on film content, and on the significance of such content — usually either in comparison to reality, again, or in terms of its possible direct influence on behavior. The beginning of this kind of work may be attributed to the first study of Jones (1942) on quantitative analysis of film content. Since then there have been more elaborate, though fundamentally similar, studies of content by researchers of the mass media of communication, considerations of various aspects of film content and trends over time (especially numerous articles in the *Journal of Popular Culture* and the new *Journal of Popular Film*), and recently, a mass of studies on television portrayal of violence and its effects.

It does not seem necessary to review these many studies here. They have a certain value in pointing out the need to set down basic identifying data about films to start with. Some of them (e.g. Jowett 1970; Safilios-Rothschild 1968) usefully summarize general characteristics of films of given sources or periods. And a few, such as the study of Marcus (1970), offer thoughtful considerations of the significance of popular films and observations that reach to covert levels of content. For the most part, however, these studies are fundamentally similar in basic approach to the less formal critical writings. That is, they also view various overt aspects of films in terms of some set of specific, separate categories which are applied to the material from outside, and they conceive of only rather simple and direct relationships between film content and behavioral reality, which are seen as quite different realms.

In sharp contrast, anthropological study of feature films, like traditional anthropology generally, is largely a matter of INQUIRY into the unknown — and hopefully discovery — as regards the films, their cultural environment and possible relations between the two, guided only by some broad principles. In the first place, the content of a cultural product so rich and complex as even an ordinary commercial film is by no means obvious at the usual viewing; this must be discerned from careful examination of the film itself.

In attempting this, ordinary terms of categorization, reflecting common cultural assumptions and usually focusing on particular details or overall impressions, may not be well suited to describing both the parts and the whole of such content. Also, an anthropological view should be concerned with what is most common and general, rather than what is special and unusual. The analysis and description of content — which is here taken broadly to include what is shown, how it is shown, and how all this is structured — in these terms is a lengthy and difficult task at best, but it is the necessary basis for all further inquiries. What does a film (or group of films) present to the eyes and ears of its audience — including both the professional observer and ordinary viewers?

It is, of course, not possible to observe and record the totality of film content or of cultural patterns, in any case. Only the film itself includes this — just as the anthropologist's field data cover only part of the living culture he studies. Even quite limited and partial studies can have valid corresponding uses. The important thing is that angle of viewing and the nature of the selectivity exercised should be known and evaluated in relation to anthropological interests in films taken as cultural productions.

Beyond content itself, anthropological film studies may extend to other matters that relate to ordinary evaluative viewing: How do films relate to their cultural sources? What is their cultural function and influence? Do films illuminate more general cultural patterns? In short, how does film content relate to reality? But the basis of such inquiries is also different in the anthropological study of feature films. At least at one important level, the reality with which anthropology is concerned is neither the raw factual details of observed behavior nor some artistic concept of truth, but is itself a cultural entity, a construct comparable in this sense to film images, though much broader — often including both these other realities.

What this approach more specifically involves may be clarified by examining next the existing body of anthropological film analysis, and then discussing its principles and practices in more detail.

A REVIEW OF ANTHROPOLOGICAL FILM ANALYSIS

Anthropological study of themes and patterns discernible on viewing feature films (with which may be grouped a few studies of similar nature by psychologists and others), and accompanying attempts to relate such observations to wider areas of culture, began in the United States during the period of World War II. At this time, there were extensive efforts toward mobilizing the knowledge and skills of social scientists to develop better understanding of the nature of various foreign societies, with the practical goal of better estimation or prediction of their members' behavior, collectively or individually.

As one part of this effort anthropologists, for the first time on any significant scale, turned their attention to study of the cultures of large contemporary societies. In the wartime circumstances, the traditional anthropological method of field work was usually not possible, and in addition there were inherent difficulties in applying this method to the study of large societies. Various means of studying national cultures using resources available in the United States were therefore explored and utilized, including interviewing foreign natives resident here, examination of written material of various types — histories, novels, descriptive and interpretative accounts by both natives and outsiders, and in particular, study of films produced by the societies in question (Benedict 1946).

Most of this pioneering work, utilizing the film resources of the Museum of Modern Art and the Library of Congress, was concerned with the films and cultures of Germany and Japan. Among the studies of which there is any published record, there is considerable variation in focus, approach, material used, and amount of information available.

For instance one of the earliest studies, Bateson's *An analysis of the film "Hitlerjunge Quex"* (1943b), concentrates on the detailed examination of a single film (except for a few illustrative references to other films), for which it is still a model. In addition to an over-all summary of the plot, this film — viewed many times for the study — is described and analyzed at length from five different but interrelated viewpoints: time perspective, political groups and background, the family of origin, the future family, and the knife (a central symbol in the drama) and death. Bateson also discusses some basic methodological issues, including film selection, checking of film observations against other sources of information, and the relationship of films to their sources. Unfortunately, only a brief account of the work (Bateson 1943a) and a summary (Bateson 1953) of the full report are readily available.

The other main work on German film was done by Kracauer. He first examined German newsreels and documentaries for the view of life expressed even in such "factual" materials (Kracauer 1942). Kracauer (1947) then considered German fictional films over the period 1919-1933, examining a considerable number of films in search of content trends relatable to, and informative about, the changing social context. This second work thus illustrates another valid and possible approach to film study, though it is nearly polar to Bateson's detailed concentration on a single film. Kracauer's work is also useful in other respects. It shows how knowledge of a film's particular production circumstances sometimes helps in understanding its content. Especially his many and varied specific observations on film content, on relations between various aspects and features of content, and on presumed relations between such observations and society are often perceptive and suggestive. By pointing to the existence and possible significance of things often not obvious, he helps expand the horizons of other observers.

However, Kracauer's work also has some serious, and perhaps corresponding, flaws. He does not rest his case on specified observations of films, German society, and spelling out the relationships perceived between these. Instead, he is given to "deep" psychological interpretations of both film and social data, to an apparently very selective and variable viewpoint, rather than consistent and systematic observation and analysis, and to sweeping (and often evaluative) conclusions about films and society.

There is less specific information available about the analytic study of Japanese films during this period. For instance, although Benedict (1946) mentions that viewing films and discussing them with informants was a significant part of her study of Japanese culture, her book contains only a few brief observations on films specifically. A World War II study, *Japanese films: a phase of psychological warfare* (Anonymous 1944), however, summarized a considerable amount of analytic observation. This report, based on twenty films selected to cover the content areas of war, relations with other nations, urban and rural life, and Japanese national and family structure, discusses a number of basic themes discerned in these films and draws conclusions about related general "psychological" (actually, cultural) attitudes. Finally, a study by Meadow (1944), though rather heavily psychological, gives fairly good summaries of seven films examined, and discusses inferences drawn from them about Japanese character structure.

After the war, interest in the related areas of the cultural study of modern nations and of film analysis continued and for a time even expanded, most notably in the Columbia University Research in Contemporary Cultures project started by Benedict and continued by Mead. The major published report on this research (Mead and Métraux 1953) includes the following material on film study: (1) a general discussion of movie analysis in the study of culture by Wolfenstein (267–280), very useful though rather psychological in viewpoint; (2) an introduction to five following illustrations of film analysis, by Métraux (281–282); (3) descriptive notes on one Italian film — among twenty examined — by Wolfenstein (282–289); (4) notes on two French films by Belo (289–290) and Gorer (290–291); (5) an analysis of seven Cantonese films, focusing on family relations and time perspectives, by Weakland (292–295); (6) an analysis of the Soviet film, *The Young Guard*, by Mead (295–297) and Schwartz (297–302), including a comparison with the original novel; and (7) a summary of Bateson's earlier study of *Hitlerjunge Quex* (302–314). Although not extensive even in total, these materials are very helpful in providing a combination of discussion of film study and a considerable variety of examples of different stages and approaches in such work.

Several additional studies, though reported separately, relate in origin to this same project. These include Erik H. Erikson's study of the Soviet film *The Childhood of Maxim Gorky* (Erikson 1950), and Martha Wolfenstein and N. Leites' consideration of plot and character in French films (1954) and trends in French films (1955). Also, there is Wolfenstein and Leites' *Movies* (1950), an examination of American, British and French films for characteristic regularities in their depiction of love relationships, family relationships, the relationships between killers, victims and agents of justice, and finally relationships between performers and observers. Though this work is subtitled "A psychological study," in its emphasis on observable patterns and crosscultural comparison it appears to be at least equally an anthropological one.

Two independent studies also appeared shortly after the time of the Research in Contemporary Cultures project. Haley (1953) presented a rather extensive analysis of patterns observable in *David and Bathsheba*, chosen for study as the most popular American film of its year, based on box-office receipts. Haley's interest in films was encouraged and may have been shaped somewhat by contact with Bateson. Nevertheless, this study related more to his own conception (Haley 1952) of films as offering audiences not escapes from, but guides to the social order, in dramatic form, by means of recurrent involvement of the audience in threatening or problematic solutions followed by standard cultural resolutions. Haley also noted how the basic pattern of the plot as a whole was often repeated in miniature, scene by scene.

The work of Honigmann and van Doorslaer (1955) in a sense is not film analysis at all, since they used as data only Indian film reviews, never seeing the actual films to which these referred. Nevertheless this study seems worth citing, especially in view of the limited body of work in this area. Their study was aimed at the identification of important cultural themes, and the large body of indigenous reviews on which it relied represent materials that generally are relevant to film analysis as at least secondary data sources.

After this, there appears to have been little or no anthropological study of fictional films for nearly ten years. Then, in the early 1960's I began to examine whatever Chinese Communist films could be found outside of mainland China. In using films for the study at a distance of a then inaccessible culture, and even more in focusing initially on the political propaganda themes in these Chinese films (Weakland 1966a, 1966b), this research clearly was reviving some of the earliest features of anthropological film study.

During the course of this long-term research, however, other features became increasingly significant: (1) The traditional culture of China had already been studied extensively by anthropologists. My study accordingly was concerned almost from its outset with observing possible relationships between sociopolitical themes in the new China films and basic themes and patterns of the traditional culture. For example, film images of foreign invasion and Chinese resistance were examined in relation to traditional Chinese family patterns (Weakland 1971a). (2) Contrasts between film themes and traditional cultural themes were observed as well as connections, with the aim of using film study as one means toward clarifying the nature of cultural change and continuity accompanying revolutionary political change. (3) Chinese films made in Taiwan and Hong Kong were also available, and were used for comparison with the mainland China films, for instance, in a study of film depiction of conflicts between love and family relationships, and their resolution (Weakland 1972).

Beyond this short list of film studies that are directly anthropological, or closely related, there seem to exist only occasional anthropologically relevant needles in the vast haystack of writings about feature films, and even such pieces are ordinarily quite brief. When it is worthwhile, such work may be tracked down with the aid of Jarvie's bibliographies.

ANTHROPOLOGICAL ANALYSIS OF FILMS: PRINCIPLES AND PROBLEMS

The most important point about anthropological film analysis is that, despite its apparently special object of study, this work relates closely to the mainstream of traditional anthropological concerns. In projecting structured images of human behavior, social interaction, and the nature of the world, fictional films in contemporary societies are analogous in nature and cultural significance to the stories, myths, rituals, and ceremonies in primitive societies that anthropologists have long studied.

There are also corresponding methodological similarities in the analysis of content, which here means both what is depicted and how, the form of portrayal as well as the subject matter.

Essentially, the study of film content is only a particular case of the more general anthropological examination of cultural material in search of themes — standard viewings of any particular aspects of life — and patterns of interconnection of such themes.[3] Some main principles of such examination have been stated simply by Benedict (1946: 6-11) and more fully explained by Weakland (1951) among others, while film analysis is discussed more specifically by Bateson (1945), Wolfenstein (1953a) and Weakland (1966a, 1966b).

Films themselves are rich and complex. Any film involves a vast quantity of information, all of which is potentially significant. For instance, while film studies have primarily been concerned with examining dialogue and depicted action, valuable information may also reside in music, sound effects and technical aspects of films such as camera usage. The thematic analysis of films, however, is not primarily a matter of correspondingly elaborate techniques. Rather, such analysis depends mainly upon two matters easy to state, but not so easy to carry out consistently in practice: direct, comprehensive, unbiased observation of the raw data, and adherence to a few basic orienting principles in making and reflecting on such observation.

The mechanics of anthropological film study are very simple and ordinary — close examination of films themselves, extensive note taking, review of what has been observed and recorded, and repetition of the whole process. But there are three difficulties involved. First, close and careful observation of films is tedious work, and this fundamental work cannot be delegated to assistants — unless they are as competent and dedicated observers as their principal.

Second, it is not easy to stick to what is actually observable, and give it the place it deserves. Again, the basic task in anthropological film study is to discern and describe the film content, deferring questions of any relationships of this to other aspects of culture till later. Since film content, either specifics or basic patterns, cannot be known in advance (if it were, there would be no point to the analysis), observable content must be taken as fundamental. One must "surrender to the data", avoiding selective emphases and preconceptions about what is important, and how it is, as much as possible. Since such preconceptions abound

---

[3] That is, while films are highly complex products technically, and maybe socially, such differences in degree should not be taken as the basis for sweeping conclusions that films must be different from all other communication media in kind.

concerning both films and cultures, and observation is tedious, this is difficult.

Third, if an observer is faced with abundant material and an injunction to avoid preconceptions as to what is significant, how does he focus and order his observation and recording at all? After setting down some record of a film's source, plot, characters, and the sequence of scenes as a start, then what? No final answer to this difficult question is possible; however, some general premises and principles sufficient to orient observation of actual film materials can be stated.

The most basic premise is that any film (or group of films from a single cultural source) will, like a culture, constitute in some form and to a significant degree an ordered whole, will exhibit a pattern made up of recurrent thematic elements related in characteristic, recurrent ways. This premise is based on the general scientific aim of building as orderly a view of the world as possible, and on successful past experience of viewing films and cultures in this way. Correspondingly, the primary task of film analysis, both in sequence and significance, is to discern such elements and relationships (unknown in advance) in the material. Certain general guidelines follow from the combination of this premise and the basic focus of interest of anthropological study.

Since anthropology is the study of man, observation of content may be focused, at least initially, on film material depicting human behavior and social interaction, especially family relationships. Even this criterion, however, may not be simple and obvious to apply; ultimately, all content must bear on these matters in some way, and such subjects may be treated symbolically or quite indirectly.

A second criterion is particularly valuable because it approaches the problem from a different and more formal angle that relates minimally to the observer and maximally to the material. It is important to note whatever aspects or elements of content the films themselves emphasize, even if these should initially appear trivial from the observer's standpoint. Such emphasis may be obvious, as in some kind of dramatic prominence; or it may be obscure, as by the recurrent depiction of something not especially striking in itself. Once a beginning has been made in discerning such emphases, it becomes equally useful to look for apparent contradictions or exceptions to these, and for anything that appears to be ignored or avoided where it might be expected to appear.

Special attention should be given to any content that appears curious or hard to understand, particularly any apparent incongruence between words and actions. Such attention to problematic aspects of content often leads to special insights, while this orientation is also serving as a valuable check on the danger of over-ready and facile "understanding" of what is observed. More generally, this danger can be controlled by avoiding hasty conclusions about content, and instead repeatedly returning to observation of the raw material — the same film, or further films from the same source — to re-check tentative conclusions against the data.

Although observations of content may usefully be made at many levels, they ordinarily tend to begin with some mixture of concrete details and rather loose general characterizations, whether of scenes, character types, plots, or whatever. As study proceeds, while an interplay between specific observation and broader conceptualization persists, refinement of both becomes possible and necessary. Close observation is needed in order to tell which details are recurrent and significant, and which are inessential. A concern with general regularities helps toward perceiving underlying, or even masked, formal similarities amid variations in specific content — to note, for instance, that heroines in mainland Chinese films commonly are isolated females, though specifically they may be orphans, stepdaughters, or even real daughters whose parents are not in meaningful contact with them.

The basic idea here, then, as in other cultural studies, is to discern increasingly general and comprehensive patterns accurately. Although the significance of details depends on their relationship to such patterns, the patterns can only be seen by first perceiving and then interconnecting significant details; the inquiry is necessarily a circular one of successive approximation. The essential patterns cannot be foreseen, or seen by overall inspection, but they do tend to become progressively more visible as the analyst (1) searches for regular, repetitive elements of content and (2) repetitive interrelations between these, especially formal ones, at increasingly general levels, and also (3) seeks to connect up with major regularities even apparent discrepancies or contradictions — usually as special cases, differing according to particular circumstances, within a more general unity. Discerning such patterns appears to be an operation for which the human mind is still better equipped than the computer!

In addition to the raw material observed (a film or films, corresponding to the actual behavior or cultural artifacts observed in other anthropological studies, and the notes made on these, corresponding to the "objective" or at least external perceptions of the anthropologist), one other kind of material on film content is important: information on the "native" view of film content by members of the culture. This may be obtained by interviewing informants who have seen the films, studying film reviews and commentaries, and so on. As long as such information is not relied on so extensively as to limit first-hand observation, it can be helpful in discerning significant details, emphases, and meanings of depicted behavior not readily apparent to "outsiders". More broadly it is important not to scant explicit views characteristic of the culture in question, while also avoiding confinement within these. Inquiry into how film content is viewed by members of the natural or intended audience also provides an initial basis for any further study of the cultural influence and significance of films (cf. Krebs' paper, *infra*).

Samples chosen for film study may vary widely. Films for study need not be great works of art, or even particularly good, provided only that they are not so badly formed and acted as to create undue vagueness, confusion, and contradiction. Very ordinary commercial films may usefully be examined, and may present advantages because of their relative simplicity of theme and presentation, or because they follow and represent the main line of film tradition closely (Marcus 1970). The choice of sample depends, first of all, on the analyst's interests and purposes; some aspects of observation will also vary correspondingly. Where a single film (or a very limited number) is chosen for study, as in Bateson's analysis of *Hitlerjunge Quex*, the emphasis will naturally fall more on intensive analysis of content and its structuring, and the film will need to be examined many times and in great detail.

When a number of films from a common source (however this may be defined) are the object of study, each film is likely to be examined less minutely, for practical reasons of time and effort, and major emphasis will be more on discerning themes and patterns common to all of the individual films observed (Anonymous 1944). One would look first for what is pervasive and fundamental; this is a necessary basis even if the analyst aims eventually to investigate more specific differences. By and large, the more varied the sample in terms of style and manifest content, the more difficult but more rewarding is this search for regularities, so long as there is some commonality of source.

One major variant of the study of a group of films involves selection of films made over a period of time, to investigate trends in thematic content, as exemplified in Kracauer's (1947) conception, regardless of its execution. This again should involve an initial concern to see what is constant — that is, common throughout the series — as a basis against which to view differences.

As was already suggested, the danger of substituting preconceptions for adequate observation is the most likely source of error in film content analysis and characterization. Such inaccurate characterization may take two different forms. One involves positive misperception, "seeing" elements of content and relationships not supported by the data. The other involves assigning too much scope or significance to accurate but limited observations, magnifying a part into the whole picture. It is important to note that this error lies in the magnification, not in the fact that the perception was partial. All analyses must inescapably be partial, though some may be more comprehensive than others. For this reason, as well as the fact that observational viewpoints may differ for justifiable reasons, analyses of the same material may produce different yet not contradictory results — valid partial views — just as may occur in field studies of cultures.

Attention has so far been concentrated on thematic study of film content in itself. Just as myths and ceremonies may be studied separately from their social sources and functions, such film content study is valid and useful, in at least three ways. Film analysis offers a readily available, interesting, and rewarding exercise in anthropological observation and conceptualization. Its application can "substitute for ... inarticulate impressions" of the style or atmosphere characteristic of a film or films, "a structured account of what has happened to produce them" (Wolfenstein 1953a). And content study is basic to any further cultural study of films. Equally, however, a basis is only a beginning. Content analysis is ordinarily seen as mainly a means toward relating films to other aspects of culture; this involves other opportunities and problems, which must now be surveyed.

USES AND PROSPECTS OF ANALYSIS

As the review of existing studies presented earlier suggests, anthropologists have been interested in film analysis largely as a means toward broader cultural study, rather than in film content itself. Yet such research is more difficult to describe and discuss. It inherently involves a wider and more complex field, so that what has been done represents a smaller fraction of the possible work, and its results are often more a matter of tentative insights and suggestive leads than of definite findings. But this only means that more careful study needs to be done, while what has been done serves in outlining general directions and possibilities.

As Bateson noted (1945), the film *Hitlerjunge Quex* was connected with Nazism in three ways: it was made by Nazis, it aimed to make Nazis (as a propaganda film), and it depicted Nazis. Putting this more generally, one can study how films are related to their makers, to their audiences, and to their depicted subject matter — which may be similar, as with that film, or quite different.

The situation is simplest when the filmmakers, viewers, and subject matter are all similar. This is also the most common case, at least if "similar" is interpreted reasonably broadly. That is, at least provisionally we may view both Hollywood filmmakers and their audiences as members of a common American culture even though their particular social positions within this differ, and consider the films they make and view as somehow, though probably not realistically, reflecting American life — just as shamans and story-tellers may be specialists, and myths are not descriptions of daily life.

Correspondingly, a very common focus of film study, in both anthropological and general critical writings, is on relating observations on films and observations on their surrounding culture. Such anthropological work commonly proceeds primarily from films toward culture — that is, film observations are used to clarify and organize observations on the culture more than the reverse, though some interplay ordinarily and usefully occurs. Further, for both areas the thrust is toward discerning general underlying themes and their patterned interrelations. As one accompaniment of this basic focus on form and organization, film patterns and cultural patterns usually are seen largely in terms of parallels and congruences, rather than inferring cause-and-effect relationships.

There are several basic reasons why fictional films should be especially useful in the study of general patterns of culture. In the first place, they are useful precisely because they are not factual. Instead, they tell a story; that is, they present an interpretation of some segment of life by selection, structuring and ordering images of behavior. We might not want to accept totally the view of Mao Tse-tung (1950) that "the creative forms of literature and art supersede nature in that they are more systematic, more concise, more typical, and therefore more universal." Yet we may recognize that even real life involves the conceptualization, organization, and punctuation of experience, and compared to daily life a fictional work represents a more highly ordered and defined unity, whose premises and patterns can be more readily studied.

For the case of large, complex, modern societies, where fieldwork could cover an extremely limited fraction of actual behavior, some such simplification appears an essential starting point. And films especially, while more limited and manageable for study — particularly repeated study — than daily life, are still rich and relevant, with several advantages over other fictional materials such as novels.

1. Films are especially likely to project important cultural views. Although films can now be made by one individual, ordinarily they are group products, involving the co-operative work of many members of a

culture. Also, since films are a mass medium of communication aimed for a wide popular audience, they are likely to present, relatively simply, quite basic and general themes rather than special or esoteric ones.

2. At the same time films are both rich and varied. Each film offers a great deal of material for observation, and films as a group deal with a great variety of subjects, so it is possible to examine how general themes and specific social situations are interrelated. Furthermore, filmmaking, like life, involves a continuation of deliberate design or control and un-planned elements — both as resultants of group interaction and because the makers cannot possibly control the reflection in films of cultural attitudes and premises operating below the level of awareness.

3. Only films provide verbal and visual material jointly. This gives an opportunity to compare what the players say they are doing with what the observer sees them doing, which may either clarify both or present revealing inconsistencies.

As mentioned earlier, a number of studies of this general type have been done. General cultural themes and patterns have been sought by analyzing films of Nazi Germany, Japan, India, France, England, the United States, and China, but the surface has only been scratched. All of these studies have been rather modest ones and there are films from many other cultural sources that have not been studied at all.

There are also several readily visible and potentially useful variants on this approach which have hardly been touched. Comparative study of films from different cultures could be applied to clarify cultural similari-ties and differences; the field is wide, but so far only approached in the work of Wolfenstein and Leites (1950) and Weakland (1972). Changes in film content could be used in studies of culture change; this idea is explicit in Kracauer (1947) and implicit in some of Weakland's work on Chinese films, but it has not yet been adequately tried out. Rather closely related, film studies could be used in the study of culture contact and adaptation; this has been proposed for Hong Kong (Weakland 1971b) but not put to practice. Over this whole spectrum, then, more work is needed, to fill in obvious gaps while helping test and refine this approach to the study of culture.

To repeat, this kind of general study of cultural patterns using film materials is based on the assumption of a fundamental similarity of filmmakers, viewers, and subjects. Most of the critical questions about such study — and even more, most critical attacks on films — relate to questioning this view, or asserting its opposite.

Critical attacks on films, to take the more specific matter first, or-dinarily rest on viewing the actual or potential audience of films (or television) as distinct and different from the makers, or from the content, or from the two in combination. That is, filmmakers may be labeled as propagandists influencing the unwary or powerless, or as commerical producers of whatever can be foisted on the public. The content thus pushed may be seen either as too fanciful or too realistic, but in both instances different either from how the audience lives, or how they should live. It is very difficult to discuss these views specifically. They rest on assumptions which are seldom examined, let alone empirically tested (which would be difficult). Instead, conclusions are drawn from them, or narrow research — e.g. on television influence — is done within them, and with a limited concept and study of the content involved.

It seems more useful and pertinent here to point out that these concerns do relate to broader problems about film content analysis and its significance. The matter of adequate conception and analysis of content itself has already been discussed. The question of the relation of film patterns to patterns of actual behavior is also significant, but far more complex even in principle than usually noted. For instance, Wolfenstein's discussion (1953b) of fiction and character suggests that impulsive behavior may be usual both in fiction and actuality, or in neither, or shown in one and restrained in the other, and that this relationship itself may be culturally standardized. In view of this, it makes little sense either theoretically or practically to make general evaluations of fictional films on the basis of their realism. Once more, empirical investigation, broadly enough conceived, would be more helpful.

Similarly, there is no general answer to the question of whether films reflect culture, or shape it. While both may be expected in all cases, only detailed studies — yet to be designed — will cast any more specific light, and the answer will vary from case to case.

Finally, probably the most general problem in film analysis and its use in cultural study concerns the breadth of applicability of findings. When film patterns are discerned, and appear to indicate the existence of similar patterns in the culture more widely — then how much more widely? The question is highly significant but once more there is no fixed answer. Beyond observing that this general problem, like the others just mentioned, is common throughout anthropology, one can only say that the more comprehensive, and the more overtly varied, the material in which the pattern appears — films, interviews with a variety of informants, books, observed behavior — the more reliance can be placed on it; yet the problem should always be remembered.

CONCLUSION

It is curious that more anthropological film study has not been done, and that less is being done than formerly. One can only speculate why this is so. Such study involves much time and effort, but this is equally true of other anthropological work. On the other hand, people who have not had personal experience of it often equate film study with movie-going, as fun rather than serious work, and accordingly make light of it. And even anthropology is subject to changes of fashion in professional interest. Probably little can be done about such matters. There is one possible factor, however, concerning which some clarification might be helpful. Since so much of this approach to film study developed in relation to contexts of international conflict, there may be tendencies to equate the two concerns — and not only has international conflict decreased since the days of World War II and the Cold War, but the study of other peoples has come to be regarded as likely to be exploitative. Perhaps it should therefore be pointed out that cultural understanding is as important in cooperation as in conflict, and this approach via film analysis can be used equally well toward understanding the cultural patterns of friends, or even of our own societies.

REFERENCES

ANONYMOUS
   1944   *Japanese films: a phase of psychological warfare.* Washington: Office of Strategic Services (Research and Analysis Branch).
BATESON, GREGORY
   1943a Cultural and thematic analysis of fictional films. *Transactions of the New York Academy of Sciences* (series 2) 5:72–78.
   1943b "An analysis of the film *Hitlerjunge Quex* (1933)." Mimeographed manuscript. New York: Institute for Intercultural Studies, and Museum of Modern Art Film Library.
   1953   "An analysis of the Nazi film *Hitlerjunge Quex*," in *The study of culture at a distance.* Edited by M. Mead and R. Métraux, 302–314. Chicago: University of Chicago Press.
BELO, JANE
   1953   "The father figure in *Panique*," in *The study of culture at a distance.* Edited by M. Mead and R. Métraux, 289–290. Chicago: University of Chicago Press.
BENEDICT, RUTH
   1946   *The chrysanthemum and the sword.* Boston: Houghton Mifflin.
BOULDING, KENNETH
   1956   *The image.* Ann Arbor: University of Michigan Press.

ERIKSON, ERIK H.
  1950   "The legend of Maxim Gorky's youth" [a study of the Soviet film
          The childhood of Maxim Gorky], in *Childhood and society*, 316–358.
          New York: W. W. Norton & Company Inc.
GORER, GEOFFREY
  1953   "Notes on *La Belle et la Bête*," in *The study of culture at a distance*.
          Edited by M. Mead and R. Métraux, 290–291. Chicago: University
          of Chicago Press.
HALEY, JAY
  1952   The appeal of the moving picture. *Quarterly of Film, Radio and Tele-
          vision* 6:361–374.
  1953   "David and Bathsheba." Unpublished master's thesis, Stanford
          University.
HONIGMANN, J., M. VAN DOORSLAER
  1955   Some themes from Indian film reviews. *Studies in Pakistan National
          Culture*, 2. Institute for Research in Social Science, University of
          North Carolina; *Eastern Anthropologist* 10 (1957):87–96.
JARVIE, I. C.
  1970   *Movies and society*. New York: Basic Books.
JONES, DOROTHY B.
  1942   Quantitative analysis of motion picture content. *Public Opinion
          Quarterly* 6:411–428.
JOWETT, GARTH
  1970   The conception of history in American-produced films: an analysis of
          the films made in the period 1950–1961. *Journal of Popular Culture*
          3:799–813.
KRACAUER, S.
  1942   *Propaganda and the Nazi war film*. New York: Museum of Modern
          Art Film Library.
  1947   *From Caligari to Hitler: a psychological history of the German film*.
          Princeton: Princeton University Press
MAO TSE-TUNG
  1950   *Problems of art and literature*. New York: International Publishers.
MARCUS, R. B.
  1970   Moviegoing and American culture. *Journal of Popular Culture* 3:755–
          766.
MEAD, M.
  1953   "Plot summary [of the Soviet film *The Young Guard*]," in *The study of
          culture at a distance*. Edited by M. Mead and R. Métraux, 296–297.
          Chicago: University of Chicago Press.
MEAD, M., R. MÉTRAUX, *editors*
  1953   *The study of culture at a distance*. Chicago: University of Chicago
          Press.
MEADOW, ARNOLD
  1944   "An analysis of Japanese character structure: based on Japanese film
          plots and thematic apperception tests." Mimeographed manuscript.
          Institute for Intercultural Studies, New York.
MÉTRAUX, RHODA
  1953   "Five illustrations of film analysis. Introduction," in *The study of cul-*

ture at a distance. Edited by M. Mead and R. Métraux, 281–282. Chicago: University of Chicago Press.

SAFILIOS-ROTHSCHILD, C.

᾿ 1968 "Good" and "bad" girls in modern Greek movies. *Journal of Marriage and Family* 30:527–531.

SCHWARTZ, VERA

1953 "Comparison of the film and novel [of *The Young Guard*]," in *The study of culture at a distance*. Edited by M. Mead and R. Métraux, 297–302. Chicago: University of Chicago Press.

WEAKLAND, J. H.

1951 Method in cultural anthropology. *Philosophy of Science* 18:55–69.

1953 "An analysis of seven Cantonese films," in *The study of culture at a distance*. Edited by M. Mead and R. Métraux, 292–295. Chicago: University of Chicago Press.

1966a Themes in Chinese communist films. *American Anthropologist* 68: 477–484.

1966b *Chinese political and cultural themes: a study of Chinese communist films*. China Lake, U.S. Naval Ordnance Test Station (NOTS, TP 4029, August, 1966).

1971a Chinese film images of invasion and resistance. *China Quarterly* 27: 439–470.

1971b Reel and real life in Hong Kong: film studies of cultural adaptation. *Journal of Asian and African Studies* (Leiden) 6:238–243.

1972 Conflicts between love and family relationships in Chinese films. *Journal of Popular Film* 1:290–298.

WOLFENSTEIN, MARTHA

1953a "Movie analysis in the study of culture," in *The study of culture at a distance*. Edited by M. Mead and R. Métraux, 267–280. Chicago: University of Chicago Press.

1953b "Notes on an Italian film: *The Tragic Hunt*," in *The study of culture at a distance*. Edited by M. Mead and R. Métraux, 282–289. Chicago: University of Chicago Press.

WOLFENSTEIN, MARTHA, N. LEITES

1950 *Movies: a psychological study*. Glencoe: The Free Press.

1954 "Plot and character in selected French films," in *Themes in French culture*. Edited by R. Métraux and M. Mead, 89–103. Stanford: Stanford University Press.

1955 Trends in French films. *Journal of Social Issues* 2:42–51.

Videotape: New Techniques of Observation and Analysis in Anthropology

JOSEPH H. SCHAEFFER

For several years I have been interested in the integration of knowledge concerning various levels of social-economic-cultural organization in an inclusive systems theoretical framework — first as an analyst of communicative behavior in a New York ghetto; then during studies of behavior associated with the acquisition, maintenance, and exchange of goods and services in a small agricultural community in Jamaica, West Indies; and recently in research on acute and long-term effects of the use of psychoactive substances in both rural and urban settings in Mexico.

Videotape technology has been advantageous in my work for several reasons. First, it permits coverage of the stream of activity in the natural setting in much of its complexity over relatively extended time periods. This coverage supplements inclusive written accounts of the activity. It complements high definition coverage of short sequences of activity, say on motion-picture film. And it provides a context for limited coverage of activity on photographs and/or audiotapes, or limited coverage through the use of other techniques.

Second, when carried out with intelligence by trained researchers, videotape coverage permits scientific rigor. Videotape records retain sample sequences of observed activity for later scrutiny. The quality and reliability of general statements concerning the activity may, as a result, be increased. Analytical operations applied to videotape records can be assessed for intersubjective reliability.

Third, videotape records permit review by scientists and informant-participants in the field to stimulate response and to increase the scope of interpretation of both general and specific sociocultural phenomena.

Fourth, videotape records can be employed to establish connections between abstractions and inferences and the observed phenomena upon which they are based. Videotape records as a constant reference point, a point of departure, permit grounded, well considered conclusions during the interpretation of original field data.

The appropriate use of videotape technology in my work, however, has not developed without thought concerning serious issues, a degree of trial and error, and a continuing effort to control an inclination to preoccupation with the technology. The issues include the ethics of detailed coverage of human activity with videotape, the field program associated with the use of videotape technology, and the implications of the use of videotape as a field tool. These issues, deserving, I think, some extended discussion, are the subject of the present paper.

ETHICAL CONSIDERATIONS

Ethical considerations in behavioral science research have been discussed in some detail elsewhere (see, for example, Ruebhausen and Brim 1965, and Westin 1967). I will mention only a few crucial points specifically related to research with videotape in the present brief statement.

The central ethical consideration in videotape research concerns the privacy of the informant-participant (hereafter called participant). Two critical issues related to privacy are voluntary consent and the confidentiality of the data. Voluntary consent implies, first, that ultimate control for involvement in research lies with the participant. Such control cannot be exercised intelligently, however, without the participant's full and clear understanding of research goals, procedures, and implications. It is the researcher's responsibility to provide an explanation of the research which permits this understanding. Second, voluntary consent implies mutual respect, confidence, and trust between participant and researcher. That is, upon consent a researcher-participant relationship is established that persists throughout the research. It must be founded in a mutual regard that the researcher may not betray.

A crucial decision in videotape research, that concerning the concealment of equipment, is related to the issue of voluntary consent. Several of my colleagues feel that a decision concerning concealment should be dictated by the research design. They suggest, for example, that research in the private domain of the psychological laboratory may permit concealment without consent. Public domain studies may permit concealed coverage without consent if research requirements are related to public interest in critical social problems. In my own work to date I have refused to conceal videotape equipment without consent. I prefer, in fact, that equipment be visible to participants whenever possible. Its appropriate use — visible or not — guarantees minimal interference with activity in most coverage situations. More importantly, the conceivable gains from research using concealed equipment without consent rarely if ever outweigh potential problems for both scientist and participant related to the concealment. Until legal authorities clarify the issue it will remain open, of course, and, to some degree, controversial.

Upon collection of videotape records, requirements concerning the confidentiality of the data become salient. Ruebhausen and Brim (1965: 1204–1205) have suggested that in any behavioral science research private data should be retained in such a manner that maximum confidentiality is guaranteed "...consistent with the integrity of the research." I would suggest more strongly that, when videotape technology is employed, the design be such that the complete anonymity of all participants be maintained. If for some reason total anonymity is not possible, comprehensive legal agreements defining limitations on the use of the data should be required. In addition, controls concerning confidentiality may be extended to participants. These may include tape destruction and/or publication review rights. If such rights are not appropriate, the scientist himself may wish to assume personal responsibility for the control of any data which could permit the identification of a participant and/or jeopardize his (the participant's) place in the community.

The other major consideration during research with videotape concerns political, social, and economic implications of the use of the data. In this regard the key question is: Can the data be used against the best wishes of participants? This question is, unfortunately, pertinent in a time when records of their activity can be turned against individuals by political whim.

The prevention of the misuse of videotape records depends upon the fulfillment of at least three requirements. First, it is important that competent, trained professionals deal with videotape during research. Second, researchers must be aware of the needs of the participants. They must consider the social, economic, and political relevance of the collected data. And they must accept responsibility for an understanding of the foreseeable implications of the interpretation of the data. Third, researchers must be willing to sacrifice the use of videotape techniques unless they are indispensable for the acquisition of information related to crucial problems. Videotape coverage of activity, especially in the private domain, cannot be justified unless no other tools permit the acquisition of necessary data.

FIELD PROGRAMS IN RESEARCH WITH VIDEOTAPE

A second important consideration for those using videotape concerns the appropriateness of the technology in specified research programs. Both the research design and the field situation affect decisions in this regard.

Design questions concerning videotape technology include the following: (1) What phenomena will be covered with videotape? Do these phenomena occur during complex, extended activity? If they do not and the research requires visual coverage, can the needs be met with photographs, photography and audiotape, 8-mm or 16-mm film, etc.? (2) What phenomena will be explored with other field techniques? Does videotape fit? Is its use redundant? Can the same information be acquired easily with less complicated techniques? (3) What will be accomplished with audiovisual devices? Certain operations employed to obtain information concerning minute details of behavior may not be appropriate with videotape; operations geared to an analysis of macrobehavior, on the other hand, may be more appropriate to videotape than to other audiovisual records. (4) How can the various techniques be employed conjunctively to greatest advantage? Rarely, if ever, will videotape be employed as the only or even the primary tool in anthropological studies: under most circumstances it will be an adjunctive tool associated with other techniques.

If answers to these questions imply the use of videotape technology then the field situation must be considered. The participants themselves may be negative toward audiovisual coverage of activity. In some urban settings in the United States, for example, research with audiovisual devices is frowned upon for sociopolitical reasons. Cultural customs in some parts of the world, e.g. Morocco, prohibit visual coverage of behavior. In these difficult situations participants may accept videotape coverage only after extended involvement in research. In some such situations participants themselves may be willing to videotape activity while refusing such coverage to researchers. Ultimately, of course, in impossible participant rejection situations the scientist may be forced to choose alternative research settings.

A second consideration regarding the research situation concerns the environment. At the time of writing, although versatile videotape equipment is available, limitations due to terrain, climate, the availability of repair shops, etc. persist. Researchers considering the use of videotape in difficult climate and terrain with no electricity should contact competent technicians before leaving for the field. Often adjustments on existing equipment can meet special requirements.

(I will have more to say on design and research setting in the case studies and the following section on conjunctive uses of visual/audio-visual technology.)

If the design requires and the field situation permits the use of videotape techniques, field procedures must be considered. One must introduce and maintain the equipment, complete necessary coverage, prepare for the storage and potential use of the data, and arrange data analyses. The introduction of equipment usually requires several steps. As implied in the brief discussion of ethics, the research "idea" associated with coverage must be raised with participants. Techniques must be described and, perhaps, demonstrated. Following the introductory period the equipment must be checked in action. Immediate reactions of participants will alter in time as familiarity with the equipment develops. The researcher should consider the progression and be willing to adjust to the requirements of the situation. Once introduced and tested, the equipment must be utilized and maintained during extended research. During this period the researcher will want to consider problems related to "appropriate coverage" and to necessary effects on both participants and other persons connected with the research. During the extended research period procedures for monitoring and recording must be considered. If a studio is to be used arrangements will be necessary. Personnel requirements must be met. Sampling procedures must be developed. During and after fieldwork considerations concerning storage and potential future use of tapes are of the utmost importance. Such factors as climate, molestation of tapes by others, potentially destructive magnetic fields during travel, etc. can jeopardize videotape records. Durability during analysis is a particular problem. Duplicates of important selected records will certainly be required. Upon successful acquisition and storage of adequate records analytical operations must be applied. If the operations require participant response to the tapes they may be completed in the field. In the studio operations can be applied to the audio and/or visual data during repeated observation by multiple observers over extended time periods.

To exemplify these points several brief case studies will be presented. The first two will cover the use of videotape techniques in urban settings. Some discussion of long-term production with relatively stationary equipment will be included in these studies. The third will cover use in a remote and rather difficult field situation. Discussions of the use of portable equipment during relatively short recording sessions will be included.

VIDEOTAPE IN URBAN SETTINGS: CASE STUDIES

The first case study is based on my research in the Project in Human Communication at Bronx State Hospital in New York City. The goal of that research was an understanding of problems related to activity in architecturally confining space among members of various cultures in an urban setting. Videotapes were produced in households, with, of course, the permission of the household members, during five- to ten-week periods. They were analyzed to determine the spacing arrangements within fixed spaces, the structure of communication associated with the use of space, and other behavior patterns in the household having to do with family life in an urban community. Videotapes were also acquired in exterior street settings to permit analysis of the structure of communication among members of the community.

Several months of ethnographic research (participant observation and interviewing) preceded the introduction of ideas concerning videotape coverage of activity. As a first step, upon the decision to introduce technology, I visited representatives of public and private community organizations and obtained informal permission for videotape research. Then, based upon a sophisticated technique carried out during demographic studies in previous weeks, I visited specified households to discuss such research. The result of these preliminary meetings was the establishment of a group of interested community "advisers" with whom I could discuss and develop the videotape coverage program.

As a second step I chose several research households in which, over a period of time, videotape technology might be employed. I visited each of these households for preliminary meetings in which the research was introduced and its goals discussed. All procedures which would involve participants in any way were reviewed including the monitoring, taping, and filming of activity in the household. I explained that visible but unobtrusive videotape cameras and microphones would cover agreed-upon public action for periods of up to ten weeks. Research personnel would monitor the coverage and tape example sequences of activity. Towards the end of the videotape periods, film equipment would be installed to permit detailed coverage of brief segments of monitored activity. I affirmed the project's position that these procedures would require the permission and cooperation of the participants. Further, participants could control coverage by disconnecting power cords and could request the removal of equipment at any time during the coverage period.

Only a brief explanation of the analysis of tapes was included in this first interview. The purpose was twofold: to indicate to household members our interest in and the implications of analyses of details of their daily activity, and to obtain permission for particular studies in the research program.

The procedures for the viewing of tape and film records were also discussed during this first interview. Participants would review all records with the understanding that requests for the destruction of "unacceptable" sequences would be honored.

Finally, legal contracts and immediate benefits to participants were discussed. A contract which guaranteed the confidentiality of the data was presented for perusal. Legal counsel concerning this contract was offered at project expense. Financial remuneration was discussed in association with the contract (though the amount was not stated in the document). The contract indicated that no hidden surveillance equipment would be employed, that only public (common) use areas would be covered, and that participants would maintain destruction rights over all audiovisual records. Written permission would be required for the display of taped situations not covered explicitly in the contract. Future use of the tapes could include immediate feedback to participant families and general feedback to the community upon the request of participants.

Before subsequent interview-discussions participants considered their involvement. Upon indications of positive response second interviews were scheduled in which detailed procedures for the placement of cameras and microphones were discussed. In preparation for these discussions I introduced portable videotape equipment to acquaint participants with the coverage capabilities of project cameras. Following the discussions I took still "mapping" photographs of potential coverage areas and separate "identification" photographs of each household member.

During successive visits to research households I observed daily activity to test tentative decisions concerning camera and microphone placement. Gradually I became better acquainted with participants and established a basis of trust in anticipation of the actual introduction of the videotape equipment. (Few placement decisions were restricted by the capability of video equipment. Cameras can be employed under relatively difficult circumstances. They are totally silent, require little power, and function at low light levels. The audio equipment was equally easy to handle.)

If building exteriors were to be used for cables or aerials, I had, of course, to obtain the permission of landlords and superintendents at some point during the interview-discussion period.

When preliminary discussions had been completed and the placement of equipment confirmed, cameras and microphones were installed. Standard procedures included the following: the equipment was checked and repaired before installation; adjustable camera mounts were constructed; a technician and I installed equipment in households at agreed-upon times. Small monitors used in the households during installation permitted precise decisions concerning coverage. When necessary, 40-watt light bulbs were replaced with stronger bulbs. Cables were run from cameras to either rooftop transmission discs or to nearby monitor studios. Microphones were installed. The entire set-up was photographed and mapped in precise measurements.

A visit to households for the adjustment of equipment followed a period in which activity was monitored round-the-clock in a nearby studio. During this adjustment interview I obtained the participants' first impressions concerning the presence of cameras and outlined plans for future coverage. Tentative conclusions concerning responses to the cameras were not surprising. Primary factors affecting camera awareness were time in the viewing area, the nature of the activity, and the age of participants. In summary: camera awareness decreased as time in the viewing area and involvement in activity increased. The younger the participant the less his continued awareness. A major secondary factor affecting camera awareness was formal education in, or perhaps more simply contemplation concerning the behavioral sciences — call it sophistication. The more sophisticated the participant the greater was his camera awareness.

Intermittent meetings and/or phone conversations with household members were scheduled during coverage periods following the adjustment sessions. These insured continued trust and confidence.

Monitor studios were established near several of the research households. They were equipped with two videotape monitors, sound systems, and switching devices attached to cables extended to installed cameras and microphones. Cables from one household were attached to a rooftop disc transmission system. Signals were received in our office studios at Bronx State Hospital (two miles away).

We geared the monitor viewing program to the total coverage of extended sequences of activity in each research household. During the early weeks a team of viewers surveyed all activity in the coverage area. Based on agreed-upon criteria each prepared a flow-chart log stating time, space, persons present, and content of activity. This information, along with any personal observations, was noted at three-minute intervals. (Whenever possible the schedule was organized so that no viewer worked more than six hours in sequence. Often two viewers cooperated to facilitate the task.)

Upon completion of each monitor week a graph was constructed from the flow-chart logs indicating the number of persons present and the activity in the viewing area during the days throughout the week. Studies of these graphs preceded the selection of example sequences of activity for recording. During final weeks the example sequences were taped non-stop from beginning to end. Eight- to ten-hour records of extended sequences of several activities were produced as well.

Toward the end of the videotape coverage period film cameras were installed. Their placement and the activity sequences to be covered had been determined during monitor periods. In most households we installed a 16-mm camera with a 1200 foot magazine. Remote control equipment in the monitor studio permitted film coverage of activity viewed on the videotape monitors. The obtrusiveness of the film camera was minimal because it was situated near the videotape camera, was run remotely, and was silent.

Upon completion of filming, film and videotape equipment was removed from the households and post-coverage contact was initiated. As soon as possible after the removal of cameras I discussed reactions with participants and indicated our continuing interest in a research relationship with them. Most participants indicated that the cameras had become "part of the furniture" during the extended coverage period. Many had accepted the cameras as a "trusted addition" to the household which, upon completion of coverage, was sorely missed!

Participants in all research households were anxious to view the records. Before display we catalogued the entire inventory and selected those tapes and films which were to be used for specific studies when viewed by participants. We arranged appropriate storage in a cool, dry, locked, well-protected area in the Bronx State Hospital studio.

The viewing brought varied reactions. Some participants watched quietly with little overt response. Some laughed and commented frequently. Others exchanged embarrassed glances as they giggled nervously. In general, responses varied according to the sex and age of the participants. The younger children often had difficulty recognizing themselves on tapes. As expected, their concentration span was limited. Older children concentrated more deeply, waiting anxiously to see themselves. Teenagers watched closely but commented infrequently. Female adults were openly interested viewers. They commented on both their own behavior and the behavior of others. Often these comments were related to activity they considered unacceptable. The adult males varied in response. Some resembled the women: others remained quiet and introspective. Cultural patterns of reaction emerged as household members from different cultures became involved in the research.

The post-film/tape procedures included the application of several analytical operations. Selected tapes from several households were employed in a study of child-rearing practices. Adults were questioned concerning such practices in Puerto Rico, among Puerto Ricans in New York, in households in the neighborhood, among friends, generally in their own homes, and on particular occasions in their own homes. Analysts applied intersubjectively reliable operations to the tapes to determine the actual practices as they were performed during daily rounds of activity. The results of the interviews and tape analysis were compared.

Several members of the seminar in etic ethnography at Columbia University, working with the guidance of Dr. Marvin Harris, analyzed selected tapes. Anna-Lou de Havenon developed operations with which patterns of dominance could be established during the analysis of command-request patterns in the household. She identified commands and requests for actors in several scenes and noted whether or not they were obeyed. Command-success ratios were established for each actor. Further analysis of this information and its representation through the use of diagraphs and matrix displays permitted substantive conclusions concerning dominance and authority in the limited sample considered.

De Havenon also analyzed food-related behavior on several taped sequences of activity to test hypotheses concerning patterns of authority and the control of food.

Sanjek and Cramer, members of the same seminar, tested three nonverbal measures of dominance and authority during tape analyses (see Sanjek 1969). These measures were: initiation of actions, control of objects, and physical displacement of other persons.

In a third seminar study, Joseph (1969) undertook a comparison of the participants' ideas concerning patterns of dominance and authority and the actual patterns determined in the de Havenon and Sanjek-Cramer studies.

A fourth member of the seminar (Kane 1969) analyzed selected tapes to determine the presence or absence of behaviors in the presence or absence of various members of the household. Conclusions were based on the assumption that authority patterns could be inferred from systematic changes in response to the presence or absence of particular individuals in various situations.

Another student, Beverly Hurlbert, analyzed touching behavior in two research households. She intended, through the use of etic analytical operations, to answer questions concerning patterns of affection between adult females and adult males on the one hand and their children on the other (Hurlbert 1970).

Several studies in the Project in Human Communication at Bronx State

Hospital were carried out with records from the videotape and film inventory. In my own work as a member of that project the primary analytical objective was a description of all behaviors as they unfold in the natural stream to provide the basis for statements concerning intracultural regularities and intercultural similarities and differences in the structure and organization of behavior. I carried out analyses of the behavior of individuals and of social and physical phenomena related to that behavior. The analytical foci included space, time, material items in the environment, sound, and the bodily movements of individuals. The operations are described in some detail elsewhere (see Schaeffer 1970).

Albert E. Scheflen and Adam Kendon analyzed videotape records to determine the systematic relationship between territorial arrangements and human behavior. During four review "passages" of each activity sequence under observation they coded the fixed architectural space, the space defined by furniture and movable objects, the position and movement of individuals in the space, the relationships among individuals in space, and the content of activity. (The Bronx project was developed by Albert E. Scheflen, a pioneer in both film and videotape analysis of therapy sessions and family gatherings. Marvin Harris of Columbia University became an invaluable consultant on the project: he has been interested in the use of videotape technology during anthropological research for many years.)

Based partially upon findings in the Bronx concerning the technology, the coverage program, and appropriate analytical operations, Dr. Harris instigated a major project in New York City to study family patterns in the domicile in two cultures. The primary research objective was the identification of family authority structures in the absence or presence of a stable male head of household. The collection of videotape records of daily activity in the domicile was related to this objective. Two white and two black families matched for marital history, income, urban birth, number of children, apartment space, religion, and education were selected for research in the following way. Research personnel searched the files of a large city agency for potential families. They discovered about 500 families meeting the above criteria and contacted them by mail. Those indicating interest in the research were interviewed by agency personnel. During these interviews project procedures and goals were described and ethical issues discussed.

Members of the Columbia research team visited families in which continued interest was evident after the preliminary interview. More detailed discussions of the project were initiated during these visits.

Portable cameras and videotape recorders were introduced for demonstration purposes.

On agreed-upon dates videotape equipment was installed in research households by a technician and a research team member. Installation was followed by monitoring in a nearby studio during two "warm-up" weeks and one taping week. The warm-up period was designed to achieve the following: the viewing of daily rounds of activity was a basis for standardizing camera selection priorities during the tape week; the maintenance of continuous activity logs; the production of videotape records of selected activity sequences at specified times to determine alterations in camera awareness over time; videotape coverage of a pre-tape-week interview involving a researcher and family members; and familiarization of the members of the viewing team with the operation and maintenance of equipment.

At the end of the warm-up period standardized operations were defined for decisions concerning the taping of activity. These were: (1) to tape only when at least one member of a defined set of family members was present and actonically or communicatively active, (2) to give coverage priority to the mother of the household based upon the assumption that inside the apartment hers was the largest set of activities involving the most household actors, (3) to give priority to other actors in the defined family set in order of age if the mother was not present, (4) to interrupt coverage of an actor for no more than five seconds to record entrances and exits of other actors, and (5) to interrupt audio coverage of priority actors if and when the priority actor was silent. The videotape recorder was turned off when none of the specified criteria were met.

Upon the removal of the cameras from each household, tapes were coded by members of a volunteer coding team from the university. Coding covered three types of request and five types of compliance expressed in both verbal and nonverbal behavior. Events were reviewed no more than five times before coding. Only those events which were agreed upon independently by several coders were accepted for inclusion in final statements. (In the first family about two-thirds of the coded events survived this concordance phase to be punched for the computer.)

As data collection approached completion researchers met to devise mathematical procedures to identify the contours of family authority hierarchies and the cost-efficiency of maintaining these hierarchies. Data matrices were employed to determine the repetition of requests, the number of fulfilled requests, the frequency of requests, the success ratio for compliance with requests, etc. Hypotheses related to these data were developed and tested.

In summary, with regard to videotape techniques in urban research, these projects indicate that in-household urban research may permit the use of stationary equipment during long-term coverage of activity. Videotape technology can be maintained by research personnel and a competent technician. Team efforts during coverage are appropriate. The scientist-participant relationship is critical and must be founded in mutual trust. Legal contracts should guarantee privacy, confidentiality, and appropriate control of data. And analytical procedures applied to videotapes may be wide-ranging and varied. They are subject to tests of intersubjective reliability.

VIDEOTAPE IN RURAL SETTINGS: A CASE STUDY

In somewhat more difficult rural research situations procedures with videotape may differ significantly from those in urban settings. My own recent work in Jamaica, West Indies, provides an example. My wife and I carried out fieldwork for a year in a small agricultural community. Our priority was a study of the effects of the use of marijuana on the behavior of human beings as members of a population in an ecosystem. Research foci included empirically measurable relationships between individuals and external elements in the environment (other individuals and material items). The immediate goal was an understanding of the significance of marijuana use in a social-economic-cultural context.

Major data collection techniques during fieldwork included standardized census interviews; extensive interviews concerning household composition, kinship networks, land tenure, occupation, income, etc.; comprehensive written records of daily activity throughout one week in each of sixteen sample households; twenty-four audiotapes (ninety minutes each), one hundred videotapes (thirty minutes each), and several films (eleven minutes each) of major activities in each sample household; and objective measurements of energy metabolism and nutrition. Other data were collected during medical surveys, laboratory studies of energy metabolism, case study visits to selected institutions, and special subject interviews and observations.

The research community was situated in hilly, shaly terrain in Jamaica's eastern Blue Mountain Range. Its population included 300 inhabitants living in eighty-five households along a winding dirt road. The primary source of income was small-scale farming — a difficult occupation given the steepness of the terrain, the unpredictable climate, and the difficulty of transportation to major market centers. The community had no running water, no electricity, and few public services.

Since coverage with videotape required work in difficult terrain with no electricity, portable equipment was necessary. I used the Sony AV3400 videorecorder and AVC3400 camera with rechargeable batteries (both thirty-minute and three-hour). A local mail carrier transported the batteries to nearby towns for daily recharging.

The field program was introduced during several months of participant observation and interviewing. The goal of the observation was an understanding of standard daily activity among participants in the community. The interviews provided necessary information concerning the significance of these activities in the social-economic-cultural context. During this preliminary period I carried a still camera and/or a small 8-mm cine-camera constantly. As a result, participants associated visual coverage with my work.

Upon completion of introductory studies the program for videotape coverage was developed. The purpose of the program was the acquisition of audiovisual records of all major activities among participants in a representative sample of marijuana-use and non-marijuana-use households. The audiovisual coverage was to supplement detailed written descriptions of daily activity and specific studies of energy metabolism.

Daily activity coverage procedures included introductory interviews, extended coverage periods, and tape viewing sessions. I scheduled the interviews with members of each of the sixteen sample households to outline the goal of the videotape work and to demonstrate the equipment. I explained that coverage decisions would depend on the permission and cooperation of the participants. Further, legal contracts would protect the use of the tapes, and participants could view all tapes and maintain destruction rights. (Interestingly, legal counsel in Jamaica suggested that direct contracts with participants might be overthrown in court. They suggested I establish contracts with project direction in the United States governing the tapes through my personal control.)

If participant response was positive, extended coverage was initiated. I observed the stream of activity of the subject participant during his waking hours for fourteen days. I listed all episodes in sequence (see Harris 1964), noted all material items related to activity, and described encounters and the content of conversation. On selected days I carried videotape and photographic equipment to produce audiovisual records of representative sequences of activity (up to 120 minutes in length). When possible the sequences included complete activities. All behaviors of all participants were framed at all times during coverage. At least three audiovisual records of each major activity were acquired with each participant (before, during and after the use of marijuana).

The portable videotape equipment deserves, I think, some comment in a brief digression since it has not been used frequently in the field. It is, first, a reliable tool. I bumped it, dropped it, lost my footing and slid down fifty-foot shale slopes with it, and soaked it in frequent rains. Still, it continued to function properly throughout the field year. It is light enough to be carried and handheld for relatively long periods in many situations — in a level yard or along a cleared road, for example. In difficult, hilly bush my strength permitted twenty- to thirty-minute records when hand use was necessary. With a monopod or tripod I covered considerably longer sequences of activity in such terrain. The equipment is remarkably capable in various settings. The camera functions adequately in relatively low light without infrared sensitive accessories. I often covered indoor scenes illuminated only by an open fire and a Coleman-type gas lantern. The compactness of the recorder and camera was an advantage in these confined indoor spaces. The battery as a source of power presented the only major inconvenience. Limited coverage in time was the result.

The videotape equipment included a small monitor which could be used to play tapes for participants. Frequent tape viewing sessions were scheduled for the participants and, upon the request of participants, their families and friends. Excitement and enjoyment marked these sessions. On occasion a videotape review method was employed to stimulate response concerning the behavior of participants in particular scenes. During brief tape studies I developed questions concerning the participants' impressions of certain details in activity. Answers were to be compared with statements based on intersubjectively reliable analyses of these details following the fieldwork.

In all cases during the fieldwork participants accepted videotape coverage without incident. Usually they were deeply involved in some activity when videotape was in use and could take no more than passing notice of my presence. As I covered particular participants in public settings, onlookers who had not seen the equipment previously often questioned me concerning its use. They accepted a brief, polite response as I continued working. Their focussed interest usually subsided within minutes.

Toward the end of the field research several nutritionists from Columbia University joined us in the field to conduct tests with a Kofrani-Michaelis gas collection device and a Lloyd gas analyzer. We asked selected participants to wear the seven-pound Kofrani on their backs and to breathe into the attached respiration tube during normal activity. I followed the participants to note the volume of consumed air in liters every thirty seconds. Intermittently I acquired air samples and transferred them immediately to an assistant in a nearby shelter. There she analyzed many of the tests on the Lloyd analyzer to determine percentages of oxygen and carbon dioxide in the expired air — that is, to make precise measurements of energy expenditure.

My wife timed and videotaped the activity tests in their entirety using the Sony portable equipment with a stationary tripod. We intended to use the tapes to relate movement in space and time to data on energy metabolism.

Upon completion of the field work three assistants and I applied analytical operations to the tapes as outlined in Harris's *The nature of cultural things* (1964), in order to relate activity to effects in the environment and to determine the number and sequence of behaviors in various activities. We also applied operations outlined in my dissertation (Schaeffer 1970) to determine the organization of behavior during work and social interaction. Patterns of behavior before and after the use of marijuana were compared upon completion of these analytical procedures.

A research associate at Bronx State Hospital carried out microanalyses of rhythmicity in movement using sample sequences from our tapes. He marked onsets and endings of movements in each of six variable body parts to the tenth of a second for participants in the taped sequences. He then compared rhythmic patterns in participants before, during, and after the use of marijuana. The findings concerning the number and organization of and the rhythmicity of movements during activity have been related to findings concerning the social-economic-cultural setting and the position of the participants as members of a population in an ecosystem (see Schaeffer 1972).

Based on these experiences in the field, on conversations with others who have employed videotape in non-urban settings, and on remarks in the limited literature on videotape in the field, several conclusions are suggested. Videotape is a valuable adjunctive tool in many field programs. Videotape techniques permit extended audiovisual coverage of activity in difficult non-urban settings. Videotape technology is reliable in the field when properly handled and maintained. Researchers should assume legal responsibility for audiovisual data. Mutual trust between researcher and participants is crucial. Review of audiovisual data by participants is often appropriate. And analytical operations applied to videotapes can be checked for intersubjective reliability.

VIDEOTAPE AND OTHER VISUAL/AUDIOVISUAL TECHNOLOGY IN RESEARCH

The above conclusions concerning videotape as an adjunctive field tool, especially with regard to its use with other visual and/or audiovisual (VAV) technology, i.e. photography or film, has interested me for some time. Reliable decisions concerning research design with videotape depend upon discussions of this conclusion. Several topics are important in these discussions: the characteristics of VAV tools in the field, the observer's influence during coverage with VAV equipment, the nature of VAV records, and the conjunctive use of VAV techniques. I will review these topics very briefly here. For a more complete statement see Collier (1967), Michaelis (1955), and Schaeffer (1970).

The important characteristics in a comparison of VAV tools are versatility, portability, and visibility. Still cameras of many types are available for research. Specialists may require records made with 11- by 14-inch, 8- by 10-inch, or 4- by 5-inch view cameras. At the other extreme, tiny Minox or 16-mm Minolta cameras may be employed. Common field equipment, of course, includes 35-mm and/or Rolleiflex cameras. Adjunctive equipment with still cameras, including camera mounts, exposure meters, flash attachments, and extra lenses, increases coverage capability.

Most still cameras are portable. They may become, as Byers (1964) and Collier (1967) suggest, appendages of the researcher. In specified situations they can run automatically and/or by remote control.

Appropriate lenses for still cameras permit coverage in practically any space. In low illumination, specially prepared films may be employed. Infra-red films, for example, are sensitive to figures in darkness illuminated from an infra-red source. Flash attachments may, of course, permit coverage in darkness. Visibility is minimal when still cameras are properly handled. They need be no more obtrusive in the field than notebooks or audio tape recorders.

Motion picture field cameras are somewhat more limited in variety in comparison with still cameras. They range in quality from 8-mm home movie type cameras to the more sophisticated 16-mm cameras employed by experienced researchers to provide comprehensive records of events. Features on this latter camera may include multi-lens turrets, external magazines for extended coverage, sound blimps, etc. Necessary adjunctive equipment may include camera mounts, exposure meters, lenses, magazines of various sizes, lights, changing bags, films, and, if sound is included, audio tape recorders, microphones, cables, and power sources.

Both 8-mm and 16-mm lenses permit coverage in various situations.

The length of film coverage is governed by the size of the magazine, camera speed, and the nature of the power source. Light problems frequently invade film work due to camera mechanism limits on possible uses of highly sensitive films.

Sound coverage adds another dimension to film research. Synchronous sound systems have been developed which permit coverage by a single researcher. Often, however, especially with 16-mm systems, a "sound man" is required to control sophisticated equipment and insure reliable results.

The visibility of film equipment is, on occasion, a limiting factor of some importance. In more complicated cameras, sound and moving parts attract attention. When these problems are overcome with sound-proof casing, size may intrude. With these cameras as well as with smaller more portable cameras, frequent reel changes and camera checks restrict the making of objective records.

(Several specific characteristics of videotape systems have been outlined in the case studies. General characteristics will be reviewed here in the context of a comparative discussion.)

Videotape systems require three components in most research situations — a camera (or cameras), a videotape recorder, and a monitor. Field cameras range in size from simply constructed, small, lightweight cameras to heavier, highly sensitive cameras. The various cameras are compatible with several $1/2$-inch, 1-inch, or 2-inch videotape recorders. During recording, camera and tape recorder can be connected directly to one another by cable. Alternatively, both may be connected to microwave devices which transmit and receive video signals. Monitors can be employed either in conjunction with or separately from tape recorders. In the latter case they are connected directly to the camera by cable.

Synchronous sound presents few problems in videotape research. Microphones can be connected to portable cameras. Sound is then transmitted and recorded simultaneously with the image on tape. If desired, microphones installed at various locations in the scene can be connected to video transmission cables.

Adjunctive equipment may include camera mounts and extra lenses. Tripods permit rapid installation but may not be necessary if cameras are to remain stationary for some time. In such cases cameras can be strapped to or mounted on poles, trees, door jambs, etc. as desired. Light meters are not required during videotape research. The image from the camera can be viewed directly on the monitor as the aperture is adjusted. Cameras adjust automatically to a certain degree when light levels change.

In comparison with motion picture cameras, the portable videotape cameras are relatively easy to handle. The lightness in weight permits control by a single researcher.

A variety of lenses permits versatility during coverage in varied spaces. Expensive cameras can be purchased which produce images in low light. Infra-red and ultra-violet sensitive tubes can be employed if required.

The visibility of videotape equipment can be minimized. The silent cameras have no moving parts. They can be placed in unobtrusive locations to transmit images to remote monitors.

Keeping in mind the general capabilities of the technology one must consider its use in research when, as Collier writes, "...the challenge is to observe with scientific significance" (1967:105). During research with still photography, film, and/or videotape techniques, the investigator influences the record. The degree of contact between researcher and his equipment during coverage is important in this regard. Still cameras must be handled constantly unless they are controlled by automatic or remote devices. As suggested above, however, portability permits constant use and consequent loss of awareness on the part of both the participant and the researcher. Motion picture cameras require less frequent handling than still cameras when prepared for coverage of particular scenes. Necessary adjustments on stationary cameras may include various camera movements, re-framing of shots, reel changes, focussing, and, if sound is recorded, control of sound equipment. Portable cameras, of course, are handled constantly. Stationary videotape cameras may remain in the scene for extended periods (weeks or even months). Adjustments may be necessary at infrequent intervals.

In most cultures influence can be reduced when portable equipment is employed if the photographer and/or cameraman maintains constant involvement with the production of records and avoids any extraneous activity. Experienced photographers, e.g. Paul Byers, Sander Kirsch, Jacques Van Vlack and others, suggest that the avoidance of unnecessary direct relationships between participant and researcher effectively reduces influence as well.

Decisions concerning content also indicate the observer's influence on the record. They are related to two pertinent questions: How much information is to be included in the frame? What phenomena are to be covered?

If the researcher wishes to focus on particular items in the environment or on micro-behaviors in specified body parts, he may limit the information in the frame with "close-up" shots. More inclusive shots can provide records of progressively wider contexts of such items or behaviors.

In standard wide-angle shots the researcher will include as much of the scene under surveillance as is necessary to provide adequate data. If, for example, he is interested in covering the interior of a house, he will want to photograph rooms in such a fashion that relationships among items can be determined. If he wishes to record interactants in a scene as a foundation for analyses of communicative behavior he will want to include all body parts of all participants at all times.

Decisions concerning the nature of the phenomena to be covered or the content in the frame need not limit the selection of equipment. A space can be "mapped" with a series of stills or a pan shot on film or videotape. Segments of behavior can be photographed in rapid sequence or covered intermittently or continuously on film or videotape.

For specific analyses, however, certain techniques are advantageous. Still photographs permit descriptions of stationary material objects. Portraits of participants are best taken with still cameras. Intermittent stills of behavior taken in rapid sequence may be useful for purposes of comparison. "Time-lapse" photographs provide important information on changes in arrangements in space over time. Stills provide useful information on color.

If details in rapid movement are of interest in relatively short sequences, motion picture records are appropriate. Less detail in extended segments may be covered with videotape cameras. Information on color can be obtained with either technique. It is more complete on film.

Decisions concerning point of view are closely related to those concerning content. Cameras can cover scenes from a variety of positions and angles. When total coverage of a confined area is required, a corner position with the camera angled down from above may be suitable. Often, however, this position produces distortions on the record. When total coverage is desired in a less restricted space the eye-level shot is usually adequate. The complete coverage of particular items may require the use of several positions and angles. Multiple cameras may be necessary when simultaneous activities among several interactants must be covered.

Whatever the requirements, camera positions which themselves produce subjective responses during analysis should be avoided. Cross-referencing shots taken with an outside camera to show the position of the research camera in the scene may be helpful.

The record will also be influenced by the researchers' decisions concerning time and sequence. In still photography specific criteria for such decisions are difficult to establish. Bateson (1942) attempted to release the shutter each time a movement occurred. In research by Collier and Buitron (1949) stills were taken as steps in technical production processes, e.g.

weaving, were carried out. For his studies of spacing, E. T. Hall takes photographs when arrangements alter among observed interactants.

In some circumstances arbitrary criteria can be established for automatic still coverage. Motor driven cameras can photograph specific scenes at set intervals, e.g. every second, every half minute, every minute, etc. Time-lapse photography with motion picture cameras is similar in effect. Frames of film can be exposed at intervals to cover patterns of movement over extended time periods. If, for example, a 1200-foot reel of 16-mm film is exposed at one frame per second, it will cover over 13 hours of activity. Time-lapse videotape coverage is similar in effect. A one-hour tape (when run at normal speed) may include information recorded at one scan per second during a seventy-two-hour period.

When film or videotape are used in the field, some of the problems associated with intuitive control in still photographic research can be overcome with records of total scenes in long sequences. During participant observation, the cameraman and/or ethnographer can usually determine segments within as well as inclusive limits of activity. He can then cover segments or total activities in their entirety.

Decisions concerning coverage must be related to questions concerning the adequacy of the record for effective analysis. What contextual data are required to ensure clarity during analysis? What factors affect the availability of the record? What tools are required for analysis?

The effective analysis of still photographs may depend upon the availability of comprehensive taped records or written accounts which provide contextual data. Motion picture film records in which extended segments of behavior are covered can be supplemented with written records, simultaneous still photographic records, and/or videotape records. When videotapes have been produced systematically over extended periods of time by remote control, information on the immediate context may be unavailable. If such information can be obtained, it can broaden perspective during analysis.

Still photographic and motion picture film must be developed before review. Still photographic positives can be developed in strips, framed into slides, or printed on paper. The first of these approaches is useful during analysis if the researcher wishes to view many pictures in sequence at relatively rapid rates. The second and third approaches are more appropriate when pictures are to be compared.

Cine film development processes vary depending upon the film type employed. When black-and-white negative film stock is used and synchronous sound is recorded, at least seven processing steps are recommended. Fewer steps are required with black-and-white reversal film.

Decisions concerning the use of one or another of these film stocks depend on the requirements of research. Under most circumstances the analyst will wish to decrease the number of steps between exposure and the production of final prints to retain definition. Reversal stock may be desired for this reason if frame numbers are to be added and few prints are required. But if the analyst expects to use many prints he will probably prefer negative film whether or not frame numbers are to be added.

Development time must be considered as well. In both photographic and film research (except Polaroid) a hiatus between recording and the viewing of data is necessary. Processes in still photography (for black-and-white film) permit the development of test strips in the field. Daylight development equipment can be used with special film to expedite field processing. Most photographic film, however, will be sent to a processing laboratory. Motion picture film must be sent to a laboratory. In the field this usually means an extended delay between recording and viewing.

Videotape need not be processed. The electronic signal is placed on the tape as the recording proceeds. Playback can follow once the tape has been rewound. As a result, the quality of the image can be checked, participants can view their behavior, and analysis can be initiated immediately after recording.

Durable records are crucial for most behavioral research. Still prints are relatively durable. They can be replaced at reasonable cost. Original negatives should be cross-referenced with adjunctive information and stored in a cool, dry, protected area. Research film prints made from master prints or negatives can be replaced as necessary. The original prints or negatives should be cross-referenced with adjunctive data and stored in unedited form in fireproof film storage centers (see Sorenson 1967). Videotape images on original tapes deteriorate relatively quickly during detailed analysis. For this reason it is absolutely necessary that master copies be stored and well protected. Duplicates can be produced by the researcher himself or an assistant with two connected recorders. These duplicates can be re-recorded a number of times from the master. To ensure permanence the tapes may be transformed to film. Improved kinescope techniques now permit the reproduction of 1-inch tapes on 16-mm film. (Techniques for the transferral of $1/2$-inch tapes are being developed.)

If analysis of recorded data is to be completed, certain equipment must be employed. Still projectors permit the analysis of slides. Stop-frame strip projectors are useful if the slides have been printed in strips. For the detailed analysis of 16-mm film records stop-frame analyzers are sometimes necessary, but regular projectors are also useful. Adequate 8-mm analyzer-projectors are available but are as yet unreliable.

Videotape recorders can be used for both playback and analysis. The facility with which the analysis can be completed is related to the size of the tape and the construction of the recorder. With $1/2$- and 1-inch machines tapes can be reviewed at the normal sixty scans per second. Stop position and slow speed controls are also available. An added advantage of the 2-inch machine at the present time is its ability to play back tapes at many times their normal speed as well as at the slower speeds. In the near future, high speed controls will be available on both 1-inch and $1/2$-inch equipment as well.

Computer technology connected to videotape equipment permits automation during analysis. Digital information can be placed on tapes on the "synchrony" lines between each scanned image without loss of information in the image. The tape itself can then be used to store and retrieve information upon request. Programs will be developed in the near future to "analyze" tapes without human intervention. Sensitizers will detect changes in degrees of light at each of many thousands of points on the videotape monitor. Computers will process information concerning those changes to indicate, say, movement of participants in a given space.

Given due consideration of the advantages of each VAV technique, their complementary use may be appropriate. Research examples indicate possible combinations.

Collier (1967) discusses complementary still cameras. Along with the standard 35-mm single lens reflex camera, the larger view cameras may be employed when contact prints which provide fine detail are required (e.g. in archaeological research). Rolleiflex cameras may be added for purposes of mapping and portraiture.

The conjunctive use of 35-mm still cameras and stationary 16-mm film cameras during field research has been discussed by Bateson and Mead (1942), Schwartz and Schwartz (1954), and Collier (1967). Mead and Bateson, in one of the first systematic attempts to use still photography and film in ethnography, shot long sequences of photographs. Intermittently they took forty-five second (or shorter) segments of film. The result was a relatively continuous record of daily events. Schwartz, Shargo (Schwartz), and Mead repeated this procedure with more sophisticated equipment. Collier discusses the use of photography as an introduction for filming. He suggests that photography can be employed both in educating participants and in researching the possibilities for filming. Peter Adair, Paul Byers, Sander Kirsch, and others have used photography to provide intermittent records during filming which can be cross-referenced with the film record during later analysis.

Photographic techniques, and videotape and film techniques, can be used conjunctively as well. In the Bronx research discussed above stills were taken to provide information on spacing, items in the environment, and participants. This information supplemented that gathered through the use of stationary videotape and film cameras.

The conjunctive use of portable and stationary film cameras may be helpful. A scene in a relatively confined space, for example, can be recorded in its entirety with cameras equipped with wide angle lenses and 1200-foot reels of film. Particular foci within the scene can be filmed by a well-trained, roving cameraman. William Heick employed two cameras in this way in his documentation of a Pomo curing ceremony (*The Sucking Doctor*, reported in Collier 1967:133–134).

Sixteen-millimeter film and videotape cameras can be used conjunctively to great advantage. In the Bronx research videotape cameras provided general records of extended sequences. They were also used to gather information on the context when intermittent films were taken. Further, videotape cameras provided an introduction to film equipment. Participants became so familiar with them that they quickly accepted the cine camera as well.

Multiple videotape cameras were also employed in the Bronx research. Stationary "close-up" cameras covered particular areas, e.g. a child's playpen, while wide angle cameras provided information on the total scene. Portable videotape cameras were used to introduce participants to the research and to record scenes which could not be covered with stationary cameras.

IMPLICATIONS OF THE USE OF VIDEOTAPE IN ANTHROPOLOGY

The third consideration related to the use of videotape in anthropology concerns the broader implications of its introduction as a research tool. Important among these are implications for investigations in the field, for analysis, for innovative research, for the presentation of results, and for teaching.

As a foundation for investigations in the field, researchers must state general goals, define specific interests, and develop appropriate procedures. The introduction of videotape may accompany improved strategies in these areas.

The description and analysis of "ideal forms" which an individual learns as a means of ensuring effective communication have been the goal of important research in anthropology during recent decades. The principle associated with this goal is that cultures are best viewed as sets of rules, as plans, or as symbolic systems which govern or organize behavior. Another goal of research in anthropology is the description and analysis of acts as they are observed to have occurred or as they can be objectively stated to have occurred by participants. Interests in precise statements concerning relations between individuals and items in their environment or concerning interaction among individuals in specified situations are related to this goal.

Videotape techniques may affect research on ideal forms. They permit the acquisition of records which, during interview-review by researcher and participant, stimulate and sharpen response. Videotape techniques are uniquely appropriate in research on the overt stream of activity. They permit the acquisition of comprehensive and precise records of such activity.

Today few anthropologists limit their concern to general sociocultural similarities and differences among widely differing peoples. Rather, they are interested in the definition of details as a foundation for the explanation of specific variables in complex systems, e.g. communication, social-structural, or ecological systems, so that intracultural behavioral regularities can be more clearly understood and subtle intercultural similarities and differences in behavior among closely related peoples can be identified. The result can be seen in research in which the precise definition of actors, the meticulous description and analysis of thought and activity, and the exact specification of the context of behavior are emphasized.

Videotape records provide necessary detail on the activity of individuals in specific contexts. As permanent records they permit analyses at various levels of focus in accordance with research interests.

Whatever the specific interests, researchers using videotape to obtain records of complex phenomena will develop sampling procedures during coverage. Three reasons may be cited: (1) as suggested in the section on ethics, videotape coverage of relatively private activity must be related to specific issues of proven importance; (2) total coverage of all activity is impractical if not impossible; and (3) the benefits of techniques associated with videotape can be fully realized if comprehensive records of random samples of activity are obtained to supplement records acquired during participant observation.

Adjustments in time scheduling and personnel will accompany the introduction of videotape techniques. The personal attachment between ethnographer and participant in the field will alter. When cameras cover activities of selected participants, continuous personal involvement may be replaced with intermittent contact. Novel roles for assistants will be created. Viewers must observe data transmitted from stationary cameras. Whenever possible, equipment must be handled and maintained by competent "field technicians." Videotape coverage by a single researcher will generate data for many analysts. As a result the ratio of observers to analysts will be altered.

Implications of the extensive use of videotape techniques related to the analysis of the record include the development and testing of sophisticated analytical operations, a demand for higher standards of proof, a revitalization of comparative research, and the adjustment of research facilities.

Two major approaches to the classification of "cultural things" have been employed in anthropology. In "emic" classifications the categorization of the data is considered appropriate only if it is isomorphic with that of the members of a particular society under investigation. In common practice in such classifications the content and context of distinguishable, meaningful segments are the same for both the scientist and the individual in a culture. The rules for determination of a segment need not necessarily be interchangeable. In "etic" classifications categories are developed prior to observation and "... depend upon phenomenal distinctions judged appropriate by the community of scientific observers" (Harris 1968:575). The distinctions need not be meaningful or appropriate to the participants.

The introduction of videotape as an analytical tool is of particular importance for etic classifications. The verification of etic categories is accomplished when "... independent observers using similar operations agree that a given event has occurred" (Harris 1968:575). The application of such operations to videotape records is appropriate. These records can be reviewed repeatedly during analysis. The intersubjective reliability of the operations can be checked. Further, although one may wish to ignore certain behaviors during etic analysis, such behaviors are not lost to the record. They may be included during later research if necessary or related to the behaviors to which etic operations have been applied.

Mathematical operations for the analysis of human behavior are increasing in importance in anthropology. Quantifiable information is now collected as a matter of routine by researchers of various theoretical persuasions. Higher standards of proof can be provided in certain of these investigations when appropriate operations are applied to videotape records. As mentioned above, computer techniques are also possible through their use. As researchers employ videotape records, in fact, they will require the development of such techniques.

Common arguments against the comparative method in anthropology may be summarized as follows: (1) the reliability of original data is often a limiting factor; (2) behaviors are interpreted apart from their context; (3) the units to be compared may not be comparable; (4) bias in analysis frequently influences results; and (5) shifting scientific interests make the reports unreliable at later times.

Videotape techniques can provide reliable records of some activity as it unfolds in the natural setting. Abstract descriptions from these records can include adequate factual data concerning exact referents. As mentioned above, precise data languages can be tested until agreement concerning the definition of comparable units has been reached, and analysts can check each other to ensure intersubjective reliability during analysis.

If sampling procedures are explicit, as implied above, sampling biases can be stated overtly during analysis. Whatever the bias in sample, the videotape record acquired by the sophisticated researcher under controlled circumstances will provide reliable original data.

Although extensive audiovisual records are subject to scientific fashion their appropriate production can alleviate its effects. If such records include sufficient data, they can be analyzed by researchers with varied interests either at the same or at different points in time.

To generalize, videotape implies the standardization of data collection and analytical procedures. Reliable comparative research requires such standardization.

Videotape records must be stored and reproduced if members of the scientific community are to use them for effective research. Videotape and film archives and libraries associated with central data banks may be appropriate in this regard. They could control the records in accordance with ethical consideration without unduly restricting legitimate research. If such institutions are not established, videotape records will remain the property of a few specialists (cf. Sorenson's paper, *infra*).

Videotape techniques will provide new ranges of data in anthropology. Based on such data, certain important strategies for the explanation of sociocultural phenomena can be given a fair test. Harris outlines one such strategy — cultural materialism — in his interpretative history of theories in anthropology (1968). Detailed studies of the relationship between cognition and behavior may follow the development of the techniques. The rules or patterns of cognitive calculus employed by individuals can be compared with actual behavior. Related debate with regard to communication and the performance of tasks may increase in significance.

Studies of particular ethnographic phenomena will be affected. Videotape is particularly appropriate for coverage of life in the domicile. Through its use the limits of research discussed by Oscar Lewis (1959, 1966), in which human observers were present in the household, and by Elizabeth Bott (1957), in which intensive interviews were substituted for first-hand observation of intra-household behavior, can be transcended.

More effective research in industrially based modern cultures will be possible. The subtle yet pervasive differences between members of urban cultures can be analyzed and discussed. Complicated behavioral arrangements in complex situations may be analyzed.

In field situations among primitive peoples the equipment can be used simply and effectively to provide extended coverage of selected, representative segments of activity with which the ethnographer is normally concerned. Specialized uses may include coverage of situations from which the ethnographer himself is excluded.

As videotape records in particular and audiovisual records in general increase in importance, the development of as yet untried publication procedures will be necessary. Sample videotape records may be distributed with written descriptive materials. Simple, cartridge-type videotape monitors such as those used for 8-mm film projection will be available for playback. Condensed records will increase in importance. Stills taken from tapes may be intensified by computers to sharpen images which are to be reproduced in book format.

Finally, the effects of videotape will be felt in the classroom. During class sessions students will be able to analyze vivid representations of phenomena from various cultures. Many points of view will be applied to the same data as discussions center on audiovisual materials in shared viewing situations. Potential researchers may prepare for field investigations by reviewing the lives of people similar to potential informant-participants. They will become familiar with physical appearance, verbal and nonverbal communication patterns, behaviors associated with activities, etc. before entering the field (cf. Hockings' paper, *infra*).

Instruction in the use and care of the equipment as well as in the training of assistants will be necessary. If the ethnographer himself does not intend to employ the techniques he may "team up" with a videotape researcher periodically in the field. An understanding of the capabilities of the instruments will be required for all concerned.

REFERENCES

BATESON, GREGORY, MARGARET MEAD
1942 *Balinese character: a photographic analysis.* Special Publications of the New York Academy of Sciences, volume two. New York: Academy of Sciences.

BOTT, ELIZABETH
1957 *Family and social network.* London: Tavistock.

BYERS, PAUL
1964 Still photography in the systematic recording and analysis of behavioral data. *Human Organization* 23:78–84.

COLLIER, JOHN, JR.
1967 *Visual anthropology: photography as a research method.* New York: Holt, Rinehart and Winston.

COLLIER, JOHN, JR., A. BUITRON
1949 *The awakening valley.* Chicago: University of Chicago Press.

DE HAVENON, ANNA-LOU
1969 "Authority patterns in Family 02." Unpublished seminar report, Columbia University.

HALL, EDWARD T.
1959 *The silent language.* New York: Doubleday.
1966 *The hidden dimension.* New York: Doubleday.

HARRIS, MARVIN
1964 *The nature of cultural things.* New York: Random House.
1968 *The rise of anthropological theory.* New York: Thomas V. Crowell.

HURLBERT, BEVERLY
1970 "Exercise in etic ethnography." Unpublished seminar report, Columbia University, New York.

JOSEPH, SUAD
1969 "Report on interviews with N and B." Unpublished seminar report, Columbia University, New York.

KANE, RONALD
1969 "Behavioral changes of siblings in Family 02 in the presence and absence of N." Unpublished seminar report, Columbia University.

LEWIS, OSCAR
1959 *Five families.* New York: Basic Books.
1966 *La vida.* New York: Random House.

MICHAELIS, ANTHONY R.
1955 *Research film in biology, anthropology, psychology and medicine.* New York: Academic Press.

RUEBHAUSEN, O. M., O. G. BRIM, JR.
1965 Privacy and behavioral research. *Columbia Law Review* 65: 1184-1211.

SANJEK, ROGER
1969 "Some aspects of authority in a black family." Unpublished seminar report, Columbia University, New York.

SCHAEFFER, JOSEPH H.
1970 *Videotape techniques in anthropology: the collection and analysis of data.* Unpublished doctoral dissertation, Columbia University, New York.

1972   "Cannabis Sativa and work in agriculture in a Jamaican community."
Unpublished report submitted to the National Institute of Mental
Health, Bethesda, Maryland.

SCHWARTZ, MORRIS S., CHARLOTTE G. SCHWARTZ
1954   Problems in participant observation. *American Journal of Sociology*
60:343-353.

SORENSON, E. RICHARD
1967   A research film program in the study of changing man. *Current
Anthropology* 8:443-469.

WESTIN, ALAN F.
1967   *Privacy and freedom.* New York: Atheneum.

The Film Elicitation Technique

STEPHANIE KREBS

This article outlines a technique rich in potential for social anthropological research — to utilize motion picture film to elicit conceptual categories of culture from members of the filmed society. Specifically, this technique employs film in structured interviews with native informants to discover how they conceptualize and categorize the phenomena of the world in which they live.

The technique itself is simple — to show an informant a carefully shot and edited film of some event or happening within his culture, and then through skillful questioning to discover how he himself structures that "slice of reality": the objects, people, ritual, or social relationships presented on the screen. Since the film can be run at normal speed, frozen at any particular point, projected in slow motion, or repeated over and over again, the researcher has maximum control over the event or set of relationships he is studying. The same film can be shown to many informants, different questions asked and a wide variety of levels of data obtained. With a film of a curing ceremony, the researcher may obtain the cosmology of the universe from the shaman, an accounting of the economics involved in the ceremony from the father of the patient, and why the cure works (or does not work) from the patient himself. The patient's grandmother may explain why the patient got sick to begin with, and point to a parti-

Research for this study was conducted in Bangkok, Thailand between August 1970 and May 1973 and forms the basis of my doctoral dissertation in social anthropology at Harvard University. Funds for this research came in part from the following sources: The Ford Foundation, The JDR 3RD Fund, National Institute of Mental Health Training Grant, the American Film Institute, and the Milton Fund, the Warren Fund, and the Comparative International Program, all three of Harvard University.

cular individual on the screen responsible for the illness. For all informants the film provides a focus frequently lacking in interviews without visual aids. To ask about an object, the researcher merely points it out on the screen. The informant MUST accept at least part of the screened event as reality, although he may correct the filmmaker-researcher: "You missed the important part; your camera should have been pointing over here to the right." In addition, in most cultures, the attraction and fascination of film as a medium provides an added incentive to the informant, particularly if the people shown and events depicted are familiar to him. Thus, if the film elicitation technique is employed skillfully, the researcher may obtain some of the most exciting data of anthropology — how members of a society conceptualize and structure the world in which they live.

In the first section below, the roots of this film elicitation technique will be traced to their origins in linguistics, ethnoscience, and earlier research using still photography and motion-picture film. The second section will describe how the film elicitation technique was developed, through recent research on how social norms and values of Thai society are communicated through Thai dance-drama. Although this section will not report specific research findings, it will indicate the problems encountered, their solutions, and the types of data obtained with each variation of the film elicitation technique. The third section will give pragmatic tips on using the technique in any study and will include a discussion of the most productive types of questions to be asked and the best projection equipment to be utilized. The fourth section will describe the qualities of a film which is well-shot and well-edited for this purpose, and give suggestions on how to obtain it. Finally, the fifth section will present possible future applications of this film elicitation technique to a variety of research interests.

1.   THEORETICAL ORIGINS OF THE FILM ELICITATION TECHNIQUE

The film elicitation technique relies heavily on linguistics and ethnoscience for its theoretical orientation and research method. First, the aims of the film elicitation technique echo basic theoretical concerns of ethnoscience and linguistics. Ethnoscience seeks to ascertain how members of a society experience, label, and structure the world in which they live (Sturtevant 1964), much as linguistics attempts to formulate the structural rules manifest in speech events. In like manner, the film elicitation technique attempts to discover how members of the filmed society perceive, describe, and pattern their world. Second, the interview procedure used in the film elicitation technique is adapted directly from linguistics, in particular, field linguistics (Harris and Voegelin 1953; Samarin 1967). To build a corpus of conceptual categories, the film elicitation technique employs such field interview procedures as "nontranslational linguistics" ("Tell me about..."); "interactive elicitation" ("What is this? Who made it? What is this part called?"); and the "word-to-text technique" ("One first elicits the names of objects and concepts in the area of the informant's competence and then asks him to talk about these things" [Samarin 1967: 83]).

The film elicitation technique also developed from earlier studies employing still photography and motion picture film. In most of these studies, the researcher used photographs or film to discover or illustrate analytical concepts of his own. The local informant had little or nothing to say about how the research photographs or films were interpreted, if he ever saw them. Nevertheless, this approach produced some meaningful studies. Most outstanding among research using still photography is, of course, Margaret Mead and Gregory Bateson's *Balinese character*, published over thirty years ago (Bateson and Mead 1942). Bateson and Mead employed rapid sequence photography (Mead 1956: 78–105), with detailed accompanying field notes, and shot about 25,000 photographs during two years fieldwork in Bali. Perusing this photographic record later became an experience shared between the two researchers, as they formulated and rechecked hypotheses away from the field. Many of these same photographs then served as data for other research, such as Mead and Macgregor's *Growth and culture* (Mead and Macgregor 1951), a comparative study of motor behavior of children in Bali and New Haven. Frances Macgregor's participation in this research adequately indicates that even without personally observing a culture, a researcher can extract valuable data directly from the photographic record itself. One reason for this is that a photograph often makes things available for study which could not or would not be consciously perceived otherwise. According to Paul Byers, in a still photograph, "we see relationships frozen that are, in life, too fleeting for our eyes" (Byers 1964:80–81). His work (Byers 1964; Mead and Byers 1968) and that of John Collier, Jr. (Collier 1967) certainly illustrate this principle well.

Unfortunately, research with motion picture film was not initially as fruitful as that using still photography. A number of studies (Bateson 1943:72–78; Erikson 1950:359–402; Wolfenstein and Leites 1950) which emerged during the forties and fifties dealt with the thematic analyses of feature films. Most of these studies were vividly colored by the recent experiences of America at war. This is not to say that the themes perceived by these researchers were necessarily incorrect, merely that their interpretations were expressed in value-laden terms. Perhaps these studies could be said to have suffered from not having a native informant handy to keep the researcher from getting carried away. Somehow the thematic interpretation of feature films left more room for free association on the part of the researcher than did the minute examination and interpretation of a large corpus of still photographs (cf. Weakland's paper, *supra*).

Later studies using motion-picture film have provided their own checks and balances within the data itself. Most of the recent important research on communication, social interaction, and proxemics (Birdwhistell 1970; Hall 1959, 1966; Scheflen 1965; Scheflen and Scheflen 1972; Watson and Graves 1966; etc.) could not have been done without film. These studies are based on extremely careful observation, counting, and rechecking, during which the film is sometimes projected frame-by-frame. Such powerful research tools as kinesics (Birdwhistell 1970) and choreometrics (Lomax 1968) could never have been developed without the aid of motion-picture film. The film elicitation technique owes a great debt to both these methods and the theory behind them—to kinesics for showing to what extent pattern exists in all communication, and to choreometrics for providing the analytic framework in which the film elicitation technique was first developed (cf. Section 2 below, and Prost's comment).

In addition to debts to the research noted above, the film elicitation technique owes much to the few filmic and photographic studies which introduced a key element into the research scheme — the native informant. In 1967, John Collier wrote: "Methodologically, the only way we can use the full record of the camera is through the projective interpretation by the native" (Collier 1967: 49). He based his statement on a number of studies, well-reported in his book *Visual anthropology* (Collier 1967), including research which he had conducted about twenty years earlier among the Otavalo Indians of Ecuador. An Otavalo Indian weaver agreed with some reluctance to be photographed weaving material ordered by the researchers. When they returned with the first set of contact prints, the weaver arranged the photos in the proper technical order, then stated that the researchers had done a bad job of recording his art. He asked Collier and his associate to shoot the sequence all over again and told them when to take each picture. In this manner, Collier and his associates obtained a truly extraordinary photographic sequence of weaving, with detailed interpretation accompanying each native-directed shot. In discussing his research, Collier suggests that a photograph gives informants something to focus on, helps establish rapport, keeps them on the topic, and makes interviewing easier and more productive. Most important, this type of interviewing with photographs helps the researcher uncover areas he never knew existed. Thus this study, and others like it, such as the aerial photography study of the Harvard Chiapas Project (Collier and Vogt 1965), were precursors of the film elicitation technique, for they sought the same goal — to discover, using photography, how a native informant structures and conceptualizes a piece of his world.

Sol Worth and John Adair (Worth and Adair 1972) used film instead of still photography to seek a similar goal. Worth and Adair believed that if they could teach people of another culture to make films they would do so "in a patterned rather than a random fashion, and that the particular patterns used would reflect their culture and their cognition" (Worth and Adair 1970: 9). To test this premise, they instructed seven Navaho in filmmaking. Worth and Adair tried to teach the basic mechanics of handling the camera and editing equipment, WITHOUT conveying American editing and shooting techniques (such as choice of subject, angle, frame, and length of shot; and for editing, order, length, and juxtaposition of takes). Although not entirely successful in this difficult endeavor (since even the most elementary mechanical instruction embodied some filmic concepts), they found that "in certain cases specific [Navaho cultural] patterns emerged DESPITE what we said in our instructions" (Worth and Adair 1972: 46). During and after the filmmaking process the researchers questioned the Navaho about their films, in an attempt to discover "how a group of people structure their world — their reality — through film" (Worth and Adair 1972: 7). They found, however, only a few Navaho cultural themes, most of which were already reported in anthropological literature, for their questioning was neither systematic nor thorough. Thus the value of Worth and Adair's study lies in their experiment of teaching members of another society to use film, rather than in working with what they produced to discover the "reality" of their world. The film elicitation technique picks up where they left off, for it provides a systematic procedure for uncovering the conceptual "reality" of the filmed culture's world.

2. THE DEVELOPMENT OF THE FILM ELICITATION TECHNIQUE

The film elicitation technique was first developed by myself during a specific study of the communication of social norms and values of Thai society through an ancient form of Thai dance-drama called Khon. Khon was viewed as a communication system derived from everyday Thai social interaction, and as such presented basic aspects of Thai life in highly stylized form. In fact, according to written materials on Thai dance, Khon was reputed to have an elaborate gesture language which communicated through dance movements the story of the drama at the same time as it was sung offstage. The aims of the research were threefold:

1. to discover whether or not Khon did communicate basic norms and values of Thai society, and if so, how;
2. to discover how native informants, both dancers and laymen, viewed Khon — how they named, categorized, and structured their dance-drama, and how they "read" the gesture language reputed to exist; and
3. to experiment with different forms of film eliciting in order to develop the film elicitation technique. This section will not report specific findings of my research, but rather will indicate how the film elicitation technique was developed, discussing the types of data obtained, the strengths, problems, and solutions in using several variations of the film elicitation technique.

Description and Preparation of Film Materials Used Initially

At an early stage in the research, a super-8-mm camera and sound-synchronized tape recorder were used to shoot several short color films of actual performance and practice sessions of Khon. The films, shot by the researcher-filmmaker, were generally composed of three-minute takes, and included a full-body view of all performers on stage at that time. After being sent to the United States for processing, the films were returned to Bangkok. During the general eliciting sessions (described more fully below), the films were projected by a super-8 sound projector which could be run forwards and backwards at normal speed or held with a single shot frozen on the screen. Unfortunately, however, there were serious technical problems with this super-8 equipment: it was difficult to reverse the projector to repeat certain sections of the footage, the machine did not start or stop easily, and it was impossible to shoot any segment of dance longer than three minutes, since all super-8 cartridges (developed for an amateur, not a professional, market) include only 50 feet of film. Informants who were dancers found it particularly disconcerting to see a dance end abruptly in the middle just because the film had run out.

Fortunately, The JDR 3RD Fund then made sufficient funds available to switch to 16-mm (professional) film size. An uninterrupted record of a complete Khon dance-drama was shot, in color with synchronized sound. The outdoor performance, presented by the finest dancers from the Thai government's College of Dramatic Arts, occurred as part of an actual cremation in a suburb of Bangkok. With the assistance of the United Nations Development Support Communication Service, I used four cameras and three tape recorders to make the record of the performance as complete as possible. The two main cameras (both Arriflexes, used by Thai cameramen) recorded an all-inclusive, constant view of the stage. The shooting of the cameras was staggered, so that while one was being reloaded the other would still be recording the continuing action. The cameramen were asked to shoot full 400 foot magazines of film (about eleven minutes' worth) without stopping, and to include, at all times, a full-body view of at least the main, and usually all, characters on stage. The cameramen performed this difficult task quite well, and generally resisted the temptation to zoom in for close-ups. Each of these Arriflexes was connected to a Nagra tape recorder, so that an accurate, synchronized, high-quality sound recording was made at the same time. I handled the third camera, a Bolex, for close-ups and cutaway shots to be used later in a more polished film of the performance. The fourth camera, another Arriflex with the third Nagra tape recorder, was focused on the audience. The Afghan cameraman in charge of this camera was asked to shoot long takes of full-body views of the audience standing watching the performance. At a later time this audience footage will be matched through its sound track to footage of the performance, for an analysis of audience reaction.

After the 16-mm film was processed, a workprint was made of all footage. The sound was transferred from quarter-inch recording tape to 16-mm magnetic tape, and a composite film record with corresponding synchronized sound was made of the whole performance, using footage from the two Arriflex cameras focused on the stage and an occasional shot from the Bolex. This composite workprint was then copied onto another piece of print stock, the sound was transferred to an optical track along the edge of the new print, and each frame of the print was numbered,[1] to aid in recording informants' responses to the film. Incidentally, this print is probably the only COMPLETE record in existence of an actual Southeast Asian dance performance.

This print formed the basis for most film elicitation interviews in the research and proved far superior to the earlier super-8 films. With the 16-mm film it was possible to employ a Steenbeck editing table instead of a projector. A Steenbeck has a small but adequate screen, reproduces

---

[1] I am indebted to Jacques Van Vlack of the Eastern Pennsylvania Psychiatric Institute for providing the frame numbers and assisting me in obtaining this print.

sound in magnetic or optical form, and projects film at normal speed, slow speed, frame by frame, or extremely fast speed for scanning purposes, forward or backward. This amount of control meant that a specific segment of film could be isolated precisely and rapidly for repeat projection. In fact, the Steenbeck was so easy to operate that one informant ran the machine himself, marking out dance structures directly.

General Eliciting

After good films were obtained, eliciting began. The aims of this early eliciting stage were to obtain a general overview of Khon, and to pinpoint the most interesting areas for future in-depth analysis. One informant was interviewed at a time, with either a super-8 film on the projector, or more satisfactorily, the 16-mm film on the Steenbeck. In this initial series of interviews, both dancers and laymen were interviewed, although the most valuable data were obtained from dancers. Interview sessions were forty-five minutes to two hours long, and were recorded on a small cassette tape recorder. Interviews were conducted in English, although Thai terms were recorded phonetically from the tape and later[2] checked by a bilingual assistant who also wrote the terms in Thai script.

Questions of identification were asked first. From the beginning I tried to elicit information without providing the categories for that information. For instance, rather than asking "What story is this?" I asked "What is happening?" Rather than asking "What is the name of this dance?" (which would assume that there was such a thing as "dance" and that it had a specific name), I asked "What is this called?" giving the informant the opportunity to interpret "this" as he wished. Of course it is nearly impossible to ask questions totally devoid of cultural loading; for instance the seemingly innocuous question "What are they doing?" implies that they are "doing" something, or if they aren't, they should be. However, some questions are more loaded than others, and for this early exploratory stage, questions which used as few researcher-defined categories as possible were desired.

But eliciting could not begin in a total vacuum. In thinking about questions for initial interviews, I drew upon data from an interesting experiment conducted by the Choreometrics Project of Columbia University

---

[2]   Although the grammatical flow of the questioning was in English, and the Thais interviewed spoke fluent English, most conceptual terms were obtained first in Thai, then translated, with the informants' help, into English.

using my own films of Khon. Alan Lomax and Forrestine Paulay, the director and assistant director of the Choreometrics Project, took certain choreometric categories, originally developed to analyze dance CROSS-culturally, and used them to analyze dance INTRA-culturally, by coding dance movements of the major characters in the films. These data proved invaluable for drawing up an initial set of open-ended questions, for it helped me to see these different character roles on a comparative basis, within a total Thai context.

The initial set of open-ended questions was adapted for each new informant's interest, fear, knowledge, and ability to conceptualize. Early in the research the assumption was made that dance-drama could be studied profitably on several different levels. Part of the initial interview with a new informant was spent in discovering the best level of questioning for that particular informant. Certain questions could be asked of dancers which could not be asked of laymen and *vice versa*. Most important, I had to remain flexible, to be ready at any moment to follow up new information with other questions designed to open up areas never before known to exist.

However, two questions, "Why?" and "What does that mean?" had to be used with great caution with both dancers and laymen. For example, an early issue in the research was whether or not dance movements had specific meanings that were recognized and labeled by Thais. To explore this matter, I selected a section of film and asked, "What does that mean?" Unfortunately, the passage first selected had no meaning for any Thai informant. But informants took interviews very seriously and felt obligated to "know the answer." To avoid losing face, several eager lay informants made up rather improbable stories. After hearing several of these, I finally realized that this question, applied to that particular passage, had no answer. So the question was changed to "Does the dance act out a story?" followed by "How? Show me how," which brought forth far more valid and interesting data. This revised question reversed roles; the researcher became the student to be taught where pattern existed in Thai dance, and the informant, no longer stuck with an unanswerable question, became the expert. Some informants actually demonstrated gestures and movements as well as pointing out where they appeared in the film.

Once it had been established that some movements could be identified and labeled as gestures by several informants, the research focused on how these gestures operated in context. I asked the most knowledgeable informant, "Do you as a dancer act out each word spoken by the narrator or sung by the chorus?" If asked initially, this question might have biased the data; however, it had already been established that some movements were seen to have specific meanings, and that this dancer was capable of dealing with such a question. To answer it, he selected a portion of film and showed me which words were acted out and which words were omitted.

Then I projected footage which the informant had not yet seen, and asked him to describe what each gesture meant. However, as an experiment, and to focus attention on the dance movements, I turned off the sound track. The informant immediately asked, "Where is the sound?" I answered "Oh, don't worry, I just turned it down for a moment, can you tell me what the movements mean without the sound?" The informant was a highly competent dancer, and had even performed this role himself. However, he hesitantly explained, since the dance had been shortened for this particular performance, he could not decode the movements without first hearing the words. So I projected the whole passage a second time with sound, and then a third time without sound. This time, having heard the sound once, the informant could decode the silent movements. Thereupon he explained an extremely important characteristic of Khon: a specific movement or gesture can have up to twenty different meanings, depending on the context in which it appears. Once the informant was familiar with the context in which the gesture occurred, i.e. once he had heard the words of the story, he could assign the proper meaning to the movement, even though he could no longer hear the words. But knowing the context was crucial to the interpretation of the gesture.

Thus, the general eliciting sessions confirmed that Khon does have an elaborate gesture language. Also, since a single gesture (a *tiibot*) may have up to twenty different meanings, the context in which the gesture appears must be known in order to interpret its meaning precisely. These two discoveries led to the *tiibot* test, which of all the research, would probably be considered the most elegant according to the criteria of ethnoscience.

The Tiibot *Test*

Having heard that each dance gesture (a *tiibot*) could possess so many different meanings, and suspecting that these clumps of meaning might represent important conceptual relationships in Thai culture, I immediately sought to obtain the names and meanings of all *tiibot* used in the dance-drama. Unfortunately, however, these gestures had never before been recorded on film or even written down in a list. Several dancers agreed that such a record should exist. So they consented to make a thirty-minute silent film with me, illustrating all basic *tiibot* used in Khon, as performed by the four main character roles: male, female, demon, and monkey.

Four dancers, each expert in one of the main character types, were selected by my chief dancer-informant to do the demonstrations. Two senior dancers directed and corrected the demonstrations, thereby ensuring that the movements recorded on film were of the highest possible quality. The dancer-informant drew up the list of all *tiibot* to be filmed; this list was constantly corrected and enlarged by many other dancers who just happened to remember something else which should be included. The dancer-informant also directed the shooting, telling me when to start and stop the camera. I filmed full-body shots of each *tiibot*, which lasted from three to fifteen seconds, depending on the particular *tiibot* and the character performing it (monkey gestures were extremely fast, male *tiibot* very slow and dignified).

After the film was processed, the dancer-informant made a preliminary identification of all *tiibot* on the Steenbeck. Then fifty gestures, as performed by one or two character roles per *tiibot*, were selected and shown to seven senior dancers for full identification. The *tiibot* were projected one at a time. After seeing each gesture the dancers wrote down (in Thai) all the possible meanings which that *tiibot* could ever have on stage. These lists were then pooled and translated into English with great care. Finally, the footage was made into a finished thirty-minute, color, silent film, with Thai and English titles identifying all gestures.[3]

As I had previously suspected, clumps of meaning associated with some *tiibot* did indeed represent important conceptual relationships of Thai culture. For instance, one gesture had the following meanings:

to respect highly	to honor
to invite (royalty or a patriarch)	father
owner of the land (i.e. the king)	deferential
in a high place	esteem
to hold above one's own head or to receive their majesties' command	most honorable

This clump of meanings obviously results from old Thai society, one of the most hierarchical of all hierarchical societies, where, on the secular level, the king was all-powerful, controlling even life itself (i.e. "owner of the land"). On the family level, the father was considered to be the top of the hierarchy. Both king and father were to be respected, honored, and

---

[3] For distribution information, contact Stephanie Krebs, 300 Highland Street, West Newton, Massachusetts 02165, U.S.A.

esteemed in the highest possible manner, and deferred to with great humility. All of these meanings are associated within this same *tiibot*, and express a set of values absolutely central to Thai culture.

Analysis of Character Attributes

Up to this point discussion has centered on employing the film elicitation technique with individual informants or a small group. However, the technique can also be employed with a large group of informants, although the data obtained are of a very different nature. Working with 200 or 300 people at the same time requires that answers must be written, not oral, and that the questions asked must be clear and rather simple. There is no opportunity to follow up an interesting response with another question, for the researcher cannot process all the responses until hours after the end of the exercise. Also, if he is working in a foreign culture, controlling the mechanics of the physical surroundings of the eliciting session can be much more difficult while working with a large group than while working with an individual.

In the Khon research, the film elicitation technique was used twice with large groups. During the general eliciting sessions, informants had frequently described main characters of the drama in fairly stereotyped fashion. In addition, the choreometric analysis of these main characters had indicated that the characters moved very differently. I wanted more information about Thai stereotypes of these characters to compare with the choreometric analysis, to see if certain characters expressed some norms and values of Thai society and not others.

Therefore the complete 16-mm performance film of $1^1/4$ hours was shown to students at a liberal arts and language college near Bangkok. After viewing the film, the students were asked to describe two of the main characters in the performance. Each student was asked his age (fifteen to twenty years old), sex, but not his name. Answers, ranging from a few words to a whole page, were written in Thai and later translated by a bilingual assistant. The answers were interesting, but difficult to work with, since students had interpreted this rather open-ended request for character descriptions in various ways.

So I made the request more specific. Using many of the words from the first group of students' descriptions, my bilingual assistant and I carefully composed a list of twenty attributes which could be applied to all major roles shown in the film. Then the same film was shown again, this time to students from the College of Dramatic Arts in Bangkok, some of whom were studying to be dancers. They were asked to rate the characters before and after the film on the twenty attributes. Thus it was possible to study (1) the original stereotypes of the characters, and (2) how these stereotypes changed after students had seen the specific episode presented in the performance film. Later these character role stereotypes can be compared with the choreometric profiles.

Eliciting with Still Photographs

Although the film elicitation technique was developed primarily through research with motion-picture film, it was also used quite productively with still photography in an analysis of the norms and values supporting the proxemic arrangement of characters on the Thai stage and in everyday Thai society. In the first instance where still photography was used with the film elicitation technique, I visited a Thai dance class and asked an informant (who was a dancer and a teacher) to direct the students so that interesting photographs could be obtained. Under the informant's supervision, the students assumed positions in several typical stage formations, such as the army waiting for its commander-in-chief. After the photographs were printed, the informant described why particular characters were shown sitting in proxemic relation to each other, and I discovered that I was eliciting many of the norms and values which govern social status in Thai society.

Next, I asked that informant to help photograph politeness and impoliteness in everyday dyadic interactions. After asking another dancer to assist him, the informant placed himself and the other dancer in carefully composed scenes. Although the resulting photographs looked extremely stiff and unreal to me, when explained by the informant they yielded much interesting data about what is consciously recognized as polite and impolite in Thai society.

Channel by Channel Elicitation

The final variation of the film elicitation technique yielded the most precise and technically complex data of all the research. Several five to ten minute segments were selected from the complete 16-mm performance film. Viewed on the Steenbeck, each segment was analyzed according to the content and form of four different communication channels operating within it: musical, gestural, proxemic, and verbal. For the gestural channel, a knowledgeable dancer-informant and I looked very closely at how gestures operated in context. Using the frame numbers shown on the film, the informant noted, named, and gave specific meanings (whenever possible) for all movements recognized as gestures shown in the selected segments. Some gestures were found to have no verbal referents, but rather expressed the feeling or relation of the "listening" character to the "acting" character in a particular passage. In analyzing the musical channel, my informant and I paid special attention to which rhythms were used for different characters. We also noted the presence of all "action tunes", songs used for certain specific characters or situations. In the analysis of the proxemic channel, we noted which door, right or left, was used for most entrances and exits of "good" characters and which was used for "bad" characters. (In Thai culture, right is "good" and left is "bad," or at least "less good.") The informant also told me why some characters' heads were higher than others in certain scenes. The informant's statements confirmed my supposition that in Thai culture status is often physically expressed on a vertical plane by the relative height of the heads of individuals in an interaction. Finally, for the verbal channel, the informant and the bilingual assistant, well-trained in Thai literature, described the multiple meanings of words used in the spoken and sung portions of the dance-drama. Thus, through channel-by-channel elicitation the dance-drama was taken apart, in order to study what was being conveyed through these four different communication modes.

Thus, Section 2 has recounted how the film elicitation technique was first developed and used in one particular study. Variations of the technique have been described, such as eliciting with experts versus laymen, with individuals versus groups, with open-ended questions versus questionnaires, and with oral versus written responses. For the benefit of other researchers, these variations have been reported in some detail, because it is difficult to design a comprehensive strategy for the full range of studies in which the film elicitation technique might be applied. Nevertheless, it is possible to formulate nonspecific guidelines for using the technique in most studies. It is hoped that the researcher wishing to employ this technique will find these guidelines (to be described below) and the preceding narrative helpful in adapting the technique to his own research interests.

3.　GUIDELINES FOR USING THE TECHNIQUE IN ANY STUDY

Having first selected the general area of study and obtained the relevant film materials, the researcher should identify the most crucial issues of the research and decide what levels of data might best illuminate those issues. If the researcher decides that some of the relevant data include how the informant conceptualizes the event shown on the screen, the first real problem looms large: How does the researcher discover the informant's conceptual categories without knowing what they are? And secondly, how does the researcher elicit those categories without using his own culture's words or concepts, thereby "contaminating" the informant?

Using some of the following questions in initial eliciting sessions with new informants may help solve these problems:

1. "Tell me about..."
2. "Does that have a particular name?" or, better yet,
    "Do any of those have particular names?"
3. "How would you describe that?"
4. "How do you think person X would describe that?"
5. "What is happening now?"
6. "What else is related to that?"

Once the researcher begins to discover some of the informant's conceptual categories, the researcher can use these categories in new questions, such as "Is that also an X, or is it something else?" In fact, a researcher should not begin any eliciting session without a good list of different types of questions. Then if one level of questioning does not produce interesting data from a particular informant, another type of question can be asked. Fifteen minutes into the eliciting session, nothing is more disconcerting than suddenly not being able to think of any more questions!

The first eliciting sessions of a new study should be exploratory in nature. Only a few informants should be interviewed. After several such sessions, the researcher will discover what makes a good informant and what issues are the most important. Then, eliciting may become much more specific and precise, and detailed information may be sought. At that point those two dangerous questions "Why?" and "What does that mean?" may be used sparingly with knowledgeable and articulate informants. Unlike linguistics which deals with a code shared by all members of a culture, research employing the film elicitation technique may deal with events regarded as falling in the domain of specialists. Therefore, if a researcher really wishes to know why a curer does certain things, he should ask not the patient but the curer himself, while showing him a particularly interesting section of film. And then the curer may or may not tell him.

Thus research should proceed from exploratory eliciting sessions with one informant at a time to more detailed eliciting about specific topics. During the final stages of the study, the researcher may wish to check data obtained from earlier interviews or his own hypotheses through eliciting sessions with large groups of informants who write answers to a few carefully-worded questions, after viewing selected portions of the total film material used in the research.

All eliciting sessions conducted with individual informants should be recorded on tape. A small portable cassette recorder works sufficiently well for this purpose. Following each eliciting session, and if possible before the next, the researcher should transcribe the tape, and adapt his questions accordingly, much as a field linguist would review the corpus he had just collected and plan his next eliciting session.

For projecting the film, the researcher wants the maximum possible amount of physical control over the material. The best machine for this purpose is the "baby" Steenbeck editing table. The screen is large and bright enough to show details clearly, and the fast forward and fast backward controls make it possible to isolate rapidly and precisely segments of film for repeat projection. Most important, a Steenbeck does not rip the film. Although I have had no experience with other brands of editing tables, they may be equally good. Many researchers doing analysis of body movement use special analyzer projectors or reconverted old Bell and Howell projectors with special hand cranks added, but I feel that a baby Steenbeck is far superior to such arrangements. A Moviola editing machine could be used, but the film would be in shreds by the end of a few eliciting sessions; and the screen size and resolution of most viewers (paired with a set of rewinds) are not adequate for this purpose. So the baby Steenbeck is currently the ideal piece of projection equipment for eliciting with one or two informants at a time. Of course a projector would have to be used if the researcher were eliciting with a large group of informants.

4. SELECTING AND PREPARING FILMS

Many films cannot profitably be used with the film elicitation technique. Alan Lomax, Ray Birdwhistell, and Jacques Van Vlack frequently have demonstrated the extent to which many other Western filmmakers obstruct the observer's view of another culture by cutting according to Western concepts of time, by zooming in on a person's face to the exclusion of 90 percent of the rest of the body, or by abruptly ending the shot because the cameraman gets embarrassed and cannot bear to watch the action any longer. Some films are so badly shot and edited that the viewer learns more about the filmmaker than about the culture presented in the film! If the researcher is eliciting in the same culture which produced the film, such a superbiased record of human behavior might be useful. In this case the informant would be reacting to the film of the event more than to the event itself. And if the researcher were studying how an informant conceptualizes film, such a film could be helpful. However, for most studies such a film document would be at worst useless, and at best misleading. So in selecting a film to use with the film elicitation technique a good rule of thumb is to find a film which places the fewest obstacles between the informant and the events shown on the screen.

Frequently the best (and sometimes the only) way to obtain such a film is to shoot it oneself or to have someone else do it under close supervision. If the researcher is preparing his own films, the following points may be helpful:

1.   Try to set up the filming situation carefully so that the act of filming does not alter the event significantly.

2.   Shoot long, wide-angle takes of the event to be studied. Focus on the main characters, but be sure to include other objects or people who may eventually be crucial to the unfolding of the event.

3.   If there is not enough film to record the complete event, shoot several long passages of action, so that the informant can describe the pattern of the event within each passage. (Some informants may then be able to report what happens in between passages as well.) Do not chop the event up into unidentifiable short bits.

4.   Do not edit or cut a shot off arbitrarily. If possible, find the natural ending of the sequence within the material itself.

If the researcher is preparing a film for use in a culture which has had no previous film-viewing experience, he must shoot and prepare the film even more carefully. In addition to the shooting and editing points mentioned above, the following should be considered:

1.   Set up the camera in one basic position and leave it there;

2.   Do not vary the angle of shooting or the size of the object being filmed;

3.   Do not zoom in or out while the camera is running;

4.   Do not edit out action.

Eliciting with film in a culture which has had no previous film-viewing experience would present many problems, for the researcher would first have to introduce his informants to the medium of film before he could even begin to elicit how they perceived the events shown on the screen.

5. POSSIBLE FUTURE APPLICATIONS OF THE TECHNIQUE IN OTHER STUDIES

The film elicitation technique could be used profitably in a wide variety of studies, such as the analysis of a curing ceremony, greeting behavior, or an initiation ritual. By filming an artist creating a painting, and then asking him carefully about each stage, the uses of certain colors, shapes, etc., the researcher could elicit the basic aesthetics of art in a particular culture.

The technique could be especially valuable for research that would benefit from different views of the same event. For instance, in a study of family therapy, a sound-synchronized film of a single therapy session could be prepared. During eliciting sessions with this material, each therapy participant, including the analyst, could be asked what he or she felt, thought, or concluded other participants really meant at key points in the therapy session. The researcher could use these data with kinesic or proxemic analyses of the same key points to obtain a many-faceted view of the dynamics of the therapy process. In the same fashion, studies of bargaining behavior in a Mexican market, of teaching in a racially-mixed school, of political decision-making in a community meeting, of the testing of a new curriculum in an open classroom, or of behavior in a group dynamics class could all find the film elicitation technique a real boon to imaginative research.

REFERENCES

BATESON, GREGORY
  1943 Cultural and thematic analysis of fictional films. *Transactions of the New York Academy of Sciences, Series II*, 5:72–78.
BATESON, GREGORY, MARGARET MEAD
  1942 *Balinese character*. New York: The New York Academy of Sciences.
BIRDWHISTELL, RAY L.
  1970 *Kinesics and communication: essays on body motion communication*. Philadelphia: University of Pennsylvania Press.
BYERS, PAUL
  1964 Still photography in the systematic recording and analysis of behavioral data. *Human Organization* 23:78–84.
COLLIER, GEORGE, EVON Z. VOGT
  1965 "Aerial photographs and computers in the analysis of Zinacanteco demography and land tenure." Paper presented at the 64th Annual Meeting of the American Anthropological Association, Denver, 1965; mimeographed.

COLLIER, JOHN, JR.
1967 *Visual anthropology: photography as a research method.* New York: Holt, Rinehart, and Winston.

ERIKSON, ERIK H.
1950 "The legend of Maxim Gorky's youth," in *Childhood and society* by Erik H. Erikson, 316–358. New York: W. W. Norton & Company Inc.

HALL, EDWARD T.
1959 *The silent language.* Garden City: Doubleday.
1966 *The hidden dimension.* Garden City: Doubleday.

HARRIS, ZELLIG S., C. F. VOEGELIN
1953 Eliciting in linguistics. *Southwestern Journal of Anthropology* 9:59–75.

LOMAX, ALAN
1968 *Folk song style and culture. A staff report on cantometrics.* Washington: American Association for the Advancement of Science. Publication 88.

MEAD, MARGARET
1956 "Some uses of still photography in culture and personality studies," in *Personal character and cultural milieu* (third edition). Edited by D. G. Haring, 78–105. Syracuse: Syracuse University Press.

MEAD, MARGARET, PAUL BYERS
1968 *The small conference.* The Hague: Mouton.

MEAD, MARGARET, FRANCES MACGREGOR
1951 *Growth and culture: a photographic study of Balinese childhood.* New York: G. P. Putnam's Sons.

SAMARIN, WILLIAM J.
1967 *Field linguistics.* New York: Holt, Rinehart and Winston.

SCHEFLEN, ALBERT E.
1965 *Stream and structure of communicational behavior.* Eastern Pennsylvania Psychiatric Institute Behavioral Studies, Monograph 1. Philadelphia.

SCHEFLEN, ALBERT E., ALICE SCHEFLEN
1972 *Body language and the social order: communication as behavioral control.* Englewood Cliffs: Prentice-Hall.

STURTEVANT, WILLIAM C.
1964 Studies in ethnoscience. *American Anthropologist* 66:99–131.

WATSON, O. MICHAEL, THEODORE GRAVES
1966 Quantitative research in proxemic behavior. *American Anthropologist* 68:971–985.

WOLFENSTEIN, MARTHA, NATHAN LEITES
1950 *Movies; a psychological study.* Glencoe: The Free Press.

WORTH, SOL, JOHN ADAIR
1970 Navaho filmmakers. *American Anthropologist* 72:9–34.
1972 *Through Navaho eyes: an exploration in film communication and anthropology.* Bloomington and London: Indiana University Press.

COMMENT *by J. H. Prost*

This paper opens a world of uses for film. There is nothing new in using film to elicit responses from informants: Darwin did it more than a century ago. The author describes how film can serve 1) as a memory device, having an actor recall his intentions as he observes something he did, 2) as a standardization tool, having people comment on the same filmed "slice of reality," and 3) as a vehicle for experimental control, having an informant respond to a film where one or another variable has been controlled, either a doctored film or a simulated portrayal. What is most intriguing with the "film elicitation technique" is that a researcher can explore the full variety of "meanings" among his informants, held individually or in concert, explore the foci of consistency and inconsistency, and show that "culture" rarely is a monolithic entity.

Audiovisual Tools for the Analysis of Culture Style

ALAN LOMAX

The electronic and chemical storage of sound and image makes available
to the scientist, layman, and student a vast but also rather bewildering
display of the varied behavioral patterns of mankind. Today the viewer
can observe the dances, work rhythms, and social interaction of most
branches of the human family and the record collector can listen to songs
and music from every corner of the globe, and yet they may emerge not
much the wiser for these experiences. Because there is no accepted method
for consistently reading out the information about culture certainly stored
in these recordings, they play a secondary, even a minor, role in social
science and in education. Too often ethnographic films merely illustrate or
supplement written accounts and analyses or serve as a substitute field
experience. It is for this reason, I believe, that the fascinating documentary
films and recordings of the past lie unused on archive shelves, while field
crews take more new footage for a public that, even in universities, remains
largely indifferent.

It is surprising that, in this age of visual and audible information
transmitted from a distance, so little has been done to describe and
compare the filmed patterns of movement and interaction, to map their
geographical ranges, and to relate them to their social and cultural settings.
This is certainly one reason that film has played a minor role, up to now,
in social science teaching and research. Even in humanities departments, in this age of global politics and unhappy cultural minorities, there
are few courses that attempt to put the life styles of the world's peoples in
perspective. At the same time, there is a growing awareness of the
interrelatedness of aesthetic pattern to social problems and of the
importance of informal, extraverbal communication systems in

understanding man's social behavior and his cultural diversity.

The contemporary breakup and destruction of mankind's varied cultural heritage is accelerating the pollution of the human environment, and it is a notorious fact that the mass media — film and the phonograph, radio and television — have hastened the process. Indeed, the camera and the recording machine have not lived up to their promise to secure a multicultural future and to make room for the development of the whole range of human expressive traditions. On the contrary, film, records, radio, and television have all, in their different ways, served to centralize culture, silence minorities, and put ersatz, marketable fads in the place of genuine style. Even with the best of intentions the Western inventors of the electronic media have used them not to foster the growth of other cultures, but to aggrandize their own. The result is an imperialism of the media which threatens the whole of man's environment — his cultural heritage.

Part of the solution is political and ethical. We must struggle for a cultural equity in the communication system as earlier generations struggled for political freedom and economic justice. Here one stumbling block is that we know so little about the relationship between culture and society on the one hand and communication on the other. Nor does the educational system, as it is presently structured, provide the answer.

Even universities are largely monocultural, concerned with teaching the values of urban civilization, especially of Western Europe and America. Those who come from other cultures — including the principal subcultures of America — to prepare themselves as teachers, eventually return to their people, armed with the authority of the college degree, to convert their brothers to Euro-American ways: they teach ballet movement in West Africa, block harmony in the Hebrides, and bel canto in Alabama. They spread abroad the feeling that the arts and the ways of their own people are somehow uncouth and inferior. Even when these Western-trained cadres set up and administer their own educational and communication systems, more often than not they use them to purvey values and standards foreign to their own heritage. The recent severe disturbances in the American school system have shown that black as well as white teachers are ill-prepared to respond to the cultural aspirations of the Afro-American.

Two reasons for this anomalous situation can be suggested. First, as long as the relationship between communication and social structure, as well as between the verbal and nonverbal communication systems, remained obscure, it has been impossible to design a panhuman or species-general rather than culture-bound educational solution. Second, the methods for describing and evaluating expressive behavior were originally devised for the European arts. The several dance and music notations are replication systems and *aides-mémoire* of service to the European performer, but inadequate for the analysis and comparison of exotic cultural styles. By the same token filmmakers, even when they are trained anthropologists, are first and foremost trained in the tradition of Western humanism and are influenced by the framework of European dramatic and visual conventions. Western documentary crews, with Western audiences in mind, normally photograph and edit the movement and interaction of other cultures to fit Western standards of tempo, length, and form. Thus even the documentary film can function to obscure, rather than illuminate, exotic cultural patterns.

This kind of visible censorship is usually unintentional and occurs outside of awareness. Usually the individual is blamed, and this is endlessly discussed by filmers. Actually the problem lies at a more general and accessible level. Each one of us lives and relates to others within the stylistic framework inculcated by our culture. Without the means of becoming aware of and controlling visible and audible preference patterns of ourselves and others, filmmaking, even by ethnographers, must continue to be culture-bound. This is where the work of cantometrics and choreometrics has, I hope, something to offer the filmmaker.

My group has spent ten years in developing a method for locating and comparing the factors that shape the audiovisual performance patterns of mankind. We are now preparing tape and film loop systems from which others can learn to use these methods. However, behind our work at Columbia University lie three decades of fundamental study of communication of which the reader should be aware.

Basic here is the discovery that all communication is a multichanneled, continuous, flowing interchange dependent upon learned and formally organized systems. In other words, communication is context-dependent. Gregory Bateson and Margaret Mead pioneered with their photographic studies which demonstrated that Balinese adult drama could not be understood outside of the context of child-rearing practices. The interplay of roles and development of dramatic action into trance by the Balinese village company reflected the peak moments of rejection and of anger in the maturational experience of the Balinese; all this was exquisitely illustrated in two parallel series of photographs (Bateson and Mead 1942).

In the 1950's the work of the structural linguists, e.g. George L. Trager and Henry Lee Smith, Jr. (1951), of Trager on paralanguage (1958), of Ray L. Birdwhistell on kinesics (1952), and of Edward T. Hall on proxemics (1959) showed that every human communicational situation was the focus of several systems as formally organized as grammar itself.

The 1956 Palo Alto conference brought anthropologists, linguists, and psychiatrists together for the first time in an intensive study of the multi-communicational content of filmed behavior. There was agreement that structures in bodily communication could be recorded that were comparable to those found in language — in other words, that the visible stream could be analyzed into small units like kines and kinemes and larger entities like words, phrases, and sentences.

In *The natural history of an interview*, Charles Hockett and Norman A. McQuown (n.d.) produced a fine-grained linguistic analysis of the vocal stream, which Birdwhistell was able to match and reproduce independently in his kinesic transcription. Further work by Birdwhistell established the existence of formal kinesic "linguistic" systems with junctures, pronominal markers, and the like, which can support or run contrary to the verbal stream. (Birdwhistell's *Kinesics and context* [1970] contains the papers that cover this whole period.)

Birdwhistell's students have continued to open up this field. Paul Byers has developed a technique for the analysis of human interaction in series of still photographs (Mead and Byers 1968). Albert Scheflen has demonstrated that the therapeutic process of psychoanalysis has a predictable structure as formal as that of a poem or a sonata (Scheflen 1965). Scheflen is now applying this kinesics technique to the study of complete filmed records of several different family traditions in an urban setting. Here the television camera runs in one kitchen for days without stopping, until it becomes a friend of the family. Review of these remarkably candid records reveals the peak moments of family interaction; these are then filmed on conventional 16-mm film to provide the definition needed for fine-grained analysis. In one of the studies of this material, Anna-Lou de Havenon has shown that the authority ranking of family members is a direct function of the amount of food each one dispenses at mealtimes.

William Condon uses the kinesics approach to study human interaction at the level of 1/25 and 1/40 of a second. Condon first makes a detailed phonetic record of the speaker in a scene. This microphonetic record becomes his base line. He then studies the speaker's bodily behavior phone by phone, frame by frame, using a stop-motion projector. He has found that the body parts of every speaker move in rhythm to his own phonation and that all those within earshot conduct their body movements in the most precise synchrony with those of the speaker. Condon has confirmed Birdwhistell's discovery that all communication is a function of social context. In order for one person to understand what another person says, he must be "in tune" with him. Condon finds that such interpersonal synchrony is far more fine-grained than that of any *corps de ballet* (Condon and Ogston 1966). Most recently Condon has discovered, in work with day-old babies, that they fall into rhythmic bodily synchrony with human vocalization, thus indicating that language learning begins kinesically long before the onset of speech.

All these studies emphasize the social nature of communication. They depend upon two frequently neglected truisms: that an act of communication must involve at least two persons interacting within the context of some socially acknowledged symbolic system, and that all acts of communication are multimodal, with two or three channels and/or levels in simultaneous and complementary operation.

Birdwhistell (1970) divides the communication stream into two main parts: (1) the informational and referential, and (2) the cross-referencing and identifying. Most studies of language and art and, in fact, most investigations in kinesics as well, have dealt with the first half of the communication system, whose prime function is to specify and define the new information that is going on the air. They have neglected the second and far larger half of the communication stream, whose function is to identify those present to each other, to define the context of the communication, and thus to keep it going. In Birdwhistell's view, this integrative activity occupies something like 90 percent of the communication space. Its prime characteristic is redundancy. Its prime function is to maintain communication. (Indeed, it is in this cross-referencing, redundant stream that the information about culture patterns may be found.) This is the aspect of communication that is of special interest to the comparativist, to the student of the performing arts, and to the maker of ethnographic films. It is these identifying envelopes of audible and visible behavior which the filmmaker captures and can present with his recording devices. If he is aware of these culturally inherited patterns of redundancy, he can record them more accurately and convey them with fewer distortions to his audience.

The comparative analysis of the performing arts can be of great advantage to the student of communication. Song and dance, like other expressive behavior, is distinguished from other types of communication by being more formally organized and more repetitive. The acts of singing and dancing are highly synchronous, joint communications, dependent for their success first of all on how strictly the actors conform to the pre-established rules of the genre. Because they are public communications, addressed to a group, they must be devoted to a message form and content simultaneously acceptable to the many. This means that the modalities of the communication must be confined to the channels and the qualities with which the audience can most strongly identify. Trager (1958) has argued that the stable and redundant features of paracommunication are societal and cultural indicators. If this be true, the principal symbolic function of the super-redundant rhythmic arts is to present and define the norms of the cultures in which they are found. This idea has been amply confirmed by our cross-cultural survey of song and dance in context. In an area that was formerly seen as elusive and hard to define, we have found rock-steady patterns of behavior which clearly and continuously differentiate both expressive traditions and the social and cultural systems they symbolize (Lomax 1968).

Choreometrics and cantometrics are empirical descriptive devices by means of which the gross characteristics of movement style (especially dance) and musical style (especially song) can be analyzed and compared cross-culturally. An example of the choreometrics rating sheet is given in Table 1. Each system is backed up by a book of definitions established during the pilot stage of the work. The experts who rated the first sample of performances made their ratings conform to these definitions as they worked. The definitions and the parameters emerged from a period of comparative work on a representative sample of material from the whole world.

Because the rating systems dealt with the relative presence or absence of visible and audible characterizers in behavior, we found that they could be taught more readily from film and tape loop than from books of coding instructions. In the case of cantometrics, for example, even when we were dealing with such matters as predominant rhythmic type or relative strength of accent, untrained coders achieved 80 to 90 percent agreement after a few minutes of work. Within a few days serious students were able to learn the whole system from the training loops. This meant that they quickly established an expert acquaintance with all the ranges of human song performance.

The human ability to recalibrate perceptual frames from context to context was here refocused on a world context and the student learned to relate his judgments to panhuman ranges instead of to those of his own culture, along scales such as the following:

Volume: (1) Soft   (2) Moderate   (3) Loud
Size of Stride: (1) Short   (2) Medium   (3) Long

Each of the rating systems produces a profile that portrays the salient characteristics of the whole of a performance style used all the way through a stretch of singing or moving. Because these profiles are numerical, they can be assembled into average or modal profiles that portray the dominant pattern of cultures, culture areas, and culture regions (see Tables 1 and 2). The speed of the rating system made it possible to dip into vast libraries of tape and film and to put together a portrait of world performance style within a relatively short time.

Table 1. Choreometric profiles of the Eskimo and the Dogon dance styles (from Lomax 1968: 249, 257)

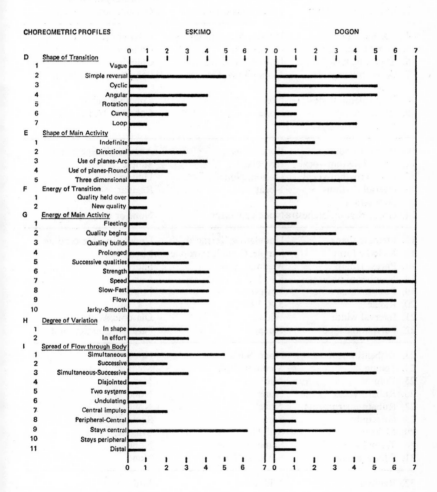

Table 2.   Cantometric profiles of North American and African song performances (from Lomax 1968: 330,332)

Cantometric Profiles	North America	Africa
Name of coding line	**Main traits**	**Main traits**
1. Vocal group	Unison, Solo	Overlap, Alternation
2. Orchestral relationship	Accompanying, None	Accompanying, Complementary or None
3. Instrumental group	1 Instrument, Unison	Unison, Some overlap
4. Vocal organization	Unison, Monophony	Polyphony, Unison
5. Tonal blend-vocal	Diffuse	Cohesive
6. Rhythmic blend-vocal	Diffuse, Cohesive	Cohesive
7. Orchestral organization	Monophony, Unison	Polyphony, Unison
8. Tonal blend-orchestra	None	Cohesive, None
9. Rhythmic blend-orchestra	None	Cohesive, None
10. Words to nonsense	Repetitious	About half repeated
11. Overall rhythm-vocal	Irregular	Simple
12. Group rhythm-vocal	Unison, None	Unison
13. Overall rhythm-orchestra	1-beat	Regular
14. Group rhythm-orchestra	None or Unison	None or Polyrhythm
15. Melodic shape	Undulating, Terraced	Undulating, Descending
16. Melodic form	Simple, Complex strophe	Litany
17. Phrase length	Medium, Short	Short
18. Number of phrases	8+, 1 or 2	1 or 2
19. Position final tone	Lowest	Lowest
20. Range	5–8, 10+	5–8, 10+
21. Interval width	Wide	Diatonic, Wide
22. Polyphonic type	None	Parallel, Counterpoint
23. Embellishment	None, Some	None
24. Tempo	Medium, Slow	Medium, Fast
25. Volume	Mid	Mid, Loud
26. Rubato-vocal	None	None
27. Rubato-instruments	None	None
28. Glissando	Some	Some, Prominent
29. Melisma	Syllabic	Syllabic, Some
30. Tremolo	Some or None	None
31. Glottal shake	Some or None	None
32. Register	Mid, Low	Mid
33. Vocal width	Speaking, Wide	Wide
34. Nasalization	Marked	Marked, Intermittent
35. Raspiness	Great, Intermittent	Intermittent, Marked
36. Accent	Forceful	Moderate, Forceful
37. Consonants	Slurred, Normal	Slurred

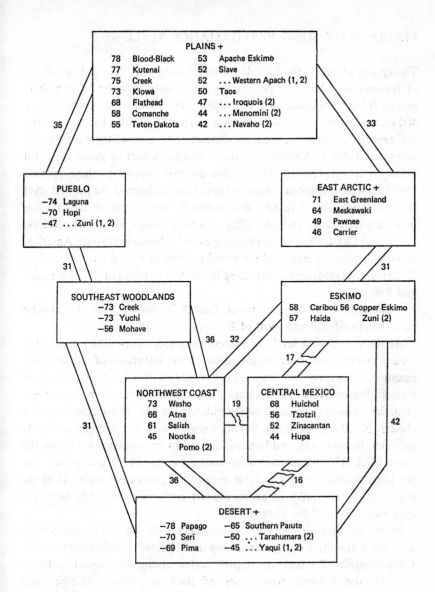

Figure 1. Residual bonds among North American areas

FINDINGS ON SONG PERFORMANCE STYLE

The system of rating the audible record of song performance is made up of features on which the performers must agree in order to win their public. It has been tested on about 4,000 songs drawn from approximately 400 cultures from all areas. The results are song profiles by culture area and region that set forth the most distinctive features of their song traditions (e.g. Table 2). A volume of these profiles, a sort of guide to world music, is in preparation. Multifactor analysis applied to these profiles produces a geographic taxonomy of considerable interest. At the first level there are three main factors accounting for a great part of the variance in style and activity and providing objective classes of similar cultures.

1. Tribal Circum-Pacific, comprising Siberia, North and South America, Australia, New Guinea, and the tribal peoples of East Asia.

2. Tropical Gardeners, comprising Black Africa, tribal India, Melanesia, and Polynesia.

3. Old High Culture, comprising East Asia, South Asia, the Middle East, North Africa, and most of Europe.

At the continental level the system produces song-culture areas that closely parallel and support the ideas of the historians of culture. For example, when forty-two song-culture profiles of North American Indians were factor analyzed, the clusters illustrated in Figure 1 were formed. (Numbers beside the culture names indicate the level of attachment to the cluster. Numbers beside the linking lines indicate the strength of bonds between the areal sets, and bonds indicated by broken lines are below the mean level.) Fifty-seven such song style areas have been established and we hope shortly to have similar results for movement style. Thus an explanatory geography of expressive art now exists to guide both the anthropologist and the filmmaker.

Steady relationships between performance style and social pattern have also been found. Conrad Arensberg and Lomax (co-directors of the Choreometrics Project) developed scales comparing social patterns through the inferred frequencies of their constituent interpersonal interactions, using the rating codes of Murdock's *Ethnographic atlas*. Correlations were established between these scales and those of cantometrics, that is, between social structure and performance style, so that one may be, in considerable degree, predicted from the other. Two main types of correlations seem to be represented in these relationships of WHOLE SYSTEMS VARIABLES — variances in the overall structures of societies — and SYSTEMS INTERNAL VARIABLES, or variance in component team structure.

A. *Whole Systems Variables*

1. COMPLEXITY: The importance of text, the precision of enunciation, and the number of types of consonants — in a word, the load of articulators in a song performance — vary directly with social and productive complexity.

2. STRATIFICATION: A high degree of ORNAMENTATION in singing is a good indicator of a complex system of social stratification.

3. POLITICAL TYPE: The most frequent leader-chorus relationship in song performance is an indicator of the level of centralized authority in the political organizations of societies.

B. *Systems Internal Variables — Component Team Structure*

4. COMPLEMENTARITY: A high degree of vocal polyphony is a sure indicator of complementary rather than one-sided interactional relations between males and females in society.

5. SOLIDARITY: The cohesiveness of choral performance varies directly with the importance of lifelong solidary group organizations in society.

6. SEXUAL TENSION: The degree of vocal tension in performance turns out to be a measure of the severity of the code of sexual sanctions in the society.

Thus singing styles are seen to be symbols for and reinforcements of the social structure in which they occur.

At each level of development we find expressive specializations that seem to reflect (a) the organizational plan, enforced by productive necessity, mediated by (b) historico-geographical conditions. Thus we speak of (a) the highly integrated communication style of (b) African village cultivators, one regional variant of a culture type found elsewhere in the world. Wittfogel's exposition of the centralized hydraulic society as a type of culture is matched by the cantometric description of an exclusive and elaborate communication style most frequent wherever hydraulic civilizations occur.

In this cross-cultural work we are indebted to the generations of field ethnologists whose work is summed up in the compendia of George Murdock, Robert Textor, Stanley Udy, Irvin Child, Yehudi Cohen, John Roberts, and John Whiting. Naroll's recent summary of this work inferentially validates our findings by showing that game styles and art styles are as reliable indicators of the state of culture as are politics, stratification, and other more standard social variables. Here Fischer's linking of elaboration in art to stratification and Roberts' correlation of game type to social complexity support our findings about song style. Expressive communication always seems to be loaded with messages about the degree and kind of complexity a society has achieved and the order of specificity it requires in its communications.

A more recent research development, however, bears more directly upon the films. By combining certain measures of social interaction from the *Ethnographic Atlas* with the cantometrics lines that describe public communications, we have produced an evolutionary taxonomy of culture independent of language. Each of its taxa are geographically continuous, each has a profile of statistically distinctive features and each falls into a slot along an increasing scale of complexity (see Figures 2 and 3).

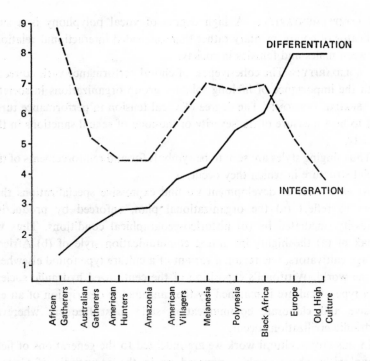

Evolutionary culture scale

Figure 2.   The weighted means of the differentiation factor (solid line) and the integrative composite factor (broken line) are plotted along the evolutionary culture scale. These are the main factors found when 71 measures were factor-analyzed over a sample of 148 world cultures (from Lomax and Berkowitz 1972).

By 1974 a set of training tapes for teaching cantometrics will be available for general distribution. It will consist of more than thirty tapes, containing excerpts from over 800 songs and a booklet explaining their use as a research tool and a teaching device. Because the tapes have only minimal verbal explanations, we hope that they will move easily across language barriers and come into general use as cultural orientation devices, as well as a method of performance analysis.

Ethnographic filmmakers have traditionally been eye- rather than ear-minded and have often treated the sound, particularly the music track, as secondary, something perhaps to be recorded later. The horrid custom of putting a composed, sometimes symphonic score to a film about an exotic

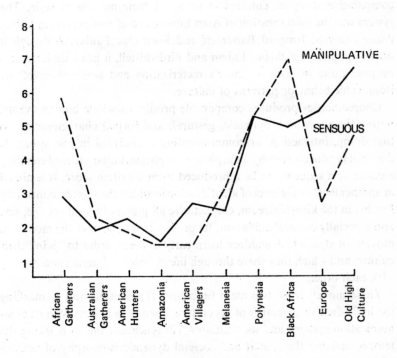

Figure 3. The two main factors of the multifactor analysis of dance style are plotted along the evolutionary culture scale; 373 dance codings from 108 of the standard Murdock sample were used in this multifactor analysis (from Lomax and Berkowitz 1972).

culture was until recently a general practice. The clash between the audible and the visible messages was painful, but a solution of the problem eluded analysis. Cantometrics now offers the filmmaker a technique for relating the structure of the musical soundtrack to the visual events in film.

CHOREOMETRIC FINDINGS

Films of other cultures have thus far served the teacher as well as the anthropologist largely as a way to supplement and illustrate observations already recorded elsewhere. A great advance came with kinesics, by which the body communication patterns of particular cultures and situations may be exactly described. Choreometrics employs film as data for a comparative study of cultures in terms of their movement style. The system was the joint creation of Alan Lomax and of two experts in Laban dance analysis, Irmgard Bartenieff and Forrestine Paulay. Although it draws upon the insights of Laban and Birdwhistell, it has a design and a purpose quite its own — the characterization and comparison of the isomorphic behavior patterns of culture.

Choreometrics produces comparable profiles of whole human events, noting their postural, dynamic, gestural, and formal characteristics, so that doing, interacting, or communicating is analyzed in one sweep. It does not produce a step-by-step, phrase-by-phrase, unitary record enabling a dance or a sequence to be reproduced from a written score. It is aimed at another level — the level of identification in which the signals, constantly flowing in the kinesic stream, characterize all present in terms of age, sex, and especially cultural affiliation. Its profiles aim to portray the models of movement style which children learn early in life in order to "join" their culture, and which they share through life in order to interact successfully with each other.

These models serve two main functions: (1) identification — marking the individual as a member of his culture when he is in tune with its communication systems and its standards; (2) synchronizing — marking the tempo, defining the spatial and societal dynamic isomorphy of activity within which the individuals of a culture can successfully mesh and coordinate their cobehaviors into effective social action — in dance, in work, and in other transactions. The principal contrastive features of these adaptive models of behavioral isomorphy are presented forcefully in the dance. Our close correlation of cultural and social features shows that these profiles mirror the cultures in which they are found.

Again, as in song performance, the dance system reinforces the order

of complexity in the survival system in a number of ways. For example, the following traits are most frequent in complex productive systems:
1. a three-dimensional, indirect approach to space;
2. rounded movement pattern;
3. high variation in movement qualities;
4. prominent use of peripheral parts of the body — hands, fingers, feet, eyes, head;
5. erect posture in walking;
6. smooth, flowing, and sustained movement; and
7. prominence of leaders and complex transformations of group organization.

On the contrary, the following are some of the movement features most frequently found among simple producers:
1. one-dimensional movement path and simple reversal transitions;
2. simultaneous use of limbs and few body parts per action;
3. relative absence of smoothness of flow and of curvilinear movements; and
4. low prominence of leading figures and little or no shift in group organizations.

These statements do not represent total presence or absence, but relative frequency in the distribution of qualities found in all human behavior.

The contrast between the multidimensional and flowing style of complex producers and the relatively more linear style of the simple producers may be a function of tool design. Simple producers must punch or hack their way straight through substances in order not to break the brittle edge of their wood and stone implements. The increasing hardness and resiliency of later tools made a curvilinear, slashing approach possible. Another remarkable evolutionary vector seems to be connected here: (1) Simple producers generally employ little articulation of either limbs or trunk; the trunk and the limbs are most frequently used as single units. (2) Articulation of the trunk in dance is a distinctive feature of pre-plough economics dependent on animal husbandry. (3) Among complex producers, foot articulation occurs frequently among the plowmen of Europe, and hand and finger articulation in the complex irrigation societies of the Orient.

There is a complexity scale of considerable interest here. As in song style, articulation seems to be a good marker of societal complexity. The articulation of the central body which appears at the middle of the scale seems clearly to stand for the sexual and the feminine; at this level females play an equal or complementary part with males in productive activity. Multi-unit trunk use is highly correlated to polyrhythm in orchestral music and to polyphony in singing. Both of these seem to be musical symbols for the complementary society, in which at least two roles can be integrated into any communication. Moreover, a sinuous and flowing quality, a successive use of parts of limbs, goes along with this multi-unit trunk style and seems to provide the baseline for the highly coordinated group dancing and work movement one finds among settled village gardeners in Africa and Polynesia and in the Americas.

One multifactor analysis of our sample in terms of these movement qualities reduces the thirty-seven movement scales to the following five general dimensions, each of which represents a describable quality of movement:

1. SINUOUS: Flowing, curved, central impulse, successive disposal of energy that permits two simultaneous rhythms and treats the trunk as two units.

2. ENERGETIC: Powerful, speedy, accelerating, centrally based and linear movement.

3. MULTIDIMENSIONAL: Varied, three-dimensional, spiraling, prolonged movement, involving many body parts, especially at the periphery.

4. LINEAR: One-dimensional, simply repetitive, direct, often jerky movement, simultaneously involving one whole aspect of the body; the trunk is treated as one unit.

5. ELABORATE: Variation, smoothly sustained and slowly unfolding, emphasizing deliberation and refinement.

Another interlinking of this matrix of similarity numbers produces a geography with two primordial stylistic zones — the Circum-Pacific and the Tropical Gardener, along with two later large territories of more complex cultures — Old High Culture and Europe.

The immediate aim of our research is to produce a geography of movement-style areas of the world that qualifies and illuminates the present culture-area system. In this way, and with a great broadening of our sample base, we hope to make movement style into a reliable tracer of detailed historical movement as well as of the overall developmental sequence of human cultures.

The choreometric coding system has, in the early seventies, grown far beyond movement analysis. Besides its coverage of body articulation, posture, stance, use of space, use of dynamics, and use of movement qualifiers, it now embodies an elaborate system for the analysis of:

(1) social choreography, (2) group dynamics, (3) leader characteristics, (4) synchronic type, (5) synchronic level, (6) rhythmic scheme, (7) use of territory and space, (8) sexual presentation, (9) leg and arm style, (10)

dynamics of change, and (11) organization of movement form.

At present there are 126 rating parameters in the system, controlled by a coding book. Multifactor analysis will certainly reduce the number of dimensions in the system.

Nowadays, an expert coder needs to spend about three hours to make an exhaustive analysis of a dance. When he has finished his work, however, he will have perceived many salient cultural phenomena. He will find that each of the main cultural taxa organizes its synchronic behavior in dance and everyday life around a small, distinctive set of features, clearly delineated by the coding system. In sub-Saharan Africa, for example, movement is frequently broken into two clear phrases, in the first of which the actors move in tight synchrony and increasing acceleration to a climax of effort, and in the second of which they recover, relax, and "do their own thing." African style is therefore characterized by peaks of high shared energy and high coordination, followed by compensatory stretches of relaxation and independence.

European song, dance, and, to a remarkable extent, everyday activity organizes several differing phrases of movement into a quatrainlike formula with a pause at the end; such a formula may be repeated with variations until the particular task is completed. If group synchrony is needed, inter-actor calibration must be far more precise. Thus European group synchrony is rigid, with exact and continuous conformity demanded in direction, focus, limb path, and timing, to produce (ideally) the image of the drill team or the famous New York Rockettes. This is only one of many examples of the kinds of insights choreometrics can offer to the ethnographic filmmaker, both while he is shooting footage in the field and when editing later on. The system can help the filmmaker shoot and cut with, rather than against, the grain of culture.

THE UTILITY OF THE CHOREOMETRIC FILMS

The choreometric rating system is hard to teach from the coding book without reference to visual examples. (This has been a continuing problem in expanding our research staff and in increasing the work flow in our studio.) For this reason we are making training films which will depict the main outlines of the coding systems, training the student to recalibrate his standards of visual judgment to those displayed in the films. The juxtaposition of visual images in a training sequence presents the contrasts immediately and unforgettably. Where the concepts are difficult, the films painlessly underline them. The student tests his grasp of the distinctions on a set of random, prerated examples. He is then prepared to improve his skill by practice.

The initial process of learning is rapid. At the end of a couple of hours of guided observation, the trainee establishes an easy relationship with two or three crucial aspects of the analytic approach. These give him a feel for some of the principal stylistic features of culture. As he proceeds with the films, he will absorb the geography and the nomenclature of culture and the system of culture regions and areas as a matter of course. Moreover, by the time he has learned how to use six or eight of the most important measures, he will be producing brief profiles that sketch expressive styles of humanity and he will discover for himself how these sets of qualities cluster to give rise to distinctive and coherent culture patterns.

The trainee comes to absorb one of the main lessons of anthropology — that every genuine tradition, no matter how strange to him, has its own clear and coherent pattern, related to adaptive problems of survival, work, and public order. Because in the filmed examples he will be looking at the activity of cross sections of societies and comparing them, he will also come to understand another basic anthropological principle: the most important human differences reside in patterns of learned behaviors, and even these differences are relative and comparative rather than absolute. Presented with the whole human spectrum in film after film, the student comes to feel at home with the species. This is one of the principal goals in undergraduate anthropology and good orientation for more serious work in the field. We feel strongly that, for those who have had this training, the overall experience has been psychologically positive as well.

About thirty pilot training films have been roughly assembled. This year two of them will be completed and made ready for distribution. The end product will have several educational purposes. It will make dance into a useful source of insights about the structure of society and the history of cultures. It will teach the student ways of finding relationships between expressive behavior, workaday behavior, and social norms. It will teach the student to observe the relationship between modes of coordination and patterns of social organization.

The student will learn how to perceive these isomorphic relationships between the expressive and the social norms across the full evolutionary range of human societies, because each training film will be made up of examples of one behavioral trait or activity from many areas and levels of culture. From the outset the student will couple the acquisition of social science concepts with the recognition and comparison of similarities and differences in behaviors he can observe for himself in the training films. Thus choreometrics will help to teach the concepts and materials of anthropology, human geography, and comparative sociology in the terms most attrative to young social scientists.

Choreometrics and cantometrics demonstrate that the patterns of song and movement style vary in orderly ways by culture area and region and that features of these expressive systems are highly correlated with important aspects of social structure. It appears that a principal symbolic function of the arts is to reinforce social adaptive patterns, supplying models that define human groups. These highly redundant models identify common cultural traditions and indicate the limits within which an individual can express himself without encountering sanctions. They reestablish interactional norms and adaptive goals in culture which make for security and stability and satisfaction. Thus film and tape analysis of expressive behavior provide a key to culture pattern, all the more effective because of the evocative power of the arts. With the connection of creative behavior to society clearly established, the basis of a fertile relationship between social science and the arts is thus open to curriculum development.

REFERENCES

ARENSBERG, CONRAD M., SOLON T. KIMBALL
  1965 *Culture and community.* New York: Harcourt and Brace.
BATESON, GREGORY, MARGARET MEAD
  1942 *Balinese character, a photographic analysis.* New York: Academy of Science.
BIRDWHISTELL, RAY L.
  1952 *Introduction to kinesics.* Louisville: University of Louisville Press.
  1970 *Kinesics and context.* Philadelphia: University of Pennsylvania Press.
COHEN, YEHUDI A.
  1961 "Food and its vicissitudes: a cross-cultural study of sharing and non-sharing," in *Social structure and personality: a casebook.* Edited by Yehudi Cohen, 312–350. New York: Holt, Rinehart and Winston.
CONDON, W. S., W. D. OGSTON
  1966 Sound film analysis of normal and pathological behavior patterns. *Journal of Nervous and Mental Disease* 143:338–347.
DE HAVENON, ANNA-LOU
  1969 "Authority patterns in family 02." Mimeographed manuscript, Columbia University, New York
HALL, EDWARD T.
  1959 *The silent language.* Garden City: Doubleday.
HOCKETT, CHARLES, NORMAN A. MCQUOWN
  n.d. "The natural history of an interview." Unpublished manuscript.

LOMAX, ALAN
  1968 *Folk song style and culture. A staff report on cantometrics.* Washington: American Association for the Advancement of Science. Publication 88.
LOMAX, ALAN, NORMAN BERKOWITZ
  1972 The evolutionary taxonomy of culture. *Science* 177:228–239.
MEAD, MARGARET, PAUL BYERS
  1968 *The small conference.* The Hague: Mouton.
MURDOCK, GEORGE PETER
  1967 *Ethnographic atlas.* Pittsburgh: University of Pittsburgh Press.
SCHEFLEN, ALBERT E.
  1965 *Stream and structure of communicational behavior.* Philadelphia: Eastern Pennsylvania Psychiatric Institute. (Revised 1971, Bloomington: University of Indiana Press.)
SMITH, BRIAN SUTTON
  1966 Cross-cultural correlates of games of chance. *Behavior Science Notes* 1:131–144.
TEXTOR, ROBERT B.
  1967 *A cross-cultural summary.* New Haven: Human Relations Area Files Press.
TRAGER, GEORGE L.
  1958 Paralanguage: a first approximation. *Studies in Linguistics* 13:1–12.
TRAGER, GEORGE L., HENRY LEE SMITH, JR.
  1951 *An outline of English structure.* Oklahoma: Battenberg. (Reprinted in 1957, Washington, D.C.: American Council of Learned Societies.)
UDY, STANLEY H., JR.
  1959 *Organization of work: a comparative analysis of production among non-industrial peoples.* New Haven: Human Relations Area Files Press.
WHITING, JOHN, IRVIN L. CHILD
  1953 *Child training and personality: a cross-cultural study.* New Haven: Yale University Press.
WITTFOGEL, KARL
  1957 *Oriental despotism.* New Haven: Yale University Press.

Analysis of Body Movement and Space

Filming Body Behavior

J. H. PROST

INTRODUCTION

There is a difference between films that illustrate and films that are sources of primary data. For the former the cameraman and editor have free license to manipulate the images. The ultimate purpose of illustrative films is to be viewed, substituting illustrative scenes for actual scenes. The viewer is the observer, seeing what the cameraman and editor create, concluding what the cameraman and editor prearrange. Documentary and visual-aid films are illustrative in nature.

Film can also be primary data. However, the photographer must have this object in mind at the time of shooting. Film may be considered primary data to the degree that the images faithfully capture one or another aspect of actual occurrences. This is possible when specific filming conditions are controlled; primary data are permanently recorded in the images and image sequences. Any editing, in the usual sense, destroys such a record.

When film is a faithful reproduction of some aspect of an original scene, it may be called a REPRESENTATIONAL film. The ultimate purpose of representational films is data retrieval. The viewer is not an observer but a participant in the operations of data collection. Representational films are permanent, primary data sources, capable of being stored and analyzed in place of the events that they portray.

The purposes and objectives of these two types of films are different and the filming procedures they call for are distinct. For example, film records structure events with a time frame. The speed of film advancement, in frames per second, furnishes a temporal segmentation of original events.

Slow motion and stop frame photography make visual that which happens too fast for the naked eye to perceive.

It might be assumed that all slow motion films are primary data films because the process of slowing action makes events available for analysis. It is not so. Motion is slowed when film speed much exceeds 16 to 18 frames per second, the slowest speeds that create image fusion in the mind of the viewer (cf. Peter M. Roget's classic paper on the persistence of vision [1824]). Speeds of 32 or 48 frames per second both give slow motion effects. A speed of 32 frames per second does not capture details that a speed of 48 frames per second reveals. For some locomotor, sport, and dance forms a speed of 32 frames per second slows the action, but movement details are lost during interframe durations. For some human activities, film speed must be 64 or more frames per second to record accurately the subtleties of activity (Marey 1895; Steindler 1955; Prost 1965; Gray 1968; Birdwhistell 1970).

Illustrative filming can slow action without regard to relations between speed of activity and speed of film. Representational filming demands a choice of proper film speed to meet the requirements of the details that are to be recorded. Mechanisms have to be adopted to ensure that the speed desired is in fact the speed attained. Many cameras do not perform at the speeds indicated on the equipment. Cameras with spring motors are notorious for changing speeds in the middle of a sequence. Representational filming must take these mechanical errors into account by calibrating the instrument, checking its performance, and supplying an external timing source for verification.

Film speed is one variable that representational filming can control. Sequencing and spatial relations are other aspects subject to control. Film furnishes a permanent record of the sequence of events, providing the photographer and editor keep the subject matter intact. For example, closeup inserts in the middle of sequences disrupt the overall field of view and break up sequences of action that would otherwise be intact. Zoom lenses offer photographers tools of dramatic effect, but at the cost of sequence continuity. A sequence of arm gestures can be destroyed with a closeup of the hands or face, by either the photographer with zoom lens or the editor in the cutting room. Once sequencing is destroyed, film changes from representational to illustrative — primary data are lost.

The spatial relations of actual scenes are reproduced on film according to rigid optical and physical laws and are therefore subject to retrieval. Changing camera positions and poorly placed shooting angles can complicate retrieval beyond correction. Camera angles chosen because they give the best scope of view or dramatic effects sometimes create distortions and foreshortenings that no calculations can untangle. Representational filming requires concern for the retrieval of data which illustrative filming can ignore (cf. Scherer's paper, *infra*).

Representational films must come with documents describing the conditions controlled. The documents must be accurate in regard to their particulars and care must be taken to ensure that the conditions under which the film was exposed can be clearly reconstructed by viewers. Illustrative films may come with titles and commentaries alone, having little pretense at being sources of precision. Libraries of illustrative films are useful and educational; libraries of representational films are fundamental to the social and behavioral sciences.

The purpose of making these distinctions is to counteract the erroneous assumption that a camera *ipso facto* "documents" action for future reference. It cannot be reasoned that because the camera is a mechanical device, it must be objective, and therefore whatever it captures is raw data. Films taken without regard for proper controls are of little more value than are verbal descriptions, perhaps even of less value, because they suggest an objectivity that in fact does not exist.

Pointing a camera at a dance scene gathers little of value if the camera speed is too slow. Artistic zoom shots of hands and feet swapped in and out of sequence do not record the dance for posterity. As use of film in the social and behavioral sciences increases, it is counterproductive for those interested in "documentation" to scotch the careful and tedious work of the many investigators who have developed the techniques of representational filming. The placement of the camera and choice of film speed are critical decisions if film is to serve as a data repository. What is preserved depends on what controls have been applied. The facile assumption that the camera "records" whatever is in its view is true only if illustrative film is being produced. The term *documentary* is really a misnomer.

A film can be illustrative for some purposes and representational for others. No photographer controls all aspects of filming sessions, and consequently the variables that are faithfully presented vary from film to film. A photographer must consciously pick his controls and supply viewers with statements identifying those variables that are suitable for analysis. The distinction between illustrative and representational filming is a distinction of purpose, rather than a dichotomy of mutually exclusive types.

A photographer chooses what he wishes to record and adjusts his controls accordingly. The same film can contain illustrative material and representational records. Primary data are the result of procedural decisions, not the automatic consequence of the mechanical and chemical properties of the medium.

Film has been used by many investigators as a primary data source for the analysis of body behavior. These investigators have developed methodological techniques that enhance the value of film records. These developments create a field of application outside the normal domain of social science "documentaries."

HISTORICAL PERSPECTIVES

The earliest use of representational films can be traced to Muybridge, Marey, and Darwin. The technical problems that these men faced were enormous. Muybridge and Marey had to design and build their own equipment, produce their own film plates, and develop their films with crude, and many times damaging, processes. The stimuli for several innovations in the field of cinematography came from the demands placed on these pioneers as they tried to develop representational techniques to record human and nonhuman body behavior.

Perhaps the first work in representational filming occurred in 1872 when Eadweard Muybridge (born 1830, Edward James Muggeridge) made his initial attempt at photographing Leland Stanford's racehorses (Taft 1955). He used a wet plate process that was too slow to make analyzable documents. From 1872 to 1877 he worked to improve his process, and by 1877 he obtained satisfactory results. Stanford was pleased with the results and supported Muybridge's work. During this time Muybridge expanded his collection on nonhuman animals other than the horse and on man himself. By 1879 Muybridge's work was well known in the United States and his fame was spreading in Europe.

In 1877 he started giving lectures, mostly in California, using his photographs as illustrations. He developed in 1880 an early model of what he called the "zoopraxiscope," an instrument with a revolving glass plate that projected pictures and produced an illusion of motion, which he used in later lectures. In 1879 he left California and spent several years traveling and lecturing throughout the United States and Europe. In 1883 the University of Pennsylvania sponsored him in a new program of photography. He used animal subjects from the Philadelphia Zoological Gardens, men from the campus of the university, women who were artists' models and dancers from Philadelphia theatres. In 1887 the university issued a limited edition of 781 composite plates, which cost about $500 per set. Pressure for less expensive editions led Muybridge to select smaller volumes. These were his books *Animals in motion* (1899, reprinted 1957) and *The human figure in motion* (1901, reprinted 1955).

From the beginning, Muybridge used the camera as an analytic device. For Stanford he examined the poses of horses in various phases of gait. His work with other animals, including man, served to expand his analysis of gait varieties. He developed a system of gait description and classification which is the classic work in the field (his system is reprinted with the edition of 1957). His analysis depended directly on his photographs. His system utilized the temporal properties of filmed motion segmentation. This was a clear case of representational filming.

In 1881 Muybridge was in Europe giving lectures. His first stay was in France. The trip, perhaps the result of urging from the French painter Meissonier, was certainly at the invitation of the French physiologist Marey (Ramsaye 1964; Marey 1895). It is known that he traded information with Marey, as Muybridge himself relates in his preface to *Animals in motion* (1957:15) that "the first demonstration given in Europe with the zoopraxiscope was at the laboratory of Dr. E. J. Marey, in the presence of a large number of scientists from various parts of the world attending the Electrical Congress at Paris."

Étienne-Jules Marey, a French comparative physiologist, was professor of physiology at the College of France, Paris, and director of the Physiological Station (cf. Plate 1). Marey described the circumstances of his exchange with Muybridge (1895:108):

After the introduction of instantaneous photography, it seemed to us that the movements of a flying bird could be analyzed by this method. We therefore asked Mr. Muybridge to make use of this apparatus to study the flight of birds. He hastened to accede to this request, and when he came to Paris, in August of 1881, he brought us several prints of pigeons photographed in 1/500 part of a second.

Marey was familiar with the use of photography before he met Muybridge, but he had not experimented intensively with the technique. Muybridge's bird photos so captured Marey's scientific curiosity that he immediately turned the Physiological Station into a photographic studio, applying photography to a variety of physiological problems.

Marey (1895) attributes the first use of photography for a study of animal movement to Onimus and Martin, who in 1865 photographed a living animal heart by continuous exposure, analyzing the systolic and diastolic positions from the coincident outlines on the plate. Marey also tells of the astronomer Janssen, who in 1873 designed an instrument to take pictures of stars and planets on a revolving photographic plate. A year later Janssen went to Japan and successfully used his apparatus to photograph phases of Venus.

The revolving plate of Janssen was identical in principle to the plate of

Muybridge's zoopraxiscope, and whether Marey got the idea from Janssen as he states, or from Muybridge's demonstration of 1881, can only be conjectured; nevertheless, Marey designed a photographic gun using the revolving drum principle. The gun was a forerunner of the modern cinematographic camera. With it Marey and his colleagues at the station photographed a tremendous variety of living phenomena. The gun was introduced in 1882, and in 1887 Marey, more for convenience than to increase his number of exposures, changed from the circular glass plate to rolls of paper film, the forerunners of roll film. By 1888 he was using celluloid.

Marey, as physiologist, was interested in the analysis of all biological phenomena, from heartbeats to limb movements. Animal locomotion fascinated him most and his best work was in this area. He developed an overall methodology, theory, and techniques, which he called "chrono-photography." He was particularly interested in the translation of motion patterns into observable, comprehensible, and analyzable pictures. His pictures of human limb movement and animal progression, showing simultaneous, overlapping phases of action, advanced the science of motion analysis, influencing not only his scientific colleagues but painters and sculptors as well (Giedion 1955). At the Physiological Station new instruments were developed to attack particular, and peculiar, problems, and a generation of "chronophotographers" was trained. Marey's most influential books were *Du mouvement dans les fonctions de la vie* (1868) and *Le mouvement* (1894).

Charles Darwin, sometime before 1872 (the date of publication of *The expression of the emotions in man and animals*), used photographs of the human face for experimental purposes. He described his own research design (1965:14):

Thirdly Dr. Duchenne galvanized, as we have already seen, certain muscles in the face of an old man, whose skin was little sensitive, and thus produced various expressions which were photographed on a large scale. It fortunately occurred to me to show several of the best plates, without a word of explanation, to above twenty educated persons of various ages and both sexes, asking them, in each case, by what emotion or feeling the old man was supposed to be agitated; and I recorded their answers in the words which they used. Several of the expressions were instantly recognised by almost every one, though described in not exactly the same terms; and these may, I think, be relied on as truthful, and will hereafter be specified. On the other hand, the most widely different judgments were pronounced in regard to some of them.

Darwin, it appears, got the thought of using photographs in this manner from the plates of Duchenne's treatise *Mécanisme de la physionomie humaine* (1862). Duchenne used his photographs as illustrations. He based his analysis of muscle function almost completely on electrical stimulation, palpation, and live observations (Duchenne 1949). Darwin reversed the logic of the illustrations and used the plates to elicit responses, thereby testing the interpretative variations in expressive faces. Darwin spawned a long line of investigators who followed basically the same method and experimental design (cf. Ekman, Friesen, and Ellsworth 1972).

Early work with representational films was hampered by technological constraints. Lenses, film, and development processes were crude, and this limited the applications of the technique (Ceram 1965). It should be stated, to their credit, that irrespective of these limitations, the photographs of Muybridge and Marey, Darwin and Duchenne, are still the most extensively used illustrations to accompany textual discussions of animal movement.

As new techniques developed, new generations of equipment and scientists emerged. The use of representational films spread over many disciplines: comparative physiology, medicine, industry, sport, and expressive (nonverbal) communication. A full discussion of the history of representational filming in these disciplines cannot be presented here, but some major contributions can be cited to illustrate the breadth of the work.

Problems haunting an investigator in one field can very often be solved quickly by reference to other fields. Unfortunately, a synthesis of all these divergent schools has not arrived, and much duplication has occurred over the years. A concerted effort should be made to pull the threads together into a more systematic field of endeavor, to the profit of both the beginner, who discovers too late that his problem has already been solved elsewhere, and the professional, who could use complementary data which, however, are stored in an obscure recess of another field less familiar to him.

In comparative physiology Muybridge's work on gait has been amplified with new analytic techniques and modern equipment (cf. Howell 1944). Following Marey, film has been used to record the dynamics of animal biomechanics (e.g. Manter 1938; Camp and Smith 1942; Gray 1944). Much of the comparative work has been excellently summarized by Gray (1968).

Applications in medicine and sport are difficult to separate because many of the data are filed under the common rubric of "kinesiology." In fact, the overlap is real as well as verbal. Carlet (1872), in Marey's laboratory, continued investigations on human walking. Londe (1891), following Muybridge's influence, analyzed human gait. In Germany, using the photographs and techniques of Anschütz and Marey, Braune and Fischer (1895) did the definitive set of studies on the biophysical attributes of human locomotion. The procession of work continued through the studies of the Ducroquets (1968), Bernstein (1967), Morton and Fullers (1952), Eberhart, Inman, and Bresler (1954), and Kondo (1960), each of whom added vital new data and imaginative techniques. Steindler (1955) gives an overview of medical "kinesiology" and supplies one of the best introductions to this literature. The works of Dempster (1961) on free-body diagrams and Hamilton and Simon (1958) on surface landmarks have helped greatly to increase the analytic capacities of body photographs.

The term *kinesiology* for many years also subsumed the use of representational film in the analysis of sport activities. Recently the term *biomechanics* has come into vogue (cf. *Biomechanics* [Wartenweiler, Jokl, and Hebbelinck 1968], *Biomechanics II* [Vredenbregt and Wartenweiler 1971], and *Selected topics on biomechanics* [Cooper 1971]). Summaries of the field and some of the applications can be found in Cooper and Glassow (1968), Kelly (1971), and O'Connell and Gardner (1972). Special attention might be given to Plagenhoef (1971). The use of stroboscopic photography is reviewed by Edgerton and Killian (1954).

In 1881 Frederick W. Taylor introduced the concept of "time studies" into the "scientific management" of industrial work. He did not use cinematography but laid the groundwork for Gilbreth (1911), who, using Amar's concepts of motion patterns (1920, original edition 1914) developed the study of work habits into a scientific field. Amar and Gilbreth both relied heavily on cinematography. Barnes (1963) and Giedion (1955) give summaries; the former is the more technical, the latter the more historical and philosophical.

Following Darwin, any number of investigations have been reported on the expressive attributes of the face. Studies on the face are well summarized by Ekman, Friesen, and Ellsworth (1972). The most important discussions of expressive (nonverbal) communication, from the standpoint of representational film, are condensed in Allport and Vernon (1933) and Efron (1941). Studies of special technical interest are those of Sainsbury (1954), Jones and Narva (1955), Hewes (1955), and Condon and Ogston (1966). The best overview is by Birdwhistell (1970), the creator of the field of "kinesics," or what, in more popular language, has come to be known as "body language."

Ethology (or comparative body language) has not yet really developed a school of representational filming but is certain to do so in the next decade. The field of expressive behavior had a late development almost surely because of the difficulties inherent in the kind of data being analyzed. Human locomotion, posture, and sport are easily subject to biophysical analyses, using physical parameters and principles in their description and calculation, whereas expressive facial and gestural behavior has not yielded to the same attack.

The use of representational film, which started with Muybridge, Marey, and Darwin, has expanded into almost all of the social, medical, and behavioral disciplines. The techniques, for example the use of high-speed photography and computers, have become sophisticated. The full range of usage for representational films has not yet been reached, and as much work will be generated in developing new equipment and innovative photography as will be produced in analyzing data. Consideration of this entire body of literature gives any researcher ample options. Cross-fertilization between disciplines ought to produce an explosion of productivity.

TECHNICAL CONSIDERATIONS

The production of the usual representational film, ignoring those requiring highly specialized apparatus, occurs in about eleven steps: choosing the camera, choosing the film, choosing the editor, anticipating the subject, arranging the environment, placing the camera, activating the camera, recording the controls, developing the film, editing the film, and analyzing the film. It should be noted that this discussion refers only to filming of body behavior, that is, external attributes of body activity. The discussion to follow is meant to draw the contrast between representational filming and illustrative filming to a finer point. A full discussion of filmmaking procedures can be found in Pincus (1969) and in technical works on photography.

The first step establishes the system that an investigator will use to photograph his scenes. The system must be appropriate for the parameters to be analyzed. Decisions at one step affect all the others. Choosing a 16-mm camera determines the kinds of editors available and establishes the system. The steps are decision points, like a feedback chain, each affecting all the others. They are listed individually for heuristic purposes. The photographer must survey his entire system and ask whether, as a unit, the system will do the job. Before he selects a camera, he must ascertain whether the characteristics of the camera will fit the objectives of the analysis, will not severely limit the choice of an editor, will not limit the filming to too few subjects. The system as a whole has to be evaluated. The total analytic capacity has to meet the research plans. The steps are examined individually for the convenience of exposition.

Choosing the camera

There are, commercially and commonly, four kinds of cameras from which to choose: still cameras, low-speed movie cameras, high-speed movie cameras, and stereoscopic still cameras. The still cameras take single exposures, as do the stereoscopic cameras. The stereoscopic cameras take two views of the same scene from focal points separated by approximately the distance between the human eyes. The stereoscopic images are viewed in a special editor that gives stereoscopic, or in-depth, perceptions of the subjects.

The still cameras take single exposures which freeze arrangements into a single image and therefore record single slices of time. The movie cameras come in two varieties: low-speed cameras with film speeds of 8 to 64 frames per second and high-speed movie cameras with film speeds in excess of 64 frames per second. Most commercially available cameras are of the low-speed variety. There are a few highspeed cameras on the market, and these are almost all made for 16- or 35-mm film. Still cameras are mostly designed for 35-millimeter or larger film. The larger film sizes give better definition to details and usually have a larger variety of accessory equipment commercially available. The regular-8 movie camera is now being superseded by the super-8 and commercial equipment for the super-8 is becoming available. The 16-mm size is the most common one now being used for representational filming with cinematography. There is a wider range of equipment available for this size than for any of the others. The 35-mm equipment is expensive and cumbersome in movie cameras. Most workers have settled on the 16-mm size as the best compromise for movies and 35-mm size for still pictures (cf. Pincus 1969).

The viewing system can be either reflex or view-finder. The reflex has been preferred because it allows through-the-lens viewing, eliminating parallax errors. The purpose behind most filming is to fill the frame as far as possible with the subject being photographed. The largest image possible is needed, and reflex cameras accommodate this far better than do viewfinder cameras, in spite of the claim that viewfinder cameras are useful for sports events. Some viewfinder cameras have parallax correction, but this must always be checked; if parallax correction is in error, part of the subject matter will be cut out of the frame.

The duration of an action must be predicted and a camera chosen accordingly. Most commercial cameras hold 50 to 100 feet of film but can be modified at some expense to take up to 400 feet. There are cameras that come with a number of magazines so that the photographer can choose his own amount of film. High-speed cameras usually hold from 100 to 400 feet of film, varying according to make and model. At high speeds the film is exposed rapidly, and unless the photographer calculates his footage carefully, the end of an action can be lost as the film plays itself out.

Most movie cameras today have single-frame exposure controls, and this makes a movie camera suitable for still frame photography. The limitations of the lenses normally used on movie cameras restrict this value somewhat, but the convenience of using only one camera for both functions has been found to offset this disadvantage.

The single-frame function in a movie camera can be useful. It has been used to substitute for a still camera, for example, in taking a large collection of facial photographs. It has been used to document overall aspects of a scene, tag film sequences, etc. Attributes of the environment and arrangements of the controls are safely recorded if they are put on the film itself. A chalkboard on which are written details about the conditions of the filming is usually used — the board can be shot with the single-frame function, tagging a motion sequence at the beginning or end and thus securing vital information.

Enough studies of human motion have been done so that an investigator can estimate the speed of the actions he is going to photograph and choose his camera speeds accordingly. Interframe durations cause actions to be lost and the choice of film speed must match the quickness of the details to be recorded.

Choosing the Film

The choice of film centers on black-and-white or color film. The graininess of a film relates to the clarity of the image: grainy films give less distinct images. Light latitude determines the amount of light that must be present for effective exposure. Usually color films have less light latitude and are more grainy. Color film that can be used under low illumination does not achieve good definition. This situation is being corrected with some of the new color films, and manufacturers can be contacted to discover the variety of films they supply.

If shooting conditions are to be under low illumination, then black-and-white film is preferable. Most investigators have used black-and-white film because in 16-mm size with high-speed cameras, the cost of color film is prohibitive. However, color film allows the best perception of details and a more vivid differentiation between shadowed areas. Black-and-white film tends to make details merge into a grayish continuum. Color film enhances depth relations and gives what appear to be less planar representations.

Color film is more expensive, and the best kinds are not suitable for personal developing. Almost all black-and-white film can easily be developed by the investigator himself. This is an advantage if a film has to be "pushed." A photographer can double the light latitude rating (ASA or DIN) on black-and-white film, making the film useful under conditions of low illumination, but increasing the ratings for example by a factor of two has to be compensated by approximately doubling the time the film is developed. Manufacturers publish instructions for "pushing" film beyond the recommended exposure limits. Most black-and-white films have greater latitudes than the ratings listed. Manufacturers supply information on the latitudes of their films and on the development compensations required.

Pushing film can give quite successful pictures. Color film can be pushed, but the problems of intercorrelating the development processes with the amount of pushing are more complex. The photographer who has his films developed by a laboratory must document carefully the conditions of exposure so that the laboratory can make the proper corrections. When film is being pushed, it is always valuable to shoot a number of extra shots or extra feet of film so that the laboratory can use these for experimentation. In fact, if movie film is being pushed, the photographer can shoot a roll which the laboratory can cut into a series of trial strips in order to determine the exact development process. If there is any doubt about the light conditions, one should always have this extra footage for experimentation. The laboratories usually do this at some extra cost; sometimes the opportunity is worth the cost. Single frames or a few feet are usually not sufficient material to work with for the highly automated laboratories — they must have entire rolls. The best practice is to shoot one experimental roll at the beginning of a session and one at the end in order to give the laboratory plenty of material on which to experiment.

There is a relation between film latitude and exposure time. The less the latitude, the longer the film has to be exposed to make an image. Where fast motions are to be filmed, long exposure will produce a blur on the film because of movement during the exposure.

Film speed and exposure time are different things. The film speed determines the number of frames exposed during one second, and the exposure time determines the length of time one frame is exposed to view. If a slow film speed is chosen, for example, 8 frames per second, action occurring in $1/8$ second or less will not be captured, in a statistical sense, in the frames. Because the exposure time determines the length of time a single frame is exposed to view, fast action is blurred by movement during exposure (Prost 1965).

The best system, of course, is one that exposes the maximum number of frames per second for the shortest periods of exposure time. The main reason video systems are not now commonly used for representational filming is that both the exposure times and the frames-per-second are slow.

One can compensate for slow film by increasing the light source (a must with video systems), creating a strobe effect to compensate for the slow exposure times, and thereby reducing the exposure times. A bright, pulsing light source, such as the stroboscopic light, gives almost instantaneous exposure times and clear, frozen-frame images (Edgerton and Killian 1954). Strobes have been used with both videotape and celluloid film. The psychological effect of the pulsating strobe, however, may be upsetting to the subjects, and consequently may be inadvisable, particularly with non-human subjects.

It has been found that it is always better to overshoot than undershoot. It is better to choose a higher film speed than desired. If too much information has been collected, film frames can be sampled, for example, by analyzing every other frame, rather than every frame. Exposure time should always be held to the minimum to reduce blurring.

These factors also interact with the depth of field. Opening the lens to get more light and a faster exposure time can subtract from the depth of field. Decreasing the exposure time to reduce blurring can reduce the light and give underexposed images. The first concern is always to get overexposure, if anything. Underexposed film cannot be analyzed because there is insufficient differentiation on the image. Overexposure is preferable to this because even if the image is washed out and the colors diluted, edges and shadows can be distinguished and some analysis can proceed.

Correct exposure, or slight overexposure, has always been recommended as the primary objective. Exposure time is a second concern. The speed in frames-per-second is the last worry. A frames-per-second speed that is slow can still sample behavior, but dark film leaves nothing to be seen. If the frames-per-second speed must be slow, then the investigator can shoot a greater amount of film and make a sampling of the details. Although details will be lost in interframe durations, taking a large sample of the same phenomena will ensure that details will appear with a statistical frequency and be captured somewhere in the collection (Prost 1965). The statistical relation between the speed of an action, the frames-per-second, and the frequency of details can be used to prove that the details would have been constant if the frames-per-second had been adequate.

With illustrative filming the quality of colors or composure of the field is emphasized. With representational filming the securing of analyzable images is paramount. With illustrative filming the film speed matches image fusion, whereas with representational filming the film speed matches the speed of the action and is almost always high-speed photography, projected as "slow motion", or frame-by-frame. Capturing actions dominates the decisions behind representational filming. Representational films are not exciting to watch. The representational film may be overexposed, devoid of color, and dull, but it is an analyzable record and ought to be judged, and appreciated, as such.

Choosing the Editor

There are two kinds of editors: commercial editors and specialized editors. Commercial editors simply project an image on a small screen for cutting. Most investigators have had to use or construct special pieces of editing equipment. Representational film requires the largest and brightest pictures possible. Most commercial editors have small screens and weak projection bulbs. Sometimes changing the bulbs will help, but this is hazardous.

There are two ways workers have overcome this problem. The first has been to use a projector instead of an editor, projecting the pictures on a prepared screen. The second has been to buy or make a specially designed editor. There are specially designed editors available for 16- and 35-mm films but not for super-8 and regular-8. Some specialized equipment for super-8 is now being marketed. Almost all recent researchers have designed their own editors. The literature has to be consulted to gain an idea of the variety of types and innovations extant.

The editor is almost always designed to show the film frame-by-frame and to have a frame counter. Most commercial editors, particularly for super-8 and regular-8, are not suitable for frame-by-frame viewing — the film passes the viewing head with a "sliding" motion and cannot be controlled for frame-by-frame analysis. Without a counter it is impossible to keep track of the frame being viewed.

The optimum editor must give a large, well-illuminated view of the image, preferably by behind-the-screen projection, because front projection means that as the worker stands between the projection bulb and screen in order to view the image, he cuts through the projection path and blanks the image. The editor or projector should have frame-by-frame and variable speed forward and reverse controls. Using projectors as editors gives front screen projection unless special viewing boxes are constructed

(Wartenweiler, Jokl, and Hebbelinck 1968; Barnes 1963; Plagenhoef 1971; Cooper 1971).

The usual case with representational films is to view the strips frame-by-frame. Single-frame (or with stills, single-slide) operations are essential. Editors have to be adapted accordingly. As with Marey's "chronophotography," the data lie in the images and image sequences. To retrieve the data, one must work on the images and reconstruct the image sequencing. Illustrative films almost always rely solely on image fusion during projection and therefore are rarely planned for frame-by-frame analysis.

Anticipating the Subject

The entire production of representational film hinges on the subject. The choices of camera, film and editor were discussed first because they render the greatest technical limitations. The material that can be photographed is dependent on the system used. It would be desirable to be able to photograph any subject, under all conditions, but many times the limitations of the system will defeat this purpose. Specialized photographic systems, such as x-ray photography and infrared photography, are being manufactured as commercial systems and vistas of research are opening. The discussion here is limited to the use of the classic film systems.

The word ANTICIPATING is meant to indicate that considerable mental effort has to be put into the design of the filming sessions. If dancers, or monkeys, are to be photographed, hours of observation have to be spent discovering their travel paths, habits, and routines. The researcher usually photographs and measures specific aspects of the environment before shooting so that movement in the environment can later be compared with actual heights and distances. Camera positions and distances from subject to camera can be predetermined so that fast focusing can be accomplished. Humans can be given travel paths, but other animals are not so cooperative. With proper anticipation, a photographer can be ready to take pictures of most occurrences and can predict directions and speeds of travel.

Here the difference from illustrative films is clear. The representational film has to be designed to sample specific behavior; the illustrative film can be pieced together with whatever is shot. The representational film must follow some design: the design explains the nature of the sample. The representational film requires not only anticipation but a program of sampling which must be revealed to the viewer; otherwise, the content of the sample cannot be comprehended. The viewer of illustrative films watches the action, whereas the viewer of representational films calculates the implications of "that" action occurring at "that" precise time. Illustrative film gives examples while representational film takes samples.

Arranging the Environment

The photographer can, before shooting, not only measure the environment but also arrange the environment. Natural objects, such as rocks, or scenery can be spaced to form natural points for distance estimations. The height and angles of backgrounds, such as trees, can be measured and markings can be arranged with colored tape. These sometimes destroy the aesthetics of the film, but they furnish the needed standards by which the action can be assessed. Under laboratory conditions complete control is possible. Under natural conditions the control must be more flexible. At ceremonies, for example, even though intrusive objects might be forbidden, the placement of appropriate objects can be prearranged or spaced. Any arrangements that help to pinpoint distance parameters are valuable. Photographing the background with distance measurements or measuring sticks in the photographs helps later when the actors act against these known backgrounds (as in archaeological recording).

The assumption that naturally occurring activities cannot be representationally photographed is incorrect. With some forethought and arrangements, many useful, but not precise, calculations can be retrieved. The speed of arm or leg movements can be estimated if a complex background is used and if the details of its pattern have been measured.

Representational films have poor backgrounds because they are photographed from angles that allow environmental objects to function as spatial markers. Spatial markers are rarely entertaining, but they serve vital purposes in the analysis of representational films (cf. Scherer's paper, infra).

Placing the Camera

Two concerns are critical in deciding where to put the camera. The first is that the camera be placed so that problems of foreshortening and other perspective distortions are minimized (cf. Miller and Nelson 1973). If arm and leg movements are to be measured, then the limbs must be photographed at known angles, so that the lengths of the segments can be used to reconstruct angular displacements. For example, when possible, side views have been preferred because the limbs are distorted least when moving in a plane perpendicular to the camera.

The second concern is with activities that cover large areas. The photographer has a problem of calculating focus. Most movie cameras either focus on ground glass or have split-image focusing, both being through the lens. It has been shown that it is best to use spots where distance settings can be made without manual focusing through the lens. With prearranged spots, focusing involves only the setting of the focus ring to the right distance. It has been shown that the focal ring distances have to be checked and recalibrated from time to time.

It is always better to photograph unexpected action from a position of certain focus than to try to focus in a hurry. If the subjects do something unusual at an unanticipated place, shoot and focus while shooting. Learn to shoot first and then focus, or the action will be over before the focusing is accomplished. When distances are measured, always notice the paths of radii of equal distances so that these can be used to help when guessing the focus for unexpected actions. With practice, guessing distances and setting the focus ring on distance markings can be satisfactory. In fact, an entire staging area can be mapped, using depth of focus and predetermined radii, so that actions at any spot can be focused on immediately. The distance markings on the lens can then be used almost entirely for focusing operations.

Activating the Camera

In representational filming, the length of the sequences should be greater than the length of the action desired. If gestures are being photographed, the sequences should contain material happening before the gesture and after the gesture so that the gesture itself is embedded in a sequence of greater length. The way a "happy" face develops, as well as the instant when the face is fully formed, is important, and the photographer must resist stopping the film as soon as the desired action point is reached, which is usually too soon. The "critical" moments of activity are important only so far as they are preceded and followed by material introducing and finishing their development. Once the camera is activated and an action is being photographed, the photographer has to resist turning to another scene because something, such as a noise, is happening there. Too many documentaries jump from person to person, for example, at a group encounter, without documenting the development of any action exchanges for any of the performers. Beginnings and endings are important. The middle, though it may contain the desired example, should not be cut to the bone.

Recording the Controls

A record must be kept at all costs, usually in the film images themselves. Film with an unknown or mislabeled frames-per-second speed is almost worthless. Shooting speeds can be calculated directly from the film in some instances, but usually films at 24 or 32 frames-per-second look so similar that without knowledge of the actual speeds it is next to impossible to tell them apart. Records must accompany the film: data sheets have to be kept. All the arrangements, measurements, conditions of shooting, etc., have to be documented for data retrieval.

The primary difference between illustrative and representational films is that for the latter records exist which identify the parameters of the film that are suitable for data retrieval. Without these records, the film is not a repository of behavioral data.

Developing the Film

Development must match the exposure conditions. If the camera settings have all been recorded, proper development should be no problem, even when pushing film (see above).

After the film has been delivered to the laboratory for developing, markings on the film cases are lost. That is why data should be kept on the film images. When rolls of similar activity are being developed at the same time, the photographer has to have a record of which is which. It is always a good practice to tag each roll with a leader and a finishing sequence of some particular object (a blackboard with a number, a picture of an unusual object, etc.) so that identification is secured. With stills, which are cut apart, there is no way to restore order if the rolls are not separately batched and if the sequences are not numbered. Some films come with marginal numbers and some cameras now number the exposures at the time of exposure. Some method has to be planned to keep the data sorted. If rolls of stills have to be kept in sequence, then the film can be developed with instructions to the laboratory not to separate and mount the stills. In this way, even still rolls can be tagged and the sequences kept intact.

Editing the Film

Editing in the usual sense does not exist for representational filming because what is captured is in the images, and efforts to separate the images or change the sequencing destroy the data. Film sequences can be clipped or separated for filing if desired, providing no sequencing is thereby lost. Libraries of clipped sequences should be started because few exist for body behavior and their value would be considerable (cf. Lomax's paper, *supra*).

Analyzing the Film

The analysis is usually a frame-by-frame process with data collection methods prescribed by the controls arranged. Storage systems have to be considered. Computers serve this function well, and most current representational film workers have turned to the computer for this very purpose.

EXAMPLES OF POSTURE AND DANCE

Two examples of representational filming will be used to illustrate two of the ways film can be used to record and analyze body behavior. The two examples given have to do with expressive posture and dance. In the case of the postural research, the problem was to examine how people structure their limb positions to express emotional categories. Specifically, how similar or different are arm positions for "happy" or for "sad" when a person is sitting or standing? Are limb positions for "angry" and "hate" similar or different? Could limb positions for "pleased" and "happy" be distinguished, and would the limb displays sort the emotional categories?

The second example is from Western ballet. A routine called *tour en l'air* was chosen for analysis. The problem was to discover what limb movements contribute to or detract from the quality of a dance performance. The routine as defined asks performers to jump straight up into the air, to turn around twice while in the air, and to land in the same spot, facing the same direction, as they were in before takeoff. This stunt was chosen because there are clearly two components to the performance: biomechanical components and expressive components. The biomechanics of the stunt are to jump high, without wobbling or tilting off center, and to land without leaning or falling over. The expressive components are to make the movements that create the jumping and turning torques as "graceful" as possible and to land without giving the impression of being off balance or of having performed a difficult trick. To the balletomane there are incommensurables which make a performance "graceful," "rhythmical," or "in good line," and this work was designed to identify these.

Postural Example

The purpose of the work was to discover whether individuals have any rules or principles that structure their performances of emotional categories. The work focused on the four limbs; the face was not studied.

Two subjects were chosen: a young girl twelve years old and an adult female twenty-six years old (cf. Prost 1973 for a fuller exposition of the project). Each of the subjects was asked to take postures that would, in her opinion, communicate a particular emotion to a viewer. The subjects were asked to express the emotional categories while standing, sitting on a chair, sitting on the floor, kneeling, or lying on the floor, in alternation. Only the standing and chair-sitting postures were sampled extensively; the others were included on a smaller scale for comparison.

The emotional categories to be portrayed were sixty different emotional types chosen from the literature on expressive emotions (Darwin 1965 [1872]; Allport and Vernon 1933; Davitz 1969). The words for the categories were read to the subjects and the subjects tried to produce a posture that would communicate that emotion. The most frequently used emotional terms were: sad, happy, afraid, sexy, angry, surprised, relaxed, tired, love, hate, sexless, sick, guilty, shy, courageous, vain, and arrogant.

The still camera was arranged to photograph the performances. The camera position, angle to the subject, distance from subject, etc., were recorded for each photograph. The pictures were taken so that the subjects could reassume the postures at a later time. The purpose of the pictures was to document the limb displays in a way that would allow reconstruction of the poses by the same subjects.

After the collection of the sample was completed, the subjects helped by retaking the poses. The positions of the various limb segments were measured from the photographs using the knowledge of the subject's body proportions, camera positions, etc. Some parameters were easy to measure directly from the photos, while others, because of foreshortenings, etc., had to be measured during the reconstructions. The photographs served as the standards by which the reconstructions were accomplished. It would have been impossible to take measurements during the actual performances because the subjects would have lost all sense of spontaneity. By using the photographs as intermediates, the subjects were free to perform without restraint.

The display of the limb segments was analyzed using the globographic method of Albert and Strasser (Albert 1876; Strasser and Gassmann 1893; Dempster 1955; Steindler 1955). The globographic method is illustrated in Figure 1. The body is conceptually broken into its rigid elements, or

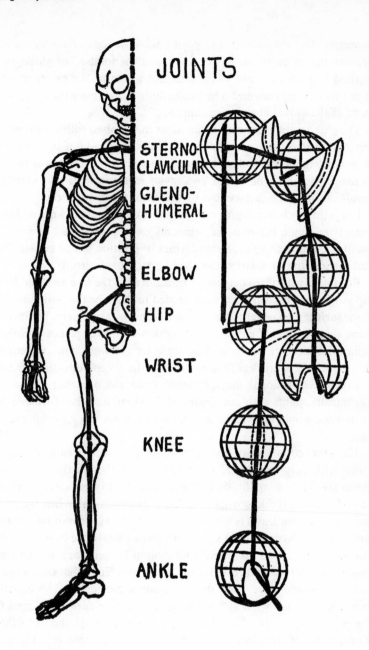

Figure 1. Composite diagram showing the human skeleton, its derived segments, and globographic constructions for the major limb joints. The maximum range of motion allowed each segment is shown on the globographic constructions. Dotted lines indicate the limits on the globe hemispheres extending behind the plane of the page and solid lines indicate the limits on the hemispheres extending out of the plane of the page.

segments. The movements and positional variations of the limbs occur because the segments are discontinuous at the joints. The globographic method is a construction which aids in translating the positions of the segments into measurements by establishing conventions for the measurement of the angles at the joint centers.

The globographic convention assumes that globes, with their centers at the joint centers, are surrounding the joints. The radii of the globes correspond to the functional long axes of the segments. Motions or positions of the segments are described by angular measurements that specify the points on the globe surfaces cut by the distal segments of each joint pair.

For joints with one degree of freedom (like the human knee and elbow joints) the angle between the segments can be measured directly. For rotations, long axis spins, a standarized 0° position has to be established and the amount of rotation can then be measured directly.

For joints with three degrees of freedom (like the human shoulder and hip joints) two measurements are needed to describe the positions on the globe surfaces: an equatorial and a meridional measurement. The measurement that is roughly equivalent to flexion-extension planes is called an equatorial measure in the globographic terminology. The measurement that is roughly equivalent to movement in abduction-adduction directions is called a meridional measurement in the globographic terminology. Technically, joints with one degree of freedom, and therefore one plane of motion, would have an equatorial measure but not a meridional measure.

The knee, elbow, wrist, and ankle joints were measured as if they were joints with only one degree of freedom, even though this is somewhat inaccurate in its simplification. The combination of equatorial and meridional moves produces what is called circumduction. When the meridional range is small, as it is with the knee and elbow, the motion can be assumed to be planar without significant distortion. In the case of the ankle and wrist, the amount of meridional motion is significant, but measuring this or reconstructing it from the films was so difficult that the meridional variables would have been imprecise for these joints. The equatorial excursions for the wrist and ankle joints could be adequately read from the photographs, therefore these alone were taken on the live subjects. The amount of error introduced by these simplifications is not large and does not detract from the measurements as they are to be used here.

The measurements taken on the limbs were: shoulder equatorial (Se), shoulder meridional (Sm), shoulder rotation (Sr), elbow equatorial (Ee), forearm rotation (Fr), wrist equatorial (We), hip equatorial (He), hip meridional (Hm), hip rotation (Hr), knee equatorial (Ke), and ankle equatorial (Ae) for both right and left limbs. The equatorial variables are roughly measures of flexion-extension, the meridional variables are roughly measures of abduction-adduction, and the rotations are the long axis rotations of the segments involved. The conventions used to establish the globe and rotational scales with respect to body planes and directions of increasing or decreasing excursions are as follows:

SHOULDER   The globe center was the joint center of the glenohumeral joint with the shoulder in a relaxed position. The shoulder is a joint complex composed of the glenohumeral, acromioclavicular, pseudoscapular, and sternoclavicular joints. This complex was handled as if it were a single joint, as if the humerus were related to the thorax by only one joint. The center was defined as lying on a transverse plane above the sternal angle, roughly midway between the sternal angle and the suprasternal notch. The center was assumed to be fixed in this position, even when the arm was elevated, elevating the scapula, clavicle, and humeral head. This approximation is a satisfactory simplification as long as it is realized that the measurements derived from it only relate the humerus to the thorax. The humeral link was always taken as a straight-line distance between the distal end of the humerus and the fixed shoulder center. In consequence, during movement the humeral link changes in length; this complication was ignored. This convention is a reasonable but not accurate simplification (cf. Dempster 1965).

The 0° mark for the equatorial measure was taken to be directly over the head. The equatorial values increase as the segment moves down in front of the body in a parasagittal plane. The meridional 0° was taken to lie medially, in toward the body, making a transverse line with the fixed shoulder center of the other side. Increasing meridional values roughly correspond to abduction of the segment. Rotation was measured from a 0° position in the frontal plane, lying medially. Increasing rotation corresponds to outward rotation of the humerus.

ELBOW   The globe center was established just below a line connecting the medial and lateral epicondyles of the humerus, roughly halfway between the two epicondyles. Instantaneous centers of rotation were ignored by the convention of fixating the joint centers (Dempster 1955). This means that no measurement could be more precise than 5° with respect to the real joint centers. As Dempster (1955) comments, this is a reasonable level of precision when using photographs or living subjects.

Because globographic motion of the elbow joint is restricted, more or less, to one plane, that is, flexion-extension, the only measure would be an equatorial one. The 0° mark for the equatorial measure was placed coincident with the functional long axis of the humerus. Increasing equatorial values correspond to extensions of the forearm.

Rotation of the forearm was measured from a 0° position with the forearm pronated until the radial and ulnar distal ends lay in a plane which, in the anatomical position, would represent a frontal plane. Increasing values of forearm rotation represent pronation.

WRIST   The globe center was fixed as being just distal to the distal end of the radius on the radiocarpal axis. The center was between the lateral margins of the wrist roughly in the position of the lunate bone. The hand segment was a line passing from this center through the third metacarpal. Motion at this joint was taken only in one plane, flexion-extension. Although circumduction is significant, it was ignored for this study. Reconstruction of circumduction positions from the photographs was so difficult that their measurement would have been meaningless. The single plane of motion was the equatorial, with the 0° mark coincident with the functional axis of the forearm, increasing values representing palmar flexion.

HIP   The globe center was fixed in the head of the femur. The 0° mark for the equatorial measurement was placed directly over the joints, halfway between the anterior superior and posterior superior iliac spines, roughly in a line with the iliac tubercle. Increasing equatorial values represent extension of the thigh. The meridional 0° was placed in a frontal plane, medially, as with the humerus, and increasing values represent abduction. Rotation of the femoral segment was measured with the 0° mark medial, in the frontal plane, increasing values representing outward rotation.

KNEE   The knee center was fixed on a line from the lateral epicondyle to just below the medial epicondyle, in the intercondylar fossa. Motion was considered for only one plane, flexion-extension because of the difficulty of reconstructing other positions from the photographs. The equatorial 0° mark was coincident with the femoral long axis and increasing values represent extension of the foreleg.

ANKLE   The ankle center was fixed at the middle of the flexion axis of the talus, which joins a point just between the medial malleolus and a point on the lateral malleolus. The foot segment axis was a line that passed through this center parallel to a plane drawn from the tuberosity of the calcaneus to the distal end of the first metatarsal. Motion of the joint was measured for only one plane of motion, flexion-extension. The 0° mark for the equatorial circle was coincident with the functional long axis of the foreleg. Increasing values represent planar flexion.

The application of the globographic system to the postural data supplied twenty-two variables describing each of the expressive postures. The total sample size was 722 poses. The poses, translated into twenty-two globographic variables for each pose, were displayed in a multidimensional field formed by the conjoint, Euclidean arrangement of the twenty-two variables. This field was examined to discover groupings in the data.

The results of the analysis showed that there was one large group in the field, encompassing all the cases. Embedded within this group were two areas of high density. One dense area was composed mostly of standing postures. The other area was composed mostly of chair-sitting postures. Lying, kneeling, and floor-sitting cases were scattered rather loosely in regions outlying the two dense areas.

The dense areas had centers that corresponded, roughly, to the standing and chair-sitting modal points, which were defined by taking the modes for each variable for each postural type. The linear distances of the cases from the standing and chair-sitting modal points are graphed in Figure 2. Floor-sitting, kneeling, and lying modes are included, although the number of cases for each of these postural types did not allow any accurate analysis of their displays.

The position of the standing mode represents a hypothetical center of "standing" habits of the two subjects. People with differing habits would have different centers. The position of the chair-sitting modal center is determined partly by the subjects' habits and partly by the biomechanical demands placed on the subjects by the chair used in the research.

The two-dimensional graph of Figure 2 distorts the multidimensional (twenty-two dimensions) nature of the real field. The points are grouped in two "tails" in the graph leading away from the centers. Actually, in the real field, the cases in the tails surround the centers like pins in a pincushion. The graph reduces the true display to its projection on a plane passing through the standing and chair-sitting centers.

The emotional categories were found to be extended groups surrounding the centers of the two dense areas. The number of cases for the other modal centers was too small to allow reasonable analysis of their displays.

The emotional groups around the two centers, standing and chair-sitting, were like the pins in a pincushion, except that each group would have been a very fat pin. Each fat pin, wider as its distance from the center increased, corresponded to an emotional category, such as "happy," "sad," etc. There were groups for the same emotions around each center, with a

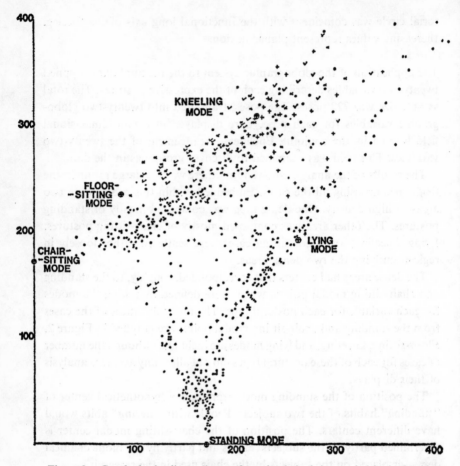

Figure 2.   Graph plotting linear distance from the chair-sitting mode (abscissa) against linear distance from the standing mode (ordinate). Postural attitudes are represented by: dots for standing, plus signs for lying, circles for chair sitting, Greek alphas for floor sitting, and checks for kneeling. The positions of the modal attitudes are indicated by large, circled crosses. Sixteen cases, falling beyond the right-hand corner, were eliminated for convenience.

few exceptions. The groups overlapped, particularly near the centers. In a few cases, e.g. "angry," there was more than one emotional group at the same center. Between the groups and at the further reaches of the display were numbers of solitary cases that did not enter the groups.

Figure 3 shows the same display with lines connecting cases in the same group. The extensional nature of the groups is clearly visible. The groups start with cases near the center and extend away from the centers with more and more distant cases. Some data suggest that distance from the centers is correlated with intended intensity by the subjects. The more

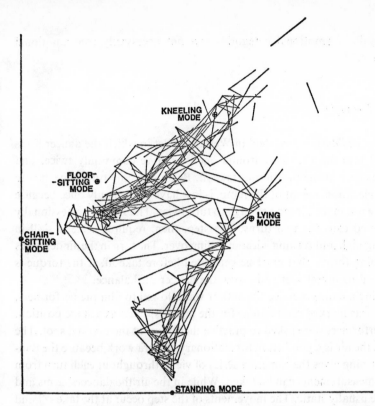

Figure 3. Same graph as in Figure 2. Lines connect cases in the same expressive group. Ungrouped cases have been eliminated. The graph shows the general orientation of the groups. Individual groups are not identifiable. Some cases enter into two or more groups, usually less that four, and they are connected by more than one or two lines.

"happy," "sad," "angry," etc., the farther from the centers. Some groups join across the area between the two tails, forming a single group, of the same emotional category, lying between the two centers.

In all, there were eighty-one groups in the field. The multiplicity of groups resulted because there were commonly two groups for each emotional category, one at each center. In some cases there were more than two groups around a center, for example, "standing angry I" and "standing angry II." These were behavioral situations where, for these subjects, there existed more than one kind of representation of a single-worded category.

The photographs were shown to other subjects who tried to guess the emotions being portrayed. The best guessing, by two subjects, one male and one female, was 25 percent correct. Using the groups and their defined boundaries in the multidimensional space, the sample was sorted, with 52 percent correct sorting. The groups represent, however, the subjects' portrayals of emotional categories and not necessarily true emotional reactions.

Dance Example

The *tour en l'air* is a *pas* 'step' in Western ballet in which the dancer leaps straight into the air, turns around once, or more commonly twice, and lands exactly in the position of takeoff. Beginners only turn once. Those whose elevation, height of the jump, is low have to turn only once because they are not in the air long enough to turn twice. The step as professionally performed calls for two turns. The step, then, requires athletic skill in jumping high and turning without falling over. The turn in the air demands a spinning torque that must be generated before takeoff. If the torque is produced incorrectly, it will throw the dancer off balance.

During a dance practice the author was allowed to film the performers. A spot was marked on the stage for the dancers to use as a stage position. The performers were asked to practice their *tours* at the marked spot. The turn in the air is a good stunt for stationary camera work because the dancer's turning gives the camera a series of views throughout each turn from which measurements can be taken. While in the air the dancers' arms and legs are usually static. The movements of the step occur at the take-off and landing, so the camera position was chosen to record these two critical instants. The purpose of the films was to estimate the joint angles from the frames of the films.

I wanted the best performances from trained professionals, but they would allow only so much interference with their regimes. The final arrangements had to be a compromise between some control of the environment and noninterference with the practice and rehearsal sessions. The subjects agreed to jump at the particular place, facing in a particular direction, but no more. Mirrors, strobe lights, etc., were not allowed. The sample was a catch-as-best-as-possible situation.

The films were analyzed for the same globographic variables as were used for the postural study except that the hip, shoulder, and forearm rotations could not be accurately estimated. This was unfortunate because rotations clearly played a vital role in the performances. However, the single camera in its stationary position could not capture a number of key rotational changes. The camera position was a flat side-view of the dancers. The limb angles at takeoff and landing were controlled most accurately for measurement. The positions during the turns were accurately assessed because the turning of the body gave many views of the limb arrangements.

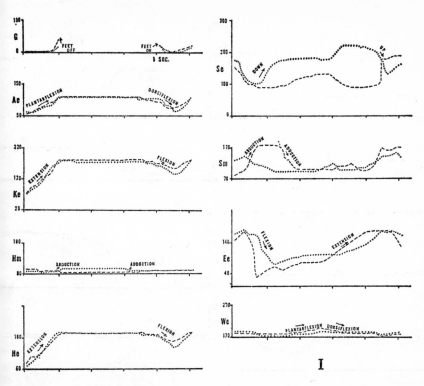

Figure 4. Eight globographic variables for performance I of the *tour en l'air*. The G curves are the angles between the foot and the ground. The right limbs are drawn as dashed lines and the left limbs as dotted lines.

Measurements of the dancers' proportions were collected with a set of standardized photographs. Limb foreshortenings and perspective distortions could be calculated from these.

The camera was placed so that as the dancers came out of their turns, they would be facing the camera head on. The spot on the stage was located next to a piece of complex scenery which served as a "grid" behind the dancer; various details of the scenery had been measured prior to the photography. If this routine alone had been the only subject of interest, some other more favorable situations might have been arranged. However, this was one of a number of dance routines that were being recorded for a collection on classical ballet. With the larger sample in mind, the author had to resist the temptation to intrude too much on the rehearsals and on the actual performances, which were then also photographed for comparison. Under the circumstances, greater control and accuracy had to be sacrificed in order to record real events.

Representational filming does not have to record everything with ac-

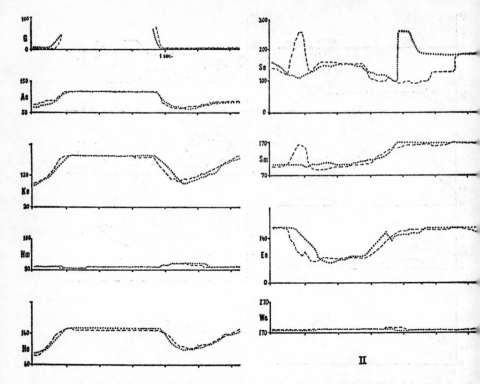

Figure 5.   Eight globographic variables for performance II of the *tour en l'air*. The G curves are the angles between the foot and the ground. The right limbs are drawn as dashed lines and the left limbs as dotted lines.

curacy, nor need the equipment always be complex, if such is not feasible. The point is that some set of variables is chosen and these variables are specifically controlled. The films are permanent records for these parameters alone.

Figures 4 through 8 are the records of the joint angles for five performances of the *tour en l'air*. Performances III and IV were done by the same subject. All the performances except V were double turns. The subject for V was unable to get high enough to do two turns and did only one turn. That subject was in fact not a professional but someone who had had dance training several years earlier and who served as a baseline for a "novice" example. The height of the jumps was about $1^1/_2$ feet for performances I and II, about 1 foot or slightly more for III and IV, and about $^7/_{10}$ foot for performance V.

The curves in Figures 4 through 8 are for the ankle equatorials (Ae), knee equatorials (Ke), hip meridionals (Hm), hip equatorials (He), shoulder equatorials (Se), shoulder meridionals (Sm), elbow equatorials (Ee),

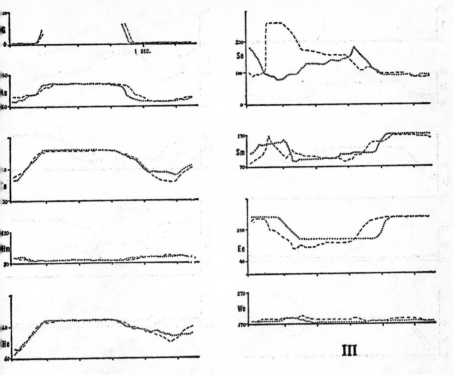

Figure 6. Eight globographic variables for performance III of the *tour en l'air*. The G curves are the angles between the foot and the ground. The right limbs are drawn as dashed lines and the left limbs as dotted lines.

and wrist equatorials (We). The G curves represent the angles of the planar surfaces of the feet with respect to the ground. The space in the G graphs indicates the time during which the dancers were in the air. Dotted lines indicate the left legs and dashed lines the right legs.

The lower limbs form a link system: foot, tibial segment, and femoral segment. From the angles for G, Ke, and Ae, the height of the hip joint from the ground was calculated. The hip joint heights are graphed in Figure 9. The graph shows the heights as percentages of the total length of the legs when fully extended. The heights are arranged according to the decreasing heights of the jump, performance I being the highest and V being the lowest jump. These charts show that subject V bent down lower in preparation for the jump than did other the subjects but did not come out of the deeper "knee bend" with the same accelerations. At the end of subject V's curves, there is a slowing of the upward push of the legs, reducing the effectiveness of subject V's application of force to the body mass. The two legs for subject V worked less in unison.

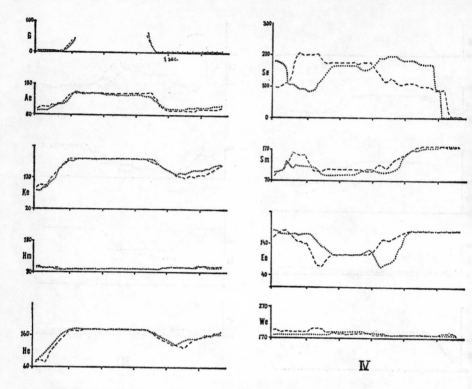

Figure 7.   Eight globographic variables for performance IV of the *tour en l'air*. The G curves are the angles between the foot and the ground. The right limbs are drawn as dashed lines and the left limbs as dotted lines.

Two interesting side issues arise in the curves of Figure 9. The differentiation of the heights for I through IV cannot be correlated with the slopes of the curves because the performances were photographed at 48 frames-per-second, a speed too slow to pick up the final instants of takeoff. If a speed of 64 or more frames-per-second had been used, the graphs could have been correlated with the heights of the jumps. Performer I was having trouble jumping straight up and tended to deviate in his flight path. The graph of I shows why. Performer I tended to jump from one leg. Performers II and III–IV (III and IV being two performances by the same dancer) had greater unison between their right and left legs and took straighter travel paths.

Reference to the graphs of Figures 4 through 8 shows that the subjects, except V, jumped primarily from the knees and hips and that the two were well coordinated. The deviations between right and left for subject I, causing wobbling during flight, also show up. Subject V jumped more from

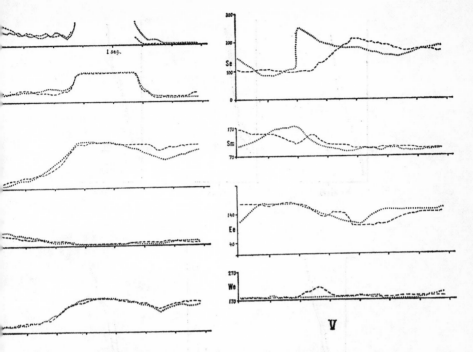

Figure 8. Eight globographic variables for performance V of the *tour en l'air*. The G curves are the angles between the foot and the ground. The right limbs are drawn as dashed lines and the left limbs as dotted lines.

the knee and ankle, and this probably explains much of the low elevation of performance V.

In the landings, subject V, having jumped lower, had to absorb less falling momentum in the lower limb joints and the He, Ke, and Ae slopes (Figures 4 through 8) for the landing are shallower. Also, subject V, perhaps because of the deep bending of the knees at takeoff, had greater deviations of the Hm measures at takeoff; this may have hindered the full use of the hips to get elevation. Performers II and III–IV had the more "catlike" landings, and part of this is due to the Hm movements. The performers let part of the force of the landing be absorbed with muscles acting to adduct the legs.

The film strips were shown to five balletomanes who commented on the "qualities" of the various performances. The landings of III and IV were considered the best. The graphs show that the slopes of the Ke and He curves are shallow for III and IV and explain the lack of "jerkiness" in these landings. Subject V also had a graceful landing, but this was accom-

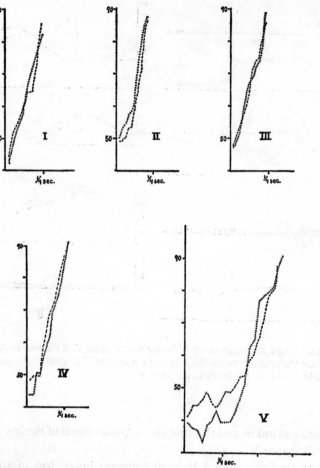

Figure 9.   Graphs showing the height of the right and left hip joints from the ground, expressed as percentages of total lower limb length, for the five performances of the *tour en l'air*. The right limbs are drawn as dashed lines and the left limbs as dotted lines.

plished by low elevation and therefore less effort in absorbing the falling momentum. The subject in III and IV took a greater part of the slowing momentum at the ankles than at the hip or knees, and this allowed the hip and knees to have their low slopes. Also, the dancer of III and IV landed with both knees and hips more in unison, giving his landing a straighter and less "tilted" appearance, requiring less adjustment at the end of the step.

From the balletomanes' comments, pinpointing the instances when "ungraceful" things happened, the real "grace" of the step was in the arms! Performer II was judged quite "mechanical" in his performance: the graphs agree. For all the dancers, spinning torque was translated to the body through one arm primarily, as the Se, Sm, and Ee curves show. Performer II made this quite evident, as the Se and Sm graphs demonstrate. The graphs for the upper limbs for performer II all show great unison between right and left, and points of jerky action, steep places on the curves, are easily read. Places of jerkiness stand out more because the rest of the curves are so tedious.

The absorption of the spinning torque left at landing is clearly shown in performer II's curve of the left limb Se. The subject in II had the arms dropped at the sides, as the Se shows. The Sm and Ee curves show places of jerkiness and long, uninteresting stretches of lack of movement. This gave the whole performance a mechanical appearance.

Performer I was considered "OK" but not "elegant." Again, one arm gives turning torque and one arm absorbs turning torque. There are places of great slope, usually in one joint or another, but these are rarely correlated throughout the limbs. This gave the performance a disassembled appearance. The arms did not end in unison and the Se and Sm graphs show distinct countermovements of the joints occurring simultaneously.

Performances III and IV were judged quite "graceful" and "elegant." Throughout both charts there are crossing lines, with movements of one joint being mimicked by similar ones of its bilateral partner slightly later. This gave the effect of leading movements with following mimicry by the other arm: it held the performances together, as with counterpoint in music. The turning torque absorbed at landing was less for subject III–IV, or at least appeared so. If the timing of the steep slopes in the graphs is compared with the position of the performer's body, it is found that many of the fastest moves occurred at such times and in such ways that the observer would not have noticed. For example, it might be suspected that performer III–IV jumped less high because of a lack of ability. This was not the case. Performers I and II jumped high in the effort to make 2 complete turns in the air. Performer III–IV really did only $1^3/_4$ turns in the air; that is, he landed before completing the full 2 turns. Performers I and II landed facing the "audience," and in order not to overshoot the landing and end sideways to the audience, they had to stop the turning torque immediately on impact. Performer III–IV landed facing about 90° away from the audience and let the remaining turning torque be absorbed against the legs in turning the body around to the audience. Thus the audience did not see the "finish" until most of the torque had been absorbed, and the process of absorption was done in a sideview to the audience, where the jerky movements were less observable. The uses of the elbows in performances I through IV are clearly distinctive and show coordinated moves with the Se variable. Performance IV was judged to be the best of all the performances in terms of "grace" and "overall quality." In terms of what the audience would have seen, the performance also had the most motions which "cut space" in large, open movements.

CONCLUSIONS

The subject of representational filming has been discussed as it relates to photography of body behavior, that is, the external appearance of the body in movement and posing. The broader subject of representational filming of social, task, and object-related behavior — how people interact with one another, perform tasks, and interact with their environments — has not been discussed.

The concept of representational filming is important because application of its principles serves to establish an appreciation of its uses. Permanent storage of analyzable films on a variety of subjects becomes desirable. The use of film for teaching purposes is expanded by recognizing the use of film as a data supplier. Phenomena that are beyond the immediacy of the classroom can be supplied as primary data through representational film; the concept of documentaries is expanded to an appreciation of the less artistic, less dramatic, but more serviceable functions of representational films. It is hoped that this brief survey will stimulate a greater recognition of what was the earliest use of the photographic processes and what is now a vital contribution to the sciences of living functions.

REFERENCES

ALBERT, EDUARD
   1876   Zur Mechanik des Hüftgelenkes. *Medizinische Jahrbücher der K.K. Gesellschaft der Ärzte zu Wien* 1876:105–132.
ALLPORT, G. W., P. E. VERNON
   1933   *Studies in expressive movement*. New York: Macmillan.
AMAR, J.
   1920   *The human motor*. New York: E. P. Dutton. (Original edition 1914.)
BARNES, R. M.
   1963   *Motion and time study*. New York: John Wiley and Sons.
BERNSTEIN, N.
   1967   *The coordination and regulation of movements*. London: Pergamon.
BIRDWHISTELL, R. L.
   1970   *Kinesics and context*. Philadelphia: University of Pennsylvania Press.

BRAUNE, C. W., O. FISCHER
1895 Der Gang des Menschen. I. Theil. *Abhandlungen der mathematisch-physischen Classe.* Akademie der Wissenschaften zu Leipzig, 21:151–322.

CAMP, C. L., N. SMITH
1942 *Phylogeny and functions of the digital ligaments of the horse.* Berkeley: University of California Press.

CARLET, GASTON
1872 *Essai experimental sur la locomotion humaine: étude de la marche.* Annales des Sciences Naturelles, Section de Zoologie 16: Article 6; Bibliothèque de l'Ecole des hautes études, Section des sciences naturelles 6: Article 6.

CERAM, C. W. [KURT W. MAREK]
1965 *Archaeology of the cinema.* New York: Harcourt, Brace and World.

CONDON, W. S., W. D. OGSTON
1966 Sound film analysis of normal and pathological behavior patterns. *Journal of Nervous and Mental Disease* 143: 338–346.

COOPER, J. M., *editor*
1971 *Selected topics on biomechanics.* Chicago: Athletic Institute.

COOPER, J. M., R. B. GLASSOW
1968 *Kinesiology.* St. Louis: C. V. Mosby.

DARWIN, CHARLES R.
1965 *The expression of the emotions in man and animals.* Chicago: University of Chicago Press. (Original edition 1872.)

DAVITZ, J. R.
1969 *The language of emotion.* New York: Academic Press.

DEMPSTER, W. T.
1955 The anthropometry of body action. *Annals of the New York Academy of Sciences* 63: 559–585.
1961 "Free-body diagrams as an approach to the mechanics of human posture and motion", in *Biomechanical studies of the musculo-skeletal system.* Edited by F. G. Evans, 81–135. Springfield: Charles C. Thomas.
1965 Mechanisms of shoulder movement. *Archives of Physical Medicine and Rehabilitation* 42: 49–70.

DUCHENNE, G. B. A.
1949 *Physiology of motion.* Philadelphia: J. B. Lippincott. (Translation of *Mécanisme de la physionomie humaine,* 1862.)

DUCROQUET, R., J. DUCROQUET, P. DUCROQUET
1968 *Walking and limping.* Philadelphia: J. B. Lippincott.

EBERHART, H. D., V. T. INMAN, B. BRESLER
1954 "The principal elements in human locomotion", in *Human limbs and their substitutes.* Edited by P. E. Klopsteg and P. D. Wilson, 437–471. New York: McGraw-Hill.

EDGERTON, H. E., J. R. KILLIAN
1954 *Flash ultra-high speed photography.* Boston: Branford.

EFRON, D.
1941 *Gesture and environment.* New York: King's Crown.

EKMAN, P., W. V. FRIESEN, P. ELLSWORTH
1972 *Emotion in the human face.* New York: Pergamon.

GIEDION, S.
   1955   *Mechanization takes command.* New York: Oxford University Press.
GILBRETH, F. B.
   1911   *Motion study.* New York: D. Van Nostrand.
GRAY, J.
   1944   Studies in the mechanics of the tetrapod skeleton. *Journal of Experimental Biology* 20: 80–116.
   1968   *Animal locomotion.* London: Weidenfeld and Nicolson.
HAMILTON, W. J., G. SIMON
   1958   *Surface and radiological anatomy.* Cambridge: W. Heffer and Sons.
HEWES, G.
   1955   World distribution of certain postural habits. *American Anthropologist* 57: 231–244.
HOWELL, A. B.
   1944   *Speed in animals.* Chicago: University of Chicago Press.
JONES, F. P., M. NARVA
   1955   Interrupted light photography to record the effect of changes in the poise of the head upon patterns of movement and posture in man. *Journal of Psychology* 40: 125–131.
KELLY, D. L.
   1971   *Kinesiology.* Englewood Cliffs: Prentice-Hall.
KONDO, S.
   1960   Anthropological study on human posture and locomotion. *Journal of the Faculty of Science, University of Tokyo* 2: 189–260.
LONDE, ALBERT
   1891   La photochromographie appliquée aux études médicales. *Internationale medizinisch – photographische Monatsschrift* 2: 9.
MANTER, J. T.
   1938   The dynamics of quadrupedal walking. *Journal of Experimental Biology* 15: 522–530.
MAREY, É. J.
   1868   *Du mouvement dans les fonctions de la vie...* Paris: G. Baillière.
   1895   *Movement.* New York: D. Appleton. (Translation of *Le Mouvement,* 1894.)
MILLER, D. I., R. C. NELSON
   1973   *Biomechanics of sport.* New York: Lea and Febiger.
MORTON, D. J., D. D. FULLER
   1952   *Human locomotion and body form.* Baltimore: Williams and Wilkins.
MUYBRIDGE, E.
   1955   *The human figure in motion.* New York: Dover. (Original, 1901.)
   1957   *Animals in motion.* New York: Dover. (Original, 1899.)
O'CONNELL, A. L., E. B. GARDNER
   1972   *Understanding the scientific basis of human movement.* Baltimore: Williams and Wilkins.
PINCUS, E.
   1969   *Guide to filmmaking.* New York: New American Library.
PLAGENHOEF, S.
   1971   *Patterns of human motion.* Englewood Cliffs: Prentice-Hall.

PROST, J. H.
1965 The methodology of gait analysis and gaits of monkeys. *American Journal of Physical Anthropology* 23: 215–240.
1973 "Expressive posture in humans". Unpublished manuscript.

RAMSAYE, TERRY
1964 "Motion pictures. I. History", in *Encyclopedia Britannica* 15:851–853.

ROGET, PETER M.
1824 Explanation of an optical deception in the appearance of the spokes of a wheel seen through vertical apertures. *Philosophical Transactions of the Royal Society of London* 1825: 131–140; *Annalen der Physik und Chemie* (1825) 5: 93–104; *Annals of Philosophy, or Magazine of Chemistry, Mineralogy, Mechanics, and the Arts*, second series (1825) 10: 107–112.

SAINSBURY, P.
1954 A method of recording spontaneous movements by time-sampling motion pictures. *Journal of Mental Science* 100: 742–748.

STEINDLER, A.
1955 *Kinesiology of the human body.* Springfield: Charles C. Thomas.

STRASSER, H., A. GASSMANN
1893 Hülfsmittel und Normen zur Bestimmung und Veranschaulichung der Stellungen, Bewegungen und Kraftwirkungen am Kugelgelenk, insbesondere am Huft- und Schultergelenke des Menschen. *Anatomische Hefte* 2 (Abtheilung 1):389–473.

TAFT, R.
1955 "An introduction: Eadweard Muybridge and his work," in *The human figure in motion.* Edited by E. Muybridge, vii–xii. New York: Dover.

VREDENBREGT, J., J. WARTENWEILER, *editors*
1971 *Biomechanics II*; volume six: *Medicine and sport.* Baltimore: University Park Press.

WARTENWEILER, J., E. JOKL, M. HEBBELINCK, *editors*
1968 *Biomechanics: technique of drawings of movement and movement analysis*; volume two: *Medicine and sport.* Basel and New York: S. Karger.

A Photographic Method for the Recording and Evaluation of Cross-Cultural Proxemic Interaction Patterns

SHAWN E. SCHERER

Several field studies in the area of human ecology have been directed in recent years at the investigation of proxemic behavior patterns. The stimulus for much of this research has been E. T. Hall's speculations on intercultural conversation interaction distances, as outlined in his book, *The hidden dimension*. Specifically, Hall has noted that peoples of different cultures not only speak different languages but inhabit DIFFERENT SENSORY WORLDS (Hall 1966:2). As a result, normal everyday conversation distances differ among culture groups. This, Hall suggests, often creates uncomfortable situations when individuals of different cultures attempt to interact socially.

Attempts to evaluate Hall's contention have, as yet, met with little success. While some studies find wide differences in spatial behavior among culture groups (e.g. Aiello and Jones 1971; Watson and Graves 1966), others find only slight variations (Willis 1966) or none at all (Forston and Larson 1968). The failure to show consistent findings is likely due in part to the lack of sophisticated techniques for monitoring and evaluating proxemic interaction data. Past studies have relied almost entirely on eyeball techniques, often obtrusive in nature, for recording human interaction distances (Aiello and Jones 1971; Hall 1955), with very little attention being paid to the use of photographic recordings. Undoubtedly, one reason for the present paucity of photographic studies is the difficulty in obtaining good photographs of dyadic groupings in the

I am indebted to Oded J. Frenkel, Anthony N. Doob, and Abraham Ross for many helpful ideas which have been incorporated in the present technique. I am grateful to Oded J. Frenkel, Elaine J. Scherer, and Lynne R. Saltzman for their assistance during experimentation stages and in the preparation of this manuscript.

horizontal plane, free from obstructions by other persons in the immediate vicinity, and yet still remaining unobtrusive.

Another problem seems to be the inadequacy of present photogrammetric methods in determining physical distance between interacting members, which takes into account the subject's angle of orientation. Since orientation has been shown to be a salient variable in evaluating individual distance (Aiello and Jones 1971; Scherer and Schiff 1973), any appropriate observational technique must necessarily take angle of orientation into consideration.

Still another problem plaguing present proxemic behavior recording methods is the lack of stringent sets of criteria and uniform procedures for obtaining reliable data. Few studies, for instance, have attempted to ensure for randomization in the selection of subjects from their samples. The incongruity among past studies could well be due to this problem alone.

Because of existing inadequacies in proxemic recording and evaluation methods, I undertook to develop a methodology that would overcome those problems just mentioned. Three pilot studies allowed for extensive experimentation with an assortment of photographic recording and data scoring techniques. The photographic procedure that is outlined below was found to be the most precise and also the most reliable method tested. This method has subsequently been utilized, with considerable success, in two independent cross-subcultural studies of proxemic behavior of Black and White primary schoolchildren observed in school playground settings (Scherer i.p.). For explanatory purposes, sections on data collection and acceptance criteria for negatives are described with reference to these recent investigations.

DATA COLLECTION

A tripod-mounted camera with a 300-millimeter telephoto lens was erected at a predetermined position in a park adjacent to the schoolyard. The location was distant enough from the play area to be relatively inconspicuous to the great majority of students.[1] Precautions were taken to ensure that only those children not aware of the observers would be included. This was accomplished by angling the camera so that the closest subjects that could be photographed were at least one hundred feet (thirty meters) away.

[1] Our studies have shown that only those subjects standing within twenty-five yards of the observation point appear to show any interest in the camera and observers.

Only dyads meeting the following criteria were selected. Subjects must (1) be relatively stationary; (2) be engaged in verbal interaction — i.e. at least one of the subjects must be observed to be moving his lips; and (3) have no physical objects or individuals obstructing their freedom of movement.

For data collection, one observer acted as photographer, the other as recorder. At the onset of a play period, the photographer began scanning the schoolyard with the camera from left to right. The recorder then called out the required dyad to scan for[2] (chosen from a prepared list of random orderings). When the photographer found a dyad (meeting the criteria outlined earlier) he stopped scanning and called out, "Now." This signaled the recorder to begin clocking a predetermined time interval, taken from a prepared list of random time periods covering from 0.5 to 3.0 seconds, in one-half-second intervals.[3] Once this period had elapsed, the recorder signaled the photographer by saying, "Now," at which time the photographer immediately clicked the camera shutter mechanism. The photographer then described the sex, approximate age, position in the yard (separated into three quadrants), and distance from the observation point. Filming proceeded in this fashion until the play period ended. During any data collection session only the recorder knew the random order of conditions[4] and the random time intervals.

If one uses the data collection procedure just described, there is no possibility for SYSTEMATIC bias to enter because human error is avoided at each stage of monitoring through both the utilization of a stringent randomization procedure and photographic recordings.

Acceptance Criteria for Negatives

Only those negatives that fulfilled the following criteria were included in the photogrammetric analysis:
1. no physical obstruction of movement evident;
2. clear silhouette of complete dyad, including all bodily parts;

---

[2] In studies referred to here, dyads were either Black or White primary schoolchildren.
[3] These time intervals are determined prior to the data collection stage and will probably vary as a function of the age and culture of interactants. In the studies referred to, fifty independent observations of break-up time for Black and White dyads indicated that mean break-up time was 1.8 seconds for Blacks, 1.6 seconds for Whites, with individual values ranging from 0.1 to 4.0 seconds. The actual range to be utilized should be determined with reference to the variance obtained.
[4] Conditions were either Black or White dyadic groupings.

3. both feet, including toe and heel points of each interactant, in clear view;
4. relatively little apparent movement; and
5. both faces clearly shown.

PHOTOGRAMMETRY

A measure of the true separation, D_t, between two interactants can be obtained from a photographic image of the pair if exact distances to each member of the pair are known. In order for the observer to remain as unobtrusive as possible, and because interactants to be observed are generally spread over a fairly wide area, the determination of exact distances is considered to be undesirable and impractical. Instead, proxemic distance scores can be obtained by using the ratio D_t/H as a measure of proximity, where D_t is a measure of average separation between members of a dyad, and H is their average height on the photographic image. This ratio is independent of the average distance of the dyad from the camera. It is, however, not independent of the orientation of the dyad to the camera. A method for taking the orientation into account is described below. Note that the ratio D_t/H is an unbiased measure of any differences between members of any two culture groups, provided that members of one group are not MARKEDLY DIFFERENT in average height from the other. This assumption seems justified.[5]

The procedure for determining the ratio D_t/H is a follows. Using the thirty-five-millimeter frames of the (negative) film, the image of a pair is projected onto the bed of an enlarger, and curves and lines are carefully drawn. Figure 1 depicts one example. The curves T_1G_1 and T_2G_2, designated here as "skewer" lines, are drawn to represent imaginary curves in a vertical plane (or nearly vertical plane) which are centrally located within the body of each subject, extending from the tip of his head to a point between his feet. In drawing these curves, the positions of the arms need not be taken into account. In practice, it is found that there is little doubt as to where a skewer curve should be drawn, regardless of the orientation of a subject to the camera. The curve is localized by the tip of the head and the neck and is drawn just ventral to the spine and parallel to it through the trunk. It tends to come nearer the leg on which most of the weight of the subject is resting.

---

[5] If we assumed the average height of members of one culture group to be greater even by two inches, this would only introduce a bias of about 5 percent into the ratio D_t/H.

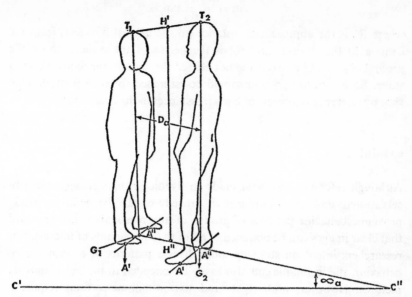

Figure 1. Geometrical parameters for determining the distance between a pair of subjects and their orientation to the camera

The points G_1 and G_2 are the intersections of the skewer curves with a line joining the midpoints (A' and A'') of the arches of the feet. G_1 and G_2 mark the intersections of the skewer curves with the ground. The angle α which the line G_1G_2 subtends from a horizontal line $C'C''$ gives the orientation of the pair of subjects with respect to the camera. D_a is the apparent average distance between the skewer curves, measured parallel to G_1G_2. When the two skewer curves are very nearly parallel, then D_a may be taken simply as the distance between them. Otherwise, D_a is calculated by dividing the area $T_1T_2G_2G_1$ by the average height of the subjects ($H'H''$).

The apparent separation D_a has to be corrected for the true angle of orientation α_t of the line $C'C''$. $C'C''$ is at right angles to the line of sight of the camera.[6]

The true separation D_t is given by $D_a/\text{Cosine } \alpha_t$. The angle α_t can be determined approximately from the apparent angle α_a (as measured from the projected images such as that depicted in Figure 1) by the relation

[6] This can be ensured by orienting the camera so that a vertical edge of its frame, as seen through the viewfinder, is parallel to a vertical line (e.g. the edge of an apartment building) in the field of view and remains in this orientation as the camera is swung from one side of the observational field to the other.

$$\tan \alpha_t = \frac{R_d}{R_h} \tan \alpha_a$$

where R_d is the approximate distance (to the nearest fifty feet) from the camera to the subjects and R_h is the height of the camera above the ground. R_h should be fixed and not altered throughout the data collection stage. R_d is free to vary and should be estimated for each photographic shot by reference to objects of known distances in the field of view.

COMMENTS

Although reference has been made to dyadic groupings only, this observational and photogrammetric procedure can be used to study proxemic behavior patterns of groups of any reasonable size, provided that clear images can be obtained of all of the interactants of interest. For researchers intent on studying more diverse patterns of human spatial behavior, the technique can also easily be extended to the use of moving pictures. However, both eight- and sixteen-millimeter films require a considerably greater initial expenditure for both film and developing than does print film.

In addition to the habitual problem of human error discussed earlier, the present method also overcomes those difficulties inherent to observational rating techniques commonly used. Because large numbers of individuals are to be observed in most proxemic investigations, experimenters in the past have been forced to make use of many different observers in each setting, and thus outcomes have been subject to the alternative explanation of differential observation styles. This, in turn, requires experimenters to run extensive reliability checks, creating unnecessary additional temporal and financial expense.

One common problem plaguing past studies seems to be the issue of exactly when the observer should make his distance judgment. Most investigators at present direct their observers to make their estimates at the first instant in time when they can "ascertain that at least one of the interactants is verbalizing to the other" (Aiello and Jones 1971:353). Despite such explicit instructions, it is nevertheless still possible that different observers tend to record their judgments at different temporal stages (i.e. one observer may wait considerably longer to confirm that two subjects are communicating), and that proxemic behavior is a function of the temporal stage of the conversation. These problems are also overcome by using the present technique.

REFERENCES

AIELLO, JOHN R., STANLEY E. JONES
  1971   Field study of the proxemic behavior of young school children in three subcultural groups. *Journal of Personality and Social Psychology* 19:351–356.
FORSTON, ROBERT F., CHARLES U. LARSON
  1968   The dynamics of space. *Journal of Communication* 18:109–116.
HALL, EDWARD T.
  1955   The anthropology of manners. *Scientific American* 162:85–90.
  1966   *The hidden dimension.* New York: Doubleday.
SCHERER, SHAWN E.
  i.p.   Proxemic behavior of primary school children as a function of their socioeconomic class and subculture. *Journal of Personality and Social Psychology.*
SCHERER, SHAWN E., MYRA R. SCHIFF
  1973   Perceived intimacy, physical distance and eye contact. *Perceptual and Motor Skills* 36:835–841.
WATSON, O. MICHAEL, THEODORE D. GRAVES
  1966   Quantitative research in proxemic behavior. *American Anthropologist* 68:971–985.
WILLIS, FRANK N.
  1966   Initial speaking distance as a function of the speakers' relationship. *Psychonomic Science* 5:221–222.

COMMENT *by J. H. Prost*

This paper raises two issues: 1) how to get unbiased samples, and 2) how to measure proxemic distances. On both issues the author gives valuable advice. The two-observer system he mentions (i.e. one cameraman and one recorder) could prove to be quite cumbersome, however. Videotape could be used instead, reducing the situation to a one-man system, the actual sampling being done on the tapes during viewing. Since videotapes can be erased and used repeatedly the cost would be minimal. Something would be lost in the definition of the video recordings but for the methods proposed in this paper most commercially available video systems would have the needed definition. With respect to Scherer's calculations of proxemic distances, it is a good idea to run a trial sample under the actual shooting conditions to see whether the method of calculations offers any more precision than outright "trained" guessing; there are some situations, for example filming with a telephoto lens combined with "crude" estimates of camera-to-subject distances, where the gain in precision is more an illusion of the geometricized formula than a reality. A trial set of values taken by several methods should identify the most efficacious strategy.

Proxemic Research: A Check on the Validity of its Techniques

ROBERT F. FORSTON

INTRODUCTION AND PROBLEM

Over a decade ago Edward T. Hall (1963, 1966) coined the term proxemics and argued for the necessity of a systematic observational and recording technique. The importance of such a system has been substantiated by its multidisciplinary use in fields such as anthropology, speech communication, psychology, and sociology. During the past decade, the number of empirical studies on personal space behavior has mushroomed. Each of these hinges on the validity of the methodology for determining the distance between the interactants. If a methodology lacks sufficient validity or reliability, the results of the entire investigation are questionable.

The techniques for determining distance between two people can be classified into three general methodologies: measurement, estimation and projection. Willis (1966) and Horowitz (Horowitz 1965; Horowitz et al. 1964) actually measured nose-to-nose distance in the presence of the subjects. Rosenfeld (1965) used a method of marking the bottom tips of chair legs with chalk. Forston and Larson (1968) took still photographs and interpolated personal space between the subjects from picture measurements of objects in the pictures of known length. Batchelor and Goethals (1972) assumed that the chairs remained stationary and that the subjects sat up straight; then, after the subjects had completed their task, the researcher measured the distance from the center of one chair to the center of another chair.

Regarding estimation techniques, several studies – Watson and Graves (1966), Baxter (1970), Aiello and Jones (1971), and Forston and Ericson

This research was supported by a Drake University Summer Research Stipend.

(1973) – have estimated spatial distances through the use of trained observers who were present during the experiment. Jones (1971) also used trained judges for estimating distances, but the judges made their determinations from slide pictures. Sommer (1961, 1962) and Albert and Dabbs (1970) employed a technique of calculating distances by placing chairs at various predetermined distances and having observers note the movement of furniture and different angles of posture.

Projective techniques, the third method of determining preferences of spatial relationships, were involved in several other studies. Little (1965), Guardo (1966), and Dosey and Meisels (1969) had subjects make placements of cardboard stick figures or of silhouette figures in relation to someone else. Horowitz (1965) and Pedersen (1971) both used forms where the subjects either drew pictures or drew circles indicating distance preference. Mehrabian (1968a and 1968b) developed a technique where a subject would react to an imaginary person in a variety of communication situations rather than to an actual addressee.

If one is in a position to make actual measurements of the distance between subjects, the question of validity of the measurement methodology is unimportant. Too many times, however, researchers find it necessary to determine personal space without the knowledge of the interactants so as not to influence or possibly contaminate the behavior of the interactants.

To date, none of the various techniques for calculating personal space has been evaluated in the literature. The primary purpose of this study was to test both the validity and the reliability of ten measurement and estimation techniques for determining distance (projective techniques will not be covered in this paper).[1] A secondary purpose was to help pin-point those methodologies for determining distances which were found to be the most accurate and reliable.

PROCEDURES

Thirty still photographs were initially taken of two interactants sitting in chairs at various distances, angles, and depths from one another. The actual nose-to-nose distances were measured by the researcher before the positions were changed for the next picture. This actual nose-to-nose measurement provided the researcher with known distances against which he could check the accuracy of the estimation and measurement techniques employed in previous studies. Slide pictures were also made from the still prints. Pictures 1 through 10 were used exclusively for training purposes

---

[1]   I believe the validity of projective techniques for determining personal space preferences is complex enough that they should be the subject of a separate study.

while Pictures 11 through 30 were used for checking the accuracy of the methods under investigation.

For the measurement technique, six conditions were investigated, using the process of interpolating personal space from picture measurements of objects of known length. The six measurement conditions consisted of three known reference objects using both prints and slides (projected on a wall). For the estimation technique, four conditions were used in comparing the accuracy of looking at a picture to estimate the nose-to-nose distance: both trained and untrained judges made estimations from prints or from slides.

MEASUREMENT TECHNIQUES

In performing the task for the accuracy of measurement techniques, three assistants were provided with a ruler with a sixty-unit-per-inch scale and with the actual distances of three natural reference objects included in each picture (the width of a door, the width of a small blackboard, and the length of a horizontal rung of a chair). The assistants were not told the actual nose-to-nose distances between the subjects in the pictures. Each assistant independently calculated the personal space from the twenty prints and twenty slides by an interpolation process; the assistant measured the picture distance of the reference object of known length and then calculated the unknown nose-to-nose distance.

The validity of personal space measurement techniques using printed photographs and slide photographs was examined with the t-test of means. Table 1 reports the accuracy and mean deviation of the measurement process using printed and slide photographs.

Table 1. Measurement technique: accuracy and mean deviation from actual distance using prints and slides

Reference objects	Prints		Slides	
	Mean deviation (Inches)	Accuracy (percent)	Mean deviation (inches)	Accuracy (percent)
Door	5.8	80.1	4.0	85.3
Chair	3.7	88.0	10.2	71.4
Blackboard	4.1	86.1	3.2	91.0
Combined	4.5	84.7	5.8	82.6

For the measurement technique using prints, the known length of the rung of a chair was slightly more accurate than that of the blackboard, but the difference in accuracy was not significantly different (t=0.42). The width of the door as a reference object was least accurate. The t-test of means revealed the following significant differences in accuracy: between the chair and the door as reference objects — P <.05 (t=1.79), and between the blackboard and the door — P=.10 (t=1.32).

Although the chair proved to be an excellent reference for prints, it was least accurate for slides. The blackboard and the door as known lengths were best for the interpolation process for slides. The mean difference between blackboard and chair data was significant at P <.025 (t=2.1), and the mean difference between the door and chair data was significant at P<.05 (t=1.88). The differences between prints and slides were statistically significant for the doors (.10>P> .05) and for the chairs (.05> P >.01); but not for the blackboards.

ESTIMATION TECHNIQUES

For the accuracy of the estimation techniques, untrained and trained judges were asked to estimate independently the nose-to-nose distance between two people from printed photographs and from slide pictures projected on a screen. The judges were never asked to estimate the distances from the same numbered picture for both the print and the slide. The untrained judges were randomly picked university students and received no training whatsoever.

The training session for the trained judges involved the following. A pool of twenty university students was shown ten slides at thirty-second intervals. During the intervals, each student independently made his estimate of the personal space. For the first five slides, the pool was informed of the actual nose-to-nose distances after each picture was shown in order to help the potential judges to improve their performance. For the remaining five slides, the actual distances were not revealed. This researcher examined the estimates of the last five slides and chose the

Table 2. Estimation technique: accuracy and mean deviation from actual distance using prints and slides

Type of Judge	Prints		Slides	
	Mean deviation (inches)	Accuracy (percent)	Mean deviation (inches)	Accuracy (percent)
Untrained	8.7	71.2	9.0	62.2
Best-trained	2.7	92.2	4.3	77.1

three individuals who came closest to guessing the actual nose-to-nose measurement to be the trained judges. Hence, although the entire pool would be qualified as trained judges, this study used only the best judges from a pool of trained judges.

The validity of the spatial distances as determined by estimation techniques using printed and slide pictures was investigated with the t-test of means. Table 2 describes the accuracy and mean deviation of the estimation process using printed and slide pictures.

The best-trained judges were clearly more accurate in their estimation of spatial distances both from prints and slides. The t-test of mean differences between trained and untrained judges revealed statistically significant differences as follows: prints at $P < .001$ $(t=3.65)$ and slides at $P = .025$ $(t=2.12)$.

DISCUSSION

For a comparison of the reliability and accuracy, Table 3 displays the rank order accuracy of the ten methods of determining personal distance from the most to the least accurate methods. Table 3 also shows the corresponding intermeasurement or interjudge reliability.

Table 3. Rank order accuracy and reliability of various methods of determining personal space

Description of technique	Accuracy (percent)	Inter-agreement reliability (percent)
E/prints/BT judges	92.2	75.7
M/slides/blackboard	91.0	97.8
M/prints/chair	88.0	96.7
M/prints/blackboard	86.1	96.4
M/slides/door	85.3	95.6
M/prints/door	80.1	94.5
E/slides/BT judges	77.1	86.7
M/slides/chair	71.4	92.7
E/prints/UT judges	71.2	69.2
E/slides/UT judges	62.2	57.1

E = estimation, M = measurement, UT = untrained, BT = best-trained.

Although the use of the best-trained judges to estimate distances from prints (92.2 percent) was slightly more accurate than the measurement technique of using slides with the blackboard as a reference (91.0 percent), the 97.8 percent reliability among those calculating the measurements was substantially higher for the latter technique as compared with the 75.7 percent reliability among the best-trained judges.

The use of estimation techniques to estimate distances will probably be risky for those investigating spatial relationships. Unless the researcher is able to select the BEST from a pool of trained judges, he may reduce the validity of his study by employing a method of determining distances which is neither highly valid nor reliable. The measurement techniques with known reference objects of sufficient length which show clearly defined edges on slides or prints proved to be quite a satisfactory method.

The mean reliability for the six measurement techniques was 95.6 percent with a narrow range of only 5.1 percent, while the mean reliability for the four estimation techniques was 72.2 percent with a wide range of 29 percent. The agreement among the best of the trained judges (81.2 percent) was considerably better than the agreement among untrained judges (63.2 percent).

REFERENCES

AIELLO, JOHN R., STANLEY E. JONES
  1971   Field study of the proxemic behavior of young school children in three subcultural groups. *Journal of Personality and Social Psychology* 19: 351–356.
ALBERT, STUART, JAMES M. DABBS, JR.
  1970   Physical distance and persuasion. *Journal of Personality and Social Psychology* 15:265–270.
BATCHELOR, JAMES P., GEORGE R. GOETHALS
  1972   Spatial arrangements in freely formed groups. *Sociometry* 35:270–279.
BAXTER, JAMES C.
  1970   Interpersonal spacing in natural settings. *Sociometry* 33:444–456.
DOSEY, MICHAEL A., MURRAY MEISELS
  1969   Personal space and self-protection. *Journal of Personality and Social Psychology* 11:93–97.
FORSTON, ROBERT F., JON L. ERICSON
  1973   Black-white nonverbal communication: personal space analysis. *Iowa State Journal of Research* 48:1–6.
FORSTON, ROBERT F., CHARLES U. LARSON
  1968   The dynamics of space: an experimental study in proxemic behavior among Latin Americans and North Americans. *Journal of Communication* 18:109–116.
GUARDO, C. J.
  1966   "Self-concept and personal space in children." Unpublished doctoral dissertation, University of Denver. (Ann Arbor, Michigan: University Microfilms.)

HALL, EDWARD T.
1963 A system for the notation of proxemic behavior. *American Anthropologist* 65:1003–1026.
1966 *The hidden dimension*. Garden City, New York: Doubleday.

HOROWITZ, MARDI J.
1965 Human spatial behavior. *American Journal of Psychotherapy* 19:20–28.

HOROWITZ, MARDI J., D. F. DUFF, L. O. STRATTON
1964 Body-buffer zone. *Archives of General Psychiatry* 11:651–656.

JONES, STANLEY E.
1971 A comparative proxemics analysis of dyadic interaction in selected subcultures of New York City. *Journal of Social Psychology* 84:35–44.

LITTLE, KENNETH B.
1965 Personal space. *Journal of Experimental Social Psychology* 1:237–247.

MEHRABIAN, ALBERT
1968a Inference of attitudes from the posture, orientation, and distance of a communicator. *Journal of Consulting and Clinical Psychology* 32:296–308.
1968b Relationship of attitude to seated posture, orientation, and distance. *Journal of Personality and Social Psychology* 10:26–30.

PEDERSEN, DARHL M.
1971 "Some personality correlates of personal space and the effects of two treatments on personal space." Paper presented at the Child Development and Family Relationships Colloquium, Brigham Young University, April 30.

ROSENFELD, HOWARD M.
1965 Effect of an approval-seeking induction of interpersonal proximity. *Psychological Reports* 17:120–122.

SOMMER, ROBERT
1961 Leadership and group geography. *Sociometry* 24:99–110.
1962 The distance for comfortable conversation: a further study. *Sociometry* 25:111–116.

WATSON, O. MICHAEL, THEODORE D. GRAVES
1966 Quantitative research in proxemic behavior. *American Anthropologist* 68:971–985.

WILLIS, FRANK N., JR.
1966 Initial speaking distance a function of the speaker's relationship. *Psychonomic Science* 5:221–222.

COMMENT by *J. H. Prost*

This paper directs itself to the problem of quantifying proxemic parameters. The issue is not whether techniques can be developed to precisely measure movements, spacing, or the like, but whether at least some form of quantification can be designed so that large samples of data can be handled statistically. With imprecise techniques, of course, estimates of the range of reliability, or the range of error, are crucial. There are powerful statistical tests at the investigator's disposal if he can once get his data into quantitative form and there are methods to handle the data even when the range of error is large. This paper offers several methods and evaluates them. One interesting application suggests itself: if a film has been shot without forethought, with regard to retrieving proxemic spacing, the investigator could shoot footage of similar situations under controlled proxemic distances and then train judges with the control film, later asking the judges to estimate the distances on the uncontrolled films. This ought to produce usable estimates. Novel approaches and new methods, as illustrated by this paper, ought to give impetus to the use of film as a data collecting medium.

The Presentation of Anthropological Information

Educational Uses of Videotape

PAUL HOCKINGS

The advent of portable videotape systems has opened up a variety of possibilities for classes in anthropology, as well as in other disciplines. Clearly, the use of videotape records can now make all the difference when a student of acting or public speaking comes to evaluate his performance. Athletes are similarly able to study and perhaps improve their behavior with the help of videotape. And, undoubtedly, the equipment can and will be applied to the study of traffic control, juvenile guidance, human anatomy, plant physiology, public relations, police methods, law court procedure, animal ethology, and much else besides.

In anthropology the videotape equipment may be used in several distinct ways. Students can use it, with relative ease, to document and analyze their domestic situation and life style. It has indeed been used in this manner by American schoolchildren in poor neighborhoods.

A related use is to replicate a field experience in the classroom. This is obviously a desirable venture in a large introductory class which, because of their sheer numbers, cannot do some sort of field project in nearby communities or small-group situations. Whether the replication is of the instructor's field experiences or of someone else's depends on circumstances: one can either present and analyze visual field notes in a class, or one can present parts of an ethnographic film and discuss these. In the latter type of usage, however, videotape offers little if any advantage over screening the original film; and may indeed lay the university open to legal action for infringement of copyright.

In teaching ethnographic and participatory filming to advanced students with little or no previous film experience, videotape offers a number of advantages. These may be loosely identified as simplicity, economy, and speed, virtues which appeal alike to student and dean.

In the first instance the portable equipment is distinctly easier to operate than sync-sound filming equipment. Lower levels of lighting are required, the loading is straightforward, synchrony between the picture and sound recording is mechanically assured, and the camera weighs very little. With these advantages, the student has been freed to concentrate on the action in front of him. Editing, too, is a quicker and simpler procedure than with 16-mm film.

Secondly, the costs of videotape equipment and training are comparatively low. An Eclair camera and Nagra recorder cost some five times what a black-and-white Sony outfit does. And since videotape can be reused repeatedly, the expenses of raw material are minimal and of processing nonexistent. This is most important, because it is when the students are beginning to master filming techniques that they need to shoot most often, albeit with the least presentable results.

And there is the third advantage of speed. If the student waits to see his film developed, finds that it looks poor, and still feels obliged to edit it with a soundtrack, this can easily be a most demoralizing experience for him, and a wastefully expensive one for his department. With videotape, on the other hand, that student can see what he has achieved a minute after he shot a scene; and if he is disenchanted with it, there is at least some likelihood that he may be able to shoot the same scene over again, right away.

Because of its cheapness and the rapidity of a playback, videotape offers some other benefits to thoughtful students. Most important perhaps is the opportunity it offers for getting feedback that will help in understanding and editing from the very people who form the subject matter of the tape. Another kind of feedback has been achieved by students in several American cities who have trained children or members of ethnic minority groups to use videotape recorders in situations where for one reason or another the middle-class students would themselves be unable to operate effectively.

In summary, then, videotape offers our students a chance to observe and interpret cultural material within easy reach of their homes. They do not merely learn how to operate a recording device, for it leads them to look for some wider significance or deeper understanding of what they have recorded. Without this, how can they get started in ethnographic filming?

Using Film in Teaching Anthropology: One Pedagogical Approach

TIMOTHY ASCH

Today's students have been brought up in a markedly different world from that in which classical pedagogical techniques were developed. Their exposure to television and the movies, radio, phonographs, and photographs, the instant communication of today's world, has led them to expect more from their education and has created a need for new teaching and learning strategies.

Over the past eight years I have been both making ethnographic film and developing techniques for using film in the classroom. This paper is a description of a course I have taught successfully at Brandeis University, with a detailed analysis of the use of one film and a suggested outline for the use of a sequence of films to demonstrate more fully the role film can play in teaching. This is followed by student evaluations of this method and a brief discussion of current film technology and how educators can make the best use of it. The paper is written for anthropologists who might wish to take advantage of new film resources and strategies for teaching anthropology.

I am grateful to Patsy Asch for help in writing this paper and to Barbara Herzstein for editing it. Napoleon Chagnon was an invaluable critic and I greatly value our collaboration. I wish also to thank Karl Heider, Paul Hockings, Thomas Hearne, Paul DeVore, Phileo Nash, Nancie Gonzalez, and Napoleon Chagnon for sharing with me their experience in using film for teaching anthropology. Ted Connant and Bill Fleming gave valuable assistance for the section on the new technology. I must also thank Peter Spier, Frank Galvin, Marilyn Wood, and Aralee Strange Mason for their assistance. Of course, none of these fine people is responsible for any of the shortcomings of this paper.

I wish also to thank the National Science Foundation for the support that enabled Napoleon Chagnon and me to develop many of the films outlined in this paper and allowed me to do the necessary research in writing it. © 1974 by Timothy Asch.

AN EXAMPLE OF THE INTEGRATION OF FILM AND ANTHROPOLOGICAL INSTRUCTION IN THE CLASSROOM

Goals of the Course

The major goal has been to give students at Brandeis an understanding of the discipline of social anthropology and appreciation of the interaction between theories and models of social behavior and ethnography, and at the same time to provide them with a sense of what it means to be a professional anthropologist. A good method for achieving these goals is to move back and forth between concrete examples of behavior seen within a developing sense of the total social environment in which the behavior occurs, and analysis and application of relevant theory. For example, I emphasize Marcel Mauss' theories of economics, of alliance and reciprocity in his book *The gift*. This important theory is demonstrated clearly to students in Yąnomamö feasting practices (as illustrated in the film, *The Feast*, and discussed in the fourth chapter of Napoleon Chagnon's book, *Yąnomamö: the fierce people*). Students see how such a theory helps them both to analyze the behavior they are observing on film and to make sense out of what appears at first to Western eyes to be exotic, aggressive chaos. The theory becomes tied to reality in the student's mind as its value is demonstrated.

Societies Studied

As a matter of strategy, I have focused on ethnography relating to three societies: the !Kung Bushmen, a hunter-gatherer society of South West Africa; the Yąnomamö, a horticultural society of southern Venezuela and northern Brazil; and the Dodoth, a pastoral society of northeastern Uganda. These groups were selected for their inherent contrasts and because of the extensive film resources available, not for evolutionary purposes. (Evolutionary questions arose, but they centered around change within a single society, such as the development of incipient political leadership in the center of Yąnomamö society, a topic of concern to Chagnon in his research.)

Particularly useful were the !Kung Bushman studies of SouthWest Africa made by John, Lorna, Elizabeth, and Laurence Marshall, also including Irven DeVore's work at Harvard done with his colleagues, and the resources on the Yąnomamö Indians of southern Venezuela studied by Napoleon Chagnon for seven years and filmed by both of us toward the end of his field studies. There are altogether about seventy-five films on these two cultures, and numerous books and articles. They represent hunters and gatherers and gardeners: examples of the development of culture in two different ecological settings.

Students examine each society fully through the literature, both ethnographic and theoretical, and through film. Comparison is encouraged only when they have developed a sense of a given society's character and thus have a context for behavior they observe within each society. Throughout the course, students observe human cultural diversity, an increasingly valuable heritage in the pressures toward homogeneity. Exposure to this diversity demonstrates to students that there are viable alternatives in human social organization.

Techniques to Involve Students

Our students are, of course, clearly products of their own society, and their behavior generally follows the normative patterns of this society. Obviously the best framework in which to develop their understanding of social anthropology is their own society, but we know that it is difficult to be objective in analyzing the social context that is most familiar. The study of anthropology can help students gain an insight into their own social relationships, but for the student studying anthropology for the first time this opportunity must be made more explicit. Therefore I include a study of aspects of our society that can be compared directly with similar aspects of one or more of the societies under study; for example, examining rituals surrounding birth and naming leads into a discussion of how the individual is incorporated into his social group. To investigate comparisons, students undertake fieldwork in their own communities.

By showing sound synchronous film, free of narration, that focuses on the behavior of an individual during a single event, students have an opportunity to engage in surrogate fieldwork. If they have studied relevant written material carefully, they are then in a position to make generally pertinent observations of the filmed behavior. By formulating and asking questions, as one might with an informant in the field, students can further simulate a field experience. As they compare their observations and conclusions with other students and attempt to resolve contradictions by reviewing both the written data and the film, students develop a method of integrating data and applying theories to new situations.

Students usually follow observations of filmed behavior in other societies with field assignments in our own society. For example, in John Marshall's ten-minute film *Debe's Tantrum*, Debe's mother wants to spend the day in gathering food. She asks an eleven-year-old daughter to stay home and take care of Debe, who is only five. The mother doesn't want to take her son because she knows she will be carrying him by the end of the day, along with the fifty pounds of roots, nuts, and firewood that she will have gathered. Debe throws a tantrum, and eventually he is taken along. Throughout the event the father lies in his hut, aloof and uninvolved. The film provides data on the structure of the Bushman family, the nature of the relationship between the members of one family, and the nature of individual roles.

Students are then asked to study an American family at a time when the mother is doing a specific job and at the same time caring for her children – preparing and serving a meal while answering her children's questions, for example. Students do fieldwork in male/female pairs and then in larger groups, comparing their data to identify apparent patterns, tensions, expectations, and contrasts within the family. Although students are encouraged to practice their skills at analyzing their observation, they are also cautioned that among professionals analysis would come only after extensive observation in many situations.

Course Strategies: A Single Film

Rather than outline the entire course, I will discuss the value of a single film in demonstrating the role kinship may play in analyzing behavior. Then I will discuss two other films, within a sequence of films that I have used frequently, in terms of the range of topics they intersect.

The Axe Fight, one of the most effective instructional films we have made, demonstrates how some of the rules of Yąnomamö social life can be generated by students from visual data and fieldnotes. *The Axe Fight* documents an explosive situation involving three lineages in a Yąnomamö village. Although the incident was recorded without preparation or an initial understanding of what was occurring, the film transmits most directly a sense of field experience to the student. It could be used as a sequence in a larger film dealing with the intersection of politics and religion and the concomitant ritual that helps to bind social groups together. By itself, it can be used as a basis for discussion of Yąnomamö social or political organization, alliance, village organization, village fusion or group solidarity, headmanship, or leadership, aggression, social controls, and the release of social tension.

After students have read Chagnon's books, *Yąnomamö: the fierce people*, and *Studying the Yąnomamö*, they see this film and pretend that they, as anthropologists recently arrived in the village, have come upon this scene. What do they make of the incident? What clues can be used to help understand this seemingly incoherent behavior? How do they make order out of chaos? Thus each student is given some appreciation of how difficult it is to interpret alien behavior.

The students recognize that they have seen an important event, but they cannot clarify the structure of that event. They then read more about it in the study guide accompanying the film. After sharing responses and questions derived from the first viewing of the film, I ask students to look at the film in slow-motion and agree to stop the film for questions. Generally, this slow-motion viewing leads to the generation of a kinship diagram showing the relationship of the key figures. Students use the diagram to analyze the behavior in the light of the ethnography they have read. Finally, they see the film again at normal speed.

Throughout the process of structuring the behavior they have observed, students inadvertently experience part of the process Chagnon went through to arrive at the theoretical model described in *Yąnomamö: the fierce people* (1968:54ff.). Social models thereby are related to observed behavior and their value demonstrated. The potential lines of fission are seen to cut through consanguineal ties as the men from different lineages who have exchanged wives defend one another. An understanding of this one incident usually generates a desire on the part of students to understand the whole social system in which it occurs.

This film is useless as a study document without background material because it has little explanation and few subtitles. But no doubt it will sometimes be used this way because it has just enough inherent structure, action, and violence to make it entertaining. This is a good example of how stereotypes can be confirmed. Viewers who rarely have been exposed to behavior that falls so entirely outside their experience will have difficulty in interpreting it as human.

Course Strategies: A Sequence of Films

The Axe Fight fits into a sequence of seven Yąnomamö films on religion and politics, beginning with mythology and ending with intervillage alliances. These films can be used in many other sequences and with many other films, but this particular sequence provides an opportunity to develop an understanding of the intertwining of Yąnomamö religion and politics. This, like any other sequence of films, demands additional readings, both theoretical and ethnographic, lectures, discussion, and possibly fieldwork. I will mention some of the materials I use; but it is important for each instructor to integrate the film material with his own reading selection and lectures. The films will have value only if they can serve the goals of each instructor.[1]

The sequence begins with a seventeen-minute film of a Yąnomamö creation myth as told by Kąobawä. The myth tells of the creation of *hekura* spirits, which are vital to the process of shamanism. It is through the symbiotic relationship between shaman and *hekura* that a man is able to cure his family and his kinsmen or kill his enemy through sorcery. Some of the cultural elements embodied in this myth are sibling rivalry, the origin of harmful magic and sorcery, the origin of spirits and characteristics of birds and other animals, the levirate, cremation, the opposition between beauty and ugliness, and the potency of blood and feces (prevelant in the mythology of almost any culture).

Shamans commonly use many *hekura* spirits, some more powerful than others. The reciting of a part of the myth is a way of substantiating for the audience, particularly those to be cured, the existence of the *hekura* as well as the relationship of the spirit to the curer.

The function of myths and the ways that they are told is first demonstrated to students cross-culturally. For example, the Yąnomamö are contrasted with societies like the Yoruba or the Bushmen, where myth can have a different function in presenting formally the history and code of ethics of a people. The Yąnomamö never tell a myth in its entirety in the linear sequence we would expect in our culture. Bits and pieces of the myth are used in a trance curing performance by a shaman who wants to establish the validity of a particular *hekura* spirit and lure it into his chest. ("I know you. I know of your origin. Come to me and we shall work together.")

We asked Kąobawä to tell his version of the complete myth without interruption, thus giving the audience an opportunity to grasp its meaning in Western terms. It also allows the viewers an intimate look at the personality of the storyteller, which would be impossible to present in a written description.

Students analyze the myth as best as they can. Then they read Chagnon's study guide, which includes this and several other important myths.

---

[1]   Study guides planned for the future are for the films: (1) *Magical Death, Children's Magical Death*, (2) *The Axe Fight*, and (3) *Yąnomamö Mythology*. The study guides will be published by Documentary Educational Resources, 24 Dane Street, Somerville, Massachusetts 02143.

In each case, a complete text is given in the original Yąnomamö, along with a direct translation, a translation into colloquial English and a preliminary analysis.

Next students see a film of Dedeheiwä, the renowned shaman of the village where most of our film was shot, telling the same myth: *The Yąnomamö Myth of Naro As Told By Dedeheiwä* (twenty-five minutes). His village is a two-week walk from Kąobawä's village and, until recently, the members of these villages had very little contact with each other. (See history of the Namowei-teri and Shamatari in *Studying the Yąnomamö*.) Students are asked to look for similarities and differences in the two versions of the myth.

By this time enough groundwork has been laid for students to understand the next film in the series, *Magical Death* (29 minutes). *Magical Death* was shot by Chagnon in 1969–1970, between two other field trips when we filmed extensively together. The film shows the first stages of contact and the formation of an alliance between two distant villages. The headman of the host village entertains the headman and his son-in-law from the guest village, and to demonstrate their solidarity inhabitants of the host village offer to use sorcery to kill their mutual enemies in a third village. This event is recorded in great detail, yet for students to understand the seemingly wild behavior that appears on the screen an introduction explaining the nature of drug-taking and curing in Yąnomamö society had to be added. This introduction precedes the main sequence, which features an extensive performance by many important shamans from the host village, led by Dedeheiwä, who attempts to kill the souls of the guests' enemies.

In the next film, *Children's Magical Death* (seven minutes), a group of boys, ranging in age from two to ten, pretend to be shamans by blowing large quantities of make-believe drugs (ashes from the hearth) into each other's nostrils. Then they act as if intoxicated, chant to their *hekura* spirits and pretend to cure. This film dramatically demonstrates an aspect of the process of socialization in a Yąnomamö village.

The sequence continues, developing the concept of alliance and reciprocity in political terms in *The Feast* (29 minutes), a film demonstrating the incipient stages of alliance formation between two recently hostile villages. Immediately after this, I show *Children at Reahumou Play* (six minutes) — children playing at having their own feast.

The Axe Fight follows *The Feast* nicely as a visual demonstration of the dynamics of village politics, intravillage alliance, and potential village fission. It can be followed by the last film in this sequence, *Kąobawä Trades With the Reyaboböwei-teri* (Asch 1972b), which demonstrates a more mature alliance between two villages important in Chagnon's ethnography. Here his latest book, *Studying the Yąnomamö*, is invaluable in understanding the entire subject of political alliance among the Yąnomamö. The seven films in this sequence can be SHOWN in three one-hour class periods or USED in six to twenty-six periods.

Throughout the sequence, comparisons can be made with the earlier studies of the Bushmen and the Dodoth. For instance, *N/um Tchai: The Ceremonial Dance of the !Kung Bushmen*, a film on Bushman curing, and the Dodoth slide strips, *Sacrifice for Sickness* and *Sacrifice for Raiding*, contrast well with *Magical Death* and provide a better understanding of all three societies. Films on the process of socialization, such as *Children's Magical Death* and *Children at Reahumou Play*, also provide excellent contrast when compared with Bushman films of children's play.

Course Strategies: The Development of Major Themes

Each film or group of films in the sequence described above can be viewed just in direct relation to the written ethnography, or can be used to explore related themes through more extensive reading assignments, lectures, and fieldwork. For example, the films *Magical Death* and *Children's Magical Death* include at least four major themes that can be explored with students: first, the close relationship between religion and politics; second, the importance of ritual, both religious and political, in binding social groups together; third, the relation between cosmology, curing practices and medical knowledge; and fourth, the reflection of the social system in the socialization process.

The relationship between religion and politics is a theme that interests many anthropologists, Chagnon among them, and the resulting literature is rich. John Middleton's *Lugbara religion*, (1960) a book more about politics than religion, provides an extension of the ideas presented in this Yąnomamö sequence. Middleton employs a case study method to define the process of fission in a segmentary lineage society. The case study focuses on a series of Lugbara sacrifices which, like *Magical Death*, John Marshall's *Argument about a Marriage* and *N/um Tchai*, and the Dodoth sacrifice slide tapes (when all taken together), are not only infused with religious ritual and meaning, but also strongly reflect the factors that influence political events. In a modest sense, my students use the Yąnomamö films and try to move from specific case studies to a formal understanding of a whole social system and an appreciation of how individuals manipulate the social order. The informal structure of the unnamed, shallow Yąnomamö lineages and their local descent groups is more clearly revealed when contrasted with the highly structured segmentary lineage systems of the Lugbara. In my course, these lineage systems are later compared with the age-grade system of the Dodoth.

The importance of religious and political ritual in binding social groups together is portrayed vividly in Bushman films like *N/um Tchai*, where the group is drawn together through dance, trance, and chanting to ward off the evil of the external spiritual world. In *Magical Death* the *hekura* spirits are called upon to help forge a new political alliance. The function of ritual is another topic where the pertinent literature is enormous.

Here again fieldwork assignments can be designed to extend the concepts into an understanding of our own society, thereby helping students to realize that their lives, too, are subject to analysis. Pertinent fieldwork could be done among religious groups in the students' own community – Catholic, Protestant, Jewish, or others, to analyze the structure and power base of these groups and the nature of the ritual through which their power and purpose is maintained, communicated, and expressed. Students could also examine the relationship of the church to the community it serves. Alternate fieldwork assignments could focus on the drug subculture and its function in American society, contrasting it with the indispensable social and religious functions of drugs in Yąnomamö society. Or they might focus on the myriad attemps to fashion new modes of communal living. Students might find, as Rosabeth Kanter argued so eloquently in her recent book, *Commitment and community*, that part of the reason these communal groups are often so impermanent is that members have little ritual that they can practice in common.

The close tie between cosmology, curing practices, and medical knowledge is a third topic easily explored in our own society and richly documented in Yąnomamö society. A Yąnomamö male may become a shaman for many reasons, but surely one of them is to provide for the health of his family. There is nothing more touching than to see a man trying all night to cure his young child. If he does not succeed, his male relatives help until finally they and the best shaman of the village focus their entire attention on curing the child. If their powers to exorcise the evil spirits causing the sickness are not successful, Chagnon reports that the sick person lies in his hammock awaiting the inevitable death that has been sent by the Yąnomamö of another village. However, the positive psychological effect of curing done by close relatives and important members of the village must have a powerful effect on the morale of the sick person. It is in obvious contrast to the often impersonal, antiseptic, "scientific" cures we practice in our own society. Both Yąnomamö and

Bushman footage could well be used by anyone studying medical anthropology. Like religion, medicine is tied to the entire cosmology of a people and to its ritual as well as its politics.

Children's Magical Death, following *Magical Death*, shows instantly the importance of play in transforming children into members of their society. An article such as Ruth Benedict's "Continuities and discontinuities in cultural conditioning" (1955) provides one conceptual framework with which to observe these behaviors. Although the literature on socialization is growing rapidly, it is only recently that anthropologists like Beatrice Whiting and her students have done fieldwork focusing on the socialization process. As the study proceeds, this aspect of the Yąnomamö films should be even more valuable. Obviously there are multiple opportunities to engage students in fieldwork on socialization within their own society (Spradley and McCurdy 1972; Maranda 1972).

Additional Film Sequences

The Yąnomamö films fit together into other sequences, most notably one that demonstrates the relationship between culture and personality and between psychology and the individual. When all films are completed, at least twelve will focus on one person, Dedeheiwä, in many different contexts. By watching this influential man interact with others in various situations, students can explore his personality for themselves. Because the films have no narration to guide the viewer and interpret the action, each student will have a different interpretation of this man and how he manipulates the rules of Yąnomamö social behavior to place himself where he wants to be within the society at any given time. Students enjoy developing, on their own, an understanding of Dedeheiwä's personality, but in later discussion many aspects of his personality can be shared by the entire class.

Students should be reminded, however, that their interpretations should be substantiated by reading and ethnographic information about Dedeheiwä supplied in the course. Moreover there is a limit, set by the information available, to which the students can generalize for themselves from the behavior they observe on film. With the combination of film and written materials, however, they have a better chance than mere book-learners of arriving at an accurate understanding of the cultural forms and social relations of an unfamiliar society.

Summary

In the course described here, I have tried to help students understand concepts by having them manipulate these concepts and work at translating them through several media of communication. The value of a concept such as alliance and reciprocity, as expressed by a range of authors, can be further demonstrated by analyzing its significance in actual behavior filmed in three different societies as seen, for example, in *The Feast* and *Magical Death, N/um Tchai* or either of the two Dodoth sacrifice slide tapes.

I have tried to show in this section the importance of integrating visual materials with written ethnography and theory. It is my feeling that in the study of anthropology what we know about human behavior and how well we have been able to analyze it depend on how well we have first been able to observe this behavior. Observation and analysis should be closely related in the study of anthropology, whether the students are graduates or undergraduates. Therefore, I feel it is important to provide a clear theoretical and ethnographic background from written sources and class discussion which students can use as a base for interpreting fieldwork in their own society. For this I find film a useful step in the process that relates abstract ideas and concepts to actual observed behavior (cf. Hockings 1972).

STUDENT EVALUATION OF THE USE OF FILM

Undergraduates in several film-oriented introductory anthropology courses at Brandeis and Harvard Universities have commented on the value of film in studying other cultures. Here are some of the comments from recent teaching.

...there are aspects of human culture and behavior that are only or best explained and complemented in visual terms. Film can create new and changing perspectives on printed materials, adding dimensions of understanding to the often impoverished ethnographic literature...Anthropological theories, methods, concepts, and images have been created, defined, and couched in language and the cognitive processes of reading. Structured by the need to translate various visually perceived phenomena, the focus on events and data has to a degree' been limited and selected by virtue of ease and suitability for print and printed thought. Film cannot only add the advantages of concrete, immediate, and real visual experience and dimensions, but also can open possibilities for the expansion of choice of material for study.

A good film gives the viewer a picture of reality which he cannot either distort or ignore, or even deny. Denial of such a film would mean a denial of reality, so in that sense film is reality. But let one not be so naive as to believe that a filmmaker could not possibly distort reality through his medium...I do not view film as pure nonfiction, but I do view it as the most positive method of teaching, when combined with written material, available to us at this time when eye-witness viewing is impossible or unattainable.

Seeing the films did give a sense of the wide and confused range of experiences one is confronted with in the field and the subsequent difficulty of discerning what is finally telling about the society as a whole. The near constant commotion that one senses on the periphery of the screen is as enlightening possibly as its focal point.

Film adds a perspective to the material. In one instant, various social segments and junctions can be fitted together and the physical environment becomes immediately identifiable. It enables the viewer to "visualize" or "deconceptua-lize" notions or actions previously out of his realm of experience. The viewer is less dependent upon an author for a translation of events, and to a great extent is free to handle the material in the fashion most beneficial to himself. Relevant time spans, in a well put-together film, whether seconds or days, are clearer and add to a better comparison of events. Also, along with the visual presentation, there is an audio one, which clarifies and explains, and which parallels that which might be presented in writing.

Seeing the film helped! – but without reading the book beforehand, I doubt whether my understanding would have been significantly enlarged. It helped by dramatizing the events I had read about – but did not add for someone who has not read the book. The film would probably be too obscure.

Two prominent psychoanalysts, Robert White and Erik Erikson, have placed emphasis on the study of children's play patterns. I have followed this argument and found Yąnomamö films added to my thinking about play...

In *Childhood and society*, Erikson describes a little girl – "What she could not have been able to say in words in many hours, she could express in a few minutes of nonverbal communication." This nonverbal communication, a major com-ponent of child's play, must be SEEN and not just read. Asch, Chagnon, and Marshall's films are so detailed that a student of play could study the nonverbal play patterns of the Yąnomamö and so draw cross-cultural conclusions.

Narration and/or subtitles are a very important part in the production of a good film. It is extremely difficult to know how much or how little information should be included, while still allowing a film the freedom to speak for itself. We learned about this when viewing the [Bushman] film, *Debe's Tantrum*, without sound. It was impossible to define kinship relationships and to be exact about what was really happening.

One method that has seemed to be very useful is that of picking scenes from the film and making them into stills to be shown at the beginning of the film with sufficient narration on who the major characters are and what, in brief, will be happening; and then to run the film with its synchronous sound [subtitles may be added at this stage for direct translations]. This was the procedure with *The Melon Tossing*. We knew exactly who was doing WHAT and WHY, due to certain relationships. When the viewer must be constantly guessing what is happening and who is doing what, the film loses its value.

Another tactic that I have found extremely beneficial has been viewing the same film more than once. We originally saw the *Bushman Stillbirth* while discussing childbirth in general – before I had any knowledge about Bushmen. Although the film had good narration, I felt at the time that it was basically a lot of screaming and rubbing on this sick, pregnant woman. My understanding of Bushman curing ceremonies was nil. Just recently we viewed this film again, and to my surprise, it was not as loud or inconsistent as I had remembered. Seeing a curing-medicine man, the rubbing of sweat onto the sick one, shouting at the guawasi – added greatly to what I "thought" a curing ceremony to be as evidenced only from reading. Through film, I understood better than I possibly could through only reading the process of curing and what the function of the medicine man means in Bushman society.

Film also allows one to view and be aware of chronological development of people and places. An ethnography of a people is probably written over a period of years from data collected during several years of research. However, the reader is vaguely aware of the passage of time when reading about a primitive people. Usually, the people appear to be living a fantasy life and can't acquire too much meaning for the reader. But when one actually sees moving pictures of real people in family, work, and environmental situations, they and their customs "come to life" and are no longer just some people in a book that one studies. In our class, we have become familiar with a Bushman woman called !Nai. Seeing her first as a child playing, then caring for her younger brother, and finally being married herself, brings into perspective many concepts previously discussed. They, too, are an actively living and growing society as is ours and have NOT been frozen in time to remain unchanged as too often the ethnographer tries to imply. Our first view of !Nai had her dressed in all-native clothing. Later her head cover and kaross were made of cloth – obviously they have had contact with Europeans, and it has and will continue to affect their way of life. We can draw a conclusion such as this one ourselves from viewing film; such concepts may then become more meaningful to the reader/viewer from having discovered them on his own than from being told that such and such was happening in a book.

For the person who is accustomed to reading exhaustive ethnographies, replete with pertinent data and stunningly clever theories, the ethnographic film is by its very nature more exciting and more informative. When the film is done well, viewing it can be nearly commensurate with being in the field; and this, after all, has been a fairly unattainable goal of classroom-taught anthropology. Of course, it is advisable to have written ethnographic material available with each film. But the principles stated so simplistically on paper become real, vital mechanisms when presented on film. One great advantage to film, then, is the realism it provides. It affords a temporal and spatial orientation impossible to reproduce through words alone. And sound is invaluable in creating an "atmosphere," including mood and rhythm.

Another major advantage is that the situations presented on film are DY-
NAMIC. One sees the progression of actions and attitudes which lead to a consequence. Movement, especially at the level of kinesics, can be captured only on
film. Most situations have certain facets which are too subtle to express adequately in a written document. Then, too, if a series of films is seen that centers on
selected individuals, these individuals become recognizable persons with dis-
tinguishing personalities and relationships.

Ideally, this set of circumstances enables the viewer to actively assimilate and
interpret the data presented, which may signify more effective learning. Furthermore, it is possible that this learning is more extensive. An anthropologist may
relate an incident to illustrate one particular principle. However, when seen on
film, the complexities of the incident are not hidden. It is therefore feasible
that, assuming that the viewer has sufficient background, the incident may be
interpreted differently; or that other aspects of the sequence may be analyzed
to illustrate other principles: one scene may communicate a variety of themes
too extensive or time-consuming to include in a written work.

This is not to say that ethnographies are not valuable. On the contrary, they
are an essential accompaniment to the films. It should be recognized, however,
that ethnographic films are probably a more flexible and effective means of
communicating anthropological concepts.

THE RELATIONSHIP BETWEEN THE STRUCTURE OF A FILM AND ITS POTENTIAL USE

Film can fulfill three main objectives: research, instruction, and entertainment. To be useful for research and instruction, footage needs an ethnographic context, with events filmed in detail so that continuity is maintained; as in archaeological research, the more the viewer knows about the
context of an artifact, the more likely it is that his conclusions will be
valid. Therefore when Chagnon and I filmed the Yąnomamö we pre-selected what we thought would be ethnographically significant and then
filmed steadily until an event concluded, attempting throughout to maintain a continuity of action. Our resulting 80,000 feet of film consists of
about sixty such events from a single village (Asch et al. 1973; Sorenson
1967; Sorenson and Gajdusek 1963, 1966).

The most important element in making valuable ethnographic film is
a close collaboration between an anthropologist and an ethnographic
filmmaker. The collaboration is most fruitful when it comes at the end
of the anthropologist's fieldwork, when he knows the language well, has
done a general ethnography, and has pursued a specialized study. It is
then that he can identify events that will be most significant and, most
important, he can predict the course the social interaction will follow in
a particular situation. If the filmmaker also has training and field experi-

ence in anthropology, and knowledge of the ethnography of the culture to be filmed, he will be able to respond with more interest and sensitivity to the guidance of the anthropologist. Mutual trust and respect are essential.

The anthropologist must inform the filmmaker as thoroughly as possible before each event. Thus when the camera is turned on, the filmmaker will respond appropriately to the action, shifting focus when necessary to capture the essence of the event by maintaining the indigenous structure. His object is to make the structure of the event the structure of the final film. This is difficult because the filmmaker as he shoots can see only the part of the event he is focusing on. The anthropologist must be observing the entire event to provide a context for the filmed behavior and to direct the filmmaker to important shifts in the interaction outside his viewfinder. Once the filming commences, however, the technical structure of the event rests primarily with the person operating the camera. Unlike Hollywood films, where a scene is filmed repeatedly from varied angles, the single-camera ethnographic filmmaker has only one chance to film his scene. The anthropologist determines which events and people are likely to display significant behavior: the filmmaker records and transmits what happens.

In the past, most filmmakers have used anthropologists simply as consultants, often expecting them to act primarily as travel guides. However, it is important for a true collaboration to exist, not only in the field, but also in the final production. Instructional films are only as valuable as the data that accompany them. A film that focuses on a single event, thereby allowing the viewer to become involved in the personalities and interactions of a few individuals, cannot also provide an analytical framework for the behavior recorded. Hence, the collaboration must continue. The anthropologist will write up his research and the filmmaker will edit the film, but the editing must be in response to insights provided by the anthropologist. Thorough study guides will be needed to make the film useful to a wide range of instructors.

The impact of our short films, or any film of this type, is often exotic and chaotic at first. Without a background in Yąnomamö ethnography, these films can easily reinforce prejudices about the savage primitive and civilized westerner. But with appropriate background, they are a powerful teaching device because in dealing with just one subject, while providing no interpretative narration, they engage the student in an active learning role. If a film is NOT seen within a broader ethnographic context, the event automatically fixes in the mind of the viewer an image that he immediately generalizes to the whole of Yąnomamö society, not in terms of

Yąnomamö patterns but in terms of behavior in his own society. Even the most sophisticated viewer will tend to integrate what he sees into his view of the world when he sees it without appropriate context.

Hence, there has been a classical pedagogical dilemma: whether to use palatable material that will bypass the prejudices of the viewer but grossly misrepresent the society, or use powerful data that more closely display indigenous behavior but can reinforce prejudice. It has been true in my experience that the more powerful material can help overcome prejudice and become valuable for instruction only in the context of a broad film resource that rests on good written material.

Before I filmed the Yąnomamö with Napoleon Chagnon, I had worked for many years with John Marshall's footage and knew many of the sequences intimately. With these in mind I made several of the Yąnomamö sequences specifically for comparison with Bushman sequences. Comparison of similar events in different cultures is an important element in anthropology, but comparison is only valid when events are truly comparable. Therefore I feel that it is important for people engaged in new film projects (particularly if making instructional sequences) to study the existing material carefully, particularly the Netsilik, Bushman, Yąnomamö and Australian films, so that they can make new material that will lend itself to cross-cultural comparison.

EXISTING FILM RESOURCES FOR TEACHING ANTHROPOLOGY

Until about ten years ago the best ethnographic films available for teaching anthropology were, by and large, images recorded by a film-maker and assembled by an editor from a large cultural panorama, as in films like *Nanook*, *Grass*, *The Hunters*, and *Dead Birds* (Heider 1972b). While some of these films were made by creative and perceptive artists and thus have great value as film art, in their relation to teaching their self-contained, highly interpretative styles do not tend to stimulate inquiry or demand analysis.

From 1953 to 1967 Rouch, the French anthropologist, departed from this style with *Jaguar*, a film about northern tribesmen in West Africa who migrate by the millions to the cities on the coast and then back to their villages in the dry, far north. To translate a study of migration patterns he had published (1956), Rouch asked three of his young informant friends to reenact such a trip. Rouch's films contrast markedly with the more general films mentioned above in which a sharply defined theme is imposed on the material and a narration tells the viewer what to look for and how to interpret what he sees.

While Rouch was in Africa doing anthropological research and experimenting with ways of adapting a cumbersome film technology to document his research, Richard Leacock was working to reshape the same technology to make lightweight, portable sound synchronous equipment to record events in American society in the period 1960–1965 (Mamber i.p.). The films he made with Donn Alan Pennebaker and Robert Drew (through their organization, Filmakers, Inc.) for Time/Life Inc., such as *Primary, Jane, Crisis* and *Cuba si! Yanki No!* are some of the best film documents of American society at a particular time.[2]

Fred Wiseman has documented American life in the 1960's (McWilliams 1970) through films which are personal statements about the effect of institutions on the individual; (cf. *Titicut Follies*, codirected by John Marshall, *High School* and *Hospital*).[3]

In the film record of American society, John Marshall's films of the Pittsburgh police probably constitute the richest ethnography available. During more than a year and a half, Marshall collected 130,000 feet of film on the events in the professional lives of a group of policemen. These films are particularly valuable today when police tend to be viewed as stereotyped actors. Marshall shows them as individuals who act within a well-defined framework, pressured by the expectations of the community and the definitions of the roles they perform[4] (Sandall 1972).

Elsewhere there are men like Jorge Preloran, an Argentinian filmmaker, who is documenting his own country. After completing his degree in film at the University of California at Los Angeles, Preloran returned to Argentina where he has made over thirty films of the many cultural groups that make up his country's population (Suber 1971; cf. Preloran's paper, *supra*).

---

[2] (1) *Primary*, (2) *Adventures on the New Frontier*, (3) *The Chair*, (4) *Eddie*, (5) *Moony vs. Fowle*, (6) *David*, (7) *Pete and Johnny*, (8) *Jane*, (9) *The Children were Watching*, (10) *Nehru*. Four other excellent films: *Synanon, Crisis, Cuba Si! Yanki No!, Happy Mother's Day* (Leacock and Chopra); (cf. Filmography, *infra*).
[3] (1) *Titicut Follies*, (2) *High School*, (3) *Law and Order*, (4) *Hospital*, (5) *Basic Training*, (6) *Essene*, (7) *Juvenile Court*. Distributed by Zipporah Films, 54 Lewis Wharf, Boston, Mass. 02110; (cf. Filmography, *infra*).
[4] (1) *Manifold Controversy*, (2) *Youth and the Man of Property*, (3) *Vagrant Woman*, (4) *A Forty Dollar Misunderstanding*, (5) *Two Brothers*, (6) *Three Domestics*, (7) *Wrong Kid*, (8) *The Informant*, (9) *Investigation of a Hit and Run*, (10) *A Legal Discussion of a Hit and Run*, (11) *After the Game*, (12) *You Wasn't Loitering?*, (13) *Henry is Drunk*, (14) *Nothing Hurt But My Pride*, (15) *Twenty-One Dollars or Twenty-One Days*, (16) *Inside Outside Station Nine*, Distributed by Documentary Educational Resources, 24 Dane Street, Somerville, Massachusetts 02143; (cf. Filmography, *infra*).

Four extensive film ethnographies, supervised by anthropologists, are available for use as instructional data for in-depth studies. First, there is film of the Australian aborigines, which includes the films of Baldwin Spencer from the early part of this century and, later, of Tindale, Mountford, Ian Dunlop, and Roger Sandall (Comité International 1970). Much of this material is a reconstruction or reenactment of aboriginal social and ritual life, but taken as a whole it is a rich resource.

Next is the material developed by Asen Balikci (Balikci and Brown 1966) and the Educational Development Center, eleven hours of film on the Netsilik Eskimos of the Central Canadian Arctic. This excellent reconstruction emphasizes ecological adaption as illustrated primarily by Netsilik technology, but many of the films include important aspects of Netsilik social life. Many attempts to reconstruct a culture on film end in disaster, but this is not true of the Netsilik project. Balikci could not have made his films five years later. The older Eskimos had seen radical changes come about in their way of life. Their contact with the modern world made it clear to them that they would be the last to have experienced the old culture. They were as passionately interested as Balikci in an accurate reconstruction; their knowledge and experience of the culture and their enthusiasm transformed the project into a collaboration. We have, then, in some of the Australian film (particularly that of Sandall and Dunlop) and the Netsilik films, images of a hunting and gathering life style in two very different environments, as well as invaluable eleventh-hour reconstructions of the heritage of mankind (cf. Balikci's paper, *supra*).

The third set of film ethnographies are not reconstructions. These are the films John Marshall made of the !Kung Bushmen, a hunting and gathering people living in small bands in South-West Africa, while on expeditions led by his father, Laurence K. Marshall, between 1950 and 1959. They constitute the most thorough film documentation of any aboriginal, preliterate group yet available. The films portray aspects of !Kung social life, politics, religion, technology, and socialization demonstrated by the members of several bands, particularly by about ten people over an eight-year period. Fifteen films are now complete, and ten more are in the editing process (Documentary Educational Resources 1973). Many of the individuals in the films are described in *The harmless people* by Elizabeth Marshall Thomas and in the monographs on the !Kung by Lorna Marshall (published in *Africa*).

The Marshall studies were followed by Richard Lee's research in 1963 on more acculturated !Kung Bushmen living not far away in Botswana. From 1963 to the present Lee's studies have been part of extensive multidisciplinary research sponsored by Harvard University and headed by

Irven DeVore. As a result, the literature available for use in conjunction with John Marshall's films is large.

Recently, Napoleon Chagnon and I returned from southern Venezuela with extensive footage of the Yąnomamö Indians which focuses on a few individuals. The Yąnomamö are village-living horticultural people with a complex social organization. Twelve sound synchronous films are now complete, and twenty-four films are in workprint optical-sound form and are available for evaluation and trial teaching. (They can be obtained from Pennsylvania State University, NAC and Documentary and Educational Resources, Cambridge.) These films have little or no narration but include translations of relevant dialogue. We plan to complete forty to forty-five films in all, depending on which sequences prove most valuable for instruction. (See Appendix 1 for a complete listing of films available and in progress.) The films will be accompanied by detailed study guides, each including a description of a specific event on film and its relationship to Yąnomamö society. The guides also will help the viewer integrate the films with all available written ethnography. Alternative ways of using the films to study Yąnomamö society, or to compare cross-culturally such topics as religion or politics will be suggested in the introduction to the guides. We do not intend that these films be used as independent data for instruction; they are closely tied to the ethnography and dependent on written material that provides a framework for interpreting the specific events.

Several film projects now in process should provide additional valuable instructional material. One is a long film on the preparation and enactment of an initiation ceremony among the Gisu of Uganda, focusing on one boy and his family over a three-week period. It was directed by Richard Hawkins and filmed by David and Judith MacDougall, with the assistance of Suzette Held (1973), an anthropologist who had worked with the Gisu for years. The project was initiated by the University of California's Program in Ethnographic Film. Recently Asen Balikci has been in Afghanistan studying the Pashtoon pastoral nomads and the villages with which they come in contact. He is now engaged in extensive filming that can be the basis of a curriculum that will show the quality of life and the relationship between pastoralists, peasants, and dwellers of a preindustrialized city in northern Afghanistan.

With these film resources now available, several of them already integrated with written ethnographies, and additional projects underway, we have the opportunity to re-examine the potential value of film for instruction and to develop techniques that make film a truly educational resource.

Occasionally commercial films are as valuable for teaching anthropology as any documentary; films such as Marcel Pagnol's trilogy, *Marius*, *Fanny*, and *César*, Sembene's *Emitai*, Satyajit Ray's *Apu* trilogy and some of Yasujiro Ozu's great films, such as *Tokyo Story*, are examples.

NEW TECHNOLOGY AND ITS USES

Present and Forthcoming Technology

My colleagues and I agree that what we have to work with now and what we can look forward to is an awkward and cumbersome technology. For great advances to be made in technology, there must be a demand for mass production. Unfortunately, because the educational market even in North America is small and will not grow appreciably in the foreseeable future, we cannot expect great technological breakthroughs. This section will attempt to show how we can make what we now have work much better for us.

TELEVISON AND VIDEOTAPE   Television has become one of the most important influences in our modern life, particularly in relation to the socialization of children. Television originally communicated the events of the world either through movies and stills or through "set-ups" in the studio (quickly preempting the magazine news medium). It now reaches out for its subject matter into our homes to see how some of us live, as in *An American Family* (1973), or into committee rooms of Washington to illuminate the process of government, as in the Watergate-related hearings. It does this through the language and immediacy of film.

Queen Elizabeth II's coronation on television was the first extensive use of live coverage of a complex event with world-wide impact. Like John F. Kennedy's funeral it made full use of the language of film to communicate the event to millions of viewers. Television has preempted film, adopting the structure of its language to communicate. It is also the medium whereby films are best distributed. Popular 16-mm educational films have been seen by more people in one evening on television than in twenty years of distribution through nontheatrical channels.

For educational uses, the best new equipment is the highly successful 3/4-inch color Sony U-Matic casette video tape player. Over 50,000 units were sold in 1972 in the United States alone. It has not become popular in schools and universities because they are waiting for a lower price. The U-Matic cassette player VP-100, which can be plugged into any television receiver, is now $1,095, and the combination recorder-player machine, the VU-1600, is $1,525. It appears that some Canadian universities, which seem to have more money and more government support than their American counterparts, are buying the U-Matics in quantity.

For people interested in designing an anthropological laboratory where local fieldworkers and researchers can use audiovisual media, the video "porta-pak" units are valuable, particularly when nickel cadmium belts are used to replace conventional portable power sources.

Three major advances in videotape technology are worth noting. The first is the new Society for Motion Picture and Television Engineers' (SMPTE) standardization for digitally marking videotape, which means simply that search and retrieval of visual data stored on tape is greatly facilitated (see Anthropology Laboratory, *infra*).

Second is a "time base corrector" which will enable 1/2, 3/4 and one inch videotape to be stabilized sufficiently to permit transfer to 2 inch (broadcast) tape or to film. The cost is still quite high: $8,000 to $12,000 instead of $50,000.

The third advance is a Kodak Flying-Spot Scanner for reproducing Super-8-mm film on any videotape.

Television technology has now reached a point where it could be used to restore old ethnographic films. Dances, for example, which were filmed at varying slow speeds could now be viewed, through television, at normal speeds.

CABLE TELEVISION   Large-scale public access to cable television in America is far in the future. One major problem is that it requires great amounts of artistic and technical expertise as well as government subsidies to work. Cable television works well in Montreal, for example, where there is adequate funding and the personnel to produce good quality broadcasting; videotapes made by private citizens have also been "aired" successfully in New York and Los Angeles (cf. Chanock and Sorenson's paper, *infra*).

CLOSED CIRCUIT TELEVISION   Some state educational systems are considering a greater reliance on teaching through television. Pennsylvania State University, with its many campuses, is designing and producing excellent programs on special topics to be sent out as "canned" video lectures. A California college system in desperate need of expanding its facilities recently decided to build a television transmitting station instead of a new campus. This new-style "campus" broadcasts to an audience of working people who keep irregular hours and older people who are not able to go to a campus. Registration, exams, and degree programs are administered in the usual manner. In terms of construction, mainte-nance, and staff this is a relatively inexpensive method of educating large numbers of people, and it provides students with access to information more easily than at a typical college campus.

A college where students never meet their professors is a frightening prospect, however. When students at Pennsylvania State were asked about their reactions to an introductory anthropology course taught by video-tape, their biggest complaint was the depersonalization of the course. Students were frustrated by not being able to talk in person to the professor who was lecturing to them. Yet a problem exists and must be faced: in many states huge numbers of students must be taught at many far-flung campuses. There are not enough good professors or the funds to pay them to meet all these needs. Much experimenting will be done using the new technology, yet it may be some time before successful solutions can be found to the problem of providing quality education to all those who seek it.

VIDEO RECORDS   Video records use a laser technology for producing the disc. It may be 1980 before this technology is fully developed. In terms of the economics involved, it will first be developed for a popular audience in the form of half-hour color discs rather than for an educational market. For any technological developments to be successful, a huge market must be anticipated. Several companies are working to develop a record, but none is available yet in the U.S.A. Telefunken in Germany is about to release its best product so far; the quality is not quite as good as the Sony U-Matic video cassette, but the record will last longer. The playback machine will be fairly inexpensive, but the recording unit will be beyond the financial reach of most institutions.

SUPER-8-MM FILM   So far 8-mm film has not penetrated into the educational market except in specialized areas in the elementary schools. For example, Education Development Center's (EDC) film-based social studies curri-culum, *Man: A Course of Study* (Bruner 1966; Dow 1972; Gonzalez i.p.), distributed by Curriculum Development Associates (CDA), uses twenty-five-minute, technicolor film cartridges. The medical profession and in-dustry have been using 8-mm technology in many professional applica-tions for some time.

The best equipment now available is the Technicolor loop projector,[5] or the new Kodak model.[6]

[5]   Technicolor 1000, 15 pounds, magnetic and optical sound, about $490.
[6]   Kodak Supermatic #60, 20 pounds, magnetic sound only, about $480.

There have been other developments in 8-mm technology. For the last five years at MIT Richard Leacock has been modifying the Nizo camera to develop a synchronous sound rig that would facilitate making documentary films on location. The price for the camera and the editing equipment is around $7,500. Just recently, Kodak brought out a good synchronous sound camera for $425, the Supermatic 200, but it is single system (putting the sound on the original film magnetically at the time it is exposed in the camera). It runs at standard sound speed but the film cannot be edited properly, or the sound transferred. It has a 200-foot magazine (cf. Leacock's paper, *supra*).

Original 8-mm film transferred at the Sony-owned Photo Cinema Lab in Japan onto a 1-inch master and then retransferred onto a 3/4-inch video cartridge for the Sony U-Matic cannot be distinguished in quality from transferred 35-mm movie film viewed on the same system. The transmission is better than the best reception from the best home television set. Sony make many of their television commercials in Japan in 8-mm and transfer the original 8-mm Kodachrome to tape for commercial video broadcast. We do not have prime quality facilities yet in North America, but good work can be done here by some laboratories.

16-MM FILM   At present most films are distributed in 16-mm form, and this will be true until new equipment is developed, probably after 1985. Equipment commonly used to make 16-mm film is the Arriflex BL and Eclair cameras with the Nagra, Stellavox, Tandberg, Sony or Uher tape recorders. Silver cadmium batteries can be used to power this equipment and although they are expensive, they last much longer on one charge than nickel cadmium batteries (Pincus 1969; Asch 1971; Lipton 1972).

New Ways of Using Existing Technology

THE ANTHROPOLOGY LABORATORY   The new technology enables us to develop a very significant tool for teaching anthropology. Students using 1/2-inch battery-run "porta-packs" [7] can undertake fieldwork assignments. If their work is good enough to be transferred to a more permanent medium, it can be put on a 1-inch videotape that can be edited and retransferred for final viewing in the 3/4-inch Sony U-Matic cassette. All these tapes can be erased and reused. George Stoney and his New York University students at the Alternative Media Center have used this tech-

[7]   Sony Video "Rover" Porta-Pak AV-3400 recorder and the AVC-3400 camera are $1,745 complete.

nique for years. For fieldwork aiming at a more permanent record of higher quality and in color, Richard Leacock's synchronous sound 8-mm rig could be used and the original transferred to the Sony U-Matic. An anthropology laboratory and editing facilities for fieldwork studies and the production of curriculum materials would cost about $35,000. If one of Leacock's synchronous sound 8-mm production units is added, the cost is approximately $42,500.

One use for such a laboratory, if it were shared by a university complex, such as New England's University Film Study Center, which serves seventeen universities, is that a film library facility could offer to the teaching public a carefully annotated film catalogue in which an entire film might be carefully indexed with digital film-edge numbers at the margin of the description. A professor could buy a blank video cassette for $30 and ask the lab to record on this cassette excerpts from ten to fifteen films that would make up a one-hour program. He could later send the cassette back to have it erased and reprogrammed. Such a complete search-and-retrieval and duplication facility could be added to the anthropology laboratory just described for a total cost of perhaps $50,000. These facilities can be a reality for any consortium of universities deeply committed to the use of media in education.

FILM TECHNOLOGY AND THE CLASSROOM   In the last eight years the educational market for new technological devices has been grossly overestimated by hundreds of companies that have either taken great losses or are now out of business. Thus perhaps a completely different approach should be taken to assess film technology. We might ask the questions: What is the role of the existing technology in communicating ideas for education? How best can we utilize the technology we now have? In the past three years I have lectured in over thirty universities and have discovered that the environment in which I work, not the technology I use, is in great need of development.

Today a university administration should be vitally concerned with proper facilities for a professor wishing to use audiovisual technology. However, an anecdote sums up a situation that is all too frequent. Some time ago I flew to New York to lecture and show a newly edited film at New York University. The anthropology secretary showed me a piece of paper proving the projection equipment for my lecture had been ordered in advance. Fifteen minutes after beginning my lecture, when I discovered that the projector had not yet arrived, I went out to get it myself. Nobody in the audience, students or professor, knew where the audiovisual services of the university were located. I phoned the main office and went directly to where I was told the equipment was stored. At New York University the building custodians operate the audiovisual equipment. There were eight of them, all playing cards in the basement of one of the university buildings. After much criticism about my direct way of handling the matter, one of the custodians brought a projector from a very dusty screened-in bin near the boiler room.

Back in the lecture hall, when we were finally able to project, the distance to the screen was so great that the image was very dim and, of course it didn't help that the windows in this audiovisual classroom were not equipped with proper blackout curtains. Besides, to get air into this stuffy room, the windows had to be opened and the interminable noise of traffic drowned out any intelligible sound that might have been made inside the room. The projector was so dirty that great globs of dust came loose from the projector housing and flitted across the image throughout the showing. The speakers on the projector were in such disrepair that the sound was garbled. When I attempted to narrate the film I found the acoustics were so bad that my most deliberate shouting was not able to reach the 200 or more students scattered about the room. The professor in whose class I lectured shrugged his shoulders and said, "Well, that's the way it is." The film had acquired a deep gouge throughout the entire print from this one performance. On the other hand, I have lectured at Boston University to over 250 students for three successive years. The Boston University Audiovisual Department has converted a synagogue into an audiovisual classroom. This classroom is usually serviced by a well-trained operator who sets up equipment in a soundproof projection booth where the high intensity xenon lamps produce a bright and sharp image. From the lectern I can stop, start and reverse 35-mm slides, and project film by operating the controls myself. There is a rug on the floor to deaden extraneous noise. The room is perfectly dark and the acoustics are so good that in the midst of all those students I have been able to hold an intimate conversation with a student ten rows from the lectern.

The question then is not the technology, but how to make the best use of it! If a university exists to teach huge numbers of students, then it must develop better ways for professors to communicate to their students. Thus it becomes crucial to the design of a new building that it be flexible enough so that one can take advantage of new technology when it becomes available. Generally, the environment for teaching in the university today is archaic. It seems we have learned little since Plato discussed the importance of the environment in the learning process.

Summary

In summary, then, I feel that 16-mm film will be the standard mode for educational distribution of film materials until after 1980, and that television, especially the 3/4-inch color videotape cassette, will only complement and later supplement aspects of 16-mm and 8-mm film production and distribution. Since there does not seem to be any technological miracle on the horizon that will improve the communication of visual images to our students, we should concern ourselves with improving the way we use what we already have.

APPENDIX 1: YĄNOMAMÖ FILMS AVAILABLE AND IN PRODUCTION (from Chagnon 1974:263–266)

1. *The Feast* (29 minutes). Winner of numerous awards. This film focuses on alliance practices and how feasting and trading create and maintain political alliances between once hostile villages. It illustrates the material presented in Chapter 4 of *Yąnomamö: the fierce people*. See review by Kenneth Kensinger (1971).

2. *Yąnomamö: A Multidisciplinary Study* (45 minutes). Also winner of numerous awards. This film describes the nature of multidisciplinary fieldwork conducted by Napoleon Chagnon and his colleagues on our 1968 expedition to the Yąnomamö area of Venezuela. The relationship between demography, human genetics, epidemiology, linguistics, physical anthropology, cultural anthropology, serology, and other medical disciplines is graphically shown through the efforts of specialists in these fields as they collect blood specimens, make dental examinations, and participate in other ways in the field work. The film also includes a brief, but comprehensive, description of Yąnomamö culture. It is useful in introductory courses in anthropology where the relationship between physical anthropology, cultural anthropology, and linguistics is given in the classroom. See reviews by Paul Baker (1972), Michael Hannah (1972).

3. *Magical Death* (29 minutes). This film focuses on the role of the shaman, Dedeheiwä, in curing his co-villagers and sending sickness to enemy villages. The use of hallucinogenic snuff is shown in its daily context. More important, this film illustrates how religion serves political ends and how a shaman can manipulate the spirit world to demonstrate his allegiance to allies. Like *The Feast*, this film focuses on one specific event and describes its development in terms of the history of political relationships between two villages that are entering into a new alliance. It is a very powerful, dramatic film and should be used in conjunction with lectures and/or with one of the mythology films described below (*Myth of Naro*). See review by Eric Wolf (1972).

4. *The Yąnomamö Myth of Naro as told by Kąobawä* (17 minutes). Kąobawä, headman of Bisaasi-teri, relates the same myth as the one told by Dedehei-wä (cf. no. 29). Equally enchanting and humorous, it provides the basis for a comparative examination of two versions of the same myth as told by knowledgeable men from different villages.

5. *Ocamo is my Town* (23 minutes). This film describes the fourteen years of activities by a Salesian priest to acculturate a village of Yąnomamö on the Ocamo River. The approach, attitude and philosophy of this missionary contrast in many ways with similar approaches made by the members of the New Tribes Mission.

6. *Tug of War* (7 minutes). A group of approximately twenty villagers play tug-of-war in a rainstorm.

7. *Children in the Rain.* (10 minutes). Some sixty children play in the rain to amuse themselves.

8. *Arrows* (9 minutes). A large group of boys engage in an arrow fight in the village clearing, shooting blunt arrows at each other to learn how to dodge arrows as well as to shoot accurately. The game ends when one of the boys is injured and falls to the ground with a minor wound on his cheek. His father breaks up the game by brusquely threatening to "revenge" his son.

9. *The Axe Fight* (10 minutes). A powerful film about a fight that erupted between the members of several different lineages. They attack each other with axes, clubs and hatchets, delivering a number of well-aimed but constrained blows with the blunt ends of their weapons. The remarkable feature of this film is that the organization of the village by lineage compo-sition and marriage alliances is clearly revealed in the contest: the fighters fall into three groups – lineal descent groups – and align themselves according to marriage bonds between the groups. This film is ideally suited for discussion of the general principles of marriage, descent, and alliance in Yąnomamö society. A detailed description of the genealo-gical relationship between all significant participants in the fight will be published in an accompanying study guide.

10. *Dedeheiwä Weeds His Garden* (15 minutes). This is a quiet, sensitive film about one aspect of Dedeheiwä's daily life. He cleans the weeds out of his maturing manioc garden and rests while his wife tenderly delouses him. About a dozen children, most of them his own, crawl over him in their play activities.

11. *New Tribes* (10 minutes). This film shows dedicated members of the New Tribes Mission attempting to teach the children of Bisaasi-teri their way of life. They describe their philosophy and methods for acculturating the Yąnomamö to Western ways and Christianity.

12. *Dedeheiwä Washes His Children* (15 minutes). Dedeheiwä takes a number

of his young children to the river and washes them carefully and patiently, while his sick wife remains in the village.

14. *Children at Reahumou Play* (6 minutes). A group of children roast meat in a make-believe house in the village clearing and share the meat with each other in a "distribution" (*reahumou*).

15. *Chopping Wood* (10 minutes). The irksomeness of daily wood collection is revealed as a woman strenuously chops a large log into kindling for her hearth.

16. *Möawä Making a Hammock* (12 minutes). The village headman, Möawä, patiently works on a hammock while his wife looks on and periodically fondles his leg.

17. *Children's Magical Death* (7 minutes). A group of young boys, ranging in age from five to ten years, pretend to be shamans. They blow large quantities of make-believe drugs (ashes from the hearth) into each other's nostrils and become "intoxicated" from this. They prance around and fall "unconscious" from their efforts.

19. *Grooming Before Dedeheiwä's House* (5 minutes). Dedeheiwä, a patient and gentle man, is respected but not feared by the village children. A group of them rest in front of his house and delouse each other.

21. *Möawä Burns Felled Timber* (13 minutes). Möawä and his wife work in the garden gathering up brush and burning it in preparation for planting crops.

24. *Collecting Rasha Fruit* (9 minutes). A young man carefully ascends a thorny *rasha* tree to harvest the fruit using an ingenious device, a pair of climbing scaffolds.

25. *The River Mishimishimaböwei* (25 minutes). An in-depth study of the use of the village water supply for bathing and drinking.

26. *Children Making a Hammock* (10 minutes). A small group of boys learn the techniques of hammock manufacture as they attempt to make a small hammock with spun cotton.

27. *Morning Flowers* (25 minutes). A portrait of the daily activities in Dedeheiwä's and Möawä's section of the village. The women and children quietly make decorations from brilliant yellow blossoms. The kinship and marriage ties between these two families are described and analyzed in the context of their daily activities.

29. *The Yąnomamö Myth of Naro as Told by Dedeheiwä* (25 minutes). This film gives the intellectual and spiritual background of Yąnomamö beliefs about the *hekura* spirits and their creation when one of the ancestors, Naro

(Opossum), initiated the use of harmful magic and killed his brother in a fit of passionate jealousy over the latter's two beautiful wives. The soundtrack contains a voice-over simultaneous English translation of the myth as Dedeheiwä tells it in Yąnomamö. It is a delightful, amusing film because the teller "acts out" the roles of the various characters in the myth as he relates the incredible and fabulous deeds they perform.

30. *Kąobawä Trades with the Reyaboböwei-teri* (8 minutes). Kąobawä and some of his co-villagers make a long trip to the village of Reyaboböwei-teri to feast with them, but by the time they arrive the meat has been eaten by the hosts. A trade follows, but without much enthusiasm because both hosts and guests are annoyed that the feast could not be held for lack of meat.

31. *Hunting Crickets* (12 minutes). A group of children perfect their archery by hunting and shooting crickets in the roof thatch with tiny bows and arrows.

32. *Doing Anthropological Fieldwork in Mishimishimaböwei-teri* (44 minutes). Many of the field methods Napoleon Chagnon describes in his book, *Studying the Yąnomamö*, were filmed in 1971. This film, in addition to illustrating the methods, also brings out the nature of the field situation and how the ethnographer relates to the members of the village in a wide range of circumstances.

33. *Bride Service* (6 minutes). One of Dedeheiwä's sons returns to the village with a large bird he bagged with his arrow, and a basketful of wild fruits. Dedeheiwä conspicuously shouts across the village for the boy's father-in-law to come and claim the food. The man sends his youngest wife, a girl of about ten, to fetch the items. They are so heavy that she cannot handle them, and she collapses to the ground amid roars of laughter from the others.

34. *Reahumou* (15 minutes). Möawä kills a tapir and presents it to his brothers-in-law, who comprise an important political bloc in the village. They cook the meat, dismember it and distribute it to the rest of the village. The women move in after the meat has been distributed, and share out the bones and scraps of skin and fat. Then the dogs arrive after the women are through and pick among the scant leftovers. A detailed examination of the kinship relationships between givers and receivers is provided in the study guide that will accompany the film.

36. *Moon Blood* (10 minutes). Dedeheiwä recites the myth of the origin of man from the blood of Moon. Voice-over English translation (Chagnon 1968: 47).

38. *Dedeheiwä's Sons Gardening* (20 minutes). Two of Dedeheiwä's adult sons plant their newly cleared gardens with plantain, manioc, and other root crops.

39. *Death of a Prominent Man* (15 minutes). One of Möawä's important agnates

from Ironasi-teri died after a visit to a distant village in 1971. Word of his death is passionately and tearfully passed to the man's brothers-in-law. A year later the brothers-in-law hold a mortuary ceremony for him and mix some of his remains (ashes) in a gourd of plantain soup and consume it.

40. *The Twin Cycle Myths* (25 minutes). Daramasiwä, a prominent man in Mishimishimaböwei-teri, tells the myth of the Twin Heroes, Omauwä and Yoasiwä (Yoawä) and their adventures with Jaguar (Chagnon 1968:46–47). Voice-over English translation. [This may be divided into two parts in the final production form.]

This is only a partial list of films to provide an idea of the resource and its scope. At least two dozen other films are either nearly complete or roughed out in preliminary editing form. These include ten films on specific myths, five films on technology and cultivation, numerous films on children's activities and several films on social activities of various kinds, such as wife-beating, raiders preparing to depart, gardening activities, and shamanism.

Finally, none of the planned general films has been described, films that will draw on footage from those listed here and other footage not described here.

APPENDIX 2: SUGGESTED USES FOR TWENTY OF FIFTY YANOMAMÖ FILMS

Below are some standard categories for studying another society, followed by a matrix (Table 1) which shows twenty Yąnomamö films and their relationship to these categories.

Ecology
Subsistence
Social Organization:
The Community
The Family
Role and Status – Life cycle for women and men
Society and the Individual – Personality and Culture
Socialization
Political Organization
Cosmology, Religion
Acculturation
Anthropological Fieldwork Methodology

Such a matrix could be applied to the film resources that deal with any society in depth such as the films of the !Kung Bushmen, Australian Aborigines, Netsilik Eskimo, or complex single films like *The Village*.

Table 1. Suggested uses for twenty of fifty Yąnomamö films

No.	Time	Title	Ecology	Subsistence	Social organization	The community	The family	Role and status: life cycle for women & men	Society & the individual	Socialization	Political organization	Cosmology and religion	Acculturation	Fieldwork
20	9	Dedeheiwä Rests in His Garden					×	×	×	×			×	
10	15	Dedeheiwä Weeds His Garden					×	×	×	×			×	×
12	15	Dedeheiwä Washes His Children					×	×	×	×				
27	25	Morning Flowers					×	×	×	×	×	×		
33	6	Bride Service					×	×	×	×		×	×	
34	15	Reahumou				×		×	×	×	×	×	×	
35	5	Wild Pig Distribution									×	×	×	
14	6	Children at Reahumou Play				×	×	×	×	×			×	
36	10	Moon Blood			×									
4	17	The Myth of Naro: Kąobawä			×									
29	25	The Myth of Naro: Dedeheiwä			×			×						
3	29	Magical Death			×	×			×		×	×		
17	7	Children's Magical Death			×	×	×		×		×			
37	20	Preparation for the Feast			×	×			×	×	×			×
1	29	The Feast				×			×	×	×			
9	10	The Axe Fight				×			×		×	×		
30	8	Kąobawä Trades with the Reyaboböwei-teri				×					×			
11	10	New Tribes		×	×									
5	23	Ocamo is My Town		×	×									
32	45	Doing Anthropological Fieldwork in Mishimishimaböwei-teri	×	×		×	×		×			×		×

REFERENCES

American Anthropologist
1965– All book and film review issues. Washington, D.C.: American Anthropological Association.

ASCH, TIMOTHY
1971 Report from the field: filming the Yąnomamö in southern Venezuela. *Program in Ethnographic Film Newsletter* 3 (1):3–5.
1972a "New methods for making and using ethnographic film." Paper presented to the Research Film Committee, African Studies Association, Philadelphia.
1972b Ethnographic filming and the Yąnomamö Indians. *Sight Lines* 5:3.
1974 "New methods for making and using ethnographic film," in *Education and cultural process: towards an anthropology of education.* Edited by George Spindler. New York: Holt, Rinehart and Winston.

ASCH, TIMOTHY, JOHN MARSHALL, PETER SPIER
1973 Ethnographic film: structure and function. *Annual Review of Anthropology* 2:179–187.

BAKER, PAUL
1972 Review of *Yąnomamö: A Multidisciplinary Study. American Anthropologist* 74:195–196.

BALIKCI, ASEN
1970 *The Netsilik Eskimo.* Garden City, New York: Natural History Press.

BALIKCI, ASEN, QUENTIN BROWN
1966 Ethnographic filming and the Netsilik Eskimos. *Educational Services Incorporated Quarterly Report* (Spring–Summer):19–33.

BATESON, G., MARGARET MEAD
1942 *Balinese character, a photographic analysis.* New York Academy of Sciences.

BENEDICT, RUTH
1955 "Continuities and discontinuities in cultural conditioning," in *Childhood in contemporary cultures.* Edited by Margaret Mead and Martha Wolfenstein, 21–30. Chicago: University of Chicago Press.

BIOCCA, ETTORE
1971 *Yanoama.* New York: E. P. Dutton.

BRUNER, JEROME S.
1966 *Toward a theory of instruction.* New York: W. W. Norton.

CARNEGIE COMMISSION ON HIGHER EDUCATION
1972 *The fourth revolution: instructional technology in higher education.* New York: McGraw-Hill.

CHAGNON, NAPOLEON A.
1968a "The culture-ecology of shifting (pioneering) cultivation among the Yąnomamö Indians," in *Proceedings, VIIIth International Congress of Anthropological and Ethnological Sciences 1968, Tokyo and Kyoto,* 3: 249–255. Tokyo: Science Council of Japan.
1968b *Yąnomamö: the fierce people.* New York: Holt, Rinehart and Winston.
1968c "Yąnomamö social organization and warfare," in *War: the anthropology of armed conflict and aggression.* Edited by Morton Fried,

Marvin Harris, and Robert Murphy:109-159. New York: Natural History Press.
1974 *Studying the Yąnomamö.* New York: Holt, Rinehart and Winston.
COLLIER, JOHN
1973 *Alaskan Eskimo education, a film analysis of cultural confrontation in the schools.* New York: Holt, Rinehart and Winston.
COMITÉ INTERNATIONAL DU FILM ETHNOGRAPHIQUE ET SOCIOLOGIQUE
1967 *Premier catalogue sélectif international de films ethnographiques sur l'Afrique noire.* Paris: UNESCO.
1970 *Premier catalogue sélectif international de films ethnographiques sur la région du Pacifique.* Paris: UNESCO.
i.p. *Premier catalogue sélectif international de films ethnographique sur l'Asie et le Moyen Orient* (approximate title). Paris: UNESCO.
CURRICULUM DEVELOPMENT ASSOCIATES
— Suite 414, 1211 Connecticut Avenue, N.W., Washington, D.C.
DE BRIGARD, EMILIE R.
1973 "Anthropological cinema." Program at the Department of Film, Museum of Modern Art, New York, May 17–July 3.
i.p. *Anthropological cinema.* New York: Museum of Modern Art.
DEVORE, PAUL, NICK LAZARIS
1972 "The Netsilik Eskimos on paper and film." Mimeographed manuscript, University of Massachusetts at Boston.
DOCUMENTARY EDUCATIONAL RESOURCES
1973 *Films of Africa, Pittsburgh, South America.* DER: 24 Dane Street, Somerville, Massachusetts 02143.
DOW, PETER B.
1972 If you were a baboon, how would you tell your mother you were hungry? *Natural History* 81 (4):22-25, 72-81.
DUNLOP, IAN
1968 *Retrospective review of Australian ethnographic films: 1901–1967.* Lindfield, N. S. W.: Australian Commonwealth Film Unit.
ENGLAND, NICHOLAS
i.p. *Music among Bushmen.* Cambridge, Massachusetts: Harvard University Press.
GONZALEZ, NANCIE
i.p. Anthropology in grade schools. *Human Organization.*
HANNAH, JOEL MICHAEL
1972 Review of *Yąnomamö: A Multidisciplinary Study. American Journal of Physical Anthropology* 36:453-454.
HEARNE, THOMAS, PAUL DEVORE
1973 "The Yąnomamö on film and paper." Paper presented at the Anthropological Film Conference, Smithsonian Institution, Washington, May. Mimeographed manuscript.
HEIDER, KARL G.
1972a *The Dani of West Irian.* Andover, Massachusetts: Warner Modular Publications.
1972b *Films for anthropological teaching* (fifth edition). Washington, D. C.: American Anthropological Association. (1973 New Hamsphire Avenue, N. W., Washington, D. C. 20009.)

HELD, SUZETTE
  1973   *Gisu homicide*. Unpublished doctoral dissertation, University of London.
HOCKINGS, PAUL
  1972   Undergraduate teaching with film. *Program in Ethnographic Film Newsletter* 4 (1):4–6.
KANTER, ROSABETH MOSS
  1972   *Commitment and community*. Cambridge, Massachusetts: Harvard University Press.
KENSINGER, KENNETH
  1971   Review of *The Feast*. *American Anthropologist* 73:500–502.
LEE, RICHARD
  1965   *Subsistence ecology of !Kung Bushmen*. Unpublished doctoral dissertation, University of California at Berkeley [Ann Arbor, Michigan: University Microfilms].
LEE, RICHARD, IRVEN DEVORE
  i.p.   *Kalahari hunters and gatherers*. Harvard University Press.
LIPTON, LENNY
  1972   *Independent filmmaking*. San Francisco: Straight Arrow Books.
LOMAX, ALAN, IRMGARD BARTENIEFF, FORRESTINE PAULAY
  1969   Choreometrics: a method for the study of cross-cultural pattern in film. *Research Film/Le Film de Recherche/Forschungsfilm* 6:505–517.
MAMBER, STEPHEN
  i.p.   *Cinema verité in America: studies in uncontrolled documentary*. Cambridge, Massachusetts: M.I.T. Press.
MARANDA, PIERRE
  1972   *Introduction to anthropology, a self guide*. Englewood Cliffs: Prentice-Hall.
MARSHALL, JOHN
  1958   Man as a hunter. *Natural History* 67:291-309, 376-395.
MARSHALL, JOHN, LORNA MARSHALL, FRANK GALVIN
  i.p.   *N/um Tchai: the ceremonial dance of the !Kung Bushmen*. Somerville, Massachusetts: Documentary Educational Resources.
MARSHALL, LORNA
  1957   The kin terminology system of the !Kung Bushmen. *Africa* 27:1-25.
  1959   Marriage among !Kung Bushmen. *Africa* 29:335-365.
  1960   !Kung Bushman bands. *Africa* 30:325-355.
  1961   Sharing, talking and giving: relief of social tensions among !Kung Bushmen. *Africa* 31:231-249.
  1962   !Kung Bushman religious beliefs. *Africa* 32:221-252.
  1965   "The !Kung Bushmen of the Kalahari Desert," in *Peoples of Africa*. Edited by James L. Gibbs, 243-278. New York: Holt, Rinehart and Winston.
  1969   The medicine dance of the !Kung Bushmen. *Africa* 39:347-381.
  i.p.   *!Kung Bushman studies*. Cambridge, Massachusetts: Harvard University Press.
MAUSS, MARCEL
  1954   *The gift*. (First published 1925) London: Cohen and West.

MCBRIDE, WILMA, *editor*
1966   *Inquiry: implication for televised instruction.* Washington, D. C.: National Education Association. (1201 Sixteenth Street, N. W., Washington, D. C. 20036.)

MCWILLIAMS, DONALD E.
1970   Frederick Wiseman. *Film Quarterly* 24:1.

MEAD, M., F. C. MACGREGOR
1951   *Growth and culture: a photographic study of Balinese childhood.* New York: Putnam.

MIDDLETON, JOHN
1960   *Lugbara religion.* Oxford: Oxford University Press.

MISHLER, ANITA
1970   *Protocol materials to teach new perspectives: the classroom as a learning community.* Cambridge, Massachusetts: Education Development Center.

PINCUS, EDWARD
1969   *Guide to filmmaking.* New York: The New American Library.

RASMUSSEN, KNUD
1931   *The Netsilik Eskimos. Report of the Fifth Thule Expedition 1921–1924* 8 (1,2). Copenhagen: Gyldendalske Boghandel, Nordisk Forlag.

ROSSI, PETER H., BRUCE J. BIDDLE
1966   *The new media and education.* Chicago: Aldine.

ROUCH, JEAN
1956   Migrations au Ghana (Gold Coast). (Enquête 1953–1955). *Journal de la Société des Africanistes* 26:33–196.

SAETTLER, PAUL
1968   *A history of instructional technology.* New York: McGraw-Hill.

SANDALL, ROGER
1972   Observation & identity. *Sight and Sound* 41 (4):192-196.

SORENSON, E. R.
1967   A research film program in the study of changing man. *Current Anthropology* 8:443–369.

SORENSON, E. R., CARLETON GAJDUSEK
1963   "Research films for the study of child growth and development and disease patterns in primitive cultures." A catalogue of research films in *Ethnopediatrics.*
1966   The study of child behavior and development in primitive cultures. *Pediatrics* 37 (1, ii):149-243.

SPRADLEY, JAMES P., DAVID W. MCCURDY
1972   *The cultural experience: ethnography in complex society.* Chicago: Science Research Associates.

STONEY, GEORGE C.
1971   Film, videotape and social change. *Journal of the University Film Association* 24 (4):108.

SUBER, HOWARD
1971   Jorge Preloran. *Film Comment* 7 (1):43-51.

THOMAS, ELIZABETH MARSHALL
1959   *The harmless people.* New York: Alfred A. Knopf.
1963   Bushmen of the Kalahari. *National Geographic Magazine* 123:866–888.

TIME-LIFE FILMS CATALOG
  1973–1974   New York: Time-Life, Inc.
WOLF, ERIC
  1972   Review of *Magical Death*. *American Anthropologist* 74:196–198.

The Use of Television in Teaching Anthropology

JAMSHED MAVALWALA

One uncompleted and six completed half-hour television tapes for teaching anthropology were produced over a period of six months in 1971 at the Instructional Media Center of the University of Toronto.[1] I functioned as an interviewer and led the interviewee through a series of questions. The tapes were directed at the level of a first year-university student with little or no idea of what is involved in anthropology; they did not aim at an audience knowledgeable in anthropology. A great many terms were not explained, under the assumption that other sources, such as a tutorial or discussion-group leader or a relevant book, would better provide clarification for the viewer.

THE SPECIFICITY OF THE MEDIUM

The use of television as a medium in anthropology is not only new, it is difficult to decide whether at this point it has been born at all or whether it is still in the gestation phase. As a medium of entertainment and communication at other levels, the full potential of television is still to be realized. It is difficult for those who have long dealt with communication in the visual media to adjust to the peculiar properties of television. It is even more difficult for those accustomed to communication only with the written word to begin to exploit the potential of television. Learning

---

[1] The tapes were later transferred by the university to Software Production, Inc., 705 Progress Avenue, Unit no. 33, Scarborough, Ontario, for distribution. They have since been registered and certified by the National Film Board of Canada as educational materials.

to transmit information via written language is a long and laborious process. In anthropology some scholars write in an exquisite style, others with florid detail; yet others link sentence after sentence together in so stodgy a fashion as to obliterate any communication flow under verbiage, even if it is grammatically correct.

If the television medium is increasingly utilized as a communication and teaching tool, we may expect to be faced with some anthropologists who will use this tool with skill, grace, and elegance, and with others who will use it mainly, or only, as a time-killing device.

WHAT IS THE USE OF THIS MEDIUM?

Television is quite different from the written language and in some ways from the other commonly used medium — film. In a written communication the anthropologist must know the use of the basic tool, the language. It is not enough to wish one's great idea onto paper. It must be written down sentence by sentence; paragraphs must be constructed, a flow maintained, certain conventions upheld. All these skills rest upon the shoulders of the anthropologist: as a group, we are not known for our ghost-writers. The result is a communication written in words, possibly embellished with some visual material. The visual material is invariably static; rarely do we come upon visual material within an anthropology communication that is evocative.

With the use of television, the possibilities expand into many dimensions. This presents more opportunities for skill, talent, and hard work, but it also presents more potential for a disastrous communication.

THE TEAM VERSUS INDIVIDUAL ASPECT

It became clear to me that a television program could be made by a team of personnel, not by the anthropologist alone. I have just been involved with the making of six television shows. I did not know at the beginning and do not know now what to do with a television studio camera: I can move it around, point it in the general direction of the action, and mechanically make it work, but I cannot use it skillfully during the filming of a sequence. I cannot handle lighting, studio sets, and the director's duties. The transmission of a few concepts to television tape takes a team. I can learn to conceptualize a program before starting it and then to do it better each succeeding time.

The anthropologist can use his conventional materials (two-dimensional diagrams, pictures, prints or slides, and film clips) and his own spoken words or written words voiced over, and then let the television personnel fashion it into a cohesive program. The use of a team is a relative phenomenon: most of us do not type our own manuscripts and we certainly do not typeset, print, bind, promote, or stand behind bookstore counters and sell them. We do not always take or process and print our own pictures.

In television the team is involved with a production that must communicate simultaneously via ear and eye to the brain of the receiver. But if the receiver is a student in a class, he is expecting information that must be regurgitated later. If a tape does everything — presents data, draws inferences, discusses issues, and comes to conclusions — it is complete in itself and leaves out the audience. In fact, it creates an "audience", not participants. The impulse is not "I would have said such-and-such in the program at that particular point" but "why did so-and-so say such-and-such?" The latter is a closure statement because so-and-so is rarely available for an answer, and the stimulation of a thought process in the observer may cease.

With television, therefore, the physical aspects of the medium are best left to the technically skilled television crews and effort is better concentrated on what one can do VIA the medium than what can be done WITH it.

THE CONTEXT

The tapes were made at the studios of the Instructional Media Center (IMC) of the University of Toronto. (I came to this university in July, 1969, and was aware of the facilities of an audio-visual section, but I did not realize that facilities for producing television programs were available.) The facilities were excellent even by professional standards and the studios were often rented by commercial television networks. As a faculty member, I learned more by accident than by design of the presence both of the studios and of funding to help to produce programs. The information came from a student seminar that visited the studios to view a television tape made by another professor. A studio official showed us around and expressed his concern over a poor, in fact almost nonexistent, response to the IMC's attempt to get faculty to advance ideas for programs. At this large university only a few faculty had come forward with any suggestions and fewer still had followed through to the actual completion of a program.

I had been on this campus long enough by then to have had some inkling of these facilities, but I cannot recall any document inviting faculty to use the facilities of the IMC. It was quite true though that even if a circular had crossed my desk, it might have aroused some interest then; but without a personal view of the studio facilities, it would not have occurred to me, someone with no prior television experience whatsoever, that it was technically possible to build up programs. The official who showed us around was merely being courteous and saw me as just another faculty member who was interested enough to come to the studios; he could have had no idea that I would participate in programs in the near future. At that point I, too, did not know.

(The studios were then situated seventeen miles from the main campus, at Scarborough College. They have since been disbanded and are being reorganized on the main campus on a smaller scale.)

I requested and rapidly received permission to produce a tape on race to be entitled *Race: Reality or Myth?* Ironically, that program has still to be completed. (As of April, 1973, it was finished but for the editing. In the meantime, six other half-hour tapes have been made and are currently registered with the National Film Board of Canada.)

PURPOSE OF PROGRAM

From the outset, the purpose of the programs was never very clearly defined, and as program after program was completed, it became clear that the visual medium can be used for many purposes in a variety of ways. What is a teaching tape? What is a half-hour television show for broadcast purposes on educational time slots or channels? When is a teaching tape or so-called educational tape considered "entertaining" enough to be broadcast on noneducational channels? Who is being taught? Only the student at the university? Only members of adult education classes? Anyone interested enough to watch? How is the teaching to be done? By stimulating the viewer via eye and ear so that at the end of the program there is more information than at the beginning of the program? By conveying information but concentrating on trying to communicate the problems inherent in the topic? Should the show raise questions or issues and leave them unanswered and unresolved? What word should one use in referring to such visual materials? A television program, a half-hour tape, a television show? In this case the term *television program* was used. It appeared to fit what was being created.

The programs tried to steer a course between, on the one hand, stimulating interest and discussion through reference to controversial issues, and on the other, transferring both factual and conceptual information. In actual practice, the programs tended to lean one way or the other. It has also become clear that the programs elicit a range of responses from class audiences. It appears that the answer to what is a good program lies in the end reaction that takes place between the viewer and the program. Very early during the showing of the tapes the viewer response appeared better if I made no explanatory remarks whatsoever beyond a brief statement about the topic covered. The viewers are generally interested not in the process of making the television tape, but in the finished product. They do not know what the original script called for, what was omitted or added at the last minute. Also, each viewer sees the tape from within the context of his own frame of reference.

I felt that the medium of television lent itself better to transmitting a sense of "person" than facts suitable for note-taking. The person providing the information was humanized by answering some personal questions, and an effort to create a sense of reality about the figures on the screen was attempted. Obviously, only degrees of success were achieved.

For teaching purposes a good television tape was seen as one that either (1) raised an issue, opened avenues of discussion, and left them unresolved with the hope that the instructor of the class would then encourage student response; or (2) offered detailed data, with the understanding that the class instructor would further reinforce this in his lectures afterwards. In both cases, wherever possible, the visual material was treated as primary and the spoken word as secondary. The dialogue was built around the slides or materials on the studio set. No formal script was written or adhered to for any of the programs. A quick reference to the programs will show that they were created by the nature and the amount of the material and by the capacity of the interviewee.

PROBLEMS IN THE ACTUAL SHOOTING

All the programs were basically in an interview format, involving only one person other than myself, and a few problems concerning participants arose. Studio-related problems were handled by the studio director and, beyond causing delays in time, did not affect me as the academic involved in the program.

One of my major problems was that because participants were often university faculty accustomed to delivering lectures to a live audience, I, as the interviewer, had to do all I could to make the person look at and reply to me rather than to the foreground. Another concern was the use of terms or remarks that were local in nature. The weather on the day we shot a particular tape might have been unusual, but a comment on the weather had to be edited out, because a class watching the tape would find it inappropriate to the stated topic.

The second hurdle was to get people to ignore the cameras and look at me while they were talking to me. I found that it was practically impossible to get a participant to remove his gaze from the large round lens of the studio cameras. A kind of hypnosis seemed to set in. It helped if the studio floor director issued specific instructions to ignore the cameras and also if I concentrated directly on the person. Removing my gaze to glance away for time signals or for a check on the monitor broke the rapport.

Another problem was voice. Reading something was fatal: a dull inflection and a monotone took over. Speaking brightly to the participant evoked a lively response. For the most part, the participants lost their nervousness in the studio within minutes of rehearsal and we could shoot a program straight through.

It also appeared better to make no attempt to establish a "proper" sitting position or to fuss over clothing (other than to advise against fabric with small checks, which tend to dance on the screen and can be distracting and disconcerting). Because we pinned microphones onto the clothing, too much movement resulted in some rustling. For at least the first three programs, I was the prime offender, with a microphone pinned onto a wool waistcoat. What a racket that caused!

When many slides are used, the participant tends to glance away at the monitor. For one show the monitor was positioned to the side, while the slides actually appeared on a large screen behind us. This meant turning our heads to look at the monitor or craning our necks to look back. We learned to position the monitor carefully within eye range so that our heads need not turn, as well as to run a quick rehearsal of the slide sequence.

There must be endless facets to running a successful twenty-eight-minute tape, but only these few that loomed large in this particular experience are mentioned here.

THE TELEVISION PROGRAMS

1. The first program, *Race: Reality or Myth?* is still unfinished. This program did not have an interview format and involved diverse material, outdoor shooting, and a search for specific photographic materials.

2. The second program, *Fossil Evidence for Evolution*, was an interview with Professor C. L. Brace of the University of Michigan. His book *Stages of human evolution* was used to begin the program and he was asked a series of questions about the fossil record, following the four stages postulated in that book. A formal set for this program contained two wicker peacock chairs. No slides were used. We had intended to make elaborate maps, charts, and diagrams, but later decided to let the program concentrate mainly on the scholar and his opinions and to have the instructor fill in with spelling of names and locations of places referred to in the program. The program was shot as a continuous twenty-eight-minute interview, which resulted inevitably in a relaxed discussion of the Australopithecines and then a hurried flurry of questions about the Neanderthals and the development to modern man.

Our use of this program has evoked student interest in these ways:

a. Students were interested in seeing Dr. Brace. He photographed dramatically well and spoke lucidly; the cameramen had a field day.

b. Dr. Brace made it clear that some aspect of his opinions had changed. I found this a good point to reinforce with those students who tended to become dogmatic believers in a particular interpretation of the fossil record.

c. Of course we hoped that the program would provoke discussion, debate, and further reading; it apparently did so. This program dealt with inferences drawn from the fossil material. It did not even attempt to show the data, which would have entailed prohibitive expense. As the tape now stands, the instructor can show fossil casts and slides of actual specimens, and can explain ways of deriving inferences from the data that differ from those discussed in the program.

3. The third program was the simplest to record, a pleasure to do, and, in my opinion, definitely the best in terms of projecting a personalized viewpoint. This program, *Being Black in Canada*, resulted from a suggestion one evening that I tape an interview with a visiting journalist for use in the program on race. The next morning, a few minutes before the program, I met Mairuth Haas for the first time. We briefly discussed the outline of the questions. Two chairs and a table were set up. Shadows on the screen at the back of the studio became a backdrop while Mairuth talked of what it was like for a black child to grow up in Canada and for a black woman to achieve success.

The program moves along rapidly, and it has to be emphasized that not all women are so elegant and that not all blacks lead such lives. What this tape does best is to destroy stereotypes, however vague, that some students in the class may have about blacks in Canada. It also brings home the point that there are race problems north of the United States border, and that they are NOT of recent origin.

I consider this a fluent interview program. It makes no pretense at providing facts and figures. It is a personal record very personally stated. I am constantly surprised at the variety of responses elicited from various class audiences.

4.   The next program was an attempt to tape an ecological picture of the Kalahari Bushmen as presented by Professor Richard Lee, then of Rutgers University. It makes extensive use of his slides and ends with a discussion of the benefits that accrue to an anthropologist who does such studies and to the people who are studied. The program discusses the onset of flooding in the rainy season, thus dispelling the idea that the Bushmen live in a permanently arid land. It also dispels a notion widely held by students that hunter-gatherers spend nearly ALL their time grubbing around desperately for food. I have used this tape to initiate two types of discussions: (1) to understand and evaluate the life-style of hunting-gathering peoples, and (2) to discuss a growing awareness in anthropology of the rights and prerogatives of the peoples studied.

5.   The next two programs were made with E. E. Hunt, Jr., of Pennsylvania State University. The first, *The Primate Puzzle*, required building a set to look like a corner of a laboratory, and concerned itself with how a bone or bones aid in the reconstruction of a long-dead fossil form. It is very much a learning program with Dr. Hunt giving a lecture on television, but on the screen he appears to be giving an interview in his laboratory.

6.   The second program with Dr. Hunt, *Behavioral Evolution*, was a straightforward expression of opinions on evolutionary processes in man examined from a behavioral aspect rather than an anatomical one. While the first program leaves the student with a residue of factual material, this program leaves the class with a residue of unanswered, somewhat controversial, issues.

7.   The last program, *The Chimpanzees are Here!*, was the result of a visit by John H. Pfifferling of Pennsylvania State University to the Gombe Stream Reserve in Central Africa. We retraced his journey to the reserve and talked about what was being learned about the chimpanzees there, the highlights of ten years' work by Dr. Jane Van Lawick-Goodall and others, and the significance and limitations of such studies for a better understanding of human evolution.

The inevitable student response is a flurry of questions. I have found it relatively easy to assign varied readings in primate behavior, particularly chimpanzee behavior, and then show this tape. The tape does not explain the features of primate behavior. It does deal with the sense of maturity that scholars dealing with primate behavior are beginning to feel about studies on the chimpanzees of the Gombe Stream Reserve.

MOTIVATION AND REWARD

What motivation is there for faculty to make television tapes for teaching purposes? At present it appears that, unlike the writing of a book for teaching purposes, creativity in the visual medium promises little in the way of a reward. In this particular case no contracts were drawn and signed until about a year AFTER the completion of the tapes! My motivation centered around an enthusiasm for the ease with which television tapes could be produced. The reason that six tape programs were completed in 1971 and none thereafter was the imminent disbanding of the studio. Participation of scholars as interviewees was easily obtained for a very nominal fee, and legal release forms required by the university were readily signed. I later realized that the Instructional Media Center itself, because of the new nature of this material, spent a great deal of effort in drawing up contracts that would be fair to all parties concerned.

I cannot help but surmise that faculty participation would have been better on this campus if there had been some recognition for making the tapes and if, at the university and departmental administration levels, means had been devised to assess and reward such participation, as is done with service in teaching and on various committees and with publications (in the written word) of a university teacher. Not all faculty write "aids to teaching" material and not all would work with television, but more talent would be forthcoming if this were encouraged at the administrative levels. The encouragement will have to come first at the level of professional recognition, and secondly at the monetary level.

Various plans are touted, but no specific system seems to have emerged. Perhaps evaluating the material created and rewarding its creators may best be achieved by conventional book publishers involving themselves with this medium as they have done in the past with such visual materials as slides and films. This immediately exposes the programs to the entire profession for critical reviews and would lead to the production of programs that the teaching market is really in need of.

ASSESSMENT

This initial production of six television tapes has brought two things into focus. First, a taped television interview interspersed with slides, film clips, and other visual material can be made within the confines of a very small budget (provided studio facilities are already available). Secondly, the problems faced are essentially minor ones.

The response from my professional colleagues was enthusiastic. If this were the determining factor, at least a dozen more tapes would be completed by now. It is also becoming evident that a single university cannot hope to sponsor successfully a program to develop teaching materials. The alternative that appears most reasonable at present is for a publishing company, outside the administrative context of a single campus, to handle the production of such materials. Publishers are in a far better position to deal with the distribution of such materials than are university systems. With a widespread distribution we will, for the first time, be able to determine exactly what does function as a good television teaching tape and what elements in this complex medium transmit information and successfully communicate a sense of intellectual excitement to students. After the initial choice by instructors (the first test) and then use by the students (the second test), an evaluative statement which is not yet available will emerge. The student is becoming a sophisticated user of visual materials. It now behooves the teachers to develop a sophistication in the production of such materials.

Research Films and the Communications Revolution

FOSTER O. CHANOCK, E. RICHARD SORENSON

The visual data of passing phenomena, preserved for restudy and re-use are vital to understanding changing man and coping with the changing world. Yet they are a resource which has only just begun to receive much attention.

Dramatic improvements in transport and communications since World War II have accelerated change throughout the world. Only a very few societies still embody those distinct independent natural experiments in the channeling and utilizing of human potential which evolved over thousands of years of isolation. Even in modern societies change is continual, and behavioral organization and human response undergo alterations perhaps even more rapidly than in isolated cultures.

Film records are essential to the detailed scientific study of such developments. Our inability to document adequately such nonrecurring phenomena is imposed by the lack of notation systems which can be used to record objectively the complexities and subtleties of human behavior as it occurs in its natural setting. Only visual records, taken at different times and in different places, can provide the data needed to examine effectively the variety of practices which emerge over time as man responds to his changing surroundings. The advantage of such records in sustaining a dynamic democratic society has been stated by Sorenson (n.d.):

Particularly in less isolated societies, perturbations, innovations, and strains continually emerge in response to new opportunities and challenges. Frequently fading, only to re-emerge in new forms, these behavioral forerunners of the future often leave no record behind to help us unravel the dynamics of the social evolution they reflect.

The unique advantage of visual records is that they make possible an ongoing public and scientific review of the dynamics of man's emerging behavioral and social repertoire in relation to the conditions which pattern his responses and adaptation.

How man fits into and copes with the world and its transformations (including those he himself generates) is of vital interest and concern to man. Visual data revealing such phenomena can uniquely inform us about that entity which concerns us most, our own species — its potential, its behavior, and its social organization. IN A DEMOCRATIC SOCIETY SUCH INFORMATION FED INTO THE PUBLIC MEDIA FACILITATES INFORMED CONSIDERATION OF ALTERNATIVES.

By bringing together two independent developments of recent years, it is now possible to tap the visual data of passing events for study and public consideration. These are:

1. The development of a research film methodology designed to preserve maximally the visual data of passing, naturally occurring human events for continued study and use (cf. Sorenson 1967, 1968).

2. The expanding capacity and flexibility of the technology of visual communication.

RESEARCH FILMS

The research film method provides identified and annotated visual records useful for continued study and use. These visual records are unedited and not in themselves "films" in the usual sense: there is no attempt in them to present a coherent statement or point of view. Not designed to demonstrate a conclusion or to impose preconceived ideas, they are intended to facilitate review and study of passing, naturally occurring phenomena. They are not constructed to conform to the aesthetic models of our age or to present worked out concepts. Rather they are designed to serve as information potential: they are ordered and annotated — but not edited, rearranged, or abstracted. Thus the name, *research film.*

Preparation of research films is not a matter of deciding what sequences to keep but rather how to make all of the exposed footage and the vast data it contains recoverable and usable. In contrast to the production of the usual motion pictures, preparation of research films principally involves order and annotation. All episodes are kept in their original chronological order and identified by time, place, and subject. Nothing is discarded. The filmer's objectives and predilections and incidental observations are included in the annotation, and, when possible, the filmed data are correlated with other related data.

Virtually any exposed film footage can become research film. As visual data resources such films can be returned to again and again either for diverse further research stimulated by new advances in science or for special productions designed to inform the public. Properly assembled and annotated, they are without equal in their ability to provide accurately identified and contextually interpretable sequences for a variety of visual needs — for research, for classrooms, and for general dissemination. A filmmaker or researcher can choose his sequences intelligently from an extensively annotated body of visual data with reference to both detailed identifications and broader contexts. This allows greater accuracy in edited special purpose films than would otherwise be possible.

The theory and method of the research film aims particularly at increasing the information value of visual records. Practical experience in collecting, preparing, storing, and using research films in a pioneer research film collection (Sorenson and Gajdusek 1966) has provided a basis on which to develop a genuine anthropological visual data center (Sorenson 1971, n.d.) and for the formulation of basic guidelines for research filming (Sorenson and Jablonko's paper, *supra*).

ELECTRONIC VIDEO TECHNOLOGY

The electronic video technology has provided a breakthrough in the study and use of visual data as well as in visual communication. Our ability to manage visual information both for research and presentation is now much greater than has ever been the case. We may review and retrieve visual information and prepare sequences for presentation with a flexibility and speed hitherto unknown. We have new power to see and understand ourselves and others; and we have new power to communicate our findings to others.

Television provides the means of disseminating information; but electronically coded videotape is the key to handling visual data for study or report. Using videotaped visual records, we may automatically retrieve preselected categories of filmed data from an archive collection and almost instantaneously copy them in the desired order for a variety of special applications. A combination of computerized indexing and retrieval with highspeed viewing equipment, including fast-forward and reverse and stop-frame capability, greatly facilitates flexible selection of visual material from visual data libraries. Different kinds of scanning are possible at several times natural speed, including multiple viewing for comparative purposes.

Video cassettes have lowered the cost and space required for copying and storing filmed data. Such cassettes can be coded and cross-indexed for rapid location of the sequences needed for scientific study or preparation of films for presentation. Aided by a computer retrieval system, a researcher, student, or filmmaker can quickly locate and review existing material. At low cost he can copy what is pertinent to his needs onto his own cassette. He may take this record home for review on his own television set or to a laboratory or studio for specialized review, analysis, or editing.

With such Xerox-like copying of motion picture sequences possible, virtually anyone may select bits from a more extensive film record for a variety of special purposes. A scientist may search for particular categories of visual data; a teacher or a group of students may assemble their own educational films; graduate students may experiment with new methods of mixed media presentation; and a scientist may inform his colleagues of his findings on passing events using report films he may assemble. Although there may be a question of copyright infringement, the variety of possibilities is great.

The visual images such people want to consider or use in their studies or projects can be retained as long as needed or desired. They can be erased and the same tape used again and again for other purposes.

Because of the electronic video technology and the enhanced flexibility it provides for studying and using visual images, collections of visual records of naturally occurring phenomena become a valuable national resource. Not only will they help feed the growing needs of the visual media for resources, but they will also extend our ability to investigate, communicate about, and deal with the changing world.

THE NEED FOR RELIABLE VISUAL DATA RESOURCES

The increasing potential of video communications is not equalled by growing visual resources, and much of the paucity of present programming can be traced to the lack of reliable and varied source materials. It is ironic that the increasing desire to use visual media in curriculum improvement, for example, has led educational institutions to buy more equipment than there is good source material to build from. Although it is encouraging to see students beginning to develop their own curriculum materials on videotape and film, this promising development is undermined by a lack of readily available, inexpensive resources.

Similarly, public television is literally starving for quality programming:

it cannot often afford the huge sums budgeted for quality documentary films. The present competitive, acquisitive approach to filmmaking, often governed by an aggressive "scoop" philosophy, is extravagantly wasteful. To rush $100,000 into a single half-hour film, financing camera crews, expedition costs, and far greater quantities of exposed film than will ever be used in the finished short film, verges on the irrational. How much better it would be to have the film from any such operation permanently available as an identified, standardized resource — not just for research but also for the varied and different kinds of generally informative films that could be generated from a large collection of such resource materials.

Much educational television today is dull — frequently because its message is too obvious and the picture does not always support the spoken message. Frequently aimed at abstract concepts of student readiness or "level", it is often so overcontrived as to be generally boring. A fundamental difficulty appears to be the shortage of appropriate, appealing visuals. Often words are used to fill this gap; they are cheap and can only too easily be used to cover scarcity and inappropriateness in visual material.

Without access to a wide range of visual resources, it is virtually impossible for the low budget educational filmmaker to break away from the model of the DIDACTIC film and its verbally oriented concepts of presentation. But with diverse, interpretable visual resources, he may begin to move toward a concept of VISUAL film. Because such visual presentation is richer in the kind of phenomenological information on which everyone has a slant drawn from personal experience, a viewer can more readily relate the insights being presented to his own sense of reality. Such films bring the educational process closer to the humanistic ideal of self-realization and personal growth (Sorenson n.d.).

Already anthropologists have pioneered in the presentation of evidence that relies more on visuals than on didactic explanation. Contextually coherent visuals seem to have a broader appeal than verbal constructs, apparently because the information is not predifferentiated (i.e. not fully run through the interpretative screen of the human mind). With greater reliance on such visual evidence, a viewer is permitted much more flexibility in seeing and interpreting than would be possible if he were simply told. Different people with different backgrounds may build their understanding on the basis of their own insights and past experience. It should not be surprising that films relying more on visuals from naturally occurring situations hold audiences of greater diversity than do "explanatory" films.

It will only be possible to exploit this potential seriously when sizeable visual resources, particularly reliably identified records of naturally occurring phenomena, become readily available. When the experimental filmmaker, the graduate student, the class, and the innovative teacher begin to have access to large visual data banks with flexible review, copying, and editing facilities, we can begin to realize more fully the power of visual images of true life as a means of learning. Only then will we begin to respond to the increasing demand for more varied and better tailored visual education.

As of March 1974, the *National Geographic Magazine* had a circulation of over 8,489,000. This is incredible for a magazine sold only by membership. Obviously the curiosity to know about the rest of the world is real, and the attractiveness and power of visual display of real life is great. In part the success of the *Geographic* reflects the generally held belief that it is accurate, that it researches its material extensively and actively culls out misinformation. Pictorial publications which have not achieved this reputation have not been so successful. This is an important lesson. Television and educational filmmakers would be wise to work with accurately identified and annotated source material.

Cable television is coming. Its needs will be great because of the diversified special audiences it best serves. Because it uses coaxial cable, rather than the limited airwaves, for dissemination, cable television has virtually unlimited channel capacity. The initial systems in the United States handle twelve to twenty channels per cable; but the new systems currently being planned provide a forty-to-sixty-channel capacity. And one can continue laying cables indefinitely!

Such a potential abundance of channels will make possible more diversified and lower cost programming than ever before. A variety of audiences with special interests can be satisfied. Mass marketing pressures will cease to push programming inexorably toward common-denominator-appeal.

The wired nation with communication satellites, cable television, video cassettes, microwave, and two-way television will soon be a reality. We will soon have at our disposal an expanded and flexible means for transmitting video information — not just station-to-home but also library-to-student, person-to-person, and resource-center-to-filmmaker.

Dependable visual resource banks are essential to this development. A communications revolution that relies on fantasy, misinformation, and contrivance will be weaker than one that can tap more solid visual data.

The research film method provides the best current answer to this need. When properly assembled, annotated, and standardized, research films, preserved in a visual data research center, provide an unequalled resource for research and public information. There is no other way to provide a wealth of accurately identified and contextually interpretable visual material for a variety of usages: for research, for curricula, and for public dissemination. With access to such a facility a filmmaker, researcher, average citizen, and student can choose sequences from an extensive, researched body of visual data with reference to detailed identifications and the broader contextual materials. Thus he can build richer presentations more confidently and with greater accuracy and flexibility than would otherwise be possible.

There is no such facility available at present; but the theory has been worked out and a model established (Sorenson 1967, 1968, 1971; Sorenson and Jablonko 1975). These guidelines for obtaining and preserving the unanalyzed visual data of naturally occurring phenomena, such as changing culture and human behavior, for continued review and use permit inquiry into the human condition to proceed hand in hand with its consideration by the public. A more useful and more powerful communication revolution is made possible because the information it uses will be more reliable.

Because of their concern with man, anthropologists have pioneered these developments, working out the methods and theory of the retrieval of data from changing culture and experimenting widely with visual techniques of revealing man to man. The possibility they have created of integrating a scholarly component into the communications revolution will make that revolution more realistic, more useful, and more democratic. A road on which scientific application joins public debate may be the rewarding route to the future.

REFERENCES

SORENSON, E. RICHARD
  1967 A research film program in the study of changing man: research filmed material as a foundation for continued study of nonrecurring human events. *Current Anthropology* 8:443–469.
  1968 The retrieval of data from changing culture: a strategy for developing research documents for continued study. *Anthropological Quarterly* 41:177–186.
  1971 Toward a national anthropological research film center – a progress report. *PIEF Newsletter* of the American Anthropological Association 3 (1):1–2.
  n.d. "Anthropological film: a unique scientific and humanistic resource." Manuscript.

SORENSON, E. R., D. C. GAJDUSEK
1966   *The study of child behavior and development in primitive cultures: a research archive for ethnopediatric film investigations of styles in the patterning of the nervous system.* Supplement to *Pediatrics* 37(1), Part II.

Mass Communication Meets the Anthropologist: A Short Manual of Some Unprimitive Thought

JAY K. HOFFMAN

During an anthropological film conference that recently took place at the Smithsonian Institution, I became aware of the ironical fact that the name of the conference — Changing Man — could not be applied to the men and women who were actually making the films, working in the field, etc. During the course of the intensive three-day event, an obvious fact became disturbing. No one ever talked about making a living — "survival" in the current jargon. Yes, members of panels eloquently and passionately suggested survival tools for peoples of the earth, but no one dealt with self-survival, and eventually I equated that with the very low esteem the anthropologist/ethnographic filmmaker has for himself. In effect, this being the second conference I had attended, it was again confirmed that here was a talented group of professionals talking to themselves, rather like a group of police commissioners talking about crime in the streets while rioting goes on around them.

I was deeply disturbed because, as a professional who deals with mass communications, I realized that getting the information about the peoples of this earth to plain old citizens was, as the saying goes, "hung up in committee." These filmmakers were busy delivering the litany of their profession, but no one was translating it now to communicate with a ready congregation of everyone from kids in classrooms to network television, cable TV, etc. And I realized that one basic reason there was such trouble in communication was the anthropologist's primitive thoughts about the commercial world "out there." True enough, I knew that most of them had shared stories with each other about distributors, networks, etc., but few if any had some hard facts. Needed was a set of simple definitions — a guideline or manual which would aid the filmmaker when venturing INTO THE STREETS (just a metaphor for INTO THE FIELD — only the natives are housed in concrete, not thatched huts).

To begin with, let's clear up NETWORK TELEVISION. For the most part, *National Geographic* has the field tied up and they produce a goodly number of programs yearly in the United States. It is not unusual for them to employ anthropological consultants — whose film does not get used but whose brains DO (if you're willing to support their particular view of mankind). If they employ you, they'll pay a fee, plus all expenses, and their film will be used both on television and in classroom. As regards the fee, check with someone else as to how much they pay. Do not take their word. As you've probably noticed, I began this paragraph with the "giant" simply to demythologize the primitive corporation. In effect, if you've been reading between the lines, what I've said is that it is likely they will consider using your expertise, but not your film(s). So, a word to the wise — if you're prepared to let their crews document a culture you have studied, be ready for a full time of it. In other words, be careful. If you're broke, be even more careful.

So what alternatives have you got? At the risk of being called wrong or a futurist, I predict that anthropology will soon have its day (and for a long time) on television — that is, if anthropologists stop dealing directly with networks or filmmakers who say they understand the "network mentality." The time has really come for the formation of a television collaborative with a pool of films available, with an administrative board, and so on. In effect, if Hollywood held out, anthropologists can, too. And eventually you'll be asked (commissioned) to make films for television — but as long as you sell out/off here and there, you'll simply be (forever) a resource for networks to make money from. The time has come to stop being flattered by being asked.

This brings us to the question of what to do if you think your particular film would make a good half-hour or one-hour "special." Can you realistically take it to a network and/or sponsor? The question answers itself if you simply watch television — not complaining that you could do a better film, but looking at the informational standards of networks — and then realize how futile your attempt would be. So we're back to zero-point, or are we? Maybe the collaborative needs an executive producer/administrator, two or three people who can be funded to organize the film material in North America.

Area number 2 is CABLE TELEVISION. As of this writing, there are over 3,000 stations in the United States and all the rumors are true. It is the medium of the future and a recent FCC ruling demands that local stations originate programming. Therefore, they'll have to look for professional material — and anthropology is one place to look — but they'll need their own guidelines set out for them by professionals who tell them how to sequence or program films, taped discussions, etc. By the way, there's no rush to sell your goods to cable T.V. Currently they're paying $25 per half-hour. Ouch! But don't fret: pornographic or "baby blue" films were getting the same until our sagacious Supreme Court came down on pornography.

We now arrive at the one area most of you are familiar with: NON-THEATRICAL DISTRIBUTION. Let it be said that here is the most sympathetic area for your films — but one which could be a little more organized and generous. As far as "organized" is concerned, you can help out by actually writing and creating the promotion copy for the flier they mail out (and the fact that they print a flier should be in your contract). Sometimes a graphically sophisticated brochure can compete with the printed material that sells the *National Geographic* films and other network material. This country's universities (its students and professors) buy "fancy" print and content, and they'll never know unless you're competitive from the beginning.

Now, as concerns "generous," try to get an advance from the distributor. Traditionally (the most perverse word in the distributor's language) you get no advance and 20 percent of gross receipts. Try not to settle for less than 25 percent of the distributor's gross sales price, but if you must, take 20 percent up to twenty-five prints sold and 25 percent thereafter. And if you feel you have a commercial winner, try getting 30 percent after 150 copies have gone into distribution.

And don't forget to try for that advance against your royalty. One good question concerns whom to contact. A fine start would be getting hold of a list of nontheatrical distributors, writing each for their catalogs, and off you go. Other questions concern whether or not nontheatrical distributors support productions while you're shooting them in the field. Now that China has opened up, the answer is "forget it." Other questions concern how much you can earn with a film in nontheatrical distribution. I'm reluctant to say, but $5,000 over five years would be nice. How about selling films in Canada or elsewhere (television again)? Here you have a better chance — with CBC-TV in Toronto and Granada Television in London. It's easier than the United States networks, but don't get enthusiastic at this point.

If this paper has presented a less than happy view of the future in communication, I am sorry. It's actually the dark before the storm — but only if ethnographic filmmakers communicate with each other along with communicating stories about other cultures. Let me assure you that the time is here for your material to be integrated into the fabric of Western life. As you see, it will take a new structure, very hard work, self-esteem, trust — but it's about time anthropologists organized their work so that it reaches out to mankind through media capable of making for effective social awareness of the world we live in.

COMMENT *by Art Brown*

Selection of Distributor

The most important thing is NOT the final terms of the distribution agreement – percentages, advance, period of time, territory, etc. – because these factors do not vary greatly from distributor to distributor in a competitive field, but rather the reputation and capability of the distributor and his attitude toward, interest in, and understanding of your film and your field. There is not a large number of distributors to consider for ethnographic films in the first place, so you should take a little time initially to talk to a few and satisfy yourself that your film will be properly presented to the intended or potential audience. Does the distributor under consideration already handle other ethnographic or documentary films? Is he visible in your field (attendance at conventions, advertisements in journals, special catalogs or other promotional material directed to anthropologists, etc.)? Does he understand your film and have a good idea of how and where to promote it? Are his advertising materials of high quality, accurate in content, and attractive? There are commercial distributors and noncommercial distributors (such as university film libraries) and agents. Generally, a commercial distributor can be expected to make more of an effort in advertising and promoting your film, to achieve a larger volume of rentals and sales, and to obtain a better price than a noncommercial distributor operating from a single location with a minimal budget for promotion and no great incentive to maximize returns. There are agents who will find you a distributor (for a fee or for a percentage of your income) or will find films for distributors (for a finder's fee paid by the distributor), but such practice usually eliminates the essential initial contact and understanding between distributor and filmmaker that is the basis for any long-term relationship, and it usually results in a smaller share of the income for the filmmaker.

Terms of Distribution

For non-theatrical distribution the percentage to the filmmaker ranges from 20 percent to 25 percent of the gross (with all expenses coming out of the distributor's share providing you have a completed film with a negative ready to go), although some few distributors offer 15 percent and an exceptional film, especially a feature-length film, might command 30 percent. Of course, the highest percentage may not always be the best deal. It takes effort and expense on the part of the distributor to bring your film to the attention of the field and build it until the return becomes significant. Television percentages (for a film which has potential for commercial and foreign television) are different. For network sales in these areas you might receive from 50 percent to 70 percent, but such sales are rare. Selling station-by-station requires as much work as selling school-by-school and the percentages are therefore comparable. Advances against the filmmaker's share are the exception, although a distributor might provide completion money if he likes a film and has enough faith in it, with such money being recouped later out of your share. Realize that the launching of even a short documentary film will require that the distributor spend a good deal of money making rental and preview prints, designing and printing and mailing an advertising piece, and getting the film previewed by potential buyers and reviewed by publications in the field.

What to Expect

The return is slow and for the usual documentary film with educational value, not very large. Many films do not earn back their production costs. (Neither do many Hollywood features.) At least, distribution income can be expected to defray part of your costs. A really useful film, however, can recoup its cost and much more from nontheatrical distribution alone over a period of years. Since the future for television use, expecially cable television, is generally optimistic, returns in the future may improve. Remember that hundreds of films are made and placed into distribution every year, adding to the thousands that schools already have to choose from in allocating their limited funds for purchase of prints. It takes an exceptional film that fills a real need to stand out.

Basic Requirements

Good technical filmmaking skills are assumed (camera work, sound recording, editing, narration, laboratory work, etc.). If you can't do the actual film work yourself (or don't feel competent to), find a good person who will work closely with you under your direction to insure a good product. Preplanning is essential, and this includes the intended audience. If you are interested only in scientific documentation, do not expect your films to hold the interest of nonspecialized audiences, no matter how fascinating the subject is to you. Although black-and-white is perfectly suitable for and may even be preferable for certain subjects, and although color costs more, you should be aware that most teachers and televison stations will prefer color. The content, of course, is the most important thing. Your film should be first of all true to its subject, factually accurate, informative, and as interesting as you can make it. Some of the very best films do not depend upon a narration to present their information, but allow it to be revealed through natural dialogue, natural sounds and music, and the images themselves.

COMMENT *by Foster O. Chanock*

Hoffman's interesting paper glances too quickly over the less glamorous media. Network television and movie theatres are fighting a losing battle with cable television. It is the fastest growing communications industry and certainly THE medium of the future. Cable's abundance of channels is forcing the industry to seek material that is not at present available. It is not really a mass medium, and it is economically advantageous for cable operators to program in as diversified a manner as possible, with appeal to special interest groups who are neglected by commercial television. (To find out more about distribution to cable television systems, you can write to the National Cable Television Association in Washington, D. C.)

Secondly, I think Hoffman underestimates the growing use of audiovisual material in American education. On all levels, film and videotape are being used as supplementary material. This too has a promising future in terms of dissemination and remuneration.

In conclusion, anthropologists should not be frustrated by the disinterest of movie and network executives. Rather, they should seek methods of distribution which are more appropriate to their audience, their experience, and the financial support available for further research.

REPLY *by Jay K. Hoffman*

Art Brown is a reputable and sensitive DISTRIBUTOR: I emphasize the word DISTRIBUTOR so the reader can understand "where he's coming from." Mr. Brown states that "the initial contact and understanding between distributor and film-maker is the basis of any long term relationship," and that is true — AFTER a deal is made. Distributors have a way of becoming friends, then getting insulted when the filmmaker tries to negotiate a stiff but just deal. Make sure that your film speaks for itself — and let an agent negotiate. There'll be fewer lunches for you — but greater and more substantial financial rewards in the long run.

Anthropological Programming in Japanese Television

JUNICHI USHIYAMA

Twenty years ago, I began work with the first television network in Japan, and since that time have been engaged in the production of documentary programs (in the broad sense) for TV networks. Last year, I established a company for such work with the co-sponsorship of a TV network in Japan. It provides about eighty hours of films per year for two national TV networks; fifty hours of which are produced by about fifteen production teams including my own one, and the remaining thirty hours are outstanding films imported from other countries.

Our purpose is the work of television journalism in a broad sense, which covers such general areas as history, ethnography, arts, and natural history. To speak from another viewpoint, however, we could say that the important role of television journalism is to mediate critically between politics and people or between the sciences and people. In other words, I hope that the films we produce influence creatively the life of the people, and at the same become a direct motivation for the producers to achieve a change toward a worldview and greater consciousness of self.

My interest in anthropology is based upon a criticism of journalism and the scholarly world. Although Japanese newspapers and broadcasting are heavily inclined to report the individual phenomena of politics, economics, and society, they are neither interested in nor concerned about the life of man in different cultures, the life-consciousness or value-ideas of people or, in general, their philosophy and *Weltanschauung*. My criticism of the streams of journalism is the basis of my attempt to introduce the life and culture of various peoples to Japanese viewers. Anthropology as the science of man embraces a strong criticism of the present academic situation in which various sciences are so diversified that they lose the understanding of man as a totality. Anthropology provides us with the clues to recover the meaning of human existence in the contemporary world. It is very unfortunate to have to state that we are the only group of television producers in Japan who are engaged in the production of documentary films with this sort of motivation.

We dispatch our teams to various countries, with a special emphasis on Asian nations. We always have more than three series of long-running serialized weekly programs on the national TV networks, which enables us to film one cultural area for several years. We never finish with one area in one film. Yasuko Ichioka, for instance, has been filming several phases of life in the Trobriand Islands: she filmed the sea-life of the Islanders centered around their fishing tradition in 1969, she filmed the Kula-ring in 1971, and she now plans to film the agricultural life centered around their traditional yam cultivation.

We always try to have the participation of local filmmakers on our film production team. So far such people have often worked as the second cameraman or sound engineer. At present we are producing an ethnographic film on the life of the Ainu, a minority group of Japan. In order for this to be as good a film as possible we are training and educating an Ainu youth as a cameraman: he will be the first Ainu filmmaker.

In Japan filmmaking has been entirely limited to those who belonged to or have belonged to the movie industry or to television journalism. There has been very little film production in the universities and research centers; we do not have a National Film Board in Japan either. Since I cannot expect improvement in the quality of film-production from this small filmmaking population, I have started appealing to the general public to produce 8-mm films. In 1973 with the co-sponsorship of big newspapers, broadcasting corporations, and our company (NAV), we started an annual national festival of 8-mm films which I hope will strengthen the above-mentioned movement. In this festival there is a competition for amateur 8-mm film production with a specific emphasis upon the folklore and family life of local communities. I do hope we will obtain good amateur filmmakers through this festival. In it we also publicized seventy-five outstanding ethnographic films of "the world", in collaboration with C.I.F.E.S.

We have always been in close association with Japanese anthropologists. In 1972 Japanese anthropologists, TV journalists and artists formed a committee called "Japanese Committee of Films on Man" in collaboration with Jean Rouch of C.I.F.E.S. One of the aims of this committee is to support the production of ethnographic films in collaboration with the National Institute of Ethnological Studies, which will open in the near future in Japan. The above Institute is expected to have an ethnographic film library which will be open to the general public.

At present we are also establishing various long-term agreements and close relationships with the governments and broadcasting bureaux of Asian countries that concern our program of ethnographic film production. In these agreements we envision: (1) the participation of local film-makers in our production team, (2) the right to use the films in their own countries freely, and (3) the establishment of a film library of various Asian cultures in the countries with whom we cement the agreement.

We have many requests to make of our colleagues. We need a list of excellent ethnographic films produced in the past throughout the world, and also information about who is producing what. We need a system for viewing all these good films; i.e. there should be at least several places in the world where all these films are available to those who want to see them. Third, we want to have the advice of anthropologists and filmmakers of various countries. And fourth, it would be very fruitful if we could produce in the future various TV series as a joint venture of filmmakers coming from various countries of the world.

The Future of Visual Anthropology

The Tribal Terror of Self-Awareness

EDMUND CARPENTER

New Guinea has been called "the last unknown." Its highest mountains are snow-covered and below these, in early morning, you walk through clouds, your breath visible. Yet tropical swamps lie immediately north and south.

Port Moresby, the capital of the eastern section, resembles a southern California town with air-conditioned buildings, supermarkets, and a drive-in theater. Four hundred miles to the west, tiny isolated bands practice cannibalism.

The bulk of the population lies between these extremes, living in thousands of tiny villages and speaking over 700 different languages.

This rainbow of regions and cultures is made all the more remarkable by the fact that, for many tribesmen, the steel axe, transistor radio, and camera all arrived together.

Several years ago the Territory of Papua and New Guinea hired me as a communications consultant. They sought advice on the use of radio, film, even television. They wanted to use these media to reach not only townspeople but those isolated in swamps and mountain valleys and outer islands.

I accepted the invitation because it gave me an unparalleled opportunity to step in and out of 10,000 years of media history, observing, probing, testing. I wanted to observe, for example, what happens when a person — for the first time — sees himself in a mirror, in a photograph, on a screen; hears his voice; sees his name. Everywhere tribesmen responded alike to those experiences: they ducked their heads and covered their mouths.

When a shy or embarrassed person in our society ducks his head and covers his mouth, we say he is "self-conscious." But why does consciousness of self produce THIS response? Does the acute anxiety of sudden self-awareness lead man everywhere to conceal his powers of speech-thought (his breath, his soul) behind his hand, the way an awakened Adam concealed his sexual powers behind a fig leaf?

Could it be that the deeper meaning these media conveyed wasn't sanitation or Westminster democracy, but self-discovery, self-awareness? Could this in part explain the riots in Rabaul and Kieta, towns where radio was part of daily life? The people in Rabaul had been in close contact with westerners since 1885, and now suddenly they were marching in the streets.

The Australian administrators were dedicated men, many of them ex-teachers and nearly all from Protestant middle-class backgrounds. They believed in democracy, cleanliness, and a personal God, and they promoted these goals via radio. Yet some of those who listened most attentively to these sermons were now in angry revolt. The administrators were puzzled and asked: what message had really come through?

WHERE THE HAND OF MAN HAS NEVER SET FOOT

It was important to us to film the reactions of people totally innocent of mirrors, cameras, recorders, etc. Such people exist in New Guinea, though they number only a handful and are disappearing like the morning mist.

To this end we went among the Biami, an isolated group in the Papuan Plateau. A few Biami men had scraps of mirrors, about the size of coins, obtained through distant trade, but my impression was that these were too small for image reflection and were treasured simply as light-reflectors.

In one village, a government patrol, searching for stolen salt, discovered a mirror carefully wrapped in bark and hidden in a thatched roof. I never learned what role this mirror had played, but I imagine it was interesting, for I saw nothing else, either in villages or jungle, that provided any means of self-reflection. Neither slate nor metallic surfaces exist and, for reasons I don't understand, rivers in this area fail to provide vertical reflections, though reflections of foliage can be seen at low angles. I doubt if the Biami ever saw themselves at all clearly.

Certainly their initial reaction to large mirrors suggested this was a wholly new experience for them. They were paralyzed: after their first startled response — covering their mouths and ducking their heads — they stood transfixed, staring at their images, only their stomach muscles betraying great tension. Like Narcissus, they were left numb, totally fascinated by their own reflections; indeed, the myth of Narcissus may refer to just this phenomenon.

In a matter of days, however, they groomed themselves openly before mirrors.

The notion that man possesses, in addition to his physical self, a symbolic self, is widespread, perhaps universal. A mirror corroborates this. It does more: it reveals that symbolic self OUTSIDE the physical self. The symbolic self is suddenly explicit, public, vulnerable. Man's initial response to this is probably always traumatic.

Added to this, mirrors reverse forward and backward: walk toward a mirror — the image moves in the opposite direction. That image, moreover, is greatly reduced. Test this yourself: with a piece of soap, outline your image on a bathroom mirror.

Mirrors have always been fraught with mystery and fear. We have the story about "Mirror, mirror, on the wall..." and our folklore warns of werewolves and vampires who, lacking souls, cast no reflections. Double-gangers are frequently associated with mirrors or window panes, and mental patients sometimes mutilate themselves while watching their reflections. Suicides committed in front of mirrors are far from unknown.

In the Congo, mirrors were placed in the stomachs or eyes of wooden judicial figures. A defendant would be forced to look into this mirror while nails were driven into the effigy. If he winced, he was judged guilty. In other words, his soul, his identity, entered the statue: he put on that statue. What made this ordeal so effective, so fraught with fear that a guilty man might unwillingly reveal himself, was that it created that intense anxiety which always seems to accompany sudden self-awareness.

When mirrors become a part of daily life, it's easy to forget how frightening self-discovery, self-awareness can be. But in New Guinea, among isolated groups, mirrors still produce that intense anxiety — that tribal terror — which so often accompanies self-awareness.

When people know themselves only from how others respond to them and then suddenly, for the first time, by means of some new technology, see themselves clearly, in some totally new way, they often are so frightened, so exhilarated, that they cover their mouths and duck their heads.

I think they do so to prevent loss of identity. New Guineans call it loss of soul, but it's the same phenomenon. It's their response to any sudden embarrassment, any sudden self-consciousness. When they first see pictures of themselves or hear recordings of their voices, this response is greatly intensified. It's as if they had vomited up an organ: they cover their mouths and duck their heads, almost as a delayed reflex, trying to prevent this.

LOVE THY LABEL AS THYSELF

In one remote village located between the Sepik River and the Highlands, we gave each person a Polaroid shot of himself. At first there was no understanding: the photographs were black and white, flat, static, odorless — far removed from any reality they knew. They had to be taught to "read" them. I pointed to a nose in the picture, then touched the real nose, etc. Often one or more boys would intrude, peering intently from picture to subject, then shout, "It's you!"

Recognition gradually came into the subject's face. And fear. Suddenly he covered his mouth, ducked his head and turned his body away. After this first startled response, often repeated several times, he either stood transfixed, staring at his image, only his stomach muscles betraying tension, or he retreated from the group, pressing his photograph against his chest, showing it to no one, slipping away to study it in solitude.

We recorded this over and over on film, including men retreating to private places, sitting apart, without moving, sometimes for up to twenty minutes, their eyes rarely leaving their portraits.

When we projected movies of their neighbors, there was pandemonium. They recognized the moving-images of film much faster than the still-images of photographs.

Seeing THEMSELVES on film was quite a different thing. It required a minor logistic feat to send our negative out, get it processed, then returned, but it was worth it.

There was absolute silence as they watched themselves, a silence broken only by whispered identification of faces on the screen.

We recorded these reactions, using infra-red light and film. In particular, we recorded the terror of self-awareness that revealed itself in uncontrolled stomach trembling.

The tape-recorder startled them. When I first turned it on, playing back their own voices, they leaped away. They understood what was being said, but didn't recognize their own voices and shouted back, puzzled and frightened.

But, in an astonishingly short time, these villagers, including children and even a few women, were making movies themselves, taking Polaroid shots of each other, and endlessly playing with tape-recorders (Plate 10). No longer fearful of their own portraits, men wore them openly, on their foreheads.

TECHNOLOGY IS EXPLICITNESS

Whenever technology makes behavior explicit, the resulting images often seem more important — even sacred or obscene. Most people swear, but when they hear blasphemy or obscenity on film or radio, action becomes artifact, and the explicit artifact offends them (or appeals to them) more than the action itself. The expletives need deleting.

We know little about this, other than the fact that it's true. Any technology, including language, can make reality frighteningly explicit, especially human reality. T. S. Eliot tells us that human beings cannot stand too much reality, by which he means, I assume, too much explicitness about reality. "A fearful thing is knowledge," says Tiresias in *Oedipus rex*, "when to know helpeth no end."

It's a serious mistake to underestimate the trauma any new technology produces, especially any new communications technology. When people first encounter writing, they seem always to suffer great psychic dislocation. With speech, they hear consciousness, but with writing, they see it. They suddenly experience a new way of being in relation to reality. "How do I know what to think," asks Alice, "till I see what I say?"

And how do I know who I am, until I see myself as others see me? "Of course in this you fellows see more than I could see," writes Conrad in *The Heart of Darkness*. "You see me."

A camera holds the potential for SELF-viewing, SELF-awareness, and, where such awareness is fresh, it can be traumatic. Using long lenses, we filmed people who were unaware of our presence. Then one of us stepped from concealment and stood watching, but not interrupting that activity. Finally the cameraman set up his equipment in full view, urging everyone to go on with whatever he was doing. Almost invariably, body movements became faster, jerky, without poise or confidence. Faces that had been relaxed now froze or alternated between twitching and rigidity.

Before we learned better, we asked people to repeat actions just observed but missed in filming. It was hopeless. Subjects were willing enough but their self-conscious performances bore little resemblance to their unconscious behavior. Among the hundreds of subjects filmed in a variety of situations, I cannot recall a single person, familiar with a camera, who was capable of ignoring it. This makes me wonder about ethnographic films generally. Even where subjects are accomplished actors, how does their acting compare with their behavior when no cameras are present? We may compliment their acting, but is it the theatrical performance we admire or their true-to-life impersonation?

When Joshua Whitcomb, a nineteenth-century actor, performed in

Keene, New Hampshire, the audience demanded its money back. It couldn't understand being charged admission. On stage Whitcomb was exactly the same as any number of local citizens who could be seen daily without charge. Said a representative in protest: "It warn't no acting; it was jest a lot of fellers goin' around and doin' things."

Since most ethnographic films profess to record just that — people going around and doing things — the question arises: do they? Or has the camera produced changes in behavior we can't see because they are so common among us, so much a part of our lives, that we fail to recognize them as alien in others? Do we take self-awareness for granted?

For New Guinea, the record is clear: comparing footage of a subject who is unaware of a camera, then aware of it — fully aware of it as an instrument for self-viewing, self-examination — is comparing different behavior, different persons.

REALITY AND SANCTITY

One day, at a marriage ceremony in the Central Highlands, we offered to photograph the bridal couple. The groom immediately posed with a male friend. We re-posed him with his pregnant bride and year-old child. Some weeks later we visited their home where we saw this photograph carefully pinned up.

Actually, the incident was infinitely more complicated than this brief account indicates. It was instantly obvious from the behavior of everyone present that the picture he had requested would have been routine, whereas the picture we took was anything but routine. It was as if we had photographed, in our society, the groom kissing the best man. All the power and prestige of the camera had been used in direct conflict with one of the deepest cultural values of this Highland society.

If I were a missionary, dedicated to promoting and preserving the Christian family, I would buy the biggest camera I could find, photograph all wedding couples and supply each with a large print, elaborately framed.

In our culture, the sanctity and reality of marriage was declared as much in wedding photographs as it was in written documents. I think the power of such pictures would be even greater in New Guinea.

Since I'm not a missionary, not dedicated to promoting alien values at the expense of indigenous ones, I offer this as an illustration and speculation, not as a recommendation.

REEL VS. REAL

In the Middle Sepik, radios are common, tape-recorders exist, and, though I saw no cameras, I met would-be camera owners (Plate 10).

Movies are occasionally shown by the government in certain villages. Without exception, the most popular films are those on New Guinea life. Villagers are aware that cameras can record their daily activities.

In Kandangan village the people became co-producers with us in making a film. The initial proposal came from us, but the actual filming of an initiation ceremony became largely their production.

In this area of the Sepik, the male initiation rite is absolutely forbidden to women, in the past on penalty of death. Our chief cameraman was a woman. It never occurred to us to ask if she might film: we assumed such a request would not only be denied, it would offend. But the Kandangan elders asked if she was good, and when told, "Yes, better than any of us," they requested that she operate one camera. Not only did they permit her inside the sacred enclosure, but they showed her where to position her equipment, helped her move it, and delayed the ceremony while she reloaded. I'm convinced she was allowed to witness this rite, not because she was an outsider, but solely because her presence was necessary for the production of the best possible film.

The initiates were barely conscious at the end of their ordeal, but they grinned happily when shown Polaroid shots of their scarified backs. The elders asked to have the sound track played back to them. They then asked that the film be brought back and projected, promising to erect another sacred enclosure for the screening.

Finally they announced that this was the last involuntary initiation and they offered for sale their ancient water drums, the most sacred objects of this ceremony. Film threatened to replace a ceremony hundreds, perhaps thousands of years old.

Yet film could never fulfill the ceremony's original function. That function was to test young men for manhood and weld them forever into a closed, sacred society. Now the ceremony, and by an extension the entire society, could be put on a screen before them, detached from them. They could watch themselves. No one who ever comes to know himself with the detachment of an observer is ever the same again.

MOMENTS PRESERVED

A still photograph moves us toward the isolated moment. It arrests time.

It exists in pure space. It emphasizes individualism, private identity, and confers an element of permanence on that image.

We used up a great deal of film during a six week stay in Mintima, a Chimbu village in the Central Highlands. It became widely known we would take anyone's photograph, free, and there was always a crowd waiting. Many walked considerable distances. I recall a policeman who walked fifteen miles, only to encounter rain, so he returned the next day, walking a total of sixty miles for one picture.

A photographic portrait, when new and privately possessed, promotes identity, individualism: it offers opportunities for self-recognition, self-study. It provides the extra sensation of objectivizing the self. It makes the self more real, more dramatic. For the subject, it's no longer enough to be: now HE KNOWS HE IS. He is conscious of himself.

Until man is conscious of his personal appearance, his private identity, there is little self-expression.

THE SEAMLESS WEB OF TRIBAL LIFE

Traditionally, New Guinea tribesmen lived within the strict confines of convention and community. They regarded themselves as integral parts of nature. They belonged to a seamless web of kinship and responsibility. They merged the individual with the whole society. They were involved with life; they experienced a PARTICIPATION MYSTIQUE. This experience is one in which they were eager to merge with cosmic powers.

Western man, by contrast, is characterized by a habit of detachment and non-involvement, a kind of uncooperative gesture toward the universe. From this refusal to be involved in the world he lives in, he derives detachment and objectivity. He becomes alienated from his environment, even from his body. He believes there is an elegance in detachment, and he values, above all else, the isolated, delimited, aware self.

All this was traditionally alien to New Guinea tribes. Such tribes were implosive. Everyone was involved with everybody, simultaneously. There was no isolating individualism, no private consciousness, no private point of view. These are everywhere alien to tribalism, and the varied tribes of New Guinea offer no exceptions.

Individualism means self-expression, private view. People who fill tribal roles have no private point of view: they share group awareness and wear corporate masks.

Traditionally the New Guinea tribesman was a conventional role player, a faithful mask wearer: wearing a mask, in this context, meant to divest, not to express oneself. Such a mask or role wasn't an extension of its wearer so much as a putting on of the collective powers of the community and environment. When the New Guinea dancer put on the feathers and flora of the jungle, he assumed the collective powers of that jungle. He manifested a corporate, not a private, point of view.

No event better illustrated the collective nature of traditional New Guinea tribal life than the sing-sing, a combination dance-song-feast usually involving more than one village.

The celebrant mixed all his senses in harmonic orchestration, opening his body and heart to everything around him. He moved with the rhythms of the group, striving to merge with social forces. But simultaneously he enjoyed a lively inner sensibility, and his attention was constantly claimed by these inner sensations. His whole psychic life was physically involved. He was always aware of his body as interposed between his inner self and the outer world, and he devoted constant attention to it.

Hence all members of a tribe adorned and ornamented their bodies. Nothing could have been more natural. The inner life imposed on every tribal member the habit of noticing and beautifying the body, which ended by being the closest object in the perspective of that person's world. And so New Guinea tribesmen created that remarkable culture of the body: adornment, cleanliness, and finally courtesy, that inspired invention which is subtle gesture.

Not only were faces and bodies painted and decorated, but those of the men were scarified. The integrity of the body was respected, design-wise, but significantly dislocated, so that what resulted was not images of deformed people, but images of figures transformed by mystical powers and significance, playing public roles.

Most sing-sings were held by firelight, though firelight wasn't really needed. Moonlight in the Highlands can be marvellously clear. But the firelight created a special effect: it made the dancing place a stage of the first order, collecting all the colors and movements into a unity. It never dispelled darkness: rather, it illuminated things within it. Forms appeared, then disappeared, merging once more with nothingness. Darkness and silence surrounded everyone.

In recent years a new type of sing-sing has come into being, sponsored and controlled by the government. These huge annual events involve great gatherings of tribesmen from throughout the Highlands, all plumed and decorated magnificently. Irving Penn took a series of extraordinary photographs at the great sing-sing held at Goroka in 1970.

As usual, he employed a collapsible-portable studio with one wall open and the camera outside, looking in. The secret of this studio was that it created its own space — a space without background.

The moment subjects stepped across that threshold, they changed, totally. All confusion and excitement ceased. Even those outside became still. A sudden intensity possessed everyone.

The same subjects who, moments before, posed comically for tourists, affecting exaggerated poses, now behaved with intense concentration. Their bodies became rigid, their muscles tense; their fingers tightly gripped whatever they touched. When Penn re-positioned them, he found their bodies stiff, in a way he never found subjects in our society.

The crowd outside, looking in, also became rigid. Chaos ceased and the scene became tableau.

If this were merely my account, it might easily be dismissed as something contrived to fit the thesis of this chapter. But I have tried to record here, as best I can remember them, Penn's own words. And the evidence is also in the photographs.

These photographs aren't anthropological documents in the usual sense. They don't record moments out of daily life. No captions explaining decorations or describing ceremonies would be relevant. Absolutely nothing that can be said about the culture or personality of the subjects is pertinent to their pictures. What holds us, fascinates us, is their stance, above all their eyes.

A camera is the ideal instrument for preserving the momentary art of body decoration and face paint. But ordinary photographs can preserve that art for us. These photographs are not ordinary. Penn has captured something so elusive, so momentary, that, were it not for the fact that the camera created it, it's unlikely the camera could record it.

And even now, with that elusive something captured and spread before us, we scarcely know what to make of it. One thing is certain: on every face, even the faces of children, there is fear. Not fear of camera or cameraman. Not ordinary fear.

If this were ordinary fear, subjects would be glancing for reassurance toward companions outside. Instead, they stare at the lens.

Nor is this the fear of those who, seeing their images for the first time, cover their mouths to preserve their identities. For participants at the Goroka Show, that was past history. Most knew a good deal about cameras. They knew their spirits were so powerful they could do more than just cast a reflection on a mirror; they could leave a permanent imprint on that mirror, an imprint that would preserve forever this moment, this man.

Bedecked in barbaric spendor once designed to strike terror into enemies, and envy into rivals, these ex-warriors asked to be recorded for posterity. Yet what we see is not terrifying expressions, but expressions of terror, combined with an exaltation that confers an awesome dignity on every subject. We see men at the very moment they voluntarily leave everything familiar behind and step forever into limbo, going through that vanishing point alone and going through it wide-awake.

When Alice went through the Looking Glass, Victorians called her a fairytale figure for children, but the coming of new media meant we would all go through that vanishing point from which none return unchanged (cf. Plate 11).

Now it was the New Guineans' turn.

Everyone who watched understood. Those outside kept their eyes on the subjects, while the subjects kept their eyes on the lens. They never looked at Penn, nor to one side, nor at those outside. Their eyes fixed unwaveringly on that single point, no matter how long the session. That point was the point men enter when they leave this world behind and step alone, absolutely alone, into limbo. That was the source of their terror and exaltation.

One sees that same intense concentration in Brady photographs; in portraits of Indians in the Old West; in Renaissance paintings of un-smiling dukes staring down eternity. Our eyebeams lock with those of strangers at some timeless, spaceless point. Those eyes stare back at us with an intensity we seldom encounter today in the portraits of our smiling leaders and graduating seniors.

Rembrandt was said to be the first great master whose sitters sometimes dreaded seeing their portraits. Perhaps one reason we could never produce another Rembrandt is that we no longer produce such sitters. The technology that hoisted man out of both his environment and his body, allowing him to enter and leave limbo at will, has now become so casual, so environmental, we make that trip with the numbness of commuters, our eyes unseeing, the mystery of self-confrontation, self-discovery, gone.

Visual Records, Human Knowledge, and the Future

E. RICHARD SORENSON

It is no secret now that there is an acute international need to document visually the remaining variety of the culturally patterned human behavior in the world which reflects diverse, sometimes unique, expressions of basic human potential. We need to act quickly if we are not to lose for all time information on a broad range of divergent possibilities in human development, particularly on those which played a part in our evolving patterns of human organization in relation to altering ecological and economic settings.

Similarly, there is critical need to document emerging developments in societies that are modernizing. We need better understanding of how man fits into and copes with the world and its transformations, including those he himself generates. These newer technologically based ways of life change perhaps even more rapidly than do isolated cultures. Our incomplete understanding of the dynamics of such change, or its sociobiological significance, frequently forces us to make uninformed and arbitrary decisions about its direction. Movement into the future would be less traumatic and more adaptive if we had greater understanding.

Annotated film records revealing the range of human behavior in its cultural and environmental settings allow a variety of studies of man's behavior, potential, and organization that otherwise would be impossible to make. Not only do such phenomenological records capture subtleties and complexities of social interaction and neuro-muscular movement unobtainable in any other way, but they also record unappreciated and unanticipated data, thus providing the possibility of sustained reevaluation of earlier deductions. The insights such records can provide into our own species and its varieties of patterned behavior could be crucial as we continue to need to make decisions about the various options life presents. We need only to look at John Marshall's law enforcement films to see the value of this kind of documentation — and this is only a bare beginning.

Here I shall suggest a rationale and movement toward realizing the scientific and humanistic potential of visual records of passing forms of human behavior and organization so that they may serve as a source of data and decision. Attention will be focused on:

1.   Developing an urgent world sampling strategy to document visually the passing forms of human behavior and organization so as to provide the fullest possible visual record of the existing range of human cultural and behavioral adaptation;

2.   Developing basic organization for the necessary national or regional ethnographic visual data centers;

3.   Establishing guidelines to govern access to and use of visual records.

THE PROBLEM

Because of the dramatic developments in communication and transport, primarily since World War II, change is now occurring throughout the world at an unprecedented and still accelerating rate. The cultural and behavioral divergence which has characterized the dispersal of man across the world from the earliest times has been reversed. We have entered a new period — one of cultural convergence in which the wide range of human variation previously developed is now rapidly disappearing under the impact of modern technology. Those few remaining isolated societies that still embody independent and unique natural developments in channeling and utilizing basic human potential are almost gone; other less isolated traditional cultures are fast following. Yet, because some of these vanishing ways of life reflect conditions important in our own behavioral and cultural evolution, and because others reveal special expressions of man's organizational capability, they are of interest. Insofar as we allow the behavioral data to vanish with the cultures embodying them, we will diminish our ability to understand our own species.

In the last decade modern equipment and new theory and methodology have been developed which permit preparation and use of visual records of naturally occurring human activity as a scientific and humanistic resource. There are strategies now which aim at maximizing the scientific potential of such visual records. By taking advantage of these developments, and by focusing effort on preserving data on the vanishing ways of life we may reduce the loss that confronts us.

In this we need not be distracted by the argument sometimes made that visual records of vanishing culture should be made as a means of renewing past practices. This does not aim at what concerns the vast majority of the peoples of the world — an improved life — nor does it take advantage of the more powerful use of such records as a possible means to increase understanding of ourselves, our potential, and our social organization.

Most anthropologists, particularly those who have been lucky enough to have done fieldwork in several parts of the world, do recognize that very few people are interested in staying as they are or going back to the way they were. It is significant that visitors, like these anthropologists, who come from technologically advanced societies usually attract a welcome and interest which is not so readily afforded strangers from less developed places. Sometimes a Western man ego-dreams about this phenomenon; but there is increasing recognition that it is not his special personal prowess or attractive personality that makes him welcome. Rather it is because he is seen as a possible source of new materials, tools, methods, ideas, or power among people who would like to improve their own lot.

Typically the human condition is one of confrontation with the new challenges and opportunities which the world continually provides. Change is inevitable; better conditions are universally desired. In every culture I have been in, throughout Oceania, and in Latin America, Asia, and Africa, I have encountered little interest in strategies to preserve old ways of life, except as a means of commercial advantage as, for example, where Westerners have taken interest in traditional art or ceremony and thereby converted its production into a means by which the local people can get the new things they really want. Virtually everyone is looking to the future. A quick way to unpopularity in New Guinea would be to suggest that these people keep their stone axes or high infant mortality rates and the kinds of cultural organization which go with them. The argument that we should make movies for their cultural renewal would be laughable to them and should be to us, for we are not likely to be receptive to the suggestion that we renew ourselves by going back to the conditions of the early industrial revolution, the sixty-hour work week, or an agrarian horse-and-buggy way of life.

While it is true that records of past events can provide models to mimic in play, song, and dance, and thereby teach us and our children about our heritage, they are not likely to attract much interest as a means of reestablishing this heritage. Such cultural renewal is reminiscent of the cultural zoo philosophy. At its worst it encourages people to remain in the backwash of history; at its best it gives moments of nostalgia to the old folks.

A more potent use of visual records of vanishing ways of life is as a source of information on man and how he has responded and developed over time, in different settings, and under different conditions. Such information, by increasing our understanding of our own species and its possible modes of response and adaptation, can contribute uniquely to an increasing and cumulative self-understanding as we adapt into the unfolding future. It can be a means to expand our developmental awareness and thus our informed power to respond and create. The world, in its dynamic diversity, continually churns out transformations in which there appears to be a sustained bio-socio-ecological evolutionary change. Man's current preeminent position seems to stem from his increasingly more knowledgeable adaptation to changing conditions. Film records which enable us to become better informed about ourselves and our organizational and adaptive possibilities would contribute to further knowledgeable adaptation. The future is where we are going. The clock doesn't run backwards.

THEORETICAL APPROACHES

Visual-records footage meant to serve as a scientific or humanistic resource may be distinguished from other kinds of anthropological film primarily by the methods and objectives which govern its production. Meant to provide a credible source of information for continued analysis and rework, record footage is different in format and use from films constructed to reveal an anthropologists' understanding of a culture or from films in which a language of visual flow is developed to communicate anthropological insight in new and more powerful ways.

A peculiar myth that has developed in recent years is that anthropological films cannot be scientific because their content is always governed by selective interests. This absurd notion ignores the degree to which selectivity and special interest underly ALL scientific inquiry. In scientific filming, as in science generally, avoidance of selectivity is not necessarily relevant. But method is crucial. In order for visual records of changing man to be a valid scientific resource, they need to be shaped by the scientific methodological considerations that govern the investigation of nonrecurring phenomena. Interpretability and verifiability must be stressed. Credibility is a key factor.

We may think of four distinct kinds of information which play a role in increasing the scientific usefulness of visual records of passing phenomena: (1) undifferentiated information, (2) structured information, (3) personal insights, and (4) time and space constants.

Undifferentiated Information

Undifferentiated information is that which has not yet been consciously perceived, structured, or organized by the human mind. Such information exists everywhere, but for cultural, technical, or biological reasons we are not tuned into all of it. At times in the course of history, as well as during crucial stages in our individual lives, becoming aware of such information allows changes in understanding and capability, sometimes leading to new schools of thought, technological breakthrough, and broadened possibilities for man's expression of himself. When such information is contained in research records, it becomes a richer source for later discoveries. Because film records a facsimile of visual phenomena by means of objective changes in light sensitive chemicals, it records considerable unseen and undifferentiated data simultaneously with collection of selected data. Strategies may be devised to increase the content of this kind of information in visual records.

Structured Information

Structured information is that mediated by the human mind. It takes its form from our habitual way of looking at the things around us according to the concepts, ideas, and values bestowed upon us by our training, as limited by the forms of mind and capabilities provided by our evolutionary background. It permits us to handle the continuous phenomena about us symbolically by organizing them into discrete categories and patterns manipulable by rules of language and logic. Such structured information permits us an intellectual grip on experience and gives us the ability to plan our own movements relative to it. It provides the basis for our discussions, conjectures, and studies, and is the "known" to which we relate discovery to learn its significance. A research record must be oriented around structured knowledge in order to be grasped intellectually.

The publicly accessible, organized knowledge of a scientific discipline is such a structure. Because they come from an extensive, interlocked body of validated data, scientifically established facts and their measured relationships furnish a basis to which other phenomena can be related and so take on meaning. However, we cannot be sure that the scientific insights we have today will be totally adequate for the research objectives of tomorrow. Thus editing or polishing visual records meant for research (as opposed to reports of research results) is to be avoided. Such structuring sacrifices much of the important undifferentiated information and thus that which we will want to discover and understand.

Personal Insights

Personal insights and predilections fall somewhere between undifferentiated and structured information and contain elements of both. The selective interests and perceptive eye of individual workers impelled by inclinations, impressions, and partially formulated ideas are a powerful force in the discovery of data and the interpretation of it. Research records influenced by such forces reflect the early stages in the formulation of ideas and data from sense impression, and make possible analysis of it as no other medium yet has. With such records, an approach to the problem of verifiability and substantiation of data coming from unrepeatable field studies becomes possible. Therefore, one must shun attempts to rework, restructure, or polish research records to fit subsequently derived ideas or generally accepted aesthetic forms. Such creative manipulation is important for many purposes, but visual records are better without it.

Time and Space Constants

Very fundamental among those structural tools that permit us to analyze and organize phenomena for their precise communication and use are our assumptions of time and spatial order. From the discovery of consistent ways to measure observed phenomena in relation to a postulated uniform flow of time and a defined geometry of space, much of our contemporary science has been built. And it is primarily on these constants that the precise communication of a scientific construct depends and upon which its validation rests. In many kinds of studies, physical and temporal separation are the critical functions, as when concepts of development, differentiation, diffusion, and communication are involved. Because of this, extensive and accurate documentation of time and place is needed in research documents. Records in which the true time sequence of the original phenomena has been disrupted, or in which the places shown are not geographically identifiable, are poorer in their research potential than those that scrupulously preserve such information.

TOWARD A WORLD SAMPLING STRATEGY

Any workable and productive world sampling strategy must be shaped by (1) the actual state of known cultural variation existing at the time of the sampling, (2) the special problems presented by different kinds of cultural situations, and (3) the availability of suitably skilled workers.

For accurate, up-to-date information on the variety, distribution, and conditions of the ways of life currently extant in the world, we have to rely on anthropologists who are personally knowledgeable about its particular regions. Checklists, schemata, and taxonomies are not sufficient. Such overviews and compendia can only develop after reflection on numerous published accounts of fieldwork. By the time these syntheses too are published, they no longer reflect either the existing state of the world or the new knowledge that has developed from its further examination and study. More reliable and useful is the more recent and sophisticated understanding possessed by specialists affiliated with various universities and research institutes who are actively investigating and learning more more about the state of human organization across the world.

A glance at G. P. Murdock's comprehensive outline and classification of world culture reveals the inappropriateness of relying on such systems as guides to a world ethnographic film sample meant to be a resource that will facilitate discovery of new knowledge and reexamination of old knowledge. This outline, although an invaluable educational tool and uniquely useful as a means of organizing cultural information for retrieval and use, does not list many groups most in need of documentation, deals poorly with marginal groups, and does not reflect newer areas of interest or inquiry. Nor does it touch on the dynamics of changing culture, an important aspect of culture which is particularly amenable to study through film records (Murdock et al. 1962–1965).

We may expect similar problems with any cultural taxonomy, simply because concepts of what exists and what is important are prerequisites to any classification system. In the study of human behavior and organization these are not yet well worked out. Thus we may classify according to various aspects of economic structure, political system, kinship organization, language, residential pattern, material accoutrement, ecological setting, song and dance style, dietary practice, patterns of aggressiveness, etc. Any qualitative or quantitative attribute which can be laid to organized human behavior may serve as a basis for classification. New knowledge, new interests, and new orientations may give rise to new taxonomic schemes.

In obtaining a world ethnographic film sample meant to be a resource for discovery, it is important to include information interstitial to and extending beyond that reflected by a schema. Simply to fill the slots of a classification system with visual samples would miss much of this and thus many things we might later find important to examine. It would tend to produce a sample reaffirming past knowledge rather than generating new knowledge.

Filming Strategies

Unlike film productions designed to communicate new knowledge to the public, visual records may not be well served by any contemporary ideas of how films are best constructed for public presentation. The ever new strategies to "turn on" audiences tend to have only a transitory appeal which may vary from audience to audience. To govern record filming by such contemporary standards of film structure would be to place too much faith in what is exciting at a given time or place.

The gathering of visual data to serve as a permanent scientific and humanistic resource must follow a different orientation. The overriding consideration here is to sample naturally occurring events as accurately and comprehensively as possible. The concern must be with data rather than with an idea of public presentation. Interestingly, such an approach is not inconsistent with later public use; for film shot so as to maximize richness of information would have to include a wide variety of angles, framing, and content. From such material an editor could construct a variety of different kinds of films for public presentation.

Because visual record filming is different from production filming, photographers or teams trained to feed the needs of the motion picture or television industry should be employed with care. Their filming techniques are most likely to be governed by the presentation requirements of those media. Furthermore, few of them would be able to stay for long periods in a particular field location; and, because they are less likely to be trained in adapting to other cultures, they are more likely to be disruptive of the natural situation. Yet collaboration with the media could be a means to support and augment otherwise more modest long-term sampling efforts.

Anthropologists trained in the use of modern equipment would be better qualified to approach the field situation effectively. Because of their training they are familiar with the problems governing scholarly study of different ways of life, and they also know something about scientific method. In addition they are likely to be in the field for the extended periods required to develop a sample reflecting seasonal or annual variations in activity.

Visual documentation is quite different from producing motion pictures or from exploiting the communicational potential of visual images. It requires its own methods. Training programs geared to this specialized need would increase the usefulness of visual records made by anthropological field workers, filmmakers, and others. Initial efforts, like those of the Anthropology Film Center in New Mexico, could provide a welcome beginning — one which could be developed in association with the programs of visual data centers.

A visual data sample of a culture could be enriched by further contributions from individuals with different interests and approaches. Just as systematically organized reporting procedures make the observations of birdwatchers of value to ornithology, amateur ethnographers, guided by principles of visual sampling, could be of value in studies of man. Particularly valuable might be the contributions made by local people trained in using the camera as a documentary tool. They would be able to provide emphases and information reflecting their own nonacademic views of themselves and their milieux. The model established by Adair and Worth, in which Navaho Indians film themselves, is a start. Even modest contributions made by such local people would measurably enhance the comprehensiveness of any visual record preserving behavioral and cultural information of a people (cf. Ushiyama's paper, *supra*).

An Approach

When considering strategies of documentation, it is useful to divide the total task into three distinguishable general cultural situations, each of which is best approached somewhat differently:

SMALL CULTURAL ISOLATES The few remaining isolated peoples of the world, who have evolved independently over thousands of years, and those small groups who represent vanishing unique expressions of human behavior and social organization, require special attention. These may change quickly, particularly after contact; frequently they are poorly understood. Anthropological field workers and concerned regional experts, trained in the use of modern film recording techniques, are better able to approach such cultures profitably. They would have the most intimate understanding of the local situation and tend to be less disruptive of it; they are likely to be familiar with the issues and stakes involved; and they would tend to remain in contact for the longer periods required for a representative sample.

PERSISTING CULTURAL VARIATION   The wider range of known, more stable cultural variation still existing in the world, including traditional folk culture, may be approached more systematically through an international concerted effort involving new kinds of anthropological documentary filmmakers, regional experts, and participating members of the cultures to be documented.

MODERN SOCIETIES   Social change in modern societies which needs to be documented in order to understand better how man fits into and copes with the changing world, can be examined profitably by a variety of concerned observers having a mastery of the modern techniques of visual documentation. Such people can enrich our understanding of emerging social conditions through special insights and expertise of many kinds while, at the same time, contributing to a visual record for re-examination by others.

THE VISUAL DATA CENTER — AN ESSENTIAL FIRST STEP

Before visual records can be assembled and made accessible for study and use, there has to be a place to put them. Centralized accumulation and annotation of visual records according to systematized indexing and retrieval methods provides the essential quantum leap from fragmentary hard-to-interpret, hard-to-locate films to a genuine scientific and humanistic resource. Without such facilities, individual anthropologists and filmmakers have no way of making their films accessible as a source of visual data to others. Very few have a way to store their unedited original films even temporarily where they will not get lost, disorganized, and deteriorate. Usually all that remains to mark the earlier existence of a much richer and more extensive body of potential visual information is one or two short films edited for public presentation, and even these may disappear over time.

Large centers are important because of the increased value a collection takes on as it becomes more extensive and because they are better able to support training, research, and collection programs. Small centers are also needed, to allow development of independent ideas and novel methods unencumbered by a single policy and established organization.

The collection, preservation, analysis, and reporting of visual information on naturally occurring human activity is the major role to which a visual data center could profitably address itself in a society interested in the further understanding of man by man. This would entail on-going investigation of technique, method, and equipment. Retrieval systems would be updated in order to keep abreast of the changing requirements of the social sciences and education. Anthropology graduate students should be encouraged and supported in efforts to make visual records during field work and to draw comparative material from the archive.

Films must be archived under optimal conditions of temperature and humidity. Original or master film documents can be protected from the cumulative damage that comes from handling and use. Prints or video-tape copies will serve the purposes of review, research, and production. Computer linked videotape equipment will eventually permit automatic retrieval and scanning of pre-selected categories of filmed data at a variety of desired speeds with Xerox-like copying of the sequences needed for research or special film productions.

An advisory body made up of professional anthropologists familiar with visual analysis could supply useful guidance on problems of access and use as well as on innovative programs and procedural modifications. Membership in an international association of visual data centers would facilitate the standardization of archiving and access procedures and the exchange and sharing of visual records.

Ideally the basic functions of an ethnographic visual data center would be:

1. *Repository and archive:*
a.   to store and preserve film records of man's varied ways of life;
b.   to maintain facilities and equipment to locate, view, and abstract specific kinds of visual data from the collection; and
c.   to provide a means to duplicate sequences required for research and education projects.
2. *Acquisition:*
a.   to undertake and support programs to document vanishing cultures

and changing patterns of human behavior; to encourage local production
of visual documents as well as those by professional groups;

b.   to accepts gifts of film for deposit;

c.   to copy undeposited orginal films before they are edited; and

d.   to purchase endangered bodies of early film.

3.   *Research:*

a.   to support the scientific study of holdings;

b.   to promote studies of the variety of filming approaches which may
be used in documentation programs; and

c.   to support studies to increase the potential of film as a scientific
and humanistic resource.

4.   *Education:*

a.   to support and conduct seminars, training fellowships, workshops,
etc. in the visual documentation of changing culture and human behavior;

b.   to support the production of educational materials from holdings;
and

c.   to support studies of new ways to use visual materials in education.

ACCESS TO AND USE OF VISUAL RECORDS

Many of those who contribute film to a visual data center will want it
to be generally available to scholars and filmmakers. Others will need
limited periods of restricted access to allow completion of their own
studies or of edited films for commercial distribution. It will also be
necessary to protect the privacy of some subjects: in particular, people who
have permitted cameras to record aspects of their lives which might em-
barrass or harm them if revealed or published must have their needs for
confidentiality protected. Similarly they should be protected from misuse
of the film records that might mispresent or abuse them.

Crediting sources is important in order to encourage documentary
effort and deposits of films. For research it goes without saying that
responsible investigators cite their sources. However, in cases of educational or public use, a formula needs to be worked out to credit depositors
in the derivative productions making use of their material.

We may consider different types of protective policy for the four major
types of possible use:

1.   *Research*: Availability for scholarly research is a primary consideration. If independent scholars from any discipline do not have
access for scientific and humanistic studies, there is little point in having

visual records. For such research use we may follow the model established by the medical profession governing a patient's privacy and the need to report new medical information: research and publication of findings are not obstructed, and identities are concealed as necessary.

2. *Professional education*: New findings, new techniques, and professional education develop hand in hand. Where material is desired for use in professional seminars associated with established institutions of higher learning, it needs to be as freely available as it is for research. Just as medical students need to see patients, or the records of patients, students in the social sciences need to see visual records of human behavior to the full degree that they are available. It is only necessary, in the case of film records, to guard against leakage into channels of more general distribution.

3. *Public information*: When the filmed material is to receive widespread distribution in schools or to the public, safeguards against misrepresentation or abuse of its subjects are particularly important. Feedback from both the social science profession and the people to be seen in the film is essential and should be solicited and heeded in this regard.

4. *Commercial use*: When it becomes desirable to make use of the filmed material in profit-making ventures, there must be prior agreement among the subjects of the films, the filmer, the commercial producer, and the center, as there would be if original footage were to be shot for the production.

SUMMARY

In the last few years, there has been increasing interest in preserving information on diverse aspects of human potential revealed by man's responses, capabilities, and organization in divergent cultural settings. This has added further impetus to a recognized need to document human culture and its transformations, simply because of the greater understanding it allows of our own species. However, the increasing rapidity with which those cultures most divergent and most in need of study have been disappearing in recent years has caught many off balance.

It is now generally recognized that systematically prepared visual records provide an unusually potent means to preserve information on naturally occurring human behavior and organization. Both the American Anthropological Association (at its 1971 annual meeting) and now the Ninth International Congress of Anthropological and Ethnological Sciences have called for urgent programs of visual documentation (cf.

Appendix to this volume). A decade of experimental efforts, particularly at the National Institutes of Health near Washington, has yielded a methodological model. The Center for the Study of Man of the Smithsonian Institution, in cooperation with the National Science Foundation, has sponsored and supported planning and organization for a broader program, and in 1974 the National Anthropological Film Center was started at the Smithsonian.

Presented here are the basic issues, theoretical considerations, and approaches which have emerged over the past decade in connection with the preservation of visual data on changing man as a permanent scientific and humanistic resource.

REFERENCES

MURDOCK, GEORGE P., *et al.*
  1962–1965   Ethnographic atlas. *Ethnology* 1–7: *passim.*

Conclusion

PAUL HOCKINGS

Of the various English handbooks now available on research methodology, only one devotes as much space as two pages (out of a thousand) to some applications of cinematography in anthropology. The others do not suggest that videotape and the movie camera have anything to offer our discipline, a view that is seemingly confirmed in the half-dozen histories of anthropology I have read, which make no mention of film. The fallacy of that position is, I trust, exposed by the present volume.

Margaret Mead has asked the question of why anthropology has been so non-visual in the past, and has answered with the perception that the scholars of this discipline have always been craftsmen with words and ideas, never with pictures and electronic technology. While that position is somewhat on the wane, there has been some justification for dissatisfaction with the work of ethnographic filmmakers, in that films have mostly been made on an *ad hoc* basis, with little cumulative impact and no theoretical contribution to the science of anthropology. In many cases, art clearly came ahead of veracity.

Of the hundred people who now work in anthropological film, a few have decried and many more have perceived the lack of direction that the subdiscipline has shown. By way of remedy committees have even been proposed to set standards by which these films should be shot and edited! Furthermore, anthropologists have reportedly been dismayed at films that touch on subjects dear to their own hearts, but which fail to use the "correct" approach and thus lay before their audiences an "uninformed" or "unscientific" view of the subject. At the same time a degree of envy is felt, I fear, at the remarkable success of a few anthropological films made by such non-scholarly organizations as Granada television or Metro-Goldwyn-Mayer.

Anthropologists nurturing these twin dissatisfactions in their breasts have for over a decade been suggesting that the ideal solution to problems, as they see them, is a fusion of the professional film company's expertise and finances with one man's favored theoretical approach to some fairly narrow anthropological topic. Such an idea is most commonly expressed as a wish that the television networks would spend their vast wealth on authenticated ethnographic documentaries instead of on the travelogues and tropical adventure films that their evening audiences enjoy so much.

Pipe-dreams such as this one, however, ignore the economic realities of film; and indeed — as Jay Hoffman implies — this ignorance of film economics has been a consistent strand in the expressed plans and wishes of those interesting themselves in anthropological film for at least the past decade. To ensure their financing, documentary filmmakers have to prepare for audiences in the tens of thousands, and television networks seek them by the millions. A specialized film that would appeal mainly to a few hundred of one's professional colleagues can never be a viable proposition unless it happens to be backed by an indulgent well-wisher; and such people are rare.

Financial and legal naiveté has also been the pitfall of certain proposals to establish national and even international archives of ethnographic film. Doubtless many of the contributors to this book have received requests from time to time to donate prints of their films or unedited footage to well-meaning institutions apparently unaware that one print can easily cost its maker several hundreds of dollars. Aside from this financial problem there is also a legal difficulty with placing films in archives. It arises from the fact that most films are copyrighted, and some are also made for "restricted" screening to audiences. The maker may well nourish doubts about how his film may be used, and whether it might be pirated once out of his hands. If it is available to viewers at the archive, what might this do to his distributor's income? But if it is not made available to viewers, what good will it do in an archive anyway? Sorenson, in the preceding chapter, offers some solutions to such problems. Yet if a well-used archive lends prints of its films to those educational institutions which cannot visit the archive; and if, further, that archive pays film-makers a royalty on rentals, how does it differ from any of the regular academic film distributors? My answer would be: not at all. In other words, a good system of distribution within a country should almost obviate the need for an archive in one of its cities. In this context it is worth mentioning technical developments in Germany which promise to provide prints of a film that look like a gramophone record, are cheap, unbreakable, and of course quite easy to mail. When played on the necessary video equipment, such a record would produce a visual image on a television viewer, along with the synchronous sound. If this system were widely adopted, it could not only make the idea of national archives somewhat redundant, but would allow any college or school to build up its own library of "pressings" at a reasonable cost (cf. Asch's paper, *supra*).

An archive that is more than a repository is nonetheless called for in Europe and North America, where usage of anthropological films is rising yearly and vast amounts of old film material remain uncared for, un-catalogued, and unknown. But the crux of the problem of non-availa-bility of certain important films on these continents is less the lack of a national or international archive than it is the poor performance of individual distributors. There are very few distributors of anthropological films who do a good job of advertising and a speedy job of shipping their wares. Some have relevant films in their collections, while potential users are not aware of the fact. The publication of Karl Heider's *Films for anthropological teaching* (now in its fifth edition) has done much to rescue teaching films from obscure shelves, but does nothing for the films that are available only in Europe, Asia, Australia, or South America. Finally, let us admit that if distribution seems poor, the films themselves are too often worthy of nothing better.

Given the expansiveness of government in almost all countries today, it is not surprising that anthropologists have suggested that national and even international governmental offices should come to the rescue of ethnographic film. I made direct approaches to UNESCO along these lines in 1969, but learned that a proposal such as that UNESCO should develop an international film archive — if indeed that were desirable — would have to come through one or more of the National Commissions to UNESCO. In many countries this channel is not an easy one to activate, at least for anthropologists. At the same time, I enquired about UNESCO's sponsorship of ethnographic films. But the policy at present in Paris is that if documentaries are to be made for UNESCO, then contracts are farmed out to the companies (mainly European) which can offer the most attractive budgets.

Discussion during the Ninth International Congress of Anthropological and Ethnological Sciences, in Chicago, made it quite clear that while a number of documentary filmmakers are devoted to recording rapidly disappearing cultures in their FILMS, an equal number of ethnologists are interested only in acquiring FOOTAGE for their own narrowly defined re-search purposes. There must of course be scope for both the archiving of uncut footage and for the production of sophisticated educational documentaries if ethnographic film is to have a meaningful future. And its future does seem assured, both by the increasing number of people who are coming into this activity and by the large numbers of new films. For example, with the initiation in 1972 of an annual Venezia Genti as part of the Venice festival, over forty new films were presented in that first year, and over a hundred recent ethnographic films were also screened at the Chicago Congress in 1973.

Away from Europe and North America the development of filmmaking and archiving facilities has not kept pace with the rapid development of national economies. The proposal made in the Appendix that regional centers for these activities be set up around the world is therefore a particularly apposite one: centers that would provide otherwise unavailable facilities to the local researcher and documentary filmmaker as well as to the visiting scholar should have very high priority in our plans to improve our documentation of the many cultures of the world.

It is several centuries since astronomers gathered their data mainly with the naked eye. Ever since the great invention of Lippershey and others around 1608, they have tended to work from observations conveniently modified by the telescope. And for over a century, they have also worked successfully with photographic plates that conveniently freeze the data of a moment. Anthropologists, by contrast, have been wary of uncritical reliance on other people's ethnographies, and have sought reassurance from cross-cultural sampling methods or even repeated visits to the field. The visible aspects and effects of behavior, recorded photographically, now hold out to us an exciting and sophisticated *modus operandi* for the future exploration and understanding of the human universe. These new methods must be applied to recording, classifying and analyzing the data, so that we may test the generalizations of behavioral science that can yet lead us to the laws of mankind.

At the same time we need to look at the broader dissemination of the knowledge our discipline has acquired. It is not sufficient to give lectures at the universities and use films solely to illustrate those lectures. We have much to teach mankind about itself; let us do so through all the visual media available to us, including television and satellite transmission. There is more at stake than the mere development of careers and the recruitment of new students. We have to produce historical documents for the future, and at the same time teach the meaning and value of cultural diversity.

Appendices

Resolution on Visual Anthropology

Passed at the IXth International Congress of Anthropological and Ethnological Sciences, Chicago, September 1973.

Film, sound, and videotape records are today an indispensable scientific resource. They provide reliable data on human behavior which independent investigators may analyze in the light of new theories. They may contain information for which neither theory nor analytical schemes yet exist. They convey information independently of language. And they preserve unique features of our changing ways of life for posterity. Today is a time not merely of change but of spreading uniformity and wholesale cultural loss. To help arrest this process, and to correct the myopic view of human potential to which it leads, it is essential that the heritage of mankind be recorded in all its remaining diversity and richness. Towards this end we propose to:

1. Initiate an immediate world-wide filming program to provide a systematic sample of traditional cultures, both urban and rural, with special attention to those isolated and unique cultures whose ways of life are threatened with extinction;

2. Locate, collect, preserve, and index existing ethnographic film records, with special attention to cultures which have already disappeared;

3. Institute an international distribution network to ensure that the people whose lives are filmed share fully in the results, and that the resulting documentation is freely available;

4. Encourage training in the techniques of modern ethnographic filming, especially for professional fieldworkers and for the peoples who are being filmed;

5. Provide an organization for the above tasks by establishing world-wide regional data centers where archiving, research, production, distribution, and training would be carried out, with special attention to the needs of the developing nations;

6.   Reorganize the present CIFES to include an international commission on urgent filming to coordinate world-wide documentation programs, to standardize indexing and retrieval methods, and to facilitate the international exchange of visual data for scientific study and education. Under this reorganization, world-wide participation would be actively encouraged and invited.

JEAN ROUCH
PAUL HOCKINGS
(Co-Chairmen)

Filmography

PAUL HOCKINGS, JUDY HOFFMAN, PAMELA JENSEN

This is not intended to be an exhaustive listing, but merely a guide as to where in North America one can obtain films discussed in this book. Distributors are identified by initials in each entry, and their addresses given at the end. All prices refer to 16-millimeter versions and are subject to increase. For a more complete filmography readers are referred to Karl G. Heider's *Films for anthropological teaching* (fifth edition, 1972), published by the American Anthropological Association, in Washington, D.C. Most of the distributors listed can supply catalogs.

ABORIGINES OF CENTRAL AND NORTHERN AUSTRALIA
1901, 1912 W. Baldwin Spencer. B & W, 34 minutes, silent. Not available.

ADVENTURES ON THE NEW FRONTIER
n.d. The Living Camera Series. B & W, 54 minutes. Distributor TLF, rental $50, sale $400.

ARAUCANIANS OF RUCA CHOROY : SUMMER
1971 Jorge Preloran. Color, 50 minutes. Distributor PF, rental $45, sale $500.

AN ARGUMENT ABOUT A MARRIAGE
1969 John Marshall. Color, 18 minutes. Distributor DER, rental $20, sale $250; PSU, rental $11.

ARROWS
1971 Timothy Asch and Napoleon A. Chagnon. Color, 9 minutes. Distributor DER.

AT THE WINTER SEA ICE CAMP
(see WINTER SEA ICE CAMP).

AU PAYS DES MAGES NOIRS

1947 Jean Rouch. B & W, 12 minutes.

AUTUMN RIVER CAMP

1964 Doug Wilkinson, Michel Chalufour, Quentin Brown, Asen Balikci and Guy Mary-Rousselière. Color, 60 minutes. Distributor UEVA, rental $18, sale $540; PSU, rental $22.20.

THE AXE FIGHT

1971 Napoleon A. Chagnon and Timothy Asch. Color, 10 minutes. Distributor DER.

BASIC TRAINING

1971 Frederick Wiseman. B & W, 50 minutes. Distributor ZF.

BATAILLE SUR LE GRAND FLEUVE

1951 (Included in *Les Fils de l'Eau*.) Jean Rouch. Color, 35 minutes.

THE BATTLE OF CULLODEN

1967 Peter Watkins. B & W, 72 minutes. Distributor TLF, rental $50, sale $400.

BEHAVIOURAL EVOLUTION

1971 Jamshed Mavalwala. Videotape, 28 minutes. Distributor SP; write for details of tape gauge and prices.

BEING BLACK IN CANADA

1971 Jamshed Mavalwala. Videotape, 35 minutes. Distributor SP; write for details of tape gauge and prices.

LA BELLE ET LA BÊTE (*Beauty and the Beast*)

1946 Jean Cocteau. B & W, 90 minutes, subtitled. Distributor JF, rental $125.

THE BILO

1936 Paul Fejos. B & W, 10 minutes, 35-millimeter. Not available.

BITTER MELONS

1971 John Marshall. Color, 30 minutes. Distributor DER, rental $25, sale $360; PSU, rental $13.

BRIDE SERVICE

1971 Timothy Asch and Napoleon A. Chagnon. Color, 6 minutes. Distributor DER.

CARIBOU HUNTING AT THE CROSSING PLACE

1970 Doug Wilkinson, Michel Chalufour, Quentin Brown, Asen Balikci, and Guy Mary-Rousselière. Color, 60 minutes. Distributor UEVA, rental $18, sale $540.

CÉSAR

1936 Marcel Pagnol. B & W, 170 minutes. Distributor CMH, rental $50.

THE CHAIR

1962 The Living Camera Series. Richard Leacock and D. A. Pennebaker. B & W, 54 minutes. Distributor TLF, rental $50, sale $400.

LA CHASSE AU LION À L'ARC (*The Lion Hunters*)

1965 Jean Rouch. Color, 68 minutes. Distributor CMH, rental $60, sale $650; UCEMC, rental $37.

THE CHILDHOOD OF MAXIM GORKY

1938 Mark Donskoi. B & W, 100 minutes. Distributor MAB, rental $35.

CHILDHOOD RIVALRY IN BALI AND NEW GUINEA

1951 Character Formation in Different Cultures Series. Gregory Bateson and Margaret Mead. B & W, 17 minutes. Distributor NYU, rental $17, sale $135; UCEMC, rental $10; in Canada, NSFL, rental $15.75.

CHILDREN AT REAHUMOU PLAY

1971 Timothy Asch and Napoleon A. Chagnon. Color, 6 minutes. Distributor DER.

CHILDREN IN THE RAIN

1971 Timothy Asch and Napoleon A. Chagnon. Color, 10 minutes. Distributor DER.

CHILDREN MAKING A HAMMOCK

1972 Timothy Asch and Napoleon A. Chagnon. Color, 10 minutes. Distributor DER.

CHILDREN OF THE TOAPURI

1971 J. Lilly and E. Richard Sorenson. Color. Archived at The Study of Child Behavior and Development in Primitive Cultures, National Institutes of Health, Bethesda, Maryland.

CHILDREN'S EVENING PLAY

1971 Timothy Asch and Napoleon A. Chagnon. Color, 9 minutes. Distributor DER.

CHILDREN'S MAGICAL DEATH

1971 Timothy Asch and Napoleon A. Chagnon. Color, 7 minutes. Distributor DER.

THE CHILDREN WERE WATCHING

n.d. The Living Camera Series. B & W, 30 minutes. Distributor TLF, rental $30, sale $200.

THE CHIMPANZEES ARE HERE!

1971 Jamshed Mavalwala. Videotape, 27 minutes. Distributor SP; write for details of tape gauge and prices.

CHLOE IN THE AFTERNOON

1972 Eric Rohmer. Color, 97 minutes. Distributor CC, rental $200.

CHOPPING WOOD

1971 Timothy Asch and Napoleon A. Chagnon. Color, 10 minutes. Distributor DER.

CHRONIQUE D'UN ÉTÉ *(Chronicle of a Summer)*
1960 Jean Rouch and Edgar Morin. B & W, 90 minutes. Distributor CMH, rental $50.

THE CITY
1939 Willard Van Dyke and Ralph Steiner. B & W, 43 minutes. Distributor NYU, rental $11; MOMA, rental $30, lease $250; UCEMC, rental $30.

COLLECTING RASHA FRUIT
1971 Timothy Asch and Napoleon A. Chagnon. Color, 9 minutes. Distributor DER.

CORRAL
1954 Colin Low and Walter Koenig. B & W, 12 minutes. Distributor CMH, rental $10; UCEMC, rental $8.

CUBA SÍ! YANKI NO!
1961 Richard Leacock and Chris Marker. B & W. Not available.

A CURING CEREMONY
1969 John Marshall. B & W, 8 minutes. Distributor DER, rental $10, sale $75.

DANCE CONTEST IN ESIRA
1936 Paul Fejos. B & W, 11 minutes. Distributor MOMA, rental $15.

DAVID
1961 The Living Camera Series. D. A. Pennebaker. B. & W, 54 minutes. Distributor TLF, rental $50, sale $400; UCEMC, rental $28.

DAVID AND BATHSHEBA
1948 Henry King. Color, 116 minutes. Distributor FI, rental $30.

DEAD BIRDS
1963 Robert Gardner, Karl G. Heider, and Jan Broekhuyse. Color, 83 minutes. Distributor CMH, rental $60, sale $650; PSU, rental $40.50; UCEMC, rental $37; in Canada, NSFL, rental $12.

DEATH OF A PROMINENT MAN
1971 Napoleon A. Chagnon and Timothy Asch. Color, 15 minutes. Distributor DER.

DEBE'S TANTRUM
1972 John Marshall. Color, 9 minutes. Distributor DER, rental $12, sale $100; PSU, rental $6.

DEDEHEIWÄ RESTS IN HIS GARDEN
1971 Timothy Asch and Napoleon A. Chagnon. Color, 9 minutes. Distributor DER.

DEDEHEIWÄ'S SONS GARDENING
1971 Timothy Asch and Napoleon A. Chagnon. Color, 20 minutes. Distributor DER.

DEDEHEIWÄ WASHES HIS CHILDREN
1971 Timothy Asch and Napoleon A. Chagnon. Color, 15 minutes. Distributor DER.

DEDEHEIWÄ WEEDS HIS GARDEN
1971 Timothy Asch and Napoleon A. Chagnon. Color, 15 minutes. Distributor DER.

LE DÉJEUNER DE BÉBÉ (*Feeding the Baby*)
1895 Louis Lumière. B &W, 20 minutes, silent. Distributor MOMA, rental $15, piano score available.

DESERT PEOPLE
1969 Ian Dunlop and Robert Tonkinson. B & W, 51 minutes. Distributor CMH, rental $22, sale $365; in Canada, NSFL, rental $8.50.

DOING ANTHROPOLOGICAL FIELDWORK IN MISHIMISHIMABÖWEI-TERI
1971 Napoleon A. Chagnon and Timothy Asch. Color, 44 minutes. Distributor DER.

EDDIE *(Indianapolis 500)*
1961 Richard Leacock. B & W, 54 minutes. Distributor TLF, rental $50, sale $400.

EMITAI
1970 Ousmane Sembene. Color, 101 minutes. Distributor NYF, rental $110, sale $1295.

EMU RITUAL AT RUGURI
1969 Roger Sandall. Color, 33 minutes. Distributor UCEMC, rental $25, sale $430; PSU, rental $12.10.

ENCYCLOPAEDIA CINEMATOGRAPHICA
n.d. Silent series; B & W. Distributors PSU, NSFL, have catalog.

THE ESKIMO: FIGHT FOR LIFE
1970 Asen Balikci. Color, 51 minutes. Distributor EDC, rental $40, sale $500.

ESSENE
1972 Frederick Wiseman. B & W, 86 minutes. Distributor ZF, rental $100, lease $750.

FANNY
1932 Marc Allegret and Marcel Pagnol. B & W, 120 minutes. Distributor CMH, rental $50.

FANTÔMAS
1914 Louis Feuillade. B & W, 64 minutes, silent. Distributor MOMA, rental $25, piano score available.

FARREBIQUE
1947 Georges Rouquier. B & W, 100 minutes. Distributor CMH, rental $50, sale $500.

THE FEAST

1968 Timothy Asch and Napoleon A. Chagnon. Color, 29 minutes. Distributor DER, rental $20; PSU, rental $11.10; NAC, rental $12.50, sale $75; UCEMC, rental $9; in Canada, NSFL, rental $7.50.

LES FILS DE L'EAU

1955 Jean Rouch. Color, 75 minutes.

FISHING AT THE STONE WEIR

1963 Doug Wilkinson, Michel Chalufour, Quentin Brown, Asen Balikci and Guy Mary-Rousselière. Color, 58 minutes. Distributor UEVA, rental $18, sale $540; PSU, rental $11.10;UCEMC, rental $30.

A FORTY DOLLAR MISUNDERSTANDING

1972 John Marshall. B & W, 8 minutes. Distributor DER, rental $8, sale $60.

FOSSIL EVIDENCE FOR EVOLUTION

1971 Jamshed Mavalwala. Videotape, 50 minutes. Distributor SP; write for details of tape gauge and prices.

GRASS

1925 Merian Cooper and Ernest Schoedsack. B & W, 64 minutes, silent. Distributor FCE, rental $55; UCEMC, rental $20; MOMA, rental $30; in Canada, NSFL, rental $12.

GROOMING BEFORE DEDEHEIWÄ'S HOUSE

1971 Timothy Asch and Napoleon A. Chagnon. Color, 5 minutes. Distributor DER.

A GROUP OF WOMEN

1969 John Marshall. B & W, 5 minutes. Distributor DER, rental $10, sale $50; PSU, rental $5.

GROWING UP AS A FORE

1968 E. Richard Sorenson. Color, 30 minutes. Archived at The Study of Child Behavior and Development in Primitive Cultures, National Institutes of Health, at Bethesda, Maryland.

GUNABIBI – AN ABORIGINAL FERTILITY CULT

1971 Roger Sandall. Color, 30 minutes. Distributor UCEMC, rental $22, sale $360.

HAPPY MOTHER'S DAY *(Quint City U.S.A.)*

1964 Richard Leacock and Joyce Chopra. B & W, 26 minutes. Distributor PI, rental $30, sale $150.

HENRY IS DRUNK

1972 John Marshall. B & W, 7 minutes. Distributor DER, rental $8, sale $60.

HIGH SCHOOL

1968 Frederick Wiseman, B & W, 75 minutes. Distributor ZF, rental $100, lease $750.

HIMBA WEDDING

1969 Gordon D. Gibson. Color, 35 minutes. Distributor SI, rental $10, sale $200.

HOME FOR LIFE

1967 Gerald Temaner and Gordon Quinn. B & W, 86 minutes. Distributor FI, rental $27, sale $350.

HOSPITAL

1970 Frederick Wiseman. B & W, 84 minutes. Distributor ZF, rental $100, lease $750.

HOUSING PROBLEMS

1935 Edgar Anstey and Arthur Elton. B & W, 15 minutes. Distributor MOMA, rental $15.

THE HUNTERS

1958 John Marshall. Color, 72 minutes. Distributor PSU, rental $25.30 (or B & W, $14.20;) UCEMC, rental $29 (or B & W, $20); CMH, rental $35, sale $500; in Canada, NSFL, rental $12.

HUNTING CRICKETS

1971 Timothy Asch and Napoleon A. Chagnon. Color, 12 minutes. Distributor DER.

IMAGINERO *(Hermógenes Cayo)*

1970 Jorge Preloran. Color, 52 minutes. Distributor PF, rental $50, sale $550.

THE INFORMANT

1972 John Marshall. B & W, 24 minutes. Distributor DER, rental $25, sale $175.

INVESTIGATION OF A HIT AND RUN

1971 John Marshall. B & W, 35 minutes. Distributor DER, rental $30, sale $300.

JAGUAR

1956 Jean Rouch. Color, 93 minutes. Distributor CMH, rental $75, sale $750.

JANE

1962 The Living Camera Series. D. A. Pennebaker. B & W, 54 minutes. Distributor TLF, rental $50, sale $400.

A JOKING RELATIONSHIP

1969 John Marshall. B & W, 13 minutes. Distributor DER, rental $15, sale $110; PSU, rental $5.50.

JUVENILE COURT
1973 Frederick Wiseman. B & W, 144 minutes. Distributor ZF, rental $100, lease $750.

THE KALAHARI BUSHMEN
1971 Jamshed Mavalwala. Videotape, 24 minutes. Distributor SP; write for details of tape gauge and prices.

KĄOBAWÄ TRADES WITH THE REYABOBÖWEI-TERI
1971 Napoleon A. Chagnon and Timothy Asch. Color, 8 minutes. Distributor DER.

KENYA BORAN
1973 David MacDougall and James Blue. Color, 60 minutes. Distributor FIR.

KINESICS
1964 Ray L. Birdwhistell. B & W, 73 minutes. Distributor PSU, rental $14.20, sale $215.

KING KONG
1933 Merian Cooper and Ernest B. Schoedsack. B & W, 105 minutes. Distributor FI, rental $75.

KINO-PRAVDA (Series)
1922 Dziga Vertov. B & W, 18 minutes, silent. Distributor MOMA, rental $20.

KULA, ARGONAUTS OF THE WESTERN PACIFIC
1972 Yasuko Ichioka and Junichi Ushiyama. Color, 67 minutes. Not available.

!KUNG BUSHMEN HUNTING EQUIPMENT
1966 John and Lorna Marshall. Color, 37 minutes. Distributor DER, rental $30, sale $400; PSU, rental $16.50.

KURU
n.d. (A comprehensive assemblage of all known cinema of kuru.) 17 reels. Archived at The Study of Child Growth and Development and Disease Patterns in Primitive Cultures, National Institutes of Health, at Bethesda, Maryland.

THE LAND
1941 Robert Flaherty. B & W, 42 minutes. Distributor MOMA, rental $30.

LAND WITHOUT BREAD (Las Hurdes; Terre sans Pain)
1932 Luis Buñuel. B & W, 28 minutes. Distributor MOMA, rental $25; CMH, rental $25, sale $240.

THE LAST OF THE CUIVA
1971 Brian Moser. Color, 58 minutes. Not available.

LAW AND ORDER
1969 Frederick Wiseman. B & W, 81 minutes. Distributor ZF, rental $100, lease $750.

A LEGAL DISCUSSION OF A HIT AND RUN
1971 John Marshall. B & W, 28 minutes. Distributor DER, rental $25, sale $250.

LION GAME
1969 John Marshall. Color, 4 minutes. Distributor DER, rental $10, sale $50; PSU, rental $4.

UN LION NOMMÉ L'AMÉRICAIN
1968 (Based on The Lion Hunters; *La chasse au lion à l'arc*.) Jean Rouch. Color, 82 minutes.

LOUISIANA STORY
1948 Robert Flaherty and Richard Leacock. B & W, 77 minutes. Distributor CMH, rental $50, lease $400.

MAGICAL DEATH
1970 Napoleon A. Chagnon. Color, 29 minutes. Distributor DER, rental $25, sale $125; PSU, rental $7.50, sale $125.

LES MAÎTRES FOUS
1957 Jean Rouch. Color, 30 minutes. Distributor CMH, rental $31, sale $385.

MANDABI
1970 Ousmane Sembene. Color, 90 minutes. Distributor GP, rental $125, sale $950.

MANIFOLD CONTROVERSY
1972 John Marshall. B & W, 3 minutes. Distributor DER, rental $8, sale $45.

MAN OF ARAN
1934 Robert Flaherty. B & W, 77 minutes. Distributor CMH, rental $35, sale $400.

THE MAN WITH THE MOVIE CAMERA
1929 Dziga Vertov. B & W, 67 minutes. Distributor MAB, rental $45.

MARIUS
1931 Marcel Pagnol and Alexander Korda. B & W, 125 minutes. Distributor CMH, rental $50.

A MARRIED COUPLE
1969 Allan King. Color, 95 minutes. Distributor MMP, rental $55, sale $750 (Canada only).

MEMPHIS BELLE
1944 William Wyler. B & W, 40 minutes, 35-millimeter. Not available.

MEN BATHING
1972 John Marshall. Color, 14 minutes. Distributor DER, rental $15, sale $200; PSU, rental $9.50.

MIAO YEAR

1968 William R. Geddes. Color, 62 minutes. Distributor CMH, rental $50, sale $680.

MICROCULTURAL INCIDENTS IN TEN ZOOS

1971 Ray L. Birdwhistell. B & W, 34 minutes. Distributor PSU, rental $13.30, sale $340.

MOANA, A ROMANCE OF THE GOLDEN AGE

1926 Robert Flaherty. B & W, 85 minutes, silent. Distributor MOMA, rental $30.

MÖAWÄ BURNS FELLED TIMBER

1971 Timothy Asch and Napoleon A. Chagnon. Color, 13 minutes. Distributor DER.

MÖAWÄ MAKING A HAMMOCK

1971 Timothy Asch and Napoleon A. Chagnon. Color, 12 minutes. Distributor DER.

MOI, UN NOIR

1957 Jean Rouch. Color, 80 minutes.

MONDO CANE

1962 Gualtiero Jacopetti. Color, 105 minutes. Distributor MAB, rental $70.

MOON BLOOD

1971 Napoleon A. Chagnon and Timothy Asch. Color, 10 minutes. Distributor DER.

MOONEY VS. FOWLE *(Football)*

1961 The Living Camera Series. Richard Leacock. B & W, 54 minutes. Distributor TLF, rental $50, sale $400.

MORNING FLOWERS

1971 Napoleon A. Chagnon and Timothy Asch. Color, 25 minutes. Distributor DER.

MOUNT LIEBIG EXPEDITION

1932 E. O. Stocker, Norman B. Tindale, T. D. Campbell, and T. G. H. Strehlow. B & W, 103 minutes, silent. Not available.

MOUTH WRESTLING

1971 Timothy Asch and Napoleon A. Chagnon. Color, 10 minutes. Distributor DER.

THE MULGA SEED CEREMONY

1972 Roger Sandall. Color, 25 minutes. Distributor UCEMC, rental $20, sale $325; PSU, rental $10.10.

NAIM AND JABAR

1973 Herbert di Gioia and David Hancock. Color, 70 minutes.

NANG YAI: THAI SHADOW PUPPET DRAMA

1972 Banchong Kosalwat and Stephanie Krebs. B & W, 20 minutes. Distributor ATFL; handling fee only, no sales.

NANOOK OF THE NORTH

1922 Robert Flaherty. B & W, 55 minutes. Distributor CMH, rental $25, sale $350; NYU, rental $31; PSU, rental $10.50; (for original silent version) MOMA, rental $30, lease $300; UCEMC, rental $21; in Canada, NSFL, rental $35.

NEHRU

1962 The Living Camera Series. Richard Leacock. B & W. Distributor TLF, rental $50, sale $400.

NEW TRIBES

1971 Timothy Asch and Napoleon A. Chagnon. Color, 10 minutes. Distributor DER.

NIGHT MAIL

1935 Basil Wright and Harry Watt. B & W, 24 minutes. Distributor CMH; MOMA, rental $20.

NOMADS OF THE JUNGLE

1959 Paul Fejos. B & W, 25 minutes. Distributor PSU, rental $5.40.

NOTHING HURT BUT MY PRIDE

1972 John Marshall. B & W, 15 minutes. Distributor DER, rental $15, sale $95.

N!OWA T'AMA: THE MELON TOSSING

1967 John Marshall. Color, 15 minutes. Distributor DER, rental $15, sale $200; PSU, rental $9.50.

THE NUER

1970 Hilary Harris and George Breidenbach. Color, 75 minutes. Distributor CMH, rental $60, sale $600; UCEMC, rental $34; CMH, rental $75, sale $680; in Canada, NSFL, rental $8.50.

N/UM TCHAI: THE CEREMONIAL DANCE OF THE !KUNG BUSHMEN

1969 John Marshall. B & W, 20 minutes. Distributor DER, rental $20, sale $175; PSU, rental $7.

OCAMO IS MY TOWN

1971 Napoleon A. Chagnon and Timothy Asch. Color, 23 minutes. Distributor DER.

PAPUA, A NEW LIFE

1971 Yasushi Toyotomi and Junichi Ushiyama. Color, 90 minutes. Not available.

PAUL TOMKOWICZ: STREET-RAILWAY SWITCH MAN

1954 Roman Kroitor. B & W, 9 minutes. Distributor CMH, rental $10.

LA PÊCHE À LA CREVETTE (*Shrimp Fishing*)

1895 Louis Lumière. B & W, 20 minutes, silent. Not available.

PEOPLE OF THE KURU REGION

1958 D. C. Gajdusek. Color, 30 minutes. Archived at The Study of Child Behavior and Development in Primitive Cultures, National Institutes of Health, in Bethesda, Maryland.

PEOPLE OF THE RIVER NERETVA

1966 B & W, 18 minutes. Distributor PSU, rental $5; IU, rental $5.75.

THE PERILS OF PAULINE

1933 Ray Taylor. B & W, 12 reels of 20 minutes each. Distributor UN-16, rental $10 per reel.

PETE AND JOHNNY

n.d. The Living Camera Series. B & W, 54 minutes. Distributor TLF, rental $50, sale $400.

PINTUBI REVISIT YARU YARU

1973 Roger Sandall. Color, 31 minutes. Distributor UCEMC, rental $23, sale $370.

PINTUBI REVISIT YUMARI

1971 Ken Hansen, Jeremy Long, and Roger Sandall. Color, 32 minutes. Distributor UCEMC; rental $23, sale $385.

PLAYING WITH SCORPIONS

1972 John Marshall. Color, 4 minutes. Distributor DER, rental $10, sale $50; PSU, rental $4.50.

PORTRAIT OF JASON

1967 Shirley Clarke. B & W, 105 minutes. Distributor NYF; rental $75, sale $1100.

PRIMARY

1961 Richard Leacock and others. B & W, 54 minutes. Distributor TLF; rental $50, sale $400.

THE PRIMATE PUZZLE

1971 Jamshed Mavalwala. Videotape, 31 minutes. Distributor SP; write for details of tape gauge and prices.

PUNISHMENT PARK

1971 Peter Watkins. Color, 90 minutes. Not available.

LA PUNITION

1963 Jean Rouch. B & W, 60 minutes.

PUSHTU PEOPLES

1963 (In five parts) Hermann Schlenker. Color. Distributor IFF, rental $15 per reel; sale: MAKING FELT, 9 minutes, $110; MEN'S DANCE, 11 minutes, $135; BOY'S GAMES, 5 minutes, $65; BAKING BREAD, 10 minutes, $125; WEAVING CLOTH, 9 minutes, $110.

LA PYRAMIDE HUMAINE
1960 Jean Rouch. Color, 80 minutes.

QUE VIVA MÉXICO! (*Time in the Sun; Thunder Over Mexico*)
1933-39 Sergei Eisenstein. B & W, 69 minutes. Distributor MAB, rental $35; MOMA, rental $40.

RACE: REALITY OR MYTH?
1971 Jamshed Mavalwala. Videotape, 28 minutes. Distributor SP; write for details of tape gauge and prices.

LES RAQUETTEURS
1958 Michel Brault. B & W, 17 minutes. Distributor CMH, rental $12.

REAHUMOU
1971 Timothy Asch and Napoleon A. Chagnon. Color, 15 minutes. Distributor DER.

LA RÉGLE DU JEU (*Rules of the Game*)
1939 Jean Renoir. B & W, 110 minutes. Distributor JF, rental $125.

RIEN QUE LES HEURES
1927 Alberto Cavalcanti. B & W, 45 minutes, silent. Distributor MOMA, rental $30.

A RITE OF PASSAGE
1972 John Marshall. Color, 14 minutes. Distributor DER, rental $20, sale $200; PSU, rental $9.50.

THE RIVER
1931 Pare Lorentz. B. & W, 30 minutes. Distributor NAC, rental $10, sale $66.50; MOMA, rental $20; UCEMC, rental $14.

THE RIVER MISHIMISHIMABÖWEI
1971 Timothy Asch and Napoleon A. Chagnon. Color, 25 minutes Distributor DER.

SAND PLAY
1971 Timothy Asch and Napoleon A. Chagnon. Color, 18 minutes. Distributor DER.

SIGUI
1969 Jean Rouch and Germaine Dieterlen. Color, 40 minutes.

THE SILENT ENEMY
1939 H. P. Carver. B & W, 60 minutes. Distributor FCE, rental $55.

SONG OF CEYLON
1935 Basil Wright. B & W, 40 minutes. Distributor CMH, rental $20, sale $250; MOMA, rental $30.

LA SORTIE DES USINES (*Leaving the Factories*)
1895 Louis Lumière. B & W, 20 minutes, silent. Not available.

SOUS LE MASQUE NOIR
1938 Marcel Griaule. Color, 50 minutes. Distributor NSFL; rental free.

THE SUCKING DOCTOR (abridged as POMO SHAMAN)
> 1964 William Heick and David Peri. B & W, 55 minutes (short version, 20 minutes). Distributor UCEMC, rental $20 (*Sucking Doctor*), or rental $10, sale $120 (both for *Pomo Shaman*). Contact William Heick, UCEMC, for *Sucking Doctor* (sale).

TARZAN, THE APE MAN
> 1932 Willard S. van Dyke. B & W, 100 minutes. Distributor FI, rental $30.

TAUW
> 1968 Ousmane Sembene. Color, 27 minutes. Distributor NYF, rental $35, sale $225.

THE THINGS I CANNOT CHANGE
> 1967 Tanya Ballantyne. B & W, 58 minutes. Distributor CMH, rental $25; UCEMC, rental $18.

THREE DOMESTICS
> 1970 John Marshall. B & W, 37 minutes. Distributor DER, rental $30, sale $380.

TITICUT FOLLIES
> 1967 Frederick Wiseman and John Marshall B & W, 87 minutes. Distributor GP, rental $100, sale $600.

TOKYO STORY
> 1953 Yasujiro Ozu. B & W, 134 minutes. Distributor NYF, rental $125, apply for sale price.

TO LIVE WITH HERDS
> 1972 David MacDougall. B & W, 68 minutes. Distributor FIR, rental $60, sale $500.

TONI
> 1934 Jean Renoir. B & W, 90 minutes. Distributor CMH, rental $60.

TRADER HORN
> 1931 Willard S. Van Dyke. B & W, 120 minutes. Distributor FI, rental $35.

TRANCE AND DANCE IN BALI
> 1951 Gregory Bateson and Margaret Mead. B & W, 20 minutes. Distributor NYU, rental $9.50, sale $135; UCEMC, rental $10; in Canada, NSFL, rental only.

TUG OF WAR
> 1971 Timothy Asch and Napoleon A. Chagnon. Color, 7 minutes. Distributor DER.

TURKSIB
> 1928 Viktor Turin. B & W, 90 minutes. Distributor MAB, rental $45.

TWENTY-ONE DOLLARS OR TWENTY-ONE DAYS

1972 John Marshall. B & W, 8 minutes. Distributor DER, rental $8, sale $60.

THE TWIN CYCLE MYTHS

1971 Napoleon A. Chagnon and Timothy Asch. Color, 25 minutes. Distributor DER.

TWO BROTHERS

1972 John Marshall. B & W, 4 minutes. Distributor DER, rental $8, sale $45.

UMBERTO D

1952 Vittorio de Sica. B & W, 89 minutes. Distributor JF, rental $125.

VAGRANT WOMAN

1972 John Marshall. B & W, 8 minutes. Distributor DER, rental $8, sale $60.

VEČNA PISEŇ (*The Eternal Song*)

1945 Karel Plicka. B & W, 72 minutes, 35-millimeter. Not available.

THE VILLAGE

1968 Mark McCarty and Paul Hockings. B & W, 70 minutes. Distributor UCEMC, rental $33, sale $510.

THE WAR GAME

1965 Peter Watkins. B & W, 47 minutes. Distributor CMH, rental $75.

WARRENDALE

1966 Allan King. B & W, 105 minutes. Distributor GP, rental $100, sale $600; MMP, rental $55, sale $600.

THE WASP NEST

1973 John Marshall. Color, 20 minutes. Distributor DER, rental $20, sale $240.

WINTER SEA-ICE CAMP, (AT THE)

1968 Netsilik Eskimo Series. Doug Wilkinson, Michel Chalufour, Quentin Brown, Asen Balikci, and Guy Mary-Rousselière. Color, 30 minutes for each of four reels. Distributor UEVA, rental $9 per reel, sale $270 per reel.

WOMAN SPINS COTTON

1971 Timothy Asch and Napoleon A. Chagnon. B & W, 7 minutes. Distributor DER.

THE WORLD OF APU

1958 Satyajit Ray. B & W, 103 minutes. Distributor MAB, rental $85.

WRONG KID

1972 John Marshall. B & W, 5 minutes. Distributor DER, rental $8, sale $45.

YĄNOMAMÖ: A MULTI-DISCIPLINARY STUDY
1968 James V. Neel, Timothy Asch, and Napoleon A. Chagnon. Color, 45 minutes. Distributor DER, rental $25; NAC; UCEMC, rental $12; in Canada, NSFL, rental $7.50.

THE YĄNOMAMÖ MYTH OF NARO AS TOLD BY DEDEHEIWÄ
1971 Napoleon A. Chagnon and Timothy Asch. Color, 25 minutes. Distributor DER.

THE YĄNOMAMÖ MYTH OF NARO AS TOLD BY KĄOBAWÄ
1971 Napoleon A. Chagnon and Timothy Asch. Color, 17 minutes. Distributor DER.

YOUTH AND THE MAN OF PROPERTY
1972 John Marshall. B & W, 7 minutes. Distributor DER, rental $8, sale $60.

YOU WASN'T LOITERING?
1973 John Marshall. B & W, 15 minutes. Distributor DER, rental $15 sale $95.

ZEM SPIEVA (*Earth in Song*)
1933 Karel Plicka. B & W, 68 minutes, 35-millimeter. Not available.

ADDRESSES OF THE NORTH AMERICAN DISTRIBUTORS

ATFL   Asian Theater Film Library
American Theater Association
1317 F Street, NW
Washington, D.C. 20004.
Phone (202)737–5606.

CC   Columbia Cinamatheque
711 Fifth Avenue
New York, N.Y. 10022.
Phone (212)751–7529.

CMH   Contemporary/McGraw-Hill Films Inc.
1221 Avenue of the Americas
New York, N.Y. 10020.
Phone (212)971–5851.
or:
828 Custer Avenue
Evanston, Ill. 60202.
Phone (312)869–5010.

or:
1714 Stockton Street
San Francisco, Cal. 94133.
Phone (415)362–3115.

DER   Documentary Educational Resources
24 Dane Street
Somerville, Mass. 02143.
Phone (617)666–1750.

EDC   Education Development Center
39 Chapel Street
Newton, Mass. 02160.
Phone (617)969–7100.

FCE   Film Classic Exchange
1926 South Vermont Avenue
Los Angeles, Cal. 90007.
Phone (213)731–3854.

FI   Films Incorporated
4420 Oakton Street
Skokie, Ill. 60076.
Phone (312)676–1088.
or:
35–01 Queens Boulevard
Long Island City, N.Y. 11101.
Phone (212)937–1110.

FIR   Film Images/Radim Films
1034 Lake Street
Oak Park, Ill. 60301.
Phone (312)386–4826.
or:
17 West 60th Street
New York, N.Y. 10023.
Phone (212)279–6653.

GP   Grove Press
Film Division
53 East 11th Street

New York, N.Y. 10003.
Phone (212)677–2400.

IFF   International Film Foundation
Suite 916
475 Fifth Avenue
New York, N.Y. 10017.
Phone (212)685–4998.

IU   Indiana University
Audio-Visual Center
Bloomington, Ind. 47401.
Phone (812)337–2103.

JF   Janus Films
745 Fifth Avenue
New York, N.Y. 10022.
Phone (212)753–7100.

MAB   Macmillan/Audio Brandon
34 MacQuesten Parkway South
Mount Vernon, N.Y. 10550.
Phone (914)664–5051.

MMP   Martin Motion Pictures
47 Lakeshore Road East
Port Credit, Ontario
Canada L5G 1C9.
Phone (416)278–2921 or –5235.

MOMA   Museum of Modern Art
Dep't. of Film
11 West 53rd Street
New York, N.Y. 10019.
Phone (212)956–4205.

NAC   National Audiovisual Center
National Archives and Records Center
General Services Administration
Washington, D.C. 20409.
Phone (301)763–7786.

NSFL National Science Film Library
Canadian Film Institute
1762 Carling Avenue
Ottawa 13, Ontario, Canada.
Phone (613)729–6193.

NYF New Yorker Films
43 West 61st Street
New York, N.Y. 10023.
Phone (212)247–6110.

NYU New York University
Film Library
26 Washington Place
New York, N.Y. 10003.
Phone (212) 598–2251.

PF Phoenix Films
267 West 25th Street
New York, N.Y. 10001.
Phone (212)675–5330.

PI Pennebaker, Inc.
56 West 45th Street
New York, N.Y. 10036.
Phone (212)986–7020.

PSU Pennsylvania State University
Audio-Visual Services
University Park, Pa. 16802.
Phone (814)865–6315.

SI Smithsonian Institution
Office of Public Affairs
Washington, D.C. 20560.
Phone (202)628–1810.

SP Software Productions
705 Progress Avenue
Scarborough, Ontario, Canada.
Phone (416)928–6520.

TLF   Time-Life Films
          Time and Life Building
          Rockefeller Center
          New York, N.Y. 10020.
          Phone (212)691–2930.

UCEMC University of California
          Extension Media Center
          2223 Fulton Street
          Berkeley, Cal. 94720.
          Phone (415)642–0460.

UEVA   Universal Education and Visual Arts, Inc.
          221 Park Avenue South
          New York, N.Y. 10003.
          Phone (212)677–5658.

UN–16   Universal 16
          425 North Michigan Avenue
          Chicago, Ill. 60611.
          Phone (312) 822–0513.

ZF   Zipporah Films
          54 Lewis Wharf
          Boston, Mass. 02110.
          Phone (617)742–6680.

ERRATUM
The following pages should have been numbered 505-527:
Biographical Notes should begin on page 505 instead of page 499;
the Index of Films should begin on page 511 instead of page 505;
the Index of Names should begin on page 515 instead of page 509;
the Index of Subjects should begin on page 521 instead of page 515.
These pagination changes should also be applied to the Table of Contents.

Biographical Notes

TIMOTHY ASCH (1932, U.S.A.). Teaches anthropology at Harvard and Brandeis Universities. Educated at Columbia and Boston Universities. Author of over forty films on the Yąnomamö of Venezuela, most of them in collaboration with Napoleon Chagnon.

ASEN BALIKCI (1929, Bulgaria). Professor of Anthropology, University of Montreal. Educated at Columbia University. Author of *The Netsilik Eskimo* and co-author of numerous films on the same culture.

ART BROWN (1928, U.S.A.). Educated at the University of Chicago, he has been engaged in filmmaking and distribution for the past 25 years. President of Radim Films Inc., an independent distributor.

EDMUND CARPENTER (1922, U.S.A.). Professor of Anthropology, Adelphi University; educated at University of Pennsylvania. Formerly taught at University of Toronto, California State University, New School for Social Research, and University of California. Author of *Explorations in communication* (with Marshall McLuhan), *Ancerca, Eskimo, The story of Comock the Eskimo, They became what they beheld, Eskimo realities*, and *Oh, what a blow that phantom gave me*.

FOSTER O. CHANOCK (1952, U.S.A.). A graduate student in communications at the University of Chicago. He is a consultant on cable television.

JOHN COLLIER, JR. (1913, U.S.A.). A photographer who, after free-lancing, worked successively for the Farm Security Administration, Standard

Oil, and Cornell University (the Vicos and Navaho projects). Now Associate Professor of Anthropology and Education at the California State University, San Francisco. Author of *The awakening valley* and *Visual anthropology: photography as a research method.*

EMILIE DE BRIGARD (1943, U.S.A.). Educated at Radcliffe College and the University of California, Los Angeles. Works as a film consultant and curator; currently preparing an illustrated book, *Anthropological cinema*, for publication by the Museum of Modern Art (New York).

ROBERT F. FORSTON (1940, U.S.A.). Educated in psychology and communications at the University of Minnesota. Now Chairman of the Speech Communication Department at Drake University, Des Moines, Iowa. Author of *Public speaking as dialogue*, *Visit into the jury room*, and several scholarly articles on communication.

PAUL HOCKINGS (1935, England). Studied anthropology at the Universities of Sydney, Toronto, Chicago, Stanford, and California (Berkeley). Has written on the Irish and the Badagas of South India, and helped film *The Village* and *The Man Hunters*. Has taught at the Universities of California and Illinois and has lectured widely in Europe, Asia, and North America.

JAY K. HOFFMAN (1933, U.S.A.). Educated at the University of Florida. Self-employed as a producer and writer. His company, Jay Hoffman Presentations, produces educational multi-media materials.

JUDY HOFFMAN (1947, U.S.A.). Studied at the Universities of Iowa and Illinois.

ALLISON JABLONKO (1940, U.S.A.). Studied anthropology at Columbia University. She now lives with her family in Perugia, Italy. Author of several papers on body movement and the documentation of vanishing cultures, particularly in New Guinea, India, and Mauritius.

PAMELA JENSEN (1952, U.S.A.). A student of anthropology at the University of Illinois, Chicago Circle.

STEPHANIE L. KREBS (1943, U.S.A.). Doctoral candidate in social anthropology, Harvard University. She is author of two films, *Nang Yai: Thai Shadow Puppet Drama*, and *Shunka's Story*.

JEAN-DOMINIQUE LAJOUX (1931, France). Research engineer at the Centre d'Ethnologie Française in Paris. Educated at the University of Paris. Author of several films, including *L'Aubrac*, *Le forgeron des hermaux*, and *Le conte du Bouc d'Aunac*, and of a book, *Rock paintings of Tassili*.

RICHARD LEACOCK (1921, England). Educated at Harvard University and now teaches film at the Massachusetts Institute of Technology. Cameraman/director who worked with Flaherty on *Louisiana Story*, he subsequently made such documentaries as *Primary*, *The Chair*, *Chiefs*, *Happy Mother's Day* and *Queen of Apollo*.

ALAN LOMAX (1915, U.S.A.). Studied at the Universities of Texas, Harvard, and Columbia and is now Co-director of the Cantometrics Project at Columbia University. Author of numerous articles and books on folklore, including *Mr. Jellyroll*, *The rainbow sign*, *Folk songs of North America*, *Folk song style and culture*, and *3000 years of black poetry*. He is editor of *The world library of folk and primitive music* (Columbia Records).

MARK MCCARTY (1931, U.S.A.). Educated in classics and film at the University of California and is now Professor of Theater Arts at the University of California, Los Angeles. Co-author (with Paul Hockings) of *The Village*, as well as numerous shorter documentaries.

DAVID MACDOUGALL (1939, U.S.A.). Educated at Harvard University and the University of California, Los Angeles; now Co-director of the Media Center at Rice University. He has made several films in the U.S.A. and East Africa, including *To Live with Herds*, *Under the Men's Tree*, *Nawi*, and *Kenya Boran*.

JOHN K. MARSHALL (1932, U.S.A.). Educated at Harvard and Yale Universities, he is now Director of Documentary Educational Resources and Research Associate in Anthropology at Brandeis University. He was director/cameraman for *The Hunters*, *Bitter Melons*, *Titicut Follies*, *Three Domestics*, and numerous other films on Bushman social life and the American legal process.

JAMSHED MAVALWALA (1933, India). Educated at the University of Delhi, he currently teaches anthropology at the University of Toronto. Author of several papers in physical anthropology and of a series of videotape programs described here in his article.

MARGARET MEAD (1901, U.S.A.). Educated under Franz Boas at Columbia University, where she has been teaching for four decades. Author of *Culture and commitment: a study of the generation gap, Continuities in cultural evolution, Male and female, Coming of age in Samoa, The changing culture of an Indian tribe, Balinese character* (with Gregory Bateson), and *New lives for old: cultural transformation, Manus 1928–1953;* also numerous journal articles and several films, among them *Trance and Dance in Bali* and *A Balinese Family.*

ALEXEI Y. PETERSON (1931, U.S.S.R.). Educated at the Tartu State University. Now Director of the State Ethnography Museum of the Estonian S.S.R. Has filmed and studied Estonian folk culture.

JORGE PRELORAN (1930, Argentina). Educated at the Universities of Buenos Aires and California (Los Angeles). Has taught at the latter institution and now makes films independently in Argentina; among them *Imaginero, Araucanians of Ruca Choroy,* and numerous others on peasant society.

JACK H. PROST (1934, U.S.A.). Educated at Northwestern University and the University of Chicago. Author of numerous papers on primate behavior, with a specialization on the evolution of locomotion; he has also taught at Duke University and the Universities of California and Illinois.

GORDON QUINN (1942, U.S.A.). Educated at the University of Chicago. Now a filmmaker with Kartemquin Films, Chicago. Co-authored *Home for Life, Marco, Thumbs Down,* and several other films.

JEAN ROUCH (1917, France). Studied at the University of Paris, and after a brief career as an engineer made four dozen films in West Africa and Paris. Best known perhaps are *Les maîtres fous, Moi un noir, Jaguar,* and *Chronique d'un été.* He is now Director of Research at the Centre National de la Recherche Scientifique and teaches at the University of Paris.

F. ROGER SANDALL (1933, New Zealand). Educated at the Universities of Auckland and Columbia. Has taught at Rice University and the American Museum of Natural History, and now teaches at the University of Sydney. Author of over a dozen films on the Aborigines of Central and Northern Australia.

JOSEPH H. SCHAEFFER (1937, U.S.A.). Educated at Oberlin College, New York and Columbia Universities, and the Mozarteum in Salzburg. Was a conductor, pianist, and musical director in New York for six years and then Field Director of the Project in Human Communication at Bronx State Hospital. He has also done research in Jamaica and the Dominican Republic, and now teaches at Marlboro College in Vermont. Author of several papers on videotape, cross-cultural communication, territoriality, and the use of *Cannabis sativa*.

SHAWN E. SCHERER (1948, Canada). Studied at York University and the University of Toronto. He is now a clinician with the Addiction Research Foundation, Toronto. Author of several papers on proxemics and drug use.

E. RICHARD SORENSON (1939, U.S.A.). Studied at the Universities of Rochester and Stanford and then was at the National Institutes of Health, while also a Research Associate at Stanford University, developing methodology for the study of passing phenomena using film archives. Author of several papers, books and films dealing with behavior in New Guinea, Micronesia, New Hebrides, Solomon Islands, Borneo, Mexico, and Nepal. Now Director of the National Center for Anthropological Film, Washington.

STUART STRUEVER (1931, U.S.A.). Educated at Dartmouth College, Northwestern University, and the University of Chicago. Has taught at the latter two institutions. He is the author of numerous papers on prehistoric American agriculture and experimentation in archaeological methods.

SOL TAX (1907, U.S.A.). Professor of Anthropology at the University of Chicago, where he was also educated. Founder and editor of *Current Anthropology* and editor of numerous books on anthropological subjects. President of the IXth International Congress of Anthropological and Ethnological Sciences. Author of *Penny capitalism* and *Heritage of conquest*.

GERALD TEMANER (1936, U.S.A.). Head of the Media Production Center, University of Illinois at Chicago Circle. Educated at the University of Chicago; formerly taught there and at Northwestern University. Co-author of *Marco, Home for Life*, and numerous other films.

JUNICHI USHIYAMA (1930, Japan). Educated in Oriental history at Waseda University. Currently President of Nippon A-V Productions; producer of *Kula, Argonauts of the Western Pacific* and other ethnographic films for television.

JOHN H. WEAKLAND (1919, U.S.A.). Educated at Cornell and Columbia Universities. Now Research Associate at the Mental Research Institute, in Palo Alto, California. Author of various papers on psychiatry, Chinese culture, and the analysis of Chinese feature films.

COLIN YOUNG (1927, Scotland). Educated at the Universities of Glasgow, St. Andrews, and California. Formerly Chairman of the Department of Theater Arts, University of California at Los Angeles, where he helped start an ethnographic film program. Now Director of the National Film School of Great Britain. Was Los Angeles editor of *Film Quarterly* for some years and has written numerous critical articles on film. Producer of *The Village, La Tirana*, and *Warao*.

Index of Films*

* Many titles have been shortened here. See the Filmography, 485–498, for fuller titles.

Index of Names

Index of Subjects